NO MORE TIME TO LOSE

The Battle of Kahlenberg and the Relief of Vienna, 12 September 1683

A. V. Exelby

'This is the Century of the Soldier', Fulvio Testi, Poet, 1641

HELION & COMPANY

Helion & Company Limited
Unit 8 Amherst Business Centre
Budbrooke Road
Warwick
CV34 5WE
England
Tel. 01926 499 619
Email: info@helion.co.uk
Website: www.helion.co.uk
X (formerly Twitter): @Helionbooks
Facebook: @HelionBooks
Visit our blog at helionbooks.wordpress.com

Published by Helion & Company 2025
Designed and typeset by Mary Woolley, Battlefield Design (www.battlefield-design.co.uk)
Cover designed by Paul Hewitt, Battlefield Design (www.battlefield-design.co.uk)

Text © A. V. Exelby 2025
Illustrations as individually credited
Maps by George Anderson © Helion & Company 2025
Colour artwork by S. I. Shamenkov © Helion & Company 2025

Every reasonable effort has been made to trace copyright holders and to obtain their permission for the use of copyright material. The author and publisher apologize for any errors or omissions in this work and would be grateful if notified of any corrections that should be incorporated in future reprints or editions of this book.

ISBN 978-1-804518-41-0

British Library Cataloguing-in-Publication Data.
A catalogue record for this book is available from the British Library.

All rights reserved. No part of this publication may be reproduced, stored in a retrieval system, or transmitted, in any form, or by any means, electronic, mechanical, photocopying, recording or otherwise, without the express written consent of Helion & Company Limited.

For details of other military history titles published by Helion & Company Limited contact the above address or visit our website: http://www.helion.co.uk.

We always welcome receiving book proposals from prospective authors.

Contents

'No more time to lose'		5
Author's note		6
Preface		7
Pronunciation note		13
Abbreviations		15
Timeline		16
Dramatis personae		19
1	Assembly of the relief force	33
2	Discussions, discussions, discussions: the Stetteldorf conference	71
3	Over the Danube and the final decisions	83
4	To the Wienerwald	98
5	Initial Ottoman preparations	109
6	These impassable mountains: the crossing of the Wienerwald	129
7	The battlefield	153
8	The conference on the Kahlenberg and the final Christian preparations	158
9	Ottoman reactions of 11 September and final dispositions	165
10	The opposing forces (orders of battle)	180
11	The Battle of Kahlenberg	207
12	Aftermath	287
13	Commentary	296
Colour Plate Commentaries		314
Glossary		317

Appendices:
I	Points of uncertainty and dispute	339
II	The Ottoman army census of 7 September and the casualty list	357
III	Ottoman discussions: did Koca Ibrahim oppose Kara Mustafa?	364
IV	Le Bègue's accounts of the battle	371
V	The 'Baden account'	378
VI	Two German accounts of the battle	382
VII	Sobieski's letters to his wife	389
Bibliography		397

'No more time to lose'

The title comes from the supposed last note sent out of Vienna to the relief force by the commandant, Ernst Rüdiger von Starhemberg, delivered on about 10 September. In full, roughly translated, the note ran 'No more time to lose, my lord, really no more time to lose' (in original German: 'Keine Zeit mehr verlieren, gnädiger Herr, ja keine Zeit mehr verlieren'). Unfortunately, the story, though dramatically appealing, is almost certainly an invention of nineteenth-century historians: there is no record in the original sources of the garrison, including the meticulous documents of payments made to messengers, that such a note was sent in the final days of the siege; and there is no record in sources from the relief army of a messenger delivering such a message. However, by 10 September, Starhemberg was communicating with the outside world by rockets launched from the tower of the Cathedral of St Stephen in Vienna; wordless though these were, as they increased in number and frequency in the dying days of the siege there could be no doubt of their meaning: No more time to lose....

Author's note

If there is sufficient interest aroused by this book, I intend to write others, covering the siege of Vienna and operations in the field before and during the siege, that together with this work will then form a coherent whole. For this reason, I have kept the background information here to a minimum. I provide a very brief 'Timeline' of preceding events, leading characters who might have been 'met before' are described in a list of 'Dramatis personae' at the start, and terminology that may be unfamiliar is defined in a Glossary at the end. I strongly recommend that users of this book not already familiar with the campaign read through the Timeline and Dramatis Personae before proceeding to the text. However, some degree of familiarity with the standard military terminology of the period is expected: the reader is assumed to know the difference between a cuirassier and a dragoon, and that the standard infantry weapon of the period was the matchlock musket with pikes supporting the musketeers.

Preface

Only two serious scholarly books have been written in English on the 1683 siege and relief of Vienna, both of them produced in the 1960s and neither by a historian interested in the deep military details. John Stoye's *The siege of Vienna* (London: Collins, 1964) provides an excellent, well-rounded and eminently readable introduction to the subject, but lacks any thorough coverage of military events, and is occasionally led by the idiosyncrasies of the sources into factual errors; Thomas M. Barker's *Double eagle and crescent: Vienna's second Turkish siege and its historical setting* (Albany: SUNY, 1967, while lacking specifics on matters such as orders of battle, is incomparably the better history from both a military and a political viewpoint, but is written in a style so full of pompous verbiage as to be practically unreadable. So, an exhaustive military history in English is long overdue. Even for those familiar with European languages, there is not as much available as one might expect. The 'official' bicentenary publication of the government of Austria-Hungary, *Das Kriegsjahr 1683*, written by the Abtheilung für Kriegsgeschichte of the k.k. Kriegs-Archiv, ought to have been definitive but was not, providing a thorough enough account but one full of errors and too rarely giving any indication of the sources of its statements, lending a spurious air of certainty to much that was debatable. Other publications of the bicentenary period were as good or better (one thinks immediately of the excellent Renner, *Wien im Jahre 1683*) but less interested in military specifics. The one publication of that period which was infused with enthusiasm for military detail was *Der Entsatz von Wien*, attributed to Karl Wilhelm Mansberg; but while he did quite well on the Christian side, indeed made a valiant and valuable effort at producing a full order of battle for the allied army out of the limited information available in the sources, he failed completely to understand the structure of the Ottoman army and filled in the gaps in his knowledge with fiction. The tercentenary in 1983 produced a spate of books in German on different aspects of the siege and battle, but no coherent study; for that, one had to turn to Poland for the magisterial study of Wimmer, although an abridged but still superb version of his study was also translated into German. Compared with other battles of far less importance, Vienna has been poorly served, and is long overdue for a new account, even one by a writer such as myself whose knowledge of Polish is limited and of Turkish non-existent. Until 2021, the most recent widely-available English account was in the Osprey 'Campaign' series, by Simon Millar, *Vienna 1683: Christian Europe repels the Ottomans*, illustrated by Peter Dennis (Oxford: Osprey,

2008), which is one of the weakest in a normally excellent series (hampered by trying to cover both siege and battle in one short book). In 2021 appeared the magnificent Michał Paradowski, *We came, we saw, God conquered: the Polish-Lithuanian Commonwealth's military effort in the relief of Vienna, 1683*, published by Helion as no.79 in this series, which is excellent generally and for the Polish side is probably the best account in English, but the book is primarily about the army not the battle, hence it deals with the battle at a different level to detail to mine, and it naturally concentrates on the Polish contribution, whereas all contingents played significant parts in the victory.

It is not even as if the battle is an easy one to understand, never needing a new study once properly covered. The relief of Vienna was an enormously complex action, and the sources available, while as plentiful as one would expect for an event of such importance, are just plentiful enough (and just vague enough) to be contradictory and confusing, especially as they were usually written by people who were not familiar with the names of the terrain features over which they had fought so that any account is full of references to locations in the manner of 'the hill next to the one we were on before'. Also, many of the sources on the German side seem to have got bored after a while, so they describe the events of the morning in some detail but then skim the rest of the day – but since they often do not provide precise times for actions, or the times they give are open to question, it is difficult to identify the point at which they start skimming. No two sources agree with each other even over significant details (Lorraine's secretary Le Bègue could not even agree with himself about the times of major features of the battle); and no two modern historians agree with each other over how to interpret those sources. However, with the exception of Barker, few modern historians have seen fit to document in detail the sources for each stage of their accounts, and too many, from the Abtheilung für Kriegsgeschichte on, have presented their undocumented accounts with far more certainty than the sources warrant. Its is surprising how modern scholars have uncritically accepted as gospel accounts from Mansberg, presented with no source cited – for example his whole section on the Saxon capture of Heiligenstadt. Therefore, I feel the time is right not only for a new study, but also for a fully *documented* study, so that the reader can grasp how reliable each statement is, can begin to understand for themselves where the sources end and the historian's interpretation begins – for there is undoubtedly a great deal of interpretation, and too often in the past it has been presented as if it comes from the sources. The reader can even tell where the particular weaknesses of this book lie, by observing how my account of the Polish aspect of the battle is dependent on the writing of just one historian (Wimmer, because his study was translated into German), supported by two other historians, Laskowski and Paradowski, and only three sources used directly (Sobieski's letters, Dupont, and Dalérac), employed more because they are in a western language than for their innate value – colourful though they are, none of them is regarded as especially reliable. A similar consideration affects the Ottoman viewpoint: I have made extensive use of the three key sources that have been translated into German by Kreutel & Teply, but my lack of Turkish prevents me from accessing further sources or the research of Turkish historians.

PREFACE

So, this is a history with a lot of footnotes. Some of them are quite substantial because, to preserve the narrative as a coherent whole without digressions of interest only to the specialist, I have also moved discussions of conflicting interpretations to the footnotes. To keep their extent under control as much as possible, however, I have also taken out of the main sequence and put into the first Appendix a number of the larger questions, and into separate appendices a number of the largest questions that warranted the most detailed consideration. Readers not interested in these debates may ignore those appendices. The same applies to the footnotes. As someone who wasted hours turning back and forth between the text of Barker and his end-notes, I make no apology for *foot*notes; when I was in my early teens and first encountered books with footnotes, often full of obscure abbreviations whose meaning totally escaped me at that time, I had no trouble just ignoring them, and the reader who does not care about the sources and the points in dispute may do likewise – but for the reader who does care, all except disputes shifted to the appendices are there exactly where they are needed instead of hidden away as end-notes. Anything, of course, is better than the absurdities of embedded citation, a system developed (I suspect) in the hope of so filling up sociological texts with interpolations that the vacuousness of the content and the incoherence of the argument are concealed from the reader.

Even with the full documentation, however, this remains a cautious history – if anyone were to analyse my word usage, I suspect that they would find the most commonly-used words are 'probably' and 'apparently', with phrases such as 'it seems' and 'I suspect' running a close second, for the sources often do not warrant greater certainty.

To support the aim of a documented study, and allow readers to make up their own minds, I have also provided translations of a number of the sources in the final appendices. Most of these are from the 'German' point of view, i.e. from the Imperialists or their German-speaking allies (although two of the most important were written in French); as already noted, my own lack of Polish has prevented me from using Polish-language sources and the only Polish source I have presented is the extract from the letters of Sobieski to his wife – taken from the well-known French translation of 1827. There is no reproduction of the Ottoman sources, available in modern German translation by Kreutel and Teply in *Kara Mustafa vor Wien*; the footnotes will indicate how important these sources are, but the German translation is still in copyright and the publisher did not respond to a request for permission to translate an extract. Despite these gaps, I hope the sources provided will enable the reader to make up their own minds about the many uncertainties in the course of the battle. All translations, whether in the text or the appendices, are my own unless specified.

It will quickly become apparent to the reader that I do not share the current fashion in the English-speaking world for ignoring the vicious nature of the Ottoman Empire, for trying to 'rehabilitate' it as a normal 'state' excluded from the community of nations only by the prejudices of the Christian world, for arguing that any attempt by historians to portray its true nature stems from the same prejudice. This is nonsense. The Ottoman Empire was from its start a robber state – today, we would call it a terrorist state – and no matter how much it tried to justify its actions with religion or to create the image of a normal state by using the proceeds of its robbery to fund art or literature or architecture, it never became anything else; the naked corruption and brutal exploitation of its period of decline were not aberrations but an integral part of its nature, qualities that had been there from the start, just better hidden from the view of more distant observers such as the English. Art or literature or architecture can never be set in the scales against the atrocities that the Ottomans committed throughout their history; but only by systematically ignoring events, events such as we will see in this book, can historians pretend that those atrocities never took place. The scope of this book does not include the worst Ottoman actions such as the cold-blooded bureaucratically-managed slaughter of the prisoners after the Battle of Párkány during the Köprülüs' War in 1663, but we will see the deliberate wide-ranging destruction of civilian property and enslaving of the population – in itself self-defeating, as this hampered the Ottoman army's ability to keep itself supplied during its siege of Vienna – as well as the casual killing of individual prisoners and the systematic slaughter of thousands of prisoners and slaves before the start of the battle.

A few notes about name conventions are necessary in a work that deals with so many nationalities. For personal names, I follow the general rule that monarchs are known by the English form of their name where one exists, unless there is strong reason to do otherwise (as with King John of Poland, whom, along with most historians, I usually call by his pre-election surname, 'Sobieski'), and the same applies to those referred to by a geographical name such as 'Lorraine'; non-royal rulers down to the level of Electors are treated likewise; otherwise, I use the accepted modern spelling of a person's name by their own compatriots – Polish spelling for Poles, German spelling for Germans and Austrians, and so on. Ottoman names are rendered in their modern Turkish form as used by English-speaking Ottomanists.

Matters become a little trickier when it comes to place names. Again, the easy part is when there is an established English name for a country, region or other locality: I always use that – Vienna not 'Wien', Warsaw not 'Warszawa', Cracow not Kraków, Buda not German 'Ofen' or Turkish 'Budin', and so on. A little inconsistency is possible: the city of 'Wien' is established in English as Vienna but the River 'Wien' is not and so remains the 'Wien'. However, I use the English word for any geographical formation, such as 'river', where this is separated from the name, unless there are good reasons not to (such as in the names of the hills of the Wienerwald, where to use Pfaffen Hill but Schafberg would be silly). Beyond this, I depart from the practice normally preferred these days: I do not use the modern name of towns indiscriminately, without regard to contemporary usage, a practice which often introduces profoundly unhistorical names into a period and effectively denies the changes that have occurred over the centuries (which, I sometimes suspect, is the whole point for some historians who prefer not to see change in history but wish it remained static and decently sociological); overall, I opt for the name used by 'those who lived there then', which reflects the seventeenth-century reality of ethnically diverse regions such as Upper Hungary with its Hungarian landlords, German townspeople, and Slovak rural population, and reminds us also of how much things may change in the world. Thus, I render the chief city of Royal Hungary as Pressburg (because the people who lived there spoke German), not Pozsony (its Hungarian name), and certainly not the much later Slovak invention Bratislava. Likewise, the chief city of what was then south-eastern Poland is spelt Lwów, not Lviv (its modern Ukrainian form) or L'vov (the Russian form that was used by historians who insisted on using the 'latest name' until the breakup of the Soviet Union complicated matters further and destroyed the foundations of the argument in favour of the 'latest form' by proving that this itself is mutable). The only exceptions to this rule are the towns of Turkish Hungary: to give these their Turkish names would be to validate the Ottoman conquest, which to me is inappropriate, and I prefer the Hungarian or German name. Also, the capital of the Ottoman Empire is Constantinople; the Ottomans themselves did not call it 'Istanbul' officially but 'Kostantiniyye' (merely a Turcised form of Constantinople), to use which would be absurd, and the Anglicised Greek name always acts as a reminder that the Ottomans held their capital by brutal conquest from its original inhabitants. When it comes to mere differences of spelling in what is clearly the same name, however, such as with the shift in German spelling between the seventeenth century and today that gives us Kahlenberg instead of Calenberg, Klosterneuburg instead of Closter Neuburg, I generally prefer the modern form; with these, there is no compelling reason to avoid the spelling that the reader will find on modern maps. Finally: I prefer 'Roumania(ns)', because the 'Romania' form is part of a historical/political claim that I do not accept.

I am less consistent when it comes to the spelling of the names of institutions and ranks. Here, there are no modern 'maps' for comparison, and it seems worth preserving older forms as a reminder that even spellings may change; thus, General der Cavalerie, not the modern General der Kavallerie. I also prefer to use the vernacular form rather than translating such titles. When dealing with the European states, there is no absolute consistency in the practice of historians in this area anyway, and, while I generally prefer not to burden the reader with terms in languages with which they may not be familiar (which is why I translate all quotations), there is often little to be gained by translating the names of institutions, at least those in reasonably-familiar German – the 'Court War Council' or the antiquated 'Aulic War Council' makes little more sense than the 'Hofkriegsrat'. However, I follow the practice of most western historians, and even that of Hungarian historians writing in English, of translating Hungarian offices and institutions into English ('Prince' of Transylvania not *fejedelem*, 'Palatine' not *nádor*); the same applies to Polish cases ('Crown Grand Hetman', not *Hetman Wielki Koronny*). While this practice is not remotely logical, it is widespread. However, when dealing with the Ottomans, there is no real option to use an English form (even if a usable translation exists, which is often not the case): experts almost invariably use the vernacular (except, curiously, when referring to the Master of Ceremonies), and anyone wanting to go from my book to works on the Ottoman Empire to know more about an office or a title will have to know its Turkish form; the one exception is the book of Kreutel & Teply, which translated offices and troop types into German – a practice which proves the validity of the general practice, for it is impossible to determine exactly what they mean by vague references to 'household troops' and the like. Overall, I hope that the reader who wishes to explore further can proceed from my book to the work of the best experts with the least confusion.

Foreign words are normally *italicised*, following accepted conventions (which are not entirely consistent); the names of corporate bodies, formal ranks and personal titles are usually not, nor are terms that have been accepted in English (thus, '*cebeci*' but 'Janissaries') or are in reality English-origin ('*timar*' but 'timariot'), but where appropriate I follow practices in expert works, as in italicising the Ottoman position of *beylerbeyi*.

Finally, I am glad of the opportunity to thank several people. I am grateful to Michał Paradowski on several fronts: for catching numerous mistakes on the Polish side, as well as adding extra information at several points, and for his contribution of illustrations. I am also very appreciative of the fine colour illustrations of Sergiy Shamenkov, and George Anderson for the maps of a very complicated action.

Pronunciation note

In a work of this kind, full of names and technical terms in many languages, it is necessary to offer at least some hints of the correct pronunciations involved, especially given increasing ignorance of even the few regular rules of English pronunciation (such as that 'kh' is not the same as 'k' but is the 'ch' sound heard in Scots 'loch'). Below is a brief selection of the main characters where different languages part company from standard English; a few cases where the language's pronunciation follows complex rules or needs further elucidation are given at specific points in the 'Dramatis personae' or Glossary. Characters where the English pronunciation will suffice, as with Polish 'ń' (where the correct Polish pronunciation would require a great deal of explanation), are omitted; for the same reason, a few other characters are given 'approximate' equivalents. Characters not listed here may be pronounced as in standard English.

pronounce this letter/combination	like this English letter/combination

German

c	normally k, as in kiss; sometimes ts (see 'z')
ch	kh (or 'ch' in Scots 'loch'), but some variations
g	g, as in get (some variations)
j	y, as in yellow
sch	sh, as in shut
w	v, as in vet
z	ts, as in gets

Hungarian

c	ts, as in gets
ö	like French 'eu'
s	sh, as in shut
sz	s, as in sit

NO MORE TIME TO LOSE

Polish

ą	like French 'en'
c	ts, as in gets
ch	kh
cz	ch, as in church
drz	d + rz (see rz)
j	y, as in yellow
ł	w, as in wet
ó	u, as in put
prz	psh, as in 'co**p-sh**op'
rz	zh (s, as in measure)
ś	sh, as in shut (very approximate!)
sz	sh, as in shut
szcz	sh-ch, as in 'ca**sh ch**eques'
w	v, as in vet
ż	zh (s, as in measure)
ź	zh (s, as in measure)

Turkish

c	j, as in jet
ç	ch, as in church
ğ	y, as in day (officially: lengthens previous vowel)
ö	like French 'eu'
ş	sh, as in shut
ü	u, as in jukebox

Abbreviations

BB	*beylerbeyi* (see Glossary)
bde	brigade
BG	Brigadier-General
bn(s)	battalion(s)
bn/g	battalion guns
CavR	Cavalry Regiment
CFH	Crown Field Hetman (see Glossary under Hetman)
CG…	Crown Grand… (Polish offices; see Glossary under Crown)
CGH	Crown Grand Hetman (see Glossary under Hetman)
Col.	Colonel
coys.	companies
CR	Cuirassier Regiment
CrR	Croatian Regiment (unarmoured regiment of Croatian origin, probably hussar style)
DR	Dragoon Regiment
FM	Feld-Marschall (Field Marshal)
FML	Feld-Marschall-Lieutenant (= Lieutenant-General; on 'Lieutenant', see Glossary)
FZM	Feldzeugmeister (= General; see Glossary)
GdC	General der Cavalerie (General of Cavalry), equal in rank to FZM
GFKC	General-Feld-Kriegs-Commissar
G-FML	General-Feldmarschall-Lieutenant (highest Bavarian rank in 1683)
G-L	General-Lieutenant (Imperialist Commander-in-Chief; see Glossary)
GWM	Generalwachtmeister (Major-General; see Glossary)
IR	Infantry Regiment
lt.col.	lieutenant colonel
P.	Pasha (see Glossary)
s-b	sancak-bey (see Glossary)
sqn(s) or sq.	squadron(s)

Timeline

(References in bold relate to brief further information in the Dramatis Personae or Glossary.)

1664 End of the previous Ottoman war, the Köprülüs' War; Hungarian dissatisfaction with the peace treaty, and selfish ambitions of magnates, led to a 'Magnate Conspiracy' against Emperor-King Leopold down to 1670.

1670 Outbreak and immediate failure of magnate revolt, with some rebels fleeing to Transylvania; but the Imperialist government blamed Hungarian Protestants for the revolt and stepped up the existing persecution of them.

1672 Rebels launched attack from Transylvania into Upper Hungary; start of the Kurucok Rebellion

1680 Imre Thököly became full commander of *kurucok* (still mainly based in Transylvania), with victories in the field but never making permanent gains.

1681 Hungarian Diet of Ödenburg: most Hungarians reconciled with Vienna, but Thököly and most *kurucok* refused. Habsburg Monarchy and the Reich faced increasing pressure from France (illegal expansion, attacks on Luxemburg etc.)

1682 February, long-delayed departure of Imperialist embassy to Constantinople under Alberto Caprara, hoping to avert war by renewing the 1664 treaty.

May, Thököly submitted to the Ottoman Empire via the *beylerbeyi* at Buda

July, Thököly started attack on Kaschau, centre of Upper Hungary; from August

6 August, Ottoman government decided on war with the Imperialists, and committed official forces to support Thököly militarily; *start of the War of the Holy League* (presence in Ottoman Empire of the embassy under Alberto Caprara made no difference to the state of war).

August–September, Thököly took Kaschau and made it capital of a state in Upper Hungary, then helped the Ottoman take the royal fort at Fülek (Slovak Fil'akovo); Thököly invested by Ottomans at Buda at vassal 'Prince of Hungary' (although continuing to negotiate with Vienna)

October–November, further *kurucok* military operations west from Upper Hungary, but no permanent gains; in the west, increasing pressure from France. Imperialists 'mobilising', though serious organisation of new regiments did not start until December.

1683 26 January, Imperialist-Bavarian alliance (directed as much against France as the Ottoman Empire)

31 March (nominal date), Imperialist-Polish offensive-defensive alliance against the Ottoman Empire

31 March, Ottoman main army started march from Adrianople for Hungary (dragging Imperialist ambassadors with it)

3 May, Ottoman army at Belgrade, and 13 May, Sultan appointed Kara Mustafa as supreme commander, with orders to take Raab and Komorn fortresses; Benaglia counted the Ottoman army at this point.

6 May, Imperialist army reviewed at Kittsee (near the Danube east of Vienna), and 9 May decided to try a limited advance into Turkish Hungary.

21 May, Ottoman army started march from Belgrade

2 June, bulk of Ottoman army arrived Esseg

end May, Imperialists advanced to besiege Neuhäusel, invested it 6 June but, on news of advance of the Ottoman army, abandoned it the next day and shifted south of the Danube to defend the line of the River Raab.

10 June, Thököly joined Ottomans at Esseg; much discussion re. plans (is often believed, wrongly, that the decision to attack Vienna was made here)

13 June, Kara Mustafa personally crossed from Esseg to Darda; from there on 14th and 15th, he and Thököly issued manifestoes calling on all Hungarians to submit (often mistaken as declarations of war).

15 June, Ottoman army crossed to Darda, and 16th, resumed march through Hungary, while Thököly left for Upper Hungary

27 June, major Ottoman strategy discussions at Székesfehérvár (German Stuhlweissenburg), often identified as the point when the decision was made to attack Vienna

1 July, Ottoman army arrived at River Raab and settled down against the fortress of Raab; but upstream, to 2 July, Hungarians guarding fords allowed Ottoman and Tatar detachments over the river; Lorraine put reinforcements into Raab and started to retreat

4 July, Ottoman army started interrogating prisoner Martelli about the situation towards Vienna, and on 6th, under strong pressure from Kara Mustafa, other commanders agreed to advance

7 July, Ottoman main army crossed the River Raab, leaving Koca Ibrahim to contain Raab fortress. Emperor Leopold and court left Vienna.

7–8 July, Ottoman advance forces broke through the line of the River Leitha and badly mauled the Imperialist 'rear-guard' (a large cavalry force) at Petronell, seriously damaging Imperialist morale, though the Ottomans were in the end driven off and Lorraine continued his retreat to Vienna.

8 July, government arrangements for Vienna during the expected siege were announced (under Starhemberg and Kapliř)

8–11 July, retreating Imperialist infantry reached Vienna; almost all were added to the garrison, while cavalry moved to the nearby Danube islands

13 July, burning of the suburbs of Vienna (to deprive besiegers of potential cover)

14 July, Ottoman army started arriving before Vienna, and opened trenches; start of the siege of Vienna

16 July, Lorraine and the Imperialist cavalry retreated from the islands to the north bank of the Danube.

Dramatis personae

Note on Ottoman names: with a few exceptions, Ottoman officials at this time had no surnames, just a given name and one or more epithets, which might be written in any order; in alphabetical lists they should be entered under their given name, and most normally are, but, for reasons unknown, expert works such as the *Encyclopaedia of Islam* instead enter *some* leading figures such as Kara Mustafa (Mustafa the Black) under the epithet, so I have chosen to enter here all Ottoman names under the first element of the generally-recognised form of writing the name as used in the text of this book.

Apafi, Michael (Mihály) (1632–1690)

Elected Prince of Transylvania September 1661 but uncontested ruler only from January 1662. In the late 1650s, Transylvania (see Glossary) had been shockingly devastated by the Ottomans for daring to seek independence, between 5 and 10% of its population being slaughtered or enslaved, and the nobility of the principality had been forced to elect as Prince a minor noble, Apafi, who lacked the private resources to maintain the power of the state, ensuring that Transylvania was henceforth weak and subservient to the Ottoman Empire. Although he did try to preserve the authority of the Prince against the power of Transylvania's magnates, Apafi remained an ineffective ruler, veering towards alcoholism as the nightmare of his position, trapped between the Ottomans, his recalcitrant great nobles, the Hungarian rebels and the Habsburg kings of Hungary, bore down on him. (As a ruler, he would normally be referred to in English works by his forename, anglicised, i.e. Prince Michael; but the princes of Transylvania are conventionally referred to by their surnames, except for the few who established short-lived dynasties.)

Baden, Hermann of (1628–1691)

Senior Habsburg officer, and President of the Hofkriegsrat. A junior member of the family that ruled Baden, but not a ruling Markgraf (Margrave); uncle of Louis of Baden. Originally intended for the Church, he had espoused a military career, and served with some distinction in the Köprülüs' War and the Dutch War, as well as acquiring political and diplomatic experience. In

1680, on the death of the great Montecuccoli, the leading military figure of the Imperialist military establishment was Lorraine, but some members of court opposed having another foreigner as supreme head of the Emperor's forces, and Lorraine had absolutely no administrative experience while Hermann had commanded several years of winter quarters, so Lorraine got only the post of General-Lieutenant and Hermann, despite his preference for field service (where he had some ability, and was not devoid of energy or original ideas), was appointed President of the Hofkriegsrat; when Lorraine commented publicly and unjustly on his unfitness for the post, they became enemies. He was hampered in organising logistical support for the army by financial difficulties; he also created problems in his efforts at advising the Emperor on policy, for he had long supported concentrating all the Empire's efforts against France and, unlike Lorraine, was not persuaded of the need to concentrate on defence against the Ottomans in Hungary until it was too late. An inveterate court schemer, he often undermined Lorraine's authority with his intrigues, though this was probably unintentional, and the hostility between the two men reached dangerous levels only in the years *after* 1683.

Baden, Louis (William) of (1655–1707)

Junior Habsburg general at this time. Nephew of Hermann of Baden, born in Paris the son of the Markgraf (Margrave) of Baden and a French-Italian princess; ruling Markgraf since 1677. Distinguished as a colonel in the Dutch War, and afterwards, as Markgraf he worked hard to oppose French peace-time expansion. Although his regiment was an infantry unit, he was himself a cavalry officer, already known for his daring, but also capable of political scheming, like his uncle. He later rose to lead the Imperialist army in Hungary with enormous distinction, but in the Nine Years' War struggled to command the Reich armies against France in the very 'political' operations in southern Germany, and had lost much of his ability by the time of the War of the Spanish Succession when he was side-lined by Marlborough and Eugene. (NB: although in modern German his name is Ludwig Wilhelm, the preferred contemporary form, even for Germans, was Louis, as in his nick-name, the 'Türken-Louis'; he was effectively bilingual in French and German, and possibly even thought in French, not German.)

Benaglia, Giovanni

In 1682, in a last-ditch attempt to avert war with the Ottomans, the Imperialists had sent an embassy to Constantinople under Alberto Caprara (a relative of General Aenio Caprara). His secretary was Giovanni Benaglia, who later wrote an account of the embassy. When war broke out, the Ottomans as usual detained the ambassador as a well-treated prisoner, and Benaglia witnessed and described the Ottoman army as it assembled at Belgrade in May 1683, creating one of our most important sources for the real organisation in the field of an Ottoman army of this period (see Bibliography).

Cantemir, Demetrius (1673–1723)

Demetrius (in Roumanian, Dimitrie) Cantemir was a member of a Moldavian princely family and himself twice later very briefly Prince of Moldavia, known primarily for a famous history of the Ottoman Empire, written mostly in exile in Russia during the 1710s; he had an insider's knowledge of the Ottoman system generally, but was certainly not an eyewitness of the events of 1683. His account of the Ottoman discussions preceding the battle is reproduced as part of Appendix III. (As an occasional ruler, technically he should be referred-to by his forename, but he is almost always cited by his surname.)

Duke see Lorraine

Emperor   see Leopold I

Heissler, Donatus Johann (ca. 1640s –1696)

Imperialist cavalry officer of uncertain origin (he claimed noble descent but may have been lying), a rising star in the Imperialist army through his huge energy and imagination as a cavalry leader. He had only acquired a regiment of dragoons and become Colonel-*Inhaber* in early August 1683.

Jabłonowski, Stanisław Jan (1634–1702)

Polish general, Crown Grand Hetman since earlier in the year. Like most Polish senior officers, a very rich and powerful noble (magnate) in his own right, he had originally been a supporter of Sobieski, under whom he had served extensively in the 1670s against the Turks; but, now that he had reached the highest offices possible, he was at this time in the process of turning against the King. However, in 1683 he served competently and diligently, recognising like all Poles the danger to his home should the Ottomans conquer Austria and the rest of Hungary.

John George III (1647–1691)

Elector of Saxony (reigned from 1680). Gained extensive military experience in the Dutch War, sometimes serving alongside Lorraine, and when after the war he succeeded his father as Elector, he founded the Saxon standing army. Head of the only Protestant contingent participating in the relief of Vienna.

Kapliř, Kaspar Zdenko (1611–1686)

Veteran Imperialist official, descended from high but badly dented Bohemian (Czech) nobility. In 1681, he was appointed Vice-President of the Hofkriegsrat (of which he had been a member since 1661), to off-set the inexperience on the board of Hermann of Baden as President; and in 1683 he was appointed head of the administration left inside Vienna when it was besieged – there have been attempts to suggest that he was in real command of the military defence, over Starhemberg, but this is not taken seriously by most historians. (Pronounced: Kaplierzh – the r-hacek is the same letter that causes the composer Dvořak to be pronounced 'Dvorzhak'.)

Kara Mehmed (d. 1684)

'Black' or 'Dark' Mehmed; Ottoman official and commander. His exact origins are unknown but there are indications he was one of the new type of Ottoman officers who were born Muslims instead of conscripted Christians, and in his case, probably from a high-status family. He was considered extremely arrogant even by Ottoman standards. He had been appointed in 1665, probably direct from training in the Palace, to head the Ottoman embassy to Vienna to bring presents promised in the Treaty of Vasvár of 1664, and subsequently held various administrative posts before his appointment as *beylerbeyi* of Diyarbekir (Mesopotamia) in 1681. See Kara Mustafa entry below on the significance of the epithet in his name.

Kara Mustafa. Pieter Stevens, 1689 (Rijksmuseum, Amsterdam)

Kara Mustafa (1635?–1683)

Kara Mustafa Merzifonlu, = 'Black' or 'Dark' Mustafa of Merzifon; Ottoman Grand Vizier (office from 1676). His origins are obscure but he was probably of Turkish Muslim descent, one of the new breed of Ottoman officials replacing the former dominance of conscripted Christians in the Ottoman elite, such as his patron Mehmed Köprülü (who was an Albanian); his epithet 'Kara' originally referred to the swarthiness of his complexion in comparison with the skin colour of the Europeans and Caucasians previously dominant in the Ottoman administration – though western obervers, appalled at his corruption and brutality, tended to assume that 'Kara' was a reference to the blackness of his morals. He had entered as a boy the household of Mehmed Köprülü when the man was a junior *beylerbeyi*, was educated alongside his son Ahmed, and rose along with the Köprülü family, holding increasingly important offices once Köprülü senior became Grand Vizier in 1656 and securing his position when he married a Köprülü daughter. Mustafa continued to rise when Ahmed Köprülü succeeded his father as Grand Vizier in 1660 (the first time the office had passed from father to son). After further administrative and military experience, including the siege of Candia and the Sobieski Wars (during which he massacred the inhabitants of the Ukrainian town of Human in 1674), on the death of Köprülü junior in 1676 he succeeded to the supreme office – given his marriage connection to the Köprülü family, he was seen as the next eligible member of the dynasty, and remained part of the extensive connections network known as the 'Köprülü household' (hence his continued use of the Köprülü Albanian guards). His first years in office were occupied with the war against Russia, fought in the Ukraine, where he wasted huge resources trying to take the comparatively unimportant town of Czehryń, finally gaining a Pyrrhic victory there in 1678. Like the two Köprülüs, he held his position secure only as long as he kept the greedy Sultan Mehmed IV satisfied, which was why he put so much effort into schemes to extort money from every possible source native and foreign, and brought intense loathing onto himself for such tricks as seizing the document containing the English trade treaty with the Ottoman Empire and forcing the English ambassador to buy it back. Despite these reasons for his conduct, he was anyway naturally domineering and tyrannical, and was widely unpopular both inside and outside the Ottoman Empire, but also a skilled politician with plenty of supporters; he would probably have held his position for many years more if it were not for the setbacks of the 1683 campaign.

Kątski, Marcin Kazimierz (1636–1710)

Polish artillery expert and infantry general. A noble of wealth but not one of the great magnates of the realm, he had dedicated himself to a military career in the artillery, unusual for Polish nobility who preferred to be cavalry commanders; the specialisation brought him recognition he might not have achieved otherwise. He had trained for a time in France, and on return home had aligned himself with Sobieski and been his artillery commander throughout the campaigns of the 1670s, including at the great victory of Chocim in 1673. (The surname is occasionally encountered in western publications in the corrupt anglicised spelling 'Konski', which approximates the correct Polish pronunciation of 'Kątski'.)

King see Sobieski

Koca Ibrahim (d. 1683)

Full name, Koca Ibrahim Arnaut Uzun Pasha (the venerable Ibrahim, the Albanian, the tall, the lord). First rose to prominence in the 1650s as a follower of Köprülü senior, who like him was an Albanian – during the era when conscripted Christian converts dominated the *kapi kulu* (see Glossary under this term), senior officials often selected their followers from other converts of the same ethnic origin, despite the supposed 'ethnic blindness' of the Ottoman system. His date of birth is uncertain, but he was considered very old and wise in 1683; he was reputed to be in his eighties then, and although this is unlikely it is not impossible (his former patron Köprülü senior was reputed to have been over 70 when appointed Grand Vizier). Ibrahim had served in the siege of Candia in the late 1660s under Köprülü junior, and had administered several major provinces before being sent to govern Hungary as *beylerbeyi* of Buda on several occasions in the 1670s; he had been there continuously since 1677 – it was very rare for any *beylerbeyi* to hold the same province for so long. He was held in high esteem throughout the Ottoman Empire, but Kara Mustafa disliked him, mostly because he was very experienced about conditions in the region and not afraid to show it – and Kara Mustafa was not the man to take being lectured kindly – but also perhaps because he was born neither a Turk nor a Muslim, was the product of an Ottoman government 'clique' to which Kara Mustafa did not belong.

Le Bègue, François (1635–1699)

Lorraine's secretary, confidant, councillor, ambassador-at-large and effectively prime minister of his 'government in exile'. Creator of one of the most important sources for the campaign; see Bibliography under Stöller.

Leopold I (1640–1705)

Emperor, and ruler of the Habsburg Monarchy (ruled the Monarchy from his father's death in 1657, elected Emperor 1658). A younger son of Emperor Ferdinand III, he had originally been intended for the Church, and only became heir to the throne with the sudden death of his elder brother in 1654, so that he was largely untrained for government when he succeeded his father in 1657. Frequently slow to make decisions, he often seemed weak and indecisive; sometimes he was, but he was also hamstrung by his situation: direct ruler of a state always teetering on the brink of bankruptcy and often paralysed by the selfishness of the aristocracies of his dominions, and elected overlord of an Empire of semi-sovereign princes most of whom acknowledged his leadership only when they felt like it. Leopold did not help matters with his firm adherence to the traditional Habsburg alignment with Catholicism; although compared with some earlier Habsburgs he was mild enough, he remained deeply anti-Protestant, weakening his already fragile position in Hungary (which was the only one of his dominions still with a Protestant majority) by persecutions and repeated failure to respect the laws enjoining toleration; the best that he could be said about him was that he was at least a sincere Christian, unlike the hypocritical Louis XIV. The weakness of his position as Emperor made it essential for him to preserve the ceremonial precedence of the rank which assured it at least some real influence within the Empire and amongst the crowned heads of Europe. As he later presided over the dynasty's stunning successes in the War of the Holy League and slowly improving position against France, while avoiding alienating most princes of the Empire (in which his avoidance of speedy decisions was often an asset), he helped recover some of the prestige that the Emperor's office had lost in the Thirty Years War.

Lorraine, Charles V, Duke of (1643–1690)

He had succeeded his uncle Charles IV as duke in 1675, but down to 1683 had never reigned over the land (despite all his efforts, he never would). The Duchy of Lorraine, French-speaking but always a part of the Empire, was already in a dangerous situation athwart the lines of French expansion, but Charles IV had made its position even worse through his staggering political ineptitude, and the duchy had been under illegal French military occupation since 1670. After a youth filled with perils created by his family's machinations, Charles junior had gone to Vienna, where he was already on good personal terms with Emperor Leopold, and entered Imperialist service for good in 1664, when he became Colonel-*Inhaber* of a cuirassier regiment, serving with distinction that year at the defence of Serinvár and especially the Battle of St Gothard. He twice stood unsuccessfully as a candidate for the Polish throne, in 1668–1669 and 1674 (on the latter occasion, as a rival to Sobieski). In 1670 he served in Hungary against the rebels, and from 1672 fought with increasing distinction along the Rhine in the Dutch War against Louis XIV, initially under Montecuccoli and later effectively as commander-in-chief when the great Italian warlord retired from field service at the end of 1675. Despite his strenuous efforts, he was never able during the war to liberate Lorraine from its French occupation, nor to get its restoration included in the peace settlement of 1678–1679; and technically, although his Lorrainer regiments were either disbanded or incorporated into the Imperialist standing army, he remained personally as Duke of Lorraine at war with France. He married in 1678 the Archduchess Eleonora Maria, a half-sister of Emperor Leopold (and widow of his first rival for the throne of Poland, Michael Wiśniowiecki), and was made *Statthalter* (Viceroy) of Tyrol. When Montecuccoli died in 1680, Lorraine was appointed to his post

Charles V, Duke of Lorraine. Pieter Stevens, 1689 (Rijksmuseum, Amsterdam)

of General Lieutenant (see Glossary), but did not get the administrative post of President of the Hofkriegsrat that Montecuccoli had also held – this went to his rival Hermann of Baden. In the political debates in the Habsburg Monarchy down to 1682, he had originally sided with those who preferred to give way to the Ottomans and the Hungarian rebels so that all efforts could be concentrated against France, but during 1682 had been persuaded by the charismatic preacher d'Aviano to see the Ottomans as the greater threat – given his personal position, an astonishing example of self-sacrifice. He had been appointed in command in Hungary against the Ottomans from the start of 1683, but had been plagued by the interference of Hermann of Baden. After failing to hold the line of the River Raab against the Ottoman army at the end of June, he had retreated to Vienna and then withdrawn over the Danube with the cavalry. He was an excellent cavalry general and a competent commander-in-chief, capable of learning from his own mistakes, but hampered by a flaw common in Habsburg officers of trying to avoid responsibility whenever he felt out of his depth by relying on councils of war or calling for explicit orders from the government.

Lubomirski, Hieronim Augustyn (1647?–1706)

Polish magnate, brave and aggressive, with great military experience against the Turks in the 1670s. Early in 1683, he was permitted by Sobieski to accept a commission by Vienna to raise several regiments in Poland to form part of the Imperialist army.

Marsigli, Luigi Ferdinando (1658–1730)

Italian official and intellectual, who had served for a few years in the Venetian embassy at Constantinople, learning Turkish and everything he could find out about Ottoman culture; in 1683, he had offered his services to the Imperialist government as a volunteer and been sent to serve in Hungary, where he was promptly captured by the Tatars and spent the siege of Vienna as a slave in the Ottoman camp. He later escaped, and became one of the Imperialists' experts on Ottoman affairs, but he was a bit of a know-all, and his opinions, which especially in military matters were sometimes not firmly evidence-based, were not always as respected as he thought they should be. At the end of his life, he wrote a monumental and not completely accurate description of the Ottoman army (see Bibliography).

Marie

In full, Marie-Casimire de la Grange d'Arquien, Queen of Poland (1641–1716); French-born wife of Sobieski (q.v.) since 1665; often referred to by the Polish diminutive by which Sobieski addressed her, Marysieńka. Sobieski loved her deeply, and was often influenced by her personal agenda far more than he should have been – even for an age devoted to minute considerations of protocol, her obsession with matters of precedence was extreme, and she was driven in addition by the desire to find royal crowns for her sons.

Mavrocordato (or Maurocordato), Alexander (1641–1709)

Greek Christian intellectual and sometime Ottoman Grand Dragoman (see Glossary sub Dragoman). Born into an extremely wealthy Greek family, he had received an excellent education, including at Italian universities, and gained a reputation as a physician as well as for his writings on theology and history, until 1673 when his learning (and the fact that he was unquestionably a subject of the Sultan) led to his appointment as Grand Dragoman, since even the Ottomans, contemptuous though they were of all outsiders, had begun to recognise the need for reliable interpreters. He was in 1683 a member of Kara Mustafa's 'party', and served not only as Grand Dragoman of the state but also as the family doctor of the Grand Vizier.

Maximilian II Emanuel of Bavaria. Pieter Stevens, 1689 (Rijksmuseum, Amsterdam)

Maximilian II Emanuel (1662–1726)

Elector of Bavaria; reigned from 1679, but regency until 1680. A young but extraordinarily ambitious, egotistical and self-willed ruler, he supported the Imperialists against the Ottomans in this campaign and later ones in Hungary – unquestionably the right thing for both Bavaria and Europe, but for entirely the wrong reasons, driven as he was by the need for personal aggrandisement. He had founded the Bavarian standing army in the couple of years preceding 1683. (Note the placing of his regnal number: he was the second Maximilian to be Elector of Bavaria but not the second Maximilian Emanuel.)

Montecuccoli, Raimondo (1609–1680)

Former commander-in-chief of the Imperialist army. Italian nobleman who had risen to high positions in the Imperialist army during the Thirty Years' War and the Northern War, and commanded it against the Ottomans at St

Gothard in 1664 (the first Christian victory over the Ottomans for a long time, though its importance was overrated) and against the French for much of the Dutch War. He was both General-Lieutenant and President of the Hofkriegsrat, and as such played a major part in turning the various Habsburg forces of the mid-seventeenth century into a regular standing army.

Sieniawski, Mikołaj Hieronim (1645–1683)

Polish Crown Field Hetman since early in the year. A magnate, he had served alongside Sobieski in many of the action of the 1670s, was experienced and able, but like all too many Polish nobles had problems with the concept of obeying orders. (Pronounced: Sheniavski.)

Sobieski, John (Jan), 1629–1696)

Since 1674 John III, King of Poland (officially, he should be referred to in 1683 as 'the King' or 'King John', but he had achieved such distinction as a military commander before his election as King that many writers continue to refer to him by his surname.) He was born into a very wealthy magnate family that was distinguished on both sides for military service and defence of Poland against the Turks – his mother was a grand-daughter of the great Polish general Żółkiewski, from whom came not only the family's vast estates in the Ukraine but also a powerful anti-Ottoman tradition stemming from his death in combat at the hands of the Ottomans at the disaster of Cecora or Ţuţora in Moldavia in 1620. After initial service against the Cossack rebels in the Ukraine in the early 1650s, Sobieski behaved (as did many Poles) rather ambiguously against the Swedish invasion of Poland in 1655–1656, but then served with great distinction against the Swedes during the rest of the war to 1660. He was increasingly in love with Marie Casimire de la Grange d'Arquien (see Marie above), a French lady-in-waiting of the Queen, even after she married another noble; and it was through her influence on him that he was persuaded to align with the King, John II Casimir, in his attempts to amend Poland's disastrously anarchic noble-dominated constitution.

King Jan III Sobieski, one of the portraits depicting him in style of the Roman Emperor. Unknown Italian painter, after 1683 (National Museum, Warsaw)

The attempts were sound, and could only have benefited Poland, but were deeply unpopular with most Polish nobles, and Sobieski found himself fighting against some of the most esteemed magnates of the kingdom; his rise to high offices, including Crown Field Hetman, owed more to these political intrigues than to military distinction, and his reputation suffered even more when in 1665 he married Marie only weeks after the death of her first husband. However, in 1667 he made his name with a brilliant victory at Podhajce against a greatly superior army of invading Cossacks and Tatars, and in 1668 he became Crown Grand Hetman. In 1669 John II Casimir abdicated and a new and inept King was elected, Michael Wiśniowiecki, as the candidate of Poland's most narrow-minded nobles, the gentry; and Sobieski plunged once more into bitter and divisive intrigues which brought Poland close to civil war, though he always defended the country's eastern borders against Cossack attacks. However, in 1672, the Ottomans, aligning with the Cossacks, invaded the Ukraine in such strength that Sobieski could do nothing against their main army (which took the important fortress of Kamieniec), although he did crush the Tatar raiding parties that tried to spread out ahead of the Turks. King Michael at once concluded a humiliating peace with the Ottomans ceding most of the Polish Ukraine, which provoked a brief civil war between his gentry supporters and the magnates, before the nobles were persuaded to settle their differences to combine against the land's common foe. In the autumn of 1673 Sobieski led a new army against an Ottoman corps at Chocim in northern Moldavia and gained a complete and glittering tactical victory which cemented his military reputation and, King Michael having died the day before the battle, secured his election as King in 1674. Sobieski continued the war against the Ottomans, often with great success in battle but always unable to achieve the total strategic victory he longed for, until he was forced to make peace at Żórawno in 1676 – a treaty all Poles loathed and were determined to throw over as soon as possible. While the Ottomans turned against the Russians, Sobieski made further efforts at reforming the Polish constitution, helped rather than hindered by French support and the activities of his vindictive and petty wife whom, for all her faults, he continued to love passionately. His French alignment had always created bad relations with the Imperialists, and he had even given military support to the Hungarian rebels in the late 1670s; but from 1681, having defeated the Russians, the Turks were starting to interfere in Hungary, and if they or their puppet princeling Thököly occupied the rest of Hungary, Poland's entire southern border was at risk, so Sobieski started a rapprochement with Vienna, which in March 1683 resulted in an offensive-defensive alliance directed against the Ottoman Empire. The time for revenge was at hand, and the Poles began to mobilise in secret, intending to launch a surprise attack on the Ottomans in the Ukraine once the heat of summer was past.

Ernst Rüdiger van Starhemberg, commander of the defence of Vienna in 1683. Pieter Stevens, 1689 (Rijksmuseum, Amsterdam)

Starhemberg, Ernst Rudiger, Graf von (1638–1701)

Military commandant of Vienna during the siege. Scion of an immensely wealthy noble family of Lower Austria with close links to the court, he had served competently but with no especial distinction in the Köprülüs' War and the Dutch War; he was most famous for having been captured by deception by the rebels when the Hungarian revolt broke out in 1670. In 1680, mainly through the political position of his family, he was appointed commandant of Vienna and colonel of the Stadtguardia regiment, the city's permanent garrison and police force. When the Ottomans arrived in 1683, he turned out to be exactly the right man to defend it: no politician, utterly devoid of charm, a man who regarded 'tact' as a dirty word, he was tough, dedicated, an excellent organiser, a first-class defender of a fortress, and impervious to political influence of the city's civilian authorities who often wished to consider the possibility of surrender. That Vienna was still there to be relieved in September was due in great part to this charmless man.

Imre Thököly. Pieter Stevens, 1689 (Rijksmuseum, Amsterdam)

Thököly, Imre (1657–1705)

Hungarian noble and rebel leader (see Glossary under *kurucok*). Only a boy at the time of the Hungarian revolt of 1670, he had fled to Transylvania when government forces besieged his dying father in the family castle at Arva. In the principality, where his family had huge estates and was thus very wealthy, he grew up into a teenage monster, driven only by the need to be the alpha-male, scheming constantly against Transylvanian politicians and other refugee rebel leaders for leadership of the continuing military struggle – despite the fact that most of the *kurucok* disliked him. He gained the desired position in 1680, at only 23 years old, and achieved some military success, but rejected all Habsburg attempts at a peaceful settlement. When the Habsburgs concluded a partial reconciliation with Hungary by substantial concessions in 1681, Thököly turned to his land's brutal enemy, the

Ottoman Empire, and in 1682 submitted to the Sultan in return for a title as Prince and military support in driving the Habsburgs completely out of 'Royal Hungary', the slice of Hungary not already conquered by the Turks (see Glossary). The massive Ottoman invasion in 1683 brought all of Royal Hungary apart from the major fortresses to submit to him, but when Kara Mustafa advanced to Vienna instead of tackling the Hungarian fortresses still held by Habsburg forces, Thököly was left in a precarious position: if the Ottomans occupied Austria, his Hungarian principality would be completely cut off from the west and its life would be short – and in such circumstances, Transylvania would soon be annexed by the Ottoman Empire, depriving him of his immense personal wealth. So, after his attempt to occupy the Hungarian capital Pressburg had been defeated by Lorraine, he spent the rest of the campaign in agonised indecision, negotiating with everyone and doing nothing.

Vani (d. 1685)

In full, Mehmed Vani Efendi (Mehmed of Van, the learned master), Ottoman court preacher (imam). An influential figure at the Sultan's court and in government, he was one of the leaders of an ultra-orthodox Islamic movement in the middle of the seventeenth century, which the government found it useful to support as a means of securing its position against the forces of dissolution that had threatened the Ottoman Empire down to 1656. Vani was a powerful preacher (he is often compared by modern historians with his Christian contemporary d'Aviano), and alongside moral regeneration he argued strongly for the resumption of the path of conquest of the fifteenth-century Sultan Mehmed II, 'the Conqueror' – he had conquered Eastern Rome (Constantinople), and the cities of Vienna and Italian Rome were seen as the natural next steps; the Ottoman government was glad to go along with such ideas since they provided support for the incessant military campaigns which were the only way it saw out of its political troubles. However, recent Ottomanists strongly doubt whether religion played a significant part in Ottoman government decisions.

Waldeck, Georg Friedrich, Graf von (1620–1692)

Head of the Reich contingent, and 'elder statesman' of the Empire. Member of the ruling family of a tiny state in west-central Germany, just north of Hesse, that had been hard hit in the Thirty Years' War, he had followed his family's Dutch connections and served in the army of the Netherlands, 1641–1651, then entered the service of the Elector of Brandenburg. At this time, his attitude was very 'Protestant' and anti-Habsburg. He played an important part in the early years of the Northern War, but left Brandenburg in 1657 when the Elector's tortuous policy caused him to align with the Poles (Catholics, and allies of the Habsburgs). In the following years, while serving various rulers and administering Waldeck on behalf of an infant relative, he began to recognise that the world no longer divided so fervently on religious lines and to see that the real threat to the Empire was now the France of Louis XIV, not the weakened Habsburg tenure of the imperial crown. He served with distinction as deputy-commander of the Reich contingent at St Gothard in 1664; in this period, he became friends with Montecuccoli and Lorraine. From 1665 to 1672, he worked for the Brunswick-Lüneburg (Hanoverian) dukes, and on behalf of the Dutch Republic against the growing French threat. When France attacked the Netherlands in 1672, he joined the service of William III and worked hard in defence of the Republic throughout the Dutch War, both in the field (where he was present at all the major battles in the Spanish Netherlands) and in diplomacy; he no longer had any objections to working with an ally of the Habsburgs. After the war, when France continued its expansion against the Reich in peace-time by pseudo-legal means, he worked hard to bring the smaller princes together for joint defence against the French, and even to align them with the Habsburg Emperor, who elevated him to Reichsfürst and appointed him Reichs-Feld-Marschall; and when the Ottoman army advanced against Vienna, he recognised that it was essential to the Empire to transfer his efforts to the east for the moment. A respected commander and diplomat, he was a little hampered by his fondness for long tedious memoranda that tended to alienate rather than convince less bureaucratically-minded generals.

1

Assembly of the relief force

The last bridge burned. On 16 July 1683, as the Duke of Lorraine, exhausted after the efforts of recent days, watched from the safety of the north bank of the Danube, the remains of the bridge over the main channel of the river in front of him collapsed. On the far side, the islands near the south bank were filled with Ottoman troops, now unable to cross to pursue him – but even further behind them and some way downstream, the city of Vienna was now isolated, cut off from Lorraine and the Imperialist field army. Vienna's fortifications were too low to be visible to the Duke from this distance, but he could make out the spires of the city's many churches reaching up to the summer sky, an apparent oasis of peace amongst the columns of smoke climbing even higher into the heavens from a multitude of points all around where the city stood, as every village and unfortified town on the south bank went up in flames. The siege of Vienna had begun.

On 14 July, the big Ottoman army and its bigger crowd of hangers-on under Grand Vizier Kara Mustafa had arrived before Vienna. While almost all of the infantry from the Imperialist field army, nearly 11,000 men in all, were left in the city as garrison, the Imperialist commander, Charles Duke of Lorraine, withdrew north of the Danube with the bulk of his cavalry, 10,000 or perhaps 12,000, to block any Ottoman moves beyond the river, and to protect the routes by which relief would arrive, against Ottoman detachments, Tatar raiders or Hungarian rebels.

Meanwhile, the Tatars and other bandits in Kara Mustafa's army spread their destruction south and west of Vienna, burning and looting villages, enslaving or killing any defenceless civilians caught in the open, but ignoring the walled towns and monasteries that they lacked the means to attack. It helped Lorraine enormously that the raiders could not capture anything with walls; in particular, they could not tackle the important permanent Danube bridge upstream of Vienna, between the little towns of Krems on the north bank and Mautern on the south. Lorraine sent a few cavalry regiments to help this and other fortified towns hold out, knowing that the bridge could be important in the assembly of a relief effort, and placed in command there his artillery commander FZM Jakob (James), Graf Leslie to assemble guns as well. A regiment or two went off to various other key points as well, for like any sensible seventeenth-century general Lorraine knew that, if you held the towns, you could always recover the surrounding countryside, but if you lost the towns, you were lost for good.

Securing the advance of the relief

Lorraine meanwhile sat on the left bank of the Danube with his still-considerable corps of cavalry and protected the great open plain of the Marchfeld behind him, against both the Ottoman army south of the river around Vienna and the Hungarian rebel leader Imre Thököly with his Magyar followers and Turkish-Tatar auxiliaries, already north of the river but away to the east beyond the River March (Morava) in what is now Slovakia. So far, the Marchfeld and the rest of northern Austria, together with southern Bohemia and Moravia, were untouched by the huge devastation that the invaders had inflicted on the villages and fields south of the river; it was essential to preserve them in order to guarantee food supplies for the relief army and ensure that the Habsburg Monarchy's already shaky tax base could provide at least some revenue in the autumn and the coming year. The Imperialist cuirassiers and dragoons, soon joined by a brigade of about 1,500 cavalry recruited in Poland for Imperialist service by the Polish magnate Hieronim Lubomirski, steadily blocked any attempt by the Ottoman main army to get across the Danube: Lorraine himself with the main body in a central position some way back from the river, a few individual regiments under energetic commanders such as Colonel Heissler (one of the Imperialists' many superb cavalry officers, only formally promoted to colonel on 26 July), watching the banks and occasionally even making forays over to the south side. It helped considerably that the river for some miles to the west, upstream of Vienna, was difficult to cross anyway: the south bank was filled with the massive block of wooded hills known as the Wienerwald, in military terms appallingly difficult terrain, and substantial parts of the north bank were covered in woods and marshes; all this made any serious crossing by the Ottomans impossible. The banks did not become clear enough for establishing bridges until Tulln, where the hills and the woods gave way on both sides, and a couple of broad islands broke up the width of the stream to make bridging even easier. Here, the little walled town on the south bank hindered any Ottoman move to exploit the situation and provided the Imperialists with a potential bridgehead to guard any crossing of their own.

Battle of Pressburg

Late in July Thököly approached the Marchfeld from the east, his rebel detachments closing in on the Hungarian capital of Pressburg. If he established himself there, he would be in a very strong position: from there he could cross the River March into Austria and not only make Lorraine's position facing Vienna untenable but also ravage the Marchfeld and threaten the flanks of Polish forces coming to help. On top of this, Pressburg, although it had no permanent bridge, was a good crossing-point over the Danube for anyone who could re-establish the boat bridges there, so it would put Thököly in a position to open direct contact with his new supporters and with the Ottoman army south of the river. Reports were already coming in to the Duke's headquarters that raiding parties were crossing the March, and that the rebels had found enough boats to begin rebuilding the Danube bridge. The rebel princeling could not be allowed to hold the city. So, on 27 July, leaving FML Johann Valentin, Graf Schulz, opposite Vienna with just two weak regiments (DR late-Savoy[1] and CrR Ricchiardi), Lorraine rode rapidly off with the rest of the Imperialist cavalry and Lubomirski's Poles to oppose Thököly, through countryside already beginning to fill with the flames of villages set on fire by rebel and Ottoman parties. A detachment of 200 of Lorraine's precious infantry, men from IR Baden and perhaps IR Grana as well, escorted by 300 cuirassiers from CR Veterani, had already been sent on ahead under Major Ogilvy to reinforce the weak loyalist garrison of the castle at Pressburg; but when these tried to enter the town late on the 26th they were attacked by *kurucok* bands, the cavalry scattered, the infantry badly hit and forced back; only 120 infantry and 80 cavalry rejoined Lorraine the next day.

On 28 July, Lorraine crossed the March some way upstream from Pressburg, well away from the rebel forces there who might have attacked him mid-crossing if he had tried it any closer, and then marched back downstream in two columns towards the city. A small *kurucok* party did try to harass one of the columns as night fell, but was easily driven off by Poles from Lubomirski's corps. Thököly's men, despite his attempts to control them, had been plundering and burning the suburbs and had started on the city as well, but they could not gain control of the castle on its hill, and when he heard that Lorraine was approaching in force Thököly quickly pulled all his forces away from the city to open ground to the north-east. There (according to the story the Ottoman commanders reported later), although his *kurucok* men totalling 14,000 together with the 6,000 allied Ottoman irregulars actually outnumbered Lorraine's 10,000 men two to one, Thököly thought that Lorraine outnumbered him, and anyway felt that his undisciplined bands could not fight the Imperialist regulars, so he repeatedly urged the Ottoman commander Abaza Kör Hüseyin, *beylerbeyi* of Erlau, to retreat before Lorraine arrived, but the Ottoman officers refused to run before they had even seen the enemy.[2] Thököly, who valued his own safety, left before dawn with his artillery, personal baggage, and the few *kurucok* infantry.

Early in the morning of the 29th the Imperialists, led by FML Louis William of Baden and GWM Ernst Peter, Baron Mercy, with all the dragoons of DRs Schulz, Styrum and Herbeville, approached Pressburg from the north, on the side nearest the March through wooded hills; as darkness

---

1   Regiment of Louis Julius of Savoy, brother of the more famous Eugene; he had been mortally wounded earlier in July at Petronell, and his regiment was in the process of being taken over by Heissler.
2   Kreutel, Richard Franz (ed.), *Kara Mustafa vor Wien: 1683 aus der Sicht türkischer Quellen*, stark vermehrte Ausgabe besorgt von Karl Teply (Graz: Styria Verlag, 1982), pp.225–226; cited hereafter as 'Kreutel & Teply'. The Turkish commander's name meant Hüseyin, the Abkhazian, the blind – though Kör could mean one-eyed, or even 'blind' in the sense of careless; see the note in chapter 5 below on Abkhazians.

NO MORE TIME TO LOSE

Fighting between Turkish besiegers and the Imperial soldiers on a bridge at a city gate of Vienna. Romeyn de Hooghe, 1684 (Rijksmuseum, Amsterdam)

faded into the grey of first light it became clear that the enemy camps were too far away to interfere with the debouchment from the defiles, so Baden and the dragoons were sent out to take control of Pressburg and then cover the deployment of the main force. Baden was a capable and energetic young officer: in very short order, he brow-beat the burghers of the city into opening a gate to him, occupied the town, threw reinforcements into the castle, and burnt the bridging materials, before taking the dragoons back out to form a screen north of the town facing the now-advancing enemy cavalry line. Behind him, first Lubomirski's Poles and then the Imperialists under GdC Aenio Silvio Caprara emerged from the defiles and formed up across the plain beyond Pressburg, facing roughly east, initially between the city and the hills, then as the second line formed up moving forward so that they had the Danube on their right, the hills on their left. Some of Lubomirski's Poles were on the right wing, joined by some or all of the dragoons once the deployment was complete and the covering line no longer needed; German cuirassiers formed the centre and left wing; and more Poles may have ended the line on the far left.[3] The whole battle-line was no more than a mile long, and formed in at least two lines, perhaps as many as four; there are hints (it cannot be put any more strongly) that Lorraine may have started experimenting with forming continuous lines, with none of the gaps between squadrons common in western tactics of the time that had allowed the Tatars to break up his formation at Petronell a few weeks earlier, but if so the 'lines'

---

3 *Das Kriegsjahr 1683: nach Akten und andere authentische Quellen dargestellt in der Abtheilung für Kriegsgeschichte des k.k. Kriegs-Archives* (Mittheilungen des k.k. Kriegs-Archivs) (Vienna: Generalstab, 1883), pp.88–89. It is not clear from this work exactly where the regiments were placed, but the 'group' of CRs Caprara, Rabatta, Carafa, Palffy and Gondola probably formed the centre, while Taafe, Mercy, Halleweil, Montecuccoli, Veterani and Götz were on the left.

referred to by his secretary must have been 'ranks', so that his whole army was no more than four deep.[4]

Nevertheless, the serried ranks of armoured men and heavy horseflesh were an impressive sight. Advanced parties of the enemy line had been skirmishing half-heartedly with Baden's covering line, but when Lorraine gave the order to advance and the whole mass started forward, the dragoons of the covering line merging into the formations at either end as they passed, the Hungarians and Turks lost what little enthusiasm they had for the fight and began to withdraw, initially in good order, towards the wood around which their overnight camp still stood. Lorraine followed slowly and cautiously; intelligence gleaned from interrogating the prisoners taken so far (probably, some of the *kurucok* captured within Pressburg by Baden) consistently if falsely put the enemy strength at 30,000 or more, perhaps as high as 40,000, and Lorraine, suspecting the possibility that his opponent had large forces out of sight, refused to get drawn into a rash pursuit, and just kept advancing steadily, never losing formation. Thököly's forces halted near their camp and for a moment gave the impression they would fight, but as the Christians drew near, Lorraine and his staff could make out clouds of dust moving to the rear at both ends of their line – and then almost the whole line turned again and began trotting away. Lorraine immediately ordered the Poles at either end of his main line, lighter and faster than his lumbering cuirassiers, to charge: on the side nearest the Danube, Lubomirski made a brief harangue to his men, had them raise a cheer, threw his hat in the air, and led them forward; on the Imperialist left, the rest of the Poles, supported by dragoons and even two cuirassier regiments, Pálffy and Veterani, threw themselves forward with equal enthusiasm. The Hungarian rebel forces broke instantly. Within minutes, they were scattered across the landscape fleeing for their lives, abandoning their camp and all their equipment that Thököly had not removed already, dragging most of the Ottoman irregulars with them – some of the Ottomans may have held together and tried to cover the rout, but this is disputed.

Armoured cuirassiers had no hope of keeping up with the light and fast horsemen, so Lorraine left the pursuit to the Poles, who, when they could be persuaded to stop plundering the camp, cheerfully harried the fleeing Turks and Hungarians for the rest of the long summer day, east along the flat land bordering the branch of the Danube (where they drove some of the enemy into the river to drown) or north-east into the hills, until Thököly's army, for now at least, existed no more. At least 600 Hungarian and Ottoman warriors were killed, only about 80 taken prisoner, and at least 1,200 ox-drawn wagons

---

4   Stöller, Ferdinand (ed.), 'Neue Quellen zur Geschichte des Türkenjahres 1683', *Mitteilungen des Instituts für Österreichischen Geschichtsforschung, Ergänzungs-Band* 13, Heft 1 (1933), pp.1–138, here p.85. On the difference between line and rank, see Glossary. The numbers and frontage give Lorraine an average of between five and six men per yard, which, since a heavy horseman could occupy over a yard in width, would have required large gaps between squadrons if the formation had been two to four lines *each* of two to three ranks.

were captured with large amounts of supplies. Christian casualties were so negligible that they were not reported.[5]

Lorraine could be sure that it would be many weeks before Thököly could re-assemble his army and persuade his shaken Hungarians to face the Imperialists again in open battle. Lorraine complimented his troops but refused to regard the action formally as a battle victory; however, the ludicrously easy rout of the Hungarian and Ottoman rabble not only cleared the threat to his flank and secured the Marchfeld from damaging raids for some time, it also gave his soldiers a valuable boost in confidence, as it proved to them that the Ottomans were not the terrifying enemies they had seemed in the initial clashes of the campaign.

Before Lorraine set off for Pressburg, he had been in discussion with the government at Passau about overall strategy, and the government had got the notion into its head that he should hold the entire line of the Danube at least as far as Pressburg, perhaps even further to the River Waag, as the best way of preserving the Marchfeld from destruction and the approaching relief forces from interference; there had even been talk in discussions within the Duke's headquarters of crossing the Danube at Pressburg, either now or when the reinforcements arrived, and operating against Kara Mustafa's lines of communication in the hope of forcing him to raise the siege. Lorraine felt that all of these ideas were impractical, but needed to deal with them, so, leaving a garrison in Pressburg, he initially marched back only to the crossing-point over the March, where he remained for a few days continuing the debate by letter with Passau. The Duke was right about the absurdity of the ideas involving Pressburg in the relief march but wrong in the belief he himself currently held that Vienna was about to fall any day and that it was necessary to relieve it very soon even if this meant not waiting for the Poles. The officials at Passau had a better understanding of the strength of Vienna's defences – and of the city's tough-minded commandant, Ernst Rüdiger von Starhemberg – and argued that it was possible to wait a few weeks longer until all possible forces had been assembled. Although Lorraine never stopped pressing for a relief operation as soon as possible, it seems that during early August he recognised that the siege of Vienna would run a normal course and, especially once he understood that the Poles were definitely on their way at top speed, accepted the government's position on waiting for all the contingents that were coming.

However, reports were now arriving at Lorraine's headquarters from FML Schulz that the Ottomans in the camp around Vienna were making very serious attempts to restore the Danube bridges there; they had already succeeded in crossing the smaller channels to the various islands and were working on the bridge over the main channel. On 4 August, Lorraine himself returned with four regiments to the position opposite Vienna. GWM Mercy was appointed to deal with the Ottoman bridging operation and, taking position on the riverbank with DR Heissler, CrR Ricchiardi, some

---

5 This account of the battle is based primarily on Stöller, pp.84–86, and *Das Kriegsjahr 1683*, pp.86–90. It is impossible to be absolutely certain about the details of the action because there are no contemporary maps.

infantry and a few cannons, he so peppered the Ottomans in their boats working on the bridge that they gave up the attempt completely. The Duke then rode back to the March and established his headquarters for the next couple of weeks at Angern, from where he could coördinate the efforts to block the renewed efforts by parties of Hungarian rebels and Turks to raid over the March into the Marchfeld – it was impossible to stop them all, but the Imperialist cavalry (in fact, most of the time it was Lubomirski's Poles) smashed any large party that managed to get over the March, and kept the raids and the damage to a minimum.[6] The Angern position also helped keep Pressburg's citizenry loyal, though this was hardly necessary any more: on 6 or 8 August (the exact date is variously given), the town of Tyrnau northeast of Pressburg, which had submitted without resistance to Thököly, was plundered and burnt by uncontrolled rebel bands, and no-one in Pressburg after that felt any inclination to submit to the rebel leader. From mid-August, the attempted raids declined noticeably after both Lorraine and Sobieski had sent warnings to Thököly that, if he continued them, their own forces in the east (the Imperialist garrison holding out in Szatmár, and Poles attacking over the Carpathians) would sack his personal estates.

Meanwhile, Lorraine continued strategy discussions, communicating with the Polish army that was now on its way regarding where it would join him, and with Passau about exactly which route the relief operation would take – he and the Emperor's ministers were by now in broad agreement that the army would assemble at the Krems-Mautern and Tulln crossing points and then advance over the Wienerwald, though, as we will see, some of the dafter alternatives were not finally scotched until early September.

As the final third of August began, Lorraine set off west to join the gathering relief army, and on the morning of the 24th was already off the Marchfeld at Stockerau preparing to march the final stage to the bridgehead opposite Tulln when the Ottomans tried again: Turkish forces under Abaza Kör Hüseyin already on the north bank way to the east beyond Pressburg, under repeated orders from Kara Mustafa to act, separated from the suspiciously inactive Thököly, headed north and made their way round by a circuitous route to enter the Marchfeld from the north-east; they were possibly joined by up to a thousand *kurucok* acting on their own initiative, but this is very uncertain. Lorraine, aware of their original moves, had ordered off a detachment under FML Lubomirski and GWM (János) Károly Pálffy; but before this could get far new reports arrived: the Ottomans had ridden across the plain to reach the left bank opposite Vienna, where they established a camp and were joined by some Turks and Tatars from the besieging army who managed to swim or ferry their horses across the river.

---

6   Paradowski, p.114, has details of a victory by Lubomirski's corps over Hungarian rebels in early August, although he locates this in 'Moravia' (exact location not specified), which I think must be a mistake: there were indeed *kurucok* raids into southern Moravia around this time, in both the areas east of the River March and to a lesser extent west of it around Nikolsburg (present-day Mikulov), but it is clear from Le Bègue's Journal (Stöller, pp.88–89) that the action was somewhere well to the south of Moravia, on the Marchfeld or in the hills to the north of it. Confusion may have arisen between 'Moravia' the province and the 'Morava', the Czech name of the March, which was a barrier the *kurucok* crossed.

All the villages in the vicinity were already in flames. Suddenly, Lorraine had a big enemy force in his rear, about 12,000–14,000 in total, 5,000–6,000 of them Turks and the rest Tatars or *kurucok* – all of them poor-quality irregulars but a serious threat to the entire Marchfeld and the approaching Poles if allowed to act unchallenged.[7] Leaving the baggage in Stockerau and hastily recalling Lubomirski and Pálffy, Lorraine turned back with his massed cavalry, officially 10,800 Imperialists and 2,000 Poles, to deal with them. He himself rode to the top of the hill to get a good view of what was happening all around. Some detachments were sent ahead to try to stop the Ottomans from burning any more villages and get some intelligence; these did engage some Turkish parties, presumably with success, as they brought back a few prisoners from arsonists for interrogation. From these, Lorraine was informed – completely erroneously – that they were part of an army of 25,000 Turks and Tatars that had crossed the March the previous night, and that Thököly was following them. The prisoners may actually have thought Thököly was indeed supporting them and believed what they were saying about him, but it is unlikely that Lorraine credited this nonsense, though even if he did, he did not allow it to influence his actions – indeed, if true it became even more important for him to crush this latest enemy manoeuvre before it got going. GWM Mercy was sent ahead, presumably with a brigade-strength detachment, to confirm exactly where the enemy camp was, and as soon as Mercy reported, the Duke formed for battle.

The Ottoman army during the siege of Vienna. Romeyn de Hooghe, 1684 (Rijksmuseum, Amsterdam)

---

7   Ottoman total numbers from Christian sources after the battle; numbers of the Turks suggested by the Ottoman account of Silahdar (Kreutel & Teply, 231). However, this put the *total* force at no more than 6,000; in addition to the general unreliability of this 'source' written well after the events by a non-participant, it is clear that he was trying to minimise the scale of the disaster by giving the Christians a serious numerical superiority which they did not in fact have. This is even more obvious with the patently absurd claim that the Turkish-Tatar force was attacked not only in front by Lorraine but also in the rear by 30,000 Imperialists coming up from Komorn, and that the Ottomans faced a total of 80,000.

Battle of the Bisamberg

The wide plain of the Marchfeld was ended at its south-western corner by the lonely lump of the Bisamberg, a wooded hill (more precisely, a group of hills) sitting near the Danube opposite the north tip of the Wienerwald on the far side of the river. Currently, Lorraine and his cavalry, riding along the road beside the Danube from Stockerau through Korneuburg, were west/north of it, the Ottomans around Jedlesee on the south/eastern side. No-one is entirely clear where the battle took place, as there are some indications that it was fought on the northern side, with Lorraine deploying just beyond Korneuburg, and other indications that the Imperialists passed the defile between the Bisamberg and the Danube at the village of Lang-Enzersdorf before deploying and fighting on the southern side. The events of the battle as far as we know them make sense only if, despite what many historians have reported, the action took place well away from the Danube, on the northern side of the Bisamberg; this is supported by the fact that no seventeenth-century general would have passed the defile at Lang-Enzersdorf with a formed enemy on the far side – at least not without his secretary making a big deal about the risks of such a dangerous manoeuvre – and by the fact that Lorraine's secretary also made no mention of any part of the Christian line resting on the Danube in his moderately detailed account of the battle, which we may expect him to have done if the river had been in the vicinity.[8] If this is so, the Ottomans, despite the suggestion in the unreliable Silahdar's account that they were almost caught unawares in their camp and fought only with the greatest reluctance, because they had no choice and the commander Abaza Kör Hüseyin refused to allow a retreat, must in fact have been advancing round the northern side of the Bisamberg, likewise avoiding the defile between the hill and the river, with the intention either of following Lorraine whom they believed to be at Stockerau or else of heading off northwards against the flank of the approaching Polish relief forces.

From this, it is safe to conclude that Lorraine deployed his 12,000–13,000 men due east of Korneuburg and advanced eastward from there with the Bisamberg to his right. The Christians formed two lines and a reserve. On the far right were posted Lubomirski and his Poles, who would be skirting the woods of the hill, then Caprara and Rabatta with the Imperialist right wing of the dragoons and what few little pieces of artillery Lorraine had brought with him, then the bulk of the cuirassiers, the left wing commanded by young Louis of Baden.[9] It seems that the Poles at least, and perhaps the whole line,

---

8   The account of the battle by Le Bègue in Stöller, pp.29–30. Christian accounts generally report or imply that the Ottomans were already on the march when Lorraine turned back; the Ottoman chronicle of Silahdar, which in other areas is evidently very unreliable, suggests that the Ottomans were peacefully camped opposite Vienna happily burning villages when the Imperialists turned back against them.

9   Thus in Stöller, p.29; it is likely that GdC Caprara, the senior cavalry officer present, commanded the centre and FML Rabatta the right of the cuirassiers. There is a suggestion, in Victor von Renner, *Wien im Jahre 1683: Geschichte der zweiten Belagerung der Stadt durch die Türken im Rahmen der Zeitereignisse: aus Anlass der zweiten Säcularfeier verfasst…* (Vienna: Waldheim, 1883), p.411, that Taafe was in command of the left, but he was only a GWM and FML Baden

formed with the classic pattern of intervals between squadrons that had been so pernicious at Petronell.[10] Lorraine himself, descending from the hill-top, joined the right wing just as the Ottoman forces struck.

Warned by Tatar scouts of Lorraine's approach, the Ottomans under Abaza Kör Hüseyin, *beylerbeyi* of Erlau, and Alp Giray, son of the Tatar Khan, had formed with the bulk of their forces in the plain but also extending a string of parties, as Le Bègue put it, in 'a line on the height extending towards the left, as if they planned to gain our flank.'[11] The secretary's statement was ambiguous, but from the context and the subsequent course of the battle it seems he meant the *Christian* left, that is, that the Ottomans were extending to their *right*, towards the hills that form the northern edge of the Marchfeld. From the names of officers killed in the action, we can deduce that the Ottoman force, in addition to the Tatars, included the *yerli kulu* of Abaza Kör Hüseyin and of a number of other junior governors of provinces in Turkish Hungary, plus some timariots from the same provinces, and many, perhaps all, of the *gönüllüs*.

As the two sides moved towards each other, forward parties skirmished all along the line, and then as they approached, the Ottoman main body detached two large bands: one of Turks which moved forward against the Christian right, where the Poles and dragoons were, and a second of Tatars which advanced against the left.[12] The first band, moving quite slowly and (if we read between the lines of the sources) trying to keep some kind of order instead of the usual Turkish wild charge, approached or went past the front of the Imperialist dragoons, who fired off their little cannons into the crowd ('several volleys' according to Le Bègue, which given the reload rate of seventeenth century artillery suggests the Turks were moving very slowly indeed), which briefly caused the Turks to waver in their advance, but then they picked up speed and charged 'with much pride' straight into the Poles. A couple of Polish squadrons were overthrown, and exploiting the gap created by this and from the normal intervals between squadrons, perhaps also a gap that arose between the Imperialists and the Poles, the Turks with 'surprising' vigour penetrated the entire first line and threw themselves against the second line. Even the fire of the dragoons, which wheeled round

---

    outranked him, though obviously he could have served *under* Baden. Other accounts give very different command arrangements; for example a version based supposedly on Lorraine's report, brought to the government by his Adjutant-General, put the Duke on the left – see Wilhelm von Janko, 'Zur Geschichte des Entsatzes von Wien', *(Streffleur's) Österreichisches Militärische Zeitschrift*, 24:3 (1883), pp.3–22, here p.7, and Georg Maria Jochner, *Zur Geschichte der Türkenkrieges im Jahre 1683: Teilnahme des frankischen Kreises an der Befreiung Wiens* (Bamberg: Historisches Verein, 1885), p.50.

10 Suggested by the events of the battle, and partly supported by an admittedly somewhat unreliable source, the account of the Conte di Frosasco, in Henri Marczali (ed.), 'Relation du siège de Vienne et de la campagne en Hongrie 1683 [by the Conte di Frosasco]', *Revue de Hongrie*, 3 (1909), pp.34–66, 169-198, 276-292, here p.286 (based on Frosasco's supposed discussion with Lorraine as to why he formed with no intervals at Párkány later in the year).

11 Stöller, p.30. The extension of the left may be a duplicate statement of the advance of the Tatars, q.v. below.

12 Stöller, p.30. In the same, p.95, it appears more that the Ottomans had an advanced line of 3,000–4,000 men which split into two parties.

to face them and fired off their muskets, initially could not stop them. Some even made it through as far as the reserve. They were aided by the fact that some Imperialist cavalrymen mistook them for retreating Poles and *let* them through the intervals. However, there were not enough Turks to affect the final outcome and the rest of the Ottoman army made no attempt to support them; having broken through the line, they found it closed behind them when they tried to escape, Lorraine himself led the dragoons in a charge, and 'few were saved'. Many senior Ottoman officers were killed, including the Ağa of the *Gönüllü*s, Gazi Bey.

The Tatar attack against Baden on the left wing was completely ineffective. Parties from the Tatar line were trying to extend northwards, obviously trying to find and get round the Imperialists' open flank, but as soon as any party made it past the flank, Baden sent some of his cuirassiers against it and cut it to pieces.

The whole Christian line meanwhile continued to advance, carefully and in perfect order – Le Bègue did not say so, but presumably it delayed while the right finished off the Turks who had penetrated there. As the Christian cavalry came close to the main Ottoman line, however, the Turkish and Tatar bands began to waver and break up... and suddenly there was no enemy formation any more, just Turks and Tatars scattering across the landscape, splitting into two main streams with one heading south-east towards the Danube crossing-points and the rest fleeing east across the Marchfeld towards the River March.[13] It was all so sudden that GWM Taafe got the impression the opening attacks must have been intended merely to give the rest of the force time to withdraw, though this was not the picture that Le Bègue portrayed.

Pursuit of those heading for the March was pointless; there was no way that the heavy cuirassiers could keep up with the light Turkish and Tatar horsemen, though they tried for a while. It was a different matter with the Ottomans fleeing for the Danube crossings, hoping to get back over the river the same way they had come; the most cursory glance would show that this was a potential trap. Some leading troops (the Croats and volunteers) were sent in immediate pursuit, the Poles followed these, and Lorraine set the rest of his army off in the same direction. Panicking as the pursuit drove in amongst them at the river's edge, the Turks abandoned their weapons and horses on the bank and threw themselves into the water trying to swim across, aided by the piles of the bridge that had been burnt by Lorraine at the start of the siege; the Tatars, accustomed to crossing rivers with their horses, mostly swam the animals across – Alp Giray, though wounded, escaped this way, as did a few senior Ottoman officers, including Mehmed Gürcü Moğrulzade, *beylerbeyi* of Grosswardein. Abaza Kör Hüseyin, already wounded in head and knee during the battle proper, was killed fighting at the water's edge,

---

13 *Das Kriegsjahr 1683*, p.105, without citing a source, says that the second group fled through Hagenbrunn. I have not found this in any source, but if true, it would confirm the location of the battle north of the Bisamberg – there is no way that Ottomans fleeing from a battle *south* of the hill towards the March could have passed through Hagenbrunn. Silahdar (Kreutel & Teply, p.232) was emphatic that the Tatars fled first, some time before the Turks gave way.

along with other officers such as the *sancak bey* of Szolnok and the *alay bey* (colonel of timariot cavalry) of Erlau; and in total the Ottomans lost around 1,000–1,200 men killed in action, drowned or captured – prisoners were still being rounded up the next day. Hundreds of abandoned horses, 25 banners and many drums fell to the Christians; such trophies were always useful for future public-relations exercises, proof of the victory and its scale.[14]

Lorraine camped the night of the 24th on the banks of the Danube where the action had ended. He was still nervous about the possibility of further Ottoman attempts to get over the river, so the next day he pulled his troops back only as far as Korneuburg, from where he could join the allies at Tulln soon enough but also turn back to block any more crossings if he had to. A few days later, at the end of August, as the leading units of Sobieski's army approached the area, the level of the Danube had fallen so low in the summer heat that the piles of the burnt bridge were easily accessible and the Ottomans used this favourable opportunity to try again to rebuild the bridge, but Colonel Heissler was sent forward with his dragoons, a battalion (five companies) of IR Lorraine and some cannon; he established a battery on an island in the river, and so ferociously bombarded the Ottoman workers that they withdrew and gave up the attempt for good. Just to be sure, Lorraine kept his massed cuirassiers and dragoons camped around Korneuburg for a few days more; they were still there when he left GdC Caprara in command of them when he rode off to meet Sobieski. There would be no interference as the final elements of the relief forces came together from the north and north-east.

The contingents

Imperialists

The effort to organise a relief force had begun almost at the same time as the siege. As the Ottomans had closed in on Vienna in mid-July, Emperor Leopold had fled upriver through Krems and Linz to Passau, where he and his ministers settled down out of reach of Tatar raids to coördinate the diplomatic effort of appealing to allies and the administrative work of supplying their contingents when they came. Imperialist forces originally left in southern Germany to face the threat from France were already pelting east along the dusty summer roads to Austria; the infantry mostly joined Leslie at the Krems-Mautern bridge, but some would join Lorraine, whose little army, still predominantly cavalry, would form the core of the Imperialist contribution to the relief effort. Even from the fortress of Raab in Hungary, technically under blockade by Ottoman forces, a couple of infantry regiments were called up to reinforce Lorraine. Hordes of noble volunteers were also heading across Europe to this crisis point for Christendom – even from

---

14 This account of the battle based primarily on Stöller, pp.30, 95. Taafe's account, which does not match it exactly, is in Renner, pp.411–412; see also notes above. Some Ottoman details taken from Silahdar's account (Kreutel & Teply, pp.230–233), on the unreliability of which, which see note above on Ottoman numbers.

France, whose government secretly favoured the Ottoman Empire, hereditary enemy of the Christian community – and most of these joined the Emperor's forces, though they were not always regarded as a useful reinforcement; they included several princes of the little state of Anhalt (pro-Imperialist at this time, despite its close links with pro-French Brandenburg), two from the family of the dukes of Brunswick-Lüneburg including the young man who in 1714 would become George I of Great Britain, two princes of Neuburg (a German dynasty related by marriage to the Habsburgs), two from the Saxon lands, two from Württemberg, two from Holstein, the Italian Marquis of Parella who brought 80 gentleman-volunteers equipped and maintained at his own expense, and last but not least the young man, not yet 20 years old, who would later become the most famous of them all, the half-French half-Italian Eugène François, prince of Savoy-Carignan, who as Eugene of Savoy would become the generalissimo of the Imperialists and their greatest military commander.[15]

Imperialist forces available to Lorraine (standard 'surnames' bolded for clarity):[16]

    G-L Charles V, Duke of **Lorraine**
    FM Hermann von **Baden**
    GdC Julius Franz Herzog von (or zu) **Sachsen-Lauenburg**
    GdC Aenio Silvio **Caprara**
    FZM Jakob Graf **Leslie**
    FML Rudolf, Graf von **Rabatta**
    FML L.W. von **Baden**
    FML Leopold Philipp Carl Fürst zu **Salm**
    FML Johann Heinrich, Graf **Dünewald**
    FML Hieronim Augustyn **Lubomirski**
    FML Charles Eugène, duc de **Croy**
    GWM Antonio **Carafa**
    GWM Karoly **Pálffy**
    GWM Don Francesco de **Gondola**
    GWM Francis **Taafe**, Viscount Taafe and Earl of Carlingford
    GWM Ernst Peter Baron **Mercy** (de Billets)
    GWM Comte de **Fontaine** & Eberstorff
    GWM Carlo Emilio San Martino Marchese **Parella**
    GWM [brevet] Prinz Ludwig Anton von Pfalz-**Neuburg** (serving as GWM)
    GFKC Seifried Christoph, Graf **Breuner**
    GQM von **Setlinger**

    and other staff named in Mansberg.[17]

---

15 Stöller, p.35; François Paulin Dalérac, *Les anecdotes de la Pologne, ou, Mémoires secrets du règne de Iean Sobieski III du nom* (Paris: Aubouyn & Clouzier, 1700), vol. 1, p.147. Eugene's late brother Louis Julius had already held a dragoon regiment in the Imperialist army (see first note above) – confusion between the two brothers explains why Eugene is sometimes described as holding a regiment at this time, when in fact he obtained one only in December.
16 See Appendix I, 1.1, for details of sources, and information on books about uniforms.
17 [Mansberg, Karl Wilhelm], *Der Entsatz von Wien am 12. September 1683* (Berlin: Rathenow, 1883), p.31.

NO MORE TIME TO LOSE

Imperial troops breaking through the Ottoman lines during the relief of Vienna. Romeyn de Hooghe, 1684 (Rijksmuseum, Amsterdam)

Infantry

The Imperialist army had not yet adopted the concept of permanent battalions; infantry regiments were recorded by the number of companies, and the companies of a regiment might be split up according to strategic needs; the companies present at the start of battle were grouped into battalions as required. By September, all Imperialist units were well below the official strengths noted below.

	No.coys/off'l strength
Grana	9 (1836)
(cmdr: lt.col. Heinrich von Samoratzky)	
Baden	10 (2040)
(cmdr: lt.col. Franz Graf von Tilly)	
Leslie	5 (1020)
(cmdr: lt.col. Giovanni Domenico Marchese Spinola)	
Croy	10 (2040)
(cmdr: lt.col. von Peterswaldt)	
Thimb	5 (1020)
(cmdr: lt.col. von Ghillany)	
Württemberg (Georg Friedrich Herzog von)	5 (1020)
(cmdr: ?) *	

Neuburg	5 (1020)
(cmdr: ?) †	
Erbprinz of Lorraine ‡	*5 (1020)*
(cmdr: lt.col. Carl Ludwig Graf Archinto di Tayna)	
Official total:	11,016
Actual:	8.500
(in battle)	8,000
Volunteers	
Parella battalion	? (300?)
Fontaine battalion	? (300)

* its Inhaber was in Vienna; regiment missing from Mansberg's list, and we do not know its commander.

† its lt.col. Areyzaga was in Vienna, and the battalion was probably commanded by its Major (Obristwachtmeister) Johann Freiherr von und zu Redern (or Rödern). Compare below under the Bavarians for what may be the same unit or perhaps a different one.

‡ Since the IR Erbprinz of Lorraine (the regiment 'owned' by Lorraine's young son Leopold Joseph) was not present in the final battle, the above list would actually give the Imperialists 10 battalions for the battle, 12 if we include the Salzburgers who were assigned to them (see the Bavarians below). This does not match the 13 battalions shown for the Imperialists in the Suttinger order of battle (to which should be added the battalion lent to the Poles, for a real total of 14); perhaps IR Beck should be counted after all amongst the Imperialists to make up the 13, or perhaps some battalions were formed from fewer than 4 or 5 companies.

Debatable units. See under the Bavarians below for IR Beck. Probably not present: IR Daun (lt.col. v. Rummel, 5 coys.) which Mansberg (p.35) puts under Lorraine; Wrede (vol. 2, p.167) says 5 companies were in Vienna, 5 companies in Prague, with no mention of any involvement in the relief.

Cavalry

The number of squadrons is not specified for regiments not participating in the battle. See Appendix I, 1.1, for discussion of the extremely unusual squadron counts.

Cuirassiers

	No.coys / off'l strength / sqn count
Sachsen-Lauenburg	10 (800) 3 sqns
(cmdr: lt.col. v. Noirquermes)	
Caprara	10 (800) 2 sqns
(cmdr: lt.col. Cavriani)	
Rabatta	10 (800) 2 sqns
(cmdr: lt.col. Carl Maria Baron da or de Pace)*	
Dünewald	10 (800) 2 sqns
(cmdr:lt.col. Paul Freiherr von Welfersheim)†	
Carafa	10 (800) 2 sqns
(cmdr: lt.col. lt.col. Gian Battista Marchese Doria)‡	
Pálffy	10 (800) 2 sqns
(cmdr: lt.col. Baron Borszita)§	
Gondola	10 (800) 2 sqns
(cmdr: lt.col. Johann Andreas Graf Corbelli)	
Taafe |	10 (800) 3 sqns
(cmdr: lt.col. Philipp Christoph Graf von Breuner)	
Mercy	5 ¶ (400) 2 sqns
(cmdr: lt.col. Wilhelm Jacob Freiherr Zante or Zandt)	
	10 (800) 2 sqns
Halleweil	
(cmdr: lt.col. Leopold Eberhard Herzog von Württemberg) **	10 (800) 2 sqns
Montecuccoli	10 (800) 2 sqns
(cmdr: lt.col. Carl Philipp Adam, Freiherr Vernier) ††	

	10 (800) 3 sqns
Piccolomini	
(cmdr: lt.col. Georg Christian Herzog v. Schleswig-Holstein?) ‡‡	
Götz	10 (800) 2 sqns
(cmdr: lt.col. Veit Heinrich Frhr Truchsess v. Wetzhausen) ‖	
Official total:	10,000
Actual:	8,100 (max.)

* Mansberg. According to Alphons Freiherr von Wrede, *Geschichte der k. und k. Wehrmacht* (Vienna: Seidel, 1889–1905, reprinted Starnberg: LTR Verlag, 1985), vol. 3, p.584, Pace was not commandant of the regiment until 1684; its commandant from 1675 was lt.col. Philipp Graf Thurn.

† Wrede, vol. 3, p.166: Peter von Welserheimb [sic].

‡ Mansberg. According to Wrede, vol. 3, p.133, Doria was not commandant of the regiment until 1684; its commandant from 1680 was lt.col. Albrecht von Lambach.

§ Mansberg. According to Wrede, vol. 3, p.555, 'Borschitta' was not commandant of the regiment until 1684; its commandant from 1681 was lt.col. Stephan Graf Götz.

| Stöller, p.29, for 24 August, gave only 6 coys., but on p.34 for 11 September the number was back up to 10. Wrede, vol. 3, p.581 explicitly says the entire regiment present at relief, though there had been only 5 companies in previous actions.

¶ Following Wrede, vol. 3, p.587; Le Bègue, whose numbering looks suspiciously repetitive, gives 10

** According to Wrede, vol. 3, p.591, Georg Friedrich, Herzog von Württemberg, but this must be an error, as Georg Friedrich, an infantry colonel, was in Vienna with half of his infantry regiment. Mansberg must be correct in this case.

†† According to Wrede, vol. 3, p.565, its commander from 1681 was lt.col. Scheller

‡‡ Wrede, vol. 3, p.145: either the Inhaber or lt.col. Warlusel or Wareusel. Compare DR Kueffstein

‖ Wrede, vol. 3, p.571: either Wetzhausen or the Inhaber.

Dragoons

	No.coys / off'l strength / sqn count
(Limburg-)Styrum	10 (800) 2 sqns
(cmdr: lt.col. Cheverelli or Chevereuil)	
Kuefstein	5* (400) 2 sqns
(cmdr: Johann Christoph Herzog v. Holstein [probably])	
Heissler	10 (800) 2 sqns
(cmdr: lt.col. Carl Graf Magni)	
Schulz	10 (800) 2 sqns
(cmdr: OWM Ferd. Max Graf von Trautmannsdorff)†	
Herbeville	*10 (800)* -
(cmdr: the Inhaber)‡	
Official total:	3,200
Actual:	2,700 (max.)
	2,100 (in battle)

* 10 companies in the Le Bègue list; 5, according to Wrede, vol. 3, p.213–214, which also gives the commandant (it was most certainly not Eugene of Savoy, as even Mansberg states)

† lt.col. von Gersdorf was 'left behind wounded' according to Mansberg; in Wrede, vol. 3, p.193, he is recorded as having been killed in a skirmish earlier in the summer. Trautmannsdorf was killed in action on the 12th according to Mansberg, though there is no mention of this in Wrede.

‡ This regiment was very new: it had been raised only in March 1683.

Croats

	No.coys / off'l strength / sqn count
Kery von Ipolykér*	8 (600) 3 sqns
(cmdr: the *Inhaber*, or lt.col. Graf von Salburg)	
Lodron	prob. 8 -
(cmdr: *the* Inhaber)	
Ricchiardi	8 (600) -
(cmdr: probably *the* Inhaber)	
Official total:	1,800
Actual:	1,500 (max.)
	600 (in battle)

* Wrede, vol. 3, p.789 makes no mention of serving in the relief; only commander mentioned is the Inhaber.

Polish corps of Lubomirski

Although the three main units of the corps were contracted to be of the usual size for Imperialist cavalry (800 men) and are sometimes given as such, the whole corps is usually described as 1,500–2,000 strong, and, since the Poles did not go in for big regiments, the 400 men specified for the *pancerni* unit may be taken as the normal strength of the other units as well.[18]

---

18   Much detail on the corps is in no.79 in this series, Michał Paradowski, *We came, we saw, God conquered: the Polish-Lithuanian Commonwealth's military effort in the relief of Vienna, 1683* (Warwick: Helion, 2021), chapter 6, including that the cavalry regiments were contracted to be equipped like Imperialist cuirassiers though also defined as 'lighter' cavalry, and an indication that at least one regiment was definitely no bigger that 400 men (p.113).

	No.coys / off'l strength / sqn count
CavR Lubomirski	? (400) 2 sqns
(cmdr: Johann von Butler)	
CavR Tetuin (Dettwin)	? (400?) 2 sqns
(cmdr: lt.col. von Modrzewski)	
DR Königsegg*	? (400?) 2 sqns
(cmdr: the *Inhaber*, or lt.col. Grocholsky [possibly])	
400 *pancerni*	? (400) 2 sqns
(cmdr: ?)	
Official total:	1,600?
Actual:	1,500
	600 (in battle)

* Wrede, vol. 3, p.650 has both Königsegg and Tetuin listed for 1683 as Inhaber and commander (no mention of Grocholsky); it says the unit was at relief. Königsegg was killed at the head of the regiment in battle on the 12th

Totals for cavalry

Establishment   17,400
Actual (maximum)   13,900
In Battle   12,300

Artillery: 70 guns recorded, probably no more than 30

The figure of 70 guns is from Suttinger and the closely related Schliz von Görz 'order of battle'; there is absolutely no other evidence concerning the Imperialist guns (nor any for the personnel), and the total of 70 seems improbable even for a government pulling out all the stops to save its capital – the contemporary norm for artillery was a ratio of between one and two guns per thousand men, and a ratio of more than three per thousand, which 70 guns would have given the Imperialists, was quite unusual. Besides, we know that the Imperialists left many of their heavier guns behind at Greifenstein, but did manage to bring up some battalion guns and even a few 12-pounders. Regarding the battalion guns, if we include the Salzburgers amongst the Imperialist infantry they had a total of 13 battalions, which, with the period's norm of one gun per battalion, gives 13 battalion guns; it is therefore highly unlikely their artillery total in the battle exceeded 30 pieces.

Overall totals

Establishment	29,516
Actual (maximum)	22,400
In Battle	20,900

On the overall totals, Le Bègue, who did not distinguish Croats and Poles, gave 8,400 'cavalry' and 2,400 dragoons (making a mounted arm of 10,800), with 8,100 infantry.[19] These figures are not absolutely identical to those above, but clearly within acceptable variations.

Schulz's corps at Jedlesee

	No.coys / off'l strength
CR Veterani*	10 (800)
(cmdr: the *Inhaber*)	
IR Salm	5 (1020)
(cmdr: the *Inhaber*, or lt.col. Franz Joachim Strasser)	
IR Wallis	3 (612)
(cmdr: the Inhaber, or lt.col. Carl Christoph Graf Schallenberg)	
official:	2,432
actual:	1,600

* Historians disagree whether it was left at Jedlesee; Wrede, vol. 3, p.598 states it was present at the relief (and names its commander as lt.col. Lorenz Graf Hofkirchen).

The following units, marked with italics in the lists above, did not serve in the relief as they were sent to Moravia with Lodron on 4 September (see below on this): IR Erbprinz of Lorraine, DR Herbeville, CrR Lodron, CrR Ricchiardi.

---

19 Stöller, p.34.

Bavarians

Bavaria had concluded a formal alliance with Leopold at the start of the year, officially intended for defence against both the Turks and France, though the young, inexperienced but domineering ruler of Bavaria, the Elector Maximilian II Emanuel (he was only just 21 years old), had further, hidden motives: his ambitions included establishing and exploiting a marriage connection with the Habsburgs, that could make his family the dominant dynasty in the Empire and might even give his descendants a shot at the imperial crown – he was already related to the Habsburgs through his paternal grandmother, a link visible in the trace of a 'Habsburg lip' in his features. In the meantime, Bavaria had already been preparing to support the Emperor with its brand-new standing army, but been caught out by the unexpected ease with which the Ottomans broke through to Vienna. Now, after a few details had been clarified in a supplementary agreement to the original alliance (Capitulation of Passau, 6 August, providing specifics on costs, numbers of troops, command arrangements, and the possibility of the Bavarians borrowing some Imperialist artillery so that they would not need to bring their own), the Bavarian forces, along with a couple of other local Reich units, just over 11,000 in total, were able to make their way quickly enough down the Danube, the infantry mostly in barges on the river itself, the 3,000 or so cavalry riding along the banks. By mid-August, these had joined the growing Imperialist corps at Krems-Mautern. They were officially under the Bavarian commander-in-chief, G-FML Christoph Hannibal, Freiherr von Degenfeld, but were also accompanied, technically only in a volunteer capacity, by the Elector, who was unlikely to keep himself in the background for very long. The standing army was new and Bavaria as a state had remained neutral in the Dutch War, but many of its officers and men had served in the Dutch War in other armies, and a few more may, like its commander Degenfeld, have had experience of fighting the Ottomans in the defence of Candia.

Bavarian troops fighting against the Ottomans during the assault on Belgrade in 1688. Romeyn de Hooghe, 1688 (Rijksmuseum, Amsterdam)

Bavarian forces:[20]

Elector Maximilian II Emanuel (technically serving as volunteer)

G-FML Christoph Hannibal, Freiherr von Degenfeld
GWM Adam Heinrich von Steinau
GWM Lorenz Ludwig von Münster
GWM Louis Marquis de Beauvau
GWM Friedrich von Rummel (or Rümpel)[21]

and other staff listed in Mansberg, pp.42-43.

Infantry

	Units / off'l strength
Infantry: electoral (5 regts of 6 coys of 192–200 each = 10 bns)	
Degenfeld	2 bns (1200)
(cmdr: lt.col. Franz Emanuel della Rosa)	
Steinau	2 bns (1200)
(cmdr: lt.col. Johann Öpfler)	
de la Perouse	2 bns (1200)
(cmdr: lt.col. Max Graf Stanga)	
Mercy	2 bns (1200)
(cmdr: lt.col. Joh. Alb. Baron Nothhafft v. Weissenstein*)	
Preising (or Preysing)	2 bns (1200)
(cmdr: lt.col. Matt. v. Seeberg)	
Infantry: attached (3 bns definite)	
Salzburg IR Steinsdorf(f)	2 bns (1200)
(cmdr: not specified)	

---

20 See Appendix I, 1.2, for details of sources and all major disputes about Bavarian numbers, including their artillery.
21 Only in the Suttinger order of battle; not mentioned in any other lists of generals. An officer of the Bavarian Kreis, not the electoral army.

NO MORE TIME TO LOSE

Bav. Kreis-IR (Col. Rummel)	1 bn (594)
(cmdr: lt.col. Peter August von Mollendorff)	
?Pfalz-Neuburg [IR?]	1 bn
(cmdr: lt.col. Rödern)	
?Imp. IR Beck†	5 coys
official:	6,000 (electoral)
	6,594 incl. Kreis only
	7,794 (incl. all attached, excluding debated)
actual:	7,500

* Until 14 July the regiment was under Berlo, which explains why it is sometimes listed under this name; it later became Leib IR.

† On uncertainties surrounding the last two units, see Appendix I, 1.3.

Cavalry (16 sqns, of 2 companies of 101 each)

	Units / off'l strength
CR Bartels (Münster)*	3 sqns (606)
(cmdr: lt.col. Joh. Baptist von Walsre)	
CR Beauvau	3 sqns (606)
(cmdr: lt.col. Heinrich Wilhelm von Lüzelburg)	
CR Schütz†	3 sqns (606)
(cmdr: lt.col. Jakob Prandler)	
CR Arco‡	3 sqns (606)
(cmdr: lt.col. Ludwig Graf von St Bonifaci)	

DR Degenfeld (2 half-regts., 'blue' & 'red')§	4 sqns (808)
(cmdrs: lt.cols. Georg Bernhard von Leoprechting &	
Ajax Dietrich von Lerchenfeldt)	
official:	3,232
actual:	3,000

* Karl Staudinger, *Geschichte des kurbayerischen Heeres unter Kurfürst Max II. Emanuel, 1680–1726* (Munich: Lindauer, 1904–1905), part 1, p.159: sub July, 'Bärtls (nun Münster)'.

† Mansberg: Johann Chr. Schüz von Schüzenhofen.

‡ Staudinger, *Geschichte*, and others: since 14 July; regiment formerly Alt-Haraucourt (and Haraucourt sometimes listed as a separate regt. present).

§ Two half-regiments, with Inhaber of both being Degenfeld.

Artillery:[22] **16 guns, =**

      6 x 6-pdrs
    10 x battalion guns [3-pdrs?]

Personnel: 3 officers, 43 constables, 220 Knechte & Schneller, & 8 other staff, 1 bridge-master & 1 bridge-thrower, 3 craftsmen w. 14 journeymen, 12 carpenters, =

official: 305
actual: 305?

Totals:
official: 11,331
actual: 10,805

Franconians

Not far behind the Bavarians were the Franconians, under the veteran Reichs Feld-Marschall and eminent imperial politician, Georg Friedrich, Graf von Waldeck. Their regiments, raised to defend the Empire against French aggression, had actually been on foot longer than Maximilian Emanuel's, and although nationalist historians are fond of sneering at the supposed

---
22   detail from Mansberg, pp.43–44. See Appendix I, 1.2.

inadequacies of these units from several different small states, they had been organised for a number of years and were in fact perfectly competent, especially since many of the officers and men were experienced from the Dutch War; their only real problem was the need for their home governments to agree on any policy, which slowed down the making of major decisions. Even with the drive of Waldeck, still capable of energy despite his 63 years, it was well into August before the various rulers had met and agreed to send their troops east, leaving their part of the Empire defenceless if France chose this moment to attack; but having decided, they wasted no further time, and their regiments were soon moving down the Danube at a fair clip, like the Bavarians their infantry on barges and the cavalry trotting beside them on the riverbank. About half of them were full regiments belonging to the small state armies of the bishoprics of Würzburg and Bamberg; the rest were real Kreis regiments, 'federal' formations each drawn together from many tiny contingents of the diminutive states of Franconia but perfectly experienced in serving together in their combined units. Including small detachments from the neighbouring Kreis of Swabia, and an attached battalion from further-afield Brunswick-Lüneburg (Hanover), they totalled about 7,000–8,000 infantry and 1,300 cavalry. It was a mark of how far opinions had changed since the Thirty Years War (for everybody except the Habsburgs and Louis XIV, that is) that the mostly-Catholic Franconians would serve alongside Protestant Hanoverians and under the Protestant Waldeck without a murmur.

At the end of August the Franconian contingent approached the Krems position, and instead of joining the Bavarians and Imperialists at the bridge, shifted south and on 6 September took up a supporting position on the River Traisen at Herzogenburg.

Franconian and other Reich forces[23]

> FM Reichsfürst Georg Friedrich Graf von Waldeck
> FML Christian Ernst Markgraf von Bayreuth
> FML Cuno Ernst Freiherr von der Leyen
> GWM Hans Carl von Thüngen

and other staff listed in Mansberg, pp.39–40.

---

23   Sources and major disputes: see Appendix I, 1.4.

Infantry (11 bns?)

	No.coys / off'l strength
Franc.IR Andlau (1st Franc. Kreis-regt) (cmdr: the *Inhaber*?)*	8 coys of 180 (1440)
Franc.IR Köth (2nd Franc. Kreis-regt) (cmdr: the *Inhaber*?)‡	8 coys of 180 (1440)†
Würzburg-Bamberg IR Leyen (cmdr: unknown)	10 coys of 150 (1500)
Würzburg IR Thüngen (cmdr: lt.col. Graf Truchsess von Waldburg)	10 coys of 150 (1500)
IR Württemberg (½ Swab. Kreis-regt Baden-Durlach)§ (cmdr: lt.col. Linth von Kirchheim)	5 coys of 200 (1000)
IR Sachsen-Hildburghausen (Sachsen-Ernestinisch)| (cmdr: lt.col. von Diemar)	6 coys of 130, (780)
IR Pallandt (½ Brunswick-Lüneburg IR)¶ (cmdr: lt.col. von Rose)	6 coys of 100 (600)
official:	8,260 (8,326 incl. staffs)
actual:	7,000

* Col. Heinrich Philipp v. Andlau; lt.col. Andreas von Imhoff

† Jochner records contradictory information abut the strength of the two Kreis regiments: both that the Kreis had decided to send only 150 men per company with 30 men remaining behind (making just 1,200 per regiment), and that the two regiments were 2,800 strong in total when they set off (Jochner, pp.34, 41).

‡ Col. Johann Wilhelm Köth von Wanschied (Johann Paul Hassel & Carl Friedrich Vitzthum von Eckstädt, *Zur Geschichte des Türkenkrieges im Jahre 1683: die Betheilung der kursächsischen Truppen an demselben* (Dresden: Haensch, 1883), p.138; Jochner, p.35); lt.col. von Erssa.

§ According to Mansberg, this was the only unit in the army equipped with bayonets, although it had not yet abandoned the pike.

| Only in Mansberg, and Hassel & Vitzthum von Eckstadt. Col. Ernst Herzog zu Sachsen-Hildburghausen.

¶ Mansberg; also Hassel & Vitzthum von Eckstadt, p.139, and Luis Heinrich Friedrich von Sichart, *Geschichte der königlich hannoverschen Armee* (Hanover: Hahn, 1860-1898), vol. 1, pp.178–179. The Hanoverian unit is mentioned by many others but often as a cavalry regiment (perhaps because both the Colonel, Pallandt, and the two Hanoverian princes who came to take part in the campaign, served as volunteers with the Imperialist CR Rabatta, giving the impression that Pallandt was a cavalryman). Hanover had no connection with the Franconian Kreis but its tiny contribution was attached to the Franconians as the most appropriate post – the duchy had not yet achieved the rank of electorate and thus its unit could not be placed with the Saxons or Bavarians. It is never made clear how the Hanoverians, who had much further to come than any other contingent, joined up in time.

Cavalry (7 sqns)

	No.coys / off'l strength
CR Bayreuth (Kreis)	6 coys of 60 (360) = 2 sqns?
(cmdr: lt.col. Graf v. Erbach)	
CR Hohenzollern-Hechingen (Würzburg)	6 coys of ?60 (?360) = 2 sqns?
(cmdr: ?)	
DR Schutzbar (Würzburg-Bamberg)	6 coys of 60 (360) = 2 sqns?
(cmdr: lt.col. Joh. Conrad Schutzbar v. Milchling)	
Dragoon Kreis-schwadron Hedesdorf	2 coys. of ?60 (120) = 1 sqn
(cmdr: ?)	
official:	1,200?
actual:	1,200?

Artillery (12 guns)[24]

    2 x ¼-Carthaunen [= 12-pdrs] (Würzburg & Bamberg)
    2 x 6-pdrs (Nuremberg)
    8 bn/g (4 each Würzburg & Bamberg)

    Personnel: 3 officers, 1 engineer, 2 fireworkers, 30 constables (qualified gunners), 24 'Handlanger', 4 craftsmen & 5 journeymen, 40 knechte, & 12 other staff, =

official:	121
actual:	100

Totals:
official:	9,647
actual:	8,300

Saxons

In northern Germany, the Habsburg envoy to Berlin Johann Philipp, Graf von Lamberg, failed to secure any aid from the important army of Brandenburg, because its ruler was in secret alliance with France and would not act to support the Imperialists even against the Turks; but at Dresden he succeeded better with Saxony, where the Elector John George III agreed readily enough to bring his army to help. The Saxon regiments, although only recently formed as a standing army, contained many men and officers who were veterans of the Dutch War, so they were a valuable addition to the relief force, although they had no formal experience in fighting the Ottomans. However, difficulties in arranging supplies for the march, especially because the chronically broke Imperialist government refused to pay the Saxons for their help and Saxony itself was not a wealthy state, delayed John George's departure until 11 August. On top of that, this was for the Saxons no easy march down a river with infantry carried on barges such as the Bavarians and Franconians enjoyed: John George, his 7,000 infantry, with cavalry probably totalling less than 3,000, and the 16 guns of his well-equipped little artillery train, would every one of them have to slog it by foot or horse-power over the mountains of Saxon Switzerland into Bohemia (the modern Czech Republic) and then south through Prague and all the way across the entire Kingdom of Bohemia to Austria. Although in terms of distance on the map, at about 200 miles, they did not have that much further to go than the south Germans, it was hard work, and redounded to their great credit that they entered Austria

---

24   Most agree on 12 guns, some saying 12 'battalion guns', which does not match the details here (from Mansberg, p.40). It is likely that the 12-pounders were left behind on the far side of the Wienerwald along with the Imperialist and Saxon heavier artillery, along with a few personnel, giving 10 guns and about 100 men in the battle.

from the north on 1 September and were approaching the Danube valley at Maissau by the 3rd.

Saxon forces:[25]

> Elector John George III
> FM Joachim Rudiger, Freiherr von der Goltz
> FML Heino Heinrich von Flemming
> GWM Christian Herzog von (or zu) Sachsen-Weissenfels
> GWM Sigmund Joachim Graf von Trautmannsdorff
> GWM Heinrich IV Graf Reuss von Plauen
> GWM Rudolph von Neidschütz (or Neitschütz)

and other staff listed in Mansberg, pp.36–37.

Infantry (12 bns of 4 coys each)[26]

	Units / off'l strength
Leib IR (Col. v. Escher)	2 bns (1182)
(cmdr: Colonel, or lt.col. Hans Rudolf von Schönfeld)	
Goltz IR	2 bns (1182)
(cmdr: lt.col. Georg v. Kleist)	
Flemming IR	2 bns (1182)
(cmdr: lt.col. Eustach v. Flemming*)	
Löben IR	2 bns (1182)
(cmdr: lt.col. v.d. Sahle)	
Kuffer IR	2 bns (1182)
(cmdr: lt.col. Hans Berhnard v. Tuppau)	
Christian v. Sachsen-Weissenfels IR	2 bns (1182)
(cmdr: lt.col. Hans Georg v. Carlowitz)	

---

25 Sources and disputes: see Appendix I, 1.5.
26 *Aufrichtige und unpartheyische Relation von der Victoria der Christen so sie beym Entsatz der Stadt Wien gegen die Türcken erhalten… zur Vertheidigung der Sächsichen Tapfferkeit* (s.l.: s.n., [1683 or 4?]), p.4, confirms 12 battalions: its says the Saxons had 6 in the first line, 4 in the second, 2 in the third. Further details of Saxon unit officers: Mansberg, pp.38–39.

a grenadier coy.	1 coy. (103 or 113)
(cmdr: Hauptmann Henri de Bose)	
official:	7,200
actual:	7,000

* Most agree, though sometimes given as lt.col. von der Sahlo. Compare IR Löben

NB: the Saxon infantry had left its pikes at home and came to Vienna equipped with muskets and *schweinsfeder*s only.27

Cavalry (regiments of 3 sqns of 2 coys = 14 sqns)

	Units / off'l strength
Leib-Regiment zu Ross (Dernath)	1 sqn (202)*
(cmdr: lt.col. Tobias v. Haubitz or Haugwitz)	
CR Goltz	3 sqns (606)
(cmdr: lt.col. de Bronne, or, Bronne de Montagu)	
CR Trautmannsdorff	3 sqns (606)
(cmdr: lt.col. v. Wolframsdorff)	
CR Plotho Frhr v. Luwelmünster†	3 sqns (606)
(cmdr: lt.col. v. Theler)	
DR Reuss	3 sqns (598)
(cmdr: lt.col. Hans Rudolph v. Minkwitz)‡	
Leibgarde-Trabanten zu Ross	1 sqn (172)§
(cmdr: GWM Neitschütz)	
official:	2,790
actual:	2,500

---

27 Oscar Schuster and F. A. Francke, *Geschichte der sächsischen Armee, von deren Errichtung bis auf die neueste Zeit* (Leipzig: Duncker & Humblot, 1885, reprinted [Munich?]: LTR Verlag, 1983), vol. 1, p.103.

* according to Hassall & Vitzthum von Eckstadt, 4 companies remained at home, only 2 accompanying the army. Schuster & Francke say nothing about this.

† Mansberg: GWM Gebhard Sigfrid von Plotho Frhr von Engelmünster (marked with [ ]); commander as listed. Hassel & Vitzthum von Eckstädt do not specify a lt.col. commander; Schuster & Francke show Plotho as the Oberst and the commander as lt.col. Engelmünster.

‡ Hassel & Vitzthum von Eckstädt, p.127, confirm that Reuss was promoted GWM of infantry on 26 August, and Minckwitz led the regiment.

§ both Mansberg and Hassel & Vitzthum von Eckstädt p.114 agree on the figures, and imply Neitschütz was the commander or *Inhaber*.

Artillery:[28] 16 guns & 2 petards, =

2 x 12-pdrs (H&V: bronze 'granatstücke' 12-pdrs [howitzers?])
2 x 8-pdr field mortars (H&V: mortars, 8-lb. stone calibre)
6 x 6-pdr bn/g (bronze)
6 x 3-pdr bn/g (bronze)

+ 2 petards

Personnel: 5 officers, 1 engineer, 17 other staff, 1 petardier, 6 fireworkers, 1 drummer, 17 constables (qualified gunners), 27 'Schneller', 5 craftsmen with 10 journeymen, 1 provost =

official: 91
actual: 80?

Totals:
official: 10,000
actual: 9,580

Poles

For the Germans, even the Saxons, the road to Vienna was comparatively easy; not so for the Poles. The Polish-Lithuanian Commonwealth had concluded a secret defensive-offensive alliance with the Imperialists at the end of March, but, although this had included clauses providing for full

---

28 Detail from Mansberg, pp.36–37, and Hassel and Vitzthum von Eckstädt, p.184; much further detail of train in *Das Kriegsjahr 1683*, p.233 and Mansberg, p.37, some further detail, Schuster and Francke, vol. 1, p.103; details of artillery ammunition brought, Hassall and Vitzthum von Eckstadt, p.184. One may assume that a few train personnel were left behind with the heavier guns at Altenberg.

ASSEMBLY OF THE RELIEF FORCE

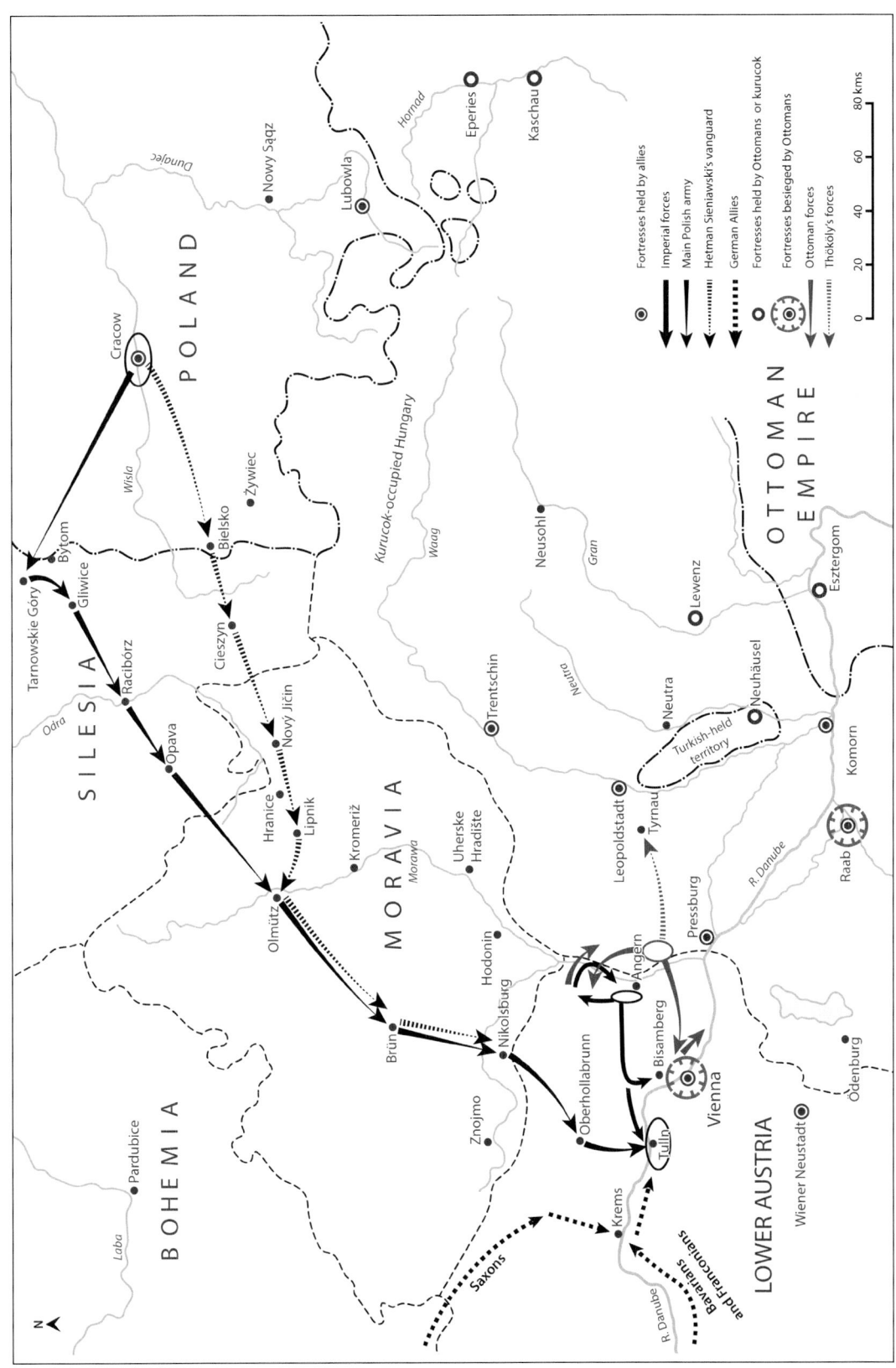

Route of the relief forces.

mutual support in the event of a threat to Vienna or Cracow, everyone at that stage had assumed that the Imperialists would hold the expected Ottoman lunge in Hungary, allowing the Poles to concentrate on their own objective, an advance into the Ukraine to recover their province of Podolia, conquered by the Ottomans a decade earlier. Therefore, the Polish standing army had been concentrated near their south-eastern border under the Crown Field Hetman Sieniawski, facing east, and the army expansion under the Crown Grand Hetman Jabłonowski was timed to be ready only for the autumn when the Poles preferred to begin operations on the open steppes – and until that time they intended to keep their alliance and preparations secret from the Ottomans so that their attack would come as a surprise. But when the Ottoman army, large enough in fact and its numbers seriously over-estimated in intelligence reports, lumbered north through Hungary, the Poles became nervous; initially, fearing that Kara Mustafa or his Hungarian puppet Imre Thököly might have designs on southern Poland, the King, John III Sobieski, started to pull the forces in the east under Sieniawski back from the Podolian border, at first only about 80 miles as far as the local centre at Lwów, then in early July 200 miles further west to cover Cracow, Poland's second city and former capital, vulnerable to attack from Upper Hungary over the Carpathians; and the recruitment of the expanded wartime army was speeded up. As the Ottoman army bull-dozered its way into Austria, appeals galloped across Europe to Warsaw for aid under the terms of the alliance, and within a few days of the Grand Vizier's arrival at Vienna, Sobieski had assured a second Imperialist appeal that he would come to the city's aid with his entire army.

Unfortunately, it was not a promise so easy to carry out. Sieniawski's force, all mounted, was already pounding across southern Poland towards Cracow, now not the city in need of defence but a jump-off point for the march to Vienna; but it would not arrive until 1–2 August. And the expansion of the rest of the army was still not completed. So Sobieski, although he left Warsaw on 18 July, the day after making his promise to the Imperialists, made only a leisurely journey south, although as he did so he started to correspond with Lorraine about the details of the relief; he only arrived at Cracow on the 29th. The first of Sieniawski's exhausted troopers, only a couple of thousand strong, camped around the ancient city a few days later, with the rest straggling in over succeeding days; and the Crown Grand Hetman, Jabłonowski, brought up the rest of the Polish army, including all the units expanded by new recruitment, on 8 August. There was no sign of the Lithuanian army which, for complicated reasons of internal Polish-Lithuanian politics, had no intention of helping Sobieski. It was the same with the Cossacks, the irregular light cavalry of the Ukraine prized by Sobieski: the agent he had sent out into the Ukraine to recruit them had failed to send back any or even submit a report, and all Sobieski had of Cossacks was a small detachment of about 150 men. The King took a few days to put his army into order, to let the corps from the eastern border rest after its heroic trek, and to ensure that preparations were in place for his army to find necessary supplies on the roads through the Habsburg provinces of Silesia and Moravia on the way to Austria. He also dispatched an envoy to Thököly to try to warn the Hungarian rebels off from attempting to interfere with his march, which would have to pass all the way across the front of territory in rebel hands.

The size of the army has been hotly disputed ever since 1683, but it seems that, out of an army of 34,000 counted in the official muster on 1 August, about 29,000 men according to official numbers (which included permitted fictional extra 'mouths' for rations) and 26,000 men in reality were in the Polish relief force when it set off. With them they brought 28 cannons, the majority of them light pieces.[29] Polish armies, accustomed to fighting in almost-deserted steppe country where living off the land was simply not an option, usually tried to carry with them as much supplies as they could, and this was no exception; the army would be accompanied by a large number of train wagons. However, to help the infantry keep up, even more wagons for carrying the foot-soldiers would be provided in stages by local civilians as the army passed. Sobieski himself was accompanied by a number of government officials and senators, present not only to allow the business of government to continue but also to keep an eye on him, for the great Polish nobles distrusted their kings. He also brought with him his eldest son, Prince Jakub, not yet 16 years old, partly to introduce the boy to army life and great affairs, partly because the King (and even more, his wife, Queen Marie) hoped that a marriage could be arranged between Jakub and a Habsburg princess on the back of the relief effort, a marriage that might help to secure the family's hold on the elective Polish crown.

On 11 August, the Polish army took the road: Sieniawski, with his original troops and a few extra detachments, was ordered to act as a flank guard for the main army against any attempt by the Ottomans or the Hungarian rebels to harass its march, and he set off directly from southern Poland, across the narrow Duchy of Teschen that formed the southernmost tip of the Habsburg province of Silesia, and thundered across Moravia. Sobieski and Jabłonowski made a side-slip back northwards before turning west, to take a route easier for the infantry and to put enough distance between them and Sieniawski for the flank guard to do its job. The main army entered Silesia on 19 August, initially not pushing itself too hard; but, as increasingly urgent appeals arrived from Lorraine stressing how hard-pressed Vienna was, Sobieski started to accelerate, and after a while formally decided to push ahead with his personal units, with the rest of the army ordered to follow and keep up as best it could. Sieniawski was also instructed to speed up and join Lorraine as soon as he could, though Sobieski soon concluded that his own political position would suffer should Vienna be saved by his subordinate and countermanded the order, leading to an acrimonious correspondence when Sieniawski took no notice and pressed on.[30]

With the Polish main army increasingly stretched out on the road behind him and especially the infantry more and more struggling to keep up, Sobieski and the royal *pułk*, himself in a coach as no horse could bear

---

29 According to Dalérac, vol. 1, pp.136–137, 5 or 6 pieces were of normal calibre for field guns, the rest so light as to be barely worth the name of cannon.
30 On the complexities around Sieniawski's position, see Paradowski, pp.119–120.

his overweight frame for very long, crossed the Silesian-Moravian border on 26 August and reached Olmütz that same evening after an astonishing day's march of 77 kilometres or 47 miles. The Poles pounded on across Moravia, past Brunn and the Raygern Monastery to the south of it, where the monks watched open-mouthed the columns streaming past their walls and Father Bernard Brulig hastened to describe the passage, the splendid cavalry and the not-so-impressive infantry, together with some astonishingly inaccurate counts of the troops, in his account of the year's events.[31] On 30 August, as Jabłonowski and the bulk of the Polish army were still straggling past the Raygern Monastery 20-odd miles back up the road, Sobieski and the men who had managed to keep up with him reached the Austrian border at Nikolsburg, and the next day entered Austria. Soon after, he was reunited with Sieniawski and the flank guard, who had not actually pushed so far ahead as to join Lorraine after all; nevertheless, the King tore Sieniawski off a strip for his ignoring the royal orders, before their forces continued together. Correspondence with Lorraine during the march had made clear that the Imperialists' preferred route for the relief was to cross the Danube upstream of Vienna somewhere around Krems-Mautern or Tulln and come at the Ottomans from the west, so from the border the Poles headed south-west towards Ober-Hollabrunn, in the direction of the bridges, instead of due south directly for Vienna. On the road later that same day, 31 August, Sobieski ran into Lorraine coming to meet him.

Both Sobieski and Lorraine had been candidates for the Polish throne in the election of 1674, and both men deeply loved wives who detested each other, so this initial meeting, despite their previous correspondence, was a little cautious as they groped for bases of understanding. Sobieski, a king even if an elected one, filthy rich and not afraid to flaunt it in clothing, gear and over-dressed servants, was unimpressed by the distinctly shabby appearance of Lorraine, the refugee duke dependent on his salary from the Emperor and currently too worn down by the burdens of the campaign to care much about his clothes; but as they rode on together, met Waldeck further on the road, and took quarters at Ober-Hollabrunn for a banquet where the wine flowed a little too freely, Sobieski started to warm to Lorraine, understood that his subdued reactions were due to a modest personality, so different from Sobieski's own ebullience, rather than any sullen rudeness, and quickly came to recognise the considerable strength of character, dedication to duty and military talents behind the quiet exterior. Lorraine, for his part, immediately recognised Sobieski's need to dominate and allowed him to play the part. It also helped that Lorraine let himself get considerably drunk at the banquet and play the fool: Sobieski was the kind of man who preferred those who could be 'one of the boys' – and no harm was done either by Lorraine's loud tipsy assertions that the Polish Commonwealth had never shown greater discernment than in its choice of its current King.

---

31 Dudík, Bela (ed.), 'Pater Bernard Brulig's Bericht über die Belagerung der Stadt Wien im Jahre 1683', *Archiv für Kunde Österreichischer Geschichts-Quellen*, 4 (1850), Heft 2, pp.255–296, and Heft 3/4, pp.397–508, here pp.424–426. Paradowski in his Appendix II (pp.205–207, reproduces and analyses Brulig's figures.

Polish King Jan III Sobieski depicted as triumphant leader during the battle of Vienna, leading his cavalry against the Ottoman troops. Romeyn de Hooghe, 1684 (Rijksmuseum, Amsterdam)

Sobieski now learnt that Vienna was not so close to falling as the nervous Imperialists, keen to hurry him along, had led him to believe. On top of this, the bridge at Tulln, necessary for the Poles to cross if they were not to waste time on a detour upstream to the permanent bridge at Krems-Mautern, was not ready: the chronically broke Habsburg government, although it had known for several weeks that it would need a bridge, had only in the last few days managed to finish assembling the materials and workers to build one – and now that the Christians really needed some dry weather, of course it began to rain, swelling the river and its surrounding marshes and adding greatly to the construction difficulties. And so the King settled down at Ober-Hollabrunn to rest the troops who accompanied him and let Jabłonowksi and the others catch up. It also gave him a few days to start developing some serious plans.[32]

---

32 I would have liked to provide here a list of the Polish army as mobilised and as it set off from Poland, but this would involve copying information from Wimmer that is or may be still in copyright, and the publisher has not responded to a request for permission to make such a copy; this is Jan Wimmer, *Wiedeń 1683: dzieje kampanii i bitwy* (Warsaw: Wydawnictwo Ministerstwa Obrony Narodowej, 1983), pp.219–230. Details of the units that reached or might have reached Vienna are given in Chapter 10 below. For references to works on uniforms, see Appendix I, 1.6.

Plate A. Saxon Cavalry of the 1683 campaign
1. Senior Officer of Cavalry
2. Cavalry Trooper

Both figures are wearing heavy buff coats, most likely made of elk or moose hide. The officer's coat has red velvet lined cuffs and is very likely one he has purchased himself. The scarf he wears around his waist denotes rank and will be of a heavily embroidered silk. Both wear *Zischägge* style cavalry helmets or 'pots' and back and breast plates for protection. The officer's body armour is supplemented by tassets to protect the thighs.
(Illustrations by Sergey Shamenkov, © Helion & Company)

2

Discussions, discussions, discussions: the Stetteldorf conference

There had been much debate in Imperialist government circles in the preceding weeks about exactly how to carry out the relief. Forcing a crossing of the Danube in the immediate vicinity of Vienna and the Ottoman army was of course impossible, and woods or marshes on the north bank on either side of Vienna, which made it very difficult for an army to even approach the river bank, meant that any potential crossing point had to be pushed further east or west. Although the Habsburgs and their ministers have a reputation for caution and sluggishness, some, including Hermann of Baden, President of the Hofkriegsrat, proposed a daring strategy: they wanted to find a way to circle round the besieging army, perhaps by going as far east as Pressburg, to cut off its line of retreat, force it against the walls of Vienna and the banks of the Danube, and crush it utterly. Sobieski had achieved just such a victory of annihilation against the Ottomans ten years earlier at Chocim and in a host of smaller battle victories, and he was equally as keen on such a plan; but with the armies already coming together in the area of Krems-Mautern and Tulln, *west* of Vienna, and with the siege pressing ever harder against the city, there was no time for fancy long-distance manoeuvring such as a march to Pressburg, while the woods and marshes of the north bank made any bridging of the Danube downstream of Tulln impractical unless one had the time to march far off to the east of Vienna.

So, the overall plan for the next stage of the campaign, over which Lorraine and Sobieski had reached broad agreement in the correspondence they had maintained during Sobieski's march, was pretty obvious: to get over the Danube, and march east towards the rear of the besieging army. There was just one physical obstacle – unfortunately, not a small one: the big jumbled range of hills and forests called the Wienerwald (Viennese Woods) that lay between the bridges and Vienna. And besides this, an even bigger mental obstacle: the small area between Krems and Tulln was filling up with alpha-males determined to maintain their position in the dominance hierarchy, in an era when no-one expected them to do anything else. Did a man who was a king but only an elected one, who had ten years before been only a private individual with rich estates but no recognised titles to his name, truly outrank a hereditary duke of the Holy Roman Empire who was also entitled to elect an Emperor? How did such a duke-elector stand against a man who was officially the ruler of a sovereign duchy but had been a refugee from that duchy almost all his life and had never ruled it – yet was also the absolute deputy in military matters of the Emperor himself? And worst of all, what would happen if the Emperor himself came down the Danube to take command himself of the attempt to save his capital? He was perfectly entitled to do so, and in fairness no-one could object if he did; and the one universally recognised fact of contemporary protocol was that as Emperor he outranked *everybody*, king, electors, dukes, the lot of them. But Sobieski wanted – indeed, for political purposes at home, desperately *needed* – to command the relief attempt and garner the prestige that would come with victory; and he regarded this prestige as the fee that the Habsburgs must pay for his assistance. The latest research suggests that Leopold's advisers, including Hermann of Baden, were very concerned for Leopold's security and wanted him as near to the army as possible but not actually with it where he might be in personal danger;[33] unfortunately, if this was true, no-one ever made it clear to Sobieski, and besides this did not exclude the possibility of a brief visit by Leopold to headquarters, which would still raise a raft of protocol questions.

For a couple of days several German commanders and their messengers trotted around in the rain between the various corps, back and forth along the flat plain of the river between Krems and Tulln, and north into the hills to meet the Poles and Saxons. Waldeck, soul of any cooperative effort and a veteran of many difficult negotiations, was especially busy. There was provisional and sometimes grudging agreement amongst the Germans that each general or ruler would command his own contingent, which could avoid some precedence squabbles but could also create a very disunited army unless they agreed to command their contingents *under a single supreme commander*, a possibility no-one mentioned for now – though the King of Poland must have been the candidate in everyone's minds. Lorraine and Waldeck agreed that Sobieski should be invited to a fuller conference, and Waldeck, an inveterate compiler of memoranda, was commissioned to draw up some kind of agenda as a framework for the discussions.

It is not clear whether Sobieski was fully informed of the scope of the discussions before he came; he may have thought he was coming only to discuss the technicalities of getting his Poles over the Danube. On 2 September, Sobieski, escorted only by a couple of squadrons of *pancerni* but accompanied by most of his senior generals, came south from Ober-Hollabrunn to Stetteldorf, a rural château at the point where the hills give way to the plain, about five miles north-north-west of Tulln (now known as

---

33　Christian Beese, *Markgraf Hermann von Baden (1628-1691): General, Diplomat und Minister Kaiser Leopolds I.* (Stuttgart: Kohlhammer, 1991), p.235. The sort of protocol questions that might arise did appear when Leopold and Sobieski did finally meet after the battle at Schwechat; see Chapter 12 below.

Gross-Stetteldorf), lying on the road that runs parallel with the Danube from Krems heading for Korneuburg and the now-ruined Vienna bridges. The same day, Lorraine came up from Korneuburg, to talk plans through with the King informally before the full conference on the morrow. He also brought with him a south-Slav messenger called Mihailović,[34] who had slipped out of Vienna through the Ottoman lines the day before with the latest reports from its dour commandant Starhemberg and his civilian colleague Kapliř, and reached Korneuburg that very day; Mihailović was presented to the King, to back up the sense of urgency Lorraine wanted to impart based on the reports, for Starhemberg, never a man to panic, and despite assuring that he would fight to the last, was beginning to warn that the Turks were dangerously close to breaking through the last of the city's defences (the report from Starhemberg warned that, on the sector of the walls of Vienna under attack, both bastions had been mined by the Turks, counter-mining was not working, and one of the bastions was so badly designed that inner defences, to provide a second line when the outer wall was ruined by the Turkish mines, could not be built). After persuading Sobieski of the danger Vienna was in, Lorraine moved on to try to thrash out the inevitable matters of protocol in advance of the main conference, in the hope that by doing so today these would not delay the important discussions on the morrow:[35] should generals of the absent Emperor or Hetmans of the present King speak first? what about the pecking order between the general of an elector, an elector himself (they knew John George would be arriving soon) and the Emperor's refugee-duke commander-in-chief? given that the right was considered the position of honour, who should sit on the right of whom – or was it best to avoid sitting completely and discuss standing? Sobieski, fed up with the pointless disputes,[36] proposed a compromise by which each national group would meet separately and then deliver its conclusions to him in a common session over which he would preside.

After a satisfactory visit, Lorraine returned to Korneuburg for the night and rode to Stetteldorf again the following morning, this time accompanied by Hermann of Baden, who had joined him from his position at Leopold's court with orders to represent the Emperor's views (including raising the questions of protocol if Leopold came to the army and met Sobieski); Hermann also had a private agenda, to try to persuade Lorraine to allow him a field command commensurate with his rank when the allied army advanced against the Ottomans – Lorraine was trying to deal with his scheming by

---

34 or Michaelowitz – the German form of his name, pronounced the same.
35 There is some uncertainty about whether this discussion took place on the 2nd or as a first stage in the talks on the 3rd. The accounts of Lorraine's secretary Le Bègue are as usual less than clear about the exact dates of the events they describe; my reading of the entry under 3 September is that the bulk of it refers to events of the previous day, with the events of the 3rd described in the entry for the 4th. See Stöller, p.32, and especially p.98.
36 At least, if his letters to his wife are to be believed; see especially the letter of 4 September in Stanisław, comte de Plater (ed.), *Lettres du roi de Pologne Jean Sobieski, à la reine Marie Casimire, pendant la campagne de Vienne* (Louvain: Vanlithout & Vandenzande, 1827), pp.47–55, for his annoyance at constant questions of etiquette. While the letters to Queen Marie were private, we must still remember that Sobieski was concerned to present himself in a favourable light to his wife as a reasonable man towering above the small-minded Germans around him.

Allied commanders after the relief of Vienna. Adam Frans van der Meulen, after 1683 (National Museum, Warsaw)

ignoring it, but the tactic could not last forever. Hermann had not been keen on the principle of each prince commanding his own contingent when he first learnt of it, during his ride to Lorraine's headquarters, but Waldeck had done a good job of persuading the President of the Hofkriegsrat that this was the best way to avoid debilitating command disputes.

That morning, 3 September, the commanders gathered in the hall of Stetteldorf Castle for their first big meeting. Present were the obese King, his Hetmans Jabłonowski and Sieniawski, his famous artillery commander Kątski, and other Polish generals, all preening themselves in their lavish costumes and sneering at the more plainly-dressed Germans; Lorraine at the head of the bevy of Imperialist officers – Hermann of Baden of course, both in his capacity as President of the Hofkriegsrat and with his military rank of Feld-Marschall, and naturally he brought his 28-year old nephew Louis William of Baden, only a Feld-Marschall-Lieutenant in rank but a reigning Markgraf, and along with them came the gouty infantry/artillery commander and second-generation Scottish immigrant FZM Jakob (James) Leslie, FML Fürst Salm who could not make up his mind if he belonged to infantry or cavalry, and a group of cavalry officers, GdC Herzog von Sachsen-Lauenburg from northern Germany and the veteran Italian professional GdC Aenio Silvio Caprara, FML Rudolf Graf von Rabatta (from Carinthia), and GWM Don Francesco de Gondola from the Italianate Republic of Ragusa (now Dubrovnik). For the Bavarians came G-FML Degenfeld, under 40 but still with fifteen years' experience of war and armies – his master Maximilian Emanuel had left home much later than the army and was planning to stop off at Linz to meet the Emperor before joining the army. For the Reichs contingent: the greybeard Waldeck. John George of Saxony and his army commander, the veteran professional soldier FM Joachim Rudiger, Freiherr von der Goltz, 63 years old and with over thirty years' military experience under his belt, leaving their hard-marching soldiers as they approached Maissau, were still riding through the pouring rain, having been misinformed initially that the conference was at Krems, and they would arrive at the castle quite late, in the afternoon.[37]

There is a story that Hermann presented Sobieski with a baton from Leopold, apparently as some kind of recognition of his supremacy; if it happened, the King thought little of the gift, since he never even mentioned it in his detailed letters to his wife.[38] Before they could get down to the agenda, they still needed to confirm Lorraine and Sobieski's arrangements agreed the day before: Waldeck despaired at the prospect of more protocol discussions but felt that the multiple meetings of Sobieski's compromise would just waste time and would have preferred to re-open the discussion on this; yet there was enough support for the compromise that it was accepted, at least insofar as the Poles and Germans met separately. The principal work was done by Lorraine, Waldeck and Degenfeld, drawing up a list of thirteen questions and the answers they desired, which Hermann of Baden subsequently presented to Sobieski in the joint session.

Although only second in the list, perhaps the most important of these was the question of supreme command: it was finally stated that Sobieski would be commander-in-chief, under the sole proviso that this was dependent on Leopold's continuing absence. The Imperialists already accepted Sobieski's supremacy, on this same condition, under the terms of their alliance, and Lorraine had personally decided not to contest the King's determination to be the alpha-male, but it was a significant step forward that the other German princes and their generals did the same. Even though they also confirmed that each prince would lead his own troops (a strong hint that the King was expected to use a light hand), the Germans thus ensured that the Poles were in a good frame of mind when their other points were discussed. The

---

37   There is some uncertainty about whether they arrived in time for the final discussions, or as the conference was breaking up. Le Bègue stated, in Stöller, p.98, that John George arrived as 'one finished', and was told of the results by Waldeck – but also says that Lorraine at the same time was informing the King, which sounds like he arrived as the separate sessions were reporting back to the common meeting. Curiously, Dalérac stated that the Elector had arrived the evening before and was present throughout (vol. 1, p.140); he also thought that the conference took place on the 4th.

38   The baton is often described as that of an Imperialist Feld-Marschall, ostensibly an honour – but one which carried a sting in the tail, for officially it could be viewed as making Sobieski junior not just to Lorraine (who as General-Lieutenant outranked all Feld-Marschalls) but even to Hermann, who had seniority within the rank. Wentzcke's description of it as a 'Feldherrnstab' (approximately, commander's staff), though no source is offered for this statement, sounds more sensible, but Hermann's biographer Beese doubts that any such presentation occurred. Paul Wentzcke, *Feldherr des Kaisers: Leben und Taten Herzog Karls V. von Lothringen* (Leipzig: Koehler & Amelang, 1943), pp.211–212; Beese, p.266 n.158

debates on the other points of the agenda would be long and fraught with the potential for explosions of offended pride, but this initial decision helped to ensure the tone remained cordial. Sobieski no doubt strenuously avoided any attempt by Hermann of Baden to obey his master's orders and discuss the protocol for a possible meeting between the King and Emperor Leopold.

After a long, exhausting day, the other points of the agenda were resolved as follows. From all reports, bizarre though it seemed, the south bank of the Danube on this the western side of the Wienerwald was clear of Ottoman troops, apart from an occasional party of Tatars scouting or searching for plunder missed by earlier raiders; so the army would simply cross the Danube, and take its route through the difficult defiles of the Wienerwald, aiming directly at the Ottoman camp and fighting through any Ottoman forces hidden in the hills or, if the hills were empty, advancing through them to attack the camp directly. According to most historians, Hermann of Baden had until this moment still entertained hopes of persuading the allies to adopt one of his ambitious wide-swinging manoeuvres to destroy the Ottomans, but this is doubted by his biographer Beese,[39] and these plans were in any case finally scotched in favour of the direct route – although Sobieski also seems to have expected the move over the Wienerwald to be carried out in such a way that he could still swing round in a narrower version of Hermann's encirclement and trap the Grand Vizier's army in an attack of annihilation, while Lorraine, more convinced that Vienna was close to falling, had the rather different intention of pushing forward through the hills to drive the Ottomans back from Vienna and open access to the city, not caring if the Grand Vizier escaped with an intact army as long as the siege had been broken. As for the specifics of crossing the Danube: all armies were to approach the bridges on Sunday the 5th, receive bread for the men and forage for the horses that day, and cross on the Monday, or Tuesday at the latest. The Saxons, who were more to the west, would use the stone Krems-Mautern bridge, join the Bavarians and Franconians already in that area, and head east along the river to Tulln; while the Poles, followed by Lorraine and the Imperialists, would use the causeways through the marshes to get to the (as yet incomplete) boat-bridge at Tulln.

Some of those present seem to have had a weak grasp of the local geography beyond the Danube, because the rendezvous for the two halves of the army was technically specified as the little River Traisen, close to Mautern, which would have required the Polish-Imperialist half to march some distance *away* from Vienna and then double back again on its own tracks; but fortunately everyone present seems to have ignored this and recognised Tulln as the real point of junction. Everyone was to be in position at Tulln ready to set off by the 7th.

For supplies, barges would be brought to Tulln and bread issued to the men, while forage for the horses could be found in the fields around; officers

---

39 pp.236–237; Beese quotes, on p.236, a foreign envoy's report from Passau in mid-August that the Hofkriegsrat had by then already agreed to the Wienerwald route, and a report by Hermann himself of the Stetteldorf discussions in which he acknowledged the pressing reasons for using the Wienerwald.

of the train were to be instructed to have eight days' worth of bread and oats to hand in the barges, which would then keep pace with the army as it moved downstream so that further supplies could be drawn from it. To secure the two bridges, and the vital magazines in Tulln, while the armies were moving down to them, a detachment of troops would be sent to support the burgher militia in defending walled Krems, and a palisaded bridgehead would be constructed on the south bank at Tulln.

Both the Imperialists and Poles were still concerned to protect northern Lower Austria and Moravia from enemy forces in the east, Hungarian rebels and the handful of Turks who had escaped from the Battle of Bisamberg. Thus around 2,000 Imperialist cavalry were to be sent off northwards to reinforce the Moravian militia, and Sobieski issued orders that 4,000 Polish soldiers from those still slogging through Moravia were to join them, plus the Lithuanians when they arrived – rather optimistically, the King thought that these must be at the Polish-Silesian border by now.

As for the matter of an 'order of battle', under which was understood both the arrangement of forces in the line of battle and the tactics they would use (the two, obviously, being closely linked), the meeting expended much time and hot air on the question but came to no agreement, other than that there should be a reserve in case the Turks, while the Christians were dragging themselves through the Wienerwald, crossed the hills in the opposite direction round the open right flank and fell on their rear. Some argued for the army acting as a single coherent unit and forming a combined battle-line, the bulk of infantry in the centre as usual, cavalry on the wings supported by the rest of the infantry, Poles forming the outermost wings on both flanks (Lorraine's secretary, Le Bègue, carefully avoided names and used the passive voice in describing the debate, but his tone implies that Lorraine himself favoured this position, though one may suspect that either sensible Waldeck or royal-minded Sobieski was behind a suggestion someone put forward that all questions of formal precedence be ignored and no regard taken of the permanent claim of the Imperialists to have the post of honour on the right).

Whatever the idea of a coherent order of battle had going for it militarily, it ran aground on the principle already so precariously established, that each prince should command his own contingent; such a command would be impossible if the contingents were split up on military lines – and without such a command, there was a risk that Saxony or Bavaria might hold their armies back even at this late stage. The matter of an order of battle was postponed until later.

With considerable confidence, the meeting even discussed what the army would do once Vienna had been relieved, and agreed on either an immediate pursuit of the Ottoman army or another attempt to take Neuhäusel (see Glossary). If the 'minutes' of the meeting are to be believed, they carefully sidestepped a remark in the agenda (probably inserted by Waldeck) that 'reflections on the Empire are not to be neglected', a strong hint that attention should be paid to the risk of French attack on Germany. The Poles could hardly be expected to join the Empire against France at such a time, so the most appropriate way to exploit any victory would be by operations in Hungary.

Late in the afternoon John George of Saxony and Goltz arrived, soaked. In the ensuing courtesies, Sobieski welcomed the Elector and apparently tried to be agreeable but, looking down his nose at the German's plain coat, probably succeeded only appearing patronising. Waldeck took the two Saxons off to a separate room to present the thoughts of the council so far. John George expressed some reluctance to acknowledging Sobieski as his superior, for reasons that are never made clear (if Sobieski's manner did not play a part, probably, John George was one of those who felt that a Duke who elected an Emperor outranked an elected King), but was persuaded by the diplomatic Waldeck to acquiesce in the common decision – and in the rest of the campaign, he would serve well away from the Poles and get along perfectly well with Lorraine, a mere duke and his undoubted junior in the recognised ducal order of precedence. After this sidebar discussion, the Saxons apparently joined the common session, and the discussions continued into the night, especially over the thorny question of the order of battle, until those present ran out of steam. Sobieski, determined to take advantage of his new position, decided to work himself on the order of battle after the meeting; it was an appropriate task for the head of the army – and it would enable him to ensure that he gave the Poles the post of honour on the right, over which he was just as keen as the Imperialists.

Text of the decisions of 3 September

Translated from the French text quoted in Mansberg, pp.25–27; the document was also published in full in other works, such as Rauchbar and Jochner, sometimes in a slightly abbreviated German translation; a modified English version is in Paradowski, pp.124–125. In this translation, I have added some punctuation where it is needed to make sense in modern English, but have retained the original's idiosyncratic use of questions marks. It should be remembered that the 'questions' were posed first by Waldeck, and the 'resolutions' came out of the discussions of the conference.

The resolutions taken at Stettendorf [Stetteldorf] the 3rd Sept. 1683

DISCUSSIONS, DISCUSSIONS, DISCUSSIONS: THE STETTELDORF CONFERENCE

To discuss	
1. The location by which one will relieve the town of Vienna	1. It was resolved to attempt the relief of Vienna between the Danube and the River Wien, all the other locations more requiring time and lacking in food and forage; in distancing ourselves from the Danube we would abandon the countryside on both sides to the enemy
2. The disposition of the armies and the command of the same	The supreme command, if His Imp. Maj. does not come, will remain to His Maj. the King of Poland, for the rest each chief will command his own troops
3. The means to subsist for each army until the crossing of the river	3. All the armies will approach the bridges Sunday so as to be able to cross Monday, or Tuesday at the latest, where they have forage and will be provided with bread
4. The location of the crossing of the river and if more bridges are needed?	4. The armies of the Emperor and of the King of Poland will cross at Tulln, and those of the Elector of Saxony at Krems to join the other allies, who are already on the other side of the river; and if it can be achieved one will make another bridge near Traismauer
5. The day of the crossing and the location of the rendezvous	5. The day of the crossing of the allies and their first rendezvous will be the Monday on the Traisen
6. The manner of the crossing and of the general rendezvous, so that the enemy will not meet us separated beyond the Wienerwald	6. The majority won the day that the enemy could not come at the allies to attack them while on the Traisen, but that the night between Monday and Tuesday the Poles will cross and draw towards the allies on the right of the bridge, so as to be able to support them while the Imperialists cross
7. The manner of obtaining bread and forage sufficiently for the expedition that one will not lose time by this and will not be forced to consume it uselessly	7. It was decreed that from each corps one should appoint officers who will receive bread and oats for 8 days in the barges, which will be placed outside the town of Tulln so that it can be brought up without difficulty

8. How to secure the bridges and our magazines?	8. That of Tulln being secured on one side by the town, one will secure it on the other by a well-palisaded work, and the bridge that one has begun establishing could under any circumstances be continued although (concluding that we have enough with two) the Krems bridge will be secured by the towns that are before it, with some soldiers joined to the citizenry, and like-wise also the magazine at Krems be secured]
9. The means to bring the food provisions after	9. One will have them brought after [the army] by water, and will take the boatmen into pay
10. The disposition for attacking the enemy and the various routes by which the corps could keep in contact, even the posts to take; to regulate the signals to be given on every eventuality; in the woods, constant patrols between the armies	10. This was postponed until one had obtained better intelligence about everything, but in general it was judged that it [the attack] should be done by the infantry, supported by some cavalry; and on the wings, covered by infantry to secure the flanks; and to secure the rear by the reserve
11. How to secure the countryside beyond, especially Prague?	11. By a detachment of two thousand horse, to be joined to 4,000 men of the King of Poland who are following and then by the army of Lithuania which must direct itself to the borders of Silesia
12. How to secure our rear, if the enemy passes by the right through the wood	12. By the reserve
13. The relief succeeding, how to exploit it for the good of the land and the public given this junction of armies; considerations of the Empire not to be neglected	13. Either by following the enemy or by attacking Neuhäusel.

The meeting broke up: Lorraine rode through the night back over the familiar route to Korneuburg, and John George took the road back east to Hadersdorf where he slept before proceeding to visit the south-German contingents at Krems-Mautern the next day. Hermann of Baden headed back to report to the Emperor at Linz, though he bumped into Waldeck on the way as he passed through Krems, and the old Reichs-Feld-Marschall, keen as ever on his paperwork, persuaded the President to check and confirm that his written record of the conference was accurate. Sobieski settled down to make Stetteldorf Castle his headquarters for a day or two more while his Poles continued to catch up; Lorraine had invited him to dine at the Imperialist camp but apparently the social niceties were prevented by the continuing rain, and Sobieski happily spent much of the next couple of days with his staff working on the order of battle.

One thing still threatened to mar Sobieski's contentment: the nagging memory that his tenure of supreme command was on the condition 'if His Imperial Majesty should not come'. Emperor Leopold might still join the army: he had already moved with his court late in August down the Danube from Passau to Linz – still a good 60 miles even as the crow flies from the nearest part of the army at Krems-Mautern, but barges could move mighty fast downstream on the powerful current of the Danube. Leopold's desire to be present with his own army when his own capital was liberated, especially after his ignominious, prestige-ruining flight six weeks earlier, was completely natural, and Leopold himself laboured under the misapprehension that his presence with the army, as the ruler universally recognised to outrank everyone, would solve precedence disputes instead of causing them – for part of being the ruler who outranked everybody was the requirement to insist on protocol that publicly confirmed this priority. Buonvisi, the pragmatic papal nuncio to the Imperialist court, recognised the danger that precedence disputes could rupture the fragile alliance and, familiar with Sobieski from a mission to Poland in the 1670s, understood Sobieski's motivation, so he advised against such a move, but many of Leopold's court and ministers, though apparently not including Hermann of Baden, supported it. Sobieski however was having none of it.

Fortunately, the King had a most unexpected ally. The Catholic Church recently under Pope Innocent XI had been active in attempting to persuade Christian Europe to come together against the growing Ottoman threat; one element in this attempt had been a little Italian monk from the Order of Capuchins called Marco d'Aviano, currently 51 years old and increasingly infirm in body, but a passionate orator who had achieved international fame since 1680 by several tours around the Empire and neighbouring lands, preaching especially on the abandonment of sins to great success before huge crowds (even though he could not speak German) and talking politics with rulers. Louis XIV, secret supporter of the Ottoman Empire, had kicked him out of France, but he had made a big impact on the genuinely religious Emperor Leopold. As the Ottoman army had pushed unstoppably into Austria earlier in the year, Leopold had sent repeated appeals to the abbot of d'Aviano's monastery in Padua that the monk be allowed to visit him again to provide spiritual support, and meanwhile corresponded at length with Brother Marco; in mid-August permission had finally been granted, and d'Aviano joined Leopold in Linz on 1 or 2 September. Together with his deep religious conviction and passionate oratory, the monk possessed – astonishing combination – a sound political head on his shoulders; he quickly agreed with Buonvisi that the Emperor must keep away from the army and lobbied strenuously against the Imperial advisers who supported going. Leopold was persuaded to issue an unambiguous acknowledgement that Sobieski was to be commander-in-chief, but the Emperor still wanted to *visit* the army, and d'Aviano was commissioned to go to headquarters and talk the matter over with the King of Poland. The monk arrived at Stetteldorf on 4 or 5 September; it is not clear what he did for the next few days, as he was documented in none of the key sources and he initially avoided mentioning the matter of a visit in his first report to Leopold – as far as we can tell, he quickly learnt that his original conclusions about the dangers of a visit were correct and was hoping that, in conjunction with the unfavourable impression that Hermann of Baden must have brought back from the Stetteldorf conference, silence would keep Leopold from coming.

If so, it did not work: on the 5th, before the first letter from d'Aviano had even arrived, Leopold decided to go downstream and orders were issued to his commissioner accompanying Sobieski, Christoph Leopold Graf Schaffgotsch, to discuss the protocol for a reception – but then was delayed, first by the ceremonial of receiving the Brunswick-Lüneburg princes (including Georg Ludwig, the future George I of Great Britain) as they passed Linz on their way to join the army as volunteers, then by his wife's going into labour and giving birth to a daughter. As soon as possible after this, Leopold set off downriver, on the 8th writing again to d'Aviano urging the monk to send his advice on what to do. The continuing silence so far achieved its desired result however that the imperial barge anchored below the cliff at Dürnstein, still a few miles short of Krems-Mautern, and waited for news before proceeding further. The court learnt that Polish officials had refused to meet Schaffgotsch to discuss the protocol of an imperial visit. On the 10th, the Imperialist general Rabatta and the diplomat Lamberg (who had been negotiating back and forth between Leopold and John George as the Saxons marched through Bohemia) arrived at Dürnstein to tell the Emperor that everyone in the army command was opposed to his coming, and Leopold, convinced at last, though in his heart he still continued to hope for better news through d'Aviano, held a final consultation with his advisers and decided to stay put. The best he could do to salvage his pride was to issue orders that, if Vienna were relieved, none of the other commanders should enter the city until the Emperor arrived. And finally on the 11th, d'Aviano wrote to him, dashing his last lingering hopes with a discouraging letter. Leopold remained at Dürnstein as the battle raged on the 12th.

Despite his silence to Leopold, d'Aviano seems to have reduced Sobieski's fears about the risk that Leopold would come. The refusal of his officials to meet Schaffgotsch to negotiate on the matter also helped. The imperial party's sudden lurch downstream to Dürnstein gave the King a nasty moment or two, but overall he was free to concentrate on military operations free from the risk of finding himself expected to bend the knee to the Emperor.

3

Over the Danube and the final decisions

In the days after the Stetteldorf conference on 3 September, as the sky persisted in pouring rain onto the area,[40] the various armies completed their preparations and continued to move together. Imperialist commissioners laboured to assemble food supplies for the Poles, since the officials of the aristocratic local government who should have taken care of the logistical arrangements had made themselves scarce. Sobieski rode down to the north bank opposite Tulln on the 4th to see for himself how the work on the bridge was progressing – not well, as rain hampered work and swelled the marshes that had to be bridged; the King had planned to send out a reconnaissance, but the weather forced its cancellation. However, at least the far bank still seemed utterly devoid of Ottoman forces.

Next morning, the skies clearing but the ground still soaked underfoot and the damp creating dreary mists, the King rode off to inspect the defences of the north bank opposite Vienna, and spent much of the day talking over with Lorraine the details of the order of battle and how the army would get through the Wienerwald. Conforming to the decision of the conference, Lorraine meanwhile sent off a small corps to help defend Moravia and the army's rear against possible incursions from beyond the River March (the Croatian regiments of Lodron and Ricchiardi, the German DR Herbeville, 300 Polish cavalry probably from Lubomirski's corps, and two battalions of IR Erbprinz of Lorraine); he also confirmed that FML Schulz would remain at Jedlesee opposite Vienna with CR Veterani, five companies of IR Salm and three companies of IR Wallis, guarding the north bank against any attempt by the Ottoman army to cross; and he set off with the rest of his massed cavalry from Korneuburg for Tulln. The Poles meanwhile were finally approaching the valley floor: although many Polish soldiers were still scattered back along the road through Moravia, the core of the army had now assembled around Ober-Hollabrunn under the two Hetmans, astonishingly including even a significant proportion of the wagon train with its essential supplies which

---

40   If the weather was the same on both sides of the Wienerwald, the accounts of the siege from within Vienna tell us that the rain continued until about two in the afternoon on the 4th.

had managed to keep up; and on 5 September, while the King was away at the Jedlesee bridgeheads, the Poles marched south past Stetteldorf Castle out of the hills and onto the plain. The main part of the army headed direct for the bridge at Tulln, but it seems that many of the train personnel and some of the seedier elements amongst the soldiers, who had already earnt an unhappy reputation for looting as they passed through Moravia, quickly spread out across the plain seizing anything they could lay their hands on. The Saxons, 20 miles to the west, had passed through Maissau and were themselves descending that day towards Krems, adopting a closed-up march formation with an advanced guard of two cuirassier regiments, and throwing out outposts whenever they halted, not through fear of Turks but to protect themselves against marauding Poles; they camped that night (5–6 September) on one of the many islands of the Danube in the vicinity, likewise for security against the Poles, but even then John George and Golz were roused in the night as panicky sentries raised the alarm when marauders approached in the dark. Some amongst the Poles tried to attribute German nervousness to their exhaustion under the burden of their efforts and despondency at the state of affairs[41], but the claim did not hold water, for, while it might have been valid for the Imperialist cavalry, *they* were not the ones panicking, and even the hard-marching Saxons had exerted themselves no more than the Poles. Fear of the unknown (especially with the Ottomans' reputation for savagery) and fear of the very real dangers from their strange allies, were more likely causes.

By the end of 5 September, the Christian army stood on the soggy banks of the Danube in two corps, the Saxons upstream ready to cross the safe stone bridge and join the Bavarians, Reichs troops and Imperialist infantry already on the south bank, the Imperialist cavalry and the Poles at Tulln looking miserably at the nightmare in front of them as labourers and conscripted peasants struggled to complete the bridges there. A junior Habsburg staff officer, Heinrich Tobias von Haslingen,[42] very experienced in warfare but in engineering possessed of nothing but boundless enthusiasm and energy, had with much effort managed to build two slightly shaky bridges over the main stream out of salt barges anchored to the river-bed and connected by planks, and was even now supervising the creation of causeways through the marshes without which the troops could not even reach the real bridges. The constructions were officially finished that night, but neither bridges nor causeways looked strong enough to carry wagons or artillery, and on the 6th, the Imperialists at first looked at the sodden marshes and suggested delaying for a day while the ground dried out more and extra work was done on the bridges, contenting themselves with sending Colonel Heissler and his 600 dragoons over the river to scout out deep into the Wienerwald as far as Klosterneuburg, a big fortified monastery on the banks of the Danube nearly half-way through the Wienerwald, which he was ordered to hold. However,

---

41   Dalérac, vol. 1, p.141.
42   The surname is often spelt Hasslingen, but his biographer Uechtritz-Steinkirch prefers one 's': O. von Uechtritz-Steinkirch, *Heinrich Tobias Freiherr von Haslingen: ein Beitrag zur Geschichte der Befreiung Wiens im Jahre 1683* (Breslau: Korn, 1883).

as the day progressed, the commanders started to imagine that the sound of artillery fire from Vienna was much louder than normal, and early in the afternoon there came the echoes of a great explosion from a mine that the Turks had fired against one of the bastions. Fortunately, the boom of cannon fire soon resumed, indicating that the city was still holding out, but Sobieski now felt that further delay was impossible, and that evening he led the way across the ramshackle bridge, preceded by his *buńczuk*, the decorated lance that served Polish commanders as a command insignium in battle, and its special guard of 100 men;[43] with the King went his household, his personal guard of haiduks and Janissaries, the two troops of *pancerni* that had been acting as his military escort recently, and a horde of Polish generals and foreign princes and noble volunteers. Once over, he took position with the entire entourage to watch as first Sieniawski and then Jabłonowski came over with their divisions, swinging right as they came off the bridge to enter the camp assigned to them west of Tulln. The noble cavalry were splendid in their armour, colourful robes, swirling lance-pennants; but when came the turn of the tatty infantry to pass in full sight of the international audience, Lubomirski, attending his King this day instead of his corps amongst the Imperialist cavalry, tried suggesting that they be left to cross under cover of darkness. Sobieski, who had been willing enough to keep his shabby foot-soldiers from the sight of Imperialist officials during the march through Silesia and Moravia, rejected such an artifice – which anyway would have further delayed setting off over the Wienerwald – and declared, proudly but untruthfully, to the foreigners that his infantry had taken an oath to uniform themselves only in captured Turkish clothing.[44] In fact, with the bridges constantly breaking and needing repair, it took the Poles all night and part of the next day, the 7th, to get all of their troops over, and even then they had to postpone bringing their train wagons across to allow their allies over. By the time the Imperialist cavalry, already grumpy at the delay, could start crossing, the rain had resumed, increasing their misery.

The only consolation was that fast-moving Heissler was already sending back promising reports. Klosterneuburg Monastery was an important post, already containing a small detachment of troops under Major Gabriel Vecchio to back up its martial monks; the Ottomans had tried four times already during July and August to take the monastery, with comparatively limited forces, and although four times they had been beaten back, a major assault at this late stage might still succeed. Heissler was very familiar with the monastery, since it had served as a base for several of his daring forays over the Danube during the summer. He was expected to hold it until the

---

43   There is some doubt about this since the *buńczuk* was technically the insignia of Hetmans, but there is no doubt that Sobieski had one at Vienna.

44   As the Poles passed Raygern Monastery, Father Bernard Brulig (Dudik, pp.431–432) had described most of the Polish infantry as well dressed and equipped and keeping good order, but also noted that many of them were 'an inexperienced, tattered, exhausted and badly-dressed folk' and, while recording their plentiful weapons, observed that 'they also kept bad [order] or even no order at all; and many of them seemed to be more like gypsies than soldiers.' (This particular passage of Brulig's is quoted, without the source cited, in Forst de Battaglia, pp.159–160.)

army caught up, in case the Ottomans decided to try to oppose the Christians within the Wienerwald – if they did and managed to take the monastery, every chance of getting through the hills to Vienna had gone out of the window. On the 6th Heissler described how he had defeated 100 Turkish cavalry round Klosterneuburg before entering the monastery; no significant Ottoman units had been seen within the Wienerwald, and prisoners taken in his skirmish, whom he sent back to headquarters, confirmed under interrogation that the mine at Vienna on the 6th, despite the ferocity of the ensuing assault, had not come close to breaking through the defences and taking the city. On the 7th, while the Tulln bridge was creaking under the weight of the Imperialist cuirassiers, Heissler sent back a further report, that he had pushed forward as far as the Kahlenberg, the last major hill of the Wienerwald before Vienna, and lit signal fires on the top as a way of telling the beleaguered city that the relief was on its way (though Vecchio had already done the same the previous day);[45] he also reported that his dragoons had skirmished for three hours with a Turkish force, which he estimated rather improbably at 3,000 strong, finally forcing the enemy to retreat with a loss of 50 dead against just three Christians wounded.

The Ottoman army facing the Allied forces as Vienna. Caspar Luyken, 1689 (Rijksmuseum, Amsterdam)

---

45   Curiously, the sources from the relief army specified fires but on both occasions the garrison reported seeing *rockets* fired from the Kahlenberg.

Lorraine had crossed the Tulln bridge on the 7th ahead of his cavalry in order to continue talking through with Sobieski the details of how to proceed and to urge that the army advance on the morrow. The Imperialist horsemen as they came off the bridge turned a little to their left and settled into the camp laid out for them all around Tulln, to the left of the Poles. Meanwhile, the Germans from the Krems-Mautern crossing upstream had been marching downriver along the open plain known as the Tullner Feld, and were starting to arrive. The Saxons, who had had to cross the bridge before joining the march, had the harder slog; shocked as they had been by the sight of 70 Turkish heads impaled on spikes over the gate of Mautern when they passed through, they were even more appalled at their first sight of the devastated, deserted countryside that was all that remained of the prosperous agricultural land of the south bank after weeks of being ravaged by Tatars; but they trailed along behind the Bavarians, the Reichs regiments and the Imperialist foot-sloggers, and most of them were appearing before Tulln by the evening of the 7th.

It was clear that the order of battle had not yet been finalised, and Sobieski caused some confusion by issuing orders as they came in that all of the infantry were to cross a little stream (apparently referring to the Tullnerbach which runs into the Danube west of Tulln) and camp together; Waldeck went to Sobieski to remonstrate, arguing that any further movement in the night would only cause confusion and the troops were secure enough where they stood, close to the Poles. Sobieski agreed and the Germans stayed put for the night. Next day, if the Hallart map is to be believed[46], all the Germans were required to undergo a further move that was not only bizarre in itself but also conflicted badly with the positions they would finally be assigned: they marched *past* the Poles and Imperialists, and camped to their left during the pause of the 8th. Assuming that Hallart is correct, this meant that the whole army was camped, with its back to the Danube and facing the Tullner Feld, in the following order: west of Tulln were the Poles; left of them and around Tulln, stretching as far as the Mühlbach rivulet to the east of the town, lay the Imperialists, their own left flank refused so that it faced the Mühlbach and the Germans beyond; beyond the rivulet, in a long line parallel to the Danube, first the Saxons, then the Franconians, finally the Bavarians on the extreme left.

The armies rested again on the 8th, while the Polish train wagons continued to struggle across Haslingen's rickety bridges. As Sobieski wrote to his wife several days later:

We had all the difficulties of the world in our crossing of the Danube. The bridges broke down under the artillery and the baggage. The

---

46 Reproduced in facsimile in Peter Broucek, Erich Hillbrand, and Fritz Vesely, *Historischer Atlas zur zweiten Türkenbelagerung, Wien 1683* (Vienna: Deuticke, 1983), opp. p.48; and as a drawn copy in *Das Kriegsjahr 1683*, Tafel III. The information contained in the Hallart map at this point has been widely accepted by historians, and Hallart later did very creditable work, but it must be noted that, since Hallart's geography on this occasion obviously leaves a lot to be desired, his accuracy on all points is open to question.

NO MORE TIME TO LOSE

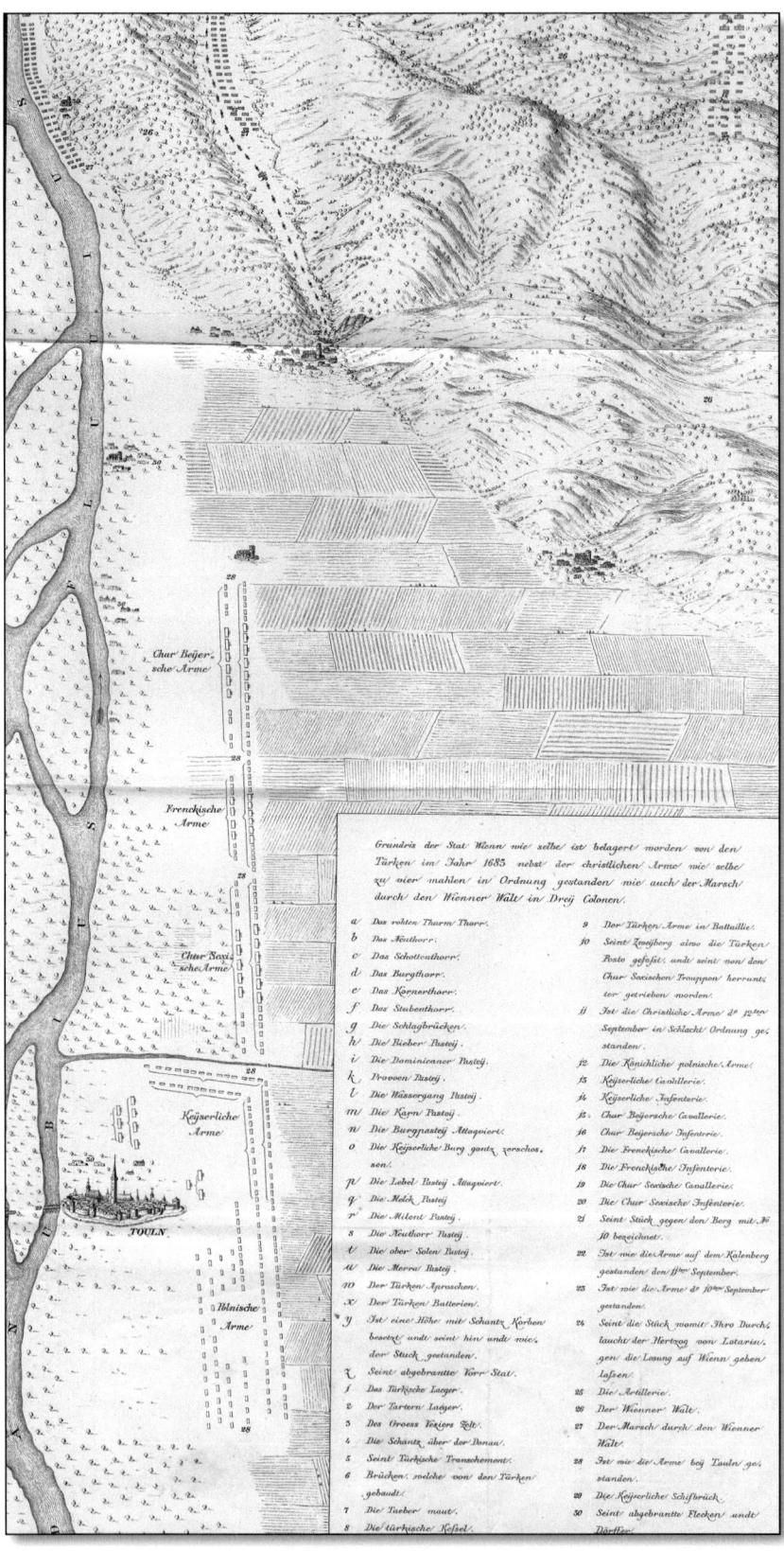

First part of Hallart's plan, from the drawn copy in *Das Kriegsjahr 1683* (see footnote).

majority of the carts had to seek fords, and luckily found some via several branches of the Danube, except for the main arm of the river, where the current was too rapid; for there is no river to compare with the Danube for force.[47]

No reason is specified for this further loss of a day, though, apart from the Poles' feeling that they ought to wait for their whole train (even though they advanced through the Wienerwald without it in the end), the day was taken up with distributing bread and other food to the soldiers (at least to the Germans), a day later than originally planned. Besides, by seventeenth-century standards the twenty-mile march of the Germans from Mautern had been a substantial effort requiring some rest; and since Sobieski sent out a reconnaissance, it is likely he was waiting for its return.

Sobieski was beginning to realise that the Imperialists could not give him information about the Wienerwald and the Turkish positions beyond in the detail that he required, so he had decided to try to use his own troops, more experienced in reporting the sorts of information he expected, though he still lacked the Cossacks who would have been the best at this sort of work – if the Ukrainian light cavalry had been present in the numbers he had envisaged, he could have flooded the Wienerwald with scouts and obtained a clear picture of the whole situation. One reconnaissance of armoured *pancerni* had already gone out from Tulln which brought in a few prisoners but no significant intelligence, and now two captains, Roman Ruszczyc and Damian Szumlański, were sent out with detachments of light cavalry from the veteran corps of Sieniawski, 100 men each, with orders to bring back reports and prisoners within 24 hours. We have no detail about the course that these Poles took, but they returned in the night of the 8th, with Szumlański mortally wounded (he died four days later) and 13 prisoners; from these, the Poles learnt that Kara Mustafa was aware of the relief's approach and had already started moving troops to face the hills and protect the rear of his camp; according to Sobieski in a letter to his wife the following day, all prisoners taken so far were in agreement that the Ottomans did not want to believe the arrival of the Poles.[48] Given Sobieski's astonishment several days later when he reached the final range of hills and saw the Ottoman camp for the first time for himself, it is very unlikely that the scouting parties penetrated far enough to give eyewitness reports of the camp; the intelligence provided almost certainly came only from interrogation of prisoners like these.

In addition to reconnaissances, the Christians were busy assembling as many guides as they could find to help them once they entered the wasteland of the Wienerwald – the Tatars had left no-one alive in the open countryside, but enough foresters and hunters had taken refuge in the town to be going

---

47 letter of 12 September, in Plater, p.65.
48 The reconnaissance is described in various works, including Paradowski, p.130; the version in Anton Dolleczek, 'Die Entsatzschlacht vor Wien am 12. September 1683', *Organ der Militärwissenschaftlichen Vereine* 26 (1883), pp.149–180 + 1 fold-out, here p.157, includes specific details of movements that the Ottomans had not even undertaken yet, and was probably padded by the author from his own knowledge of subsequent events. Plater, p.60, for Sobieski's remark to his wife.

on with. A bigger concern was supply, especially for the horses: armies could carry grain to make bread for the humans, and soldiers could carry enough baked bread to keep them going for a few days, but the horses, if they could not have fresh grass, required huge amounts of bulky hay and straw, far beyond what could be transported; the Christian army was top-heavy in cavalry and had an extraordinarily large number of mounts, but the valley south of the Danube here had been sacked systematically by the Tatars – the steppe folk not only destroyed the villages and killed or enslaved the population, they also burnt all traces of agriculture, and the fields from which Sobieski and Lorraine could have expected to feed their horses over the next couple of days as they approached the Wienerwald contained nothing but rain-soaked ash. The resources of the north bank were already being eaten up, the horses of the army beginning to go short; and Sobieski was looking out with foreboding across the valley floor at the Wienerwald, full of wooded, *grassless* hills.

During the pause, Lorraine went to attend religious services.[49] Marco d'Aviano held a great religious ceremony for the King and most of the generals (despite occasional suggestions that this was a multi-denominational ceremony,[50] it is unlikely that Protestants such as Waldeck or John George of Saxony and his officers were present): the monk blessed the congregation for the coming operations, they took communion from his hands, and he said Mass and delivered one of his famous passionate sermons, ending in an emotional call on the congregation to declare their complete confidence in their god and leading them in calling out repeatedly 'Jesus Maria!' – the phrase that would be adopted as a battle-cry when they reached the Ottomans on the 12th. After the service, d'Aviano retired with Sobieski for a private audience in which he informed the King of his conversations with Leopold at Linz, stressing how he had urged the Emperor not to even approach the theatre of war, let alone try to join the armies. A nasty moment arose when household officials of the Imperial court were reported to have arrived in Tulln to inform the King that Leopold was on his way and would enter Tulln by nightfall; d'Aviano quickly smiled and assured Sobieski that he did not believe it, that it must be a joke, that Leopold, despite his fervent desire to meet the King and view the army, would not arrive without a formal Polish invitation and so would not come beyond Krems (and indeed, as we have noted already, Leopold came to a halt at Dürnstein, just short of Krems).

Lorraine had heard also about the arrival of the household officials, and, accompanied by Waldeck, John George, and the other generals, hurried

---

49 The location of this is unclear. Le Bègue (Stöller, p.99) said that Lorraine went 'from' Tulln, and Sobieski's letter of the 9th to his wife (Plater, p.57) suggested that the private audience was held half an hour before crossing the Danube, from which we may infer that Sobieski had rejoined the rump Polish camp north of the river at this time and that the service took place there. However, even the date is not entirely certain: Sobieski seems clear enough in referring to 'yesterday' (8th) but his letters to his wife were not intended to be perfectly accurate historical records; Le Bègue, as usual, could be read as describing events of the day before his dated entry. However, the 8th seems the most logical date.

50 e.g. Wentzcke, pp.214–215. Stöller, p.99, names only Lorraine and Sobieski, with the others joining them *after* the ceremony to discuss the military plans.

to see the King, officially to discuss military matters but almost certainly first of all to reassure him. Once it became clear that d'Aviano had calmed Sobieski's apprehensions, the discussion turned to the matter of finalising the formation to be adopted and questions of command, and the exact routes to be taken into the Wienerwald.[51] Sobieski, as commander-in-chief, had prepared and now presented his plan, a document he called an 'Order of Battle' – not a complete listing of units and their hierarchical relationships as we now understand the term, but a general arrangement of the different corps and an indication of how they were to fight once the Christians made contact with the Ottomans. Respecting the principle that each prince was to command his own contingent, Sobieski had made no detailed rules about the organisation within each corps, although he stepped over the boundary to make a few minor alterations. According to this Order of Battle, the allied army would advance as follows: the Poles would form the right wing, under the direct command of Crown Grand Hetman Jabłonowski; the Imperialists would form the centre or 'corps de bataille', under Lorraine; the armies of Bavaria and Saxony would form the left wing, under the two electors; the Reichs troops under Waldeck would form an extra corps on the extreme left, intended, once they made contact with the Ottomans beyond the Wienerwald, to push directly along the Danube both to outflank the Ottoman right wing as part of the battle and to open a route into the city to throw in reinforcements in case the battle should go badly. Sobieski proposed lending four or five squadrons of his heavy winged hussars to the Imperialists, in addition to the *pułk* of Hieronim Lubomirski (four squadrons of *pancerni*, presumably expected to join the several regiments of Lubomirski's corps already in the Imperialist army), and would also lend a few squadrons to the left wing. The artillery was to be divided up, and if the electors did not have enough, Lorraine was to give them some from the Imperialist park – the Saxons had a good artillery train with them and had no apparent need of more guns, so here Sobieski was probably just incorporating into his plan the arrangement that the Imperialists already had with the Bavarians in the Capitulation of Passau to supplement their artillery from Habsburg arsenals. To ensure as smooth a passage of the Wienerwald as possible, the infantry all along the front of the army would take the first line, keeping clear of the cavalry who were to follow; if they tried to march in formation together, the woods and defiles were bound to cause confusion. Sobieski also expected that the infantry would help clear broken ground to facilitate the cavalry's advance (Polish infantry were always equipped for such a role); he did not state this in the Order of Battle, but mentioned such an intention in his letter to Queen Marie the next day. When they reached open ground beyond the Wienerwald, the cavalry would move up to take position in gaps between the infantry battalions, and the King explicitly stated that he expected his winged hussars to charge first. Hopelessly over-estimating the size of the army in relation to the extent of the ground on the far side of the Wienerwald, he declared that forming in the usual three lines (two battle-lines and a smaller

---

51 On questions surrounding this council, see Appendix I, 3.1.

reserve) would extend the front so much that the right wing would have to pass the River Wien, an obstacle that should be used to protect the flank instead of splitting the army, and that therefore the army should adopt a deeper narrower formation, four lines deep, three full lines and the smaller fourth as the reserve.[52]

Sobieski's plan met with universal aversion. Reasons for disagreement are hard to find in the sources, but there are remarks in Le Bègue's entry in his 'Diary' for the 8th on this topic which suggest that the old questions of regal precedence were still playing their part, and a compromise had to be reached.[53] The position of greatest honour was on the right (this notion dated back to classical times, at least as far as the Roman Republic), and the troops of the senior monarch were always entitled to this post, with those of the next-senior monarch entitled to the left wing and the unfortunates at the bottom of the status stakes entitled only to the centre. Leopold as Emperor outranked everybody, and was universally entitled to the right; his General-Lieutenant, whatever he felt in person, could not abandon his master's claim to precedence. But Sobieski wanted the right, and in his favour had good military reasons that even the Imperialists acknowledged, in addition to the fact that he was the senior ruler *present* with the army. From the sources, there is no evidence of any heated arguments, and since the King made no complaint on the subject in his letter to his wife first thing next morning, we may assume that the changes were agreed relatively cordially, especially as on the primary point of status the King got his own way – undoubtedly it also helped enormously that Lorraine was continuing to acknowledge Sobieski as supreme commander, visiting him every day to receive the parole, and even John George had started doing the same since the Saxons had joined the combined army. So one of those typically dotty compromises of status-obsessed ages was arranged:[54] Sobieski could have his right wing with the Poles, but the Germans would then pretend to themselves that he constituted a separate army, and would form themselves with their own centre, left and right: Lorraine himself would command the left wing, comprising the bulk of the Imperialist troops, reinforced by the Saxons under John George; the centre would be formed from the Bavarian and Reich forces, under the overall command of Waldeck; and a small right wing was created of Imperialist cavalry under GdC Julius Franz, Herzog von Sachsen-Lauenburg (Saxe-Lauenburg), officially comprised of eight regiments of cuirassiers, two of German dragoons and one of Croatian cavalry, but all of them were under-strength and formed in action only about twenty-three squadrons in total. Thus, troops of the Emperor held *both* the right and the left; the Emperor's prestige was secure. After all this petty arguing, it was no problem at all for Sobieski to agree to give up on his four-deep idea and

---

52 See Glossary for the distinction between 'ranks' (rows of soldiers within regiments) and 'lines' (rows of regiments).
53 Stöller, p.100
54 This sort of compromise can seem so ludicrous to modern eyes until one works in a corporation and discovers that the same spirit of trivial competition for marks of status is alive and well today in the twenty-first century.

accept a more traditional formation of two lines and a reserve; probably, the Imperialists, familiar with the distances involved on the far side of the Wienerwald, convinced him without difficulty that his concerns about the River Wien were unfounded – and even in the new formation, the Christian army's right flank would not in fact stretch anywhere near the Wien. Equally uncontroversial was the decision to leave a detachment to guard the bridge at Tulln, the trains to be parked there and unnecessary gear to be left on the left bank and islands: every man was needed to relieve Vienna, but if nifty Tatars got round the Christians' rear and destroyed their reserve supplies or even used the bridge to cross to the north bank and spread devastation across untouched northern Austria, it would be a disaster whether Vienna had been relieved or not, so a number of men would have to be spared. About 2,000 were appointed to remain behind, half Germans and half Poles.[55]

The text of Sobieski's original Order of Battle (which was *not* followed in the action) is as follows:

> The *corps de bataille* will be composed of Imperial troops, to which we will join the cavalry regiment [*pułk*] of the Marshal of the Court [Lubomirski] and four or five squadrons of our men-at-arms [hussars], in return for which one will give us some dragoons or some other German troops. This corps will be commanded by monsieur the Duke of Lorraine.
>
> The Polish army will occupy the right wing, which will be commanded by the Grand Hetman Jabłonowski and the other generals of this nation.
>
> The troops of messieurs the Electors of Bavaria and Saxony will be on the left wing, to which we will also give some squadrons of our men-at-arms and of our other Polish cavalry, in place of which one will give us dragoons or infantry.
>
> The cannons will be divided up; in the case that messieurs the Electors do not have enough, monsieur the Duke of Lorraine will provide them with some. This wing will be commanded by messieurs the electors.
>
> The troops of the Circles [*Kreise*] of the Empire will extend along the Danube with the left wing, falling back a little on their right [i.e. with the extreme left getting ahead of the rest of the line], and that for two reasons: the first, to worry the enemy about being charged in the flank; and the second, to be within reach of throwing a great aid into the city, in the case that we are not able to drive off the enemy as soon as we hope. Monsieur the Prince of Waldeck will command this corps.
>
> The first line will be only infantry with the cannons, followed closely by a line of cavalry. If these two lines were mixed, they would undoubtedly get tangled up in passing the defiles, woods and mountains; but as soon as one will have reached the plain, in the intervals between the battalions, which will be ordered to allow this,

---

55 We are not informed of further details. Dolleczek, 'Entsatzschlacht', p.156, gives the names of some regiments, but these are the same as units sent off north under Lodron.

> the cavalry will take post, especially our men-at-arms [hussars], who will charge first.
>
> If we put all our armies in only three lines, that will extend more than one and a half German leagues,[56] which will not be to our advantage, and it will be necessary to cross [i.e. extend beyond] the little River Wien, which we must actually keep on our right wing; this is why we must form four lines, and this fourth will serve as a reserve corps.
>
> For greater security of the infantry against the first effort of the Turkish cavalry, which is always very strong, one would do very well to use 'Spanische Reiter' or *chevaux-de-frise*, but very light, so that they can be carried comfortably and at each halt thrown down before the battalions.
>
> I beg all messieurs the generals that as the armies descend the final mountain and enter the plain, each will take his post as it is indicated in this present order.[57]

Other than the need for the Imperialists to hold the right, reasons for the new order of battle are not specified in the sources, but are easy to deduce: Lorraine recognised that the ground on the right once they reached the far side of the Wienerwald was far more open than that on the left, and thus more suitable for cavalry; it was for this reason that he had been prepared to let Sobieski have the overall right, and it made sense to put next to the Poles the bulk of his heavy cavalry, especially as the Reichs contingents were comparatively weak in horse and the left wing would be facing difficult terrain beyond the Wienerwald where cavalry would be of limited use. Lorraine himself wanted to be on the left because, as hinted in Sobieski's Order of Battle, here next to the Danube was the best route for breaking through the besiegers and pushing them back from Vienna, or even, if the battle went badly, of just getting reinforcements into the city, and this was what he saw as his primary objective, not grandiose attempts at a battle of annihilation. Having secured the point of protocol about the right on his master's behalf, the Duke saw no need to command there himself, leaving it to a comparatively junior general.

There was also a small anomaly in the positioning of the two electors: Bavaria was technically the senior secular electorate,[58] outranking Saxony, and Maximilian Emanuel might have been expected to insist on the post of

---

56 The German league was officially about 7.5 km., or 4.6 English miles; the Germans themselves rarely used 'league', but counted in German 'Miles', which were about the same as the league. Sobieski's statement translates as just under 7 English miles, which is a tolerably accurate estimate of the distance between the Danube and the River Wien at the point where the foothills of the Wienerwald end, though an optimistic one of how much frontage the Christian army of at most 70,000 men would cover.

57 Translated from the version in Philippe Dupont, *Mémoires pour servir à l'histoire de la vie et des actions de Jean Sobieski III du nom roi de Pologne, par Philippe Dupont, attaché à ce prince en qualité d'ingénieur en chef de l'artillerie* (Warsaw: Nakładem Świdzińskich, 1885), pp.130–131; there are German translations in *Das Kriegsjahr 1683*, pp.237–238, citing Coyer, and Renner, pp.416–417 (source not cited), also a different English translation in Paradowski, p.126.

58 It had been given the senior electoral position, taken from the Palatinate, as a reward for siding with the Catholic Emperor in the Thirty Years' War; the Palatinate got *an* electoral hat back at

second honour with Lorraine on the left, instead of being lumped with the common herd in the post of least honour in the centre; probably, Maximilian Emanuel had shot himself in the foot with his attempt at false modesty in pretending he had come to serve only as a volunteer, for this meant he was not present in an official capacity and did not 'count' in status calculations, so, although at some point after he arrived in camp that night he did raise a tentative claim to command the entire centre instead of Waldeck, this was firmly rejected and all he could expect formally was to be placed with his soldiers in the centre under old Waldeck. It may also be relevant that the new arrangement placed John George as far away as possible from the Poles; poor Sobieski had tried again in his ebullient patronising way to charm the stockings off the Elector of Saxony when his army reached Tulln the previous day, and he would take John George with him on his review of the army the following day, but all he could achieve was civility, and nothing he did could efface the bad impression created by his uncontrollable marauding camp-followers on the dour, disciplined Saxons. Lorraine needed plenty of infantry, of which the Saxons had 12 excellent battalions, their quality impressing even Sobieski; and the Duke knew that he could expect obedience from John George (the Elector had served under Lorraine in the Dutch War when heir to the Saxon electoral hat and got on with him well enough); so he gladly welcomed the northerners into his wing.

Later on the 8th, the King reviewed the entire army from one end to the other, his last chance to see his combined force before it set off, and with him he took John George of Saxony, still trying to win the Elector over and still ruining it all as he disparaged in his mind the Saxon's plain tents and lack of a lavish entourage, even his attire, so staid to eyes accustomed to Polish flamboyance.[59] Nevertheless, they rode together down the lines that dull day: the massed ranks of all the Germans mostly in their dreary grey and buff and metal, relieved only by a small block of red from the Saxon IR Leib and a larger block of blue from (some of) the Bavarians as well as (possibly) some of the Franconians and the Imperialist IR Baden, with the brilliant colours of the regimental flags fluttering overhead, and the occasional splash of red and gold from a senior officer's coat; then the glorious splendour of the showy Poles; while behind the inspecting generals and in front of the inspected troops lay the deserted Tullner Feld, marked only by the burnt-out shells here and there of villages that had been flourishing communities only a couple of months earlier, before the Tatars came; and beyond the plain, the dark wooded hills of the Wienerwald. Occasionally, a small Tatar party of horsemen would float in and out of the hills, scouting from a very cautious distance or trying to find some final booty in the already-ravaged land. It was the nearest the Ottoman army came to opposing the crossing of the Danube.

---

the Peace of Westphalia, but it was a new position and the treaty formally confirmed Bavaria's precedence.

59   The review is explicitly mentioned in Sobieski's letter to his wife dated 5 a.m. the next morning (Plater, pp.59–60); Le Bègue made no reference to it, but such a parade would have been seen as almost a necessity, if only to allow the soldiers to learn to recognise their commanders and each other's banners so that they would know each other in battle.

NO MORE TIME TO LOSE

Battle of Vienna. Published in Rome by Giovanni Giacomo De Rossi (National Library, Warsaw)

Morale in the Christian army was good. Most of the Imperialists were veterans by now. The other German-speakers were not necessarily experienced against the Turks, but they were all in well-trained corps, usually with plenty of combat experience from the Dutch War, and contained at least a few officers, like Waldeck and Degenfeld, who had faced the Turks before. Some soldiers in the newer contingents were still a bit nervous, panicky sentries raising the alarm in the night at shadows or lurking Polish marauders, imagining that the Tatars were upon them; but already the word must have started going round from the Imperialist cavalrymen, veterans now of two complete victories over the once-terrifying enemy, that the Ottomans were nothing to fear after all. The Poles, familiar with their country's long tradition of victories in battle against the hereditary enemy, and many of them veterans of the most recent of those victories under their esteemed King, were full of enthusiasm for action and utterly confident of success.[60] Everyone had now seen what the Tatars had done to the Tullner Feld; the army was united

---

60   see the opinion of a Polish noble quoted in Otto Forst de Battaglia, *Jan Sobieski* (überarbeitete Neuauflage, Graz: Styria Verlag, 1982), p.175. The Poles had suffered some strategic disasters, including the near-trap at Żórawno in 1676 which had brought them to the peace treaty with the Ottomans that they loathed so much; but this could not detract from their many glittering tactical successes, especially under Sobieski.

in its hostility to the barbarous enemy, and even the traditional religious antipathies between Catholic and Protestant were muted – astonishingly, given the Habsburgs' deserved reputation for religious bigotry whatever the circumstances, we hear for now no complaints of any interference in the religious services of the Protestant Saxons. Marco d'Aviano may have played his part, both in creating the sense of unity amongst the Catholics through his preaching and in discouraging harassment of the Protestants – Sobieski himself remarked, with just a hint of surprise, that the monk was no bigot.[61]

---

61   Plater, p.57.

4

To the Wienerwald

The Wienerwald

In front of the allies lay the Wienerwald. One of the outlying ranges of the eastern Alps, the mountains that occupy so much of southern Austria, this chain of heights, roughly wedge-shaped on the map, stretched from south-west to north-east in the direction of the Danube, broad at the base where it left the Alps, narrowing to a point at its northernmost tip where came to an end hard by the bank of the river. It was the northern section that interested the allies, broadly the chunk separated from the root by the little River Wien (in German, Wienfluss, literally the River Vienna). This was the only watercourse of any significance in this part of the Wienerwald; it rose in the west side of the range and, fed from the north by several significant streams including the Mauerbach, flowed east to reach the Danube just by Vienna the city. Genuine mountains were limited to the range south of the Wien, but even in its final stages north of the little river as it approached the Danube, the Wienerwald contained many substantial hills, the majority of them (as its name implied) wooded, serious obstacles the lot of them, all jumbled up with few clear passages through from one side of the range to the other. The hills were sparsely populated: a few scattered villages, isolated huts of foresters and wood-cutters, a modest single-storey Carthusian monastery at Mauerbach protected by nothing more than a garden wall, all of them deserted now for their inhabitants had been killed or taken off by the Tatars, or else had fled. Just one big settlement existed at this northern end of the range, one oasis of safety against Ottoman raiders: the fortified monastery of Klosterneuburg, perched on the north-eastern side on the banks of the Danube.

To the north-west of the hills lay the long narrow plain of the Tullner Feld, through which ran the Danube. The river then curved round the tip and hugged its north-eastern side, passing Klosterneuburg, before parting company to turn eastward and head for the Hungarian plain. Roughly where the river turned away, there was a basin of lower open ground, formed on two sides by the eastern hills of the Wienerwald proper and on the south (beyond the River Wien) by a lesser outlying hill, the Wiener Berg, with the Danube itself closing the basin to the north-east. In this basin lay Vienna, and round it the Ottoman army; once the allies had passed the last of the hills, so they thought, they were on open ground fit for deploying and fighting. The allies had to get from the Tullner Feld on one side of the Wienerwald to the basin on the other.

There was one big problem: the overall watershed of the Wienerwald this far north was to the west; most streams leaving the hills did so on the chain's eastern side, so that was the side with the most openings; there was not enough ground for any streams on the western side to develop into more serious watercourses before they flowed out of the hills onto the Tullner Feld, and so few openings had been cut in the row of heights on that side. And this was the side facing the allies; even getting *into* the Wienerwald would be difficult.

Two potential routes sprang immediately to mind. The first and most obvious lay along the northern edge of the hills, close by the bank of the Danube: a road ran from the Tullner Feld, passed between the tip of the Wienerwald and the river, through a gap often very narrow indeed, and, when the basin opened up on the far side, headed pretty directly for Vienna. Far to the south lay the second alternative: the valley of the River Wien, which, if the Christians could reach its upper levels, would allow them to descend this comparatively easy natural roadway to join the Danube hard by Vienna. The most obvious way to reach its upper levels would be to march almost due south from Tulln to Ried, from where a comparatively short climb over intervening hills would put them at the head of the Gablitz, one of the Wien's tributaries; or, if the allies preferred not to go so far south, they could try to find a way through to the valley of the Mauerbach, which they could descend to its junction with the Wien. Between these two alternatives, the only route that seemed militarily viable was to find through all the winding passes and valleys or over the forested hills to the head of the valley of the Alsbach stream, which would allow troops to deploy at the end and advance out of the hills in tolerably good order.

None of these routes was ideal: the road along the Danube seemed so easy, especially since it would allow supply barges to move alongside keeping the soldiers provisioned at all times, and in fact offered the only obvious way *into* the Wienerwald from the Tullner Feld. Lorraine had already sent Heissler ahead to secure the first part of it by occupying Klosterneuburg. However, it was narrow, a 'defile', a feature that would force the army to stretch out in a narrow column many miles long, and seventeenth-century commanders had a horror of defiles at the best of times – even more so here, where a nimble enemy was positioned just beyond the defile, and could either prevent the Christians' debouching from the defile or could attack the column's exposed flank from the hills. Any classically-educated general in the allied army would have taken one look at the pass, thought immediately of how a Roman army had been annihilated by Hannibal at Lake Trasimene in just such circumstances, and rejected it as a primary route. The river road could still be used in a support function, and would be; but it was not the way to get the army through the Wienerwald. The route through Ried or the Mauerbach and then the valley of the River Wien, assuming one could find a way to reach it from the Tullner Feld, seemed better – perhaps a little longer on the map than the Danube route or going straight through the Wienerwald, but this should be more than compensated by the greater speed and ease with which an army could move once it reached the easy valleys, and the debouchment from the defile onto the Danube basin, while potentially hazardous, was a lot less risky than the one by the Danube road because the Wien valley was so much wider. It also brought an army using it almost across the Ottoman line of retreat and offered potential for trapping the Ottoman army as Sobieski and Hermann of Baden desired. We will see in a moment that some in the Christian headquarters seemed to be considering this route. The difficulties here were two-fold: the ease of the final stages might be counter-balanced by the difficulties of entering the upper Mauerbach if they chose this route in, which might take longer than they dared allow (the alternative, Ried, was no further from Tulln than any of the other points north of it); and more importantly, if they descended the Wien in column of march (whether they had entered it via Ried or the Mauerbach), they would be separated from their major supply line, the Danube, by miles and miles of forested hills. As for the final route, the Alsbach, it was too small to be considered a *primary* means of access to the Vienna basin, but could and would be used as part of a wider plan.

Relief army in the Ottoman camp. Johan Martin Lerch, after Justus van der Nypoort (Wien Museum Inv.-Nr. 31092, CC0)

In fact, what the Christians had decided to do in the discussions of the 8th was not to approach the battlefield in column and deploy, using one or other of these routes, as contemporary commanders would normally have expected; they were going to cross the northern part of the Wienerwald on a battlefield frontage. To say that they would advance in order of battle would be claiming too much, because the hills and tortuous valleys would make it impossible to keep anything like a proper formation, but there would be no single narrow column or columns advancing strung out for miles along a single access route. It was intended that corps would occupy as wide a front as possible as they advanced, sometimes bunching into valleys, expanding again over hills, broadly keeping to the arrangement of the final order of battle: Imperialists and Saxons on the left, Bavarians and Franconians in the centre, then Sachsen-Lauenburg and the phoney little right wing of Imperialist cavalry, and the Poles in the most exposed position on the far right. The left wing could use the Danube road for some of its units, or for the guns and heavy equipment, but would not be strung out along the road in a vulnerable column, and the rest of its units advancing alongside it over the hills just in from the river would prevent any ambush; the river would also protect the flank of the army on this side. The Poles might conceivably exploit part of the Mauerbach route; they would have to see. Some troops would use the Alsbach, but by then the army would be deploying along a wide front by any means possible, not by a single debouchment that would be so easy for the Ottomans to block.

Lateral communications along the line would be very difficult; if the Turks attacked in force before the allies reached the Vienna basin, it would next to impossible for any corps to come to the aid of its neighbours in a timely fashion. At least the various reconnaissances had confirmed that no Ottoman forces were present in the first half of the hills, and none were present yet even in the second half; had enemy troops been entrenched in those awful defiles, or along the ravines or in commanding positions on the hills, getting through would have been impossible. No-one expected the march to be easy; no-one knew how hard it would actually be.

One thing the allied commanders did not know yet: how they were to get into the Wienerwald from the Tullner Feld, where only the Danube road offered an entrance into the hills whose exit they knew for sure; no-one wanted to march off into some comfortable-looking valley only to discover it was a dead end or led them in the wrong direction. Scouts had not yet found the answer to this question; when they did, there would still be enormous difficulties due to trying to pass such rough terrain on such a wide front. The Wienerwald had numerous paths, it is true, for connecting its scattered villages, but these paths were mostly for foresters, hunters and wood-cutters, operating alone or in small parties, and even the best of the tracks were intended only for an occasional village cart; nothing was designed for the movement of 60,000–70,000 men and 30,000 or more horses, a hundred or so pieces of artillery and scores of great military wagons all together. Most of the troops would have to go cross-country, where even at the best of times a traveller had to contend with steep slopes, often made more difficult by scree or by cuttings carved by streams, and of course the ever-present thick woods and scrub – and now, with the days of pouring rain recently, the group was slippery underfoot, the streams often so swollen that wagons and guns could be got over them only by stopping and building bridges.

Despite Sobieski's naïve initial belief that the army would extend beyond the River Wien if he did not adopt a deeper formation, it would not actually come anywhere near the Wien as it crossed the hills, and this meant that the advance had one big tactical drawback: the right flank was in the air. Lorraine and the left wing would be anchored on the Danube; he was fairly safe from the danger of substantial Ottoman forces getting round the flank and attacking him from the side and rear. Not so the Poles: their right flank was open, covered by no other forces and no natural obstacle – potentially a disaster, for no-one could imagine that an enemy would fail to exploit such a mistake. Unless Sobieski continued to believe that his forces *would* extend to the River Wien very soon after they entered the Wienerwald and that the little river would provide an anchor for his flank, which seems unlikely as the Imperialists had already disabused him at least of the first misapprehension,[62] then the King must have known that he was risking military suicide. Did he have private knowledge that the flank was safer than it seemed? We noted above that, in addition to prestige as a reason for demanding the right, Sobieski had good military justifications for doing so. What were they? There was much talk of dodgy deals involving the Tatars; from prisoner reports, these folk were expected to be on the Ottoman left and would therefore be facing the Poles if they held the right. A Polish diarist of the campaign, Mikołaj Dyakowski, recounted a tale of how Sobieski, in the final campaign of his previous war with the Ottomans, at Żórawno in 1676, had formed a secret pact with the then Khan of the Crimea, Selim Giray. Supposedly, during peace negotiations with the Ottoman commander mediated by the Khan, Sobieski had sworn personal brotherhood-in-arms with Selim, each of them promising never to serve again against the other; thus, if Poles faced Tatars now, the Tatars would avoid action rather than break the oath, and the Polish flank would never be at risk.[63] Aside from the inherent improbability of the story (that either of these rulers would or could commit their peoples to such a cease-fire, or that the Tatars would ever take any notice of anything that would interfere with their desire to loot), and aside from the unreliability of its source (Dyakowski is now recognised as thoroughly untrustworthy), there is one big flaw in it: Selim Giray was not the current Tatar Khan – he had been replaced in 1678 by Murad Giray, who still held the Khanate and commanded the Tatars in Kara Mustafa's army. Murad could not be held to a personal oath sworn by his predecessor. Nevertheless, there is still something very fishy about the complete failure of the Khan and his followers to do *anything* against the Christians.

We will look at this from the Ottoman perspective shortly, but it is worth mentioning here that there *is* an indication of secret deals, again not completely trustworthy but still better accredited than the Dyakowski story. Before the allies crossed the Danube, various shifty characters had been appearing amongst them from Imre Thököly, hinting at his willingness to change sides but actually playing the rebel leader's old game of spying under

---

62 One would have expected the Imperialists to have disabused him of the second notion as well, if he held such an idea; every man on the Imperialist staff must have known the Wien and its inadequacy as a military obstacle. However, since they failed to fill him in on another obvious geographical mistake (on which, more anon), it is all too possible they failed in this case as well.

63 The story as reported by Dolleczek, 'Entsatzschlacht', pp.155–156. Other writers have picked up on the story from Dyakowski, and most historians these days take it with a pinch of salt. Sobieski's actual conduct at Żórawno, where he had tried sowing dissension between the Tatars and the Ottoman commander by opening a negotiation with the former and then letting the latter know of it, was hardly likely to have endeared him to the Khan sufficiently that Selim would have made him a blood brother.

the cover of diplomatic initiatives – and amongst these, a message had been delivered from Michael Apafi, Prince of Transylvania, offering to mediate peace between Emperor Leopold and the *Khan*. Since the offer is mentioned by Sobieski himself,[64] we must believe at least that it was made; but was it genuine? The Prince of Transylvania was not in the Ottoman camp with the Khan or the Grand Vizier, he was seventy miles to the east sat in front of Raab with the limited Ottoman forces investing the fortress, very thankful to be out from under the eyes of Kara Mustafa. However, there was much to-and-fro between the two camps, as well as messages flying back and forth between the Ottomans at Vienna and Thököly on the north bank; if the Khan had wanted to send a message back to Raab with a request for Michael Apafi, and if Apafi had surmounted his terror of Kara Mustafa sufficiently to forward a message to the Christian leaders, it was perfectly feasible. Khans of the Crimea had made informal approaches like this before as the first stage in mediating peace between their Ottoman suzerains and enemy powers (as vassals of the Sultan rather than his subjects, they were not necessarily committing treason in doing so). A delicate approach like this, at one further stage removed than usual from the principals involved, had all the necessary attributes of deniability – if the offer were exposed, Murad Giray could accuse Apafi of inventing it, or could claim that he was merely putting out feelers to find out whether Leopold was prepared yet to cede his capital; but the Christians were bound to read between the lines of the offer – and Murad was sure to have realised this before he wrote – that the Khan was hinting that he had had enough of the campaign, that he had no intention of fighting to the end, and that if allowed to leave the theatre of war without being himself attacked, his Tatars would not attack. Such an idea was inherently credible anyway: the Tatars were prepared to fight sometimes, but they much preferred looting, destroying and enslaving the helpless, and once they had got plenty of booty, their main interest was in getting home with it, not in fighting on for a pile of stones that, as nomads, they had no interest in conquering, and that would benefit only their suzerain the Ottoman Sultan.[65] If the Tatars were reluctant to fight anyway, then the best means of reinforcing that reluctance was to put the Poles opposite them: the Poles were very well equipped and organised to deal with Tatar tactics, and the Tatars knew it; and the Poles had many times smashed the Tatars in action in recent years – and the Tatars knew it. So, the flank might not be at risk at all, but even if the approach through Apafi of Transylvania was a fake (it was well within the range of Ottoman methods to throw out false diplomatic hints like this to keep their enemies off balance), and there were Tatars waiting to strike in the Wienerwald, the Poles would deal with them better than anyone else could.

---

64 In his letter of 4 September to his wife: Plater, p.54.
65 Mansberg, p.79, although he rightly suspects the Dyakowski story, does not mention the approach through Apafi, and speculates rather that Sobieski, a past master of diplomatic intrigues, may have managed to buy off the Khan with money or promises of future favours. It is not impossible, though if he had done so, one might have expected Sobieski to crow about such cleverness to his wife – and he did not.

NO MORE TIME TO LOSE

The local population pays tribute to the Ottoman and Tatar armies marching towards Vienna. Romeyn de Hooghe, 1684 (Rijksmuseum, Amsterdam)

The risk of Tatar attack was not the only danger for the Christians in choosing to cross the Wienerwald as they did. They had chosen this route because the alternatives – taking circuitous but easier paths – seemed too costly in time, but if they became bogged down in the hills for longer than expected, as was indeed to happen, the Wienerwald could turn out to be a deadly mistake. Added to that was the danger of what would happen to the army if it were defeated by the Ottomans in the Vienna basin: such a defeat would of course be a disaster anyway, as it would inevitably be followed by the fall of Vienna and all that that implied,[66] but a defeated Christian army would have the Wienerwald at its back, and unless its infantry survived the battle in sufficient numbers to allow it to get into the woods where it could well protect from pursuing Ottoman cavalry the retreat of the rest to Tulln and the north bank, then the entire army – the defence of Austria, Bohemia, southern Germany, and Poland – would be trapped, annihilated.[67]

However, it was too late for the allies to change their minds now.

From Tulln to the edge of the Wienerwald

Previously, Sobieski had been keen to advance and had been held back by Imperialist caution; now that they were over the Danube and provisions had been distributed, it was Lorraine who itched to moved out and wondered nervously why the King seemed so uninterested in setting off for the Wienerwald. Perhaps he was unaware of the reconnaissance that Sobieski had sent out from his Polish forces and whose report the King was awaiting, which was a fair reason for delay. Maybe, however, he was aware of it but felt the Polish party had gone in the wrong direction, or else he concluded that more needed to be done to prod the King into action by getting intelligence

---

66 The consequences if Vienna had fallen are discussed in Chapter 13.
67 Dolleczek, 'Entsatzschlacht', p.151.

that his advance would be safe; he may also have begun to understand how, while his own appointed route through the hills was safe enough (one flank secured firmly by the Danube, the other covered by the rest of the army, while the superbly capable Heissler sat ahead holding the fortified post of Klosterneuburg preventing any possibility of surprise), the Poles when they first entered the hills would be advancing with a completely open flank, liable to be swamped by Turkish or Tatar hordes which, since there was no sign of them on the open plain, must surely be lurking in the woods ready to pounce – Lorraine was at this stage unaware of Sobieski's reasons for believing he would be safe from Tatar attack. So, Lorraine sent out a big scouting party of his own, towards the right, going over ground that the Poles would be covering during the advance. Although other reconnaissances were in progress, concentrating especially on trying to find routes for moving artillery (even as the armies set off no-one knew for sure exactly where they would enter the Wienerwald), soon after the arrangements of the order of battle had been agreed on the 8th, the Duke sent out one of his trusted cavalry officers, GWM Ernst Peter, Baron Mercy de Billets, a brave general and a recognised 'partisan' (leader in small-scale actions). Mercy, an exiled Lorrainer like the Duke, was assigned a force of about 1,200–2,000 cavalry,[68] composed of his own Cuirassier Regiment and that of Hallewyl, plus some or all of the Saxon CR Goltz under the command of its lieutenant-colonel, Bronne, yet another Lorrainer. If Le Bègue is to be believed, Mercy was to explore the Wienerwald far out on the right flank, to push as far as Mauerbach, a village with a modest Carthusian monastery (almost certainly abandoned) about half-way down the stream of the same name, and to try to discover from there what movements the Turks were making in their camp. This is odd, since one cannot see Vienna or the Ottoman camp from Mauerbach – although Mercy's reports would concentrate on information gleaned from prisoners captured on what was going on at the siege.[69] Perhaps the most likely explanation relates to Lorraine's concern about Sobieski's refusal to start moving: he was taking measures himself to get intelligence, especially about movements out from the Ottoman camp into the hills, i.e. whether there were any Tatars lurking in the hills on the open flank of the intended march, or about pathways for artillery, to convince the King that it was safe to advance into the hills.

Whatever his exact orders, Mercy set off; and he had hardly disappeared into the darkness of the hills beyond the plain before Lorraine was again urging on Sobieski the need to start soon, and worrying why the King suddenly preferred to sit and do nothing. By first thing the next morning, 9 September, with the weather promising a clear day, Lorraine had had enough: at daybreak, the Imperialists set off. They marched not forward across the plain but almost east parallel to the Danube; if the positions in camp shown on the Hallart map are correct, they had to move first past the rest of the Germans. The ground underfoot was still soggy from all the rains, but the

---

[68] At full strength, the regiments would have totalled 2,000; I strongly doubt that they were at full strength, and incline to the lower figure.
[69] See Appendix I, 4.1, for discussion of the puzzle of Mercy's mission.

artillery and its ammunition wagons could take the road directly along the river, avoiding churning up the ground used by the infantry and cavalry, so the columns advanced steadily enough without getting bogged down. Barges full of food and extra ammunition coasted along the river keeping pace with them on their left. As the day progressed and scouts continued to send in reports about the state of paths within the Wienerwald, the Imperialists began to spread out, forming several small columns that would reach the edge of the hills across a front of several miles. Normal procedure would have been for the quartermasters to go ahead to lay out the camp; it seems likely that Lorraine went with them to set up his headquarters well before the troops arrived (he would definitely do this the following day). The march to the foot of the Wienerwald was about seven miles, a comfortable distance on open, level ground; the Imperialist soldiers, even the infantry, would not have found it too strenuous, and it seems likely that they were at their target positions by early afternoon.

It appears that the Germans of the centre, and perhaps even the Saxons who were supposed to join Lorraine, did not start off at the same time; the Poles certainly did not. Maximilian Emanuel had only arrived in his barge first thing that morning, and Hermann of Baden soon after; both of them had to present themselves to the King, and, although Hermann had obtained the field command in the Imperialist army for which he had been scheming, he showed no great inclination to join Lorraine and take it up, but spent part of the day with Sobieski at Tulln, discussing with the King and the remaining generals the necessary measures for the march, and then sharing a mid-day meal. Lorraine's staff speculated about the reasons for this failure to move: some thought that it was because the Polish generals felt their train was essential to their army's subsistence and were still waiting for the last of it to cross from the north bank, others suggested that Sobieski was still worried about the possibility that Leopold might come down and join them.[70] The former is possible, the latter unlikely. As for supply: the barges on the Danube would be able to supply Lorraine's left wing and possibly the centre but not the Poles away on the right. On the danger of an imperial visit: Sobieski had only that morning reported to his wife how his concerns on that front had been eased, and if the matter had still been on his mind, it would undoubtedly have poured out in his next letter (which complained about Haslingen's bridges but said not a word about Leopold). The most likely explanation seems to be that Sobieski saw no point in setting off until the routes into the Wienerwald had been chosen – Lorraine's route was clear enough even if details remained to be determined, but if the Germans and Poles were to advance when they still did not know exactly where they would heading, they could waste time and energy tramping around the plain to no purpose.

Lorraine's concern about Vienna increased as his Imperialists marched along the Tullner Feld for the hills. Mercy had sent back his first report: whether his orders had been to find routes or Tatars or Ottoman movements,

---

70 Stöller, p.100.

he appeared to be doing none of it, but trying to find out what was happening at Vienna by unreliable indirect means. He sent to Lorraine first a report that he could still hear firing from the city but it was now mostly small-arms fire rather than artillery fire – which *could* be taken as indicating the attack was in its very last phase, with the besiegers too deep in the fortifications to be hit by defending cannon or else all defending artillery destroyed. Then Mercy sent back a prisoner he had taken, who had described in some detail the major assault the Ottomans had thrown at Vienna on the 8th; the account was not necessarily accurate, but Lorraine was not to know that, and it was the only significant intelligence that he had; the prisoner's claim that the Ottomans had gained for a while a lodgement on one of the bastions, even if they had lost it again soon after, indicated that an end of the siege could not be far away.[71] Lorraine, having interrogated the prisoner himself through his interpreters, sent the man on to Tulln to be delivered to Sobieski with another appeal to get moving. Still the King would not budge.[72]

Finally, enough reports came in for the generals at Tulln to have a reasonably clear picture in their minds of the hills, allowing them to choose the two routes by which they thought they would at least be able to get their artillery into the Wienerwald and through it. More work would be needed on the morrow to find other paths for the infantry, but for now, this was sufficient. About two hours after that dinner with Hermann of Baden and the others, leaving the agreed detachment behind to guard Tulln, the rest of the army set off:[73] the Bavarians and Franconians at a slightly steeper angle away from the Danube than the Imperialists but still very much with the river to their left, their march columns heading for the hills to put them on the right of the Imperialists; the Poles heading further away from the river, almost south-east, merely crossing the width of the plain instead of marching along it, less than five miles, so that, although they started last and had to let their wagons keep up, they had no trouble reaching the edge of the hills along

---

71 Le Bègue's 'Account' (Stöller, pp.32–33) and 'Diary' (Stöller, p.100) are contradictory: the former describes intelligence of Ottoman attacks of 4 and 6 September on the Löbel Bastion, the latter, an assault on the 8th on the Burg Bastion. In fact, the besiegers attacked the Burg Bastion on the 4th, and the Löbel on the 6th and 8th. Both versions mention the Turks' having briefly made a lodgement on the walls, and undoubtedly this was the key element, the fact that Lorraine at once focused on.

72 There are as usual irreconcilable inconsistencies in the sources. Le Bègue's 'Account' (Stöller, p.32) was emphatic that Lorraine set out at daybreak on the 9th, and even states that this was with all the Germans (this latter claim is not supported by other accounts); his 'Diary' (Stöller, p.100) was equally clear that Mercy's reports came in during the day and that Lorraine sent the prisoner *back* to Sobieski at Tulln. However, the 'Diary' then refers to Sobieski refusing to budge himself but giving Lorraine permission to march with all the Germans and even to enter the Wienerwald and occupy positions that would secure the general march. Was the King giving Lorraine permission for the advance of the Imperialists that he had already done without orders? or was he allowing the other Germans to set off after the Imperialists? or had Lorraine personally set off but without his Imperialist troops, who only now set off to catch up with him?

73 From the 'Baden account' (see Appendix V), in Philipp Röder von Diersburg, *Des Markgraf Ludwig Wilhelm von Baden Feldzüge wider die Türken…* (Karlsruhe: Müller, 1839–1842), Urk., p.14. This is partly supported by the Franconian account of Schliz von Görz, in Johann Newald, *Beiträge zur Geschichte der Belagerung von Wien durch die Türken im Jahre 1683: historisch Studien* (Vienna: Kubasta & Voigt, 1883–1884), vol.2, p.99, which also gives emphasis on this day to the work of reconnoitring routes, though the two accounts are not completely compatible.

with everyone else as dusk was coming down. The Imperialists and Germans camped along the line centred at the village St Andrä, their left extending to Altenberg at the point where the road along the river enters the narrow pass caused by the Wienerwald's approach to the Danube, their right extending to make contact with the Poles at Königstetten. Sobieski's forces lay from Königstetten along as far as Tulbing.

If the Christians had looked very carefully off across the plain to the south as they advanced, they might just have made out in the distance a small party of horsemen watching them for hours, motionless. Finally the group wheeled and disappeared into the hills, well clear of the Polish line of march. Even if they had seen the little group, they would not have recognised it, but this was the Tatar Khan, and watching the Christians set off was to be his sole contribution to the battle.[74]

Lorraine had not been idle in the afternoon while waiting for the allies to catch up with him. More scouts had been sent into the hills in front of him to explore paths suitable for troops, and learn more about the practicality of moving the guns through. He had also himself reconnoitred the Danube road: as noted above, seventeenth-century commanders detested defiles, but this one had added disadvantages, obstacles such as barriers of cut-down trees created by Christian inhabitants over the summer as part of their desperate attempts to stop the movement of the Tatar raiders. The road was still too important to be ignored, so Lorraine appointed FZM Leslie to deal with it, gave him 10 battalions of infantry, two dragoon regiments and a detachment of cavalry and sent him along the road to start clearing the barriers and then take positions from which he could cover the movement of wheeled traffic on the road. The artillery was ordered to follow, and keep going all through the night, so that it would have a head start on the rest of the army.

---

74 See Chapter 5 below, section 'The Khan and the Tatars', on the question of the authenticity of this. Even if untrue, it seems that the Ottoman command was aware of the Christian advance, and must have known about it from Tatar observers; and since no-one in the Christian army remarked upon them, they must have been small, distant and quiet.

5

Initial Ottoman preparations

On the far side of the Wienerwald, in the Vienna basin around the besieged city, what were Kara Mustafa and the Ottomans doing?

The siege of Vienna had already taken much longer than expected, but the Ottoman progress, while slow, had been steady, and an end was in sight. During the night of 2–3 September, the Burg Ravelin, the forward defence for the main wall at the attacked sector, reduced to a pile of rubble, had finally fallen, and the Ottomans could proceed to drive their trenches and mines against the main defences behind: the Burg or Palace Bastion, the Löbel Bastion, and the curtain wall between them. Driven by the first news of the gathering relief force, Kara Mustafa desperately pushed his trench commanders hard; they exploded mines and hurled ferocious attacks against the Burg Bastion, and, when these failed, on 6 September they turned their attention on the Löbel Bastion instead. From the 7th, in addition, approaches were driven forward heading for the curtain, almost the last line of defence.

Success seemed so close, but the relief force was approaching. Kara Mustafa had been aware during most of the siege of the need to block any Christian army assembling; he expected the Tatars ranging beyond the Wienerwald to give him plenty of warning of any bodies of troops coming down the Danube from the west, while his Hungarian puppet princeling Thököly and the Turkish-Tatar warriors assigned to support him had been commissioned to break through onto the Marchfeld and prevent forces coming down from the north. After the last attempts on the north bank had finally in late August been so conclusively smashed at the Bisamberg – in full view of the Ottomans on the south bank, helpless to aid their compatriots – for about a week Kara Mustafa seemed to give up and concentrate every effort of his army on taking Vienna as fast as possible, before relief could arrive. Even as it became clear that the relief would not come over the Danube from Lorraine's base at Korneuburg

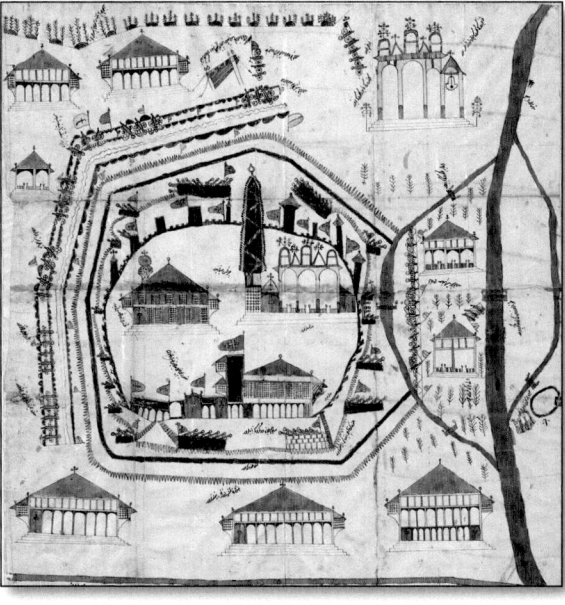

Ottoman plan of the siege works around Vienna in 1683. (Wien Museum Inv.-Nr. 52816/1, CC0)

but would cross the Danube and assemble beyond the Wienerwald, no troops were sent over the hills to hinder the crossing. It is sometimes suggested that Kara Mustafa actually expected the Tatars to block any Christian forces trying to cross the Danube by the Krems bridge; but while the Grand Vizier sometimes showed considerable ignorance of military affairs, it is incredible that he would have been so ignorant as to have expected the irregular Tatar cavalry, unfitted by weapons, training or tactics to such a task, to do any such thing. However, the Tatars could have harassed the Christians' march and greatly slowed it down. The Grand Vizier probably thought that enough Tatars were present on the Tullner Feld beyond the Wienerwald to give him full intelligence of Christian movements, and to slow any advance of the relief force for days; he apparently had no idea just how few Tatars there were on the far side of the hills.

The first wake-up call came on 4 September. Lorraine was only just leaving Korneuburg for Tulln, and the Poles had not even come down out of the hills to the river valley, but the Tatars had caught a Christian soldier and brought him in to the Grand Vizier for interrogation – an unreliable means of getting intelligence at best, but without sufficient Ottoman scouts beyond the Wienerwald and none north of the Danube, the best available. Kara Mustafa got a nasty shock: the prisoner claimed that 85,000 Germans and 35,000 Poles and Lithuanians were in the relief army, two-thirds of the total (80,000) being infantry. No doubt the brave man, knowing his hours were numbered, set out to scare the Ottomans as much as possible in the hope that such reports would cause them to raise the siege; and no doubt Kara Mustafa did not accept the numbers quoted at face value; but here was evidence of a big army already dangerously close. According to the Italian Marsigli, at this time a prisoner in the Ottoman camp, the significant news was that Sobieski himself was at the head of the relief force, and this created a ripple of alarm bordering on panic that ran throughout the entire Ottoman army.[75] Kara Mustafa's mind turned at once eastwards to Raab: an Ottoman corps had been left blockading the Imperialist fortress when the main army marched past it to attack Vienna; in command was Koca Ibrahim, *beylerbeyi* of Buda, a veteran Ottoman official, reputedly over 80 years old (see Dramatis Personae), who was much too ready to give advice that Kara Mustafa did not want to hear, and in July the Grand Vizier had been only too glad to leave him behind. But his substantial corps was now needed. Orders immediately went out from the camp to Raab summoning most of the troops there to Vienna: Koca Ibrahim was instructed to bring the units of *kapi kulu* he had been assigned, his own *yerli kulu* and most of the other troops there, leaving only Mustafa of Mitylene, *beylerbeyi* of Silistria, with his household troops and the unreliable forces of Transylvania, to maintain the blockade of Raab

---

75 Luigi Ferdinando Marsigli, *L'état militaire de l'Empire Ottoman, ses progrès et sa décadence = Stato militare dell'Imperio Ottomanno…* (Hague: Gosse & Neaulme, 1732), vol.2, p.120. Marsigli stated that it was the news of Sobieski's presence at the head of the relief army which caused Kara Mustafa to send for Koca Ibrahim, which gives the lie to suggestions that the Ottomans did not believe Sobieski had come with the relief force.

and protect the Ottoman lines of communication. Until these reinforcements arrived, not a man would stir out of the camp to go foraging.[76]

The census of the army on 7 September

While waiting for Koca Ibrahim to arrive, Kara Mustafa decided to conduct some kind of muster or census of the entire forces available to him in the theatre of war. For the troops in camp this was carried out, or at least completed, on 7 September. From this exercise, he seemed to have 168,000 troops and potential combatants at his disposal, the majority of them in the camp around Vienna or now pounding the road from Raab, but with a few units elsewhere, such as the remnants of the detachments originally sent north of the Danube and now lost somewhere beyond the River March.

The list produced by this 'muster', which is reproduced, and analysed in detail, in Appendix II below, achieved considerable fame: it was captured by the Christians after the battle, translated, and not only incorporated into the 'Account' of the campaign written by Lorraine's secretary Le Bègue but also published in various contemporary descriptions of the campaign. Hocke mentioned that the list was found in Kara Mustafa's captured chancelry after the battle and recorded in the diary of the Imperialist envoy Kuniz, who had been a prisoner in the Ottoman camp throughout the siege[77]. It has been accepted, often uncritically, as a reliable count, even a count of the Ottoman army *at* Vienna, although even its contemporary editors recognised that this was not the case. Despite a few errors and inconsistencies in the various versions, there is no reason to go so far as to believe the document was a complete fabrication (there are far too many correct details of provinces and the names of their governors that can be confirmed independently from Ottoman sources, and a forger was hardly likely to have given such unexpected figures as the extraordinarily low number of timariot *sipahi*s), although the original translator may have made some mistakes in the numbers, because the chancery script used by Ottoman bureaucrats has always been notoriously difficult to decipher. The reproductions in Christian works now form the sole source, because the original document has never been found by modern researchers.

It was probably the Christian transcribers, accustomed to the western practice of a 'muster', who assigned that term to it; it is more likely that the count was created by Ottoman bureaucrats from their records than that it originated in a formal muster which verified the presence of the soldiers counted. Even as a genuine document, however, and even if its western editors transcribed correctly the difficult Ottoman bureaucratic script (especially the numerals), the muster still gave a misleading picture.

---

76 Marsigli, vol. 2, p.120.
77 Nicolaus Hocke, *Kurtze Beschreibung, dessen was in wehrender türkischen Belägerung der kayserlichen Residentz-Statt Wienn… passiret* (Vienna: Voigt, 1685), p.200.

Firstly, there were those forces which, as even the contemporary editors recognised, were elsewhere in the theatre of war: Koca Ibrahim would soon join the Grand Vizier, true, but he had left some Turks behind at Raab, along with the Prince of Transylvania, and the listed figure of 6,000 for his contingent of *yerli kulu* was in any case improbably high; Imre Thököly, likewise seriously over-estimated at 15,000, was lurking somewhere beyond the River March, along with the remnants of the Turks who had been assigned to him, probably including most or all of the *gönüllü*s, listed at 5,000 – if Kara Mustafa had any Hungarian troops at all in his camp, there were only one or two thousand of them. Deducting Thököly, the *gönüllü*s and the rest would take a good 30,000 off the total.

Secondly, there was the count of 20,000 camp personnel who were considered potential combatants – an absurd idea, as if men who had never lifted a sword before could be armed and put in the line against disciplined western regulars. Other contingents could not be counted on for different reasons: the 6,000 Roumanian forces of Moldavia and Wallachia were not considered front-line troops by the Ottomans even if their reliability was assured – and it was not. These bring the total down by another 26,000, leaving 112,000.

Finally, and most importantly, there was the grave suspicion attached to most of the figures even of the contingents genuinely present in the camp before Vienna, especially when compared with the careful counting of the Ottoman army at the start of the campaign by an eyewitness, Benaglia, who had seen it at Belgrade in May (see Dramatis Personae and Appendix II), or with the figures quoted a few days after the muster for certain contingents by two Ottoman diarists.[78] More Janissaries were recorded as present on 7 September than had paraded at Belgrade in May, although the corps was known to have suffered very heavy casualties during the siege; and the figures for other corps of the *kapi kulu* likewise seem inflated. The *yerli kulu* of the individual pashas showed in all but a couple of cases a similar discrepancy. For example, the substantial contingent of Kara Mehmed Pasha, *beylerbeyi* of Diyarbekir (Mesopotamia), was listed in the muster list at 6,000, but by Benaglia in May at 1,500 (and at about the same time the Ottoman minister Mavrocordato gave him 2,500), while the Ottoman diarists on 9 September recorded 2,000. The lower figures are generally more probable: the majority of *beylerbeyi*s, and all *sancak-bey*s, were not expected to bring into the field anywhere near 1,000, only a handful of the most senior *beylerbeyi*s had revenues sufficient to maintain several thousand household soldiers, the salary for Diyarbekir was within the normal range,[79] and 6,000 was about

---

78 The latter are too rounded to be considered perfectly reliable, but still provide a dependable enough benchmark.
79 Ottoman *beylerbeyi* salaries are recorded in various works; I use here that of Evliya, who put Diyarbekir at 1.2 million *akçe* (the hugely devalued Ottoman unit of account) per year, at the upper end of the 'normal' range. See Evliya Çelebi, *Narrative of travels in Europe, Asia and Africa in the seventeenth century* [translated anonymously from the German translation of] Joseph von Hammer-Purgstall (London: Oriental Translation Fund, 1834-1850, 2 vols., reprinted in one volume, New York/London: Johnson Reprint, 1968), vol. 1, p.89 (the author is identified as 'Evliya Efendi' in the work). It would be useful here if we could compare the *salaries* of the

the limit for the Grand Vizier himself. Pretty much the same can be said of the Tatars, listed in the census with 20,000 men; at the most (see Appendix I, 5.3), they had about 15,000, probably nearer 10,000 – and although Kara Mustafa was not to know this on 7 September, few if any of them would fight at all in the battle. Specific figures are given in the lists in Chapter 10 below, but overall we can determine that Kara Mustafa had no more than 65,000 troops at hand, 75,000 including the Tatars.

This leaves us with the question: where did the discrepancy come from? Vaelckeren, himself a senior official in the Imperialist army, suggested in his history of the siege, in which he published a version of the muster, that the manner of conducting the muster facilitated fraud, and the numbers were *deliberately* inflated to encourage Kara Mustafa to fight: the rest of the army wanted to see him go down in defeat and thus be rid of his tyranny.[80] This beggars belief. Many senior officials and commanders in the camp, perhaps a majority, loathed Kara Mustafa for his arrogance and tyrannical treatment of subordinates (they cared a lot less about his tyrannical treatment of the Empire's Christian and Muslim subjects), but the Grand Vizier also had his supporters, who were more likely to have reported truthfully, and who would have revealed to him any deliberate deceptions – as his enemies would have known before they even considered such a scam. Besides, supporters or enemies, few of them would have intentionally courted defeat not only for their empire and their religion but also for themselves, their household troops and their reputations, merely out of spite for Kara Mustafa. Apart from the Tatar Khan, no Ottoman commander gave any indication in the final battle of any desire to lose. Slightly more probable is that some of the provincial governors and officers of the *kapi kulu*, terrified of what would happen to them if it were revealed to the violent Grand Vizier how weak their contingents had become, delivered absurdly inflated figures – not intending to create a defeat, but out of a desire to save their own skins. One can imagine even those who were supporters of Kara Mustafa being prepared to tolerate a deception on such grounds. Most of this remains pure speculation, however.

It is not even clear whether the Grand Vizier was fooled: Kara Mustafa had many faults as a commander, true (he had made some serious strategic mistakes in his conduct of the campaign, and would commit a cardinal one in a few days), and he was as capable of self-deception as most humans, perhaps more so than the average, but he was not a complete idiot. He was familiar enough with the Ottoman system and the way it worked or did not

---

beylerbeyi and the Grand Vizier, but I have never found any record of the Grand Viziers' salaries in this period – the nearest I have found are informal reports of suspect figures from the late sixteenth century, well below the amount awarded to *beylerbeyi*s.

80   Johann Peter von Vaelckern, *Relation or diary of the siege of Vienna…* (London: Nott & Wells, 1684), pp.92–93; also put even more explicitly in Christoph Boethius, *Ruhmbelorberter, triumphleuchtender und glantzerhöhter Kriegs-Helm Dero Röm. Kaiserl. auch zu Hungarn und Böhmen Kön. Maj. und dero… Bunds-Verwandten wider den… Türckischen Tulband…* (Nuremberg: Lochner, 1686–1698), vol. 1, p.140. This version of Vaelckern is a translation from Latin original, *Vienna a Turcis obsessa…* (Vienna 1683); there is also German version, *Wienn von Türken belägert, von Christen entsetzt* (Linz, 1684). On the mechanism of the muster, see the discussion in Appendix II.

NO MORE TIME TO LOSE

Ottoman army during the siege of Vienna. Artist unknown, 1683 Wien Museum Inv.-Nr. 212825, CC0)

work; he knew perfectly well about the various units that were elsewhere in the theatre of war and the contingents that could not be trusted, he knew the huge casualties that the *kapi kulu* corps had suffered during the siege, and he knew the normal range of numbers of troops that a *beylerbeyi* or *sancak-bey* was expected to bring into the field. Everything Kara Mustafa did in these days suggests, not a commander supremely confident in the huge size of his army but a man who was very concerned about the numbers and the prospect of fighting the relief army. The inclusion of the 20,000 servants in the list as potential combatants indicates how worried the Ottoman high command had become, for the Ottoman government was normally keen to preserve the distinction between members of the *askeri* arms-bearing class and the tax-paying *reaya*. On the 7th, Kara Mustafa even had his Grand Dragoman (chief interpreter), the Greek Alexander Mavrocordato, make an approach to the captive Imperialist envoy Kuniz, the second in recent weeks (a similar but less official feeler had been put out on 29 August through the Prince of Wallachia).[81] Mavrocordato claimed he was acting on behalf of the Hungarians who were desirous of mediating between the Emperor and their new suzerain the Sultan, but no-one believed for a moment that the approach came from anyone but Kara Mustafa. The Grand Dragoman asked Kuniz whether he had authority to negotiate a peace treaty; Kuniz replied that he had not – apparently quite crossly, remarking on the number of times he had already answered this question throughout the campaign. He suspected some kind of trick, but since he was not allowed by the Ottomans to communicate with the outside world, the approach can hardly have been intended by Kara Mustafa as some kind of deception, and can only be a further indication that

---

81 The approach is recorded in Kuniz' own diary, as quoted in Renner, pp.307–308 fn., and in the diary of a member of his staff in Friedrich Firnhaber (ed.), 'Diarium, was sich vom 7. Juny anno 1683 biss zu End der Belagerung Wienns bei der Türkischen Armee zugetragen', *Archiv für Kunde Österreichischer Geschichts-Quellen*, 4 (1850), pp.496–507, here p.505. Renner had doubts about the reliability of the former source; the publication of the second seems to dispel such doubts.

the Grand Vizier had no confidence in the outcome of the military operations and was seeking alternative paths out of the situation.

The one thing Kara Mustafa did not do was send troops forward to face the relief army. No Ottoman units went into the Wienerwald to fight the Christians in the hills, nor went beyond it to the Tullner Feld to get reliable information on what was happening there.

Initial discussions

On 8 September, shortly before mid-day, Koca Ibrahim arrived in the camp with his forces: his own *yerli kulu* (which may have included some provincial timariots), some Janissaries, *cebeci*s, and the four junior regiments of the *Sipahi*s of the Porte (two regiments each of *ulufeci* and *gureba*); the numbers are variously given at 8,000 and 13,500, with the lower figure the more likely.[82] Assuming the order summoning him on the 4th had arrived early on the 5th, his men had been three days on the road from Raab, marching at about twenty-five miles a day – smartly enough for a corps which, although predominantly mounted, included many foot-sloggers.

Ibrahim found the Ottoman camp filled with a slightly unreal atmosphere. That morning, a prisoner had been taken, a German captured by the outposts of the Egyptian troops (where this was, the sources do not say, but most of the Egyptians had been serving during the siege on the Prater Island) trying to sneak through the lines into Vienna with a letter for Starhemberg;[83] the letter had been translated (though since the key points would have been in cipher, it is unlikely the Ottomans derived very much benefit from it), and the prisoner brought before Kara Mustafa for interrogation, where he no doubt confirmed the Christian army's crossing of the Danube. Despite this, Kara Mustafa went out into the siege trenches to encourage the troops and workers there through his presence and speeches, clearly hoping to speed up the fall of the city before relief could arrive; he spent the afternoon watching as two mines were exploded under the Löbel Bastion and a ferocious assault lasting two hours was thrown against it – and when that failed, a second was attempted a little later, with no better effect. It was only then[84] that the Grand Vizier decided to send out a detachment under Ömer Deli Bey, the recently-

---

82   Kreutel & Teply, 182, with most modern historians offering some version of this. On the numbers of men, the Ottoman diarists in this translation say nothing, although Wimmer (*Wiedeń*, p.304 n.4) suggests 8,000 is the quoted figure but he inclines to the higher; Stoye and Necati incline to 8,000, Barker to 13,500, with none of them citing a source for their preference.

83   On prisoners and their intelligence, including the man captured later in the day: Kreutel & Teply, pp.182, 183, 235–236. The Master of Ceremonies stated that the letter contained intelligence of the greatest importance for the army of Islam, but failed to give specifics, and I suspect that he did not have any. His account is definite that it was the second prisoner in the evening who reported on the situation at Tulln; Silahdar's account could be read as indicating both prisoners did so, and this is more likely.

84   if the sequence in which the Master of Ceremonies wrote down events is an accurate reflection of their course; since most of the time he tried conscientiously to record events in the correct order and, if not, at least specified times, we must assume that the sequence is correct.

appointed *sancak-bey* of Karahisar, to obtain some reliable intelligence on the moves the Christians must be making now that they were on the south bank of the Danube (Kara Mustafa was unaware that the Christians had wasted the day as much as he had). Ömer and his horsemen had barely disappeared into the hills when Kara Mustafa called a meeting at his 'bunker' in the trenches for initial discussion of what the army should do, especially whether it should continue the siege or, leaving a token force to keep the garrison of Vienna contained, turn against the relief army. All of the viziers and other *beylerbeyi*s with the army, plus the Janissary Ağa Mustafa Pasha Bekri and his deputy the *kul kahyasi*, came back out of their positions in the trenches or forward from the camp for the council. The sources record only the bald statement that the council decided Kara Mustafa should withdraw from his bunker in the trenches to his great palace-tent complex in the main camp, at the point known to later generations of Austrians as 'auf der Schmelz'. In the approaches, one *beylerbeyi* (Binamaz Halil of Sivas) was replaced with another (Şişman Mehmed of Karaman), for no readily apparent reason, and just one officer, Deli Bekir Pasha, *beylerbeyi* of Aleppo, pulled out of the trenches, presumably to form the basis of a defence against the relief army.[85] Given the situation, the absence of any decision to suspend the siege operations and the trivial withdrawal of forces from the siege works could only mean that Kara Mustafa's desires had broadly prevailed: he himself was moving back to the camp to oversee measures against the approaching relief army, as was appropriate for the commander-in-chief, but the siege would continue at full effort.

In the evening of the 8th, before Kara Mustafa had moved to the camp, Tatar scouts from beyond the Wienerwald brought in a 'hat-wearing' prisoner (a formulaic Islamic term of abuse for a German), only recently captured, probably from one of the reconnaissances being sent forward by the Christians, who gave the first truly significant details about the allied army: it was fully over the Danube, and about to set off in order of battle and full readiness, leaving its baggage behind at Tulln. The prisoner also threw in the spurious detail that Christians had 200 light and heavy guns with them.[86] Kara Mustafa did nothing for the rest of the night; early next morning, as agreed, he moved with his entire staff and household to the palace-tent complex 'auf der Schmelz', and here summoned a fuller council of war.

The council of war of 9 September

To Kara Mustafa's huge and obscenely luxurious tent that morning came in response to his summons various senior officers: *beylerbeyi*s of vizieral rank, Abaza Sari Hüseyin, *beylerbeyi* of Damascus and the senior vizier in the Ottoman hierarchy present in the army, Kara Mehmed of Diyarbekir, as well as the lower-ranked Binamaz Halil of Sivas, plus the *Ağa*s of the *Sipahi*s

---

85 Kreutel & Teply, p.183.
86 Kreutel & Teply, pp.183, 235–236.

and *Silahdar*s (two of the seniormost cavalry officers of the army), and the commanders of the *cebeci*s and *topci*s. Infantry officers who had participated in the discussion the previous evening, such as the Janissary Ağa, were not present, and nor was the Khan, but most conspicuously absent from the list of attendees was the high-ranking *beylerbeyi* of Buda, Koca Ibrahim – Kara Mustafa clearly still had no intention of hearing his unwelcome advice.[87] The reasons why the *cebeci* and *topci* commanders were summoned but not the Janisaary Ağa are not stated; it may be that their technical opinion was desired on the feasibility of continuing the siege, though given Kara Mustafa's known wishes, it is unlikely they would have dared express an opinion against continuing.

Discussion lasted only an hour or so. In light of the latest intelligence of the Christian advance, it was no longer possible to do nothing about the advancing relief army, and the meeting concluded by deciding, in keeping with Kara Mustafa's wishes, to continue the siege with most of the foot-soldiers already in the trenches, while 'all the Pashas' would prepare to oppose the relief army with the cavalry of their households and provinces. The Grand Vizier expressed a desire to 'go' into the field with the cavalry, but was persuaded by the rest of the council to remain in his tent complex, 'to stand firm, in the heart of the padishah's army, like a mountain of stone' – almost certainly, the wish to command in the field was formulaic and insincere, and the other officers picked up on Kara Mustafa's real desire to concentrate on the siege.

Although the Ottoman diarists do not say so explicitly, it seems that the council started the process of assigning commands; at least, as soon as it was over, Abaza Sari Hüseyin Pasha rode off to take charge of 'the area assigned to him' (the left wing), while most of the other officers remained behind in Kara Mustafa's tent for a brief period, for reasons not specified, before mounting to accompany him on a careful and detailed reconnaissance of the Christian approach routes through the Wienerwald.[88] According to the Master of Ceremonies, reconnoitring 'right and left', they 'looked closely and abundantly into the routes on which the approach of the infidels was to be expected…'. If they had gone too deeply into the Wienerwald, they would have run into the Christians entering the hills on this day, some of whom were already in the Kierling-Altbach valley, and, since we know they did not, it is likely that the reconnaissance encompassed only the chain of hills directly surrounding the Ottoman camp, from the Danube as far as the Alsbach or even the River Wien, concentrating especially on the passes

---

87   The list of attendees is in Kreutel & Teply, pp.183–184; with the decisions on p.184 and the persuading of Kara Mustafa to remain in his tent on p.185. Older European histories, whose view of the position in the Ottoman camp was dependent on the suspect account of Cantemir, included Koca Ibrahim amongst the attendees since Cantemir gave him a leading role in debates; some modern historians, even Wimmer, *Entsatz*, p.174, put him there as well, while even Barker, p.319, who recognises his absence, suggests that he managed somehow to present his opinion anyway. The issues surrounding the whole question of Ottoman councils of war are discussed in Appendix III.
88   Kreutel & Teply, p.184.

between the heights, all the streams and their valleys that formed approach roads leading directly out of the Wienerwald at the Ottoman camp.

From the organisation of the field force that Kara Mustafa ordered on his return to camp, the reconnaissance must have concluded that the biggest threat lay on the side nearest the Danube, with the main road along the river and the passes over the Kahlenberg chain. It was only reasonable to assume that the Christians would make some use of the Danube road, and would want to exploit the advantage offered by having the river secure their flank. However, Kara Mustafa may also have received definite reports during the reconnaissance (or very soon after it) from vedettes to the north in the Weidling valley, who by now must have been aware that Christian forces were descending the Kierling-Altbach valley, heading for Klosterneuburg and thus for the Danube. Such reports would have made it imperative to concentrate on the right.

Initial Ottoman deployment of 9 September

After the reconnaissance, Kara Mustafa retired to his tent complex in the main camp, conforming to the decisions of the council of war, and, while Ottoman officials prepared the written instructions for the governors who would serve in the field army, the Grand Vizier settled down to keep watch over both the siege works and the troops 'outside', constantly sending out 'informants' on both sides 'here and there' to bring him up-to-date reports on what was going on. His location was much closer to the city than to most of the approach routes, and his attention continued to be focused on the progress of the siege, where work in the approaches continued unabated.

At the same time, however, the forces assigned to face the relief army were beginning to move into their new positions facing the hills. Around noon, the observers on the tower of St Stephen's Cathedral inside Vienna, looking beyond the siege works at the huge semi-circle of Turkish tents around the city, reported large numbers of troops moving away out of the camp's far side, heading towards the hills, especially on the northern flank, towards the Kahlenberg chain. Behind them, workers and other troops struck the tents they had left, loaded them up together with all their belongings and provisions onto camels and wagons, and moved the lot to new camp positions along the foot-hills near where the field forces were now posted.

On the left, Abaza Sari Hüseyin[89] *beylerbeyi* of Damascus, with his Syrians, the timariots of the Asian provinces, and some other troops, had taken up his position immediately after the council of war, facing the southernmost

---

89 Hüseyin the Abkhazian, the Blond. Abkhazia was a small region on the outermost limits of the Ottoman Empire in the Caucasus (today it is mostly in Georgia). In the seventeenth century Abkhazians had started entering Ottoman service (the *kapi kulu*) voluntarily; 'Abaza' was a fairly common epithet by 1683. The region was backward, and Abkhazians were regarded by Ottomans of true Turkish or European origin as stupid, the butt of jokes equivalent to the 'Irish' jokes of the English and 'Belgian' jokes of the French. It is hardly surprising that he was 'blond': the Caucasus is after all the region from which we take the formal name for 'white' people.

INITIAL OTTOMAN PREPARATIONS

sector of the hills, probably concentrating especially on watching the exit of the Alsbach valley, the most obvious debouchment from the Wienerwald. Even after he was joined by the Tatars later in the day, this was a weak corps covering a wide front of two to three miles, and it is unlikely he extended in force as far as the River Wien, although he probably placed outposts watching the Wien valley.[90]

Much stronger was the right wing,[91] which was organised as soon as Kara Mustafa got back from the reconnaissance. Koca Ibrahim *beylerbeyi* of Buda was placed in command here – however much Kara Mustafa disliked him, he was a very senior officer, a *beylerbeyi* of vizieral rank, who, although his long experience lay more in administration and diplomacy than in military campaigns, had the official authority and personal reputation to hold together a big corps (at the very back of his mind, Kara Mustafa may also have held the thought that, if anything went wrong, Koca Ibrahim was the man he most wanted to take the blame). Ibrahim was assigned 23,000 men, mostly light *yerli kulu* cavalry but with a core of regular *kapi kulu* troops: 5,000 Janissaries, and the four junior regiments of the *Sipahi*s of the Porte that he had brought from Raab.[92] It is possible that some elements of this wing only joined Koca Ibrahim over the following couple of days; although the Ottoman diarists list Hizir *beylerbeyi* of Bosnia amongst the forces initially assigned to the right wing, the Master of Ceremonies also stated that Hizir was only moved across from his original camp on Prater Island on the next day, 10 September. Also placed in this area, though not apparently directly under Koca Ibrahim, was a formation designated the 'advance guard', 5,400 *yerli kulu* under Kara Mehmed *beylerbeyi* of Diyarbekir, another vizier with a lot of experience of high office but too little of it in high command in the field, though he had some natural military ability. Apart from the household troops of Ibrahim himself, of Hizir Pasha the *beylerbeyi* of Bosnia (another very senior official), and a few minor governors, all the troops of Koca Ibrahim's command and the advance guard were Asian in origin.

The right wing took positions at the north end of the camp, broadly facing north and north-west, its right flank resting on the arm of the Danube known then as the Canal (on which Vienna itself lay), and extending left until it made contact with Abaza Sari Hüseyin; as yet, there was no separate 'centre'. We do not know the right wing's exact positions on this first day, but it was certainly holding the lines of the streams that run west-east down from the hills here to the Canal and form effective barriers against anyone coming

---

90 Silahdar (Kreutel & Teply, p.237) did state that Abaza Sari Hüseyin stood on the banks of the Danube. This is impossible.
91 The Ottomans were aware of the concept of the right as a post of honour, and in the 'classical' period of Ottoman military organisation (down to the mid-sixteenth century) they had respected it in their own way: during campaigns in Europe, provincial forces of Europe held the right wing, while in Asia, the troops of Anatolia had the right (the centre, as the real key to their formation, was held by the *kapi kulu*). The practice had fallen out of use for many years, and, although here in this European campaign a *beylerbeyi* of a European province commanded the right while a *beylerbeyi* of an Asian province commanded the left, the bulk of both their forces were Asian.
92 See below on the Ottoman Order of Battle for full details of Koca Ibrahim's wing. For the Master of Ceremonies on Hizir: Kreutel & Teply, p.185.

NO MORE TIME TO LOSE

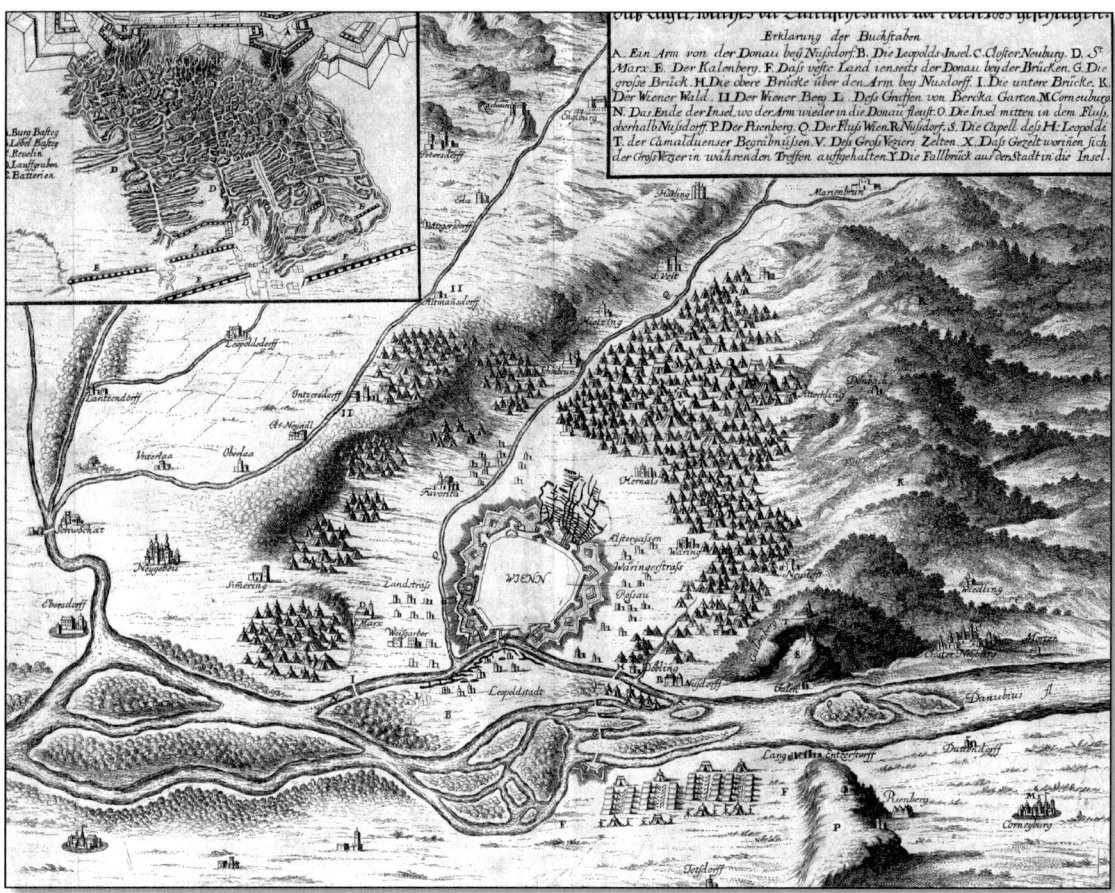

Turkish siege of Vienna in 1683. Published in Frankfurt in 1691 (National Library, Warsaw)

down against the camp from the north. In all probability, Koca Ibrahim took as his main position the ridge on the south bank of the Krottenbach-Döblingerbach, where entrenching work was already beginning. Parts of his own force may have been pushed forward of this line to other streams beyond, and Kara Mehmed with the advance guard lay even further forward, on or beyond the Nussberg, with posts pushed forward as far as start of the woods of the Kahlenberg chain. The Ottoman army already had small outposts in the ruined buildings on top of both the Leopoldsberg and the Kahlenberg.

No-one had recorded any discussion of numbers in the council of war, and, since dispositions were to be in constant flux over the next couple of days, it is impossible to say categorically the total numbers assigned to the field army at this stage; we have only the figure for Koca Ibrahim's right wing, of 28,400 including the advance guard – compared with most reports of Ottoman numbers, this is reliable, but even so it probably represents some degree of exaggeration. It is very unlikely that, even after the arrival of the Tatars, the whole field army amassed more than 40,000 on this day, the 9th. Although the majority of the troops were mounted, the *yerli kulu* were capable of fighting on foot as skirmishers, and Koca Ibrahim had that solid core of Janissaries – although it is often stated that most of the Janissaries remained in the siege works, the 5,000 assigned to the right wing must have represented the majority of those still surviving.[93]

In circumstances such as the Ottomans faced, a western army would have long since established a systematic set of entrenchments facing the open country, known as lines of circumvallation, to protect the camp and act as a significant barrier against any relief attempt.[94] Such lines were not part of Ottoman practice, but the Turks were aware of the concept of entrenching a camp (they had done so at Chocim in 1673, though it had done them no good then), and they now set to with the spade, though in a rather disjointed and unenthusiastic fashion. On Koca Ibrahim's right wing, the village of Nussdorf was partly fortified as an advanced post, and a rough-and-ready line of trenches and artillery positions thrown up along the line of the Krottenbach-Döblingerbach ravine, covering the northern end of the camp. We know for sure of one battery of six guns at the left end of this line, and there were probably similar positions further downstream. Just to the south of this line, somewhere between the villages of Döbling and Gersthof, the workers, either now or on the 11th,[95] established some kind of redoubt; the exact lines of this work have never been established, but since the district *subsequently* came to be known as the Türkenschanz (Turkish entrenchment), and the hill here forms a natural bulwark, its general location is assured. We should not imagine that the redoubt covered the entire area of the park that presently fills the area; it sat behind the Krottenbach defences, and while it may have been fortified to some degree on this side to act as a second line, it faced primarily west and west-south-west, covering the exit route from the hills of the Währingerbach, and its main fortifications were undoubtedly on this side. For lack of any other name, we will follow here the practice of all historians of the battle and adopt for this redoubt, inaccurately but descriptively, the later name of Türkenschanz. For now, the redoubt seems to have been part of Koca Ibrahim's sector, but from the start the Ottomans probably intended it would become the core of a centre yet to be formed. Beyond the Türkenschanz, across the several miles of more open land to the River Wien, there were no entrenchments that we know of; whether Abaza Sari Hüseyin elected not to entrench or lacked the men to dig in, we do not know, but given the extent of front he had to cover and the apparent belief of the Ottoman high command that this was the least-threatened sector, the omission was probably by choice.

---

93 Benaglia had recorded 15,000 Janissaries at the start of the campaign; the Ottoman casualty list of 7 September actually gave Janissary deaths as 10,000, which would suggest none at all were left in the trenches – the list is clearly inaccurate, but nevertheless the Janissaries had lost many thousands during the nearly two months of siege.

94 Modern historians are fond of sneering at the practice, paying too much attention to the small number of cases where exceptionally able or lucky commanders of relief forces managed to break through such lines. In fact, they were a very successful technique, and it is worth remembering that even Clausewitz stressed their usefulness (in a critique of Napoleon's conduct of his siege of Mantua); see Carl von Clausewitz, *On war*, Book 2, Chapter 5, available in numerous editions, or his *Die Feldzug von 1796 in Italien* (translated into French as *La campagne de 1796 en Italie*, never translated into English), Chapter 48.

95 see below, chapter 9.

The placement of artillery followed the pattern of entrenching, with a bias to the right and centre. Sixty light guns and two of the bigger pieces known as 'columbrines' (probably 8-pounders)[96] were taken from the camp or use in the approaches and deployed with the field army, almost all of them either on the right wing (on the Krottenbach-Döblingerbach line or in front of it) or in the centre at the Türkenschanz.[97] The predominance of light pieces is striking: Kara Mustafa had no intention releasing any of his limited number of heavy guns from the siege works for use against the relief force.

The Khan and the Tatars: Murad Giray's inaction

Khan Murad Giray had not been present at the council of war. He and his Tatars, having failed to do a thing about the Christians' crossing of the Danube at Tulln, should have been busy observing and harassing the advance of the infidels across the Tullner Feld and into the Wienerwald. In fact, he had apparently sat quietly with his immediate entourage somewhere beyond the hills and watched as Lorraine and Sobieski set off, doing nothing; a few parties of Tatars had certainly kept watch on the Christian advance and would continue to do so, but the Crimeans, from Khan down to humblest raider, had been astonishingly quiescent, and many Ottomans were deeply suspicious about this inactivity. Silahdar[98] (who was not even present at Vienna, but wrote his history as a re-working of other accounts some years later) recorded a little story of how Murad on this day sat on his horse, in a classic pose of detached equestrian arrogance, watching as the Christians crossed the bridge, and when asked by his imam why he did not attack the vulnerable crossing, launched into a tirade against Kara Mustafa: he accused the Grand Vizier of personal disrespect to him as Khan and of ignoring his advice, and, while acknowledging that he, Murad, *could* act effectively against the Christians, refused actually to do a thing against them. According to this story, he declared that he had repeatedly recommended that Kara Mustafa do something about the approaching relief, that he had urged the Grand Vizier to draw enough artillery out of the siege works to deliver a proper battle in the field or begged him, if he would not do this, to let the Crimeans go home in safety before the Christians reached Vienna; but Kara Mustafa would have none of it, had even written back to him letters full of abuse, with references

---

96   In Turkish, 'kolumburna' or 'kolonborna', though 'columbrine' is a valid form as the word was Italian in origin. As with all Ottoman artillery terms, experts can never agree on what exactly the name meant; I follow Rhoads Murphey, 'The functioning of the Ottoman army under Murad IV (1623–1639/1032–1049): key to the understanding of the relationship between centre and periphery in seventeenth century Turkey' (unpubl. PhD thesis, U. of Chicago, 1979), p.134, in his definition which gives the piece a shot of about eight pounds.

97   The Master of Ceremonies (who provided the numbers of cannon) said only about the placement that they were put 'opposite the three ways on which the infidels would in any case advance' (Kreutel & Teply, p.184). It is not clear what he meant by this, and the positioning of the artillery has been described following what we learn of it from the battle itself.

98   Kreutel & Teply, pp.237–238; compare pp.213–214 for the story of how Silahdar's account was composed.

to Tatars eating 'stinking horse flesh'; and so Murad did not care if he was committing treason against his overlord and his religion.

Many details of the story do not ring true.[99] However while the words may have been put into Murad Giray's mouth by Silahdar, there is some substance behind the story, firstly in terms of Ottoman *suspicion* of Murad, and secondly as an indicator that those suspicions were to a substantial degree justified, that Murad Giray and his followers were definitely up to something and that they had understandable reasons for doing so. Many in the Ottoman army *expected* the Khan to have done much more to disrupt the Christian army during such a dangerous operation as crossing the Danube up to and including the 8th. In fact, the Khan and his depleted Tatar horde would have found it very difficult to act effectively against the Danube crossing, which the Christians had secured very thoroughly; the suspicions of Kara Mustafa's entourage on this point, while understandable, were not justified. However, Murad had also done nothing to hinder the allied advance across the Tullner Feld, where Tatar harrassment could at least have forced the Christians to slow their march to a crawl, and he had so far done nothing but observe the Christians once they entered the Wienerwald – and indeed that was all the Tatars would ever do in the coming days. There is no doubt that the Ottomans had good cause for serious reservations about Khan Murad Giray. We know how little the allies saw of Tatar riders as they crossed the Danube and set off; and we have the strong suspicion that Murad Giray had given hints to the infidels that he might not participate in any battle. Tatar sources themselves, such as the chronicle written by Mehmed Giray (a member of the royal clan, and probably a brother of Khan Murad), also support the impression that Silahdar was on the right track in suspecting some degree of treachery from the Crimeans, if not from the Khan himself.[100] It was easy enough to see why. Kara Mustafa, who bullied anyone within his reach, made enemies easily; but the Khans were not subservient officials of the Ottoman Padishah who could be browbeaten with impunity, they were proud rulers of a state which claimed an ancestry far older and mightier than that of the house of Osman. The Girays as a clan had been giving Khans to the Crimea for centuries, and even at the best of times regarded Kara Mustafa as an oik, or as Mehmed Giray the chronicler put it, an 'obstinate vulgar backwoodsman of humble origin'[101] – not an entirely accurate statement, but close enough when viewed from the lofty lineage of the Girays. A wise Grand Vizier did not treat the Girays with the contempt he might show to a *beylerbeyi*, and a wise Grand Vizier received the opinion of a Giray Khan with some respect even if he did not follow it; but Kara Mustafa was not a wise Grand Vizier, and he could

---

99 See the detailed discussion of this point, and of the other questions surrounding Tatar inaction, in Appendix I, 5.1 and 5.2.
100 Most of what follows is from the article by Markus Köhbach, 'Der Tārīh-i Mehemmed Giray – eine osmanische Quelle zur Belagerung Wiens durch die Türken im Jahre 1683', *Studia Austro-Polonica*, 3 (1983), pp.137–164. Mehmed Giray's chronicle is not especially reliable, but firstly provides a confirmation of the overall tone of hostility amongst the Tatars to Kara Mustafa, and secondly may corroborate other witnesses, or the inferences we may draw ourselves from events.
101 Köhbach, p.151; the quote comes from a passage describing events of late 1682.

not control his temper. Murad had already tried warning Kara Mustafa once recently about the gathering relief force; Kara Mustafa's refusal to take any notice had so infuriated Murad that he left camp on some unspecified raid (it is possible that this refers to his departure to the Tullner Feld to watch the Christians and do nothing), and relations between the two men reached their nadir.[102] Murad Giray's complaints to his imam about abuse from the Grand Vizier, while the words are obviously designed by Silahdar to show Murad in a bad light, do have a ring of truth about them: the Khan was clearly very, very unhappy about the way he had been treated, and, from Mehmed Giray's chronicle, we can see that many other Tatars shared his hostility. Given that the Tatars were only in the field for booty anyway, it would have surprised no-one but Kara Mustafa to find that the Crimeans had no inclination to fight.

The diplomatic niceties could still be observed. Some time in the afternoon of 9 September, Murad rode back into the Ottoman camp with his entourage, and paid a call on Kara Mustafa in his tent complex. Kara Mustafa received him civilly. Murad informed the Grand Vizier that the Christians were coming, and warned him that, the way the infidels were marching through the Wienerwald, he expected them to arrive at the Ottoman camp by Sunday (in which he was exactly correct).[103] They discussed with elaborate formal Oriental courtesy for some time the details of the situation and the measures to be taken, dined together, then Kara Mustafa thanked the Khan and gave him a fine sable-fur coat, as if (said Silahdar, his pen dripping with sarcasm) he had done the Empire a great service. Murad then rode west out of the Ottoman camp with his 200 'booty-seeking Tatars' to his assigned position in the line of battle (the left, alongside Abaza Sari Hüseyin) and set up his tents there.[104]

Two hundred Tatars? This brings up to the final mystery surrounding Crimean involvement in the final battle: how many of them were present on 12 September? Obviously the figure of 200 represents only the Khan's personal retinue and escort, but it may not have been very far off the real total.[105] There are strong indications that the bulk of the Tatar army had packed up and left Vienna well before the battle started; only a recently-arrived detachment of 500–600 under Hacci Giray, another member of the royal clan, is mentioned as playing any part in the battle by the Tatar chronicler. The Ottoman battle-line may have been joined by the Tatar scouting parties currently still in the Wienerwald, though it is just as likely that these followed the rest of the Crimean army off into Hungary before the battle started. Khan Murad may have had as few as one or two thousand Tatars with him on 12 September.

---

102 Köhbach, p.154.
103 Accounts of the Master of Ceremonies and Silahdar (Kreutel & Teply, pp.184, 238). The former is more neutral in tone; the latter, naturally after the story he had recounted about the diatribe to the imam, is hostile. It is possible that the prediction of the date the Christians would arrive was added after the event by the antipathetic Silahdar, but I cannot see any reason why he would do so.
104 Kreutel & Teply, p.184.
105 see Appendix I, 5.3, for full discussion of this point.

Adjustments 9–10 September

The Ottomans did not sit still once they had made these initial dispositions: changes continued to be made right down to the battle, as Kara Mustafa reacted to fresh intelligence coming in or merely to his increasingly nervousness about the approach of the relief army, and the Ottoman Grand Dragoman Mavrocordato grew quite scathing about the way the troops were worn out by too much marching here and there.[106] During the afternoon and into the following day, the camps on the Prater Island were being broken up and most of the troops there were being moved into the great main camp around Vienna or to join the field army beyond. During the morning of Friday the 10th, ignoring the previous day's decision to sit tight at his tent complex in the camp, Kara Mustafa was out reconnoitring the entire vicinity of the camp, and soon after his return at noon, a report was delivered from Kara Mehmed, commander of the 'advance guard' towards the Kahlenberg chain, that the Christians had advanced to just three leagues away and were approaching by two routes along the river and 'above the camp' inland (which sounds like Kara Mehmed had identified the Christian left wing and centre but knew nothing of the Poles). The Grand Vizier ordered his entire household and personal troops, together with the two senior regiments of the *Sipahi*s of the Porte, the *Sipahi*s and *Silahdar*s, to form up and hold themselves ready for action. It was also at this time, according to the Master of Ceremonies, that Hizir *beylerbeyi* of Bosnia finally moved across the Canal from the Prater to take his place in Koca Ibrahim's command with his 2,000 *yerli kulu*, his place on the island (which to some degree covered Koca Ibrahim's right flank) being taken by the much smaller contingent of Ahmed Şeyhzade, *sancak-bey* of Saruhan (300 *yerli kulu*), the less dependable Roumanian vassal troops of Moldavia and Wallachia (6,000 at most between them) and two *ağa*s of Kara Mustafa's household (presumably with small detachments of his personal troops).[107]

Much movement was also visible, to the watchers in St Stephen's and amongst the various Ottoman camps south of the River Wien: some tents were struck as part of the general move into the greater security of the main camp, others were moved to the slopes of the Wienerberg.[108] The general pulling-in continued on the 10th, though some camps south of the Wien apparently moved back to their original positions.[109]

---

106 Kreutel & Teply, p.87.
107 Kreutel & Teply, p.185. Ahmed (his epithet means 'the sheikh's son') had been formally appointed to Koca Ibrahim's right wing, as had Hizir, and these changes were probably adjustments within the right wing.
108 Hocke, p.187. On the final point, Hocke refers to camps at Gumpendorf and 'Hunds-Thurn' being moved; the former is on the Wien and represented a slight move 'outwards', away from Vienna; the latter is not identified (it is unlikely to have been a reference to the Hundskogel, a point in the southern Wienerwald, view of which for the watchers in St Stephen's would have been blocked by the intervening hills).
109 Hocke, p.189.

NO MORE TIME TO LOSE

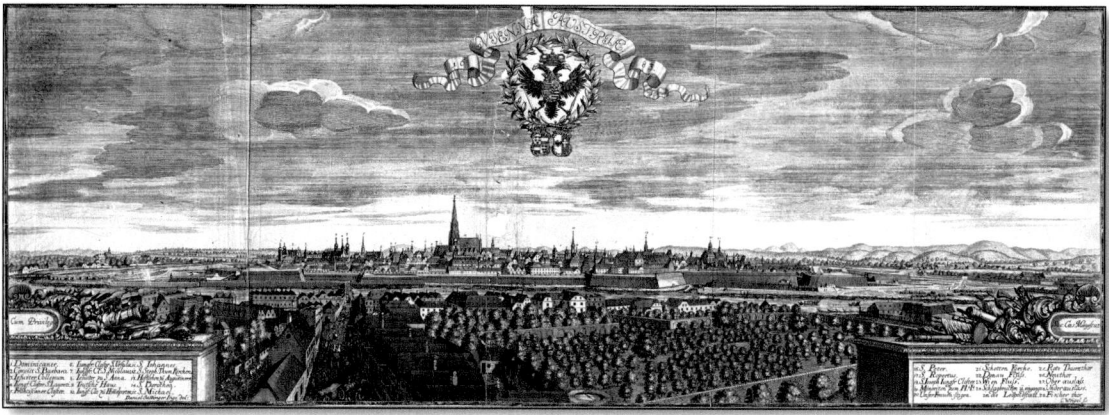

Panorama of Vienna in 1683. Daniel Suttinger, made before 1690, published in 1702 (Wien Museum Inv.-Nr. 19514, CC0)

Meanwhile the endless work of supplying the big army continued unabated.[110] Large numbers of foragers had followed the troops of the field army to their new positions on the 9th, with horses and wagons laden with hay and straw – for Ottoman horses had to eat as much as Christian ones did. Meanwhile the latest in a long series of food trains arrived in camp, sent by Hungarian lords as part of the price of being allowed to submit to the Ottomans in July and spare their lands from devastation; as usual, the wagons were ordered to set up a market at the Executioner's Tent (ominous location) with orders to sell only at the customary market price. On the 10th, the foragers went back out again south of the Wien on their eternal round of mowing.

Did Kara Mustafa hold more discussions in these days? Later historians sometimes referred to further councils; usually, they are the historians who accept the Cantemir's version of the final days of the siege, and sometimes seem simply to be muddling his story, stretching his account of a single dispute between Kara Mustafa and Koca Ibrahim over several days. Certainly, the Ottoman diarists recorded no council of war after the initial one-hour debate on 9 September. However, Kara Mustafa was not a decisive sort of commander, he was the sort who needed to talk things over a great deal[111] – and the sort who would want plenty of meetings onto which he would be able to shift the responsibility if anything went wrong. It is inconceivable that no discussions of any kind were held. There may well have been no formal councils of war, but Kara Mustafa must have talked over the situation with his immediate entourage whenever new intelligence came in. He would probably also have discussed options with those who accompanied him on the long reconnaissance that filled most of the morning of the 10th; and since that reconnaissance took him all round the areas occupied by the field army, he would have had to meet Koca Ibrahim, and the crusty old *beylerbeyi* of Buda would have been able to present his obnoxious views on how the Grand Vizier was doing everything wrong. This is all speculation, but the idea that Kara Mustafa sat in splendid silence for days after the council of the

---

110 On the foragers: Hocke, pp.187, 189. On the Hungarian supply wagons: Kreutel & Teply, p.185.
111 At the crucial stage in the early campaign when the Ottoman army sat at Raab debating whether to besiege Raab or continue to Vienna (see Timeline), there were many discussions.

9th, while reports continued to come in suggesting that his army was in an increasingly dangerous situation, is not probable.[112]

Despite encouraging reports from the siege trenches that the approaches continued to be pressed forward, Kara Mustafa's nervousness increased during the evening when more intelligence came in. Tatars in the Wienerwald captured 20 prisoners, presumably Christian stragglers, or members of an incautious scouting party; with the short-sighted brutality typical of the Ottoman-Crimean system, the Khan had nineteen of them killed before sending the twentieth on to Kara Mustafa to be interrogated – thus ensuring that there could be no corroboration for anything the unfortunate man told them.[113] (It is possible that the Khan left Kara Mustafa with only one prisoner out of sheer awkwardness, pretending to provide him with a source of intelligence while greatly reducing its value – but we do not need to seek hidden reasons; this sort of stupidity was common in Ottoman campaigns.) By this last man, the Grand Vizier was told that the Christians were advancing by two routes (in this case, the two routes probably refer to the original entry points of the allies into the Wienerwald at St Andrä and Königstetten), the Poles under their King with 40,000, Germans under their Emperor with 30,000 infantry and 40,000 cavalry, between them dragging a total of 200 light and heavy guns; they would attack the Ottoman camp on the morrow. This information, inaccurate though it was in fact, chimed in very closely with what other prisoners had said; Kara Mustafa swallowed it hook, line and sinker. Alarmed, he had the entire army stand to arms and kept it sleepless and in readiness throughout the night, right through until the grey of dawn. The Janissary Ağa was pulled out of the trenches at the head of a number of his Janissaries, with other infantry available on his call if required, to protect the entrances to the trenches against any enemy attempt to enter them; presumably Kara Mustafa feared Christian troops might slip unnoticed through his camp in the dark – a somewhat improbable risk, if he had been able to think clearly about it. At some point during the night, the *beylerbeyi* of Rumelia, Arnaut Hasan Hocazade, was also pulled from his post in the siege works to join the field army, apparently with some of the timariots who had been serving dismounted in the trenches for much of the siege.[114]

It is not impossible that all these outrageous exaggerations of Christian numbers were not actually presented to the Grand Vizier at the time, but were fictions added to the accounts of the Ottoman diarists *after* the final battle, as

---

112 See Chapter 9 below for the question of a council of war on the 11th.
113 The captures and the result of the interrogation: Kreutel & Teply, p.186.
114 Kreutel & Teply, p.186. The exact statement of the Master of Ceremonies runs: 'advanced with the *sancak* of his left wing out of the ditch to outside'. Although the position is not clear, it seems that at some point *during* the siege (it had not been so when the siege started) the left-hand side of the Turkish approaches had become the 'Rumelian sector', and it is presumably to this that the 'left wing' refers; the reference to *sancak* (on which, see Glossary, 'Sancak-bey') is assumed to indicate that he commanded timariots rather than his *yerli kulu* – dismounted timariots had certainly done a lot of service in the trenches during the siege. Hasan (his names mean Hasan the Albanian, son of Hoca) had only been *beylerbeyi* of Rumelia for a couple of weeks, having received an astonishing promotion to from the lowest gubernatorial rank, Neuhäusel, to this the highest.

a way of attempting to excuse the disaster. Certainly, even in their records of later days they never corrected the erroneous impression that the Christians had brought 110,000–120,000 men and 200 guns to the battle, though it is impossible they could have continued to believe in such figures after the battle. The Grand Dragoman Mavrocordato managed to get the numbers about right, at 20,000 Poles, mostly elite cavalry, and 50,000 Imperialists and their auxiliaries, mostly infantry.[115] Admittedly, Mavrocordato's account was written some time after the event, when he had had time to reflect, and so might not reflect what was known at the time; but on the other hand, although at the time of the siege he was a trusted official of Kara Mustafa, by the time he wrote he had not the slightest motive to try to excuse the Ottoman defeat by playing with the numbers, and for all we know he may have recorded honestly what the Ottoman headquarters knew about the approaching Christians. The question cannot be resolved with certainty. The best we can say is that everything about Kara Mustafa's known actions, from the summoning of Koca Ibrahim to Vienna up to the keeping of the army unnecessarily under arms all that night of 10–11 September, suggests a man deeply concerned about the scale of the threat he was facing, very possibly a man who thought that he was seriously outnumbered – though if he did, it makes his mistake in continuing the siege even worse.

While the Ottoman troops grumbled at their posts during the night as they tried to stay awake, behind them in the beleaguered city swarms of rockets burst up into the dark sky. No-one on either side needed a cipher book to understand the message that Starhemberg was sending the relief force: no more time to lose….

---

115 Kreutel & Teply, p.87.

6

These impassable mountains: the crossing of the Wienerwald

The allies enter the Wienerwald: Friday 10 September

By the end of 9 September the allies had reached the edge of the Wienerwald. Lorraine, who had already been doing so much of the reconnaissance work and making the decisions about the routes, rode back along the line of the hills to Königstetten late in the evening,[116] to confer with Sobieski, and perform the little respects such as taking the word of the day from him that appeared to acknowledge his recognition of the King's primacy and so absurdly pleased Sobieski. No doubt he couched the decisions he had already taken in terms of reports and proposals to his commander-in-chief, for the same reason; but there is equally no doubt that Sobieski let him get on with it when it came to the routes – he was the stranger here, the Imperialists knew (or ought to know) the lie of the land, and he had to trust them. Unless the army were to change its plans completely and try to cross the Wienerwald well to the south, Lorraine and his scouts had in fact found the best access points into the hills – even today, St Andrä and Königstetten are the only points in this northern part of the Wienerwald where proper roads enter it, while the secondary access that the Poles would use a little further south at Tulbing offers only a marked path. The Germans on either side of St Andrä would have a comparatively undemanding task ahead of them: the route into the hills, formed by the opening created by the little stream Hagenbach which rose in the hills and flowed north to the Danube, was easiest here, no serious

---

116 Le Bègue dated his Diary entry that night from there; see Stöller 100. Regarding Lorraine's responsibility for the routes, it must be admitted that the Franconian account of Schliz von Görz (Newald, vol. 2, p.99) stated that Sobieski *chose* the entrance on the right, implying some involvement in the decision; but, given that the army was supposed to be advancing in formation and that King had already insisted on holding the right, the statement seems redundant. Lorraine ensured that routes had been found; the Poles automatically took the one on the right.

trouble for any of the light artillery or equipment using the defile, while for the troops going cross-country, only a fairly short stretch of wooded hills faced them; once over the watershed, they would enter the comparatively open upper reaches of the east-west running stream the Kierling (sometimes known as the Altbach in its lowest reach), which runs into the Danube at Klosterneuburg, about six miles from St Andrä as the crow flies.

No such easy passage awaited the Poles advancing from Königstetten and Tulbing: hills covered in woods, over the hills mere paths slick with the recent rain, endless swollen streams, and, except maybe along the Weidlingbach, no wide clear valley to help them but many winding passes that would scatter their columns and hinder lateral communication for them even worse than the rest of the army; it would be very easy for their columns to get lost or end up following routes that were slower than others available. Foresters, hunters and other local inhabitants familiar with the terrain had been assembled by Lorraine and were now distributed as guides. It seems that, since the Poles would have so much more need of them, the majority of these were assigned to the right wing, including the chief among them, the Imperial Forester Christian Pötzlberger, head of the dynasty's Forest Office at Anzbach.[117] Everyone knew that it would take them two or more days to reach the Vienna basin, so the rendezvous for the following evening was established, for the Imperialists and Germans at least, as the left bank of the Weidlingbach, the next stream south after the Kierling-Altbach.

Once the preparations for the next day had been approved, Lorraine returned to his troops camped around St Andrä. First thing on 10 September, the allies set off. The soldiers carried just three days' supply of bread with them; the supply wagons had been left at Tulln, and only troops near the Danube would be able to draw further food from the barges on the Danube. At least the rain was a thing of the past: the weather during was cool, perhaps even chilly, but bearable.[118]

As expected, the left wing had a comparatively easy day. A detachment, including Lubomirski and his brigade of Polish cavalry, went off north along the edge of the hills via Greifenstein to join the Danube road and follow Leslie round that way to Klosterneuburg. Apparently, the heavier Saxon guns set off after them but stopped at Altenberg.[119] The heavier Imperialist guns

---

117 Renner, p.417, with the correct office identified on p.273. It may be significant that both Pötzlberger and the only other guide named by Renner, Leonhard Suttner, were men whose area of expertise lay *outside* the sector through which the Poles were to advance: Pötzlberger's office was well to the south-west, and Suttner came from Greifenstein up by the Danube, so the Poles may have been getting less experienced advice than they thought. However, Sobieski recorded with the Imperialist government his praise for Pötzlberger's skill and hard work, and the Forester received a small cash bonus as his reward.

118 Mansberg, p.61, refers to sharper cold than this, and a heavy storm, and others occasionally follow him in this. No storm is mentioned in other sources, or in the diaries from Vienna on the other side of the hills – a really bad storm would surely have been extensive enough to have extended to or passed the city. It is possible that Mansberg mis-dated the high *wind* (no indication of a full storm) that Sobieski described in his letter to his wife of 12 September and that he timed to mid-afternoon on the 11th.

119 It is sometimes suggested that the Saxons left their entire artillery behind here, but Hassel and Vitzthum von Eckstädt, p.146, is explicit that only the heavier guns were left (for the Saxons,

THESE IMPASSABLE MOUNTAINS: THE CROSSING OF THE WIENERWALD

Relief of Vienna. Justus van den Nijpoort, 1694 (Rijksmuseum, Amsterdam)

and equipment wagons likewise made it no further than Greifenstein; the reason is never made clear, but it seems that Leslie had not managed to clear the road of its obstacles sufficiently to allow the passage of the bigger wheeled vehicles. Meanwhile, the soldiers of the bulk of the left wing shouldered their muskets and pikes and set out up the hills in front of them. At St Andrä itself, the natural pass was left for the lighter Imperialist and Saxon battalion guns, ammunition wagons and other equipment accompanying the regiments; these entered the defile then turned left to cross the Römerbrunnen Pass into the valley of the Rambach stream and thence into the Kierling valley. The troops themselves took the dreadful paths, or made their own, over the hills to the Kierling-Altbach valley, the only difficult part of the day for them, and then marched down the valley through Gugging and Kierling villages heading for Klosterneuburg.[120] The valley opened up onto the pleasant open

---

this meant four pieces), and indeed we know from accounts of the battle the Saxons had their battalion guns with them in action. It is never stated why the four guns (from the official lists, two howitzers and two 'field mortars') did not follow the road round, but the stopping of the heavy Imperialist equipment just ahead of them was probably decisive, though the Saxons may have simply concluded these pieces would be so ineffective in the coming battle that there was no point in dragging them along.

120 That the defile was left for the guns and wheeled transport is nowhere stated in the sources, but, like the exact course taken immediately after leaving St Andrä, can be deduced from various other statements, including that the left wing was camped along the hills as far as Altenberg. It would have been impossible for 20,000 men to make it through a narrow bottle-neck like the defile and still reach the positions they occupied by night-fall; the soldiers must have crossed the hills. The ease of the march for the Imperialists is shown by the brevity of Le Bègue's entry in his Diary describing it – a single sentence of two lines (Stöller, p.100).

round hills encircling their destination, with the monastery's lofty towers reaching up to the sky and, from the tops of the hills that allowed them to see over the forests of the north bank of the Danube, the glorious vista over the river of Korneuburg town and the whole wide-open Marchfeld beyond. As they approached Klosterneuburg, they saw a few detachments of enemy troops in the low ground to the south of the monastery, the only Ottomans the Imperialists encountered this day; these immediately withdrew before them, vanishing into the woods of the Kahlenberg chain to the south. Some time before evening came down, Lorraine and his staff were at the head of the march, and he established his headquarters for the night in an advanced position at the burnt shell of the village of Weidling, on the little river of the same name south of the monastery complex, looking south at the lower open hills directly before him and then the final row of hills facing the Christians, the heavily wooded Kahlenberg chain. Heissler, no longer needed to protect Klosterneuburg, was sent forward with his dragoons from the Weidling to the Kahlenberg again, presumably to ensure that the Ottoman scouts had really withdrawn and to have another look at what the Ottomans were doing in the Vienna basin beyond. Behind this 'front line', the troops began to fill up the open spaces with their camps for the night, most of them in the lower Kierling valley but some, including the Saxon infantry of the first line, went a little further and took position on the Buchberg, the open hill south of Klosterneuburg and behind Lorraine's headquarters in Weidling. Some of the wagons may have taken a little longer to catch up and enter camp, but on the whole the Imperialists and Saxons were comfortable enough.

Not so the Bavarians and Franconians, and Sachsen-Lauenburg's Imperialist cavalry: their day was more difficult. It would probably have been better all round had they delayed setting off for a few hours to let the Imperialists and Saxons clear the passes, then followed them into the Kierling-Altbach valley and swung in onto Lorraine's right at the end of the day; but the army was committed to the advance on a wide front. Like the left wing, the centre sent any wheeled equipment out from St Andrä up the Hagenbach, and where the Imperialist and Saxon vehicles turned left over the Römerbrunnen, the Reichs ones kept on going south up the increasingly difficult ravine of the Hagenbach, the soldiers keeping pace in the hills on either side.[121] Probably somewhere near the village of Kirchbach, as they approached the stream's source, the various columns split: the infantry turned to their left and headed across the wide expanse of the Kierling Forest (sometimes known as the Klosterneuburg Forest) to the upper valley of the Rotgraben, which they then descended until it joined the little River Weidlingbach, near to Lorraine's headquarters at Weidling. If accounts of where they camped that night are correct, however, a large

---

121 Wimmer, *Entsatz*, p.178, explicitly states that the centre left its guns at the edge of the Wienerwald. This is unlikely: the Bavarians, at least, are known to have had artillery with them in the battle (though admittedly the references are more equivocal than those proving the Saxons had theirs); if any guns were left behind, they would have been heavy pieces, with the battalion guns continuing to accompany the regiments. The artillery would have had a hard task getting through the Kierling Forest, but may have accompanied Sachsen-Lauenburg instead for this part of the journey.

part of the force was actually moving through the Kierling Forest *north* of the Rotgraben, so that some came out of the forest to join the Saxons for the night on the Buchberg and others camped as far away as the Freiberg, north of Klosterneuburg.[122] While the foot were dragging their way through the forest, Sachsen-Lauenburg took the united cavalry of the centre and his right wing straight across from the headwaters of the Hagenbach to the headwaters of the Weidlingbach, and presumably descended the valley some way; the location of his camp for the night is unknown. Thus, the two halves of Waldeck and Sachsen-Lauenburg's command had avoided the height of the Tafelberg by going round it to north and south.

If the centre found the going difficult, the Poles on the right had by far the worst day. Apparently they knew this before they started: provisions had been shared out from their wagons before they set off from the camps around Königstetten, the last serious food supply they would receive until after the battle; and then most of the wagons themselves, for which Sobieski had delayed so long while they crossed the Tulln bridge, were sent off north along the edge of the plain to the depot that was forming almost by accident at Greifenstein; only some ammunition vehicles followed the regiments. A few of the heavier field guns from the train were sent round to St Andrä to follow the Imperialists into the Kierling valley,[123] and Sobieski's personal train may have gone with these, leaving the King with nothing but what could be carried on a couple of mules. But the Polish infantry commander, Kątski, an artillery specialist in origin, refused to abandon the majority of his pieces, and took steps to ensure they would not fall behind: the train was broken up, and each of the eight brigades of infantry (formations barely bigger than a western battalion) had its two battalion guns assigned to it from the start, together with one or two light field guns and all the ammunition wagons, with clear warnings that they were responsible for keeping it all with the army. Acutely aware as they were how few infantry they had, the Poles probably felt that they needed every artillery piece they could bring to help cover the shortfall.

The main part of the Poles formed two divisions, under the Hetmans: the left under Crown Field Hetman Sieniawski, while Jabłonowski, as Crown Grand Hetman the senior of the two, had (of course) the right. The infantry brigades and their assigned guns were divided equally between the two columns, while the army's six regiments of dragoons had (Wimmer thinks) been sent a bit further south to take a different route entirely. Sobieski himself accompanied Sieniawski's division, and his great royal *pułk*, which in the battle would form the centre, probably went with him.

The entry-point at Königstetten was itself less easy than the Germans had enjoyed at St Andrä with its opening cut by the Hagenbach: merely a path or two up into the hills around the 1625 foot tall Tulbinger Kogel. Sieniawski and Jabłonowski set off promptly, each in several columns, using the paths

---

122 Thus in Staudinger, *Geschichte*, vol. 1, p.169; the positions sound wildly improbable, but information on the position of the centre at nightfall is scarce.
123 Wimmer, *Entsatz*, p.178, clearly states that the heavy guns went round by the Kierling and the Poles took their battalion guns with them; others suggest they were dragging their battalion guns *and* some other light field pieces.

past the Kogel to head for Kirchbach in the upper Hagenbach valley, less than three miles away as the crow flies (the point at which Waldeck and Sachsen-Lauenburg were also aiming and from where they and their Germans would turn east and south-east). Some of the Polish infantry were sent ahead to act as pioneers, cutting trees and levelling paths to make it easier for the cavalry and artillery following; the rest of the infantry, with the extra work of pulling wagons and cannons, began to fall behind the cavalry. Descriptions of the march lack sufficient detail to be certain, but it seems that Sieniawski on the left was soon in the lead, with Jabłonowski gradually falling behind instead of keeping pace with him. It is likely that Sieniawski was following the path that in modern times would become the main road, and perhaps also the valley of the Eberhardsbach to the north – the valleys and hills were wooded, but at least his division had valleys to follow, and the hills were lower. Jabłonowski, south of this, would have had no choice but to use the tiny valley of the Marleitenbach, even today nothing more than a path, and the nameless tracks on the lower slopes of the Tulbinger Kogel massif. On top of the terrain difficulties, Jabłonowski's division ended up responsible for dragging most or all of the ammunition wagons in addition to their assigned share of the cannon, so his troops had a harder slog of it and were soon falling even further behind.

Conditions were dreadful: 'through mountains that to human understanding, on account of the narrow paths, the stones and the thickness of the woods, seemed impassable,' as Kątski recorded in his diary.[124] By nightfall, Sieniawski and his division had reached Kirchbach and, though hungry and tired, were able to spend the night sleeping on the ground in the woods around the burnt village, possibly even beyond it as far as Hintersdorf village and the western edge of the Kierling Forest (although not clearly confirmed in sources, the progress that Sieniawski was to make on the next day suggests a more advanced start point than Kirchbach for at least some of his troops).[125] The bulk of Jabłonowski's cavalry was apparently beginning to draw level with them during the night and could rest, but the Grand Hetman's infantry did not sleep: all that night, they were dragging the train over each stream or rock or steep incline in turn, harnessing extra horses to individual cannons and wagons, attaching ropes or inserting levers to add their own weight to the effort, then once that obstacle was passed, unharnessing the animals and moving back to the next vehicle in line to do it all over again.[126] Even by noon the next day, the 11th, Jabłonowski's infantry had not reached level with Kirchbach where Sieniawski had spent the night – and Sieniawski himself was well behind the Germans next along the line, Sachsen-Lauenburg's Imperialist cavalry, who were ahead in the Weidlingbach valley. As for the Polish dragoons: if Wimmer's assumption is

---

124 Quoted in Wimmer, pp.178–179.
125 *Das Kriegsjahr 1683*, p.245, even puts the Polish overnight positions as far as Kierling. Not only is this inherently improbable, it is also much too far east for subsequent Polish moves.
126 Wimmer, *Entsatz*, p.179, quoting Kątski's diary. Dalérac, vol. 1, p.143, also referred to the difficulties and the need to use levers; his statement that very few cannons arrived, and those only the lightest, has often been taken as applying to the whole army but actually referred only to the Poles.

correct, they went south from Tulbing and climbed a steep path west of the peak of the Tulbinger Kogel and then, south of the hill, turned east and led their horses single-file along the track known as the Tulbinger Steig, even today no more than a path for mountain bikes, or perhaps they used the easier valleys a little more to the south.[127] Unencumbered by artillery and wagons, and lightly equipped compared with the armoured hussars and *pancerni*, the dragoons kept up well enough despite this circuitous diversion. The allied left wing and centre had generally advanced about five miles during the day; the *leading* units of the Poles had barely managed three, some as little as one mile.

Some accounts suggest that the Poles were already starving. This seems a little extreme, since food, ostensibly for several days, had been distributed only that morning; perhaps not all of the soldiers had received their share, and maybe the Polish infantry, known for its profligacy, had scoffed the lot before setting out. Certainly, the day's exertions for the foot-sloggers had been enormous, and they would have needed more than just bread anyway to replace the huge number of calories spent dragging guns and wagons uphill. Jabłonowski's infantry in particular, slaving for more than twenty-four hours without a break, must have been close to collapse by the 11th. Kątski's insistence on bringing the artillery and ammunition was already costing the Poles dear. It was even worse for the animals, for there was no way the army could carry the enormous bulk of food that every horse required daily, and there was no fresh grass to be found in the wooded hills traversed so far; by the end of the 10th, some horses were already reduced to trying to eat leaves off the trees. At least the march had been unhindered by the enemy: like the Imperialists, the Poles saw only occasional small Ottoman scouting parties, Tatars probably, who watched from a distance and, though their presence kept the Poles on edge, made no attempt to interfere with the nightmare march.

Mercy rejoined Lorraine from his reconnaissance during the day. We have no definite information on what he reported, but presumably he filled in the intelligence gathered about the routes through the hills on the right, and his skirmishing with Tatars confirmed that they were present but no large body of Ottomans was hidden just ahead ready to pounce.

The night of 10–11 September

As Sieniawski's men descended to Kirchbach, Sobieski left them and rode off with his staff, son and personal infantry guards westward, through the southern side of the Kierling Forest (probably picking his way through the tail of the Germans of the centre) towards Kierling and then Klosterneuburg. Given Sobieski's huge girth, it is unlikely they were moving very fast, and the

---

127 Wimmer, *Entsatz*, p.179, explicitly states that the dragoons followed the Tulbinger Steig, and his map shows Poles using a route labelled thus – but the Tulbinger Steig on his map is too far south at this point: in actuality, the climb hugs the south side of the Tulbinger Kogel peak, comes out at Hainbuch near the headwaters of the Hagenbach, then heads south-east past the Heuberg.

foot-slogging guards would have had no trouble keeping up. Although it is sometimes suggested the King was merely playing his role of commander-in-chief and reconnoitring the hills still to be crossed all along the line, it is hard to believe that he did not intend also to confer with Lorraine. The Duke himself had not settled into his headquarters at Weidling but was still out on his horse reconnoitring (he would remain in the saddle most or all of the night); the two leaders met on the slopes of the Buchberg between Klosterneuburg and Weidling, and had a brief discussion – it was too informal to be called a council of war, though some other senior allied commanders seem to have joined them.[128] Lorraine pointed out to the King the Kahlenberg chain before them, the route that the Imperialists and Saxons would be following the next day into the chain, and the positions he intended to be in by the next night; he also drew Sobieski's attention to the small Ottoman outposts in the ruined buildings atop the Kahlenberg and Leopoldsberg that had been discovered by Heissler's reconnaissance, which could be serious obstacles to the advance, especially if the troops there were reinforced.

The hill-tops were significant, the Turkish detachments weak, and Lorraine was keen to take the one and drive out the other as soon as possible, but at first he seems to have accepted Sobieski's argument that any such action this early would be counter-productive: only small detached forces could be sent forward to the task, and they would be separated for hours from the main body as it struggled to catch up (it would indeed take the army all of the 11th to reach the crest of those hills), and a premature action by isolated parties might encourage the Ottomans to counter-attack in force, re-take the unsupported posts and hold them in greater strength – thus starting the battle with a set-back for the Christians, which would do the army's morale no good at all. Sobieski, who in light of the complete Turkish failure to oppose the crossing of the Wienerwald was beginning to entertain hopes of surprising the Ottoman army completely in its camp,[129] possibly feared as well that any premature attack would give the game away. He *may* also have had a hidden extra motive for this argument: a desire to prevent the left wing and centre from getting too far ahead of the Poles as they fell behind. Whatever the precise reason, it was agreed that for now forces would be placed to contain the Ottoman outposts so they could do no harm: Heissler's dragoons were already up on the heavily wooded slopes of the Kahlenberg facing the ruined monastery, the King (who was preparing to spend the rest of the night in this sector) sent his little company of haiduk guards (100–200 infantry) to help Heissler keep watch, and a little later, once the blue-coated guards had crossed the Weidlingbach, two Saxon battalions were ordered to march after them as supports (John George sent two battalions of an unspecified regiment of the first line, together with their two battalion guns).

---

128 Le Bègue's Diary (Stöller, p.100) suggests that at least part of this discussion took place early the following morning; the 'Account' (Stöller, p.33) is less clear, and the majority of other sources are against the secretary on this point.

129 Janusz Woliński, 'König Johan III Sobieski und die Schlacht bei Wien 1683', in *La Pologne au XIIe Congrès International des Sciences Historiques à Vienne* (Warsaw: Państwowe Wydawnictwo Naukowe, 1965), pp.49–62, here p.58.

The Turkish posts were to be taken the next day once the main army was closer.

Meanwhile, the generals had finalised the arrangements for the next day. Enemy posts were now in sight; hitherto the army, specially the Germans, had been marching in a way that *broadly* reflected the order of battle, but using columns of march through the valleys; now, it was necessary to advance in something much more like battle formation, or as close to it as the terrain allowed. At least for the left wing and centre, this the army would now do: the units would form themselves into the three lines of the formal order of battle and advance in something resembling this, each 'line' probably in fact a line of small columns and naturally bunching into denser columns where forced by the terrain, but ready to fight at short notice. On the extreme left the Danube would cover the flank well, and the army's heavy equipment such as the ammunition wagons could follow the road along the river south from Klosterneuburg and *round* the Leopoldsberg. The Poles would try to catch up, to come up into line on the right of the Herzog von Sachsen-Lauenburg and his Imperialist cavalry. The trials of the day had convinced Sobieski even more of the importance of infantry in this broken ground, and he obtained the loan of four German battalions to help his Poles; the four were taken equally from the main German-speaking contingents (one Saxon, one Imperialist, one Bavarian, one Franconian), and presumably set off from the Buchberg this night or early the next morning to head up the Weidlingbach valley to join the Polish wing.[130] There was also talk of 10 Imperialist squadrons being shifted across from Sachsen-Lauenburg's command to reinforce the Poles, though it is unclear if anything came of this.[131] It may also be at this time that Sobieski delivered the promised squadrons of his armoured hussars to the left wing in return for this loan of infantry.[132]

Sobieski spent the rest of the night with the left wing, probably resting in the camp on the Buchberg; the two electors, John George and Maximilian Emanuel, sent detachments of cavalry to help guard his tent.[133] Lorraine meanwhile, seemingly inexhaustible ('He does not eat or sleep, and always takes the greatest care, he personally checks the posts…' reported d'Aviano in a letter to the Emperor),[134] remained in the saddle for most of the night,

---

130   See Appendix I, 6.1, on the loan of the four battalions.
131   Annemarie Thiel, 'Johann Heinrich Graf von Dünewald', unpubl. PhD thesis, U. of Vienna, 1941, p.48, and Newald, vol. 1, p.208, claim that four cuirassier regiments from Sachsen-Lauenburg's command (Dünewald, Rabatta, Pálffy and Gondola) did join the Poles. Schliz von Görz (Newald, vol. 2, p.99) mentioned 10 squadrons going with the four battalions. Since the named units were on the far flank of the Imperialist 'right wing', next to the Poles anyway, they may have received orders to support the Poles or even join them.
132   Since we have no clear indication of these having served there in the battle, we might doubt whether they arrived, or even left the Polish army, but Le Bègue did describe them as following the Imperialist cavalry under Caprara (Stöller, p.33).
133   Plater, p.66.
134   d'Aviano to Leopold, 11 September, reproduced in Renner, p.420 and fold-out; also in German translation, without source cited, in Wentzcke, p.215 and Hans Urbanski, *Karl von Lothringen: Österreichs Türkensieger* (Vienna: Amalthea, 1983), p.135. The latter argues, unconvincingly, that Lorraine was doing all the 'donkey work' of a second-in-command, implementing the plans whose broad strokes Sobieski had laid down.

continuing to explore the access routes for his wing, especially around the Kahlenberg – urged on no doubt by the sight in the night sky to the south of the swarms of rockets sent up by the garrison of Vienna in mute appeal for immediate help. He could not get out of his mind the Ottoman outposts on the two hill-tops: the detachments sent ahead to the Kahlenberg seemed capable of containing the post there well enough for now, but he had nothing on the Leopoldsberg. Admittedly the slopes of the latter were much steeper, much less likely to be used by his own troops in advancing or by the Ottomans in any counter-attack, but the Chapel of St Leopold in Turkish hands would still be a threat that could not be ignored as he went past, and, since it was marginally nearer, it ought to be taken first. Around 2 a.m., ignoring Sobieski's recommendation, he had the Leopoldsberg occupied by 300 troops, *apparently* with no opposition – presumably, the Ottomans, exposed and isolated, withdrew as the Christians approached.[135]

After several more hours reconnoitring the hills, at about 5 a.m. Lorraine returned to the camp, heard mass, and went to inform the King of what he had done during the night. Meanwhile, behind him, things were moving on the Kahlenberg of their own accord. The Saxon reinforcements had reached Heissler about 2 a.m., and there are hints that in the darkness the Christian soldiers on the slopes may have helped scare off some Ottoman troops heading to reinforce the post. Before day-break, a handful of Imperialist musketeers, together with one of the companies of noble volunteers that had formed to serve in this historic campaign, moved in and after a brisk skirmish drove the Turks out of the ruined monastery. The Saxon battalions were immediately put in as garrison, and orders were issued to get at least a handful of light guns posted there. In the grey half-light of dawn, they thought they saw Turkish forces below approaching from the forward Ottoman positions on the Nussberg, but these turned back once it was clear the hilltop was firmly in Christian hands. The posts had fallen, and there would be no dangerous unsupported fight with the Ottomans over them after all.[136]

---

135 There is a great deal of confusion over the events of this night, especially, much muddling of the forces placed overnight to contain the Kahlenberg with the action of the following morning. In light of this confusion, I have followed Le Bègue, who was absolutely explicit in both the Diary and the Account (Stöller, pp.33, 100) that Lorraine occupied the *Leopoldsberg* post during the night, with the exact time specified in the Account; he mentioned no opposition, and the version in the Diary can only be read as an unopposed occupation. However, he also mentioned no action against the Kahlenberg; but if the Leopoldsberg post had been taken at 2 a.m., the action described by others a few hours later must have been at the Kahlenberg.

136 The story of the detachment (60 musketeers of IR Croy, volunteers under Parella) comes from Mansberg, p.63; no source is cited, and other historians who recount the story seem to have taken it from him; I have not found this in any other source. Mansberg actually has Parella and co. taking the Leopoldsberg first, then the Kahlenberg; see the previous note on this. Some nineteenth-century historians recorded a story that signals were made to Vienna from the Kahlenberg this morning as soon as it was light enough to see, including a big red flag with a white cross on it, but if any such signals were made, they were not seen in Vienna, and this seems to be a confusion with the events of the following morning.

THESE IMPASSABLE MOUNTAINS: THE CROSSING OF THE WIENERWALD

To the crest of the Wienerwald: Saturday 11 September

Lorraine had a last discussion with Sobieski, pointing out to him again the routes the left wing would take. The Germans were forming up in full order of battle in the bottom of the lower Weidlingbach valley, all the generals in their proper places,[137] and before they set off Marco d'Aviano blessed the chiefs and the entire army.[138] Sobieski then recalled his haiduks and left to return to his Poles, who were getting worried about him after such a long absence, and the army set itself in motion. As the morning mists dried up in the growing warmth of the sun, the sky promised a typical hot early-autumn day, though there would be one or two bouts of poorer weather later.[139] Despite the difficulties of the previous day, morale was high, the troops willing to work hard to overcome any obstacles. Concerned not just about the dangers from the Ottomans as they drew closer to the Turkish camp but also about the risks to the soldiers in this unknown and increasingly broken terrain, the commanders issued strict orders that troops were to keep together, to avoid scattering at all costs,[140] but despite this, the occupation of the line of the crest would be a muddled affair, units in different parts of the line reaching the top at different times due to variations in the terrain they had to traverse.

Broadly, the pattern of the previous day was repeated. Lorraine, John George, and the Imperialists and Saxons of the left wing, while finding the going tougher than on the 9th, had the easiest time of it; Waldeck and the Bavarians and Franconians in the centre had further to go and no Danube road to help them; the Poles, from a position to the rear, with furthest to go anyway and the most awful terrain in front of them, fell even more behind.

Medal commemorating two victories against Turks besieging Vienna: in 1529 and in 1683. Made by Johann Kittel in 1683. (Wien Museum Inv.-Nr. 37942, CC BY 4.0)

---

137 It is notable that Le Bègue chose this day, the 11th, to record in his diary the generals accompanying each corps (Stöller, p.101), probably an indirect acknowledgement that the army was now seriously shaking itself into order ready for action.
138 On this, see Appendix I, 6.2.
139 As with the 10th, later historians refer to bad weather later, in this case a thunderstorm with rain, that does not appear in the sources, unless it is a reference to the high wind described for the afternoon by Sobieski (see below).
140 Renner, p.420.

Left wing

The left wing set off from the lower Weidlingbach, heading for the two main heights of the Kahlenberg chain, the Leopoldsberg and the Kahlenberg itself. They used two 'routes', a separation that has sometimes led to the erroneous belief that they were operating in two 'columns', even that the Imperialists and Saxons formed separate national columns. The first route did indeed require a column: much of the cavalry followed the Danube road. The second 'route' involved going up the jumbled slopes and ravines that led up to the Kahlenberg chain, using what Le Bègue called 'the great path of the Chapel St Leopold', which can only mean the saddle between the Kahlenberg and the Leopoldsberg and the slopes of the Kahlenberg itself[141] – there are no indications that anyone attempted to cross the steep-sided Leopoldsberg proper.

The entire cavalry of the left wing was under GdC Caprara, a veteran Italian professional soldier with nearly thirty years' experience in the service of the Emperor, an excellent cavalry officer but a man often cantankerous, difficult to get on with. Under him was a whole international set of good cavalry commanders from the polyglot Imperialist army: FMLs Louis William of Baden and Fürst Salm[142] (Germans) and the Pole Hieronim Lubomirski, GWMs János Károly Pálffy (Hungarian), Francis Taafe Earl of Carlingford (Irish, with strong links to the house of Lorraine), and Mercy, the Lorrainer.[143] Most of them had distinguished experience behind them from the Dutch War of 1672–1679, though Pálffy had spent those years in action against the Hungarians of the Kurucok (Thököly) Revolt. Caprara's authority also extended over the Saxon cavalry, and although Le Bègue did not deign to mention them, he had some junior Saxon generals under him as well: GWMs Sigmund Joachim Graf von Trautmannsdorff, Heinrich IV Graf Reuss von Plauen and Rudolph von Neidschütz.[144] The wing comprised, of Imperialists, six or seven regiments of cuirassiers and two of dragoons; the Polish brigade of Lubomirski (three mounted regiments smaller than the Imperialist norm, plus some *pancerni*), to which had probably been attached the 'real' Polish units lent by Sobieski, a few squadrons of winged hussars; and of Saxons, units making up four regiments of cuirassiers, and one dragoon regiment.[145] The dragoons of the left wing had already been ordered to clear the road forward of Klosterneuburg and around the Leopoldsberg,

---

141 Stöller, p.33.
142 To give him his splendid full name, Carl Theodor Wildgraf zu Daun and Kyrburg, Rheingraf zum Stein, Fürst [Prince] Salm. Salm is mis-identified by Mansberg as Leopold Philipp, apparently because this name was mistakenly put on his patent as Inhaber of the IR late-Trauttmansdorf. Although he held an infantry regiment and appeared in one version of the final order of battle in command of a small infantry brigade, it seems he served as a cavalry general (it was not unusual for infantry *Inhaber*s to serve as cavalry commanders: the same situation applied with Louis William of Baden), and would rise later to the rank of General der Cavalerie.
143 List from Stöller, p.33, with a briefer version, pp.100–101.
144 Although all of these appear to have been cavalry officers, some or all of them would be drafted as infantry brigadiers for the battle.
145 As with all the following description, full details of all units can be found in Chapter 10 below.

and occupy it to secure the troops following.[146] Along the road came part of Caprara's cavalry, along with the heavy equipment. Their comparatively slow progress is easy to explain: they could not forge ahead, but had to keep level with the rest of the wing stuck in the hills, so although they had a much easier day than anyone else, they advanced no faster. Those horsemen who were not assigned to the road were formed up *behind* the infantry and followed them through the broken terrain to the Kahlenberg.

Lorraine's infantry was now officially under his scheming political opponent, FM and President of the Hofkriegsrat Hermann of Baden. Hermann had shown enough competence during his field service in the Dutch War of 1672–1679 to be trusted not to make a complete mess of the command. His subordinate generals were not quite such a stellar cast as served under Caprara (the Habsburgs had long been better at producing top-class cavalry commanders than infantry ones) but they could do the job: the Scot FZM Leslie with his joint infantry and artillery responsibilities, the 32-year old Belgian FML Charles Eugene, duc de Croy, who had achieved some distinction in Danish service during the Baltic phase of the Dutch War, and a couple of GWMs, the obscure comte de Fontaine (probably another Lorrainer) and the rather more prestigious Prince Ludwig Anton von Pfalz-Neuburg, son of the heir apparent to the Elector Palatine and brother-in-law of Emperor Leopold, who was acting as GWM without a formal commission – 'performing the function' of GWM as Le Bègue put it (presumably, the Imperialists were so short of infantry generals that they needed a temporary promotion to cover all the brigades). When it came to the infantry, Le Bègue overcame his snobbish feelings about the Saxons enough to mention three of their generals: the commander-in-chief was of course the Elector John George, but under him was the old war-horse FM von der Goltz, FML Hans (or Heino) Heinrich von Flemming, another officer with plenty of recent experience behind him from the Dutch War, and GWM Christian Herzog von Sachsen-Weissenfels (though Le Bègue could not get *his* first name right), only 33 but a veteran of the Dutch War. Given the fact that the big Imperialist infantry regiments were not yet organised into permanent battalions but had their companies distributed willy-nilly amongst armies, to be formed into battalions of variable size when necessary, it is impossible to be entirely certain about the number of tactical units Lorraine had available (see also Chapter 10 below), but it appears that the Imperialists, together with the Salzburgers serving with them, mustered 14 battalions, 13 after deducting the battalion lent to the Poles. John George's Saxons were a bit more modern in this respect and their six regiments had two battalions each; with one battalion lent to the Poles, this gave them a total of 11 battalions, giving Lorraine a grand total of 24 battalions. He also had a couple of small battalions of noble volunteers, including the young man who would later rise to be the greatest military commander of the age, Prince Eugene of Savoy.

---

146 according to the 'Baden account', in Röder, vol.1, Urk., p.15. Since one of the Imperialists' two dragoon regiments of this wing (Heissler's) was apparently otherwise engaged on the Kahlenberg, one of these DRs must have been from Saxon or from Lubomirski's corps.

The Imperialist and Saxon infantry struggled up the slopes that led to the Kahlenberg chain, followed by cavalry. Despite the orders to keep to formation, the terrain frequently broke up their line, sometimes so badly that soldiers were shouldering their muskets and almost climbing rather than marching in order. But the Christians' luck held: there were no Ottoman forces in the hills to exploit the situation. Due to the order of battle for the entire Christian army, the Imperialists were more to the left, the Saxons to the right (in the overall order of battle, the Saxons were technically towards the centre from the Imperialists, not 'on the right'), and according to one Saxon account[147] the terrain in front of the Elector's troops happened to be more open, so that while the Imperialists sometimes had to advance in single file through the ravines, the Saxons could march on a wider front and often found themselves drawing ahead of their allies. In obedience to the orders about keeping together, they constantly had to stop to let the Imperialists catch up. As they climbed on, they increasingly found a gorge separating the two forces.

Nevertheless, all the troops were making steady enough progress, with the Saxons rather encouraged by their awareness that they were well ahead of the Franconians to their right. Around 11 a.m., Lorraine and John George joined the advanced troops in the burnt Camaldulensian monastery on the top of the Kahlenberg, and established their headquarters amongst the ruined buildings; from here, they could see everything that was going on in the Vienna basin below. Apparently, they were in advance of the main elements of the first line, which was now continuing the Imperialist-Saxon race up and around the Kahlenberg. The Saxons, approaching the top of the Kahlenberg on its western side, sent a patrol of 30 musketeers ahead as a scouting party; this reported back the rather alarming news that it could see the Ottomans below forming up in order of battle, as if ready to attack, and the Saxons speeded up trying to reach the peak before the Turks – only to discover when they reached it that the Turks were actually a good distance away (between half a mile and a mile) and making no attempt to advance against the hills.[148] Mightily relieved, the Saxons extended to their left to restore contact with the Imperialist troops now around the monastery. The rest of the first line caught up bit by bit with their commanders at the top of the hill or in the saddle towards the Leopoldsberg.

This was their target point for the day, and along the crest-line they came to a halt: the rest of the army to their right was nowhere in sight. For protection in case the Turks attacked, *chevaux-de-frise* were put together

---

147 *Aufrichtige und unpartheyische Relation*, 5; also published in the contemporary news collection, *Theatrum Europaeum, oder, Aussführliche und warhafftige Beschreibung aller und jeder denkwürdiger Geschichten…* (Frankfurt am Main: Görlin, 1691), vol. 12, p.520.

148 Thus in the Saxon account in *Aufrichtige und unpartheyische Relation*, pp.5–6, also in *Theatrum Europaeum* (Schuster and Francke, vol. 1, p.105, appear to refer to the same event but give the patrol an officer and 20 musketeers). Since John George was already in the monastery and could be expected to warn them of any danger, the story does not seem completely credible. However, the Saxons had been the most nervous of the new contingents at Krems-Mautern and Tulln, so perhaps they were still jittery, inclined to overreact slightly without relying on the Elector to inform them of any danger approaching.

and positioned, and, where the ground allowed amongst the trees, crude entrenchments hastily thrown up. Skirmishers, especially from the noble volunteers keen for personal distinction, descended the southern slopes to engage in sporadic clashes with the Turks at the foot who seemed inclined to dig in there. The head of the cavalry column on the road, level with them on their left, was also clashing with the light Asian riders opposite them – nothing serious, and casualties were minimal (see below). Behind the skirmish line, Lorraine ensured that his troops occupied the upper levels of the seven or eight 'avenues' that provided access down the wooded slopes to the open ground at the bottom, avenues that would be essential on the morrow.[149] As the afternoon progressed, some troops were set to working on improving the routes down, clearing trees and levelling the ground where they could, to make the descent as easy as possible. Meanwhile, the lines of infantry behind the first, and the cavalry following at the rear, continued to arrive throughout the afternoon – some stragglers not even making it until the night. The artillery was finding it even more difficult.

Despite Lorraine's orders of the previous night, no-one had managed to get any artillery to the monastery yet, but around 4 p.m.,[150] by dint of doubling and tripling the teams of horses pulling them, a few battalion guns (two Saxon, one Imperialist) were dragged up the Kahlenberg, placed in front of the monastery, and opened fire on the Turks below. At that range and from such an elevation, they can have done little real harm,[151] but in conjunction with the skirmishing volunteers, they seem to have made life uncomfortable enough for the screen of enemy troops at the bottom, light *yerli kulu* from Kara Mehmed's advance guard, to cause them to shift positions several times and then eventually give up and pull back completely out of range. A couple more light pieces may have joined the little battery on the Kahlenberg – the number of battalion guns there is variously given at four and six. The rest of the artillery was still struggling: Lorraine was now directing his energy to organising efforts to improve the access routes, and doubling and tripling of the teams allowed the rest of the battalion guns and some of the lighter field pieces to be brought up the steep slopes in dribs and drabs, but the work went on well into the night; the Imperialists eventually gave up the effort altogether with the 12-pounders and left these behind.[152]

---

149 *Das Kriegsjahr 1683*, p.247, claimed that Lorraine and John George addressed their soldiers at the top. This is mentioned in no source, and it was certainly not Lorraine's style to indulge in such histrionics.
150 The time is never made clear in sources from the relief army, but watchers in the city (Hocke, p.192; Johann Georg Wilhelm Ruess, *Wahrhaffte und gründliche Relation über die den 14. Julii Anno 1683 angefangene, den 12. Septembris aber glücklich auffgehobene Belägerung der Kays. Haupt- und Residentz-Stadt Wien* (Vienna: Ghelen, 1683), p.70) recorded first noticing artillery fire from the crest at this time. According to Vaelckeren, p.97, however, the garrison did not even see the troops appearing on the Kahlenberg until about an hour later.
151 Dalérac, vol. 1, p.150, said about guns on the Kahlenberg on the 12th that they could not reach the Turks at all due to the distance and elevation (round-shot artillery acted against personnel like a bowling ball, and thus depended on a comparatively low flight path, level to the ground at the target).
152 Stöller, p.35.

The centre and Sachsen-Lauenburg's right wing.

The centre and right wing set off from positions further up the Weidlingbach than the left wing, possibly with some units hurrying to catch up from overnight camps further to the north. We have a lot less evidence for them than for Lorraine's troops, but we know that they had a more difficult time of it than the Imperialists and Saxons.

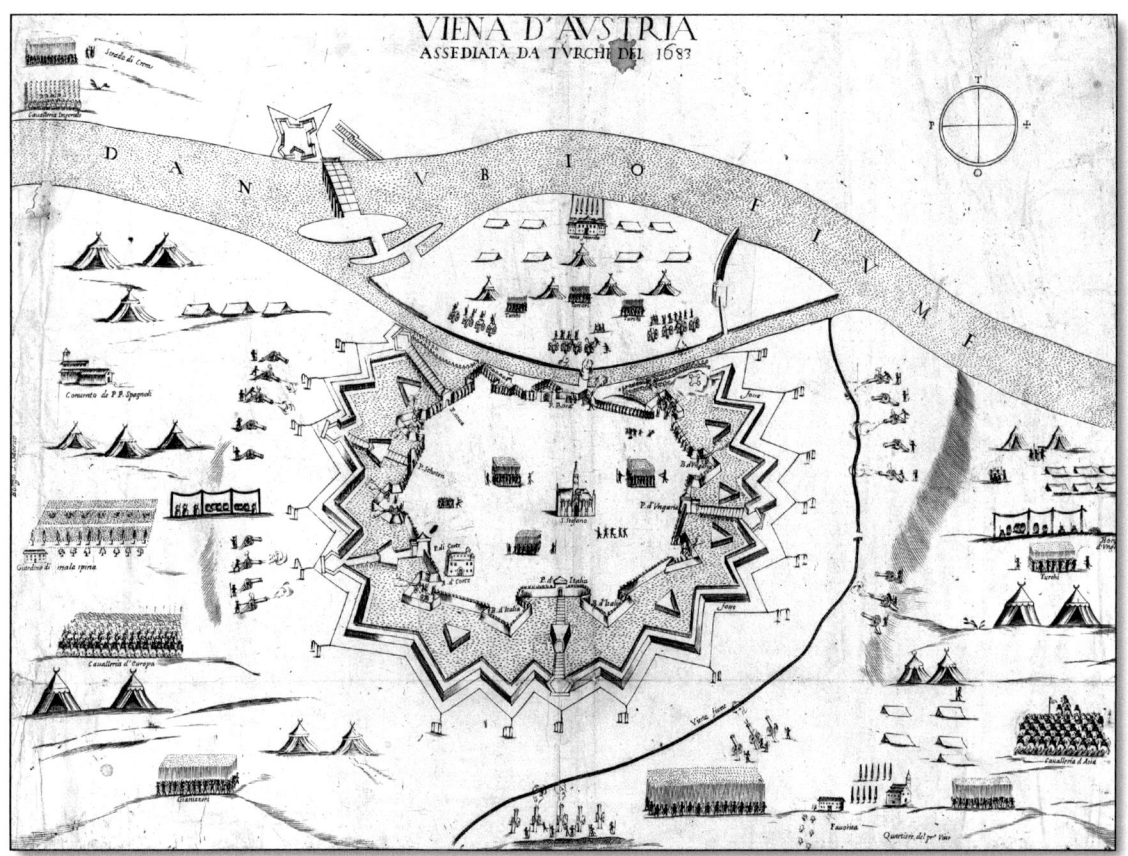

Vienna besieged by Turks. Author unknown. Like may contemporary illustrations, this is complete fiction. (Wien Museum Inv.-Nr. 8675, CC0)

Old Waldeck was in overall command of the centre, comprised of two main contingents: the Franconians on the left, Bavarians on the right. If Le Bègue is to be believed,[153] Waldeck commanded only the infantry of the Germans, their cavalry having at some point been joined to Sachsen-Lauenburg's Imperialist cavalry division – though apparently this was not a view of the command structure that Waldeck himself shared, and it remains possible that Le Bègue got this point wrong, and that the cavalry of the Reichs

---

153 Stöller, p.33. Le Bègue was not present with the centre, and since Lorraine was not technically commander-in-chief he had no oversight of it and his secretary had no direct evidence of what was going on there, though here, in his 'Account' written up at some point after the battle (no later than 1684) he might have obtained such evidence from others.

contingents, posted on the right of their line *next* to Sachsen-Lauenburg, remained under Waldeck's command.

Under Waldeck, FML Cuno Ernst Freiherr von der Leyen commanded the Franconians, with the assistance of GWM Hans Carl von Thüngen. We know little about von der Leyen other than that he was an officer of the episcopal Bamberg-Würzburg forces who had served with no great credit as a GWM of the Reichs forces in the Dutch War (his one claim to fame was that he ruined the blockade of Philippsburg in late 1675 by withdrawing from his assigned posts around the fortress, on the excuse that he could not keep his forces supplied where they were).[154] Thüngen, however, 35 years old, came from a long-established noble family of Franconia, and, after a period of delinquency in his youth, he had gained wide experience in the Dutch War, first serving with the Lorraine troops and then with the Franconian Kreis contingent, which he rose to command by the end of the war, so he was a very experienced and competent soldier (after 1683, Thüngen continued to serve with distinction throughout all the ensuing wars, until his death, still in harness, in 1709).

The Bavarians were officially under G-FML Degenfeld, whom we have already met, although they were accompanied by the Elector Maximilian Emanuel, and no-one was fooled for a moment about who had the final say in any important decision. Degenfeld was assisted by GWMs Adam Heinrich von Steinau and the more obscure Rummel or Rümpel. Steinau was a 30-year old professional soldier of slightly unclear origins who had gained plenty of military experience in the Dutch War (in which he had served in Imperialist forces) before joining the new Bavarian standing army in 1681.

As for GdC Sachsen-Lauenburg and his cavalry: like Caprara on the left wing, he had a group of solid professionals under him: the Imperialist FMLs Rabatta (Carinthian), who had served in the 1670s first in Hungary against the rebels and then throughout the Dutch War, and Johann Heinrich Graf Dünewald, of a noble family from western Germany, who had served in the Swedish army in the early 1660s before joining the Reich forces in the 1664 campaign against the Ottomans in Hungary, where he acquired great credit at the Battle of St Gothard, before obtaining an Imperialist cuirassier regiment in 1670 and thereafter fighting, both in Hungary and the Dutch War, with very great distinction. As GWMs, Sachsen-Laueunburg had the Gondola from Ragusa and the Italian Antonio Carafa, experienced in the Dutch War and the Hungarian revolt respectively.

The Franconian cavalry was under FML Christian Ernst Markgraf von Bayreuth, who, since he outranked the Bavarian cavalry generals, had authority over the Bavarian horse as well. Bayreuth was a competent and tolerant forward-looking ruler of his little principality, with good service in the Dutch War behind him as a senior officer of the Kreis troops, and he would continue to serve with credit through the 1690s, though his reputation would be ruined in the War of the Spanish Succession. The Kreis contingents were not top-heavy like some armies, and he had no Franconian generals

---

154 Beese, p.141. He may also have been the 'von der Leyen' who served as General-Quartiermeister in the contingent of the League of the Rhine at St Gothard in 1664.

subordinate to him in the cavalry, but under him were the Bavarians GWMs, Lorenz Ludwig von Münster and Louis, Marquis de Beauvau; we know little about Münster but Beauvau was a French nobleman who had aligned with the house of Lorraine and served with Charles V's uncle, Duke Charles IV, before entering Bavarian service in 1673 – because Bavaria had kept out of the Dutch War, his recent military experience was probably limited. Overall, the Bavarian infantry including the Kreis battalion mustered 11 battalions, 10 if the unit lent to the Poles is deducted; their four regiments of cuirassiers and two half-regiments of dragoons, officially smaller than Imperialist cavalry units but after the strains of the summer campaign probably as large as Lorraine's depleted regiments, made 16 squadrons. The Reichs contingent had 8 or 11 battalions, and a meagre 7 squadrons. Sachsen-Lauenburg commanded 8 cuirassier regiments, 2 of dragoons and 1 of Croatians, all under strength and formed tactically into just 24 squadrons.

The Germans of the centre struggled through terrain every bit as difficult as that faced by the Imperialists and Saxons – and they had no Danube road to send their heavier equipment along, so *everything* had to be dragged through the woods and up the hills. Broadly, the troops under Waldeck were intending to go over and round the height known as the Vogelsang, the next hill in from the Kahlenberg (from what we know of their positions on the 12th, the extreme left of the Franconians was heading for a position near the head of the Wildgrube ravine, where they would make contact with the Saxon right), while Sachsen-Lauenburg took the cavalry over the next height along, the Hermannskogel. The hills were higher than those facing Lorraine (the Vogelsang rose to 1,693 feet, the Hermannskogel to 1,780 feet), the gaps between them less clear-cut, the woods as tough or tougher without even ruined monasteries and chapels to break them up. It is probable that the cavalry had a particularly tough day, as did those responsible for dragging the battalion guns. The leading units of the Germans may have been at the Vogelsang, technically in line with the leading units of the left wing, at about the same time, 11 a.m., and Sachsen-Lauenburg may have been approaching the Hermannskogel at about that time, but the majority of the Reichs troops were all strung out back through the woods as badly as the Imperialists and Saxons, and it would be night before they were over the two heights. And that was not the end of it: before them, especially for Sachsen-Lauenburg, separated from the Vogelsang-Hermannskogel line by the headwaters of a stream, sat the great block of the Latisberg (also known as the Cobenzl or Kobenzl) barely lower at 1,614 feet. There was still a way to go yet. They were out of sight of the left wing, and had lost contact with the Poles to their right.

Poles

The Poles, as noted above, started from points some way behind the Germans and Imperialists: Sieniawski had reached Kirchbach, while Jabłonowski was drawing level with him to the south with some of his units but his infantry in particular was falling even further behind. And, not only had the Germans and Imperialists marched further on the 10th: due to the shape of the Wienerwald and the angle of their march, they had put themselves in a

THESE IMPASSABLE MOUNTAINS: THE CROSSING OF THE WIENERWALD

Crossing the Wienerwald.

much better position for the 11th than the Poles – whereas Lorraine, when he set off from the Weidlingbach, had less than a mile and a half before him up to the crest of the Kahlenberg chain, the Poles, who had hitherto been heading roughly east but who now had to turn more south-east and incline to their left more to bring them back into line with their allies, faced over four more miles of woods and hills before they could reach the crest-line, in blistering heat from which even the shade of the woods offered little relief. The stretching of the Polish army, the distance between its leading units and those at the rear, grew even greater on this day; the distinction between the two columns of Sieniawski and Jabłonowski became blurred. Contact with the rest of the army (Sachsen-Lauenburg) would be lost for part of the day.

The route for the Poles would take them over the first watershed from Kirchbach village and the headwaters of the Hagenbach stream to the headwaters of the Weidlingbach, several miles above the point lower down the valley from which Sachsen-Lauenburg and Waldeck would be setting off. They would then descend or cross the upper Weidlingbach valley, navigate several more (though at least slightly lower) hills, such as the Simonsberg and Sauberg, and face the final watershed, climbing or going round the last row of hills that separated them from the Vienna basin: the Dreimarkstein (next along from the Hermannskogel, a target for the left column), then the Gränberg and, furthest south-west, the Rosskopf. When they set off, Sobieski was still absent, away at the left wing conferring and playing at commander-in-chief, and some of the Poles were beginning to get worried, junior officers to mutter about bad omens, when his absence exceeded twenty-four hours and a few Tatar parties could be seen lurking in the woods to the left from where he was expected; but before panic could set in, they caught sight of Sobieski's bulk approaching at the head of his haiduk guards.[155] Tatar scouts continued to pop up at various points throughout the day, just watching,[156] but even if they had been inclined to interfere they were few in number, and were in fact easily kept at bay by the Polish light cavalry and the little detachment of Cossacks under Colonel Apostoł Paweł Szczurowski – though the successes of this band only made Sobieski bewail even more that his agents had not managed to procure more of them from the Ukraine.[157] To the relief of everyone from the King down, the awful day passed without the slightest enemy interference.

---

155 Sobieski to his wife, 12 September, in Plater, p.67. A little later, Sobieski mentioned that he rejoined his army around noon, which, if true, rather undermined his claim to have been away for a total of 26 hours.
156 Dalérac (vol. 1, p.143, reproduced in Paradowski, p.134) recounted a rather unlikely story, that a Tatar party of 30 horsemen ran into the head of Jabłonowski's column under BG Dönhoff, and the Tatar leader, instead of fighting, calmly asked Dönhoff for news; on being told that the Christians were part of the Polish army under the King, he laughed and said he knew this for a falsehood as it was known that Lubomirski had brought Polish reinforcements to the Imperialists. Aside from the story's inherent improbability, against it is the fact that the Ottoman senior officers were fully aware of Sobieski's presence – though they may have tried to conceal this from the rest of the army by spreading the Lubomirski story.
157 The identity of the colonel has long been obscure – even Wimmer only knew him by his first name; but he has been fully identified by the Polish historian Marek Wagner, as noted in Paradowski, p.99 and note 163.

The difficulties were not uniform: the pattern that showed up with the rest of the army – that the march got worse from left to right – was preserved with the Poles. Sieniawski on the left had a marginally better day than Jabłonowski. The woods here must have been more open, because today the Crown Field Hetman was able to have some of his cavalry lead the way, although, since the infantry was later reported to camp in a position ahead of the cavalry, this cannot have been universal. His main force crossed the hills beyond Kirchbach into the valley of the upper Weidlingbach, descended it past the straggling village also called Weidlingbach (not to be confused with Weidling further downstream) then swung to their right, striking south up out of the valley for the final row of hills. Detachments of cavalry continued even further down the valley before turning, extending far to his left and re-establishing contact with the Germans around the Hermannskogel. Sieniawski's infantry spent the night on the Dreimarkstein, with the bulk of his cavalry behind on the Sauberg; from what transpired on the next day, it is likely that any troops on the Dreimarkstein were on its *northern* side, with the bulk of the hill still before them. At some point in the Weidling valley, the Poles had come across and promptly seized a herd of Turkish cattle being pastured by unsuspecting train folk from the Ottoman camp, which provided at least some of them with food.[158] If true, the story also indicates that pasturage was available in some parts of the Wienerwald, so the equally hungry Polish horses must also have *occasionally* found some kind of sustenance.

Jabłonowski's column struggled again: it started out behind Sieniawski, and many of its men, especially the infantry, were completely exhausted before they even began. The day did not make things better for them. Once they passed the hills around Kirchbach, they faced yet more steep slopes and swampy stream bottoms over and through which they had to drag their cursed guns and ammunition wagons, hunger gnawing ever more fiercely at their guts. As the day wore on and their strength wore out they began to abandon equipment. When they got over the first range into the Weidlingbach valley, apparently well into the afternoon if not already the evening, some of the shattered artillerymen and train personnel discovered near a village (probably Weidlingbach itself) some of the characteristic half-buried 'wine cellars' of the area, and were soon mutinous under the influence of the wine; Jabłonowski had to send in several hundred cavalry to smash all the barrels they could find so that the roistering could be stopped and the workers driven back to their drag-ropes.[159]

Sobieski and his household had called a halt to 'dine' about the same time, also somewhere in the Weidlingbach valley, but all they had was bread and water, the bread all that could be carried on the backs of a few mules.[160]

---

158 Dupont, p.134, and Dalérac, vol. 1, p.143, with Wimmer, *Entsatz*, p.182, accepting the story. There is a hint in Sobieski's letter to his wife of 12 September (Plater, p.67), which may confirm the story. One is left wondering how they found time to cook the meat without delaying the march, but methods can easily be imagined.
159 Dolleczek, 'Entsatzschlacht', p.160.
160 Dalérac, vol. 1, pp.144–145. This source actually suggests that the only water they had was from the canteens of Bavarian soldiers, which sounds unlikely.

As night fell, the troops could go no further and camped or just collapsed where they were, spread out over a wide area. Some of the cavalry had made it out of the Weidlingbach valley, either over the Simonsberg and the slopes to the south or (more likely) ascending the little ImReitergassel valley to the west of the Simonsberg to avoid the hills altogether, and had just about reached the woods on the northern side of the Gränberg – still well short of the target crest line. Most of the column had not even reached this far, and the artillery had not yet made it out of the Weidlingbach valley; Jabłonowski accepted that it would be impossible to move the guns through the dark for a second night, and obtained permission from the King to leave them where they were until daybreak.[161] The cavalry spent the night camped 'greatly in disorder' in the woods, while the infantry, occupying the only open ground, surrounded itself with *chevaux-de-frise* against possible surprise attacks in the darkness.[162] A few Poles may have been at the hill-tops, since they claimed to have lit fires to signal to the city that relief was at hand – though they were later to be told that due to the nature of the ground these had never been seen.[163]

All this while the Polish dragoons, out on the far right flank, had been pushing forward on their separate route, and apparently breaking the pattern, for they had a much easier day than Jabłonowski's men. They were probably still following the Tulbinger Steig as this path, leaving the Tulbinger Kogel, wandered through the valleys to the south-east until it brought them, after a journey of four miles of no great difficulty, to the Rosskopf. Here they formed for now the anchor-point for the right end of the Polish line. Since the path wandered on across the northern side of the Ross-kopf and beyond it back along the front side of the final hills, Sobieski ordered the dragoons to block it in case the Turks tried to use the path to come at them and the flank of the army as it descended.[164] Beyond the dragoons were only a couple of squadrons of cavalry under Rafał Leszczyński, detached by Sobieski as a flank guard just in case there were thousands of Tatars lurking in the woods beyond ready to pounce on the open flank.

As the day wore down towards evening for the increasingly shattered Poles, their struggle was made a little more difficult when the wind picked

---

161 Wimmer, *Entsatz*, p.182, at this point makes a very odd assertion about Polish movements on this day: he states that the heavier Polish guns, which had been sent round via Kierling, were arriving at the pass between the Kahlenberg and the Vogelsang (i.e. the Wildgrube ravine). No source ever mentions seeing Polish guns here.
162 Dalérac, vol. 1, pp.145–146.
163 Dalérac, vol. 1, pp.147–148.
164 Wimmer, *Entsatz*, p.181. According to others (the Polish historian Otton Laskowski, *La campagne de Vienne, 1683* (Warsaw: Institut des Sciences Militaires, 1933), p.25, with Barker, p.318, apparently following), the dragoons were actually used to block a threat way off on the opposite flank of the Polish army: Sobieski, fearing that the Turks might be able to get over the saddle between the Hermannskogel (Sachsen-Lauenburg) and Dreimarkstein (Sieniawski) and thus split the allied army, even attack the scattered Polish forces still in the Weidlingbach valley, had dragoons occupy the saddle and fortify it. Either Wimmer was wrong in his statement that the entire dragoon force of the Polish army was on the extreme right (for they could hardly have made it across the entire front of the Polish army from its right to its left, any more than Sobieski would have ordered such a move when there were troops already close by to do it) or Laskowski was wrong, either in the action or in attributing it to dragoons.

up in their faces and increased to such a gale that the horsemen could barely turn their horses into it. For a while, there was muttering amongst the ranks of the more superstitious of the Polish soldiers that the Grand Vizier Kara Mustafa, reputed a dark magician of great vigour, had summoned the 'aerial powers' against the Christians.[165] Apparently, the wind soon dropped away again, or else more rational minds calmed the fears of the soldiers, for Sobieski had no qualms about leaving the Poles again soon after to return to the left wing for more discussions. However, all was not well with the King: at some point during the day, he had either glimpsed the terrain beyond the last hills himself, or more likely had had reports of it from scouting Cossack parties, and the news had been worrying enough for him to send out his French engineer Dupont to get a fuller picture for him. He now had that fuller picture, and, as he rode along through the Germans heading to meet Lorraine, Sobieski was not a happy man.

---

165 From Sobieski's letter to his wife, in Plater, p.67. The letter was *started* at 3 a.m. on the 12th and stated that the wind arose ten hours before, which would put it at 5 p.m. on the 11th; however, Sobieski was not being very precise in the details he gave his wife, and besides we have no idea when in relation to the 3 a.m. dating of the huge rambling letter the remark about the wind was made. Presumably the wind at least provided some relief from the heat of the day.

Plate B. Saxon Infantry of the 1683 campaign
1. Musketeer, *Leibregiment zu Fuss*, Guards Infantry Regiment
Red coat, white cuffs and hose, grey breeches
2. Musketeer, Regiment *Sachsen-Weissenfels*
Grey coat, yellow cuffs, breaches and hose. This musketeer is equipped with a *'swine feather'* rest that acted as a defensive measure against cavalry.
(Illustrations by Sergey Shamenkov, © Helion & Company)

7

The battlefield

As noted in Chapter 4, Vienna sat in a basin formed of the arc of the easternmost chain of hills of the Wienerwald, closed to the east by the Danube and to the south by the River Wien and the lower heights of the Wiener Berg beyond. This final chain, separated from the pack of the Wienerwald by the valley of the Weidlingbach, was no gentle falling off to the basin but comprised hills as tall as any in this northern section of the Wienerwald: sturdy heights 1,500 feet or more above sea level, 900 feet or more above the level of the city. We have already met many of the hills from the sides facing away from Vienna, north and west: the Leopoldsberg nearest the Danube, then steadily rising in height through the Kahlenberg and the Vogelsang(berg) to the Hermannskogel, at 1,778 feet the highest point in the chain, with the sturdy outpost of the Latisberg or Cobenzl standing in front of the last two. This northern section of the chain was known as the Kahlengebirge, or Kahlenberg chain, a term applied most especially to the two nearest the Danube, the Leopoldsberg and Kahlenberg. From the peak of the Hermannskogel the height gradually fell off a little through the Sauberg, the Dreimarkstein and Gränberg (with the Simonsberg to their rear), and soaring up again to the Rosskopf-Exelberg complex before declining again – just a little – westward towards the Mauerbach and the River Wien. Even when one had passed the chain itself, there lay a further row of slightly lower hills as outliers towards the city: nearest the Danube the Nussberg (Nut Hill), lowest and most open of the lot, then the impressively-titled Krapfenwaldl (though a mouthful, the name means simply 'hook-woodlet'),[166] and after a gap, to the south the hills Pfaffen Berg, Michaeler Berg, Schafberg, Heuberg (itself actually taller than the Leopoldsberg) and the Galitzin Berg.[167] The lower slopes of these on the western side extended well out towards the city's

---

166 in present-day German, 'Krapfen' means a doughnut, but this usage is unlikely for the hill in the seventeenth century.
167 There is an extraordinary variety in spelling for some of these hills, and in whether the 'berg' is merged with the name or treated as a separate word; for example, this last hill may be spelt Galitzin, Gallitzin, Galizin, or Gallizin, all of these with 'berg' either suffixed or added as a separate word. I have generally followed the most recent Austrian practice.

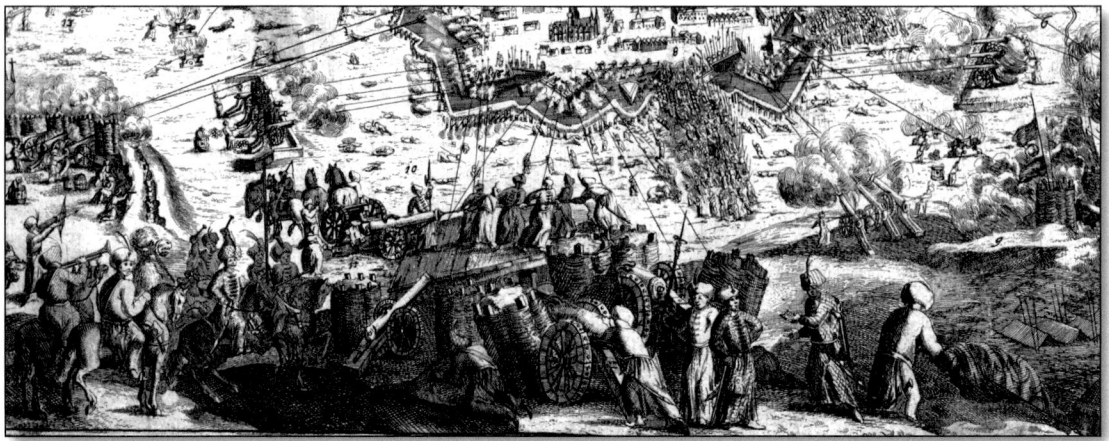

Ottoman artillery during the siege of Vienna. Artist unknown (Wien Museum Inv.-Nr. 212950, CC0)

suburbs, providing country that was usually rolling, occasionally still broken and awkward.

We should pause a moment to concentrate on the two peaks nearest the Danube, that would be so prominent in the opening stages of the battle: the Leopoldsberg and Kahlenberg. Most of the hills were bare of habitation, but these two had ruined remnants of human presence: atop the Leopoldsberg, the remains of the Chapel of St Leopold (Leopolds-kapelle) from which it took its name; on the Kahlenberg, the burnt shell of the church and little monastery of St Joseph, of the Camaldulensian order of monks – technically, the Camaldulensians (or Camaldulians) being a hermit order, it was a hermitage or 'eremia', but since contemporaries always referred to it as a monastery, that will do for us. The Chapel of St Leopold had been a ruin for many years, possibly since the first Turkish assault on Vienna way back in 1529, certainly by the time the Turkish traveller Evliya visited Vienna in 1665 with the great Ottoman embassy of that year sent to confirm the Treaty of Vasvár. St Joseph's, on the other hand, had only been founded by the Habsburgs earlier in the seventeenth century, and it had been burnt by the Tatars as they savaged all the land around Vienna two months earlier – the white-robed monks themselves had skedaddled back to their order's home in Italy well before the Ottomans arrived, though according to legend one ancient brother, too old to withstand the burdens of travel, had at his own wish remained behind and was slaughtered kneeling before the altar by the Tatars before they set fire to the place. Rather confusingly, the hill nearest the Danube had once been known as the Kahlenberg, and the next one in, after the establishment of the Camaldulensian foundation on it, as the Josephsberg; these names were still in use as late as 1672 when the famed Austrian topographer Vischer produced his series of plates depicting the region; but by 1683 it appears that the modern names had become reasonably settled, and since contemporaries usually specified that they were talking about 'the hill with the monastery', it is most of the time clear enough to which they were referring.[168] The Leopoldsberg was officially the

---

168 The Franconian official Schliz von Görz, for example, was explicit in referring to the height with the monastery as the Kahlenberg.

lower of the two (though it is often depicted as the higher), but much steeper, especially on the Danube side where its slopes plunged at a forty-five degree angle the 850-odd feet from its peak to the narrow gap where the road ran along its base beside the river. The Kahlenberg, although higher than the Leopoldsberg, as heavily wooded and as broken under foot if not more so, had gentler slopes, and would be the hill of choice for Lorraine to descend to the basin. On both hills, the woods extended only part of the way down the slopes, eventually giving way to patches of open ground before the vineyards started, all before the valley floor between the Kahlenberg chain and the Nussberg was reached.

The hills themselves – the main chain in its entirety and all of the outliers except the Nussberg – were heavily wooded; not always continuously forested, but the occasional breaks and glades offered no real tactical relief from the obstacle of thick undergrowth and trees – mostly deciduous trees, at this time of the year still with their full clothing of green. The woods stretched quite a way down the inner slopes towards Vienna, and, where they gave out and there had once begun more open land that might have been suitable for formed infantry and especially cavalry, now there were vineyards all along the foothills, vineyards with hedges or fences or embankments or walls in addition to the vines themselves, extending the difficult terrain even nearer to the city. These were rarely shown in contemporary engravings. They may not have covered every hill: there are hints[169] that the Nussberg may have been open. However, most accounts seem clear enough that there were plenty of obstacles across the Nussberg which can only have come from vineyards. Only very close to the suburbs was there genuinely open ground, and most of that had been filled already by the vast semi-circle of the Ottoman camp. As Le Bègue described the situation facing Lorraine:[170]

> From the exit of the wood as far as Vienna, there was almost an hour and a half on the ground in a very difficult terrain, cut by vineyards, ravines and hollow ways, which went on, always descending, until a short half-an-hour from the city. This vineyard ends by a big ravine [the Nesselbach] which covered the enemy camp on the side of Heiligenstadt.

The vineyards often had extra-tough barriers facing the hills, intended to keep out the wild animals of the Wienerwald that the inhabitants could not kill because these were protected, preserved for hunting by the imperial family. The vineyard defences below the Kahlenberg were particularly strong, an embankment formed of scree removed from the vineyards and topped by plank fencing, providing not just an obstacle to the Christian advance

---

169 Hocke, p.194, noting in his account of the battle that the Imperialists did not reach 'the vineyards' until about mid-day, suggesting that the Nussberg may have been quite open and he was referring to the vineyards on the city side of it (the Imperialists reached the vineyards below the Kahlenberg much earlier). However, the whole sentence in which this statement occurs is full of ambiguities, including even the possibility that 'gegen Mittag' might not mean 'towards noon' but 'to the south'.
170 Stöller, p.36.

but a good defensive position for the Ottomans, effectively a defence work proof against musket-fire. It is sometimes suggested that this *Wildzaun*, or wild-animal fence, extended right along the line of the hills, but there is no evidence that it formed a continuous coherent barrier – just the strong line at the foot of the Kahlenberg, and diverse fences on various other slopes. There was also a separate screen or embankment across the Nussberg, known as the Eichelhofweg (Acorn-Court Way). None of these are shown on any map or contemporary illustration, and their exact location remains uncertain.

Vineyard fences were not the only obstacles. As noted above, the watershed of the northern Wienerwald lay on its western side, giving plenty of room for streams to develop on the eastern slopes; whereas on the west only the paltry Hagenbach left the range, here numerous streams ran out of the hills, heading for the Danube or, more often, its Canal arm, often in stony deep beds and sometimes in sharply cut ravines. High up in the hills where the streams arose, the ravines were especially deep, adding to the terrain difficulties for the Christians as they struggled to make it out of the woods. In the north, these streams ran in the main directly *across* the path by which the Christians (here, Lorraine) intended to advance, and offered the Ottomans excellent lines of defence, though even here the Christians might find themselves outflanking the upper ends of the barriers via the next hills to their right. As the line of the hills curved round to the south, this defensive advantage disappeared, the streams ran out from the hills through the Ottoman camp, parallel to the line of advance of the allies, forming merely another nuisance to the Christian advance rather than a position the Ottomans could defend, and eventually avenues facilitating the Christian advance. For the historian, there is the added obstacle of the often-extraordinary number of names these rivulets managed to pick up in their short lives. From the north, starting at the foot of the Leopoldsberg, they were: the little brooks Waldbach and Schäblergraben that ran into the Danube at the village of Kahlen;[171] the much more considerable Schreiberbach, which arising up in the saddle between the Kahlenberg and the Vogelsang (where its ravine was called the Wildgrube) passed between the Nussberg and the Krapfenwaldl (the valley here known as the Muckenthal) before skirting the southern slopes of the Nussberg through the substantial wine-producing village of Nussdorf to enter the Danube just at the point where the Canal arm splits off from the main channel; on the far side of the Krapfenwaldl, two small brooks, the Steinbergerbach and the Reisenbergerbach, which merged as they reached the lower slopes to become the Nesselbach (occasionally known as the Grinzingerbach, after a village on its middle course), to flow through the village of Heiligenstadt to the Canal; then the Erbsenbach and Krottenbach (also known under its original and more revealing spelling of Croatenbach, meaning Croats' Stream), which merged just short of Döbling to become the Döblingerbach – the main Ottoman entrenchments were in this area; beyond this, the Währingerbach, which, perhaps embarrassed by its inability to acquire more than one name,

---

171 This was the name by which it was known in 1683; by the nineteenth century the name had expanded to the cumbersome Kahlenbergerdörfel, though in the twentieth this was pulled back a bit to Kahlenbergerdorf.

failed to reach the Canal on its own but joined its sibling stream to the south; the Alsbach, arising south of the Gränberg and descending between the Heuberg and Schafberg to become the most substantial of all these streams, with its valley heading like a wide avenue straight at the heart of the Ottoman camp; then beyond the Alsbach, only the obscure little Ottakringerbach, often forgotten, that got lost amongst the suburbs of Vienna, crossed the broad dry space before the substantial course of the River Wien. Most of these streams, and especially the Alsbach, had a definite exit-point where they left the hills, a point where the defile became open level ground, where any troops descending the valley could be prevented from debouching out onto the open by a determined opponent.

Villages littered the slopes and valleys. All of them were currently burnt husks, having been visited by the Tatars before the siege of Vienna even began, but many (not all) were built on the highest ground in the vicinity, some bump in the valley or else the last outlying slopes of a hill, and this, coupled with the fact that some contained substantial stone buildings that had survived the flames, could turn them into significant defence-points. Some had extensive walled gardens around them, orchards and vegetable patches for the inhabitants or sometimes former pleasure gardens for the enjoyment of the city inhabitants – all destroyed of course, but still capable of adding to the villages' defensibility. In fact, the Ottomans used only a handful of them. We have already mentioned a number of the villages to the north of Vienna, along the Danube and Canal. More to the west of the city, 'villages' nearest the Danube were in fact the suburbs of Vienna, already within the Ottoman siege works, and here the overall pattern was of a line of villages strung along the middle of the open ground (Hernals, Ottakring and so on), another line at the points where the valley streams finally met the open ground (Gersthof, Dornbach), and more settlements further up near what we might call the heads of the valleys (Neuwaldegg, Pötzleinsdorf, Neustift, Sievering).

In all this, the biggest problem, the thing that made Sobieski so cross, was the broken nature of the ground beyond the crest. He had been expecting for weeks now, based first on the maps that the Imperialists had sent to him during his march from Poland and then on discussions with Lorraine and his colleagues, that once the army had reached the final chain of peaks (from the Leopoldsberg to the Rosskopf), the ground was open and easy, the slopes tending gently down to the level of Vienna, perfect ground for his cavalry-heavy army on which to make the smashing knock-out blow he had set his heart on. Now, he found before his Poles more hills (from the Nussberg to the Galitzin Berg) with yet more ravines and woods, and beyond them he could see, or his engineer Dupont had told him about, the vineyards, hedges, hollow ways, all the broken ground that would have to be crossed before his hussars and *pancerni* could form for a decisive charge. In all, there was about three more miles of hell for the leading Poles on the Gränberg, even more for those strewn back through the Wienerwald. The timetable to which he had been working was thrown completely out of kilter.

8

The conference on the Kahlenberg and the final Christian preparations

As Sobieski's overburdened horse puffed up the Kahlenberg to the monastery, Lorraine and John George were busy looking out over the Vienna basin. With them, or soon to join them, were Waldeck, probably Hermann of Baden, perhaps Maximilian Emanuel and other generals.[172] Again, there was no formal council of war, but naturally, in the pauses as the battalion guns banged away around them, they discussed informally the position of the enemy and what to do on the morrow. The view from the top of the Kahlenberg was magnificent: the entire basin lay before them, brilliantly lit by the golden light of the westering sun as it leaned down towards the tree-studded hill-tops behind the Poles. All around the city, starting from below them and stretching off round to their right, was the huge semi-circle of the brightly-coloured Turkish tents, marching off towards the River Wien more than six miles away, with another camp on the Wienerberg beyond it; and even on the Prater Island to their left they could see more tents – although the Ottomans had been evacuating many of their forces from the island, some Turkish troops and the unreliable Roumanians remained there, at the northern end covering the right flank of the field army. Vienna itself, almost five miles away to the south, was shrouded in smoke from all the artillery fire coming from the Turkish siege pieces and the defending guns; only the tops of church towers could be seen, especially the great 450-foot spire of St Stephen's Cathedral, soaring up out of the murk like ships' masts in a fog, along with occasional rockets streaking skyward from the garrison. With the smoke, it would have been impossible for them to tell exactly how the Turkish siege works were progressing, but the city's desperate situation

---

172 It is very likely that Sobieski picked up Waldeck and Maximilian Emanuel as he passed through the centre on his way to meet Lorraine, but this is nowhere stated in the sources. Sobieski did however stress to his wife (Plater, pp.65–66) his continuing good relationship with the electors and the frequency of their contact, as well as the friendship between Maximilian Emanuel and their son, Prince Jakub.

was obvious enough even without Starhemberg's mute appeals by rocket. Directly below them, Ottoman troops were boiling out of their camp like ants, shifting here and there as they settled into positions for battle facing the hills, while their outposts were already skirmishing with Lorraine's own. With such an excellent view, it was easy for the Christians to tell that the Ottomans were fielding about 20,000–30,000 men against them on this side.[173] Behind the outposts and the forming troops the watchers on the hill could make out entrenching work being done around the facing parts of the camp; while way off to their right, on the Ottoman left, facing where the Poles would eventually descend, they could see what appeared to be hordes of light cavalry coasting around the land in front of the hills and woods – but no fortifying.[174]

Sobieski joined Lorraine, John George and the others at their vantage point. The King when he arrived had no interest in the Ottoman moves: he was too annoyed about the terrain. He had been planning for a battle on the 12th, tomorrow, when he would deploy his massed cavalry for the final blow, for the encircling move and the great decisive charge in the eastern style of his experience that would drive the enemy against the Danube and annihilate them. But the dreadful terrain that was revealed below, especially before his Poles, made it look as if he would have to change plan completely: now, it would take the army another whole day if not two just to reach the open ground where they could deploy, a whole day if not two in which they would have to alter their whole style of combat and resort to the careful style of the west – the style of such archetypes of caution as the Genoese-born Spanish commander who came to Sobieski's mind at this moment, Spinola, who had fought against the equally careful Dutch seventy-odd years before in the fortress-studded Netherlands – and descend step by step, from post to post, winning ground from the Turks bit by bit, first the intervening hills and then the vineyards and villages one by one, until they could reach the open terrain beyond and deploy properly for the charge. Now they needed artillery even more, to support this difficult operation, and must wait for it to catch up before they could even start to drive for the open ground. Dupont had come with Sobieski and argued strenuously that the chosen fronts were not suitable for attack at all (if his enemy Dalérac is to be believed, he made an embarrassing scene in front of all the Imperialist generals with the vigour

---

[173] The 'Baden account' (Röder, vol. 1, Urk., p.15) mentioned that it was easy to estimate the Ottoman numbers from the extent of their camp – although the writer carefully avoided specifying a figure. Although the Ottoman camp had been shrinking as camp followers departed or moved beyond the Wien, the size of the camp would still give an exaggerated notion of the size of the army; but Lorraine and Sobieski could see equally well the numbers of troops being fielded against them. However, Dalérac (vol. 1, pp.146, 151) twice stated that only about 10,000 Turks were sent to face Lorraine; either he was down-playing the numbers facing the Imperialists so as to belittle their success on the morrow, or the Christians really could see only that many at the foot of the Kahlenberg this evening.

[174] Dupont, p.135, thought the forces that he could see on the Turkish left wing were Tatars. We cannot be sure whether the Tatars were even present, but we do know for sure that Abaza Sari Hüseyin and his light cavalry were already in position on that wing.

of his objections);[175] as he had been sent to see the intervening ground at closer quarters, his opinion carried great weight with the King, and the issue teetered in the balance for a while. It appears that he was arguing not just about the ground in front of the Poles but also that before the left wing, perhaps even pushing for a complete change in direction by the allies – if so, he can only have meant that the allied army should shift to its right, to the more open country nearer the River Wien, but this would have taken far too long. Sobieski, despite his disappointment about the problems his own people would face, was in the end less convinced by this, and was persuaded by Lorraine, with no great difficulty, to agree that the entire army would continue on the path it had chosen, and that Lorraine himself would start descending the next day. All the generals present approved of the plan. Admittedly, the King thought that, with the Turkish forces coming out of the camp opposite the left wing and giving every impression of offering a tough fight tomorrow, Lorraine would be lucky if by the end of the 12th he had occupied 'the first heights at the exit of the wood along our front', that is, the Nussberg;[176] so the left wing was unlikely to make any more progress than the right, and the Poles – with Sobieski at their head – would still play the decisive part in the eventual battle and gain the prestige.[177] The King cast his experienced eye over the terrain before his Poles and selected the positions where they could camp on the 12th and 13th, noted the points that the Ottomans were holding with their cavalry and dragoon-style *yerli kulu*.[178]

Jan III Sobieski and Charles V during the battle. Leonhard Losche, 1683 (Wien Museum Inv.-Nr. 8685, CC0)

Lorraine in fact had every intention of driving right through to Vienna on the next day if he could, had started making his dispositions for an early start; but he let the King go on believing what he wanted, and as evening descended and a thousand Turkish camp fires burst into life in the gathering darkness below, the gathering broke up with cordial sentiments on all sides, agreeing to meet again the next morning for a council of war at which they would make more definite decisions. The good mood was helped by a cautious feeling of optimism: the Ottoman forces in the field were strong (although Sobieski in his letter to his wife that night lightly pooh-poohed

---

175   Dalérac, vol. 1, p.148. Dalérac is extremely hostile to Dupont and may have overstated the case, as no-one else mentioned any embarrassing scene.
176   Stöller, p.36. Schliz von Görz (Newald, vol. 2, p.100) broadly concurs that Sobieski ended by agreeing with Lorraine.
177   See Appendix I, 8.1, on these discussions and Le Bègue's down-playing of Sobieski's involvement. NB: according to some accounts, it was at this point that Sobieski requested the loan of four German battalions, which I conclude occurred earlier (see Appendix I, 6.1).
178   Dalérac, vol. 1, p.149.

those facing Lorraine as 'fifty-odd squadrons with a few thousand Janissaries') but hardly overwhelming, nothing like the huge numbers some of them had been half-expecting.[179] Even if the advance to contact would still take a couple more days, the open Turkish camp, the lack of serious fortification defending it – for no-one regarded the entrenching work the Ottomans were doing now as a serious obstacle – the absence of other precautions, the complete failure of the Ottoman forces to defend the hills so far and their continuing passivity in their night positions at the foot of the Kahlenberg chain, all pointed to a careless and foolish enemy commanded by an inept general. No-one doubted that the fighting would still be very tough, and Lorraine had reservations about how big a success could be achieved, but some kind of victory now seemed a realistic expectation.

As Sobieski remounted his unlucky steed and set off again along the paths that would take him back to the Polish wing, it is probable (though not stated by the King or any other witness) that he took with him two important impressions. Firstly, it cannot have escaped his attention that the Ottomans seemed to be concentrating heavily on their right, against the allied left; the forces facing where the Poles would come down were so far few in number, lightly equipped, and devoid of even the weak entrenchments being dug opposite Lorraine and Waldeck. At the moment, it looked as if the Turks had no idea that the entire Polish army would be descending on their left wing. This would obviously change in the ensuing days, but the weakness of that left undoubtedly reinforced Sobieski's hopes of a great victory of annihilation, for it seemed clear that his forces could smash the light screen facing them and turn in on the rest of the Ottoman army, trapping it.[180] Secondly, he must have seen the Alsbach valley off to the right, must have recognised its importance: the only significant debouchment from the hills where the Poles would be descending, the only way his mass of cavalry would be able to get out of the hills sufficiently in formation to act effectively.[181] The Alsbach was going to be very important tomorrow.

Lorraine believed that Vienna could not wait one or two days. He had always believed that it was better to drive the Ottomans off and break the siege than to spend more time seeking a position from which a victory of annihilation might be gained, at the risk of delaying until Vienna had already

---

179 The size of the Ottoman camp and the number of its hangers-on made it difficult to form an accurate impression of the size of Kara Mustafa's army. Nevertheless, Lorraine had been camped on the far side of the Danube from it for two months, and must have begun to realise it was nowhere near as big as it seemed; and Sobieski knew from extensive personal experience how big Ottoman armies were in reality.
180 However, it seems that Laskowski, *Campagne*, p.25, was overstating the case when he suggested that Sobieski planned to attack the Turkish bridges on the River Wien so as to cut off the Ottoman line of retreat at that point. The view from the Kahlenberg must have convinced him of the extra time that this would add to the already-extended timetable (distance for Poles to reach the plain by marching forward: about three miles; distance for Poles to reach the Wien: nearly six miles for the main body at the Gränberg – a little less for the dragoons on the flank, but they could not act alone).
181 Gustav Schröder, 'Der Kampf um Wien 1683: sein Verlauf und seine Bedeutung für die Geschichte des Festungskrieges', *Archiv für die Artillerie- und Ingenieur-Offiziere des deutschen Reichsheeres* 47. Jhg., = Vol.90 (1883), pp.305–382, here p.373.

fallen – if Vienna fell into their hands, the Ottomans might easily thumb their noses at any attempt to trap them in the field, and even if they *were* defeated in a great battle and a shattered sacked Vienna subsequently recovered by the Christians, the damage to the Habsburgs' prestige from even a temporary loss of their capital would be irreparable: Hungary would be lost forever, their authority in the Empire broken… and lurking in the wings as always was Louis XIV ready to grab any spoil he could, including the crown as Holy Roman Emperor. And with the fall of the Habsburg Monarchy went any hope the Duke of Lorraine would have of regaining his French-occupied homeland. So, Lorraine intended to do his damnedest on the next day to push through along the Danube:

> His plan was [Le Bègue noted], in the enterprise of tomorrow, to drive along always close to the bank of the Danube, and to attack the enemy camp by their right. It was for this reason, and because of the cut-up terrain, that he put on this left a great body of infantry, and that he remained always at the head of this wing which advanced first against the enemy.[182]

Although anything beyond this is conjecture, it is clear that Lorraine intended to fight the Ottomans opposite him, to defeat them if he could, but above all to penetrate far enough to establish communication with the city, throw in reinforcements, and place his army so as to protect supplies from the wagons on the road and barges on the river as they passed behind it into the city. Once there, now with the city to protect his flank, he could continue the battle against the Ottoman army in the hope of forcing it back over the Wien and raising the siege for good. In his view, there was no way he could afford to wait one or two days more for the Poles to reach the plain, and that seemed the only alternative. Even if victory was a realistic expectation, no-one at this stage expected an *easy* fight or an Ottoman collapse on the same day – the abysmal Ottoman performance at Pressburg and the Bisamberg might have suggested such a possibility, but those had been defeats of Tatars, Hungarian rebels, and the dross of the Ottoman army, while before them was its cream, expected to fight to the last.

So, smiling and agreeing with Sobieski, Lorraine kept his intentions to himself, and once the King had gone, took himself off in the deepening darkness down the hill to reconnoitre personally the terrain at the foot of the Kahlenberg, where his troops would be leaving the cover of the woods

---

[182] Stöller, p.36. The Diary (Stöller, p.101) has less to say about Lorraine's intentions, but is clearly enough in agreement, that Lorraine intended to advance forward from the Kahlenberg and take post against the Ottoman forces facing him, especially as he had noticed that they were concentrating their forces so heavily towards the Danube. The 'Baden account' in Röder, originating in the entourage of Hermann of Baden, says nothing about the plans; it seems that most officers took it for granted that Lorraine would simply advance to contact the next day. The only alternative voice is from the Franconian, Schliz von Görz (Newald, vol. 2, p.100), who seems to suggest that nothing was decided at all, a final decision being deferred until the morning, especially because the artillery was not yet up and they needed to wait for it. Perhaps Lorraine was keeping his intentions secret not just from Sobieski but also from the other Germans.

and encountering the Ottomans in the open ground beyond. Returning from this, he ordered Leslie to prepare some of his infantry to 'establish a post' (in seventeenth-century military jargon, taking up a fixed position and probably entrenching it) at the exit of the wood during the night, and to build a battery (see Glossary) at the forward edge of the wood, ready to receive some guns and cover the debouchment and advance of the troops the next morning. The exact location of the battery is unknown, but since the saddle between the Leopoldsberg and the Kahlenberg was a key route by which the Imperialists would be coming down, it was probably placed on the lower slopes of the Kahlenberg, on the Leopoldsberg side facing towards the Nussberg and the Danube, so that it could cover the debouchment there.[183] Leslie, who was not known for exerting himself when he could avoid it, put the comte de Fontaine in charge of this task, and initially assigned only two battalions to do the hard labour, holding back on sending more troops until the work was completed and (if Le Bègue's less than clear Account is to be believed) until the artillery had been brought forward at last and could be put in; men from the two battalions may also have been used as draft mules in dragging the field guns the final stretch of the hill to the position. Aware that the Ottomans were throwing up field fortifications which, however weak they were, might require artillery support to be stormed, and knowing that they had left their 12-pounders behind, the commanders in this sector were very concerned about bringing up the rest of their artillery to support the attack in the morning, still doubling and tripling teams to get the cannons one by one over the hill. In fact, it would be nearly 6 a.m. before the Imperialist guns were in position.[184]

While the drivers and appointed battalions laboured with the guns, and a few tardy regiments struggled to catch up, the rest of the army got what sleep it could amongst the trees. The units of the left wing were mostly along the crest-line of the Kahlenberg chain, the centre coming up to the crest next along but with further to go before it reached open ground, the Poles still not even at the crest. It was a mild early-autumn night. There was no moon, so anyone up and about could not see the city below, but Starhemberg was still flooding the sky with rockets broadcasting his appeal for urgent assistance, and there was no hiding the ring of camp fires below the Christians, along the foot of the Kahlenberg chain for the troops of Koca Ibrahim or throughout the camps to the Wien and beyond. The soldiers of the left and centre were still in good condition, the Poles less so, especially as they had little or no food; but all of them from the Danube to the Rosskopf remained filled with a great determination to do their utmost. Lorraine neither ate nor slept that night but constantly toured the posts and explored the ground, his eyes like those of his other generals on the watch fires of Koca Ibrahim's troops below, puzzled and worried about what the Ottomans were up to, for no-one could

---

183   For what it is worth, we can note that the Hallart map shows a battery on the lower slopes of the Kahlenberg, facing roughly in this direction – interpreting this map is not helped by Hallart's extreme concertina-ing of the hills, and this battery is easily confused with another shown very close to it but which must be on the Nussberg, facing south, towards Grinzing.
184   Stöller, p.101.

quite believe that the enemy would fail to contest the woods, would simply let the allies get out to the open ground, as the position of the fires and the lack of apparent Ottoman movement suggested – the Ottomans must surely be up to something. Sobieski meanwhile had returned to his Poles, and spent the night amongst Sieniawski's infantry of the Polish left wing,[185] presumably not going any further because he intended to return to Lorraine's wing in the morning, both for the agreed final discussions and because he recognised that, with the Ottoman troops below the Kahlenberg chain, the action there would quickly get interesting tomorrow and he wanted to be present. There was not much more that the King could do that night, especially as he did not expect his Poles to be in action tomorrow, but the noise from some artillery fire from the Turkish camp kept him awake,[186] so around 3 a.m. he settled down to write another of his interminable letters to his wife, describing the events of the past few days since the crossing of the Danube and grumbling about how hungry he and his soldiers were.[187]

Slowly, beyond the distant hills to the east, the sky began to turn from black to pale grey.

---

185 Wimmer, *Entsatz*, p.183. This seems the most likely location, despite the fact that he told his wife he spent the night 'on the extreme right' (Plater, p.69); had he done this, it would have taken him much longer to return to Lorraine's wing.

186 It is not clear to what he was referring; he wrote 'One can see all the Turkish camp, and the cannon do not let one shut one's eyes' (Plater, p.69), which presumably refers to the sound of artillery fire from the siege works but could mean anything. It was not normal for cannon in the seventeenth century to fire during the night (the cannon's recoil every time it was fired made it impossible to hit a target if the gunner could not see it) and the diaries of the siege do not give any indication of night firing; but Kara Mustafa may have had his gunners make occasional shots during the hours of darkness merely for the sake of harassing the garrison.

187 The letter is in Plater, pp.64–70; see Appendix 8.

9

Ottoman reactions of 11 September and final dispositions

Actions on the last day before the battle

Ottoman troops, except those still working on the siege, had spent the night of 10–11 September under arms expecting an attack at any moment. There are indications that Koca Ibrahim sent some of his own wing forward during the night in an attempt to reinforce and hold the posts on the Kahlenberg and Leopoldsberg, but this move was forestalled by the Christians' occupation of the two peaks, and the advance was cancelled.[188] Early in the morning of the 11th, Kara Mustafa had the army form up in order of battle; his own personal forces, including his entire household and the *müteferrika*s and *çavuş*es, accompanied by the famed court preacher Vani Efendi, were drawn up fully armed and armoured before the treasury tent. Then a report arrived from the *beylerbeyi* of Maraş, Ömer Deli, that the infidels had withdrawn (where he got this erroneous impression from, we do not know; maybe he had lost sight of the Christian centre as it moved around the hills and thought that it had retreated). The Grand Vizier kept the troops waiting for an hour or two longer, before finally giving the order to stand down: all men were to return to their tents, but to continue to hold themselves ready for action.[189]

Meanwhile, the effort against Vienna resumed: although the garrison thought the work on mining had slackened significantly (in fact, the mines in the curtain were ready to be loaded with gunpowder), the Ottomans manned their heaviest guns and the bombardment of the surviving defences rose to a

---

188 Known from reports from the Christian side. The Ottoman diarists were at Kara Mustafa's headquarters, and once they recorded the forces assigned to Koca Ibrahim, seem to have thought little more of him, and what he did can only be ascertained from Christian reports of what they saw.
189 Kreutel & Teply, p.187. All details of the initial Ottoman response, including all quotes, are from this source unless specified otherwise.

The Ottoman army in the march. Painting from the end of 17th century, based on 16th century engraving (National Museum, Warsaw)

new height. The cannon thundered away for about two hours as the sun rose in the sky towards noon.

Not all Ottoman officers were as clueless as the *beylerbeyi* of Maraş. Receb, *sancak-bey* of Tarsus, brought in a couple of prisoners who were interrogated and then decapitated;[190] no-one bothered to record what they said, but it is likely that they had been captured in skirmishing near the Danube with the head of the cavalry column on the road, and gave Kara Mustafa a first indication that the Christians were definitely still approaching. A little later, around the middle of the day, the Ottomans of the right wing and advance guard began to see that significant bodies of troops were appearing, first on the road along the Danube and then on the crest of the Kahlenberg and the slopes either side, with their advanced parties already pushing down the hill and skirmishing with the Turks, or, as the Ottoman diarists put it, 'the godless infidels, like enraged pigs, attacked the battle-bands of Islam'. Kara Mehmed's troops threw themselves into action against a party of 200–300 men (probably the companies of noble volunteers who led the Imperialist skirmish line), and claimed to inflict heavy casualties, though they brought in only two heads, the traditional Ottoman means of securing a financial reward for killing an enemy;[191] the *sancak-bey* of Székesfehérvár, Mehmed

---

190 Kreutel & Teply, p.187. Receb is not mentioned in any of the lists of forces, and was probably serving with his provincial superior, the *beylerbeyi* of Adana, in Kara Mehmed's advance guard facing the Kahlenberg chain.

191 There was no guarantee, of course, that the heads, for which Ottoman warriors could expect a cash bonus, came from Christian soldiers killed in fair fight; they could have come from

Bey Atlibeyzade, sent in one young prisoner to headquarters but the unfortunate youth was unceremoniously handed over to the executioner – with the enemy in sight, there seemed no longer any need to interrogate prisoners.

There could now be no doubt that the relief force had arrived. Kara Mehmed hastened to report to the Grand Vizier. Kara Mustafa immediately had his retinue draw up again in full gear, then summoned the Janissary Ağa[192] from the siege works and ordered him to get dug ditches 'at the field of action before the artillery', which *probably* meant the position in the centre, and may indicate that work on the Türkenschanz began only today. Soon after, Kara Mustafa's *kethüda* Ali Ağa Gürcü (the Georgian), advanced with the Grand Vizier's personal troops to the assigned position, at the Türkenschanz, while Kara Mustafa himself even now remained at his palace-tent complex. Meanwhile, the warriors of Koca Ibrahim's wing boiled out of their camp in their formless bands, 'marching here and there' (as the Baden account put it) seeking advantageous positions on eminences covered by bushes or ditches.[193] Some may have gone forward and reinforced Kara Mehmed's line nearer the woods, in action with the Christian advance parties. Lorraine's secretary, watching from the top of the Kahlenberg, described them thus:

> The troops that they had advanced consisted of cavalry and another type of soldier who fought almost like our dragoons, on foot and on horse, but rather on foot than on horse [not surprising, when one considers the terrain]. Of these latter, the number was quite large. They had brought out of their camp only a little infantry, without cannons, in all this detachment that they placed against us.[194]

As noted above, at about 4 p.m. the Christians opened fire from the top of the Kahlenberg with a few battalion guns. Although the distance must have been much too great for their fire to have done any real damage, the Turks withdrew well out of range, and subsequently lit their fires and settled down for the night beyond cannon-shot – probably camping in a line across the northern slopes of the Nussberg.

So far, the Ottomans had observed only the Christian left wing under Lorraine; they had not seen a sign of the centre under Waldeck, any more than Waldeck's men had seen hide or hair of a Turk on this day, but the positioning of Kara Mustafa's household troops at the Türkenschanz, well back from the Kahlenberg chain, *suggests* that the Ottomans knew to expect more infidels in this sector – although the placing there could equally well

---

unfortunate prisoners.
192 He had already been called out of the approaches during the alarm on the 10th (see above); presumably he returned to the siege effort after the alarm was over, and was now called out for the second and last time.
193 Röder, vol. 1, Urk., p.15.
194 Stöller, p.36; a similar account with less detail, Stöller, p.101. Dalérac, vol. 1, pp.152–153, also stressed in his account of the battle that the Christians faced only cavalry and 'dragoons'; he said they saw no Janissaries at all – we know this to be inaccurate, but it indicates how small a part the Janissaries played in the battle in the eyes of many in the allied army.

have been with a view to using them as a final reserve for Koca Ibrahim. At first sight, the Türkenschanz position can seem ineffective, until one remembers that the shape of the Wienerwald on this side meant that the Ottoman centre at the Türkenschanz was not much further from the foothills than Koca Ibrahim was from the Kahlenberg. Unlike the right wing, which could use the open-topped Nussberg and its surrounding streams and villages as an excellent defensive position, the centre could not hold the foothills near it, as these were wooded, and the streams offered not obstacles to a Christian advance but avenues to facilitate it. As for the Poles, the Ottomans must have known they were approaching based on reports from the few Tatar parties that had been observing Sobieski's march, but facing them was only Abaza Sari Hüseyin and the weak string of the left wing, supported by however many Tatars had remained to fight in the battle.[195]

The deployment to the foothills was not the only movement within the Ottoman camp. Observers in Vienna noticed a great deal of activity as the afternoon wore on, striking of tents and loading of camels and pack-horses, and a great deal of confused movement back and forth. The merchants, slave-dealers, sutlers, and all the other horde of camp-followers and hangers-on of the Ottoman army had decided that the omens were not good for their continued existence if they remained outside Vienna, and were packing up to cross the River Wien and head for Hungary. Their departure thinned the camp out rather than altering its overall shape, for right up to the end of

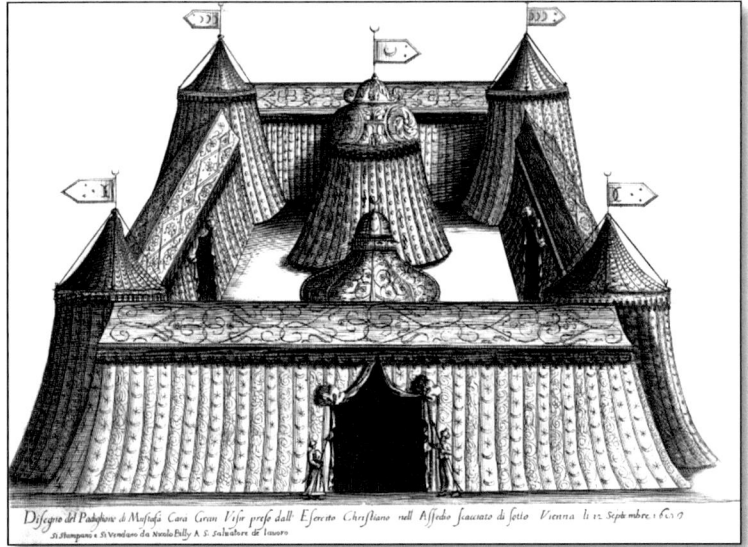

Kara Mustafa's palace-tent complex, captured at Vienna by Polish troops. (Wien Museum Inv.-Nr. 37989, CC0)

195 Dalérac, vol. 1, p.146, records under the 11th a rather odd story that Sobieski had deliberately 'informed' Kara Mustafa of his approach by interrogating two prisoners, a Turk and a Tatar, very closely, then letting them go, so that they could report to their leader the Polish advance as eye-witnesses; such a report is not recorded from the Ottoman side, and this was in any case a very odd thing for Sobieski to do if his desire was to trap the Ottoman army. The story is probably untrue (Dalérac is not regarded as a very reliable source), but just possibly the stratagem was aimed at the Khan, not the Grand Vizier, as part of Sobieski's attempts to ensure he did not have to face the Crimeans.

the battle the Ottoman camp maintained its extent from the Wien to the Döblingerbach. It may have been this withdrawal of the non-combatants that Cantemir misinterpreted and described as a desertion of a quarter of the Ottoman army on the eve of the battle – though it is possible that some armed contingents did also make off around the same time, for we hear nothing of the reduced Hungarian detachment in the battle, and the Tatars may have left at this moment. The departure of the non-combatants would hardly weaken the army's effectiveness in battle, in fact its effectiveness might even improve a little with the removal of all the clutter from the camp. But the combatants were aware of how important all these non-combatants were in the supplying of the army; and besides, if thousands of men and women were leaving for safety, this was bound to give a severe knock to the morale of the battle-bands of Islam.

If Kara Mustafa hoped by remaining at his tent complex in the main camp to keep the siege effort going, he failed, for soon after noon, with attention drawing towards the hills, the bombardment slackened off – the Ottoman cannon did not actually fall silent, but their fire fell away to a mere nuisance, probably kept up merely to discourage the garrison from launching a sortie. Although the miners had reported that they had dug five mine-channels into the main wall, each four ells or about fifteen feet deep, which would soon be ready for loading with powder so that they could be blown up to open breaches in the enceinte, nothing was done about loading them. Though the artillery fire would resume on the 12th, the siege had come to an effective standstill pending the result of the attempt at relief. Nevertheless, Kara Mustafa kept troops in the siege works: those of the Egyptian infantry who had not been assigned to Koca Ibrahim, the *yerli kulu* of a small number of *beylerbeyi*s (see chapter 10 below), some volunteers from other corps, most of the *topci* gunners, and the *cebeci*s and miners, who were not trained to fight in a field battle. In total, they amounted to about 10,000 men, or 15,000 at most.[196] This number may not have included unarmed workers in the trenches and mines, prisoners and slaves and the like.

Kara Mustafa has often been heavily criticised for this failure to concentrate every armed man against the relief army (even his subordinates did so; see 'The final council of war' below), and the more we understand just how weak the Ottoman army was in comparison with the huge numbers of combatants usually attributed to it, the bigger the mistake seems. However, only a small fraction of the troops left in the siege works would have been effective in the field anyway, for the *cebeci*s and miners were not really battle troops (although they could fight, and Koca Ibrahim had been assigned some *cebeci*s); and, given that the Grand Vizier had already committed the original cardinal mistake of not giving up the siege several days earlier and advancing to engage

---

196 It is extremely unclear who was left in command of these troops. Western works often refer to the *Kul kahyasi* (second-in-command of the Janissary corps, sometimes referred to as the *Kul kiaya*) or the *Kiaya bey* or *kethüda bey*, apparently unaware that this second title was a different official entirely, the Grand Vizier's deputy. In fact, both the *Kul kahyasi* and the *Kiaya bey* are recorded by the Ottoman diarists as serving in the field army, at the centre. For the various officers left in the trenches, see Chapter 10 below.

the allied army well away from Vienna, leaving him to fight a battle with an armed fortress directly to his rear, there was little else he could do, because, had he denuded the siege works of troops, he would not only have risked the garrison coming out and destroying his trenches and batteries, he would also have risked finding it attacking the rear of his army at a critical point of the battle – a dangerous prospect, for although the Vienna garrison had lost heavily during the siege, it still amounted, as Kara Mustafa knew from spy reports, to about four or perhaps five thousand troops, not counting civilian companies. Kara Mustafa should have given up on the siege days before and gone to meet Sobieski and Lorraine well away from the city, abandoning his siege works and taking up the siege again if he won in the field (though it is psychologically easy to understand why he did not do so, and as we will see shortly he did have what he thought were good reasons for not doing so); but having chosen not to do so, he had put himself in a position where he *had* to leave some troops facing Vienna to contain the garrison – and once that was allowed, there was no reason why they should not spend their time profitably and continue the effort to take Vienna… so the bombardment of the city and the mining work would continue on the 12th.

The final council of war

Discussions amongst the Ottoman commanders about how to fight the approaching Christians almost certainly continued down to the end of the 11th, although the evidence is contested.[197] Late on the 11th, feeling increasingly uncertain about the situation and knowing the effect that the departure of the non-combatants was having on morale, Kara Mustafa finally called a council of war that included the detested *beylerbeyi* of Buda; he may have been prepared at last to consider listening to Koca Ibrahim's advice, though equally there may have been, at the back of his mind, the realisation that he might need a scapegoat after tomorrow and thus had to involve Ibrahim in the decisions so that he could be blamed.

Koca Ibrahim felt that the army was too weak for it to be divided or for it to attempt to defend the too-extensive camp; in the debate, he argued in favour of raising the siege and taking the entire army to face the relief force, occupying the near edge of the woods and cutting down trees to form an abatis, a continuous barrier of interlocked trunks and branches that could be a nightmare to penetrate. Deep earthwork entrenchments behind this would strengthen the army's position even further.[198] Supported by cannon placed

---

197 See Appendix III for full discussion of the issues and a quote of Cantemir's account of the great final debate. I argue there that, although even the existence of this final discussion is now doubted, and Koca Ibrahim's recommending of actions that were now impossible suggests that if it did take place it occurred before the evening of the 11th, the overall picture of the debate as summarised in the text is probably true.

198 Cantemir's account (see Appendix III) mentions only an abatis; the La Brune version (Jean de La Brune, *La vie de Charles V duc de Lorraine* (Amsterdam: Garrel, 1691), p.279) included entrenchments. The subsequent write-up of the causes of the defeat by the Master of Ceremonies,

all along such a barrier or in a big battery, the Ottoman forces could hold off the initial attacks of the Christians and then, when they were shattered by repulse after repulse, send detachments of cavalry round to fall on their open flank, the right.

Entrenching activity like this was exactly the sort of action expected by the Christians, who were so puzzled by Koca Ibrahim's inactivity during this evening, and historians considering the effectiveness of the idea will immediately think of the carnage the French were able to inflict on Marlborough's army from such defences in 1709 at the Battle of Malplaquet. However, Koca Ibrahim and the right wing had already lost access to the near edge of the woods near them, so that the crucial part of the Ottoman army could not have done what he suggested even if Kara Mustafa had agreed, though the centre and left might still have done so. Nevertheless, Ibrahim's idea found widespread support amongst the other officials present, but Kara Mustafa would have none of it: he had already in effect decided to continue the siege (as above), and refused to consider changing the decision. His reasons were not always coherent, for he argued both that the enemy was superior in force to the Ottomans and that he was weaker, but the overall thrust of his argument was that if the siege were abandoned now, it could not be resumed later and the prize, whose fall was now only a few days away, would be lost completely. He had two main reasons for thinking this: while the Ottoman army was away fighting the relief force the garrison would ruin the siege works forcing the Ottomans to start again almost from scratch; and with the shaky morale of the army, even if the Ottomans won the battle it would be difficult if not impossible to persuade the troops to resume the gruelling siege work. There was even a risk, he felt, that if the siege works were abandoned, the troops would be so demoralised by this abandonment of their months of hard labour and blood that they would fight poorly in the battle against the relief force. In fairness to Kara Mustafa, it must be acknowledged that, as discussed in the previous section, by the 11th he was indeed in a position that *required* containing the city's garrison.

The majority of the council remained unconvinced; they acknowledged that the *kapi kulu* troops, especially the Janissaries, notoriously had limits to what they could be pushed into doing and a reputation for turning against their officers who did try to push them too far, but argued that this could usually be overcome by persuasion and bonuses; and they stressed that the Christians, fighting not just for a single city but for the defence of all Christendom, would be making the most powerful effort they could muster against the Ottomans and it required the Ottomans to use very man available to oppose them. None of this had any effect on the Grand Vizier: like all those who call meetings for the purpose of passing on responsibility without the slightest intention of listening to any advice, he ended by insisting that he alone was responsible to the Sultan for the conduct of the campaign and his

---

while it made no mention of these discussions, did argue that the army should have entrenched, and in such a way as to allow cavalry counter-attacks when the Christian assaults were repulsed.

opinion alone was what counted.[199] This killed the debate: the Grand Vizier was the Sultan's absolute deputy, and if he was expected to confer with other officers and ministers over major decisions, he was under no requirement to pay attention to their advice. The last council broke up, and the various Ottoman officers returned to their posts to await the dawn. No attempt was made to entrench the near edges of the woods.

According to our sources, neither Kara Mustafa nor anyone else mentioned several further flaws in Koca Ibrahim's proposal. Firstly, there was the reason we have noted above, that some troops had to be left in the siege works to prevent the field army from being attacked in the rear during the battle. Secondly, the *beylerbeyi*'s idea of an abatis was predicated in part on the need to defend a position less extensive than the Ottoman camp – but any abatis, if it was not to be outflanked, would have to be every bit as long as the camp. Perhaps Koca Ibrahim was thinking only of the Christians in sight facing him, of entrenching only the woods at the front of the Kahlenberg chain, and was unaware that the Poles were approaching to his left and would not only block any flanking counter-attack against repelled Germans but would eventually outflank any abatis line he created facing north. Thirdly, there was the fact that the Ottoman army was no better suited for what Koca Ibrahim proposed than for what it actually did on the 12th: it lacked the sufficient numbers of experienced infantry necessary to defend a long line of entrenchments, and its numerous light cavalry, while effective in counter-attacking a repulsed enemy under normal circumstances, would find it very difficult to do so in the woods of the Wienerwald. Even if the Ottomans had thrown up entrenchments at this stage, these would not have been as devastatingly effective as they were at Malplaquet – and even there, the attacker took the entrenchments and won the battle, albeit despite appalling losses.

These were not the only reasons for Kara Mustafa's making the decisions that he did. It is interesting to compare the situation at Vienna with only other major military operation Kara Mustafa had commanded before, the siege in 1678 of the Cossack-Ukrainian town of Czehryń (modern Chyhyryn) in what was then the Polish Ukraine. Czehryń was never mentioned in the accounts of the discussions that have come down to us, but it may tell us about the military lessons Kara Mustafa might have thought he had learnt about such a situation, for the Ottoman attack on the Cossack stronghold bore several resemblances to the situation he found himself in now. In 1678, the Cossacks were supported by the Russians, and the besieging Ottoman army had faced both a fortress and a field army – albeit not a relief force but a Russian army entrenched from the start in contact with the fortress. Despite the extraordinary difficulty of his situation, Kara Mustafa had (after bouts of vacillation) besieged Czehryń and taken it in the teeth of the Russian army.

---

199 The Sultan had formally appointed Kara Mustafa as *serdar* or *seraskier* (absolute commander-in-chief) at Belgrade on 13 May. There may have been a solemn sultanic document or *hatti-sherif* containing this appointment; nineteenth-century historians often suggested Kara Mustafa dragged out such a document when his wishes were questioned, but this is not explicitly mentioned in the Cantemir account.

The victory owed far more to luck, to Czehryn's wooden fortifications which had burnt so easily, and to Russian unwillingness to risk everything for what was to them a comparatively unimportant border town, than to the Grand Vizier's military ability, but it seemed to prove for Kara Mustafa that it was possible to besiege a town while at the same time fighting off a field army. He had done it once; he could do it again. Kara Mustafa was hopelessly wrong, but he thought he had reasons for believing he was right.

Ottoman morale

The morale of the Ottoman army on the eve of battle, its readiness for the coming fight, has been much debated. There is comparatively little disagreement on the situation with the auxiliaries, much more on the situation with the core units of the army.

The auxiliaries certainly were not to be relied on. The Moldavians and Wallachians, unwilling Ottoman vassals, were untrustworthy, and the Ottomans knew it too. If there were any Hungarians left in the camp, they could not be expected to fight well (if at all) against their co-religionists either – many Hungarians might hate the Habsburgs and be prepared to fight against the Germans on their own, but they had had a summer of devastation to remind them why the Ottomans were the real enemies of their land and people. As for the Tatars, most of them had probably left the army already, leaving only a small band of warriors determined to fight; even if they had not gone home, their readiness to fight was barely above nil, and besides, their effectiveness in a field battle against disciplined western troops or the trained Polish cavalry was strictly limited.[200]

The position with the main elements of the Ottoman army was less clear-cut. Obviously morale was not at rock-bottom, because most elements of the army would fight long and hard during the battle the next day. But there is a world of difference between soldiers who fight because they are convinced they will win and those who fight only because it is their duty while they labour under the conviction that they are going to lose; and it seems that Ottoman morale was nearer the latter than the former.

Conditions in the camp were not good. Men assigned to the siege itself had been working extremely hard under great stress while suffering appalling casualties, as the siege dragged on far longer than originally expected; most were exhausted. The recent heavy rains had only made things worse, in the trenches and amongst the tents. Sickness was widespread in the camp and getting worse daily – Ottoman camps had once been thoroughly sanitary places, but standards had slipped in the seventeenth century, and it was in any case impossible to preserve hygiene amongst the thousands of hangers-on who filled the camp, so disease ran rampant through the army. Food

---

200 The Imperialist cavalry had been trounced at Petronell by the Tatars, but largely through panic created by surprise when first faced with Tatar tactics. They had learnt since how to deal with Tatars.

supplies were always short: wagon trains of provisions were being delivered all the time from Turkish Hungary or by the cowed Hungarian lords and towns, a final one arriving in the camp on the 11th, but they could never bring enough for the army and its horde of hangers-on – a couple of times during late August, the camp had been close to starvation. Kara Mustafa tried to keep some supplies back to build up a reserve, either as a sensible precaution against future crises or in order to be able to stock up Vienna when it fell into his hands, but these wise measures only provoked hostility to him amongst the ranks, for it looked like he was hoarding food for his own use – and he certainly never shared the men's privations. When food deliveries went short, the army could not live off the land near Vienna either, for the Tatars had destroyed all available food supplies for many miles around when it sacked the countryside during the early days of the siege – never was the short-sightedness of Ottoman methods shown more clearly than in this – and the only untouched region from which provisions might have been drawn, the Marchfeld, had been forbidden to them throughout the siege by the determined actions of the Duke of Lorraine in blocking any attempt to get over the Danube. If the food situation was bad for the men, it was worse for the horses: foraging parties did occasionally manage to go out into the surrounding countryside to find grass, but never in sufficient numbers to keep the many thousands of animals fed properly, and they were having to go ever further off to find fields or meadows that had not been burnt by the Tatars or eaten up already. Besides, foraging had to be curtailed even further as the infidel army approached and men had to be kept in the camp ready for action. Many (probably the majority) of the Turks' horses were in poor shape. In addition to all this, most of the merchants and sutlers packed up and left during the 11th, which not only lowered spirits with its unspoken declaration that they considered defeat inevitable but also told the men remaining that their supply situation would soon get very worse, for what there was of the army's provisioning beyond Hungarian deliveries was dependent on these civilians.[201]

On top of the physical conditions, dissatisfaction and despondency had spread throughout the ranks. Only a couple of weeks before, the entire army had witnessed the slaughter on the slopes of the Bisamberg of its brethren who had tried to establish a hold on the Marchfeld, and everyone was aware of the similar rout at Pressburg a month before. Although historians are fond of referring to the Ottoman army's belief in its invincibility, this was not actually the case: the Ottomans certainly disregarded their defeat at St Gothard in 1664, which they viewed as a trivial skirmish, but they faced tough times in the Ukraine Wars (when they took Czehryń in 1678, it was their second attempt, the first the year before having failed ignominiously), and had been defeated several times in the Sobieski Wars of 1672–1676 against Poland –

---

[201] A Polish slave who escaped on the 11th from the Ottoman camp into the city reported that there was 'an inexpressible fear' amongst the Turks (Ruess, p.70). The evidence of such escapees is not always reliable, but his report may accurately reflect the morale amongst the train personnel and camp followers, amongst whom he would have been dwelling, rather than that of the front-line troops.

they had forced the Poles to peace at Żórawno only by the most strenuous efforts. And the Lion of Lechistan, the man who had beaten them so often, and destroyed them so utterly at Chocim in 1673, was now heading towards them out of the hills. Older hands amongst the men might have remembered Candia: the Ottomans had certainly taken the great Venetian fortress on Crete in 1669, but also that it had taken over twenty years of war and nearly three years of continuous siege to do it. Although the *kapi kulu* were officially a disciplined standing army, there were considerable restrictions on how deep their discipline went, and they had a long history of violent objection to service they had taken a dislike to, even turning on commanders who had displeased them. Kara Mustafa was right to be concerned about how the troops would react to being forced to re-do the siege work if he raised the siege to concentrate against the relief army.

However, the Grand Vizier had himself contributed to the problem. At the best of times, Kara Mustafa was not an inspiring leader like Sobieski; he spent much of the siege in luxury in his palace-tent complex, and even when he visited the trenches to try to encourage the men with words and rewards, his use of an armoured litter was not calculated to create respect. Far worse than this, however, was when he hit the men in their purses: the Ottomans were all enthusiastic slavers, and although centuries earlier in the days of the Empire's expansion a tax known as the *pencik* (originally a fifth of all slaves, later a cash payment) had been levied by the state on every captured Christian sold as a slave, this had been abandoned nearly two centuries before, so when Kara Mustafa tried to revive it in the camp, at the comparatively substantial rate of one zecchini a slave (about equivalent to twenty days' pay for an entry-level Janissary or ten days' worth of revenue from the income of a basic timariot's fief), he brought huge resentment down upon his head from both the Ottoman troops who did pay and the Tatars who refused flat-out to pay it.[202] The *pencik* probably played its part in the dissatisfaction which brought the bulk of the Tatars to do so little as the Christian army approached; the Ottoman soldiers, who could not just pick up and depart like the Tatars, were left fuming with hostility against their commander. (The tax also contributed to Ottoman supply difficulties, for, once the men had paid the tax, they could hardly be forced to get rid of all the slaves that filled the camp with useless mouths – until the morning of the battle, when it was too late.) Towards the end of August, about the same time as near-riots amongst the troops over food shortages, there had even arisen in the Ottoman camp, perhaps in reaction to Kara Mustafa's resurrection of the antique *pencik*, a demand that the siege be called off after 40 or 43 days because of an alleged ancient rule that Islamic warriors were required to serve against the infidel for no longer than this period.[203] The claim was fatuous, for many Ottoman campaigns had lasted far longer than 40 days, and the siege of Candia that

---

202 Marsigli, vol. 2, pp.120–121. The tax is not mentioned by the Ottoman diarists, but Marsigli was a prisoner in the Ottoman camp during the siege and therefore an eyewitness.
203 This appears to have originated in reports by Kuniz smuggled into Vienna, as cited in Renner, 306, and Newald, vol. 1, p.182; it is also in the diary kept by the man of Kuniz' staff, in Firnhaber, pp.503–504.

ended fourteen years previously had run continuously for nearly three years – but logic never plays a big part in such situations, and the dissatisfied Ottoman soldiery, close to revolt, was merely resorting to any legitimate-sounding excuse it could find that might end the misery. Kara Mustafa had been compelled to call on the court preacher, Vani Efendi, to use his famous oratory to persuade the troops to give up the demand and stay for a few days longer. Afterwards, the Grand Vizier vigorously spread rumours through the camp about how close to surrender the city was, how the relief army had been defeated and scattered, even that the Emperor Leopold had died, as well as distributing rewards and punishments along with repeated promises of great plunder when the city fell – anything to persuade the troops to stay and see the operation through to the end. The rumours, or else the arrival of provisions that alleviated the food shortages for a while, perhaps aided by the fact that a week later the Burg Ravelin fell and the besiegers could at last see the prospect of a victorious end to the siege, seem to have done the trick, because the 40-day demand never re-surfaced that we know of and most of the Ottoman soldiers, unhappy though they were, continued to work in the trenches right to the end – although the captive Imperialist envoy in the camp, Kuniz, maintained his belief that if Lorraine were merely to re-establish communications between Vienna and the outside world over the Danube islands, the entire army would revolt against Kara Mustafa, and at the very end of August some of the Egyptian troops did withdraw from the trenches against orders and may even have gone home.[204]

This gives an idea of the spirit of the Ottoman army as Lorraine and Sobieski drew near. Exhaustion, sickness, hunger, and a profound hostility to their commander bordering on mutiny, did not necessarily constitute complete dejection, they would not prevent the army from fighting and even from fighting with vigour, and they did not lead inevitably to defeat; but they were not conditions that helped put an army into the right frame of mind when it was going into a difficult major battle. They certainly did not help an army that was going into a major battle with most of its troops of indifferent quality, fighting in circumstances where their few good attributes – their mobility and speed – could not be put to use.

There have even been suggestions that in the final weeks of the siege the Ottoman army from the top down was filled with a spirit of fatalism created by all these difficulties, a belief that nothing could be done that would have any effect on the outcome of events, and it was this fatalism that lay behind the complete failure of the Ottoman army to make any significant reaction to the approach of the relief army.[205] This is going too far. It is true enough that in many respects Ottoman statesmen and soldiers did share the Islamic belief in predestination and did suffer the common consequence of this, that it led to a failure to attempt to deal with difficult situations (for example, it was the reason for the Ottoman Empire's consistent failure to take any steps

---

204 Since the Egyptians had only brought 3,500 troops to the army, and a significant proportion of them was assigned to the field army while others were reported as serving in the trenches to the end, this cannot have been *all* of the Egyptians, as is sometimes implied.
205 La Brune, pp.278–279.

whatsoever to hinder the spread of plague in its dominions). But there was no fatalism about the efforts that the Ottomans made against the city in the final days of the siege; the real problem was personal, in that command of the army was held by a poor decision-maker, Kara Mustafa, who, when presented with awkward situations that required a firm and decisive response, preferred to stick his head in the sand and continue with the course he had been following to date, doing nothing about the new threat until it was too late.

The final Ottoman positions and plan

The overall Ottoman disposition had not changed significantly from the arrangement ordered on the 9th. Koca Ibrahim commanded the big right wing facing the Kahlenberg chain, broadly occupying the ground below the Kahlenberg and Leopoldsberg, and ready to hold the several stream-lines behind this, back to the entrenchments of the Krottenbach-Döblingerbach which protected the northern end of the camp. Either amongst Koca Ibrahim's forces or more likely in front of them were Kara Mehmed and his advance guard (there are strong indications he was not under the direct command of Koca Ibrahim); possibly his units were concentrated on the extreme right, nearest the river. Protecting the right flank of Koca Ibrahim (as it protected the left flank of the Christians) was the Danube, and, if the Ottomans were pushed back far enough, the Canal. Beyond the Canal, at the northern tip of the Prater Island, was posted the small corps of *yerli kulu* of Hasan Defterdar, *sancak-bey* of Hamid, a unit from the right wing, about 400 Ottoman troops, together with the 6,000 or so untrustworthy Moldavians and Wallachians – although he must have known that their princes were in contact with the enemy, it is to be assumed that Kara Mustafa hoped these would fall on Lorraine's flank over the Canal if the Imperialists drove Koca Ibrahim past them, but nothing is heard of them in the battle, and if the Roumanians actually stayed to the morning of the 12th, they disappeared very soon after without firing a shot. South of Koca Ibrahim and the right wing was the small Ottoman centre around the Türkenschanz, facing roughly west to the hills, approximately at the point (did they but know it) where the Polish left wing would be coming out. South of this was the over-extended left wing of Abaza Sari Hüseyin, facing west and officially covering the three miles to the River Wien and the Ottoman camps on the hills beyond it – though only if the Tatars had been present at their maximum likely strength, giving him 20,000 men in total,[206] could Hüseyin really have been extended over such a wide front with sufficient men to form a battle-line deep enough to fight (at four men per yard); if the Tatars had left already, he had only about 4,000 for certain, and can have had no more than 5,000–7,000 men if he is allowed a reasonable share of the troops whose location is unknown, giving him just one to two men per yard if he tried to cover the entire distance, an

---

206 The maximum number of Tatars that could have been present was 15,000, although 10,000 was more likely – and as noted above, I believe most of these had already left the battlefield.

obvious impossibility (compare this with the five to six men per yard that, at the worst interpretation, Koca Ibrahim had, or the seven to eight men per yard in the Allied army at Blenheim in 1704). It is reasonably certain that the left wing tried to cover about half of the distance to the Wien, no further than the village of Ottakring. Probably, the Ottomans had a rough idea of where the Poles were and knew that their most southerly exit route would be the Alsbach, so that, although Abaza Sari Hüseyin's left flank was in the air, it was under no serious threat at the moment. However, there *was* that big gap of a mile and a half between his flank and the Wien, a mile and a half of unprotected ground that was the Ottoman army's line of retreat should it be defeated; and it would take only a small shift of direction by Sobieski and the Poles to put them in the gap, across that line of retreat and trapping the entire Ottoman army – exactly the situation Sobieski had been longing for. What were the Ottomans thinking of?

Unfortunately, we have no clear idea of the Ottoman plans for the battle. From the Ottoman diarists we hear not a word. Cantemir does tell us that when Kara Mustafa took command of the centre on the day of battle he 'orders them at least to stand firm, and repel the first shock of the enemy.'[207] Taken together with what the Ottomans did on the 12th, this suggests that that was all there was of an overall plan: a generally passive defensive, to wait for the infidel attack and hope to throw it back, sometimes with strictly local tactical offensive moves, while behind them the siege works were garrisoned and pressure kept up on the city by maintaining the bombardment, Kara Mustafa clearly still hoping that Vienna would fall imminently and that once this happened all his troubles would be over. Sobieski's biographer Otto Forst de Battaglia described a grandiose Ottoman plan involving the right wing fighting a holding action against Lorraine and the Christian left while large cavalry forces on the left wing, supported by a flanking attack by the Tatars from the south, would deliver the decisive blow against the Poles as they descended from the hills.[208] There is not a shred of evidence to support this, and much evidence against it, for by no stretch of the imagination could Abaza Sari Hüseyin's wing be regarded as a large cavalry force capable of delivering a knock-out blow against the Poles – even if the Tatars were included at full strength, his wing was substantially inferior in numbers to the 28,400 of the Ottoman right wing and its attached advance guard. The Turks knew perfectly well that the Poles were approaching and were familiar with them as tough opponents, yet they concentrated the bulk of their forces to the north, away from the Poles, facing the only enemy currently visible, Lorraine and his Imperialists. Perhaps Kara Mustafa was unaware of just how weak his left wing was – since the Ottoman diarists had recorded from the 9th in some detail the forces assigned to the two wings, this seems unlikely, unless the Grand Vizier seriously over-estimated the strength of the Tatars, and perhaps more likely is that Kara Mustafa really was doing nothing more than concentrating against the visible enemy and trying to

---

207 Demetrius Cantemir, *The history of the growth and decay of the Othman Empire…*, transl. by A. Tindal (London: Knapton, 1734–1735), vol. 2, p.310.
208 Forst de Battaglia, p.173.

pretend to himself that the enemy out of sight did not exist. It seems that Forst de Battaglia imagined the plan he described, influenced by a desire to play up the role of the King. Forst de Battaglia may have been slightly nearer the mark when he referred to the Ottoman camps beyond the River Wien as 'reception positions'; we do not know exactly what the Ottomans intended by these camps (they are not mentioned by the Ottoman diarists), but they do have a feel of being intended as fall-back positions, as if headquarters seriously expected to fail to repel the Christians and believed that positions were required where they could rally the army and cover its retreat.

10

The opposing forces (orders of battle)

Ottoman order of battle

Figures, in descending order of reliability, are: in **bold** from the Ottoman diarists, in (parentheses) from the Benaglia list at Belgrade in May, in [brackets] from the 7 September 'muster', with question mark for informed guesses based on comparing the different sources with casualty figures for the siege and the usual sizes of Ottoman corps. See Appendix II for a breakdown of the sources for this list.

The names and numbers here, apart from types of soldier explicitly identified such as Janissaries, do not represent coherent units. In most cases, the numbers from the author Silahdar listed against officials, especially the *beylerbeyi*s, are given in Kreutel & Teply with the unhelpful German translation 'Pforten- und Provinztruppen', sometimes 'Hoftruppen'. More useful is the Benaglia list, which, except for Rumelia and Damascus (and an anomalous reference against Buda), for *beylerbeyi*s listed only *yerli kulu*; only a few officers at *sancak-bey* level were in his list, those too with smaller numbers of *yerli kulu* – but far too few to match the figures for *sancak-bey*s below. A *sancak-bey* normally brought his own immediate retainers based on his high-value benefice under the traditional timariot system, but, although there were wide variations, these retainers were normally in the range 50–120, so the numbers below probably include the other timariots of their provinces – admittedly, at much lower levels than expected under the official system. (Against this is the fact that the official head of the timariots of a province was an *alay bey*, and the presence in the suspect 7 September 'muster' of the mysterious 'Villa or Dilly Ağa of the timariots' with his alleged 5,000 men.) I believe that the numbers against *beylerbeyi*s can be read as 'mostly *yerli kulu*, maybe with some timariots', while those against sancak beys can be read as 'mostly timariots, maybe with some yerli kulu'; overall, the majority of these named-official units would have been *yerli kulu*. The structure of the Ottoman army at this period is covered more fully in my forthcoming title on the 1684 campaign, *Wilfully run our head against the wall*.

THE OPPOSING FORCES (ORDERS OF BATTLE)

Forces facing the relief

Right wing (Koca Ibrahim)

Advanced guard (Kara Mehmed)			
Kara Mehmed Pasha BB of Diyarbekir	2,000		
Binamaz Halil BB of Sivas	1,500		
Deli Bekir BB of Aleppo	1,000		
Deli Emir BB of Adana	900		
	=	5,400	
Main force (Koca Ibrahim Arnaut Uzun Pasha of Buda)			
Janissaries		5,000	
Cebecis		1,500	
The 4 junior regiments of the *Sipahis* of the Porte		3,000	
Ömer Deli, BB of Maraş		1,200	
Mehmed Şişman BB of Karaman		1,000	
'Troops of Damascus'		600	
Hizir BB of Bosnia		2,000	
Hüseyin P. Kadizade s-b of Bolu		300	
Arab Ali P. s-b of Teke		200	
Ahmed P. Şeyhzade s-b of Saruhan		300	
Quartermaster Hüseyin (or Hasan) P.		150	
Troops of Egypt (under the 'bey of Cairo')*		1,000	
Hasan P. the treasurer, s-b of Hamid [on the Prater; see below]		400	
Ahmed P. of Aydin†		500	
Mehmed Harmuş P. of Menteşe		200	
Ali Şeyhzade P., BB of Neuhäusel		500	
Dilaver Deli P. s-b of Kaysariye		150	
Abdülmümin P., s-b of Içel		200	
Sahib Deli Ömer s-b of Karahisar		200	
Hüseyin Bey Can-Arslan-Pasha-zade, s-b of Kangiri [Çankiri, in Anatolia]		150	
Koca Ibrahim Arnaut Uzun P., BB of Buda		4,000 (2,865)	
Mehmed Bey, s-b of Beyşehir [in Karaman]		150	
Mustafa P., s-b of Hercegovina		300	
(Veli Bey, s-b of Vize		150)‡	
		=	28,400

Extra troops known to have served here:			
Ahmed Osmanpashazade P., BB. of Anatolia	[1,000]		
Osman Oğlu, s-b. of Kutahya [see Appendix 1, 11.1]	1,000] (510)		
	=	1,510?	

* Ottoman Egypt technically had *sancak-bey*s but they were a completely different type of official from those in the rest of the Empire, owing more to the 'emirs' of the Mameluke past of the province, and often referred-to as just 'beys'.

† There is a possibility that this may have been the same person as Ahmed of Saruhan; if so, the Ottoman diarists slipped up.

‡ Only present in the Silahdar version of the list.

Centre (Kara Mustafa)

Kara Mustafa, his court & Janissaries [Arnauts/Bosnians]	[6,000] 1,500?		
Mustafa Bekri, Janissary Ağa [Janissaries]	??*		
Osman Ağa of the *Sipahis* (the two senior regiments)	[9,000] 4,000 max.?†		
	=	7,000?	
		=	36,910

* No figure available. 15,000 Janissaries had been at Belgrade; 5,000 were now under Koca Ibrahim, and 10,000 had been listed as killed during the siege, so one might imagine that not too many were present here, but Kreutel & Teply, 188, is explicit that a strong detachment Janissaries was here at the Centre under the Janissary Ağa. I would make a guess at 1,500.

† only two regiments present in the centre, though these were the two that were normally the strongest; see Appendix II.

(Paradowski, pp.138, 140, refers to the Ottoman force here including 'Levantine infantry'; no such category existed in the Ottoman army – but the quote on p.140 indicates that this refers to '*levend*s', an extraordinarily elastic term that most often referred to a form of militia, especially naval, but could also be used for fire-arms–equipped 'mercenaries', including those of the *yerli kulu* – in particular, such mercenaries who served the state directly as opposed to a *beylerbeyi* could be called *miri levend*; and, although the term is not normally used for them, the household troops of the Grand Vizier, as effective head of the state, could be considered as serving the state directly.)

THE OPPOSING FORCES (ORDERS OF BATTLE)

Left wing (Hüseyin of Damascus and Tatar Khan)

Abaza Sari Hüseyin P. BB of Damascus	[3,000] (2,300)		
Tatar Khan, Murad Giray	1–2,000?		
		= 4,300?	
			= 41,210

(The figure for the Tatars is based on the conclusion that most had already departed; see Appendix I, 5.3. The Necati map adds to the left wing the troops of various smaller *eyalet*s; many of the units under 'Location unknown' below probably belong here)

Other forces available to Kara Mustafa at Vienna

On the Prater:			
Hasan of Hamid	**400**		
Şerban Cantacuzeni, Prince of Wallachia	[4,000]		
George Duca, Prince of Moldavia	[2,000]		
		= 6,400	
			= 47,610
Known left in siege or assumed to be:			
*Topci*s (gunners)	[1,500]		
*Cebeci*s (armourers)	[4,000] 1,000?		
Egyptians (*Misirli*)	[3,500] 1,000?*		
Miners (*laguncilar*)	[5,000] 2,000?†		
Celeb Hasan P., BB of Jenő	?? 500?		
Volunteers of the *Sipahi*s and *Silahdar*s [*serdengeçti*s?]	?? 500?		
(The numbers for the last two lines are pure guesses.)			
		= 6,500?	
			= 54,110

* There were 3,000 Egyptians at Belgrade; 1,000 had been assigned to Koca Ibrahim, and, although we do not know the casualties during the siege for the Egyptian rank and file, they were probably heavy; there is also the possibility that some Egyptians had gone home. Thus, 1,000 is probably an absolute maximum.

† Given the admittedly improbable casualties of 16,000 specified for this corps (see end of Appendix II), this figure is extremely unlikely. The number of 2,000 is a pure guess.

Location unknown

Villa or Dilly Ağa of the timariots	[5,000]		
Çirkeşli Celeb Hasan Efendi BB of Temesvár*	[1,000] (900)		
Hasan Arnaut Hocazade BB of Rumelia†	[6,000] (4,500)		
Ahmed, s-b of Tire	[600]		
Ali, s-b of Ankara	[500]		
Aslan, s-b of Nicopolis	[1,000]		
Hasan, s-b of Nigde (in Karaman)	[500]		
Ali, s-b of Brusa	[300]		
Hasan, s-b of Chernomen (Turkish Çirman, in Bulgaria)	[300]		
		=	[13,600]‡ = 10,000?
		=	64,110§

* see Appendix 3 below for the appointment of the very reluctant Hasan. The Benaglia figure is the number of troops at Belgrade for his predecessor, Ahmed.

† Stated in Kreutel & Teply, p.186, as leaving the siege trenches to join forces against the Christians, but no specifics; widely given as reinforcing Koca Ibrahim; see the events of 11 September. In the Benaglia list, his corps was listed as including the timariots of his province.

‡ In Benaglia, the 4,500 for the *beylerbeyi* of Rumelia is the total for the *beylerbeyi and ten beys subordinate to him*; this means that units further down the list such as Nicopolis and Chernomen probably should be included in the 4,500. It is unlikely the troops in this section should number more than 10,000, and may well have been a lot fewer than this.

§ or 74,110 if all Tatars were present, which as noted in Appendix 1, 5.3, I do not believe.

THE OPPOSING FORCES (ORDERS OF BATTLE)

Not counted

Servants not in pay but capable of bearing arms	[20,000]
(unfit for service or left)	
Hungarians under Nadasdy & Draskovich (see Appendix 3)	1,000–2,000?

Forces elsewhere in the theatre

At Raab	
Mustafa P. of Mytilene, BB of Silistria	[1,500] (1,080)
Michael Apafi Prince of Transylvania	[6,000]
North of Danube with Thököly (definite & probable)	
Ahmed P. Kethüda Sarhoş BB of Erlau	[600] (570 + 400 Janissaries)
Mehmed Gürcü P. Moğrulzade, BB. of Grosswardein	[600]
Timariots of Erlau & Grosswardein	??
Thököly & Hungarians	[15,000]
Gönüllü	[5,000]*

* The Ağa of the *Gönüllü*s had been killed at the battle of Bisamberg; it is likely that he had his entire corps with him at the time, since *gönüllü*s, volunteers serving for booty and an opportunity to distinguish themselves in such a way as to win a *timar* or a position in the *kapi kulu*, were best suited for service in the field.

These figures give a total for Kara Mustafa at Vienna of about 64,000 men, or 74,000 if the Tatars were present in full force; the number should probably be reduced even further, since the 6,000 Roumanians were too unreliable to be counted. Such a low total may seem surprising for those who have encountered historians who quote much higher figures, both for this battle and for Ottoman armies generally; but is a reasonable figure, and comes close to the numbers estimated for the Ottomans by reliable and thoughtful eye-witnesses such as Starhemberg the commandant of Vienna (less than 60,000, not counting train and other non-combatants) or Kuniz the Imperialist envoy imprisoned in the Ottoman camp (70,000). Ottoman numbers had always been greatly exaggerated, partly by westerners through mis-understanding of just how many non-combatants trailed round after an Ottoman army, partly by the Ottomans themselves through their willingness to claim huge numbers for their forces – they had a cultural predisposition to grandiloquence, but they also found such exaggeration a useful psychological weapon. However, it is astonishing that anyone ever accepted some of the absurd figures quoted for the Ottomans: totals such as 200,000 or 250,000 or even more were quite ridiculous,[209] for an army so large could never have fed or watered itself – Vienna itself had a peacetime population of 50,000–60,000, and communications around the city, provided the Danube was included, were capable of feeding that many mouths, no more, so the notion that an army four or five times that number, with no established food network and no access at all to the Danube for food deliveries, could have fed itself for two months, is quite absurd. Likewise the figure of 168,000 provided by the 'muster' of 7 September, often accepted by nineteenth-century historians, was inherently improbable, even before its inaccuracies are considered (see chapter 5 above, and Appendix II). The most careful modern historians incline towards figures matching those given here: Wimmer gives the Ottomans 65,000 facing the relief army and 10,000 in the siege works, for a total of 75,000, though he was counting neither the Tatars nor the Roumanians in this; Barker gave very similar figures.[210] Of modern historians only Sobieski's biographer Otto Forst de Battaglia erred on the high side, giving Kara Mustafa 90,000 facing the relief army and 25,000 in the siege works.[211] Not only did Kara Mustafa simply not have access to so many men, it was also impossible for 25,000 men to have occupied the siege works – the Ottomans were only attacking on a two-bastion front, about 600 meters wide, and although within that front they had row after row of trenches, nevertheless the 10,000 men normally agreed for the siege corps would have found things quite crowded, let alone 25,000.

Christian order of battle

The Christian order of battle, at least as far as the German-speakers are concerned, is not as uncertain as the Ottoman, though it is still insufficiently documented. Staff officers of the period usually showed an almost maniacal desire to create plans of camps showing orders of battle, but there were no camps in the Wienerwald, and staffs of the allied army were far too busy in those days of early September 1683 to spend time drawing up such documents – especially since any attempt to put the exact structure of the army into writing would have threatened to revive all the disputes about precedence and bring down the delicate structure of fudges and half-unspoken agreements under which the various rulers had agreed to serve together. So, apart from the records of the allies listing their contingents, there are only two significant sources for the order of battle of the allied army, which have been the basis for most lists produced in the intervening centuries: a graphic produced by the Saxon engineer Suttinger, issued as part of his map of the battle, containing

---

209 Sobieski himself (Plater, p.74) suggested 300,000. His letter to his wife was intended for publication in full or part, and any such statements were part of his attempts to puff up the scale of his victory.
210 Wimmer, *Entsatz*, pp.173, 175; Barker, pp.321, 430 n.105.
211 Forst de Battaglia, pp.173–174.

THE OPPOSING FORCES (ORDERS OF BATTLE)

a generalised version of the order of battle, and lists and notes included in the Diary and Account of Lorraine's secretary Le Bègue, which were almost certainly used by works such as the nineteenth-century official Austrian publication *Das Kriegsjahr 1683* even before their publication in 1933. The original Suttinger is reproduced in various publications, most clearly in Broucek, Hillbrand and Vesely, pp.52–53 (which also usefully shows the modified *Kriegsjahr* version alongside), or Toifel. [212] Neither Suttinger nor Le Bègue is fully trustworthy. The geographical oddities in and omissions from Suttinger's map do not inspire complete confidence in his overall reliability, though he obviously had less scope for mistakes in an order of battle, and he received substantial support from the publication in 1883 by Newald of the 'Relation' of the battle by the Franconian Kreis official Johann Freiherr von Schliz genannt von Görz, which included an appendix with the 'Forme de la Bataille' that, while comparatively slight, agrees with Suttinger in most details except for a few differences in numbers, all but one of them minor (the major one involves giving the Franconians six battalions in the third line, for a total of 13 battalions in the Kreis forces; on this, see Chapter 1). The French title of the document hints that it may have been copied down from an original drawn up by Sobieski, who was using French as the only common language understood by all the allied army's commanders. So, with certain corrections Suttinger can be accepted as giving a good picture of the overall structure of the army, at least as far as concerns the German-speakers – his knowledge of Polish organisation was obviously sketchy. Le Bègue on the other hand gives us several lists, principally of the Imperialist regiments present, ostensibly with much more detail than Suttinger, but he seems to have been less than meticulous when it came to such detail and his lists not only completely omit some regiments known to have been present but also give unreliable figures for the regiments he does include; the constant repetition of the neatly round figure of '10 companies' for every Imperialist cavalry regiment, in particular, is bound to excite suspicion. In any case, it is very unlikely that all of Lorraine's cuirassier and dragoon regiments were at full strength even at the start of the campaign, let alone after the disastrous retreat from the Raab defences in early July and the summer of successful but strenuous campaigning since.

In any case, the two sources are not fully compatible with each other, and even less compatible with the records of the allied contingents – the allies, setting out from peaceful homes with well-ordered contingents, were able to document fairly precisely the troops they sent, but the issue was then further confused by a few shifts between contingents (the Salzburgers moved from the Bavarian contingent to join the Imperialists, a few battalions were lent to the Poles) and the detaching of various corps (Lodron went to Moravia, some soldiers were left behind at Tulln and Greifenstein). Given the weakness of Le Bègue's listings, it is also necessary to take into account the statements of Imperialist regimental histories, published or unpublished, as summarised in Wrede. The best attempt at a full order of battle was made

---

212 Carl Toifel, *Die Türken vor Wien im Jahre 1683* (Prague/Leipzig: Tempsky/Freytag, 1883), Beilage IV.

two centuries after the relief, when the Prussian staff officer Mansberg put together a complete graphical order of battle in the traditional style for the late seventeenth century, and coupled this with a detailed listing of the regiments of all contingents.[213] He failed to get the Poles right, though he was in good company there; but for the rest of the relief army, although he made a few mistakes and some assumptions that are impossible to agree with,[214] he set the standard for any further work. So here are produced two versions of the order of battle: a semi-pictorial version based on the original graphic of Suttinger, mostly as interpreted by *Das Kriegsjahr 1683*, backed up by Schliz von Görz, to show how a contemporary put it, with some corrections and modifications plus the placement of generals in their appropriate positions; and a list based on the graphic and listings of Mansberg, with a smaller number of changes and corrections.

(Note: there is no indication in any order of battle of Hungarian troops in the army, except insofar as the Kéry Croatian Regiment technically counted because Croatia was part of the Crown of Hungary, and CR Pálffy had a Hungarian *Inhaber* and may have included some Hungarians in its ranks (but probably did not);[215] otherwise, Hungarians are usually not mentioned at all, though see Appendix II on the faint possibility a few may have been in the Ottoman army. It is generally accepted that the Palatine of Hungary Pál Esterházy was present with the relief army, probably with Lorraine and his staff. On whether Esterházy might have been accompanied by any troops, see Appendix I, 10.1.)

The Poles are a more difficult question altogether. We have a key source for them, in the documents of the muster of 1 August held before the army left Poland to join Lorraine; the muster listed every unit and counted every man in them, and, within the normal limits imposed by seventeenth-century bureaucratic corruption, seem to have been pretty reliable – much more so than the Ottoman 'muster' of 7 September. Unfortunately, the speed with which Sobieski force-marched his troops across Silesia and Moravia to Austria, even in an army so strong in cavalry and so experienced in using wagons as troop transports, left many men trailing back along the road, with some still catching up weeks and even months later. Some whole units may have fallen behind; other units would have been below their full strength; but we have no documents to give us detailed information on the one or the other. Like the Germans, the Poles had other things on their mind in early–mid-September than compiling lists. According to the muster, about

---

213 Mansberg, foldout sheet, and text, pp.30–47.
214 To cite just one example: he gives the Duke of Sachsen-Weissenfels as commander of a brigade of Saxon cavalry of the first line – even though Sachsen-Weissenfels was an infantry officer, who is recorded in Saxon histories as being in action with the infantry of the first line. We will see in the account of the battle however that Imperialist cavalry generals could command infantry formations, so it is not impossible that the same applied to Saxon ones, especially as the Saxon contingent was rather short of junior infantry generals.
215 CR Pálffy was originally raised in 1672 from 'Croats and Hungarians', though the former probably predominated even then; by the time it was converted into a 'German' cuirassier regiment in 1675, it is unlikely, though not impossible, that the unit contained many Hungarians. Wrede, vol. 3, pp.554-555.

THE OPPOSING FORCES (ORDERS OF BATTLE)

Triumph of King Jan III and Emperor Leopold I. Giuseppe Maria Mitelli, 1683 (National Museum, Warsaw)

34,000 Polish troops had been assembled on 1 August, and Polish historians think 26,000–29,000 set off from Poland (see Chapter 1 above); according to Le Bègue, 3,000 infantry and 12,000 cavalry crossed the Danube, for a total of 15,000.[216] Between these two alternatives, there is much room for debate. A few historians of the nineteenth century hostile to the Poles even tried to drag the Polish total below 15,000, but these were being unfair; Le Bègue himself was almost certainly trying to down-play the role of the Poles in the relief and thus inclined to under-estimate their numbers – and he may also have been making an honest mistake, for Sobieski, despite what he said at Tulln, may well have sneaked some of his shabbier infantry units over the Danube under cover of darkness, so that Le Bègue did not even see them. I am inclined to agree with Wimmer that the real total was around 20,000.[217] Some of these may have fallen out of the ranks in the Wienerwald due to exhaustion during the march through the hills, but the determination of the whole army was so high, there cannot have been enough of these to make a significant difference to the overall figure. However, none of this helps be sure of very much regarding the names of units. Wimmer himself provides some lists, but his own figures elsewhere do not match precisely (for example, he names 20 *chorągiew*s of hussars out of the 25 mustered on 1 August, but

---

216 Wimmer, *Wiedeń 1683*, p.230 for the final total; Stöller, p.34.
217 *Wiedeń 1683*, pp.235–236; also in his *Entsatz*, p.131. Dalérac, vol. 1, p.147, also gave the Poles as 'not' 20,000, i.e. just short of this.

elsewhere stated that 23 *chorągiew*s of hussars fought in the battle.[218] So the best we can do for the Poles is to list the units known to be present, fleshed out with details from the 1 August muster, which for the hussars and *pancerni* not only listed all *chorągiew*s with their strengths but also indicated to which *pułk* they were assigned (unfortunately it omitted some *pancerni* and did not give the *pułk*s for the light cavalry at all). In the list below, units shown in clear were listed by Wimmer as definitively in the battle; those in square brackets *may* have been present, but we do not know. The numbers of men are from the 1 August muster and are purely indicative, to give an impression of the normal sizes of the squadrons or battalions in the Polish army – the infantry in particular, although not as weak as Le Bègue thought, were almost certainly well under strength, and Polish foot regiments were normally quite weak by western standards anyway, so each brigade should be thought of as a battalion-sized formation.[219] Information on generals is unclear; names have been placed with troops only when absolutely certain, the rest are listed at the end (see also the Suttinger order of battle, next).

---

218 For the lists of units in the battle, see following note. For Wimmer's contradictory numbers see his *Entsatz*, p.131. This gave in total for the cavalry: 23 hussar units making 2670 men, 3 arquebusier units making 530, 53 pancerni units (out of 84 in the muster) making 5,100, 26 light cavalry squadrons (out of 28 in the muster) making 1,900, and 6 dragoon regiments plus an extra company [Marcin Kątski's free company?] (out of 9 regiments and a free company in the muster) making 2,800, for a grand total of 13,150. I have reservations about the numbers of light cavalry: Brulig's list of the Polish army passing Raygern Monastery (Dudik, pp.424–426) *could* be read as describing the light cavalry as 'Cossacken' or 'zu pferdt', with 'reütter' (older form of modern German 'Reiter', cavalryman) restricted to the armoured hussars and *pancerni*, in which case it suggests that most of the light cavalry did not even pass Raygern until after the battle.

219 Extracted from Wimmer, *Wiedeń 1683*, pp.325–327, modified, supplemented or noted from the same, pp.219 ff. (the muster of 1 August). This has been in varying degrees supported by other histories: the article of Adam Przyboś, 'Die Waffenbrüder König Jans III. Sobieski im Jahre 1683', *Studia Austro-Polonica*, 3 (1983), pp.241–256; *Das Kriegsjahr 1683*, pp.234–236; Mansberg, pp.47–54; Dolleczek 'Polnische Armee', pp.127–130; also Dolleczek 'Entsatzschlacht', pp.174–175 (citing Kochowski, Daleyrac and Rubinkowski, although German accounts of the late nineteenth century were mostly following the work of the Polish historian Kluczycki). Where variant spellings are possible for a name, Wimmer's Polish edition has always been preferred. Regrettably, Paradowski does not provide full order-of-battle details for the Poles; the nearest is his Appendix IV (pp.210–215), which lists the official strengths (usually very different from those here) for most Polish cavalry units at the start of the 1683 campaign alongside almost-always identical figures for the start of the 1684 campaign.

THE OPPOSING FORCES (ORDERS OF BATTLE)

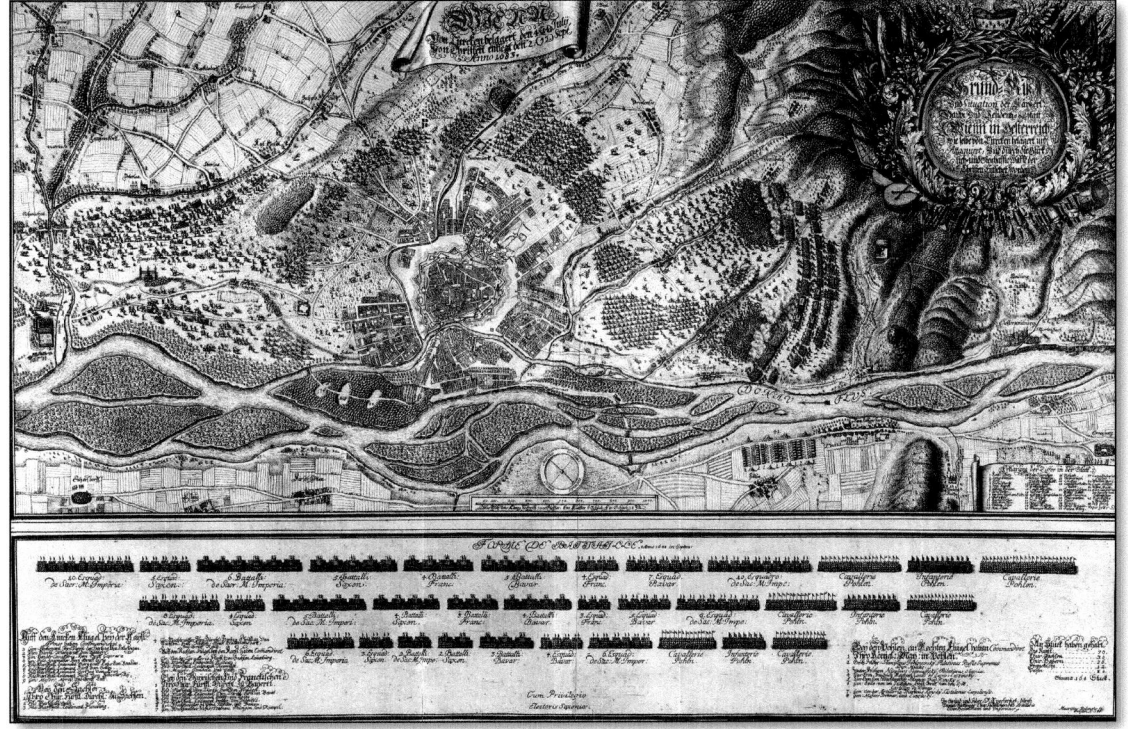

The 'Suttinger' order of battle (see text); drawn by Daniel Suttinger, engraved by Moritz (Mauritius) Bodenehr, 1688. (Wien Museum Inv.-Nr 57188, CC0)

The Suttinger-based order of battle

From the Suttinger print; with placement of generals (whom Suttinger listed separately) generally but not always according to the version in *Das Kriegsjahr 1683*, and modified to separate Sachsen-Lauenburg from Waldeck into a distinct 'right wing' (though I am almost certain that both *Das Kriegsjahr 1683* and Mansberg got it wrong in putting Dünewald under Sachsen-Lauenburg); the Poles are also shown according to *Das Kriegsjahr 1683*, not Suttinger who merely drew them as undifferentiated blocks of cavalry and infantry. Suttinger and *Das Kriegsjahr 1683* disagreed occasionally on the number of battalions or squadrons; I have selected what seems to be the correct number in each case. Where groups of units are listed directly below another, they should be regarded as placed to the right of the former (e.g. the 10 Imperialist squadrons of Baden's brigade were on the extreme left wing with the 5 Saxon squadrons next in. NB: according to Hassel and Vitzthum von Eckstädt (p.144), John George III directly commanded the Saxon *cavalry* of the first line, and he mostly remained with them. I have omitted the otherwise completely-unknown 'GWM Buttler' who pops up in the *Das Kriegsjahr 1683* version in the 3rd line of Sachsen-Lauenburg's wing.

NO MORE TIME TO LOSE

CinC
King John III Sobieski of Poland

	Left wing Lorraine		Corps de bataille FM Waldeck		Right wing GdC S-Lauenburg		Extreme right wing CGH Jabłonowski CFH Sieniawski	
1st Line			John George III of Sax.	(Maximilian Emanuel of Bavaria)				
GdC Caprara	FM Hermann of Baden	FM Goltz		GWM Münster			BG M. Matczyński	BG Stan. Potocki
FML LW Baden	FML Croy	GWM Sachsen-Weissenfels	FML Bayreuth	GWM Beauvau	FML Dünewald	BG Zamoyski		
=========	=====	=========	=========	=========	=========	=========	=========	=========
10 Imp. sq. (1) 5 Sax. sq. (2)	6 Imp. bns (3)	5 Sax. bns. (4)	4 bns Reichs (13) 5 bns Bav. (14)	4 Reichs sq. (15) 7 Bav. sq. (16)	10 Imp. sq. (20)	4 inf. bdes	Hussar division	Pancerni
2nd Line			FML v.d. Leyen		FML Rabatta		Gen'l M. Kątski	
FML Lubomirski	FZM Leslie	GWM Neitschütz	GWM z.Fuss Steinau GWM z.Fuss Thüngen		GWM Pálffy		BG Comte de Maligny BG J. Gorczynski	
=========	=====	=========	=========		=========	=========	=========	
8 Imp. sq. (5)	5 Imp. bns (7)	4 Sax. bns (8)	4 bns Reichs, 4 bns Bav. (S: 3 Franc.) (17)		8 Imp. sq. (21)	4 inf. bdes	6,000 dragoons	
			3 sq. Reichs, 5 sq. Bav. (18)					
						BG Butler		
						BG Dänemark		
4 Sax. sq. (6)								
3rd line								
GWM Mercy		GWM Trautmannsdorf	FML Degenfeld					
GWM Taafe	FML Fürst Salm	GWM Reuss	GWM z.Fuss Rummel		GWM Gondola		C.G. Camp Mstr M. Chełmski	
=========	=====	=========	=========		=========		=========	
6 Imp. sq. (9) 3 Sax. sq. (10)	2 Imp. bns (11)	2 Sax. bns (12)	3 bns Bav. (19)	4 Bav. sq. (19)	6 Imp. sq. (22)		15 hsr & *pancerni* sq.	

THE OPPOSING FORCES (ORDERS OF BATTLE)

The Mansberg/Wimmer order of battle

Each brigade, from left to right, and within each brigade, from left to right, numbers in parentheses at the start of each brigade match brigades in this list to the Suttinger order of battle above; due to the divergences between the two versions, a few numbers appear twice. There are *irreconcilable differences* between Mansberg and the assignment of generals in Suttinger and *Das Kriegsjahr 1683* as shown above.

The 'Germans'.

Lorraine's wing.		
(informal advance guard)		
	GWM Fontaine	
		Parella (1 bn)
		Fontaine (1 bn) (both 'international volunteers)
1st line		
	(1) Louis Wilhelm von Baden brigade (Imperialist)	
		Heissler DR (2 sqns)
		Styrum DR* (2 sqns)
		Halleweil CR (2 sqns)
		Mercy CR (2 sqns)
		Caprara CR (2 sqns)
	(2) Christian von Sachsen-Weissenfels brigade (Saxon)	
		Reuss DR† (3 sqns)
		Leib CR (1 sqn)
		Trabanten ‡ (1 sqn)
	(3) Croy brigade (Imperialist)	
		Croy IR (2 bns)
		Baden IR (2 bns)
		Grana IR (2 bns)
	(4) Flemming brigade (Saxon)	
		Flemming (2 bns)
		Goltz (1 bn)
		Leib (2 bns)

NO MORE TIME TO LOSE

2nd line		
	(5) Lubomirski brigade (Imperialist-Polish)	
		Königsegg DR (2 sqns)
		Tetuin Cavalry (2 sqns)
		Lubomirski Cavalry (2 sqns)
		Pancerni (2 sqns)
		Polish hussars (3 sqns, under ? Chrzanowski)§
		Jan Oginski (?)
		Jan Gninski (118 men)
		Jan Cetner (100 men)
	(6) Trautmannsdorff brigade (Saxon)	
		Trautmannsdorff CR (2 sqns)
		Goltz CR (2 sqns)
	(7) Leslie brigade (Imperialist & Salzburg)	
		Steinsdorff IR (2 bns, Salzburg)
		Daun IR (1 bn)
		Lorraine IR (1 bn)
		Leslie IR (1 bn)
	(8) Reuss brigade (Saxon)	
		Grenadiers (1 coy)
		Kuffer IR (2 bns)
		Weissenfels IR (2 bns)
3rd line		
	(9) Taafe brigade (Imperialist)	
		Piccolomini CR (3 sqns)
		Taafe CR (3 sqns)
	(10) Neidschütz brigade (Saxon)	
		Plotho CR (3 sqns)
	(11) Salm brigade (Imperialist)	
		Thim IR (1 bn)
		Beck IR (1 bn)
	(12) ?? brigade (Saxon)	
		Löben (2 bns)

THE OPPOSING FORCES (ORDERS OF BATTLE)

Centre.		
1st line		
	(13) v.d. Leyen brigade (Reichs)	
		Pallandt bn. (Hanoverian, 1 bn)
		Württemberg IR (1 bn)
		Von der Leyen IR (2 bns)
	(14) Degenfeld brigade (Bavarian)		
		La Perouse (2 bns)
		Degenfeld (2 bns)
	(15) Bayreuth brigade (Reichs)	
		Schutzbar DR (2 sqns)
		Bayreuth CR (2 sqns)
	(16) Münster brigade (Bavarian)	
		Red dragoon sqn (2 sqns)
		Münster CR (3 sqns)
		Blue dragoon sqn (2 sqns)
2nd line		
	(17) Thüngen brigade (Reichs)¶	
		Andlau IR (1 bn?)
		Thüngen IR (2 bns)
		Hildburghausen IR (1 bn)
	(17) Steinau brigade (Bavarian)	
		Preysing IR (2 bns)
		Steinau IR (2 bns)
	(18) ?? brigade (Reichs)	
		Hedesdorf drag. (1 sqn)
		Hohenzollern-Hechingen CR (2 sqns)
	(18) Beauvau brigade (Bavarian)	
		Arco CR (3 sqns)
		Beauvau CR (3 sqns)

3rd line			
	(19) Rummel brigade (Bavarian / Bavarian-Kreis)		
		Mercy IR ** (1 bn)	
		Kreis-regt Rummel (1 bn)	
	(19) ?? brigade (Bavarian / Reichs)		
		Hamilton sqn of Kreis cuirassiers (1 coy.)	
		Schütz CR (Bavarian, 3 sqns)	

<u>Sachsen-Lauenburg's right wing.</u>

1st line			
	(20) Rabatta brigade (Imperialist)		
		Rabatta CR (2 sqns)	
		Sachsen Lauenburg CR (3 sqns)	
		Kueffstein DR (2 sqns)	
		Schulz DR†† (2 sqns)	
2nd line			
	(21) Dünewald brigade (Imperialist)		
		Montecuccoli CR (2 sqns)	
		Gondola CR (2 sqns)	
		Carafa CR (2 sqns)	
		Dünewald CR (2 sqns)	
3rd line			
	(22) Pálffy brigade (Imperialist)		
		Kéry CrR (3 sqns)	
		Götz CR (2 sqns)	
		Pálffy CR (2 sqns)	

* Mansberg puts Kueffstein here; accounts of the battle suggest that Kueffstein may have been under Sachsen-Lauenburg and DR Styrum should be here; but this is not certain – there are also indications that Styrum *was* in the right wing.

† The 'Saxon account' in *Aufrichtige und unpartheyische Relation*, p.10, also in *Theatrum Europaeum*, puts the Saxon dragoons in the second line.

‡ Mansberg's pictorial 'Schlachtordnung' in a foldout puts this in the third line with CR Plotho, but the squadron counts quoted otherwise do not match this. In any case, as will be seen below in the account of the battle, the Elector used them as his personal guard, regardless of their formal position.

§ The three hussar *chorągiew*s and their commander specified in Mansberg, p.49; two of the squadrons are identified in the 1 August list (Cetner's as part of the royal *pułk*) but there is no trace in the list of Ogiński, and since the Ogińskis were Lithuanians and the Lithuanian army had not even left Poland, this is doubtful. Le Bègue confirmed (Stöller, p.33) that 'some' squadrons had been joined to Lubomirski's corps by Sobieski.

| According to Suttinger, 5 battalions. Since Suttinger under-estimates the number of Franconian battalions next to the Bavarians in the line, the figures become more sensible if we simply shift one battalion along from the Bavarians to the Franconians.

¶ Only 3 battalions according to Suttinger.

** According to Dauer, p.47, the Mercy IR actually had 1 battalion each in the first two lines.

†† see previous note on Kueffstein DR.

The Poles

Right Flank Guard (Crown Standard-Bearer Rafał Leszczyński)					
(exact composition unknown; compare his *pułk* below, and note in Chapter 11 section 'Advance and deployment of the Poles'.)					
Right Wing (CGH Jabłonowski)					
	Cavalry:				
		Hetman's *pułk*			
			Hussars		
				Jabłonowski	200
				S. Małachowski	118
				W. Leszczynski	91
				[J.D. Krasiński	128]
				[F. Bieliński	118]
			Pancerni:		
				Jabłonowski	192
				F. Dzieduszycki	90
				J. Słuszka	98
				A. Chodorowski	95
				J. Stadnicki	104
				M. Rzewuski	119
				[S. Czarniecki	121]
				[A. Sierakowski	118]
				[S. Ledóchowski	91]
				[J. Szumlański	88]
				[S. Grudziński	60]
		K. Wiśniowiecki's *pułk*			
			Pancerni:		
				Wiśniowiecki	145
				[J. Mniszcha	117]
				[J. Gyżycki	100]
				[A. Radliński	73]
				[S. Witwicki	90]
		S. Bidziński's *pułk*			
			Pancerni:		
				Bidziński	134
				S. Tarły	96
				[S.S. Łaźiński	91]
				[M. Ubysz	100]

THE OPPOSING FORCES (ORDERS OF BATTLE)

		R. Leszczyński's *pułk*			
			[Hussars]:*		
				Leszczyński	133
			Pancerni:		
				[J. Rokitnicki]	65]
				[W. Łubieński]	100]
			Light cavalry:		
				('several chor.')	??
		M. Zbrożki's *pułk*			
			Pancerni:		
				[Zbrożki]	128]
				[J. Skarżyński]	100]
			Light cavalry:		
				(unknown no. of chor.)	??
		A. Miączynski's *pułk*			
			Pancerni:		
				Atanezego Miączynski	136
				[Andrzej Miączynski]	78]
				[Stanisław Miączynski]	72]
			Light cavalry:		
				(unknown no. of chor., possibly up to 7)	??
		Jabłonowski Arquebusiers			100
		Total: 4 chor. hussars, 20-22 *pancerni*, 13-14 light			
	Infantry (BGs Dönhoff, Zamoyski):				
		Dönhoff or 'Royal' brigade			
			King's Guards (Ernst Dönhoff; Col. Bernsfejer)		597
			Crown Prince Jakub (Col. Otto Seswegen)		545
		S. Morstin brigade			
			Queen's Gds (Morstin; Col. Gerard Tegenhoff)		380
			Wacław Szczuka (Col. Weretycz)		276
		E. Łącki brigade			
			Łącki (Col. Franciszek Lanckoronski)		290
			Wacław Leszczyński (Col. Tobiasz Knobelsdorff)		308
		F. Gröben brigade			
			Gröben (lt.col. Jerzy Guttry) [fig. specif. is full strength]		380
			Jabłonowski (Col. Jakub Berens) [off'l strength 590]		580
			J.D. Krasiński (Col. Tyburce Żórawski)		300
		+ 1 Imperialist, 1 Saxon and 1 Bavarian battalion (probably ½ IR Neuburg, possibly ½ IR Goltz, probably ½ IR Mercy)†			

		Dragoons (BGs Louis d'Arquien comte de Maligny, Jan Górzyński):‡		
			Guards of the King *pułk* (Col.: Franciszka Gałecki)	600
			Guards of the King [2] or Maligny's *pułk* (Col.: Maligny)	355
			Jabłonowski's *pułk* (Col. Jerzy Taube)	568
			Bidzyński's *pułk* (Col. Jan Koszkiel)	600
			Chełmski's *pułk* (Col. ?)	302
			A. Potocki's *pułk* (Col. ? (not listed at all in Wimmer)	?
Centre (King John III Sobieski)				
	Cavalry:			
		King's *pułk* (cmdr: Kazimierz Prusinowski, *starost* of Horodła):		
			10 chorągiew husssars:	
				King's	159
				Prince Jakob's	184
				Prince Aleksander's	149
				M. Zamoyski	150
				S. Prażmowski	108
				J. Wielopolski (formerly Morstin)	131
				M. Warszycki	135
				J. Lubomirski	124
				S. Branicki	144
				M. Cieński	71
			10 chor. *pancerni*:	
				[King's	190]
				[M. Sapieha	92]
				[M. Daniłowicz	118]
				[M. Warszycki	112]
				[W. Prażmowski	90]
				[J. Lubomirski	140]
				[J. Koniecpolski	107]
				[S. Druszkiewicz	105]
				[A. Rzeczycki	105]
				[M. Zamoyski	120]
		Royal Regt. of Arquebusiers (a.k.a. Guard Drabant-Reiters); Col.: Jan Górzyński§		293
		[Cossack detachment; Col. Apostoł Paweł Szczurowski]		150]
		[are also references¶ to an unspecified number of 'royal Tatars' (light cavalry)]		
	Infantry:			
		Guard Janissaries		
		Guard Haiduks		
		(Numbers are uncertain, as the small royal guard units were maintained by the king out of his own pocket and did not appear in the muster of 1 August, although a new company of Janissaries was listed. Many historians** give one company of Haiduks ('Hungarian infantry') and one of Janissaries, at about 100 men each for a total of 200; some suggest that more may have been present.)		

THE OPPOSING FORCES (ORDERS OF BATTLE)

Left Wing (CFH Sieniawski)						
	Cavalry:					
		Hetman's *pułk*				
			Hussars:			
					Sieniawski	200
					S. Dąbski	97
					S. Lubomirski	120
					J. Myszkowski	96
					[W. Urbański	112]
			Pancerni:			
					Sieniawski	200
					S. Opaliński	108
					F. Makowiecki	100
					[M. Czartoryski	121]
					[K. Łużecki	131]
					[A.M. Sieniawski	134]
					[S. Cetner	81]
					[M. Bogusz	117]
					[M. Grudziński	118]
					[F. Koryciński	120]
		A. Potocki's *pułk*				
			Hussars:			
					Potocki	121
			Pancerni:			
					[Potocki	111]
					[A. Modrzewski	119]
					[Stan. Potocki	86]
					[N. Żaboklicki	111]
					[W. Bykowski	81]
		Szczęsny (Felix) Potocki's *pułk*				
			Hussars:			
					Potocki	120
			Pancerni:			
					[Potocki	107]
					[M. Wasilkowski	92]
					[H. Lanckoroński	99]
		T. Karczewski's *pułk*				
			Pancerni:			
					[Karczewski	114]
					[A. Dymidecki	91]
			Light cavalry:			
					(unknown no. of chor.)	??

		M. Radecki's *pułk*			
			Pancerni:		
				[D. Zabokrzycki]	100]
				[W. Stępkowski]	85]
			Light cavalry:		
				(unknown no. of chor.)	??
		Total: 6 chor. hussars, 16-18 *pancerni*, 12-13 light			
		Sieniawski's Arquebusiers (1 sqn)			197
	Infantry (BGs Jan Butler, Jan Dennemark):				
		J. Butler brigade††			
			Butler (Col.: the Inhaber) [off'l strength 180]		179
			Kątski (Col. Henryk Henrykoswki) [at off'l strength]		590
		J. Dennemark brigade			
			Dennemark (lt.col. Salomon von Sacken)		346
			A. Potocki (Col. Jan Cetner) [shown at full strength]		380
			H. Lubomirski (Col.: ?) ‡‡		343
			Maligny (Col.: Franciszek Kożuchowski)		321
		K. Zamoyski brigade			
			Kaz. Zamoyski (Col. Aleksandr Domaradzki)		254
			M. Zamoyski §§ (Col.: Wilhelm Dobszyc)		340
			J. Gniński (Col.: Teodor Frank)		311
		Eliasz Krauze brigade ‖			
			J. Wielopolski (Col.: Eliasz Krauze) [shown at full strength]		390
			M. Sieniawski (Col. Aswerus Wrzospolski) [off'l strength 590]		453
			W. Dönhoff (Col.: Otto Fabian Felkersamb) [off'l strength 390]		399 [?]
		+ 1 Franconian battalion (possibly IR Köth von Wanscheid)			

* Wimmer, *Wiedeń 1683*, p.325 actually says his squadron of *pancerni*, but there is no trace of such a *pancerni* unit in the 1 August list.

† Mansberg p.57, incl. n.34. Since the regimental history of Mercy's (later the Leib Regiment) did not mention serving with Poles, I doubt the last name (Dauer, p.47, says that when the army set off Mercy's 'apparently' had one battalion in each of the first two lines, and mentions no change in this).

‡ In addition to the usual mis-representation of the Polish dragoons as 6,000 strong, there is much disagreement over the regiments and their colonels. The colonel of the first regiment (here following Wimmer) is sometimes shown as Jan Górzyński. *Das Kriegsjahr 1683* (p.235) and Dolleczek, Anton, 'Die polnische Armee im XVII Jahrhundert: ihre Einrichtung, Gliederung und Kampfweise, mit besonderer Berücksichtigung der... bei dem Entsatze von Wien betheiligt gewesenen polnischen Truppen', *(Streffleur's)*

Österreichisches Militärische Zeitschrift 24.iii (1883), pp.105–130, here p.129, give the 6 regiments as: King's, Queen's (Gałecki), Georg Taube, Friedrich Strem, Johann Kokel (or Koskel), Andreas Chełmski.

§ Górzyński is sometimes (e.g. by Mansberg, p.53) given as commander of the guard infantry detachments.

| Placement here conjectural. The Cossacks were not in the 1 August list; their strength is usually quoted by historians as about 150, but sometimes as high as 200.

¶ Wimmer, *Entsatz*, p.215. Compare Brzezinski, Richard, *Polish armies 1569-1696*, colour plates by Angus McBride (Men at arms 184, 188) (London: Osprey, 1987), vol. 2, p.12.

** *Das Kriegsjahr 1683*, p.235; Dolleczek, 'Entsatzschlacht', p.174; Mansberg, p.53; supported by the slightly ambiguous statement in Wimmer, *Wiedeń*, p.327. Brzezinski however states (vol. 2, p.12) that both the extant companies of Janissaries were present, and Brulig (Dudik, p.425) did report seeing pass Raygern on 30 August one unit of Haiduks at 100 men and two units of Janissaries making 200 men.

†† Mansberg, p.53, defines this formation as the 'artillery *pułk*'; he says it was a permanent formation for artillery protection, and that the *pułk* was under 'Colonel Butler & Lt.Col. Fink', then says there were 28 guns under Colonel Herychowski & Lt.Col. Rutkowski. *Das Kriegsjahr 1683* & Dolleczek 'Entsatzschlacht' define the Kątski regiment as 'zur Geschützbedienung'; Dolleczek 'Entatzschlacht', p.175, says the artillery was under Kątski overall, but directly under Col. Fink. None of this is mentioned in Dolleczek 'Polnische Armee' (p.129).

‡‡ according to *Das Kriegsjahr 1683* & Dolleczek 'Entsatzschlacht', the Inhaber; no colonel mentioned in Mansberg or Wimmer (1 August), and Lubomirski, with his position in Lorraine's wing, was hardly likely to have commanded it himself.

§§ Not in the lists in *Das Kriegsjahr 1683* or Dolleczek, 'Entsatzschlacht'.

|| Mansberg (p.53) adds to the Krauze brigade the regiment of the 'Untermarschall' of Lithuania, colonel unknown; there is no trace of such a regiment in the 1 August list recorded in Wimmer.

Artillery:
28 guns (5 or 6 field guns and the rest very light, according to Dalérac[220]).

Serving with the Imperialists.
See Lubomirski's brigade above.

Generals (where not already listed).[221]
> Crown Grand Guard Stefan Bidziński (sometimes shown as one of the BGs of light cavalry; see below)
> Lieutenant-General of the 'Germans' Ernst Graf Dönhoff (see above as BG)
> Crown General of Artillery Marcin Kazimierz Kątski (= *starszy nad armatą*; ? – compare Suttinger order of battle)
> Crown Military Guard Michał Zbrożek (*strażnik wojskowy*)
> Crown Grand Camp-Master Marcjan Chełmski, (*obozny wielki*; shown by Wimmer as a MG)
> Crown Military Camp-Master Tomasz Karczewski (*oboźny wojskowy*)
> Crown Grand Master of the Horse Marek Matczyński (*koniusz wielki koronny*)

Major-Generals/Brigadiers (other):
> Eliasz Łącki
> Kazimierz Zamoyski
> Fryderyk Gröben
> Szczęsny (Felix) Potocki[222]

Many of the 'brigades' listed above appear to have been commanded by colonels, but even allowing for this, this list is by no means complete.

Supposed Brigadiers of light cavalry:
> Stefan Bidziński (see above)
> 'Montreoski' (no trace)[223]
> 'Mioszenki' (possibly a reference to Miączyński's *pułk* ;
> see Right wing)
> Crown Clerk Stefan Czarniecki (*pisarz koronny*)

---

220 vol. 1, pp.136–137. Father Brulig at Raygern counted 30 'great pieces' going past with Jabłonowski on 30 August; his figures are wildly inaccurate for the numbers of soldiers, but it is reasonable to assume he was able to count cannon more accurately.

221 From Wimmer; *Das Kriegsjahr 1683*, 234; and Dolleczek, 'Polnische Armee', p.127; with additions and corrections based on accounts of the battle. References to the brigadiers of light cavalry from Mansberg, p.52; the same names (with some differences in spelling) are identified in *Das Kriegsjahr 1683*, p.235, and Dolleczek, 'Entsatzschlacht', p.174, as colonels of big regiments of 'Vlach' or 'Cossack' regiments not otherwise appearing in reliable works.

222 *Das Kriegsjahr 1683*, p.239, puts Potocki the *starost* (sheriff) of Halicz as a general in its crude version of the order of battle; but the *starost* of Halicz was Stanisław Potocki, a young officer (24 years old) commanding a *chorągiew* of *pancerni* in the *pułk* of his father Andrzej (who was at home); his uncle Szczęsny, *wojewoda* (provincial governor) of Cracow, aged 53, was far more likely as a general officer.

223 a couple of captains of light cavalry *chorągiew*s at the 1 August muster are potential matches: Wojciech Mąkolski and Jan Modzelowski; see Wimmer, *Wiedeń*, p.226, and Paradowski, p.81.

THE OPPOSING FORCES (ORDERS OF BATTLE)

Similar names are sometimes listed as colonels of light cavalry regiments: Miszlinewski, Semen, Butyko and Ystrycki (or Yskrzycki). None of these names, nor anything like any one of them, appears in Wimmer or Paradowski.

Numbers summary

Allies

Contingent	Infantry	Cavalry	Artillery	Totals
Imperialists	14 bns, incl. Salzburgers 8,000, + 600 vols.	48 sqns (Lorraine & S-L.) 12,300, incl. Lubomirski but excl. Poles lent by Sobieski	70 (official) 30 (probable) personnel n/k	20,900
Bavarians	11 bns incl. Kreis 7,500	16 sqns 3,000	16 guns 305 personnel	10,805
Saxons	12 bns 7,000	12 or 14 sqns 2,500	12 guns 80 personnel	9,580
Reichs	8 or 11 bns 7,000	7 sqns 1,200	10 or 12 guns 100 personnel	8,300
[German non-Imperialist total	31 or 34 bns 21,500	35 or 37 sqns 6,700	38 or 40 guns 485 personnel	28,685]
Poles	3,000 (according to most); 7,650 (Wimmer)	14,000 (according to most); 10,350 cavalry, 2,800 dragoons, = 13,150 (Wimmer) Others give anywhere from 12,000 to 17,000.	28 or 30 guns 150 personnel.	17,000 (most); 20,950 (Wimmer)
Totals	33,100 or 37,750 (depending on nos. of Poles) 44 bns excl. Poles	33,000 86 sqns excl. Poles	96 or 98 guns 635 personnel (+ Imp.)	66,735 or 71,385 (depending on nos. of Polish inf.) + Imp. arty

NB: the battalions lent to the Poles are still counted here with their parent contingents.

Ottomans

Location	Infantry	Cavalry/uncertain	Artillery	Totals
Right wing	6,500	3,000 regular, 18,900 irregular, + 1,500 extras		29,900
Centre	1,500 (guess)	4,000 regular, 1,500 KM hshld		7,000
Left wing	-	4,300 irregular (if only 2,300 Ta.) or 14,300 (if 12,000 Ta.)		4,300 or 14,300
Prater	?	?		6,400
Siege works	6,500			?
Location unknown		10,000		10,000
			60 light guns 2 8-pdrs	
Totals (if most Ta. gone)				64,100
Totals (if Ta. present)				74,100

Plate A. Ottoman Kapi Kulu Sipahi Cavalryman
Illustration by Sergey Shamenkov © Helion & Company.
See Colour Plate Captions for further information.

Plate B. Ottoman Janissary
Illustration by Sergey Shamenkov © Helion & Company.
See Colour Plate Captions for further information.

Plate C. Polish Infantryman
Illustration by Sergey Shamenkov © Helion & Company.
See Colour Plate Captions for further information.

Plate D. Polish Winged Hussar
Illustration by Sergey Shamenkov © Helion & Company.
See Colour Plate Captions for further information.

Plate E. Imperialist or Bavarian Grenadier
Illustration by Sergey Shamenkov © Helion & Company.
See Colour Plate Captions for further information.

Plate F. Imperialist Cuirassier
Illustration by Sergey Shamenkov © Helion & Company.
See Colour Plate Captions for further information.

Plate G. Ottoman Timariot Sipahi Cavalryman
Illustration by Sergey Shamenkov © Helion & Company.
See Colour Plate Captions for further information.

Plate H. Ottoman Balkan Yerli Kulu Infantryman
Illustration by Sergey Shamenkov © Helion & Company.
See Colour Plate Captions for further information.

11

The Battle of Kahlenberg

Beginning of the battle on the left: the fight for the exit from the woods

Few men in the Christian army got much sleep that night. Around 4 a.m., while it was still dark, Sobieski finished his letter to his wife and prepared to come across to the left wing again, and all along the line religious services were held for the soldiers.[224] Once these were finished, the troops began to move into their positions ready for resuming the advance, and awaited orders, except for those men still hard at work under Fontaine constructing 'Leslie's battery' on the lower Kahlenberg to support the debouchment from the woods.

The battle was certain to begin on the left wing, where Lorraine commanded his 13 battalions of Imperialist infantry, 2 battalions of volunteers, and 24 squadrons of Imperialist cavalry, all of them comparatively under-strength, together with the 11 battalions and 12–14 squadrons of Saxons, all of these at or close to full strength.[225] The cavalry were mostly in a column on the road along the river, the extreme flank of the whole allied army; the infantry, and many if not all of the dragoons, were on the hills 'inside' them, the Emperor's troops of course on the left, nearest the cavalry, and the Elector's to their right, towards the centre of the order of battle, stretching as far as the head of the Wildgrube ravine, theoretically in contact with Waldeck's corps. No-one was in proper battle-formation yet, as the ground still made this impossible.[226] Although this is nowhere stated in the sources, it seems that the bulk of the Imperialist infantry was concentrated in the saddle between the Leopoldsberg and Kahlenberg, some units perhaps stretching out to their left across the lower slopes of the Leopoldsberg towards the cavalry column but not in real military 'contact' with it; the steeper slopes of the Leopoldsberg

---

224 The services, for the German-speakers at least, are usually timed at 4 a.m.; a Bavarian letter a few days later (Newald, vol. 2, p.96) referred to services held by d'Aviano at 3 a.m.
225 This is not counting the one battalion of Saxons lent to Sobieski.
226 Schliz von Görz, in Newald, vol. 2, p.100, makes clear that the action started before the army was in a regular order.

made them impractical for a formed advance, and the Imperialist infantry would come out of the saddle, covered by Leslie's battery, and extend to the Danube once out in the open.

Lorraine was determined to fight today, but no-one on the left wing was expecting the action to start quite this early, for it was yet dark and the last of the artillery was still being dragged over the saddle to join the troops just beyond the crest-line;[227] so far no guns had even been placed in Leslie's battery. However, during the night the Turks had heard the noise of the construction of the battery at the edge of the wood and of the troops being sent down the hill to do the work and support it, and they had decided to stop it. Around 5 a.m., before light had touched the sky, an advanced force, probably detached from Kara Mehmed's corps, assembled under cover of a small height, sometimes identified as the Nussberg but more likely to have been the lesser unnamed hill between the Nussberg and the Danube, south-west of Kahlen. If the 'Baden account' is to be believed, there were about 1,200 men in the body.[228] It is not clear who their commander was, but he may have been the strangely-named Osmanoğlu Pasha, *sancak-bey* of Kütahya.[229] They advanced through the dark vineyards on the northern foot of the Nussberg across the low ground towards the rising slopes of the Kahlenberg and the battery; here, they reached the toughest of the barriers erected by the Austrian villagers against depredations by wild animals, an embankment topped by planks which some witnesses described as a palisade – showing not only that it formed a serious obstacle in the eyes of experienced military men but also that the wooden planks were placed vertically in the ground with a gap between each (no-one would have used the word 'palisade' if it had been in the style of a rail fence). From behind the cover of this, they began to pepper the labouring German soldiers with wild musket-fire – not very effective at long range and in the dark, but a hindrance nevertheless.[230] Fontaine had his men stop work and assembled them in formation in front of the battery, making about two battalions in total, probably including some of his noble volunteers; and these began to fire back at the Turks behind their barrier.

By this time, the sun was rising, and, although a light autumn-morning mist appeared at about the same time, Lorraine and the other commanders watching from the monastery on the Kahlenberg were soon aware that other Turks were deploying as well, moving up from their night camps to form a continuous line on either side of the forward detachment, towards the Danube on their right and on their left the Schreiberbach and beyond

---

227 Le Bègue in his Diary (Stöller, p.101) states that it arrived at 6 a.m. – but this version, in contrast to his Account and to most other witnesses, puts the start of the action at 7 a.m.; it is more likely that his sequence of events is correct but the exact times are wrong, especially as he clearly puts the arrival of the artillery before the start of the action.
228 The 'Baden account', in Röder, vol. 1, Urk., p.16. The writer actually said 1,200 *Janissaries*; as he was not apparently one of those who called *all* Turkish infantry Janissaries, this might be an accurate indication.
229 On the identification of Osmanoğlu, see Appendix I, 11.1.
230 No source actually refers to Turkish *fire*, only to their harassment of the work from the embankment; but they could only have harassed by missile weapons, and firearms predominated over the bow by this period. Likewise, no-one explicitly states that Fontaine returned fire.

it the Krapfenwaldl, so that they appeared to be trying to 'gain the flanks' of Fontaine's little brigade. Fontaine however kept his men far enough back from the embankment that, with his rear close to the woods behind him, his flanks were under no serious threat; Le Bègue noted that he gave himself 'room to be able to take some measures to prevent himself from being enveloped by the enemy',[231] which implies some deliberate formation, perhaps one with the two ends of his line curling back to the edge of the woods. Neither side could have been losing many men as they continued to pop away at each other in the mist. Nevertheless, Fontaine was under increasing threat.

Relief of Vienna, with monarchs and main commanders leading the troops. Emperor Leopold I and Sultan Mehmed IV, despite not being present, are also depicted here (middle of the top row). Joachim Wichmann, after 1683 (Wien Museum Inv.-Nr. 31208, CC0)

Lorraine reacted promptly: several battalions from the regiments closest to this point were ordered down from their night positions, under FML the duc de Croy, to support Fontaine directly, and about the same time or very soon after (it was now about 6 a.m.), a general advance was ordered of the entire left wing, by making the agreed signal of five cannon-shots from the guns on top of the hills.[232] Croy quickly united with Fontaine and was soon extending his front to left and right matching the Turks, with more Imperialists heading to join his left and Saxons to join his right towards the Wildgrube ravine. The Belgian duke decided to attack the Turks behind their palisaded embankment, and his half-dozen or so battalions moved forward clear of the woods and over the open ground, their musket-fire increasing in intensity as they advanced. The two sides never reached close quarters for hand-to-hand combat, but, as Le Bègue observed, 'The thing

---

231 Stöller, p.37. From this point, quotes from Le Bègue will not be specifically referenced, because his Account and Diary are translated in full in Appendix IV.
232 There is some doubt about exactly when this five-shot signal was made; it may have been a little later, after the final discussions with Sobieski; but Le Bègue was absolutely clear that Lorraine put the left wing in motion *before* the talks with Sobieski, and if this is accepted then a signal later would have been pointless.

was carried out with such vigour that the enemy, not being able to hold off this effort, abandoned their post and withdrew behind another screen, where was standing the main body of their troops.' This left the Imperialists now holding the line of the palisaded embankment. During this push, Croy took a musket-ball right through the shoulder and he was forced to withdraw for a while to have the wound dressed, so Fontaine resumed command of this detachment and, observing that the Turks seemed inclined to counter-attack, rode up and down the line encouraging the men and taking whatever measures were necessary to hold the embankment. But the Turks did not come out across the vineyard to attack them after all; they stayed put behind their new screen (probably a hedge), watching as the Christians continued to advance carefully out of the woods in the strengthening light to join the ever-widening line; and they peppered away at Fontaine's men, who, poking their matchlock muskets through the gaps between the upright planks of the palisade, replied with equal enthusiasm but, what with the two barriers and all the vines between them, to very little effect. There may have been a little skirmishing amongst the intervening vines by the boldest spirits on both sides keen to distinguish themselves, especially for the Christians by the bravest or stupidest amongst the hundreds of noble volunteers.

Already from first light, the Christians could hear in the distance, beyond the Turks in front of them, the heavy boom of the siege cannons before Vienna, as the Ottoman artillery resumed its relentless bombardment of the crumbling final defences of the city. This noise in the distance would be their constant accompaniment for the rest of the day, a perpetual reminder of the reason they were fighting and of the need for immediate action. Within the city, the defenders, for their part, were preparing last-ditch retrenchments in case the Ottomans broke through the breaches, while the garrison and militia companies were kept in readiness all day, and Starhemberg did his part by directing the fire of the city's long-range cannons onto the rear of any Ottoman forces assembling for the battle that they could reach. Eager watchers directed their gaze towards the hills and, from the moment they were able to see that far, detected the troops appearing out from under the trees of the Kahlenberg and would watch their steady advance during the morning.[233]

The battle had begun almost without anyone deciding it. On the Ottoman side, Kara Mehmed of the advance guard had sent in to headquarters a report that large numbers of infidels were advancing over the hill nearest the

---

233 The view of Lorraine's advance from within the city is described by many diarists; for example, Hocke, p.194, and Ruess, p.71. Some nineteenth-century historians again added the tale of a flag hung out from the monastery and other signals made by Lorraine this morning; the flag does not appear in the sources, and, given that Lorraine and his staff would have known that their advance would be visible as soon as it was light, it is unlikely they would have bothered. The garrison's firing on the rear of Ottoman troops is from Vaelckeren, p.98 (also quoted in Renner, p.431); *Das Kriegsjahr 1683*, p.230, manages to have the artillery fire directed against Ottomans assembling at Laimgrube, a suburb of Vienna close to the Wien, well to the south of the battle lines – if there was any firing here, it was only against those packing to flee.

Danube against him,[234] but the news had already spread throughout the army – a shiver of alarm ran through the camp as the cry was passed from mouth to mouth 'The infidels are close!' and many of those still in the main camp, soldiers or those camp-followers who had not left already, began to pack their most precious things ready to flee, rather than joining the battle-line. Dalérac, who was not inside the camp, reported seeing large numbers of equipages with pack-horses and camels being moved off over the Wien towards Raab, and claimed, presumably from information gleaned from prisoners after the battle, that the move was led by the principal pashas, who were the first to get their belongings off, so that much less than expected of the rich Ottoman harnesses and other personal gear would be found in the camp later by the Christian soldiers.[235] Kara Mustafa issued orders to kill all infidel prisoners in the camp, a sign of just how insecure the Grand Vizier's headquarters felt;[236] some Ottoman masters declined to kill their slaves, especially amongst those who were already preparing to leave the camp for Hungary, so that a number of prisoners, Marsigli included, avoided this death sentence, but perhaps as many as 10,000 unfortunates were slaughtered or left for dead with ineptly-inflicted wounds.

Meanwhile, Kara Mustafa prepared to fight. Some of the *yerli kulu* of Koca Ibrahim and Kara Mehmed were already in action, but by no means all of the big right wing; now, however, the rest of them poured out of their overnight camps and moved towards the developing battle, or into position further back lining the various streams that blocked Lorraine's path to Vienna; Marsigli, watching from a couple of miles to the rear inside the main Ottoman camp, described their turbans covering the lower hills like a white carpet.[237] Kara Mustafa himself mounted with his sons and his staff and entire household, along with Vani Efendi, and probably the Khan as well; unfurling the Standard of the Prophet, and accompanied by the big *Sipahi* and *Silahdar* regiments of the *Sipahi*s of the Porte, they rode forward from the palace tent complex to join the Janissary Ağa and his troops already in position at the Türkenschanz entrenchments, the central point of the overall Ottoman line. Here, as the sun rose in the sky promising a hot day, Turks set up to keep the Grand Vizier cool a rich red sunshade or baldachin, a kind of small side-less

---

[234] The Master of Ceremonies (Kreutel & Teply, p.188) stated that he reported 200,000 Christians; this may have been an exaggerated figure added after the defeat to excuse it (for the Ottoman diarist can have written his account no earlier than the night after the battle), or it may have been the customary Ottoman hyperbole, which Kara Mustafa would have known how to interpret.

[235] Marsigli, vol. 2, p.432; Dalérac, vol. 1, p.153. Marsigli does not restrict the alarm to those in camp, but since he was positioned well inside the main siege camp, opposite the city's Schotten Gate, he cannot have been a close witness to events in the forward camps of Koca Ibrahim and Kara Mehmed; and the watching Christians, who had a good view of these, made no mention of any troops moving away from them; so Marsigli must be taken as describing only the situation in the main camp. Renner, p.432, appears to quote Marsigli that the panic was so great, only the unfurling of the Standard of the Prophet persuaded enough troops to face the enemy; I have found this in neither his *Stato militare* nor his *Autobiografia*.

[236] Cantemir, vol. 2, p.310. The order is not mentioned by the Ottoman diarists and has often been doubted, but the relief army later found the bodies of many of the slaughtered prisoners in the camp, or those still living with severe wounds; see below.

[237] Marsigli, vol. 2, p.121.

tent, and Kara Mustafa settled down to make himself comfortable – he spent the first part of the day drinking coffee with his two sons and the Khan as he watched the developing struggle on the right wing.[238] All eyes turned to the north and the Kahlenberg chain, where the infidel forces seemed to be forming a crescent formation as they came out of the woods 'like a flood of black pitch'.[239] While this was going on, the regular cavalry peeled off to form to the right and left of the Grand Vizier's post, and the rest of his troops joined the Janissaries in front at the entrenchments. The Ottoman diarists, supporters of the Grand Vizier, were at pains to stress that his position was within artillery range of the infidels, a disingenuous assertion, for, although he would be under fire by the end of the day, at this point of the morning he was a good two miles away from the nearest deployed Christian artillery, the battalion guns accompanying the Imperialist infantry now coming out of the woods of the Kahlenberg chain, and two miles did not count as 'within range' of such guns even if there had not been so many hills intervening. The Ottoman artillery of the Türkenschanz would be silent for several hours yet. After a pause watching the developing action on the distant hills, Kara Mustafa sent forward some reinforcements under his *kethüda* Ali Ağa Gürcü (Ali, the master, the Georgian): according to the Ottoman diarists, these comprised the official known as the *serçeşme* (see Glossary), several *ağa*s, and the 'retinue' (almost certainly a reference to Kara Mustafa's own *yerli kulu*).[240] It is not clear how soon these came into action against the Christians, but since they had a couple of miles to go to the battle-line, we may safely assume that it was not immediately.

Fontaine and his battalions were still holding the line of the palisaded embankment, with more and more Imperialists and Saxons coming down the slopes and out of the woods to join them. Lorraine, still at the monastery atop the Kahlenberg, sent messengers off to Waldeck at the centre and Sachsen-Lauenburg at the phoney right wing urging that they start their own advance now as well and 'come out of the wood by the avenues which were at the head of their camp' – Le Bègue actually recorded that he sent *orders*, but given that the Duke was not formally the superior officer of Waldeck, to him at least he can only have made suggestions (unless Lorraine, in Sobieski's absence and using his rank as the Emperor's General-Lieutenant, was trying to act as local commander-in-chief of all the Germans).[241] Correctly, Lorraine also sent off to inform his nominal superior, Sobieski, of the steps that he had taken so far, but was then informed that the King was already on his way to the monastery with his household and some other Polish magnates for the agreed final discussions, and so decided to go out

---

238 For the coffee: Dalérac, vol. 1, p.157, citing later prisoner reports.
239 Kreutel & Teply, p.189; a common cliché for Christian troops in Ottoman writing.
240 Kreutel & Teply, p.189. The text indicates that the reinforcements were dispatched 'after' half an hour – but given the undetailed description of the action (not surprising, given the distance at which the diarists were observing events), it is unclear which specific event this was half an hour after.
241 In the order of battle, Lorraine was not in command of Sachsen-Lauenburg either – but Sachsen-Lauenburg was an Imperialist officer commanding Imperialist troops, and Lorraine was commander-in-chief of the Imperialist army.

and meet him on the way. They met – we do not know exactly where – and rode back to the monastery together, Lorraine filling in Sobieski on what he had done and the dispositions of the left wing he had now made. Once on top of the Kahlenberg, Sobieski could again get a perfect view of the entire battlefield, below and stretching off round to his right where the centre and his Poles would appear. He could see clearly, confirming the impressions from the previous evening, that the Turks were holding the Nussberg in great force below them against Lorraine, with the several streams behind the hill protecting their camp like so many lines of entrenchments; that they were occupying several villages such as Grinzing, Sievering and Pötzleinsdorf in the manner of outposts for their centre at the Türkenschanz, facing the area in which Waldeck and Sachsen-Lauenburg would appear; and that they had their left wing in the open ground south of the Türkenschanz, with forward positions on the hills Michaeler Berg, Schafberg and the tall Heuberg. There was again no formal council of war – it was far too late now for that, and besides Sobieski was still not really expecting the final battle involving his Poles to take place today – but the King as supreme commander approved all the actions that Lorraine had taken on his own authority, and there was probably a brief conversation with the Duke about his plans for the rest of the morning; Sobieski, having won the main point of holding the supreme command of the army and the marks of recognition that went with it, and having learnt that Lorraine possessed a sound judgement, was not inclined to balk now at Lorraine's independent actions provided they did not interfere with his own overall plan – and looking at the dense Ottoman formations at the foot of the Kahlenberg chain, he fully expected the Duke to be busy all day down there, leaving him plenty of time to get his Poles out onto open ground for the killing stroke tomorrow.

After this brief conference, Sobieski entered the ruined chapel of St Joseph's Monastery on the Kahlenberg to hear mass, while Lorraine, who had probably heard mass with Marco d'Aviano earlier at 4 a.m. at the same time as the rest of the Germans, went off to join the main line of the advancing Imperialists.[242] Amidst the devastation that the Tatars had left when they sacked the building, an altar was built up from stacked drums and d'Aviano officiated for the King and his household. After the ceremony, Sobieski knighted his son Prince Jakub. (Although every other indication suggests that Sobieski did not expect the Poles to make their attack this day, this ceremony does give a contrary impression. Perhaps he thought that *preliminary* hostilities might begin today, or that there would be no time for these day-of-battle rituals if combat began first thing on the 13th.) Sobieski and his party did not return immediately to the Polish army, for they knew that it still had a long way to go before it could enter the action; instead, they descended to one of the valleys around the Kahlenberg where some baggage wagons had been brought up, and in a tent there enjoyed the first decent meal they had had in several days, while, not long after they had started eating, the increasing sound of musket and artillery fire from beyond the

---

242 See Appendix I, 11.2, on the question of this mass.

Kahlenberg told them that the battle was for the left wing well and truly under way. After the meal, Sobieski conversed briefly with his entourage and companions in arms about their past successes, referring especially to Chocim, the great victory of which he was so proud and whose completeness he hoped to repeat here: 'The same enemy that we defeated at Chocim stands facing us. We are admittedly in a foreign land, but we are not fighting for a foreign cause. We fight for our homeland and for Christianity, not for the Emperor but for God.'[243] Talk of past victories was a natural way to keep morale high, but the fact that Sobieski felt the need to make these comments shows that there was lingering dissatisfaction amongst some Polish senior officers about the campaign. Breakfast over, the King returned to the top of the Kahlenberg to see how the fight was going.

Below, the infantry of the left wing, principally its first line, had continued to move out from under the trees into the open and join the expanding line just forward of the wood's edge, while the second line persevered in its struggle down through the trees. As far as we can tell, the Imperialists in particular were still primarily coming through the 'defile' of the saddle between the Leopoldsberg and Kahlenberg, appearing behind the already-formed line and peeling off to right and left to join its ends. Even when they reached open ground, the foot-soldiers had to step carefully, for the slopes were still steep, especially for those on the left on the Leopoldsberg or for the Saxons in the Wildgrube ravine. The Saxons may have been some way behind the Imperialists,[244] and Goltz was preparing to construct a battery for a few cannons to help cover his troops' advance over open ground. Some battalion guns were beginning to make it out of the woods to join the Imperialist line.

Once in the open, the Imperialists were careful to form a continuous front, without any of the gaps between battalions that would have been regarded as normal in a battle between two western armies, for they had learnt to their cost in the actions at the start of the 1683 campaign that Ottoman fighters would make wild unformed attacks that could easily penetrate any gap in the line and immediately wreck the formation. On the far left of the line GdC Caprara added two dragoon regiments, the Imperialist DR Heissler and the Saxon DR Reuss, almost certainly serving dismounted at this point, and probably with young FML Louis of Baden as their direct commander; these extended the line as far as the foot of the Leopoldsberg below the chapel on the peak.[245] This indicates, first that the line was already stretching across the middle part of the gully of the Waldbach stream that runs down between the Kahlenberg and the Leopoldsberg to the Danube at Kahlen, and secondly, there was still a substantial gap between the end of the line and the road by the Danube. From what happened later, we may infer that the dragoons might have been refused slightly from the main line, their front angling back gently towards the left, at an angle to the main line no acuter than forty-five

---

243 quoted in Forst de Battaglia, p.176.
244 The Saxon publication *Aufrichtige und unpartheyische Relation*, pp.6–7, clearly states that the Imperialists were further down the slope than the Saxons.
245 The dragoon regiments and their locations are named by Le Bègue; in some histories, the regiments are named as Heissler and Styrum, both Imperialist.

degrees, so that their left flank rested on the woods behind and they faced towards Kahlen; in this way they would have been able to cover the open flank against a growing threat on that side. Such a disposition would have given the whole line a bow shape, and could have been what the Ottoman observers away at the Türkenschanz described as a crescent formation. It is not stated who was in command of the whole line at this stage: FM Hermann of Baden was for the moment remaining with the other seniormost officers atop the Kahlenberg, FZM Leslie as the senior infantry officer ought to have been commanding but was busy overseeing the final moves of the artillery, FML Croy had been wounded, and FML Louis of Baden was apparently concentrating on the dragoons, so GdC Caprara, despite the fact that he was a cavalryman, was clearly the highest-ranking officer present and must be assumed to have been in overall command at this point.

Fight in the Ottoman camp. Engraver known only under monogram G.W.W.B. (Wien Museum Inv.-Nr. 98032, CC0)

Ottoman troops were not only joining the bands at the hedge, facing Caprara and Fontaine and the new Imperialist main line across the width of the vineyard, where apparently Osmanoğlu still commanded; the Turks still held the village of Kahlen on the river-bank, and some bands were massing in the gullies of the little streams Waldbach and Schäblergraben and the country between, taking pot-shots up-slope at the flank of the Imperialist line where the dragoons were posted. (This makes clear that the Imperialist forces on the river road had not yet made it past the Leopoldsberg, otherwise they would have been able to clear away these bands harassing the dragoons.) Alert Imperialist officers may already have spotted that the Ottomans, behind their hedge and in the hollow ways beyond, were building themselves up for a general counter-attack on the whole Imperialist-Saxon line. Around 8 a.m., Caprara ordered Heissler's dragoons to attack the nuisances in the gullies, which probably implied a left-leaning direction of advance diverging slightly from the main line; and the Imperialist infantry were soon after ordered to cross the palisaded embankment in order of battle (no-one indicates how they managed this feat) and advance straight ahead, or as Le Bègue put it in his Diary, 'to attack the Turks in the little valleys on the right'. Baden led the dragoons forward, but before the infantry line could get going, Osmanoğlu launched his counter-attack.

The Ottomans threw a three-pronged offensive against the infidels, though calling their incoherent masses 'columns' is overstating the case.[246] They were apparently reverting to a crescent-formation attack, in earlier times a classic tactic of the Turks, as it had been of many horse-archer peoples before, but one that the Ottoman Empire had not used in battle for centuries, and the poorly-trained Ottoman *yerli kulu* may have been falling back on this basic form for lack of the ability to try anything more complicated. Firstly, some forces joined the skirmishers harassing the dragoons in attacking towards the vulnerable left flank of the Imperialist line (Le Bègue's Diary referred to Heissler's being ordered to attack a 'battalion of Janissaries, which were the most pushed forward on the left', which might indicate Janissaries were present, but could come from the standard assumption of western observers that all Ottoman infantry were Janissaries). Secondly, a big force advanced over the Nussberg to join the existing line against the Imperialist infantry; if the indications that this set off from the Nussdorf area are correct, they came over the river side of the hill and were intended to coöperate with the first prong in hitting the vulnerable left end of the Imperialist line, probably in conjunction with a frontal attack by the troops at the hedge. Thirdly, a mass of *yerli kulu* advanced up the Schreiberbach valley, towards where the Saxon infantry battalions were still coming down; it is not known if they were aware yet of the Saxons in the Wildgrube ravine, and if they were not, the push was probably aiming to hit the Imperialist infantry line on its apparently-exposed right flank. It is just conceivable that this last force comprised, or included, the household troops of Kara Mustafa under his *kethüda* Ali Ağa Gürcü, that had been sent forward from the Türkenschanz.[247]

Louis of Baden and the dragoons were almost immediately in trouble as they pushed forward down the gully of the Waldbach stream and towards that of the Schäblergraben, for his left flank was already open and, the further he advanced, the more his right separated from the main line and became exposed too. Hermann, watching keenly from the monastery on the Kahlenberg above, could see that the Turks were being constantly reinforced,

---

[246] This counter-attack is undoubtedly the most uncertain part of the account of the battle; it could be placed at almost any point in the couple of hours between 8 and 10 a.m., and indeed there are some intimations in various accounts, including those of the Ottoman diarists, that do suggest the Imperialists were a lot further forward than the palisaded embankment when they were hit by it – and that, therefore, their battle-line must have been even more bowed forward than described here (without such a bow, the Ottoman attack from Kahlen would not have been possible). My placing the counter-attack at this point is dependent on Le Bègue's two writings, especially the Account – admittedly an extremely brief description, which could refer to anything, but it is the only event in Le Bègue coming even close to the counter-attack, and there is no doubt that his event is placed soon after leaving the tree-line and well before reaching the Nussberg.

[247] The account of the Ottoman diarists (Kreutel & Teply, p.189) is not really detailed enough about the exact time of Ali's dispatch from Kara Mustafa's headquarters to be sure which part of the action Ali Ağa Gürcü took part in, but this is one possible match; see below for another. By the time of these events, 8 a.m., Ali would have had time to reach the front line unless he was sent much later than appears from the diarists' account.

and that several detachments were running along hedgerows out of Louis' sight trying to gain his flanks and surround him. The threat to his nephew galvanised the Feld-Marschall into action, and he hurried down and across to help, ordering infantry in the woods to follow him as he passed, and even picking up FZM Leslie on the way.[248] Turkish musketry was especially hot in this area, though not apparently very effective; the arriving infantry, and perhaps some more dragoons as well, stiffened Louis of Baden's line, and soon enabled it to resume its advance, steadily pushing the Turks back over the gully of the Schäblergraben. It was probably about now (although this is nowhere stated in the sources) that the head of the Imperialist column on the river road appeared, making Kahlen untenable for the Ottomans and finally providing enough troops to extend the Imperialist line to the Danube and make it secure at last.

At about the same time or soon after, just as Lorraine himself was coming down to join the ordered advance, the main Turkish forces hit the Imperialist infantry line at or in front of the palisaded embankment. Although the fighting here was tough (a Saxon account described the Ottomans attacking 'furiously', and if the rather general account of Schliz von Görz is to be equated with this phase as it seems, they threw themselves forward so furiously that at some points they broke through to hand-to-hand combat with the Christians), and the Ottoman warriors may on occasion even have driven the Imperialists from the palisaded embankment back towards the edge of the wood, we do not know much for certain about this clash.

We know a lot more about the Ottoman attack up the Schreiberbach towards the Wildgrube ravine. Goltz, as noted already, was up at the front building a battery to cover the Saxon advance, and his first-line infantry under GWM Sachsen-Weissenfels, grey-coated except for the red of the Leib IR, were somewhat to the right-rear of the Imperialists, but already in the open (presumably, the tree-line was further up the slope at this point). Here, too, however, there was a barrier behind which his leading troops could form, very similar to that protecting the Imperialist battalions: 'along the foot of the hill a screen of stone, man-high, was placed, and on this a board partition of wood was found, which the battalions of the first line had used very conveniently to their advantage.'[249] Suddenly, the Saxons saw in the valley below them a great mass of Turks advancing up towards them, at the same time as the Imperialists further down and to their left came under the fierce assault of the Ottoman central force. Goltz quickly perceived the importance of bringing the Saxons into line with the Imperialists, and hurried his soldiers over the great fence and further down the slope as fast as they could go – 'neck over head' as the German expression put it – without regard to formation. This scramble was probably made a little easier by the fact that none of them had to carry cumbersome pikes, just their matchlock

---

248 Hermann's aid, from the 'Baden account', in Röder, vol. 1, Urk., p.16. If Hermann really arrived in time to be any help, the infantry that he picked up must have already been close to leaving the woods anyway.
249 *Aufrichtige und unpartheyische Relation*, p.6. The following account of the Saxon action is largely based on this work, pp.6–8.

muskets and *Schweinsfeder* spears. Towards the bottom, enough men were assembled to form two battalions which were quickly posted to prevent the Ottomans gaining possession of a gully or 'hollow way' that would have been very advantageous to them – probably a reference to the 'bottom' between the Kahlenberg and the Nussberg;[250] spears would have been jammed into the ground pointing towards the Turks, and behind them the musketeers prepared for firing. As the rest of the Saxons caught up, they were shoved into line with these two battalions. Seeing this rapid movement, the Ottomans halted their advance up the hollow way, and their infantry took cover wherever they could find it and began taking pot-shots at the Saxons, who easily held firm under this initially-ineffective harrassment. After a while, it became clear that the biggest threat was the Ottoman attack towards their left (since the Schreiberbach force was now pinned down before the Saxons, this was probably from Osmanoğlu's centre force), at the point where the little company of 100-odd Saxon grenadiers now held the link with the right flank of the Imperialist line, which here was holding a fence.[251] As the attack on this junction became hotter, the Saxon first line began a leftward swing in order to face the Ottoman horde – but of course, as it did so, it moved its own right flank into the open towards the Ottomans in the bottom. Here, the *yerli kulu* had got themselves pretty well established in cover, protected by bushes and stones, and their fire was increasing nastily against the Saxons, exposed 'from foot to neck' in the open.

At this point, the Saxons looked over to their right and saw above them there on the far side of the Wildgrube a great swathe of pale grey coats, the leading Franconian infantry, stationary in the open; immediately, GWM Reuss sent over to the commanding officer there, FML von der Leyen, to request that he move his battalions down to block moves that the Turks were making via the Schreiberbach to get round at the Saxon rear. If the Franconians had moved down, the Christians could have formed a continuous line as far as the Krapfenwaldl hill and beyond, leaving no gaps or flanks to be exploited at this point. Von der Leyen refused: Kreis officers tended to be very reluctant to act on their own initiative, and he declined to budge, stating that he had the most explicit orders from Waldeck his commanding officer not to move from the spot without instructions direct from himself, Waldeck.[252] In fairness to von der Leyen, we should also note that such a move would have involved a left-ward drift of his line, separating it from the Bavarians, and if

---

250 This is my interpretation; many historians have read this as a reference to a continuing Ottoman advance up the Schreiberbach into the Wildgrube ravine, but later statements in the *Aufrichtige und unpartheyische Relation* do not make sense if this interpretation is accepted.
251 It is not clear from the Saxon account whether this was the same palisaded embankment held from the start by the Imperialists, or a different barrier.
252 *Aufrichtige und unpartheyische Relation*, pp.7–8. The officer to whom the appeal was made is always identified by historians as FML von der Leyen, but the Saxon account specifically refers to 'the commanding Major General', and the Franconians had only one GWM, Thüngen. The Franconian history by Jochner (p.72) sniffily doubted the Saxon story, or hinted that von der Leyen may have misunderstood Waldeck's actual orders. Von der Leyen may have been influenced by an experience in the Dutch War: during a blockade of Philippsburg he had withdrawn his troops due to lack of supplies on his own authority, and had got himself into trouble for it; this could well have made him determined to follow orders to the letter.

the Bavarians tried to compensate and keep contact with the Franconians, the whole centre would have found itself inclining to the left, opening up a dangerous gap further along the line. There are some indications (not mentioned in the Saxon account) that the Hanoverian battalion in von der Leyen's brigade went to help the Saxons anyway, with an attack over the Schreiberbach that relieved the pressure on the Saxons just long enough for Goltz to make his own response.[253] Goltz anyway, swallowing his annoyance at the rejection, ordered the Saxon second and third lines to move up to where the first line had been standing before it started its swing, facing rather towards the Ottomans in the Schreiberbach valley, so that the Saxon infantry as a whole formed 'a single [line] with two fronts' – apparently meaning a kind of V-shaped formation, the point roughly towards the south-east, one side facing the Ottoman attack on the centre, the other side facing the bottom to the south and perhaps curving back facing the Schreiberbach. The first line remained enfiladed from the point of view of the Ottoman troops in the bottom, who from their covered positions kept up a heavy fire on the Saxons to which they could not themselves reply.

With casualties mounting, Goltz had had enough: the time had come to drive the Turks from their 'advantage'. After a short review of the enemy position (in the circumstances, it is impossible that the 'recognoseiret' of the Saxon account can have meant a reconnaissance closer than provided by Goltz moving up to look over the heads of the front line of soldiers), he ordered the Saxon infantry to advance. They took the Turks 'in front and flank', by which the Saxon account probably meant that the first line took Osmanoğlu's centre force in the flank (almost certainly in conjunction with Imperialist pressure on its front) while the second and third lines attacked the Turks in the bottom frontally. The Ottomans were quickly thrown into confusion and began retreating towards the Nussberg. Forward came the Imperialists as well, and the kink in the Saxon line was evened out as the whole left wing began to press forward after the Ottomans, over the bottom and up the Nussberg beyond, striving to prevent the Ottomans from rallying on the hill and finding enough time to dig in. There are suggestions in the Saxon account that their infantry may have been in advance of the Imperialists' at this point; they may well have pushed ahead and gained an initially exposed forward position on the hill, where the Imperialists quickly joined them before the Ottomans could rally and counter-attack.

---

253 Mansberg, pp.90–91; Wimmer, *Entsatz*, pp.187–188. Mansberg and Wimmer suggest that it was here that Pallandt met his death, killed by a shot from a Turkish *yerli kulu* musketeer; this conflicts with other accounts that put Pallandt fighting with the two Hanoverian princes with the Imperialist CR Rabatta.

The left wing: the Nussberg, Nussdorf and Heiligenstadt

Lorraine and the left wing had won their exit from the woods and were now on the first phase of their drive for Vienna, shaking themselves into the formations and tactics that they would be using for the next few hours, starting with the Nussberg before them, technically open (unwooded) but littered with vineyards and their enclosing hedges and embankments.[254] The Duke himself had joined the troops at the front, while the Elector John George of Saxony was apparently accompanying the cavalry still coming up to join the left flank – at some point, the column on the road must have passed the Leopoldsberg and deployed to help occupy the village of Kahlen, though this is nowhere mentioned in the sources, and there are only hints that the cavalry joined the main line later (see below); for the moment, infantry units were continuing to join the line and extend it leftwards towards the security of the Danube. Already there was room behind them for the second line to come out of the woods and form up properly behind the first, and as the advance progressed it created yet more space for the remaining Imperialist troops. Croy, his wound dressed, returned to resume direct command of the first line of the Imperialist infantry, and would remain at his post for the rest of the day; Caprara returned to his responsibilities with the cavalry. Leslie had by now got most of the Imperialist artillery down the hill and out in the open, so the infantry had their battalion guns; these were now placed in front of the infantry, not in intervals between the battalions,[255] for Lorraine and his colleagues were still determined to allow no intervals between units that could be exploited by wild Ottoman 'rush' tactics. Where the terrain did not provide embankments, hedges or fences to help in the defence against Ottoman charges, the battalions deployed their *chevaux-de-frise* in front of them, moving these forward when they advanced;[256] or if they had the *Schweinsfeder* instead, stuck their boar spears in the ground pointing towards the enemy whenever they halted to face an attack.

The advance began; from what we know of later events, the time can be estimated at around 9 a.m. It was a careful, painfully slow process – they hardly came on 'like wild pigs' as the xenophobic Ottoman diarists put it[257] –

---

254 See Chapter 7.
255 The placement *before* the infantry comes primarily from witnesses within Vienna: Hocke (p.194), and possibly Vaelckeren; Ruess, p.71, mentions the advance with both infantry and cannon firing-and-advancing, but is less explicit about the placement of the artillery. However, the Baden account from the relief force also briefly supports this: 'the duke formed the [order of] battle and making the cannons march at the head he had this army advance…' (Röder, vol. 1, Urk., p.17). As for Vaelckeren: there is no mention of the tactic in the English edition I have consulted, but Renner, pp.430–431, quotes a substantial chunk from the German edition which is absolutely unequivocal, down to the jumps forward of 40–50 paces.
256 these are specifically attested by the Ottoman diarists: Kreutel & Teply, p.189.
257 Kreutel & Teply, p.189.

for every care had to be taken to keep the line intact amongst the vineyards and gullies and scrub of the Nussberg and its surrounding terrain.[258]

We need to dismiss from our minds the idea given by contemporary prints and paintings of great hordes of Turks swirling around the Christians at close quarters, for the action, though 'hot' in contemporary terms, was rarely like that. The Ottomans faced the Christian line in a dense enough mass, it is true – with the reinforcement sent by Kara Mustafa and the inclusion of Kara Mehmed's advance guard, Koca Ibrahim theoretically had a good 30,000 troops here on a front of no more than a mile and a half, making 11 men per yard even before their horses are taken into account (although this density itself makes the 30,000 figure more than suspect, and Koca Ibrahim would not have tried cramming them all into his front line anyway). However, they were not in constant contact with the Christian line: their normal 'resting' position was probably well out of musket range of the German infantry, that is at least 100 yards away, perhaps with skirmishers in front firing on the advancing Christians; every now and then individual groups or parties, perhaps sometimes as large as the entire household corps of an individual governor, would psyche themselves up for a forward rush trying to find a weak spot in the solid line – Marsigli, watching from the Ottoman camp, described how they 'went up by platoons, some of them advancing, others retiring';[259] less often a more serious attack would be made by a much larger body of men.

This general distance allowed the Christian tactics to work, but also the tactics reinforced the tendency of the Ottomans to keep their distance: the battalion guns, already loaded, would be dragged forward of the infantry, perhaps as far as 40–50 paces (this comparative mobility enabled by the greater ease of moving single cannon amongst the rows of vines than that of moving whole battalions while maintaining strict formation), the guns would fire off their blast of canister shot against the Turks – presumably, if any Ottoman party was heading for them, concentrating on that, otherwise aiming for the great mass of troops further off – and waited for the advancing infantry to catch up; if the canister fire did not make the Turks recoil further back, the infantry would now be in range and it would open up with its musket-fire, until the enemy mass gave ground again to pull out of range or was provoked into attacking. If the guns were attacked while pushed forward and the single hail of canister did not deter the Ottomans, there would be no time to reload, so (we assume) the gunners ran for their lives back to the main line, by then not too far away, and dived under the protection of the *chevaux-de-frise* or the infantry's pikes as they were lowered, while the musketeers blazed away over their heads. The Turks when they charged might fire off some initial shots but would normally resort to their traditional

---

258 This paragraph is based on a combination of evidence (the descriptions from the witnesses within Vienna and from Le Bègue of the method of advance, Marsigli's brief but crucial description [see following note], and certain specific events of the advance) and an interpretation of this evidence in light of the weapons and tactics available to either side.
259 Marsigli, vol. 2, p.121; quote translated from the French text – the Italian text has slightly different wording with the same broad sense.

tactics, rush headlong in a terrifying mass screaming wildly 'Allah! Allah!' and struggle to break through the *chevaux-de-frise* and pikes to get to close quarters, all the while under steady musket fire from the infantry beyond; and most of the time they would get no further, their morale would crumple under the withering hail of shot and back they would run again, leaving the gunners to return to their cannon and the infantry to resume their steady advance. Occasionally, one of the attacks broke through the defences and made life very unpleasant for the infantry for a while, maybe even required temporary support from the second line, but at no point was any attack big enough and successful enough to threaten to rupture the whole formation. Although many of the Ottoman *yerli kulu* had and used firearms (we know from named officer casualties amongst the Christians that they sometimes inflicted quite substantial losses),[260] they cannot have used these extensively, or else were astonishingly ineffective in using them, for if they had used musketry effectively, the Christian tactic with the battalion guns would have exposed the gunners terribly and soon left the cannon with no crews at all.

Every now and again, the Christian advance reached a barrier – a hedge or fence or embankment (later in the day, after crossing the Nussberg, it would be the half-entrenched streams such as the Schreiberbach) – that provided the Ottomans with some cover and gave them the courage to stand against the blaze of shot, and the action ground to a halt briefly as the Christian fire swelled to force them back, or until the pikes were lowered and the grey-coats surged forward to push the enemy back physically. According to Le Bègue, the first line 'never stopped making a continuous fire of musketry mixed with that of artillery', but we should not take this too literally, for not only would continuous musketry have made it impossible for the artillery to conduct its bound-and-fire without being shot down from behind, but also the musketeers would very quickly have run out of ammunition. Le Bègue probably meant that along the line, at any minute at least one platoon or division of musketeers was giving fire. It is psychologically likely, though not mentioned explicitly in any of the sources, that the vigour of the Ottoman rushes declined during the morning as time after time they failed to break the Christian line and to stop that inexorable advance; it is even more likely that the confidence of the Imperialist and Saxon infantry increased every time one of these rushes failed, and every time a blast of canister or musketry made the huge Ottoman right wing give just a bit more ground.

The Nussberg

Such was the general method to be employed as the left wing set off up the Nussberg. For the Imperialists, the advance was slow and tough, with some casualties (lieutenant-colonel Tilly of the blue-coated IR Baden was severely wounded by a shot in the upper thigh, and we may guess that along the line a

---

260 See below re. casualties in the battle. Some historians are fond of reinforcing the drama of the action here by stressing the heaviness of the casualties; given that the Christian losses in the entire battle were quite modest, casualties in this stage of the action cannot have been extreme.

few hundred rankers fell) but it was steady.[261] Things were less straightforward for the Saxons. Their battalions on the left adjoining the Imperialists formed part of the general advance of the left wing, but those units facing the 'bottom' had a more difficult time of it. If we understand correctly the vague descriptions of the Saxon account,[262] the latter, the battalions formerly of the second and third lines, were facing the bottom between the Kahlenberg and the Nussberg with the Schreiberbach on their left, perhaps with their line even refused back up towards the Wildgrube ravine. Although the rest of the left wing was now pushing ahead across the Nussberg, here some Ottoman detachments had established themselves in what the Saxon account called a ditch in the bottom; this *may* have been a reference to the Schreiberbach, here running along the left side of the bottom from the Saxon point of view, or it may have been an unmarked ditch in the bottom itself, but whichever it referred to, it seems to have been at the point where the bottom met the Schreiberbach valley, with the comparatively open ground beyond of the lower Schreiberbach as it curved round the western side of the Nussberg. The Turks in the ditch were firing continuously on the Saxons, hindering them from advancing further. Eventually, the Saxon commander here detached some men from one end of the line to go forward and take the Turks in the ditch from the flank; this they did, quickly driving the Turks off, and the delayed Saxon battalions were now able to advance across the bottom and along the western slope of the Nussberg to come into line with their comrades as part of the general advance. At some point as they drove across the hill, the Saxon contingent received a visit from its ruler: John George rode up, excusing himself for not participating in the action on the grounds that he could not leave 'the left wing' where he commanded, and publicly praising the generals who had been leading his battalions in this sector.[263]

At some point during the crossing of the Nussberg, the left wing reached another 'screen', one 'which extended almost from the Danube as far as opposite the Camaldulensian [monastery]' (Le Bègue); and here, at about 10 a.m., having apparently for the moment driven the Ottomans off down the far side by its fire and secured a brief respite from the lunges, it

---

261 The Saxon account *Aufrichtige und unpartheyische Relation*, pp.9–10, refers to events during this advance involving what appears to be a premature advance by two battalions under Croy, and an attack by the Saxon dragoons, brought up and dismounted by Louis of Baden. However, the writer himself admits that he was not an eyewitness of these actions and that he is reporting them second-hand; and they appear to be a garbled version of the events earlier in the day, when Croy first took command at the palisaded embankment and Baden led the dragoons forward against the harassing Turks in the gullies.
262 *Aufrichtige und unpartheyische Relation*, pp.8–9. The rest of this paragraph is the best sense I can make of the imprecise descriptions in the Saxon account, but the possibility cannot be excluded that the 'bottom' here refers to the Schreiberbach and the battalions of the second and third lines were actually pressing over it to occupy the Krapfenwaldl hill. It is even possible that the Saxon account is here describing events later in the day; it jumps considerably from detailed description of the gaining of the open ground early on to the actions of the afternoon, leaving the reader none too clear over exactly where to place in time the events here; my interpretation is heavily dependent on the translation of a subsequent time-check, 'gegen 2. Uhr umb Mittag', as 'towards 2 hours [lit., the second hour] before mid-day', which squarely places these events prior to the 10 o'clock pause that preceded the storm of Nussdorf.
263 *Aufrichtige und unpartheyische Relation*, p.9. See Appendix I, 11.3, for discussion of this point.

halted briefly.[264] We do not know exactly where this screen was, but Barker identified it as the Eichelhofweg, a line based on a track running diagonally across the Nussberg, barely at its crest.[265] The angle of this track seems odd for a line on which the Christians would have halted, for it would give them a pronounced rearward inclination to their right, and would imply that their left, which was still 'open', was pushed further forward, when we might expect it to be held back. However, the angle could match the delayed start of the majority of the Saxon infantry; and there is certainly a strong implication in Le Bègue's writings that the left wing halted just as Nussdorf came into view, that is, as it breasted the top of the Nussberg. Wherever it took place, during the halt or just before it, finally the gap to the Danube was closed as GdC Caprara extended the line to the riverbank (almost certainly with more dragoons from the road column); the remaining infantry had now left the woods of the Kahlenberg chain and was filling up the ground behind the first line, while the rest of the cavalry was swinging in from the road to form up *behind* all the foot-soldiers, for it was now clear that the continuing advance would be a matter primarily for the infantry. Leslie brought up some guns to the top of the Nussberg and from there opened fire on Nussdorf, joined by a couple of Saxon battalion guns that were dragged up with their infantry.[266] All the while, Sobieski continued to watch events from his position at the monastery on the Kahlenberg.

Lorraine meanwhile sent across to Waldeck, 'who was appearing already on the first heights to the right', and to Sachsen-Lauenburg, 'who also had exited from the wood', urging them 'to continue their march until they had come into line level with us, and to advance extending to the right until they would be in reach of supporting the Poles at the exit from the defiles of their route, which was on the right of the whole army' (again, Le Bègue refers to Lorraine sending *orders* to both, and again, we must interpret this as a certain degree of licence on the secretary's part given that the Duke had no official authority to command Waldeck, although he certainly had such authority over Sachsen-Lauenburg).[267] It is none too clear exactly where the centre's battalions were at this point, but they were obviously some way back forming an entirely unintentional echelon from the left wing, and their left-most elements, the Franconians, were as we have seen above not in contact with the Saxons yet, so they were perhaps no further forward than the tree-line

---

264 The gaining of the Nussberg is sometimes placed by historians as early as 8 a.m., but this timing is impossible to square with the explicit statement of Le Bègue or with the time it must have taken the slow-moving left wing to get so far from the tree-line where it had started.

265 Barker, p.324. He does not cite any source for the identification.

266 *Das Kriegsjahr 1683*, p.252; *Aufrichtige und unpartheyische Relation*, p.10. There are suggestions from Saxon sources that the Saxon artillery was not very active in the battle: at the end of the campaign, the six 6-pounders reported firing only 37 shots in total, and the six 3-pounders, only seven (Hassel and Vitzthum von Eckstädt, p.171). However, this report did not mention canister shot fired; and besides, the miserly Imperialists, while refusing to feed the Saxons free of charge during the campaign, had promised free ammunition (to supply them or replace what they used), so the figures may represent only what the Saxons did not get replaced.

267 Wimmer, *Entsatz*, p.188, interprets this as Lorraine getting Sobieski, the nominal commander-in-chief, to issue the orders. This is possible, though Le Bègue makes no mention of any intermediary.

on the southern side of the Latisberg (Cobenzl), probably not as far forward as the Krapfenwaldl,[268] and certainly nowhere near being in action with the enemy. If they were as far back as the Latisberg, and if the Saxons had no troops across the Krapfenwaldl either, Lorraine's concern to hurry Waldeck along is understandable, for this left a gaping hole between the right flank of the left wing and the point where the centre began. One might be astonished that the Ottomans made no attempt to exploit such a hole, except that the rearward inclination of the left wing's line along the Eichelhofweg starts to make more sense in this context, for the angle covered the gap rather well, leaving the left wing with no open flank that the Ottomans might attack, because the open end of the line was so far back – while the centre was still so far behind that its theoretically-open left flank was under no real threat at all unless the Ottomans were prepared to go past the left wing and enter the woods, something they had consistently shown themselves unwilling to do.

The allied cavalry breaking into the Ottoman camp. Franz (Frans) Geffels, between 1683 and 1694 (Wien Museum Inv.-Nr. 40132, CC BY 4.0, Photo: Birgit und Peter Kainz)

Lorraine now took position with the first line of the left wing ready to resume the advance. Again, his main concern was to ensure that the entire line remained intact, with no gaps appearing as it advanced, and the junior generals were instructed they 'should re-establish order in the places where it was broken by the difficulty of the passages, and that one should keep up there by all means a steady advance making a continuous musket and cannon fire' (Le Bègue). While the preparations were being made, John George of Saxony came back from his visit to his own infantry and joined Lorraine, and 'remained always at his side in the most exposed positions', as Le Bègue was at pains to stress.

The advance resumed: the left wing set off down the south side of the Nussberg heading for Nussdorf and the lower west-east section of the Schreiberbach. As before, the artillery would leap-frog forward to blast away

---

268 though *Das Kriegsjahr 1683*, p.253, does think some of them had advanced this far.

at the Ottoman masses while the infantry laboriously marched forward intent on maintaining an unbroken formation, all the while harassed by Ottoman skirmisher fire and intermittent lunges at the barrier of *chevaux-de-frise*. As Le Bègue drily put it: 'One advanced in this manner albeit quite slowly, as much through the difficulty and unevenness of the ground as through the enemy opposition.' It seems likely (though this appears nowhere in the sources) that, if the line did indeed start out inclining back on its right along the Eichelhofweg, the inclination was evened out during the advance; it could be at this stage, rather than earlier, that the battalions of the Saxon second and third lines caught up with their confrères and gave the right end of the line enough strength to push forward, perhaps even extending it across the north-south section of the Schreiberbach to the Krapfenwaldl, so that the entire left wing was finally on a parallel line, facing south.[269] On the far left, Colonel Heissler was ordered with his dragoon regiment to drive some 'Janissaries' from an entrenched position (almost certainly amongst the gardens before Nussdorf near the river); Heissler at first dismounted his entire regiment, but then thought better of this and remounted half of it, formed up, and launched a joint foot-mounted attack on the entrenchment. The Turks immediately fled. Heissler and the dragoons, their blood up, pursued, but got carried away, went too far and ran into a large body of assembled Turks (2,000, according to the source) and were forced to retreat back over the entrenchment.[270]

At some stage during this advance, perhaps developing out of the repulse of Heissler, the Ottomans possibly tried another counter-attack, in all probability a three-pronged push again – a push on each flank and the centre, feeling out the weak points while fixing the main body.[271] The attack, especially that on the river side, was probably formed of Syrian troops taken from Kara Mehmed's advance guard, driven back from their original positions around Kahlen.[272] Depending on how one reads the Ottoman diarists, the reinforcements sent by Kara Mustafa under Ali Ağa Gürcü may have arrived here and formed part of the left prong. There are suggestions of artillery support from the few heavy guns that the Ottomans had placed at the Türkenschanz, but given that this was still well over a mile away from

---

[269] Mansberg, p.89, suggests that the Ottoman resistance had been broken in part by the deaths of two senior *beylerbeyi*s, those of Anatolia and Sivas. In fact, according to the biographical information in the Kreutel & Teply index, the current holders of both these offices lived for many years after 1683.

[270] Mansberg, p.89 and n.57 (quoting a news publication of 1684). See Appendix I, 11.4, for discussion of this point.

[271] This counter-attack is not mentioned at all by Le Bègue (in which the nearest event would be the vigorous defence on the right overcome by the Styrum Dragoons, and 'considerable resistance' at Nussdorf), the Baden account, either of the Saxon accounts, or any other source that I know of; it appears only in the accounts of various nineteenth-century historians (especially Mansberg, pp.92–93), and those who follow them. Even then, the histories suffer from considerable confusion between this counter-attack and that earlier in the morning. What follows can be regarded only as a highly speculative 'best guess' based on suspect secondary information; from what is in Le Bègue, the Ottoman 'counter-attack' might have been only an especially vigorous defence at three points.

[272] See Appendix I, 11.5, for discussion of who commanded this.

the action, and that the heaviest guns there were probably no more than 8-pounders, this is extremely unlikely; any artillery support came from guns that Koca Ibrahim may have placed in own entrenchments nearer the battle-line, and even these would have been operating at very long range.

Whatever the artillery support they had, the three attacks took the usual Ottoman form, of delivering a ragged blaze of musket fire at a distance too great to be truly effective, followed by a furious charge seeking to get to close quarters and create gaps in the solid line or find its weak spots. The central attack did bring the advancing infantry to a halt, and may even have forced the two battalions of IR Grana, that were getting very close to Nussdorf itself, to withdraw some way back up the Nussberg (if this was so, the units of the line on either side must have bowed in to keep contact with it, or else the gap was very quickly plugged by battalions of the second line, for we hear of no breakthrough by the Ottomans). Before long, the Imperialists had rallied and were driving forward again, may even have penetrated briefly over the lower Schreiberbach, well beyond the level of Nussdorf, before being forced back over it by the large forces of Koca Ibrahim beyond.

On their right nearest the river was where the Ottomans came closest to success, perhaps aided by the presence in the opposing line of dragoons (who probably did not carry *chevaux-de-frise* even when dismounted) and cavalry (who certainly did not). Here at least, some of the Ottomans seem to have acted mounted. If they could break through by the river and deprive the Christian front line of the safety the river gave its left flank, the whole line might be in trouble. Ottoman infantry and cavalry poured out of Nussdorf, and the situation looked grim for DR Heissler and for the left end of the line. More dragoons were pulled in, including at least one regiment of Poles from Lubomirski's corps, but its colonel, Casimir Freiherr von Königsegg, was struck down by a Turkish horseman whose sabre went right through the protective iron cross or horse-shoe in his hat into his skull (he died a few days later), and the regiment was badly mauled. Despite the difficulties of the ground, the Caprara Cuirassiers were moved out from where they had been placed behind all the infantry, as well as more Poles from Lubomirski's corps. John George of Saxony brought up his two little guards units, the one-squadron strong Leibgarde-Trabanten zu Ross and the single squadron of the Leib Regiment zu Ross (cuirassiers) that had accompanied him to Vienna, and personally led them into the mêlée, driving against a push by more Syrian cavalry; the Elector was wounded by an arrow in the cheek, and a Druse horseman was raising his lance to run him through when John George turned on the man, one blow from his sword breaking the lance and a second parting the Druse's head from his body. At this point, Lieutenant-Colonel Hans Rudolph von Minkwitz, commander of DR Reuss, dragged the blood-covered Elector from the fray. All these heavy horsemen, perhaps reinforced by yet more Saxon cavalry from the rear lines, finally halted the Ottoman counter-attack here and forced it to give way; its energy quickly dissipated; and the Turks pulled back to Nussdorf. The left wing's river flank was secure again.

On the Ottoman left, facing the Saxon infantry, the Turks also gave the Christians a hard time. This is the only part of the counter-attack that has direct support from the major sources, for Le Bègue, admittedly referring to an event *after* the fall of Nussdorf and describing it in terms of resistance to the Christian advance rather than a counter-attack, says: 'There was the same [resistance] on our right to occupy, on the same line [as Nussdorf], a height held by the enemy who, by the vigour of their defence, had shaken one of our battalions, but having been supported by the Styrum Dragoons which Graf Dünewald sent there, this battalion rallied, it then occupied this height and one continued to advance.'[273]

Despite the brief danger to parts of the first line, the counter-attack had had little chance of success. Even with the prong nearest the Danube which seemed to come so close to victory, if the Ottomans had noticed just how deeply the Christians were stacked up behind that first line, they might have saved themselves the trouble, for even if the first line had collapsed, only if the morale of all the lines behind had given way could they have made a significant impact.

Departure of Sobieski for the right wing

After his breakfast, Sobieski had remained all this time at the monastery up on the Kahlenberg with his entourage, watching the battle of the left wing developing below. He had sent somewhat redundant orders to his Poles to advance (they had actually been on the go since 6 a.m.) but otherwise remained for a while convinced that the main battle would be on the 13th and that he might as well stay where he was playing the role of supreme commander. However, the sight of the reinforcements sent across by Kara Mustafa from the centre, and other bodies of troops that were apparently being drawn to this side (one thinks here perhaps of the *beylerbeyi* of Anatolia, not initially assigned to Koca Ibrahim's right wing but nevertheless mentioned as serving here), suggested to the King that the attention of the Ottomans was being so very firmly drawn away from their left, where his own army would be appearing, that the Poles might have an easier task breaking through to open ground than had been anticipated. It is also probable, though not recorded in the sources, that he had begun to realise how far Lorraine was advancing – much further than anyone had expected, and with every indication that the left wing would continue to steam-roller on at the same steady pace for the rest of the day; if the King did not rethink his plans, he might find that Lorraine had stolen the glory of the victory from under his nose, before the Poles were in position to fire a shot, and that would never do. So, after hearing mass for the second time, late in the morning – it must have been somewhere around 11 a.m., certainly before the fall of Nussdorf – Sobieski set off to rejoin his own troops, accompanied by a number of German aides de camp assigned to him by Lorraine that he intended to use

---

[273] It is not absolutely impossible that Le Bègue was here referring to operations of the 'right wing' of Sachsen-Lauenburg, rather than the right of the left wing; but if so, it is unclear to what hill he was referring, which of 'our' battalions had been shaken, or how events so far away could have contributed to 'our advance'.

to keep control of the battle and carry his orders.[274] There was no need for any great urgency, however, for from his vantage point on the Kahlenberg he had not yet seen the Poles emerge from the woods, so he did not hurry: to avoid burdening his horse with his enormous weight on the difficult ground, he walked down the hill aided by his servants and then continued on foot heading south-west, passing between the Vogelsang and the Latisberg (that is, behind the advancing centre under Waldeck) and only then mounted – for, acutely aware as he was of his public image, he would have known that he needed to be on horseback by the time he reached the Poles.[275]

Coincidentally, soon after Sobieski left the Kahlenberg, the drift of Ottoman troops towards their right was reversed; Kara Mustafa knew that the Poles were coming, and, as we shall see later, was beginning to move some forces away from the right and towards the left, to face them when they deployed.

Nussdorf

The counter-attacks had been beaten off, after two hours of fighting the Christians finally had the Nussberg in their possession, and their line held the north bank of the lower Schreiberbach facing Koca Ibrahim's hordes beyond; Nussdorf's hours were numbered. Yet it would not be taken without a tough fight, for its houses were big, substantial buildings, some of them several storeys high, and it was surrounded by walled gardens and yet more of the seemingly unending vineyards, all too solidly built for the Tatar sack of the village in July to have done major damage – it seemed made for defence. In this sprawling redoubt was a large garrison of Ottomans: more Syrians from the advance guard, probably many of Koca Ibrahim's substantial corps of real Janissaries, and some troops identified as Egyptians or Egyptian Janissaries (*misirlu*) under the *beylerbeyi* of Aleppo, Deli Bekir Pasha.[276] The entire left half of the Imperialist line as far as the Danube, supported by Leslie's guns, was drawn into the battle for the key position, and inside, the Turks made use of all the houses, cellars, ditches, fences and garden walls to fight for it tooth and nail. We do not have very much detail on the struggle here, for most of the witnesses who wrote accounts of the battle seem to have been elsewhere; Lorraine must have been off facing the Ottomans over the Schreiberbach, for his secretary merely recorded that the left 'took from them the village of Nussdorf, after a quite considerable resistance.'

---

274 A number of historians report Sobieski's group of foreign adjutants; the story seems to originate with Dalérac, vol. 1, p.150, which says the aides were given by Lorraine. One wonders if they received private instructions from the Duke first.
275 Exact sequence from Wimmer, *Entsatz*, p.192; slightly different version in Mansberg, pp.96–97. Dalérac (vol. 1, p.144) asserted that Sobieski spent fourteen hours continuously in the saddle – a claim even Sobieski himself did not venture to make.
276 His name is often rendered at this point as Ebu Bekir or variants of the same; Deli Bekir (mad Bekir) is the name in Kreutel & Teply. It is possible that these were local Janissaries from Syria, perhaps Damascus, rather than *misirlu*.

The pause

The time was about noon, or probably somewhat later, nearer 1 p.m.; nigh on half of the autumn day had passed, and the left wing had advanced a couple of miles from its starting positions towards Vienna, but it still had a good three miles to go ahead of it, three miles full of massed Ottoman troops. Nevertheless, here along the course of the lower Schreiberbach in line with Nussdorf, Lorraine called a halt. The main reason, according to both Le Bègue and the Baden account, was that the Poles were still behind, not even in sight yet.[277] While Lorraine was determined to push on to Vienna this day, he was not stupid enough to do so without support, and though Waldeck and the centre were now coming level with the left wing, he would undoubtedly have preferred to have the Poles on the field, if only to provide a distraction for the Ottomans, drawing troops away from those facing him and to ensure no open flank for the new left-and-centre line of battle, for although the Christian forces were advancing along an arc, concentrically, so that they were getting closer to each other, this was counter-balanced by the tendency of the centre's cavalry to contract the line by pulling in behind the infantry, and there was still open space beyond Sachsen-Lauenburg, leaving the Ottomans still with the possibility of taking the cavalry division there from the side and rolling up the whole line from Sachsen-Lauenburg to Lorraine. The Ottomans had already twice made counter-attacks that showed their willingness to seek out the flanks of an enemy; there was no need to offer them an opportunity on a platter. Almost all historians add to this reason for the pause, the valid point that the troops were exhausted, badly in need of a rest after what for some of them was six hours of continuous fighting, under a hot September sun, sweltering in their thick coats while carrying heavy muskets and pikes and their personal equipment, in addition to the ponderous *chevaux-de-frise*.

Lorraine and his officers may also have used the delay to do some further re-jigging of the formation – Ruess, watching from Vienna, noted that the troops were put into 'correct battle order' at about this time;[278] it is difficult to be sure what was meant by this, but it probably involved sorting out the over-extended Saxons, putting their second and third lines back in their correct positions behind the first. One might imagine that it also meant the cavalry being pulled forward to its correct position on the left of the infantry line, but this is doubtful: the terrain ahead was even less suited to cavalry action than the Nussberg had been, and most if not all of the Imperialist and Saxon cuirassiers almost certainly continued where they were, behind the infantry, with dragoons completing the left flank. That flank, once the line passed Nussdorf, would not rest on the Danube proper, but on the narrower

---

[277] Stöller, p.38; Röder, vol. 1, Urk., p.17. Each source mentions only one halt, but there is a distinct impression that they are not the same halt; one suspects a brief halt along the lower Schreiberbach as clearly described by Le Bègue and another longer one, the one described by the Baden account, after taking Heiligenstadt. There may in fact have been a lot of stop-starting in the German advance from this point; see below for uncertainty over the time of the famous decision of Lorraine and Goltz to continue to Vienna.

[278] Ruess, p.71.

Canal that separated the Prater Island from the mainland and led south to the ramparts of Vienna.

Despite the tiredness, morale was high: according to the Baden account, the impatient soldiers would only rest by leaning on their weapons, and all the time every face was turned to the west watching eagerly for the first sign of the Poles. Le Bègue did take a moment to look across the hills in the same direction and admire the scenery, even enjoy a touch of smugness: 'The soundness of this advance, that of our order of battle, and the situation of the area which made our troops appear as if in a type of amphitheatre, presented to the viewer in this movement a great and formidable object, and I have no doubt that it appeared so to the Turks, and that it was one of the causes of the victory.'

Advance of the centre

Waldeck and the centre, with Sachsen-Lauenburg's right wing closely attached, had spent the night where they had collapsed; most of them were on the correct side of the hills (the Vogelsang and Hermannskogel respectively) but they covered a wide area undoubtedly stretching back across to the wrong side. The eight or more battalions of Franconian infantry under FML von der Leyen on the extreme left, on the eastern side of the Vogelsang, were not too far from the headwaters of the Wildgrube ravine near the Saxons, and were in the open from comparatively early on, but the rest of them – Degenfeld and Maximilian Emanuel with the 11 battalions of Bavarian infantry, the 16 squadrons of Bavarian and seven of Franconian horse under Bayreuth, and the 24 squadrons of Imperialist cavalry – were still in the woods with the Latisberg and then the foot-hills before them, and, due to the shape of the battlefield and the Ottoman positions on it, even once they left the woods, most of them had much further to go before they reached the Turks than did the left wing. As far as we can tell, the bulk of the cavalry started out together on the right, perhaps with some of the dragoons pushed further forward of the rest, but Waldeck still firmly regarded the Reich cavalry as part of his command.[279]

Waldeck's troops almost certainly did not start quite as early as the left wing, but they were in motion well *before* 8 a.m. (the time given for their start by the Polish historian Wimmer). While Lorraine's troops had only to descend the Kahlenberg to reach open ground, most of the centre had more than a mile to go through the thick woods and trackless terrain, over or round the Latisberg, all the way dragging their battalion guns, those in front constantly stopping to let those to the rear catch up. As noted above, the Franconian infantry, or part of it, appeared out of the woods and formed up quite early, some time soon after 8 a.m., apparently on the upper slopes

---

279 Wimmer, *Entsatz*, p.191, claims that the centre was followed for a while by the heavier Polish cannons that had spent the night in the saddle between the Kahlenberg and the Vogelsang and which, despite the best efforts of their teamsters, were still unable to rejoin the Polish army; on this, see above, Chapter 6, section 'To the crest of the Wienerwald'.

of the Krapfenwaldl, but there halted waiting for the rest of the line to come level with them, and refused to go to the assistance of the Saxons without direct orders from Waldeck. The Bavarians and the horse still had some way to go. According to the historian of the Franconians, they were under constant harassment by Turkish infantry,[280] but this is recorded nowhere else, and there is no evidence from the Ottoman side that troops had been pushed so far forward into the woods – indeed the Ottoman council had explicitly agreed not to do so (though it is not impossible that Koca Ibrahim, who in the debate had wanted to occupy the near edge of the woods and been overruled, chose to ignore orders and to send some infantry in, especially once it became clear from his fighting with Lorraine just how dangerous to the Ottoman warriors the Christians could be once they formed up in the open). Indeed, the Saxon account recorded indignantly that as late as 10 o'clock 'not the least' had been heard from the centre.[281] During the advance, it became increasingly impossible to preserve the correct order of battle, and much of the horse – at least the Bavarian and Franconian troopers under FML Bayreuth, but probably not at this stage Sachsen-Lauenburg and his Imperialists – dropped back behind the foot to follow it in three or more lines, but some cavalry units remained mixed up amongst the infantry.[282]

The Ottoman army retreating from their camp at Vienna. Artist unknown (Wien Museum Inv.-Nr. 33324, CC0)

It was probably around 9 a.m. when the rest of the centre broke out of the tree-line into the comparatively open ground on either side of the Latisberg, at the upper reaches of the streams that would become the Nesselbach and the Döblingerbach, and set off through the vineyards that covered the lower

---

280 Jochner, p.75.
281 *Aufrichtige und unpartheyische Relation*, p.10. This is dependent on the translation of '2. Uhr umb Mittag' as '2 hours before middday' – but if the 'before' is incorrect, it puts the centre even later getting into action.
282 Johann Georg von Rauchbar, *Leben und Thaten des Fürsten Georg Friedrich von Waldeck*, [ed. by] L. Curtze and A. Hahn (Arolsen: Speyer, 1867–1872), vol. 2, p.268; Wimmer, *Entsatz*, p.191, follows.

THE BATTLE OF KAHLENBERG

Battle from before dawn to early afternoon.

hills before the main Ottoman positions. Here was where they finally began to face opposition: detachments of Turkish infantry, probably most of them *yerli kulu*, nestling in the vineyards, firing on them from every wall or fence or embankment, falling back to the next obstacle back whenever they got too close, and most of the time in terrain far too broken for any cavalry to be deployed to drive them away for good, though there are some vague suggestions that at one point during the advance two Imperialist cuirassier regiments were deployed to drive off some of the enemy skirmishers somewhere in front of the Latisberg.[283] The advance would take several hours, but it would not be especially difficult, for the detachments of Turkish infantry facing the centre were not large in number, and no source mentions any big counter-attacks with larger bodies of troops such as those that were hurled at the left wing. Generally, the centre adopted the same methods as the left wing: slow careful advances through the vineyards taking great care to keep the formation closed and intact, battalion guns leap-frogging ahead driving off the Ottoman detachments where necessary. It appears, though we cannot be certain for the exact movements are never defined, that the Franconians were descending the Krapfenwaldl, their left towards the Schreiberbach but still some way behind the Saxon right, heading broadly for Grinzing;[284] while the Bavarians to their right were coming off the western side of the Latisberg and probably heading over the hill 'Am Himmel' for the upper Erbsenbach and Sievering. By about noon, most of them were on the last down-slopes, the city side of the last hills or in the upper parts of the stream valleys leading onto the flank of Koca Ibrahim's position.

The overall shape of the Christian line was beginning to change, and precisely how to interpret the vague descriptions of the centre's moves depends on how one understands the change was taking place. The Germans (Lorraine's and Waldeck's two corps) had started out the day broadly on an east-west line facing south, but with a slight southward bend towards the western end, Waldeck's corps. As the morning wore on, that bend might have become more pronounced as the centre swung in more to face the north-west–facing Ottoman defences while the left wing preserved its south-facing orientation. However, it seems more likely that the Bavarians were considerably more delayed by the woods than the Franconians, and that the wood-line for them was further south; once the former found themselves

---

283 Rauchbar, vol. 2, p.269; Jochner, pp.73–74, follows. It is not at all clear where these two Imperialist regiments came from; the implication seems to be that they came from the left wing, but, although Rauchbar was based closely on Waldeck documents, his history is not a source and we cannot read too much into his exact wording. The two regiments may have come from the left wing against Turkish infantry on the Krapfenwaldl, though if so, the event must have been quite late in the morning, after the Imperialist cavalry had slotted in behind the wing's infantry; or they may have come from Sachsen-Lauenburg, perhaps some of those cavalry mentioned as mixed amongst the infantry.

284 Most accounts say something like Schliz von Görz, that the centre took the height next to that which the Imperialists and Saxons had taken; the Imperialists and Saxons had taken the Nussberg, making the Krapfenwaldl the next one over – but if the Saxons had extended to the Krapfenwaldl, as is possible (though not likely) from the vague Saxon account, the next hill along would be the unnamed hills to the south-west, the outliers of the Latisberg, pushing the Bavarians even further across. This latter option is hard to square with other events of the battle.

in the open, they were somewhat in advance of their neighbours and the latter, now behind both the Bavarians and the Saxons, began to move south skirting the middle Schreiberbach so as to catch up and slot in between these two. When these came level with the left wing during the pause at Nussdorf around noon or 1 p.m., the bend in the overall line had evened out and the orientation of the whole left wing and centre was pretty much south-facing except perhaps the Bavarians who may have faced south-east, their line across the upper Erbsenbach.[285]

Heiligenstadt, Grinzing and Sievering

The pause lasted a 'good half hour' if the Baden account is to be believed,[286] probably somewhat longer. Eventually, around 2 o'clock, the anxious eyes directed to the west caught sight of the distinctive long pennants that the Polish hussars carried on their lances, emerging from the trees in the distance. The Poles were still a long way back from the Ottomans, but nevertheless a great cheer went up from the waiting German soldiers, and some of them, carried away by enthusiasm, even rushed forward in disordered crowds towards the enemy, until their officers caught up with them and drove them back to the ranks with blows from the flats of their swords. Once order had been fully restored, the German advance resumed.

Lorraine and the left wing crossed the lower Schreiberbach. The main Ottoman strongpoint in front of them was the village of Heiligenstadt,[287] astride the Nesselbach, and the task of taking this fell to the Saxons.[288] The Elector's troops, still tired despite their rest, faced difficult terrain with yet more vineyards and their usual accompaniment of fences, embankments and ditches, which the Ottomans used to good effect to hamper their advance even before they reached the village. At one stage during the advance, a

---

285 This is heavily dependent on the sense of Le Bègue's Account: 'The King being still behind, the army halted quite close to [level with] Nussdorf, until the Duke noticed that we were everywhere just about level, he continued his march, and our left, advancing, took without much resistance the post that the enemy held at Heiligenstadt. The Prince of Waldeck on his side obliged those facing him to withdraw.' This gives a strong sense (but is not explicit) that Lorraine resumed his advance after the pause along the lower Schreiberbach when the centre came into line with him (not when the Poles appeared).

286 Röder, vol. 1, Urk., p.17. The pause, according to the Baden account (not Le Bègue, or at least, only very obliquely) ended when the Poles came into sight, which is generally reckoned to be around 2 p.m. (see below). Compare the suggestion above that there may have been two or even more pauses.

287 This is another of the parts of the battle that have caused endless confusion; see Appendix I, 11.6, for discussion.

288 What follows is largely taken from Mansberg, pp.94–95 (which is followed by most more recent historians), except ignoring Mansberg's assigning of the event to the same time as Nussdorf's fall. Mansberg cites no source for his account, and the possibility cannot be excluded that it is largely or entirely invented. Mansberg doubts whether the 'Janissaries' sent as reinforcements were real Janissaries; he is right under normal circumstances to doubt any western identification of Ottoman infantry as 'Janissaries', but has chosen the wrong point to make it, because the dispatch of the troops by the Janissary Ağa inclines the balance of probability in favour of their belonging to the corps.

big counter-push of screaming warriors brought the Saxons to a standstill and even drove them back for a distance before it ran out of steam (since the Saxons lacked pikes, and *may* have been using their *Schweinsfedern* as stakes rather than to form *chevaux-de-frise*, it would have been easier for the Ottomans to do this to them than to the Imperialists); a couple of battalions, probably the IR Löben, were pushed especially far back and were put in a particularly dangerous situation; if the local Ottoman commander (the 'Ebubekr' referred to by Mansberg, who was probably Deli Bekir *beylerbeyi* of Aleppo) had possessed any real military ability, the whole Saxon infantry could have been in peril, but he did nothing to exploit the situation, contenting himself with concentrating (as Mansberg put it) 'like a bull' on blocking whoever was directly in front of him without regard to anything else. The Saxons rallied, reformed, resumed their advance; they recovered the lost ground and broke into the village. The fight here was probably a lot less tough than it had been at Nussdorf, as Le Bègue recorded baldly that the left wing 'took without much resistance the post that the enemy held at Heiligenstadt'. Kara Mehmed had appealed to the command centre at the Türkenschanz for reinforcements; some infantry reinforcements were sent to the front line by the Janissary Ağa (which makes it probable that these were genuine Janissaries), but they declined to put themselves in the doomed village, perhaps recognising it as a death-trap, and took position instead in some entrenchments along the Nesselbach between Heiligenstadt and Grinzing. The Saxons, breaking over the Nesselbach through Heiligenstadt and out the far side of the village, turned to take the entrenchments in the flank and rear, trapped the Ottomans, and slaughtered them.

As for the Imperialists, they must have been marching along between the Saxons and the Canal, driving back in the usual manner the Ottoman forces facing them, until they too broke over the Nesselbach. Beyond the Canal to their left was the Prater Island, still technically in Ottoman hands but held only by limited Turkish forces, most of the Ottomans who had spent the siege on the island having withdrawn before the day started (there is never any mention of the Moldavian and Wallachian forces who had been posted here, and we may assume that these had departed long ago). With the bulk of Koca Ibrahim's forces being driven past them on the mainland, the few Ottomans in the meadows at the northern end of the island and the ruined suburb of Leopoldstadt further south, opposite Vienna, were preparing to retreat, and, according to one not entirely plausible story,[289] their first preparation was, about the time Heiligenstadt was falling, to massacre all the Christian slaves yet in their hands. The cries of these prisoners as the slaughter began reached across the Canal to the ears of Elector John George, presumably at

---

289 Recorded in Mansberg, p.96, again with no source cited. The story is riddled with holes. It is very unlikely that the Ottomans were keeping prisoners in the meadows at the northern end of the island, and if they killed them in the Leopoldstadt, their cries were unlikely to have carried up to two miles to John George on the level of Heiligenstadt, especially not amidst the din of battle. Furthermore, the Canal, which was normally navigable, was only fordable at times of very low water, and the heavy rains in the region recently would suggest rather that the Canal would have been swollen, making any fording of it less than likely. The best that can be suggested is that the story belongs somewhat later in the battle.

this moment accompanying the Saxon dragoons on the left of the line, and he plunged his horse into the waters of the canal, initially followed only by his immediate staff, trying to rescue the unfortunate captives. Soon enough, the Poles of DR Königsegg followed, and together these scattered the Turkish detachments and managed to save the lives of the majority of the prisoners.

The Franconians and Bavarians had been advancing as well. They took Grinzing and Sievering, apparently without much difficulty – Le Bègue only bothered to record that 'Waldeck on his side obliged those facing him to withdraw.'

The Christian line was now along the south side of the Nesselbach. Unfortunately we do not have an exact time recorded anywhere for the fall of Heiligenstadt and the crossing of the Nesselbach; all of the sources, so full of detail about the exit from the woods and the advance over the Nussberg in the morning, had lost interest by now, bored with the slow but steady advance of the Germans, and much of the afternoon passed by for them as a fast-moving blur while their attention, like that of the German soldiers, was directed more to the south-west, watching the Poles. It was the same for the Ottomans: immediately after the fall of Heiligenstadt there seemed to be motions in Koca Ibrahim's lines that suggested he was planning to come out and make a counter-attack on Lorraine and Waldeck (as Le Bègue put it, 'the enemy troops who had formed up in their camp made some movements which seemed to intend come at us'), but with the Polish debouchment becoming ever more obvious, the aggressive inclination dissipated and Ottoman troops began to move rapidly and in large numbers towards their centre and left wing to face the Poles.[290] The combativeness of the Ottomans of Koca Ibrahim's wing may well have been declining already as their morale sank under the effect of the defeat of every attack they threw at the Christian line, of the inexorable advance of that line driving them back now for three miles (the tale of the reluctant Janissaries of Heiligenstadt supports this); but at this point, whatever the reason, opposition facing Lorraine and Waldeck was definitely easing off. Nevertheless, Lorraine, seeing the pressure the nearest Poles were under as they struggled to break out onto level ground, decided to ease that pressure on them and continue his own advance.

As the left wing's battalions approached the line of the Döblingerbach-Krottenbach, they had already advanced a good mile from the Schreiberbach, and even with the reduction in fighting which enabled a faster progress, the advance to and the capture of Heiligenstadt must have taken them at least an hour, probably more, so now the afternoon was already wearing on as they approached the next stream-line, the last before the Ottoman camp. There are indications that some Turkish warriors were on the northern side of the stream, perhaps in some kind of skirmisher cloud, but beyond, the Germans looked at Koca Ibrahim's line of crude entrenchments on the slopes beyond, and were aware of the Türkenschanz a bit further on (the Türkenschanz was probably not directly visible from the present point of view of the Christian generals, but Lorraine and his fellows had to have known it was there from

---

290 Both Le Bègue and the *Aufrichtige und unpartheyische Relation* make clear that very substantial forces were moving off to face the Poles.

their surveys of the battlefield from atop the Kahlenberg earlier in the day). There must have been another pause as the generals considered, and once again all eyes turned towards the Poles.

Advance and deployment of the Poles

The Poles were a long time coming. Lorraine started the day a few hundred yards from the front line of the Ottomans facing him; the Poles started it with more than two miles to go, over hills and through thick woods (so dense that the watchers in Vienna later claimed to have seen them only by catching sight of their lance-pennants when using telescopes from observatories high up in the tower of St Stephen's)[291] – though when they came out, along the axis of the Alsbach valley, they would be much closer to the main Ottoman camp than Lorraine was when he started, and potentially in position to carry out the action Sobieski yearned for, of trapping and annihilating much if not all the Ottoman army.

Some amongst the Germans, anxious to see the Poles in action supporting them and unaware of the nightmare march so far of their allies through the Wienerwald or of the original plans of their commanders, were inclined to think harshly of the Poles and their apparently sluggish advance, but the reality was very different. The Wienerwald had been at its worst for the Polish army from the start – no comfortable camps around Klosterneuburg for them. They started the 12th with most of them (the dragoons at the Rosskopf excepted) barely out of the Weidlingbach valley, let alone at the crest line of the last row of major hills: Sieniawski was a bit further forward, his infantry on the northern side of the Dreimarkstein but most of his cavalry behind on the Sauberg; Jabłonowski's column was even further behind, and, although some of his cavalry had made it to the northern slopes of the Gränberg, the majority of his troops were still strewn back as far as the upper Weidlingbach valley. Ahead of them, the routes were no easier, as thousands of men and horses, half-starved and already exhausted from two days of this, struggled to get through the woods and over or round the great hills, constantly dragging the infernal cannons that Kątski refused to leave behind. Cavalry, for much of the time at least, had to dismount and lead their horses. It did not help that (a point often forgotten but already stressed above) no-one in the Polish army was anticipating the real battle would take place today, for, when Sobieski left before dawn to go and meet Lorraine for further discussions, he was still expecting the 12th to be filled with the advance to contact ready for battle on the 13th, and he preserved this belief for a substantial part of the morning as he enjoyed his leisurely breakfast and returned to the top of the Kahlenberg to watch Lorraine's progress. So when the Poles set off on the 12th at around 6 a.m. – a good half an hour after dawn, and by military standards not an especially early start – they were not being sluggardly, for they did not expect to be fighting this day; given the exhaustion of the men and horses after their

---

291 Dalérac, vol. 1, pp.147–148, citing information given by Starhemberg to the King.

exertions of the previous two days, it was a perfectly reasonable time to get going. It would also have been reasonable if they had not pushed themselves too hard during the morning, but in fact, given the distance they had to go and the difficulties of the terrain, it seems that they drove forward as fast as could be expected.

From that 6 o'clock start, the infantry of both divisions were in the lead again, Sieniawski's over the Dreimarkstein, Jabłonowski's over the Gränberg, clearing the way where necessary for the following cavalry, guns and ammunition carts. Somewhere amongst the eight weak brigades of Polish infantry were the four borrowed German battalions. Again, Sieniawski's men were having a slightly easier time of it than Jabłonowski's, for some of the Polish left wing were far enough forward not to have too far to go, while the right division not only had to advance but also to extend further to its right to ensure that the subsequent advance down the Alsbach was covered from both sides; but it was a terrible morning for all of them. Kątski in his diary stressed the difficulty of the passages, so bad that some of the carts had to be left behind, but his determination kept the artillery, and with it the whole army, moving steadily forward, overcoming every obstacle.[292] As the sun rose in the sky above them, the temperature soared, but still they pressed on. Then, as already described, fairly late in the morning, away at the left wing on the Kahlenberg Sobieski began to realise that Lorraine's successes below him meant the battle could well be over by the 13th and the Poles would be needed on the field *today*; so he started sending off messages to the right wing urging it to get a move on,[293] and soon after set off himself, though not so very fast, to join them. On his arrival, he threw all his efforts into urging his soldiers, especially the infantry and artillery, to keep going, not to rest for a moment; there is not much evidence that he paid serious attention any more to acting as commander-in-chief of the rest of the army.

As early as noon (according to Le Bègue) the left wing of the Poles had come level with Sachsen-Lauenburg, who was probably advancing south from the Hermannskogel on the right of the Bavarians.[294] However, we do not really know exactly where Sachsen-Lauenburg was at this time, and besides Lorraine's secretary was none too reliable when it came to times.[295] Most

---

292 Wimmer, *Entsatz*, p.192. The Polish part of the battle is recounted primarily from the work of nineteenth- and twentieth-century historians, the most notable being the authoritative study of Wimmer; Dolleczek is also valuable, if used with a certain amount of caution, because he makes quite a number of mistakes in his identifications of streams and hills; Laskowski likewise, with similar reservations; Mansberg is also useful. In cases of doubt or disagreement between historians, I have usually sided with Wimmer. Paradowski, published long after this text was first written, is generally in line with Wimmer and in one area provides a particularly valuable different interpretation (preparation of the final charge, under the sub-section 'Strike to, strike dead').

293 Only thus can we interpret the odd reference in Le Bègue's Account late in the morning that the King 'sent orders to his troops to march' (shortly before he left to join them). Sobieski must have known that his army was on the move by now, so such orders can only have been to hasten their advance, not to start it.

294 Wimmer's map erroneously puts in his path a non-existent hill called the Heuberg (the only Heuburg was south of the Alsbach).

295 The Diary appears to put the Poles coming into line even earlier: 'The King of Poland who saw from the height of Kalenberg the order of march of the German troops, their firmness and the

historians put the Poles reaching the crest line of the last row of major hills at about 1 p.m.: Sieniawski and the left wing on the Dreimarkstein, Sobieski around the Gränberg with his big royal *pułk* that would form the army's centre, Jabłonowski and the right wing (apart from some leading forces that may have already reached the upper end of the Alsbach valley north-west of Neuwaldegg) now extended as far as the Rosskopf. This extension to the right brought the dragoons, initially out there as a flank guard, into contact with Jabłonowski, and it seems that they were re-integrated into his division, subsequently advancing on its left covering the southern flank of the advance down the Alsbach. As a detached flank guard, this left only Rafał Leszczyński's little *pułk*, no more than a couple of squadrons of *pancerni* and a few of light cavalry,[296] which today was sent by Jabłonowski further out, apparently to scout the Ottomans positions in and beyond the River Wien – now that it was reasonably clear there were no significant Ottoman troops in the Wienerwald from this point south to the Wien, it became important to know what was going on a bit further afield. The only significant forces in their path were the Tatars of Hacci Giray, 500–600 strong at most (see Appendix I, 5.3), positioned somewhere in the Wien valley in the vicinity of Mariabrunn; Leszczyński's cavalry, secure in their long experience of dealing with Tatars, had no worries against so few of them.

Descending from the peaks to open ground

The Poles on the last row of peaks still faced the task of getting over the lower hills and down past the belt of vineyards to the better cavalry ground at the bottom, where Abaza Sari Hüseyin and the bulk of the Ottoman left wing waited for them, still a good couple of miles away. In that intervening difficult ground, however, Hüseyin had advance units holding various strongpoints, some of them quite deep into the foothills: up the Alsbach possibly as far as Neuwaldegg, in the village of Pötzleinsdorf sitting in a bowl almost hidden at the head of the Währingerbach valley, and on the hills between these; and someone – if not Hüseyin, then either the centre under Kara Mustafa or the far left of the right wing of Koca Ibrahim – had put troops in the village of Neustift at the head of the Krottenbach. However, these detachments were not for the moment very strong, for Abaza Sari Hüseyin's wing as a whole was comparatively weak (see Chapter 10 above) due to the initial concentration of forces against Lorraine. Down from the peaks set off the Poles, at the start at least with infantry still in the lead, now with the battalion guns able to provide at least occasional support. Kątski, with huge effort, had managed

---

retreat of the Turks, quickly went to his army, with the result that towards eleven o'clock the entire army had descended and was in order of battle, on the same line as Nussdorf. After this the general advance began, the enemy always retiring under the musketry of our infantry….' However, times specified in the Diary agree with no-one else's times, not even Le Bègue's own Account; and besides these words, when read carefully, do not necessarily include the Poles.

296 Wimmer, *Entsatz*, p.194; a couple of squadrons of hussars and pancerni (one each?) according to Dolleczek, 'Entsatzschlacht', p.154; according to Paradowski, p.138, 'a few banners of *pancerni* and Wallachian light horse'. Leszczyński's force is elsewhere given as light cavalry only. Events described in less detail, Laskowskii, *Campagne*, p.27.

to get a few of the slightly heavier field guns up to the forward slope of the Gränberg, only to discover that they were hopelessly out of range of any Ottoman forces, so on down the hill they were dragged by the long-suffering gunners and infantrymen.[297] Ottoman bands meanwhile threw themselves at the advancing lines trying to bring them to a halt, but they were too small at first, and if they were not halted by a blast of canister from the battalion guns or a volley of shot from the muskets, they were too weak to make it past German pikes or Polish *berdysz* axes. The advance ground on downhill through the trees and into the more open land of the foothills.

On the left, Sieniawski's division – perhaps because it was already a little ahead of the rest and the land in front of it was less wooded, certainly also because it had less far to go – began to draw effectively ahead of Jabłonowski, sufficiently far that the nineteenth-century Habsburg officer-historian Dolleczek could identify his wing as an 'advance guard' of the whole army.[298] As the force pushed down through the woods south of Neustift heading for the open, it branched into two 'columns': one, on the left, skirting Neustift towards Pötzleinsdorf, and the other, on the right, inclining a bit further south heading for the Michaeler Berg and the Schafberg beyond. The left column, probably passing the ground that would later become the village of Salmannsdorf, crossed a ravine near the source of the Krottenbach (west of Neustift) and came under fire from some Janissaries posted there – not a particularly strong detachment; supported by the canister fire of their battalion guns, the Polish infantry pushed forward wielding their *berdysz* axes, and drove the Turks from the height beyond. Resuming its advance, the column followed them, and when it reached the Pötzleinsdorf basin, it ran into the first serious opposition: reinforcements were now being moved to the Ottoman left from their centre and right, and a large number of Janissaries – allegedly several thousand, about one thousand is a more likely number – probably sent upstream from the Türkenschanz, were now holding the village and its surrounding gardens and vineyards, clearly under orders to defend it at all costs. They had no artillery, but they were well ensconced amongst the walls and embankments and using their muskets effectively enough; and there were too many of them to be left behind, for if the Poles went past them, they would cut the Poles off from the Germans and be in a position to attack either of these in flank and rear whenever they chose.

Fortunately, the Poles had help at hand: to their left, they were now in contact with Sachsen-Lauenburg, or at least with the two dragoon regiments at the head of his division, Schulz and Kueffstein. Sobieski, having supervised the start of the advance of the royal *pułk*, appeared here on the Polish left and directed two Polish infantry brigades (each about the strength of a normal battalion) to attack the strongpoint in the hollow and drive out the Turks.

---

297 Mansberg, p.97. Most writers suggest that he got the guns firing from there, but Mansberg is right – the only Ottomans to which he would have been able to establish a line of sight from there would have been Abaza Sari Hüseyin himself two or more miles away; the nearer Ottoman detachments were not only still out of range but also out of line of sight.

298 Dolleczek, 'Entsatzschlacht', p.164. Sieniawski's wing in the army was not identical with the 'advance guard' he had commanded during the race across Moravia.

When this was repulsed with heavy casualties, more battalion guns were called up, then the Imperialist dragoons. Eventually, perhaps as late as 3 p.m., the village fell to the Christians, the Janissaries were killed or driven back, and the left column could continue, now moving down the Währingerbach in steady contact with Sachsen-Lauenburg, who was apparently descending the Krottenbach. As for Sieniawski's right-hand column, it had inclined more to the south, coming alongside the big royal *pułk*, and these two divisions, the preponderant cavalry increasingly pushing to the fore as the ground opened up, headed together for the Michaeler Berg, where Ottoman resistance was still weak and easily brushed aside, then on towards the Schafberg. It was reputedly these divisions, appearing in the open somewhen around 2 p.m., that were seen by the eagerly-awaiting Germans of the left wing and centre and provoked the great cheer of welcome.[299] (We do not know where the treeline was on this part of the battlefield, but it appears that the same situation applied in 1683 as in the late nineteenth century, when the Michaeler Berg was wooded and the Schafberg was not.) The Schafberg was more hotly defended by the Ottomans, though in terms of skirmisher lines and small bands of *yerli kulu* disputing the vineyards and fences rather than a stand-up defence by a large coherent force; the hill cost the Poles a number of casualties, including Lieutenant-Colonel Aswerus Wrzospolski, the commander of Sieniawski's own infantry regiment, before they gained undisputed possession of it.

Kątski meanwhile, encouraged by the King and both Hetmans, was struggling to have some of the heavier guns brought up to the front line; calling on the last reserves of strength in the Polish foot-soldiers, and in the end only by abandoning the limbers so that the pieces could be dragged by main force on their own, one by one, across the broken terrain, he managed to get three cannons up onto the Schafberg, where at least they had a clear line of sight to the Ottoman left wing and the camp beyond. Sobieski was up here, and, impatient and wildly over-optimistic, gave the gunners as their first target the red baldachin of Kara Mustafa, between one and two miles away;[300] he even offered the considerable sum of 50 silver pieces to any gunner who could hit it. Unfortunately, getting the guns up had not involved bringing their ammunition carts as well; the cannons had few balls, and no wadding (without which round-shot artillery could not be fired effectively). A French

---

[299] Wimmer, *Entsatz*, p.193; Barker, p.328. This is not entirely convincing: from the present position of the Germans behind the Schreiberbach and westward of this, there is no clear line of sight to the Michaeler Berg and Schafberg; higher hills intervene. The first sighting of the Poles may have been later, or the Poles may have been a bit further forward of the Schafberg by 2 p.m. It goes without saying that we have no completely reliable times assigned to any of these events in the sources. Paradowski, p.138, agrees on 2 p.m. as the time for the occupation of the Michaeler Berg and the link-up with the Germans, but does not mention their being cheered by Germans further-off.

[300] The tent is sometimes identified as the great palace-tent complex, but that was at least two and probably nearer three miles away. The guns did have a clear line of sight on the baldachin, and it was at least closer; Dalérac, i, 158, was quite clear that the target was the sun-shade at the Türkenschanz. As for the currency offered: Dalérac quoted 'écus', a French silver coin; Sobieski might have used such a coin to his foreign engineers but would have been more likely to have had and offer Polish *złoty* coins; some historians give the German *thaler* instead; all three coins (écu, złoty, thaler) were of silver and *very roughly* equivalent value; see Glossary under 'Thaler'.

officer of Sobieski's household, Dalérac, suggested trying wads made from various items from a French engineer – gloves, a wig, his cravatte, even a large bundle of newspapers he had in his pocket.[301] Some shots were eventually got off, but since no-one saw fit to record their effect, it is safe to assume that they carried nowhere near as far as the target, and that Sobieski soon lost interest and left Kątski to oversee the bringing up of real ammunition and the use of the guns for their proper purpose, against armed Ottoman troops facing the Poles. Sieniawski's troops ploughed on down the slopes towards the main Ottoman positions with the guns now firing over their heads.

Jabłonowski and the right wing of the Poles, advancing from the Gränberg-Rosskopf area south of the Alsbach valley, and apparently down the valley itself as well, kept broadly level with the King's *pułk* and Sieniawski's right-hand column on the northern side. As with Sieniawski, Jabłonowski's infantry at first led the way, clearing routes for the following cavalry, including a stiff fight when they ran into the first Ottoman forward post at Neuwaldegg village, and an even stiffer one at Dornbach, which controlled the exit from the valley to the level ground. More infantry regiments from Jabłonowski's wing were drawn into the fierce struggle for Dornbach. 'At this new ousting of the Turks,' Kątski recorded in his diary, 'many of our people fell, or were shot down wounded, yet the enemy could in no way restrain the pugnacity of the soldiers, who hurried forward blindly as if to a dance.'[302] With this village in Polish hands, the valley behind was free and safe for the cavalry to descend and get itself into some sort of order ready for the attempt at debouchment.

To Jabłonowski's right, under the command of Louis de la Grange d'Arquien, comte de Maligny, brother of Sobieski's Queen, were the dragoons, who covered his flank on this side as far as the Heuburg. The dragoons crossed the Heuberg and then moved on towards the lower slopes beyond, close to Dornbach, joining the Crown Grand Hetman's infantry there and also ready to support the debouchment from the Alsbach. And beyond the dragoons came Rafał Leszczyński's little flank detachment. At some point during the day (the time is never specified, but was probably in the afternoon after the occupation of the Heuberg), Hacci Giray's Tatars in the valley of the River Wien made a fairly feeble lunge north towards the Galitzin Berg, but were parried easily enough by Leszczyński's *pułk*, perhaps supported by the dragoons. There are no details of the clash, but it could well have happened either as suggested by Wimmer's sketch map of the battle (with Paradowski's map following), with the Poles descending the valley of the Halterbach stream to hit the Tatars on their left flank as they moved north, or as his text describes, with an indecisive attack on the slopes of the Galitzin Berg, easily repulsed. All Tatars knew what their chances were against Polish cavalry – too many of their brethren had been killed in the Sobieski Wars for them to

---

301 Dalérac, vol. 1, p.158; also quoted in Mansberg, p.98 and n.63. Technically Dalérac said that he made the suggestion *to* the French engineer. The French engineer referred to was almost certainly Dupont; since these two did not get on, Dalérac's suggestion may have been intended purely sarcastically, or even invented after the battle to try to trivialise his enemy's role in the battle.
302 quoted in Wimmer, *Entsatz*, p.194.

be under any illusions, and whatever Hacci Giray's personal commitment to the fight, his men would have scarpered in very short order. Leszczyński moved on to hold the eastern lower slopes of the Galitzin Berg, facing the Ottoman camp, still guarding the outermost flank of the army and ready to support it out on the plain.

Before we proceed to the debouchment from the Alsbach, it is worth considering another small mystery of the Polish advance: where were the four borrowed German battalions? As noted above, one battalion each from the Imperialists, Saxons, Franconians and Bavarians had been assigned to Sobieski by Lorraine and Waldeck, probably on the night of 10–11 September. Sobieski had been very pleased to receive them, and not only because they increased his infantry strength considerably (each was as strong as or stronger than a whole Polish infantry brigade); when he wrote to his wife in the small hours of the morning of the 12th, he remarked that they 'serve with a docility that I have never seen in ours' especially since the Polish infantry seemed interested only in getting into the Turkish camp for plunder[303] – though given the effort the Polish infantry had been putting into moving their guns, the criticism seems unfair. Most historians put them on the Galitzin Berg by the afternoon of the 12th, or if not there then on the Heuberg – always, at least, on the right or southern bank of the Alsbach, there supposedly to help cover the debouchment. This is improbable for two reasons. Firstly: even with a start on the evening of the 10th, with most of them setting off from as far away as the Buchberg it is very unlikely that they made it so far – they might during the 11th have made their way up the Weidlingbach valley smartly enough, but afterwards they would have had to march much further than the Polish infantry moved in the same time, including over all the same ground that the Poles found so difficult. Even if the Germans had abandoned their battalion guns, and thus not been so hampered as were the Polish foot-sloggers by being called on to act as draft animals for the artillery, it is still stretching credulity to imagine they could have got so far so fast. If the loan of the four battalions was as late as is sometimes suggested (evening of the 11th), their march all the way to the Galitzin Berg becomes even more unbelievable. Secondly: even if they reached the Galitzin Berg or the Heuberg, what were they doing there? Army historians of the late nineteenth century viewing the battlefield in the light of their everyday experience, which included the rifle with an effective range of 1,000 yards or more, probably saw nothing wrong in the idea of four battalions managing from these positions to cover the debouchment from the Alsbach; but infantry of 1683 had the matchlock musket which was considered not worth firing at more than about 100 yards, and with these ranges, even from the very lowest slopes of the Heuberg or the Galitzin Berg and even if they had succeeded in dragging a few battalion guns with them, there was nothing they could do to support the debouchment from there – to achieve anything, they would have had to step out into the open ground in the face of the entire Ottoman left wing. (Cavalry might have been able to do it, for they could charge out

---

303 Plater, p.70, with similar comments earlier, p.66. It must be admitted that earlier in the same letter (Plater, p.66), Sobieski had remarked that the four battalions 'form the right wing'.

against the flank of any Ottomans blocking the debouchment – but for a mere brigade of infantry this would have been suicidal.) The only practical placement would have been where the Polish infantry actually stood, around Dornbach – and no-one has ever suggested that they were there. Mansberg had enough sense to recognise the absurdity of the Heuberg/Galitzin Berg placement, but substituted one of his own every bit as ludicrous when he put the four battalions on the top of the Gränberg (along with the equally misplaced artillery) to 'cover the debouchment' from there.[304] The most likely placement for the four is suggested by references (to which we will come later) indicating that the Franconian battalion was on the Schafberg, on the *north* side of the Alsbach; assuming that all four battalions served together and that therefore the other three were close by, this leaves them with less far to travel, and puts them in the thick of action where they could contribute effectively. It also puts them close to the person who wanted them most: the royal *pułk*, with its huge concentration of heavy cavalry, had almost no infantry support, apart from the piddling little guards companies, for the Polish infantry had all been assigned to the two Hetmans – but Sobieski had recognised the quality of the borrowed German foot-soldiers. Where more likely to find them placed by the King than close to his own *pułk*, providing it with the best possible direct infantry support during its advance to open ground?

The reconnaissance charges and the deployment

As the afternoon wore on, perhaps as late as 4 p.m., the Poles began to reach the edges of the really difficult terrain and enter ground which, though still sloping and in many places littered with vineyards, was open enough for them to start forming up, at last beginning to create a single coherent line of battle fully adjoining that of their German allies.[305] For Sieniawski and perhaps part of the royal *pułk*, this involved coming out on a relatively broad front, rather as Lorraine and the Imperialists-Saxons had done; for Jabłonowski and the rest of the royal *pułk*, it involved debouching from the Alsbach valley. Before Sieniawski's extreme left were the Türkenschanz and the Ottoman centre, but before the rest of the Polish army they could see Abaza Sari Hüseyin and the slim lines of the Ottoman left wing, drawn up facing them on the level ground, stretching beyond the Alsbach perhaps as far as Ottakring, with the vast extent of the Ottoman camp to its rear. Reinforcements were visible

---

[304] Mansberg, p.97.
[305] There is considerable disagreement over both the exact time of this deployment, and whether it preceded or followed the Zbierzchowski charge. Many put the time much earlier, at about 2 p.m.; I follow Wimmer, *Entsatz*, p.195, in preferring 4. Regarding the relationship to the deployment: Wimmer puts it before the charge, others after; it seems reasonable that both may be right – that the deployment started, Sobieski sent out a reconnaissance to make the situation clearer or distract the Ottomans, and the deployment then completed. (A few historians, including Laskowski, put the Zbierzchowski charge as a first step of the final Polish attack; while not impossible, this seems unlikely, although from Le Bègue's writings it seems that there was no great interval of time between Zbierzchowski and the final attack.)

pouring across to join Hüseyin's corps from the Ottoman right wing, beefing up his comparatively weak force while denuding Koca Ibrahim.

Although the worst terrain was now behind the Poles, Sobieski, watching the Turks through a telescope (probably still from his earlier position on the Schafberg with Kątski's guns), even now could not be sure about the exact nature of the ground in front of them, what more dangerous obstacles were concealed amongst the vineyards and embankments that might hinder an effective advance by his massed cavalry. At some point during the deployment process, a number of small Polish companies were sent forward to test the opposition and the ground before them. This use of what was effectively a 'forlorn hope', a suicide mission, was a fairly standard Polish practice. In the present circumstances it may have had an additional advantage, over and above the reconnaissance aspect, of distracting the Ottoman main line, drawing its attention off while the bulk of the Polish troops performed the difficult and dangerous task of getting out into the open and formed up – unlike Lorraine and the Imperialists and Saxons, they had no perfectly-placed palisaded embankment to provide them with some degree of cover and disrupt any attacks, and they were facing an enemy army fully alert and deployed, unlike the limited forces that initially faced GWM Fontaine and FML Croy.

First to go out was a squadron from the royal *pułk*. Soon after 4, Sobieski ordered forward a *chorągiew* of just under 150 winged hussars, the one officially belonging to his younger son Prince Aleksander, under its field commander, Lieutenant Zygmunt Zbierzchowski.[306] Zbierzchowski may have been supported by one or more other squadrons[307], but this is not reliably attested. Out from the Alsbach defile the little band rode towards the long lines of Abaza Sari Hüseyin's command, Polish armour glittering in the afternoon sun, a streaming blizzard of black and yellow over the hussars' heads from the huge long pennants on their lances in their squadron's colours. Forward they went, roughly south-east in the direction of Kara Mustafa's great palace-tent complex 'auf der Schmelz',[308] for at least 400 yards, before

---

[306] The source on this action for almost all historians is primarily the Polish diarist Dyakowski, who is not always regarded as trustworthy. For this reason, Mansberg, pp.98–99, doubted whether the attack took place at all, but it has been accepted as fact by all other writers, including both Wimmer, *Entsatz*, p.19, and Forst de Battaglia, p.178. Paradowski quotes an account by a rare Turkish witness, Cebeci Hasan Esiri (p.140), vivid though written decades later, and analyses the account of a Polish near-witness, Wojciech Stanisław Chróściński (pp.140–142); however, on p.43, Paradowski had stated that Hasan Esiri did not take part in the campaign himself. 'Zbierzchowski' [pronounced 'Zbiezh-khovski'] is the accepted modern spelling of the commander's name; in the nineteenth century it was rendered as 'Zwierchowski'. He held the provincial office of *podkomorzy* (lit., chamberlain; head of a local court resolving estate disputes) of Łomża, a small royal free town in Mazovia – such an office indicates he was of middle nobility, well-off but not in the same class as the magnates who monopolised state offices. The squadron had 149 men in the 1 August muster, but according to personal communication from Michał Paradowski, the real strength would have been about 130–135 men.

[307] Dolleczek, 'Entsatzschlacht', p.165. Le Bègue also referred to 'several squadrons' of hussars, but included in this would be the Potocki reconnaissance sent by Sieniawski, so this statement is not conclusive.

[308] The exact path of the charge, even whether it was north or south of the Alsbach, is unclear; I believe the southern option is the more likely, especially given explicit references to the Grand

they crossed a ditch and approached the Turkish front line. As Lorraine's secretary, watching from the left wing a few miles away, recorded, they 'charged with great vigour, lances lowered, to attack the Turks frontally.'[309] Although it seemed to Le Bègue that they 'overthrew at first those who were opposite them', in fact, the light cavalrymen of that part of the Ottoman first line facing Zbierzchowski recoiled, reluctant to face the armoured and heavily armed hussars with the fantastic decorations and great fluttering pennants that made them seem even bigger than they already were. The second line did likewise. But now Zbierzchowski was deep inside the Ottoman battle formation, isolated. He rode on, apparently avoiding some Ottoman reserves that showed some inclination to tackle him, but as he swung south to pass near the palace-tent complex and then back towards his own lines he ran into some tougher opposition, and more and more of Hüseyin's men were closing in on him from all sides; the squadron had to fight his way back out. Sobieski had closely observed the charge through his telescope, until the clouds of dust raised by the horses of both sides obscured everything in the Ottoman lines; the King raised his necklace-crucifix to the sky with a brief prayer, and the squadron came out of the dust, wheeling to come home, clearly identifiable not just by its pennants but also by its company banner of black-yellow with a white Polish eagle.[310] Ottoman cavalrymen were pelting after it, may even have cut down a few of the slower hussars, but more Polish cavalry rode out from the still-deploying lines and drove off the pursuers, allowing the remains of the squadron to rejoin the royal *pułk*. Of the hundred-and-a-half who had ridden out, according to the standard accounts a good third were left behind on the field – 19 *towarzysze* of the front rank and 35 or 36 of their *pocztowi* retainers.[311]

Sieniawski sent out a similar reconnaissance charge north of the Alsbach, possibly on his own initiative, though since these charges were a standard Polish tactic, he was hardly going out on a limb, and such action was in all likelihood entirely within his authority as Crown Field Hetman and commander of the left division. There are also indications however that he

---

Vizier's tent (the little baldachin at the Türkenschanz was hardly likely to have been visible enough as a target point, so this can only mean the great palace-tent complex 'auf der Schmelz'), and Sieniawski would not have bothered making his own reconnaissance north of the Alsbach if Zbierzchowski had already done it for him there. As for the distance covered: it must have gone a lot further than 400 yards if it went anywhere near the tent complex.

309 It is not impossible, however, that this description refers to events involving Sieniawski's corps.
310 This detail largely from Dolleczek, 'Entsatzschlacht', p.165. If the description of the pennants is 'true' and not merely colourful detail added by Dolleczek, then it *may* reinforce the impression that the squadron had not seen such close action as is sometimes portrayed – the big Polish hussar lances were designed to shatter on first impact, so any hussar still with his pennant at this stage had technically not fought with a Turk; however, Michał Paradowski has argued in personal communication that men of the second and third ranks might legitimately have retained intact lances.
311 Dolleczek, 'Entsatzschlacht', p.165; however, Paradowski, p.142, points out that the King in a letter a month later put the losses at 12 *towarzysze* (it is possible that the standard figure represents the losses for the whole campaign). Nevertheless, this represented significant casualties, but comparatively light ones given the circumstances – as with the charge of the Light Brigade at Balaclava in 1854, Zbierzchowski would have left every man dead on the field if he had been facing competent enemies.

would have had trouble *not* carrying out such a charge, because the Poles of his wing were restless, eager to get into action, difficult to restrain; and besides, there were signs that the Ottomans facing them, increasingly reinforced from the centre and Koca Ibrahim's wing, were psyching themselves up for a serious attack that might fall before they could fully deploy in the open. So the Hetman ordered forward the hussar *chorągiew* of Szczęsny (Felix) Potocki, from the *pułk* of the same, under the command of a junior officer called Krzysztof Skarbek, towards the Türkenschanz; to this, without orders, joined a *chorągiew* of *pancerni*, those of Szczęsny's young nephew Stanisław Potocki from the *pułk* of Andrzej Potocki;[312] the Crown Court Treasurer Andrzej Modrzewski also joined them, either on his own or with his *pancerni chorągiew* likewise from Andrzej Potocki's *pułk*. The start-point of the lunge is unclear: it is sometimes given as the Michaeler Berg, quite a long way back, which, with the target of the Türkenschanz, gives the impression that the charge might have run down the Währingerbach past Pötzleinsdorf; but more likely is that it started from wherever the tree-line was on the Vienna side of the Schafberg, and ran down the gentle lower slopes of the hill before it reached level ground. Before the Potockis was terrain far more broken than that which had faced Zbierzchowski, and much of it was occupied by Ottoman parties of Janissaries and dismounted *yerli kulu*; during their long advance through the vineyards and ditches and embankments, they were under constant harassing fire from these skirmisher detachments, which nevertheless avoided any contact and by feigned or real flights drew the Poles further on, so that the two squadrons had suffered heavy casualties even before, somewhere around the village of Gersthof, they ran into formed bodies of Ottoman soldiers, Bosnians and the household troops of the Grand Vizier.[313] As further Ottoman bands began to pile in around them, making their situation increasingly look like a trap, more of Sieniawski's battle-hungry cavalrymen allowed themselves to be drawn towards this area or were committed by the Hetman, to help disengage the Potockis. Back they came, the disengagement charges not very effective, for they were still hotly pursued as they went swinging in a wide bow to the north across the Währingerbach valley until they ran past the front of the Bavarian infantry whose musket fire finally persuaded the Ottoman horsemen to give up the chase.[314] Amongst the dead they left behind was Stanisław Potocki, killed by a powerful horizontal sword-cut which cut through his chain-mail neck-guard and into his skull; his half-decapitated body was found later, with no sign of the upper portion of the head.[315] Nearby was the body of Modrzewski.

Sieniawski and his eager men would not give up. Down the hills came a new limited attack, 2,000 cavalry under the Polish court official Marek

---

312 See Appendix I, 11.7, on the Potockis, including the 'Felix' vs. 'Szczęsny' question.
313 The Bosnians were probably amongst those moved across from facing Lorraine – their *beylerbeyi* was originally under Koca Ibrahim.
314 Since this would have taken them right past the front of the Türkenschanz, it is not the most obvious route the Poles would have chosen to retreat.
315 This is the standard account, based on Dyakowski; but Dalérac (vol. 1, p.157), reported he was killed by a musket shot that went through his mail armour (admittedly, identifying him indirectly, not by name).

Matczyński, Crown Master of the Horse.[316] They advanced partly from Pötzleinsdorf down the Währingerbach valley, and partly over the same crumpled extended lower slopes of the Schafberg that the Potockis had traversed. The Ottomans were pushing more and more troops in the area they were aiming for (probably, on either side of Gersthof, facing roughly northwest), and had even put 16 cannon in front of those on the southern side of the village, near the foot of the Schafberg slope – given the calibres of the guns they had assembled in the Türkenschanz just behind, it is safe to assume that these were light pieces. As Matczyński's men cleared the vineyards and began to build up speed, they received a salvo from these cannon – but there was only time for the one, and it was not enough to stop the Poles, who lowered their lances and drove through the guns into the waiting Ottoman troops behind. The first Turkish ranks were overwhelmed by the charge, but gradually the Poles were brought to a stop as they lost momentum due to the sheer density of the Ottoman masses still in front of them; and while those masses to their front were fighting them to a standstill, more troops were coming at their left, passing in front of the Türkenschanz or issuing out from it (Mansberg refers to Janissaries and *Silahdar*s attacking the Poles,[317] which seems plausible enough). Matczyński's command began to waver, then gave way, and suddenly they were fleeing back the way they had come, with thousands of jubilant Turkish horsemen on their heels.

It was a bad moment for the Poles; if the Ottomans broke through here, at the hinge with the Germans, the Christian army might just conceivably be split. Some of Sieniawski's infantrymen that were well forward on the slopes were ridden down, either by the fleeing cavalry of Matczyński or by the Turkish pursuers. Far away on the left wing, even the watching Goltz recognised the critical nature of the situation and, according to the Saxon account,[318] sent a message to the generals of the centre urging them to send reinforcements to the Poles – 'the Franconian Major General' was willing to go, but was barred from moving by orders from Waldeck who refused to brook any interference in his command. But Sobieski was on hand at the top of the Schafberg: he ordered the remaining Polish infantry brigades, and the Franconian infantry battalion (which was fortuitously standing on the northern slopes of the hill at that time) to open fire on the Turks, which broke the pursuit and allowed the cavalry to get behind the infantry where Sieniawski could rally them and start reforming their shattered ranks. The Turkish cavalry then turned on the infantry, who were now joined by the

---

316 This operation is one of the most obscure in a battle full of obscurities; see Appendix I, 11.8.
317 Mansberg, p.100. Mansberg provides some names of senior Polish officers killed in this clash, but since he includes in this list 'Montreoski', his version of the name of the commander of the attack, some doubt attaches to the reliability of the information (both officers who might be a match for 'Montreoski' were present at Párkány in October: Matczyński, the real commander, and Miączyński, the putative commander, the pronunciation of whose name, 'Mionchinski', makes him the most likely match for Mansberg's corrupted form).
318 *Aufrichtige und unpartheyische Relation*, pp.10–11 (the placement at this exact point in the afternoon is based on interpretation of the source). The claim is a little odd, but if true suggests that at this time the centre was still so far behind and so mired in difficult terrain that it could not see what was going on with the right wing.

remaining three German battalions.[319] Three times the disordered Ottoman bands threw themselves at the infantry holding steady behind their *chevaux-de-frise* and their lowered pikes; three times, they were stopped by the barriers and mown down by the blaze of musket fire that undulated up and down the line. Before the Ottomans could psyche themselves up for a fourth charge, help for the hard-pressed infantry thundered down from the north. First the two gallant Imperialist dragoons regiments Schulz and Kueffstein drove over the Währingerbach valley and ploughed into the right flank of the Ottoman horsemen; they were not strong enough to rout them, but the attacks on the infantry stopped while a bitter mêlée developed. The dragoons suffered heavily; Major Trautmannsdorf, in command of DR Schulz, was killed, other officers went down, and many dragoons[320]. However, they had bought time for their heavier brethren to advance: FML Rabatta brought some of Sachsen-Lauenburg's cuirassiers over the Währingerbach on the tracks of the dragoons, including his own regiment, and these managed to catch the Ottoman cavalry again on an exposed side. Rabatta's own cuirassier regiment as it advanced attracted a lot of fire (presumably, from the guns around Gersthof or above in the Türkenschanz) because it had at its head two figures in bright red coats, which the Ottomans knew was a colour indicating great nobles of the Christian world – and they were right, for these were the volunteer princes of Brunswick-Lüneburg, including Georg Ludwig, the future George I of Great Britain.[321] But the Turkish shots missed the two princes, and the armoured cavalry, despite some casualties, smashed into the Ottomans and began to drive them back. Rallied Poles from Matczyński's battered command joined in the counter-attack, and Waldeck apparently at last sent in some of the Bavarians as well to help.[322] Finally the Ottomans broke to flee; Kara Mustafa rode out and tried to rally them, but nothing could halt them until they reached their lines around Gersthof and under the guns of the Türkenschanz plateau.

Despite the unfortunate course of the follow-on attack of Matczyński, the two reconnaissance-charges had done their work: they had given the Polish commanders a working idea of the true nature of the terrain before them, and demonstrated how tough a response they might expect from the enemy – very tough before Sieniawski, feeble before Jabłonowski. Whether intentionally or not, the two charges, combined with the final outcome of Matczyński's attack, had also broken Ottoman willingness to oppose the Polish deployment. At some point during the Matczyński charge, Abaza

---

319 Wimmer, *Entsatz*, p.198, specifies the Franconians; most German accounts (at least, those that mention the Matczyński attack) suggest that all four borrowed German battalions were involved, which seems sensible enough, even if those accounts do still manage to place them way across the battlefield on the Galitzin Berg or the Heuberg.
320 Trautmannsdorf, from Mansberg, p.101. Mansberg also names another officer, but from DR Styrum, which was *probably* not here because (despite Le Bègue's Diary) it was recorded in action with Lorraine.
321 Sichart, vol. 1, p.447. It was probably around this time that Pallandt was killed.
322 Suggested by Le Bègue's Account. It is possible that Le Bègue's 'several Bavarian battalions' actually referred to the four battalions lent to the Poles and the reference to Waldeck was based on the secretary's assumption that the commander of the centre must have been ordering them.

Sari Hüseyin had unfurled near the centre of his wing, probably somewhere near the Alsbach, a huge red banner, 20 feet by 16 feet, decorated with gold symbols and inscriptions, attempting so it seems to encourage his men to fight harder;[323] but this could not stop the Ottomans of the left wing, shortly afterwards, from spontaneously pulling back from their forward positions to a line much nearer their camp, between Weinhaus/the Türkenschanz and Ottakring, ceding to the Poles the ability to get out onto the open ground unopposed.[324] There was no retreat by the Ottoman centre around the Türkenschanz, but here too any inclination to move forward again to stop the Polish deployment had vanished. The Poles meanwhile, seeing Hüseyin's banner, mistakenly believed it was the Standard of the Prophet and that it marked an Ottoman declaration to die fighting – Sobieski again distracted his artillery from their proper purpose by getting them to aim for this out-of-range symbol – though it was in fact merely a traditional Ottoman command flag as granted to senior officers. Despite the false impression conveyed by the banner, the balance of morale was clearly tipping in favour of the Poles, and the experienced Polish commanders did not fail to notice the moment: Sobieski cried out that the Ottomans were lost, sent aides across to Lorraine requesting him to send reinforcements with all speed, and ordered the hussars to advance.[325]

While Sieniawski's men had been suffering on the Schafberg, Jabłonowski had been building up his cavalry in deep formations at the broad exit from the Alsbach defile, just downstream from Dornbach, with Maligny and the dragoons continuing to cover the right flank of this position from the lower slopes of the hills to the south. The ground in front of them was not truly open or even level yet, for there were still the outlying slopes of the hills and these continued to be clogged with vineyards and their enclosures; but it was good enough ground on which to form up. Now, with the Ottoman left wing pulling back, was the right moment to come out, and out came Jabłonowski and the massed cavalry of his right wing and the royal *pułk*, out from the defile onto the fields immediately before it, peeling to right and left in all their

---

323 Time of the unfurling, from Wimmer, *Entsatz*, p.199. There are hints in other histories (e.g. Dolleczek, 'Entsatzschlacht', p.167) that it may have been deployed a little later, as part of an attempt to prevent the left wing pulling back. The Germans would capture several more such massive banners during the subsequent war. See Chapter 11, 'Booty' section, including the note on Sobieski's dispatch of the banner to the Pope, for the its subsequent fate. The main known surviving reproduction from the period is in Feigius (Johann Constantius Feigius, *Wunderbahrer Adlers-Schwung, oder fernere Geschichts-Fortsetzung Ortelii Redivivi et Continuati: das ist, eine aussführliche historische Beschreibung von mancherleyen vorgefallenen Staats-Händeln… und von allem was von anno 1664 in politicis und civilibus so wohl bey dem Käyserl. Hof zu Wienn, als in Ober- und Nider-Ungarn, auch Sibenbürgen… vorgefalle* ([Vienna]: Voigt, 1694), vol. ,1 plate opp. p.94, with description, pp.94–95); it did also appear in other dodgier publications, and is also described in Boethius, vol. 1, pp.168–170, and a nineteenth-century reproduction is in Toifel. Unlike other captured banners, this one has rarely been reproduced in modern works.
324 According to some, e.g. Stoye (p.262) and Dolleczek, 'Entsatzschlacht' (p.167), there was a general flight. For the left wing as a whole, this seems an over-reaction; only those parts of the left wing that had been in action along with the Ottoman centre against Sieniawski were likely to have fled.
325 Dalérac, vol. 1, 158–159. Dalérac gives an indirect description of Sobieski's words, not an exact quote: he 's'écria, que c'étoient des gens perdus' – he cried out, that they were lost folk.

feathered, armoured splendour to form up in line of battle, with Sieniawski's men coming down to link up to their left. Including Sieniawski, the line extended from near Gersthof and the Währingerbach on the left, where it was in contact with the Germans, to somewhere south of the Alsbach on the right.[326] Not all of Sieniawski's wing joined the new formation, however; on his left, the northern end of the line nearest the Währingerbach, the Poles remained formed as before, with infantry continuing to lead the struggle towards the Türkenschanz. At the southern end, although no history ever says so, it is likely that the 2,800 dragoons came out to complete the line and cover its southern flank, perhaps facing or just north of Ottakring – Sobieski and Jabłonowski could see the shallowness of Abaza Sari Hüseyin's wing and knew that he did not have enough troops to send off on a flanking attack that would pose any real threat to the end of their line, while Rafał Leszczyński had guaranteed that there would be no Tatar harrassment from the south. Between 7,000 and 10,000 Polish cavalry (not counting the dragoons) were in this great formation or in the process of joining it. There were two main lines. In the first were most of the winged hussars, the élite of the Polish army, about two and a half thousand men, each *chorągiew* the usual two or three ranks deep, with substantial intervals between each *chorągiew*. About 100 paces behind these, in the second line were the much more numerous *pancerni* squadrons, perhaps themselves in two lines with the first facing the intervals in the hussar line and the second covering the intervals in *that* line. Behind this chequer-board layout, the infantry formed up, both the Poles and the four borrowed German battalions, to 'receive' the cavalry if it was defeated. There was also some kind of cavalry reserve – we know that at least two squadrons of hussars, the *chorągiew* of the King and that of Prince Jakub, were left in reserve, presumably behind the infantry, and there may have been a few of *pancerni* held back as well; the light cavalry squadrons were probably placed with the reserve as well. Westerners noted how deep the overall formation was compared with what they were used to – 'more depth than front' said Le Bègue, though in fact it was hardly much deeper than the formation adopted by the left wing all day. (This is the standard account, but see below for a different version according to Paradowski.)

Morale was high. The bulk of the cavalry faced Abaza Sari Hüseyin's left wing; not only could they see the weakness of the forces opposing them but also they had observed for themselves how reluctant the Ottomans troops were to face them. Even for Sieniawski's troops on the left who had just had to fight so hard, they had been allowed in the end to deploy without further molestation; the battle was clearly going their way. And they were now ready for the sort of fighting the Poles knew they were very good at.

To their left or left-rear, the Poles were supported by another great mass of cavalry, Sachsen-Lauenburg's Imperialists and, a bit further on, the

---

[326] The exact point where the line ended is never made clear. Suttinger's picture-map of the battle shows the Polish line stopping short of the Alsbach; despite Suttinger's frequent geographical errors, this may give us a hint that there was not enough going on beyond the Alsbach to command attention. However, the marginally more ridiculous Hallart map puts the Poles well beyond the Alsbach.

THE BATTLE OF KAHLENBERG

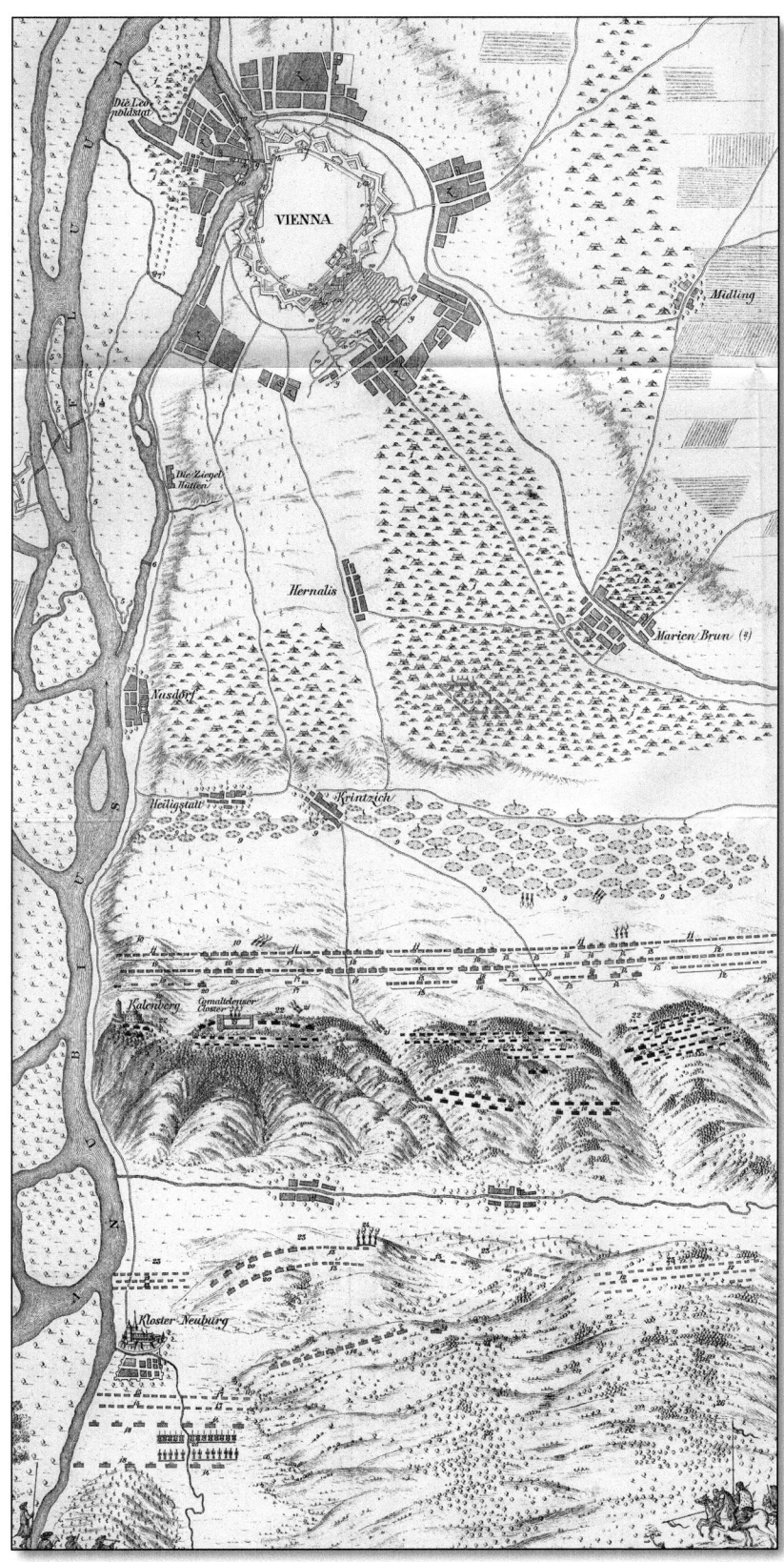

Second part of Hallart's plan, from the drawn copy in *Das Kriegsjahr 1683*. See Chapter 3 for the first part of this and comments on Hallart.

Bavarian and Franconian cuirassiers and dragoons under FML Bayreuth. The Imperialists had perhaps as many as 6,000 in their 11 regiments totalling 24 squadrons; Bayreuth had 3,000 Bavarians and 1,200 Franconians in 23 rather smaller squadrons. Although this made a good 10,000 horse, giving a grand total of cavalry in this part of the field of 20,000 (a figure which carried Wimmer away into describing the subsequent actions as 'one of the greatest cavalry attacks of history'),[327] the Reichs troops were already, as we have seen, rather pushed behind their infantry than on its flank; Sachsen-Lauenburg, in whole or in part, may have initially flanked the Poles, standing between them and the Bavarian infantry, but when the advance resumed, as we will see, its concentric nature meant that there was less and less room in the line, and the German cavalry was pushed out of the line to the rear, so that it supported the German infantry and the Poles from behind.

Final attack

The 'decision' to press on

With the entire Christian army now, some time before 5 p.m., out of the woods and fully formed up in a proper single line of battle stretching from the Canal near Heiligenstadt to the Alsbach and beyond, the moment of truth had come: should they press on or wait for a fresh start on the morrow? If anyone seriously considered this question, they did not think about it for very long. As already recorded, Lorraine and the left wing had around or before 4 p.m. resumed their advance after Heiligenstadt in the hope of easing the pressure on the Poles of Sieniawski by preventing the Ottomans from sending even more troops from their right wing across to face the Poles; by the time the Polish line had deployed, the Imperialists and Saxons were approaching the Döblingerbach-Krottenbach line, or had reached it and paused again waiting to see how the Poles would fare – no later than 5 p.m. and, as we shall see, perhaps as early as 4. While Sieniawski's forces were fighting back and forth with the Ottoman centre, according to the Saxon account:

> … the Duke of Lorraine, together with other Imperialist generals, came to the Saxons on the forementioned hill and observed the action on the right wing right to its end, and as one saw the enemy flee, the Duke of Lorraine asked the Field Marshal Goltz whether one was satisfied with the honour and great advantage that had been won over the enemy this day; to which Field Marshal Goltz gave the answer: As it appears that the enemy is terrified, so he thought it good that one should pursue them and further prosecute the victory. The Duke of

---

327 Wimmer, *Entsatz*, p.201.

Lorraine said to this, 'Marchons donc' [let us march then] and together with the other generals with him rode back to the Imperialists.[328]

According to an anonymous Saxon manuscript,[329] Goltz added that he was an old man and looked forward to having decent quarters in Vienna this night. However, the whole incident was probably a piece of man-management by Lorraine, giving the Saxons the impression that he was involving them in the decision-making, either out of courtesy or due to the need to ensure that he kept them willing – Goltz' humorous reply suggests that the veteran war-horse understood the situation perfectly well and did not take the offer of a choice too seriously either. For there can be no doubt that Lorraine had been determined from the start to do as much as he could on this day to relieve Vienna, and with sunset in mid-September falling at around 6.30 and darkness perhaps half an hour later, the day still had at least two hours of daylight left, with the constant incentive in his ears of the incessant bombardment of Vienna still going on ahead of him; it is highly unlikely that, no matter how hard the day's fighting had been for the soldiers, the Duke seriously considered stopping, abandoning the momentum that had been built up during the day and giving the Ottomans a night to repair their obviously shaky morale, to entrench their positions even further.

The same applies to Sobieski. Some historians[330] have suggested that even up to this point the King was still thinking, now that he had occupied the foothills, of halting for the night and making the final decisive attack on the following morning, and only changed his mind at the last moment. This is unlikely. Sobieski had late in the morning changed his mind about an attack on the 13th; by the time he rejoined the Polish army from the Kahlenberg, the decision had been made that the attack would take place today. If the King had been motivated when he left the left wing solely by concern that Lorraine might win the battle without him, more serious reasons had taken over by now: his forces, deployed and ready to strike, were facing a wavering and increasingly confused enemy, with a couple of hours of daylight left; even if the Poles could be persuaded to sit down and rest for the night (the eagerness of Sieniawski's men to get stuck in made this improbable), they would find it very difficult to make a camp secure against Ottoman sneak night attacks when the two sides were so close; and in the night, anything could happen – the Ottomans might entrench, might call up reinforcements or slip significant forces round into the Wienerwald to attack his flank or rear, might very well strengthen the left wing (already being reinforced) that needed to be weak if he was to encircle their whole army, worst of all might decamp over the River Wien and avoid altogether the noose that he wanted to slip round their army's neck, especially if Lorraine kept up his own advance

---

328 *Aufrichtige und unpartheyische Relation*, p.11. The hill mentioned cannot be identified with certainty; from the context of the text, it could be read as the Nussberg, which is highly unlikely. The mention of the enemy fleeing, which seems to refer the repulse of those attacking Sieniawski, puts the discussion with Goltz at somewhere between 4 and 5 p.m.
329 quoted by *Das Kriegsjahr 1683*, pp.257–258.
330 e.g. Barker, pp.330/332.

until nightfall – and it had been clear all day that the morale of the German troops was high and nothing would prevent them from continuing their own advance if they elected to do so. Sobieski wanted his decisive victory, and he could read a battlefield very well; if the thought of stopping for the night ever entered his head, it had gone by the time of the Ottoman left wing's nervous withdrawal a little earlier, when he had cried out that the Ottomans were lost.

There may well have been a brief period at that moment somewhen around 5 o'clock when, from Lorraine facing the Döblingerbach past Waldeck before the Türkenschanz to the Polish dragoons beyond the Alsbach, the whole Christian army was halted, preparing for the final push; but if so (and I doubt this), it did not last very long.

Final Ottoman positions and attempted counter-measures

The Ottoman army had preserved its overall arrangement, but the proportions had radically changed. Koca Ibrahim still commanded the right wing, but this was a badly depleted formation, no longer nearly half of the army; apart from the casualties of eleven hours of continuous fighting and those who inevitably would have slunk away as the battle went from bad to worse, he had lost thousands of troops moved across to the centre and left wing, either by orders from the Grand Vizier or of their own volition. What remained of the right wing held the entrenchments along the Döblingerbach, up as far as where this line overlapped the centre at the Türkenschanz; the field fortifications were feeble, but the stream in front appeared to the advancing Imperialists like a ravine, a substantial obstacle, and the shape of the hill beyond made it difficult to see the Ottoman defences clearly until one had crossed the ravine and climbed the hill, though it also meant that the artillery studding the line would be unable to fire properly at the advancing Christians. There is in Le Bègue's Diary a suggestion (it cannot be put any stronger than this) that the Ottomans had by now lost contact with the 'Danube' (the Canal), that is, that their line had become so shrunken, it no longer reached right to the water, and was open to be outflanked at any time.[331] The rest of the army, the centre and left wing, now contained the bulk of the Ottoman troops, perhaps as many as two thirds.[332] In the centre, Kara Mustafa still commanded at the Türkenschanz, with men in the entrenchment on the hill and bunched up in positions before it and around or behind Gersthof, facing on one side Waldeck and the Reichs troops, on the other the northern end of Sieniawski's line. Here was where the Standard of the Prophet really stood. A little earlier, 16 Ottoman cannons had been in position south of Gersthof; it is not known if these were still in service, or whether they were out of commission after they had been overrun by Matczyński's first charge, but we

---

331 Le Bègue said, describing in brief terms the general advance from the level of Nussdorf: 'the enemy always retiring under the musketry of our infantry, which forced them to abandon the Danube and make an effort against the right wing, where the Poles had only cavalry.' This might only refer, however, to the drift of Turkish troops to their left, and the consequent thinning of the whole wing nearest the Danube.

332 It is hard to equate with the events of the final attack in the centre the claim by *Das Kriegsjahr 1683*, p.257, that the centre was now almost denuded of troops and held only by artillery.

hear no mention of them in action in the final stage of the battle. It is unclear whether the Ottomans still held Gersthof itself; since it lay below the edge of the hill on which their centre now primarily stood, I believe they did not. On the left was Abaza Sari Hüseyin and the left wing, over-extended and thin even with his left flank stretching only as far as Ottakring but filling out all the time as troops moving across from Koca Ibrahim were fed into the line.[333] Like the Poles opposite him, his southern flank was effectively in the air, but with the Poles deploying out of the Alsbach, they were in no position to catch him with a flank attack.

Superficially, the Ottoman position still had some advantages: the line of the Döblingerbach-Krottenbach, with its 'ravine' and entrenchments on the slopes behind. But that was the last line of defence from the north: behind it stood what Christian witnesses called the 'first camp', the section of the Ottoman ring of tents between the Döblingerbach and the Währingerbach. For the rest of the Ottoman army, streams cut into its position all along the line; even the Türkenschanz, on its moderately commanding hill, was dominated by nearby lower slopes of the foothills, so that if the Christians brought up some artillery, they could with ease make it completely untenable. And like Koca Ibrahim's wing, the rest of the line was now pushed back close to the camp; it had for a primarily-cavalry force very little room for manoeuvre, no space in which to rally and reform if anything went wrong.

There are occasional suggestions that Kara Mustafa ordered counter-attacks, either on the extreme left wing alone or on both wings, to try to stop or at least hinder the impending attack, only to be thrown back yet again by a blaze of infidel musketry. The sources have no trace of this, although earlier in the afternoon after the capture of Heiligenstadt the Imperialists had thought the Ottomans were preparing a counter-attack on them (see above), with which this might be confused. Certainly, as we will see, Ottoman morale on Koca Ibrahim's wing was so bad that any counter-attack there was now beyond their capability.

Who broke in first?

The question is one that has vexed historians ever since 1683; on it could be said to turn the issue of who, ultimately, 'won' the battle for the Christians: Austrians, south-Germans, or Poles. Had Lorraine already broken through Koca Ibrahim when Sobieski began the final great Polish attack, or did the Polish attack make it easier for him to get over the Döblingerbach?

Given the extraordinary imprecision and inconsistency of the times specified in the various contemporary accounts that make it impossible to match them all up exactly with each other, we may never know for sure. Le Bègue was quite explicit about the sequence of events in both the Account and the Diary, but there is always a subtle bias in his version of events in favour of his master, so on its own his version cannot be accepted. However, there

---

[333] Many historians put the line extending as far as Baumgarten on the River Wien, or to Breitensee not far short of it. The Ottoman camp behind stretched all the way to the Wien, but Abaza Sari Hüseyin did not.

is one key feature of the battle that pushes the balance down firmly in favour of one side: the fact that so many Ottomans from the right wing, including Koca Ibrahim himself, managed to escape. If Sobieski had broken Abaza Sari Hüseyin first, the Poles must soon after have been in the southern part of the main Ottoman camp, squarely across the line of retreat of Koca Ibrahim and his troops. There was admittedly a moderately wide gap beyond the camp before the Ottoman siege works began, but this was filled with the ruined suburbs of the city and littered with all the detritus of a great siege; it would not have made an easy line of retreat for thousands of fleeing Turks, even if we allow that the Poles in the camp would have voluntarily stood by and let them go past unhindered, watching go with them all Sobieski's hopes of a victory of annihilation. Over three miles separate the Döblingerbach where Koca Ibrahim made his last stand from the River Wien, beyond which lay comparative safety for the fleeing Ottomans. Three miles past the Poles, with no attempt by the Poles to interfere, to trap them? It is inconceivable. Kara Mustafa's attempt to fight a holding action around the palace-tent complex was undoubtedly intended to gain time for as many of his troops as possible to get past the Poles and over the Wien, but the action here did not last long enough to have allowed all of Koca Ibrahim's men to get past, and besides it was really only holding the Poles up along a small front – no real obstacle to Polish penetration of the camp on either side. The escape of Koca Ibrahim, the absence of a massive entrapment of the bulk of the Ottoman army by the Poles, argues strongly for a collapse and retreat of the northern sector starting some time *before* Sobieski gave the word for the winged hussars to charge, thus confirming the sequence of events recorded by Le Bègue. Maybe the watchers in the city[334] who timed the final attack by Lorraine as early as 4 p.m. were actually nearer the mark than Le Bègue who put it at 5. Maybe Le Bègue was correct in timing the Imperialist entry into the Ottoman camp at 5 and the final Polish attack that broke through Abaza Sari Hüseyin's lines somewhat later. However, against all this, we must observe that the Ottoman centre, in the Türkenschanz-Gersthof area no more than a mile nearer the Wien than Koca Ibrahim, was almost certainly still fighting when the Poles started their attack – unless Sieniawski's infantry attacked well before the great hussar charge, which Wimmer explicitly denies, the Turks must have still been in action here when the hussar charge hit, and would have had to make it past the front of the Poles for at least two miles – just as awkward as for Koca Ibrahim's men, if the Poles were then or shortly after in possession of the Ottoman camp.

Although historians down to the nineteenth century generally allowed national bias to influence their conclusions – according to German-speakers, Lorraine broke through first; according to Poles, Sobieski did – today even Wimmer, writer of the definitive recent history from the Polish perspective, has conceded that Lorraine's drive over the Döblingerbach preceded the Polish attack, indeed precipitated it (see below).[335]

---

334 Hocke, p.194; Ruess, p.71.
335 Paradowski, pp.143–144, while not stressing the point, acknowledges it. This is not to say, however, that the Polish contribution to the victory was not important. On this point, see

Lorraine and the rout of Koca Ibrahim

So, by 5 p.m. at the latest, perhaps as early as 4 p.m., Lorraine with the Imperialist and Saxon infantry set off to cross the Döblingerbach, still in the careful order of battle, fully closed up. The attack turned out to be a lot easier than expected. Le Bègue, starting from the point of the stabilising of Sieniawski's line after the Matczyński repulse and including the advance south from the Nesselbach, put it thus in his Account:

> After this success the King continued his advance with all the army, the enemy for their part resisted in all the different posts that they had occupied. The fire of their musketry and of their cannon did us some damage, but our troops not being shaken advanced always and continued to gain ground. However the Duke having got close with the left to the enemy camp so as to distract the effort that they were making on the right, the Turks formed up in order of battle at the ravine before their camp, and, turning several pieces of cannon against us, they fired with them several shots and gave the impression of wanting to hold this post [the line of the Döblingerbach], which was the strongest of all the ground and which served as a retrenchment for their camp. But their firmness did not last long, and our people having advanced to musket range, they abandoned this ravine at five o'clock in the evening, and we seized the opportunity to get over it without hindrance and to enter their camp.

The Baden account broadly supports this description, of a moderately tough defence *before* the ravine, followed by almost complete failure to defend the height and the camp beyond:

> They made a great noise at our arrival and came up in disorder sword in hand, seeming as if they wanted to fall right amongst our battalions; but not being able to sustain the fire of our infantry and of our pieces, they were overthrown and forced to retrace their steps in confusion faster that they had come, knowing that they were abandoning to us this height, the same as the one where their camp was positioned.

The Saxon account described it slightly differently:

> The Saxon infantry thereupon immediately advanced down the hill, with the Imperialists following, and the whole [order of] battle began to move. Those Turks which were still in the bottom, as they saw this, retired to their first camp, and one saw, that they had assembled many thousands above at their camp on the left side, where was a great open field. On the corner of this height the enemy had thrown up something rather like a redoubt, and placed in it 6 bronze cannon, from which they gave fire on those advancing, but always shooting too high.

Chapter 13 below.

> One held it assuredly for certain at this time that the enemy would dispute this height, as nothing was to be seen from the bottom of what was happening on the height. Both the Imperialists and the Saxons steadily advanced to the height, and everyone was busying himself climbing this while keeping in good readiness to fight. Finally as one got to the top expecting to meet the enemy, they had already cleared off, retreating for the last camp.
>
> The Saxons were thereby the first [in], and therefore they also received the 6 bronze guns as booty, as their standards had been the first to be seen flying in the enemy camp.

So when the Christian left wing had climbed the heights south of the Döblingerbach, Koca Ibrahim's men were already withdrawing south through the tents of the northern end of the Ottoman camp; amongst the tents, the withdrawal degenerated into a rout, and soon the Ottomans of the right wing were heading for the main camp beyond and then the River Wien.[336] The only uncertainty is the six-gun battery mentioned so proudly by the Saxon account: it is tempting to see this as a reference to the Türkenschanz, and some historians have done so, but the Türkenschanz was the next step *beyond* this line that the Saxons were attacking here, and besides, if the Saxons could not see properly from the bottom what the Turks were doing on the heights directly in front of them, they certainly could not see the Türkenschanz any more than the Ottomans could have fired on them even so ineffectively. It may refer to a redoubt on the left end of Koca Ibrahim's line, probably on the Krottenbach west of Döbling village, and therefore somewhat north of the Türkenschanz, though in this case it is hard to see the Saxons describing it as part of the field 'on the left side', which from their point of view meant Koca Ibrahim's *right*.[337]

Koca Ibrahim and the Ottoman right wing were no more. Up to this point, Lorraine had apparently been sticking with his original intention, to push on keeping the Canal to his immediate left, until he reached the counterscarp of Vienna itself. Now, however, he changed his mind: the entire left was ordered to swing to its right, inward, away from the Canal, and march through the camp in that direction, 'without a single soldier breaking ranks to plunder the baggage that the enemy had left scattered around, nor their raised tents' (Le Bègue). His precise aim with this move is less clear, but was probably intended to support the allies: the day was clearly now won,

---

336 Hocke, p.194; Ruess, p.71.
337 Slight support for the former interpretation is provided by the Suttinger map; idiosyncratic though Suttinger's geography was (in this same section of the map, Nussdorf and Döbling are almost within spitting distance of each other, with no sign of Heiligenstadt at all), as a Saxon he might be expected to try to get the Saxon trophy guns correct, and indeed there is an Ottoman gun emplacement, the only artillery portrayed on the map, some way up the Döblingerbach, on the edge of the slope facing north, right opposite the point in Lorraine's line where we would expect the Saxons to be… with exactly six tiny cannons visible. Although technically the position could equally be meant to portray the Türkenschanz (of which there is no other trace on the map), and what appears to be the Saxons might equally be the Reichs corps of the centre, the number of guns being the same as those the Saxons captured cannot be a coincidence.

Vienna bound to be relieved, so pushing on to establish contact with the city was no longer so pressing, and he could afford to turn in to help the centre and right wing, where the Türkenschanz (probably) and Abaza Sari Hüseyin (certainly) were still holding out; Le Bègue certainly *implies* that his aim was to frighten the rest of the Ottoman army (and states that it did so). Perhaps he had finally been convinced of the value of Sobieski's desire for a victory of annihilation and was prepared to move inwards to act as the anvil on which the Poles would smash the remaining Ottoman forces. Or perhaps the reason was entirely prosaic, and the tents of the Ottoman camp were so densely packed nearest the Canal that it was easier to advance further away from the river where tents were presumably more scattered, allowing the left wing to preserve its formation as it passed through them.

Waldeck and Sieniawski against the Ottoman centre

Waldeck and the allied centre resumed their advance at the same time as Lorraine. On one side, the centre maintained contact with the left wing, remained roughly level with it, but on the other side, the right, the Bavarians, after passing Sievering, had been pushing ever further southward – as we have already seen, in contact with the Polish left flank near the upper Währingerbach after helping them in the action around Gersthof.[338] Sachsen-Lauenburg and the cavalry were increasingly squeezed back behind the infantry as the semi-circle of the Christian line closed in on the Ottomans. Kara Mustafa faced them from his headquarters in the central entrenchment of the Türkenschanz, but this was not the sole Ottoman defence here: their line ran probably from the Krottenbach, where it had been in contact with the right wing, around the edge of the 'plateau' on which the Türkenschanz stood and therefore in front of the Türkenschanz, to curve round in a great horseshoe-shaped arc following the line of the Währingerbach towards Weinhaus. The right-hand part of the line faced north and north-west towards the Reichs troops; the left-hand part faced west and even southwest, towards the Bavarians and the Poles of Sieniawski's left. Artillery from at least three points in the circumference was bombarding the allied centre as it closed in (apparently concentrated to the north of the Währingerbach, since they are specified as firing on the Bavarians); Ottoman artillery was quite slow-firing, so we should not think of this as a hail of cannon-balls, rather an occasional blast, and we should also remember that the calibre of most guns was small. Janissaries along the Währingerbach side, almost certainly supported by some of these guns, were meanwhile blazing away with their muskets at the Poles, inconveniencing Sieniawski considerably.

---

338 Account of the centre's action based primarily on Wimmer, *Entsatz*, pp.202–203; and Mansberg, p.108, including the 'Franconian manuscript' (actually part of the Schliz von Görz account) quoted in n.75; with some value to be found in Rauchbar, vol. 2, p.270. The Bavarian military histories provide some details, but do not give the impression that they have fully understood the lie of the field in the centre. No-one can agree on exactly when the Türkenschanz fell; I have followed Wimmer on the time, as his version seems the most credible.

About the time that Lorraine and the left wing were driving over the Döblingerbach and throwing Koca Ibrahim's troops into rout, and as Sobieski was ordering the *first* of the great Polish attacks, the Reichs forces were closing in on Kara Mustafa, still under the bombardment of the three batteries. The right flank of the Ottoman line here was already in the air, due to the departure of Koca Ibrahim's men, and Waldeck ordered the Franconian generals FML von der Leyen and GWM Thüngen to push three battalions forward against that flank, while Degenfeld, accompanied by his spirited Elector, led forward the Bavarians in a frontal attack on the sector nearest the Währingerbach (presumably, the rest of the Franconians fixed the Ottomans in front of them across the lower Krottenbach). Although no Polish involvement is mentioned by the German accounts, Sieniawski was also sending forward some of his infantry brigades to deal with the Janissaries on the heights. Disturbed by the flanking move of the three Franconian battalions, and aware that their friends to their right were already in flight, the north-facing Ottomans easily gave way. The Bavarians advanced through the slow storm of cannon-shot, and as musket-fire from the Janissaries joined in, they climbed the slopes leading up to the plateau, calmly and steadily, without hesitation. Sieniawski's brigades closed in from the southern side. Ottoman morale was already plummeting with first Koca Ibrahim's men fleeing behind the centre and now part of the centre joining the flight under the pressure of the Franconian attack; as the Master of Ceremonies put it, with the enemy storming forward on all sides 'there vanished from every one of them the strength and desire to struggle and fight, and there appeared the indications of that confusion which always leads to a defeat.' Now, faced by the apparently unstoppable advance of the Bavarians, the remaining Ottomans began to waver, abandoning their weak entrenchments, including the artillery, as they gave ground.[339] Nine cannon fell into Bavarian hands and, according to one version, were turned by the Bavarians against their original owners. On across the plateau drove the Bavarians and Franconians, keeping good order, steadily firing with matchlock and battalion gun – much, we may imagine, like the progress of the left wing over the Nussberg earlier in the day; 'the army of Islam was showered like rain with shot from the cannons and muskets of the enemy,' the Master of Ceremonies recorded.[340]

Kara Mustafa was in despair. His right flank had collapsed completely – Koca Ibrahim had appeared before him at the baldachin while the battle still raged, and the Grand Vizier heaped vituperations on him for failing to defeat the infidels, then ignored him.[341] Now, the Poles were pressing Abaza

---

339 Unusually, we have support for this point from both sides. The Schliz von Görz account (Newald, vol. 2, p.101) described the Turks, as the Bavarians stormed forward despite their fire, as 'wavering' (*wankelhaft*); for the Master of Ceremonies, see Kreutel & Teply, p.190.
340 Kreutel & Teply, p.190.
341 Mavrocordato, in Kreutel & Teply, 88. Given this statement, it is highly unlikely (no matter how psychologically believable it is) that Kara Mustafa actually handed command of the army to Koca Ibrahim (as some historians claim, following the Baden account in Röder, vol. 1, Urk., p.18) so that the venerable *beylerbeyi* of Buda could be blamed for the defeat later – though of course Kara Mustafa may have *claimed* later that he did transfer command. The rest of this paragraph is based primarily on the Master of Ceremonies' account in Kreutel & Teply, p.190.

Sari Hüseyin hard on the left, and no-one could expect the left wing to hold out much longer. Polish troops attacking on the Währingerbach side even appeared to be driving for the Standard of the Prophet. Kara Mustafa finally mounted his horse, and, joined by Vani Efendi, formed up the cavalry still with him, the *Sipahi* and *Silahdar* regiments of the guard cavalry, and whatever was left of his household troops, to his right and left, and prepared to stand firm, perhaps even hoping to launch a desperate counter-attack with this cavalry reserve (the location of this is unknown, but may be presumed to have been behind the Türkenschanz proper). But the Germans continued their advance, in the same sort of solid line blazing with fire that had proved so unstoppable throughout the day. Turkish morale collapsed completely. On either side of the Grand Vizier, masses of men turned their horses and fled, most heading straight back to their tents in a desperate hope to be able to pack up their goods before the Christians caught up or before Abaza Sari Hüseyin and the left wing finally collapsed under the Polish onslaught. Kara Mustafa struggled back through the masses of fleeing Turks through the camp, heading for the great palace-tent complex, accompanied only by his immediate entourage, who carried the Standard of the Prophet. Orders were sent to the Ottomans in the siege works to evacuate the works and join the general retreat.[342] He may have been accompanied by the Khan, and if so the story in western sources[343] may even be true that the Grand Vizier turned to him with an appeal for help only to be told that the Tatars knew the King of Poland and the only way to save oneself from him lay in flight; but according to Mavrocordato the Khan had already fled the field from a position on the left wing (perhaps with Hacci Giray's little band) well before this.

Behind them, the Reichs infantry halted, knowing they could never catch up with the fleeing cavalry, and the lines opened up to let out their own lumbering horsemen who would now lead the continuing advance;[344] the Bavarian CR Arco was first into the Ottoman camp. Maximilian Emanuel or Degenfeld had issued orders that the regiments were not to break ranks, and were to leave only a watch guard to 'take possession' of those parts of the camp they had won; and the sturdy professionals obeyed to a man – despite all the provisions and riches that they could see around them as they penetrated amongst the luxurious Ottoman tents, not a soldier left the ranks.

As Kara Mustafa and his party made their way south through the chaos of the camp, here and there enemy riders were beginning to appear amongst the tents to their right: Sobieski had struck.

---

342 According to Mavrocordato (Kreutel & Teply, p.88), this order was only issued when he reached the palace-tent complex; according to the diarists (see below), he was far too busy there to issue orders. By this stage, Kara Mustafa was not really capable of rational decision-making, but it does seem unlikely that he and his entourage would have ridden *past* the siege works and then tried to send orders *back* to them in the teeth of the rout and pursuing Christians.

343 Dalérac, vol. 1, p.159; Plater, p.78. Sobieski's story, written to his wife as a form of self-praise, is hardly reliable, and Dalérac's account may have been based on a published version of the King's letter.

344 such, at least, is the conclusion from the tradition that CR Arco was first in (from e.g. Renner, p.437); this cannot have been so if the centre's cavalry had still been following the infantry, as previously.

NO MORE TIME TO LOSE

Climax of the battle.

Strike to, strike dead: attack of the Polish cavalry

Sobieski was probably still on his vantage point on the Schafberg when he saw Lorraine's crossing of the Döblingerbach and the collapse of the right wing. Not only was it *possible* to fight the battle today, it had now become *essential* for the Poles to strike if the King was not to be left a humiliated spectator of another man's victory or of an Ottoman withdrawal over the River Wien during the night escaping the trap he had planned for them. So down the hill the King rode to join his massed cavalry formed up at the bottom of the Schafberg, stretching from where Sieniawski's left was in action around the Türkenschanz plateau south across the Alsbach. Slowly and calmly he rode; the careful progress projected an air of confidence to the soldiers, passed on an impression that the Ottomans were not enough of a threat to be worth hurrying – with a bit of luck (he may well have thought) they would not notice that the overburdened royal horse could hardly go any faster.

Because of the heat under the blazing sun, the King had decided to go without any armour – given his bulk, this would have been intolerable – and was wearing civilian clothing that stood out very clearly amongst all the metal and mail of the hussars and *pancerni*: a *kontusz* (a robe with large skirts and split sleeves) in a deep sky blue colour, over a white silk under-coat or *żupan*; on his head, a fur-edged *kołpak* bonnet with a spray of feathers held in place by a clasp with a huge and enormously valuable gemstone; in his hands, nothing but the *buława*, the big heavy ceremonial mace used by Polish generals as one of their insignia of command, gilded and with its onion-shaped head encrusted with jewels.[345] The steed itself was a perfect specimen, a magnificent chestnut horse, richly caparisoned with all the fussy ostentatiousness that Poles loved. Behind him on one side rode a herald bearing a big ceremonial shield showing the coat of arms of the Janina clan, to which the Sobieski sept belonged; on the other, a hussar bearing his *buńczuk*, the second insignium of command, a lance with some kind of decoration on it – for the supreme commander, a spray of falcon's feathers – designed to allow the general's position to be seen from any part of the battlefield. Always image-conscious, the King had made sure that everything about him declared his community with his soldiers – every part of his attire was distinctively, loudly Polish. However, beside him rode his teenage son Prince Jakub, and there the image was completely different: Sobieski wanted to arrange a marriage for Jakub with a Habsburg princess, which might help make permanent his family's hold on the elective Polish throne, and since he knew how royalty of the west looked down their noses at the 'backward' Poles, Jakub was smartly dressed in a *western* manner, with a coat and breeches, a helmet, and the sort of old-fashioned body armour that west European generals still occasionally wore even though it recalled the styles of the Thirty Years' War. No-one was going to sneer at Jakub Sobieski for a

---

[345] Most historians record some version of the description, based on a contemporary work produced by Sobieski's PR machine, Kochowski; but only Wimmer, *Entsatz*, p.201, says he went without armour because of the heat, others suggest that the armour was under the clothing.

hick – and it did no harm that the get-up would protect the royal son and heir quite well should any enemies come his way.

(What follows is the standard account, with a dramatic charge by the winged hussars, but Paradowski presents a more nuanced version, with the Poles partly organised into mixed 'squadrons' of hussars and *pancerni*, not all of which participated in the grand charge – some units were held back in reserve, meaning that the usual figure quoted for the hussars of 2,500 is probably too high. This strikes me as very credible, but the reader will need to review Paradowski and make up their own minds on the point.)[346]

Around 5 p.m., with about an hour and a half to go before sunset, Sobieski put himself at the head of the massive chequer-board of cavalry units;[347] he raised the *buława*, the heart-exalting trumpets and great bloodbeat-heavy kettle-drums began to sound, and slowly the huge body of horsemen began to move forward.

For all their feathers and armour and their medieval noble arrogance, the Poles were professional soldiers – and this was not Hollywood[348] – so there was no hugely dramatic and hugely ineffective onslaught with riders starting to canter and then build up to a furious gallop hundreds of yards from the enemy; even on level ground, the norm was to charge only from about 50–60 paces. Hindered by the last of the vineyards and their hedges and ditches,[349] the cavalry's advance was at first slow, but gradually picking up speed, always careful to preserve formation; it ignored occasional artillery fire from the Ottoman left wing ahead or striking its left flank from the Ottoman centre, it ignored sporadic musketry from Ottoman skirmishers (who presumably either fled after firing or were ridden down), and only as it reached the

---

346 Paradowski, p.144; on the use of 'squadrons', a term not otherwise encountered in Polish organisation except as a translation for *chorągiew*, see Paradowski, p.63. In personal communication, Michał Paradowski has suggested that, with two units kept in reserve and casualties from earlier in the action, the number of hussars was probably around 2,200–2,300.

347 This timing from Wimmer, *Entsatz*, pp.200–201; Paradowski's account of the final attack (pp.144–146) does not specify an exact time but places it after events timed at 4 (Abaza Sari Hüseyin's unfurling of a great banner) and before those at 6 (the point at which it became clear the Ottoman army was broken), so roughly 5 can be inferred. Forst de Battaglia, p.179, put the charge as early as 3.20, and Dolleczek, 'Entsatzschlacht', p.168, at around 4. One Polish historian, Laskowski, *Campagne*, p.30, did put it even later than Wimmer, at 6 p.m. – but this was around the time the Poles entered the Turkish camp.

348 There are three elements of warfare in the horse-and-musket era that films invariably show with spectacular inaccuracy: artillery fire (they just have to show explosive shot), fortresses (artillery fortification always looks like a medieval castle), and cavalry charges (always shown charging at full gallop from ludicrous distances). The normal method of a hussar charge is described in Richard Brzezinski, *Polish winged hussar, 1576-1775*, illustrated by Velimir Vuksic (Warrior, 94) (Oxford: Osprey, 2006), pp.44–45.

349 Many accounts refer to a ravine as an obstacle during this advance. No such ravine is visible on the detailed nineteenth-century map reproduced in *Das Kriegsjahr 1683* or mentioned elsewhere. There may have been some kind of ravine *parallel* to the line of advance. However, the most likely explanation is that the 'ravine' comes from a misreading of Dalérac, i, 159: 'Il [Sobieski] fit avancer les Houssars, ausquels on a vû descendre une ravine à toute jambe, parmi les murailles & les terrains escarpez, où un homme à pied auroit eu de la peine à se tenir.' At first sight this appears to refer to a ravine after the hussars started their advance, but it is actually describing the conditions they had been facing before they started their advance, i.e. their descent of the Alsbach valley.

long, comparatively narrow stretch of open ground between the end of the vineyards and the start of the Ottoman camp did it start to build up to battle speed – still taking great care to preserve formation. At some point as they entered the plain, Sobieski himself halted on a slight elevation and let the cavalry continue.

Most accounts tell nothing of what the Ottomans were doing as the Poles approached; the implication is that Abaza Sari Hüseyin's *yerli kulu* received the charge while stationary. However, this would be unusual, and it is possible that, light cavalry though they were, they tried to advance to meet the wall of horseflesh and armour bearing down on them. If any of them had tried to face the charge dismounted, out in the open with no obstacles to protect them, they would have been simply ridden down, for the Ottomans did not employ pikes or mobile barriers for defence against a cavalry charge, and as infantry they certainly could not amass the concentrated sustained musketry fire that was the only other way infantry would have had even a hope of stopping the Poles. It is also possible that the formation was already 'shedding from the rear'; Le Bègue noted after the Imperialists' turn-in on the Ottoman camp that 'This movement being seen by the Turks who were facing the Poles, succeeded in disconcerting them, and, afraid of being taken in flank, they began to withdraw', which probably refers to the Ottomans facing Sieniawski but may also suggest that the men of Abaza Sari Hüseyin, especially those on the right or in the rear ranks, aware of the Christians coming in on them from behind, were also beginning to drift away, even before the Poles struck.

Now was the moment for the charge. Hurling to the sky their battle-cries of 'Jezus Maria ratuj' (Jesus and Mary stand by us) and 'bij zabij' (strike to, strike dead), the hussars clapped spurs to their horses' sides for the last handful of yards. Down came the forest of lances with the great multi-coloured pennants that flapped and fluttered in the faces of the Turkish men and horses as they increased speed, and at last they crashed into Abaza Sari Hüseyin's light cavalry. Nothing could withstand them. Of 2,000-odd hussar lances, reputedly only 20 were left unbroken within moments of hitting the Ottoman line. Any Ottomans facing the gaps in the line were hit by the *pancerni* behind, but these were few – thousands of Poles had no need even to draw their swords. The Ottoman line recoiled under the great hammer blow, some men backing towards the line of tents where the ground rose a little, others – perhaps the majority – drifting southward, towards the extreme left wing and the prospects of either gaining the Poles' flank or a safe flight over the Wien.

Thoroughly professional, the Poles halted, reformed, prepared to attack again. Sobieski had seen the drift of the Ottomans to his right, and, while Jabłonowski had the dragoons advance out towards Ottakring, the King ordered the depleted *chorągiew* of Prince Aleksander to advance in the direction of the centre of the Ottoman camp, that is, likewise to the south (heading towards or over the Alsbach).[350] For the second time that day, the

---

350 The second charge by the Prince Aleksander hussars is omitted by some historians, and put in a variety of places by others, usually as some kind of second reconnaissance charge preceding the

valiant little band of hussars rode out alone, and was the first to strike into the leading edge of the confused Ottoman masses. Their comrades this time were not far behind; the hussar line again charged, against both the forces in front and following the Prince Aleksander squadron southward. The long lances were gone already but they drove into the Ottomans with drawn swords, the *yerli kulu* fought suicidally for a few moments, and then it was all over. Around 6 p.m., the entire Ottoman left wing collapsed, panic spread like wildfire, every man turned to flee, and the battle was won.

End of the battle

Rout of the Ottomans and occupation of the camp

Nevertheless, the fighting was not yet over. Some of the Ottoman cavalry that had been moving to the south were advancing to meet the dragoons around Ottakring; Hacci Giray and his band of Tatars may have made a brief appearance here as well[351]. The Poles easily routed their opponents, and here too they headed into the huge Ottoman camp after the fleeing Turks. Some detachments were pursuing wildly but the Polish advance for the moment remained careful and organised – Ottoman feigned flights to draw out an enemy into breaking formation were too well-known for the Polish commanders to be willing to order an all-out pursuit yet, especially as the speed of the collapse of Abaza Sari Hüseyin's wing seemed suspicious.

By now, Kara Mustafa and his entourage from the Türkenschanz had reached his palace-tent complex[352]. Small groups of Poles were already at the

---

main hussar charge. Having a second reconnaissance clashes with the general impression given that the hussar charge was delivered as a single block. I have followed Wimmer, *Entsatz*, p.202, in the placement of it *after* the first charge; and I have assumed that the consistent statements of the target as the centre of the Ottoman camp can only mean the area of Kara Mustafa's palace-tent complex, which was viewed as the centre even though geographically it was not, and which was to the south of the Polish position (although it was so far from the position of the royal *pułk* that he can hardly have been expected to reach it).

351 A possibility suggested by the Ottoman diarists (Kreutel & Teply, p.190), though not too much can be read from this very vague statement, primarily intended to blame the Khan for his lack of action.

352 For this section, I follow primarily the Ottoman diarists (Kreutel & Teply, p.190–191); the briefer account of Mavrocordato (Kreutel & Teply, p.88) is broadly supportive except in its placing of the order to evacuate the trenches this late. Kara Mustafa's departure from the palace-tent complex is timed by the diarists at 'one and a half hours before sundown', which would put it at 5 p.m., rather earlier than the 6 p.m. established from Christian sources; 'sundown' may have been a poetic turn of phrase for 'dark', which occurs somewhat later. There is no reference to a wagenburg in the Ottoman sources, however; this comes from Wimmer, *Entsatz*, p.203, and *Das Kriegsjahr 1683*, p.259, though the latter's placement of this defence measure is odd. Western accounts describe a slightly more hysterical response by Kara Mustafa, including an appeal to the Khan (who replied that against Sobieski there was no option but flight) and tearful embraces with his two sons before leaving; Dalérac, vol.1, pp.159–160, cites a letter from the Prince of Transylvania to Sobieski as his source for this, but Apafi was miles away at the time in the camp at Raab, and although he might have heard stories of the events from eye-witnesses

Executioner's Tent, and a Polish flag had been placed at the Treasure Tent where the army's cash reserves were normally kept – the collapse had been so sudden that there was no opportunity to move the money out. Mavrocordato was scathing about the responsibility of the *hazinehdar* (treasurer), whom he blames for the failure to get more than 10,000 gold pieces off in safety;[353] but Kara Mustafa had elected to stand and fight without moving any of the valuables or equipment to safety, and provided no leadership during the day as to when the point had been reached that the cash should now be moved. The Grand Vizier made some attempt to organise a last resistance to cover the retreat: he ordered some wagons to be formed into a redoubt, a 'wagenburg', and approaches amongst the tents blocked by any chests that could be found, and using these measures his remaining personal troops, especially his red-coated Arnaut (Albanian) lifeguards, held out briefly against the Poles before they were overwhelmed and annihilated. Kara Mustafa himself, lance in hand, led some of his household and officials into the fight around the palace-tent complex, perhaps trying to recover the cash from the Treasure Tent; around him, his privy scribe and many *ağa*s and pages were killed or wounded, while other pages (especially those who were former prisoners or conscripted Balkan Christians, forcibly converted) hastened to submit to the Poles, and slaves were scrambling to get out of the tents with whatever valuables they could lay their hands on – whether to escape with it for themselves or carry it back to Hungary for their master, no-one could at the moment tell; and a red rage began to take him over, the desire to die rather than survive such a day (as the diarists put it) or face the consequences of his own ineptitude (as seems more likely).[354] Amidst the swirling combats with the Poles many of those surviving from amongst his household were calling on him to retreat to Raab, and finally the Ağa of the *Sipahi*s, Osman Ağa, desperate at the need to save as many Muslims as possible and to preserve the Standard of the Prophet, struggled to penetrate the fog surrounding the rational part of Kara Mustafa's mind: 'Master, be merciful! Everything is lost, but your life is the soul of the army; if you sacrifice yourself, the army of Islam must in its totality be destroyed. Please, let us still break out!'[355] Perhaps it was these words, perhaps it was that the *Sipahi* commander at the same time took hold of the Standard of the Prophet and prepared to take it off the field; whatever the reason, Kara Mustafa turned and left the palace-tent complex by its 'back door' and joined the stream of men and horses heading for the River Wien. It was about 6 p.m. Around him, Turks, aware of the growing numbers of Poles amongst the tents, were desperately trying to pick up the most portable

---

after they reached Raab, such accounts might well have become seriously distorted by then. We have already seen a version of events that shows the Khan's departure *before* this point.
353 Kreutel & Teply, p.89.
354 Mansberg, pp.107–108, describes the Grand Vizier being wounded over the right eye by a blow that threw him from his richly caparisoned horse, so that he was saved only by the sacrifice of 'his *kiaya* Ahmed Pasha, the leader of his guard' (actually Ahmed Ağa); this action is not mentioned by the Ottoman sources, but nor is Ahmed Ağa the Grand Vizier's *kethüda* mentioned after the battle.
355 Kreutel & Teply, p.191.

of their possessions before they joined the flight, though many gave up the attempt and rode south glad to escape with their bare lives.

Delayed a little by Kara Mustafa's rearguard actions and still suspecting some kind of trick, the Polish army continued carefully to press forward, and, shortly after Kara Mustafa had left his palace-tent complex by the back door – certainly no later than 6.30 – Sobieski, guided by one of the turncoat pages from the Grand Vizier's household, entered it by the front.[356] Accustomed as the Poles were to the Ottomans' combination of splendour and savagery, nevertheless they gawped and shuddered at the sight that met them: gawped at the fabulously rich tents and hangings and carpets, at the baths and artificial gardens with little fountains still incongruously burbling away amongst the chaos, at Kara Mustafa's richly-caparisoned ceremonial horse that had apparently been kept ready for a triumphal entry into Vienna and that his servants now delivered to Sobieski, even at a brightly-plumed parrot tearing around the interior of the tents that the Poles could not catch; shuddered at the carnage all around of the slaughtered prisoners, dead, dying and hideously wounded – predictably, the Poles were most affected by the sufferings of the attractive, so were especially struck by the fate of a three-year old boy of 'extraordinary' beauty whose head had been cut open by a sword-cut across the mouth.[357] The Turks had even killed an ostrich, captured in a Habsburg zoo at the start of the campaign and now slaughtered out of sheer spite to prevent its being recovered by its original owners.

More handfuls of former Christians were abandoning their Ottoman masters and coming to join the allies, many of them well-dressed and -mounted,[358] but otherwise, in front of the Poles, the last of the Ottomans were streaming away through the tents towards the River Wien; it was now too late to cut off their line of retreat. Sobieski seems to have forgotten by now all about his hope to trap the Ottoman army and annihilate it; at least, if he felt any annoyance at the disappointment of his great plan, he kept it firmly to himself. Ordering the soldiers to keep strict formation and threatening penalty of death for any who broke ranks to plunder, Sobieski posted his dragoons to guard the palace-tent complex and had the rest of the Polish army enter the camp and swing round to face the River Wien, in case the Ottomans were reforming amongst the tents on the Wienerberg or in the hidden ground beyond it ready for a counter-attack.[359] Some, perhaps all, of the Polish army and the neighbouring German cavalry crossed the Wien to the Wienerberg.[360] there, they were able to confirm that no Ottomans

---

356 The time of 6.30 was specified by Dalérac and accepted by Forst de Battaglia. Le Bègue in his Account however put the King's entry into the camp at around 7, stressing that this was just after Waldeck entered it with the troops of the centre.
357 Plater, p.75; Dalérac, vol.1, pp.160–161. One assumes that the child was dead, though both these sources are ambiguous on the point.
358 Plater, pp.71–72.
359 Dalérac, vol.1, p.161, especially stresses Sobieski's concern that the Ottomans might rally behind the Wien and, if they could catch his forces once the formation was broken, by a sudden counter-attack deprive him of the victory. Barker (p.333) suggests that he feared an Ottoman return as at Chocim in 1673 – but there had been no such last-minute counter-attack at Chocim.
360 Dolleczek, 'Entsatzschlacht', p.169, says that Sobieski halted the army in order of battle for the night on the Wienerberg; the sources give no clear information at all on where the Poles spent

were lurking ready to surprise them, but Sobieski remained cautious. As darkness fell, a small force was sent on after the retreating Ottomans, more as a reconnaissance than a proper pursuit: the *pułk* of Miączynski (between one and three squadrons of *pancerni* and up to seven of light cavalry) and the *pancerni*-captain Remigian Strzałkowski (forces unknown, perhaps from the royal *pułk*), totalling around 2,300 cavalry. Their horses exhausted, unfamiliar with the terrain and trying to find their way in the darkness, these quickly managed to get lost beyond the Wienerberg and halted to rest while sending back to the King early the following morning with a request for reinforcements. The veteran Imperialist partisan commander, FML Johann Heinrich Graf Dünewald, a tiger in the saddle despite his 63 years, did slightly better: whether on orders of Sobieski or his own initiative, he took out in the same direction some German cavalry (details unknown; the force is sometimes described as 'light cavalry', which in the Imperialist army meant dragoons, although one might have expected Dünewald to take his own cuirassier regiment as well), and hit the Ottomans hard at some point beyond the Wienerberg, inflicting casualties and taking prisoners, and almost certainly helping to ensure that the Ottoman army continued its flight to Hungary at top speed.[361]

Turkish prisoners and battle loot in front of the Emperor and allied commanders. Artist unknown, after 1684 (Wien Museum Inv.-Nr. 19746, CC0)

the night, but the general impression is that the bulk of them were *probably* on the north side of the Wien, not on the Wienerberg, although Sobieski's keenness not to be caught amongst the tents would support the move beyond the Wien since there was no clear ground on the Vienna side of the river.

361 The story of Dünewald's action is variously reported, usually vaguely or with obviously exaggerated details; even the clearest account, in Thiel, pp.49–50, must be viewed with some caution. The difficulties are compounded by the problem of where the action took place: it is usually located at 'Enzersdorf', which is a small town 13 miles east of Vienna, and must therefore have taken place the next day – but this might be a misspelling of Inzersdorf, a village only just

Apart from these small-scale moves, Sobieski halted for the night. For the King himself, 54 years old and seriously overweight, a reaction was certainly setting in after the stress and exertions of the day on top of a sleepless night before, and as for the troops and horses, they finally had to pay the price for pushing themselves so hard over the past three days; they could go no further. Sobieski was still uncomfortable about the ease with which Abaza Sari Hüseyin had collapsed and nervous about sneak Ottoman attacks (he wrote to his wife the following night, 'The victory had been so sudden and so extraordinary that in both the city and in our camp we were always being alarmed; one kept thinking one was seeing the enemy coming back at any moment'), so he issued orders for the entire army to remain under arms throughout the night; but this was observed only by the Germans, for now that it was dark the Poles, not as accustomed to such strict discipline, were soon slipping away to start searching through the Ottoman tents – after three days of hard slogging with little or no nourishment, they may have at first left the ranks just to search for any kind of food, but once they had started, it was not long before full-blown plundering was under way, especially with all the treasures they had seen in and around the palace-tent complex of the Grand Vizier, the cash and jewels and gold plate and robes rigid with precious metals and stones. They quickly degenerated into unseemly indiscriminate looting: the Imperialist envoy Kuniz, held captive for so many months in the Ottoman camp, had barely realised that he had been abandoned by his Turkish guards and that he was safe at last, when Poles burst in and he and his staff were plundered more thoroughly than the Ottomans could have done; for a while, despite the presence of the Polish-Imperialist general Lubomirski, their lives were actually in danger[362] – after such a battle, it was bound to be difficult for the exhausted and adrenaline-drenched soldiers to make careful distinctions between friend and foe amongst those they found in the enemy camp, especially in the absence of a common language, but if the story about Lubomirski's presence is true, he really ought to have been able put a stop to it.

Clearing of the approaches

Lorraine had broken the resistance in front of him at some time before 5 p.m., and started swinging in to his right away from the Canal, perhaps to take the remaining Ottoman forces in the rear or act as an anvil against which Sobieski could trap them. The speedy collapse of both the centre and then the left wing of the Ottoman army made such a move redundant, and, still under orders that no-one was to break ranks to plunder the tents, the allied left wing resumed its steady advance in order of battle through the

---

beyond the Wienerberg. Dalérac, vol.1, p.161, has no mention of a pursuit by Dünewald but claims he was busy starting the pillaging early by seizing the tents of the *beylerbeyi* of Egypt.

362 Newald, vol. 2, p.122, and n.5 on pp.122–123. The Polish resident at Constantinople before the war, Samuel Proski, had also been detained by the Ottomans and was in the camp; presumably, he managed to avoid problems with his compatriots, since he could easily convince them that he was not Turkish.

camp towards the city where, astonishingly, the Ottoman bombardment was continuing – at this stage, Kara Mustafa had not yet issued the order to the troops in the siege works, or else the order had failed to get through in all the confusion, and, although some of the Janissaries (presumably those in positions with a good view of the battlefield) had retreated as soon as they saw the Christians approach the Ottoman camp,[363] the batteries were still firing solid shot at the walls and bombs over them into the city, the workers still labouring away in the trenches preparing the great mines that were expected to blow sky-high the city's last defences.[364] To Lorraine's right, the allied centre continued to march south through the Ottoman camp, perhaps joined by elements of the left wing;[365] but the advance through the tents was taking too long for Lorraine. If Dalérac is to be believed[366], Lorraine had already sent to Sobieski to request permission to clear the trenches and had received a refusal, Sobieski still being more concerned to concentrate against a possible counter-attack over the River Wien by the Ottoman army; even if such a request was made, Lorraine made it only for form's sake, and he certainly took no notice of any negative answer.

At some stage between 6 and 7 p.m., as the left wing was approaching the suburbs on the north side of the city, FML Louis of Baden was ordered to form a task force from a number of crack units and move ahead of Lorraine's main body, through the suburbs, to make contact with the garrison at the Schotten (Scottish) Gate on that side, and in conjunction with it continue round to the south around the ditch and clear the Ottoman siege works.[367] Picking up some regiments that had hitherto been under the command of GWM Mercy, Baden assembled CR Hallewyl, DR Heissler, the Saxon DR Reuss, and the one battalion of IR Württemberg in the relief army, perhaps some other infantry as well. He may also have been supported by some or all of Lubomirski's corps of Polish cavalry and dragoons. As they advanced into the gathering gloom, the Ottoman bombardment was continuing as fiercely as ever, and the city replying just as hotly with cannon, musket and grenade from the walls in front of and neighbouring the approaches. With night descending and the smoke from all this firing hindering visibility, plus the terrific noise, Baden has his regiments strike up with their drums and trumpets to draw the attention of the garrison to his approach, so that it was almost like a ceremonial march. As they approached the palisades that

---

363 suggested by Le Bègue, in the Account: 'the body of Janissaries who were there [in the trenches] did not have the opportunity to complete the retreat that they had already begun as soon as they saw us approach their camp.'
364 It is sometimes suggested that Janissaries in the approaches had actually been making assaults during the battle. No such assaults are recorded in the diaries of the besieged; Le Bègue mentioned one in the Account and the Diary, but given the silence of witnesses from the city I assume that this must be a mistake.
365 This is not clear from the sources, but is safe to assume, and receives a small degree of support from the description of Silahdar (Kreutel & Teply, p.240), who states that at this point the infidels formed two columns, one of which continued along the Danube and took the approaches while the other occupied the Ottoman camp.
366 vol. 1, p.162. The request is not reported at all by Le Bègue, who referred (Account) only to an exchange of compliments and an attempt by Lorraine to discuss the arrangements for pursuit.
367 The time of this is variously given: see Appendix I, 11.9.

ringed the counter-scarp (the outer side of the ditch), the Schotten Gate was opened, and a detachment from the garrison came out through the Schotten Ravelin to join them – at this point, with contact established between the garrison and the relief force, the siege of Vienna was symbolically over. The joint force turned to its right against the flank of the Ottoman siege works, forming up apparently with DR Heissler on the side nearest the city, practically on the glacis. Presumably all of the cuirassiers and dragoons were dismounted. Finally waking up to the threat, the Ottoman troops in the works turned a few of the siege guns on the advancing force and opened fire, getting off several shots before the Christians closed with them and broke into the tortuously winding Turkish trenches. Here there was still tough action, some Ottomans fighting ferociously to hold up the Christians while their fellows escaped behind them, and much musket-fire by the dragoons was mentioned by Le Bègue.[368] From the city, the Imperialist GWM Carl Ludwig, Graf de Souches, led a further sortie out over the breaches direct into the trenches, but the Turks knew all the convoluted turns and side-branches of their approaches better than the Christians, and the few men still left in the approaches now escaped from the trenches without difficulty; Souches' men, to their considerable annoyance, found not a single living Turk in the approaches – but every last piece of Ottoman artillery fell into the hands of the Christians.

About 600 Ottomans, Janissaries, miners, workers and gunners, were killed in the approaches.[369] The rest had made it out in time, but only those who had fled promptly on receiving Kara Mustafa's order or earlier would have been able to join the flight over the River Wien unimpeded; now, there were thousands of Poles and German cavalry securely across their line of retreat, and more marching past to the west, so that any escape route was securely blocked. Some who tried to get out were cut down; some undoubtedly managed to slip away in the dark; others tried to hide amongst the ruins of Vienna's suburbs, and, broken and hungry, over the next few days were caught or came out and surrendered.[370] If Silahdar is to be believed, muleteers and camel-drivers who had taken their animals out to pasture several days before brought them back to the camp at the end of the day, unaware of the defeat,

---

368 Hocke, p.198, from within the city, thought that the combat was merely 'some little skirmishing with the Janissaries', while the *Aufrichtige und unpartheyische Relation*, p.12, described 'substantial resistance' and referred to heavy casualties amongst the Saxon dragoons. The latter was based on those who were present; the former, on witnesses watching from a distance, from within the city; the fight was probably fierce, at close quarters, but not long-lasting, and too scattered amongst the trenches to appear much from a distance.

369 The figure is from the Schliz von Görz account (Newald, vol. 2, p.102), and has been accepted by most historians. Barker, p.338, citing a contemporary account to which he does not provide a clear reference, suggests that 3,000 Turkish sick and wounded found in the camp the next day were burnt alive by garrison troops (although without orders, and Starhemberg punished the ringleaders afterwards). Silahdar (Kreutel & Teply, p.240) claimed that 10,000 sick, wounded and exhausted Turks left behind were killed – but since whoever he got his account from would have already been several miles from the field at the time, his claim cannot be taken too seriously, though the story might have been passed on to him by one of those who did escape.

370 Mansberg, p.110; news reports recorded in Dudik, pp.445, 447.

and were all captured by the Christians;[371] while the story seems absurd at first, it is worth remembering that from a few miles away the sounds of the battle would have been no different to the normal sounds of the siege, so the drivers' lack of awareness of the action is not so improbable.

The end

Still the Germans plodded on, past the rear of the approaches that Baden had cleared, still heading south through the dark, still preserving their ranks, still making sure that not a man stepped out to plunder – which, as Le Bègue proudly noted in his Diary, 'was obeyed'. According to the Saxon account, it was only at this point that for the left wing the cavalry was fully moved forward to advance in front of the infantry, ready for pursuit.[372] However, there was still no pursuit launched. As the evening wore on, certainly no later than 10 p.m.,[373] the Germans ground to a halt, exhausted; most of them had been on the go continuously for up to seventeen hours in the gruelling late-summer heat, and some who had not had a chance to rest the previous night had been working, marching and fighting for more than a day. Exactly where they stopped is never made too clear; Le Bègue in his Account referred to 'this part of the camp which was between the Danube and the River Wien, the enemy having retired beyond this river', which can only mean somewhere in the southern part of the main Ottoman camp, north of the Wien – especially as no-one ever refers to the bulk of the Germans crossing the Wien on this day.[374]

Even now, Lorraine's enthusiasm had not run out. Sobieski had set up a tent somewhere beyond the Ottoman camp, where Waldeck and some of the other German commanders were already coming to congratulate him[375] and d'Aviano was twittering with joy about having seen a white dove hovering over the armies during the battle; the Duke himself sent a message to compliment him on the victory – 'as if we owed it to his presence', Le Bègue acidly commented – and to ask about measures for the pursuit the following day. The King, refreshed by food and drink that Starhemberg sent out after midnight,[376] and so busy basking in the glory and the praise that he had apparently forgotten all about his desire for a victory of annihilation,

---

371 Kreutel & Teply, p.240.
372 *Aufrichtige und unpartheyische Relation*, p.12.
373 The hour specified in Le Bègue's Diary. Given the secretary's strange time-keeping at this point of the day, not too much reliance can be placed on this. Schliz von Görz (Newald, vol. 2, p.99) said the battle lasted until 9 p.m.
374 The Wien enters the Canal at almost right angles, so on neither side of it could anyone be accurately described as 'between' it and the Danube. Vienna actually fills the angle on the north side, so that it is not easy to imagine an army west of Vienna being described as between the Wien and the Danube, but the absence of any reference to crossing the Wien seems conclusive.
375 It is however unlikely that the German soldiers of the centre and even their commanders flocked to surround and cheer Sobieski the moment the Turks gave way, as the King claimed to his wife (Plater, p.76).
376 Dalérac, vol. 1, p.162. Dalérac has Sobieski spending the night at the foot of a tree; on the following night (p.169), he has Sobieski establishing himself in the Grand Vizier's palace-tent complex.

generously returned the compliment by declaring the success due to both Lorraine and the German troops, but avoided any decision about a pursuit, evasively replying that he would discuss this with Lorraine on the morrow after a religious service of thanks (which practically guaranteed no movement before the 14th).

And so the Germans, disciplined to the last, settled down to spend the night where they stood, while all around them, hour after hour, they could hear the Poles plundering the Ottoman camp for its foodstuffs and valuables.

The cavalry had arrived in time; Vienna was relieved.

Casualties

Allies

It should come as no surprise to any-one at this stage to learn that there is no agreement over the figures for casualties. No official figures were produced except for a few Reich units, and contemporary western reports varied wildly between 500 and 4,000 dead and wounded, often depending for the most part on how strongly the writer wished to emphasise the ease of the victory over the infidel, but also influenced by other factors such as whether they had bothered to include the Poles. The earliest reports of the victory that flew around Europe may have been issued before anyone had been able to tot up the butcher's bill,[377] or repeated one general's statement of the losses of his own contingent as a statement of the whole army's casualties. There is also the problem that the different contingents had fought with differing intensity (the Bavarians and Franconians in the centre had had a much easier day of it than the Imperialists, Saxons and Poles), and even within contingents, different regiments or divisions had faced varying opposition and suffered different casualties accordingly (to mention just the most glaring examples, there is the difference between the extremely tough fight for Sieniawski's Poles compared with the devastatingly easy success of Jabłonowski and the royal *pułk* in the final cavalry charge, or the fact that little of Waldeck's centre behind its first line and none of its cavalry was ever in action, likewise 80 percent of Sachsen-Lauenburg's troopers never had a chance to draw pistol or sword). These differences make it unwise to try, as Mansberg did,[378] to extrapolate from known reliable figures for a few Saxon battalions. Certainly, for the scale and importance of the day-long battle, the allies had suffered comparatively lightly: Le Bègue stressed the low casualties, the Irish-Imperialist cavalry general Taafe noted 'Never victory of so great importance

---

377 Hocke, for example, said (p.201) that the total was not more than 600–1,000; 'barely 1,000' was the figure in the news reports reaching the Moravian monastery of Raygern (which was still watching the tail of the Polish column go past) (Dudik, p.457); 'around 600 in all the army', recorded Dalérac, vol. 1, p.163. Le Bègue in his Diary (not a public document at the time) went as low as 200 Imperialists and 150 Poles.

378 Mansberg, p.112.

cost so little blood',[379] and even the highest suggested numbers give a casualty ratio of just 6%, or less if the army was larger than 66,000; but the lower figures in the area of 500 (0.75 percent) are simply impossible to believe.[380]

Despite the weakness of the method, it is worth considering the specific figures available for the Bavarians and Saxons, if only because there are no other equivalents available. Mansberg cited an unspecified report of the Saxons covering the six battalions of three of their infantry regiments, IRs Kuffer, Flemming and Leib, which gave 66 killed and 38 'heavily' wounded, for a total of 3 percent (2.9 percent, to be exact); the reference to 'heavily' wounded indicates that the count was not complete, but on the other hand the regiments included in the report were probably deeply involved in action, more so than others of the Saxon contingent, these two factors broadly cancelling each other so that the percentage may be accepted as a *rough* average for the overall contingent, giving 287 casualties in total for the entire corps (which matches reasonably closely the figure of 200–250 estimated for the Saxons in the Bavarian study of Diani cited by Staudinger). As for the Bavarians, Mansberg cited another unspecified report that their five infantry regiments recorded 31 officers and NCOs and 123 men killed or died of wounds, again making around 3% (actually around 2.6 percent) – but with no mention of the wounded. The Bavarian officer-historian Staudinger, on the other hand, recorded[381] that the Bavarians reported 65 infantry and 36 cavalry killed (1.7 percent) since the army set off, and noted besides that when the contingent advanced into Hungary a month later it left 672 sick in Vienna of which very few were wounded; this would suggest that there had been few wounded in the battle who did not recover soon enough to march with their comrades, but still unjustifiably excludes all the wounded from the count. Against this, however, we need to remember that the Bavarian infantry fought in the battle while the Bavarian cavalry did nothing but lead the final advance through the camp. Taking the two figures for the Bavarians into account and allowing for the wounded, it does seem that this lightly-involved contingent suffered around 3 percent overall, even if we remain suspicious that they really suffered as badly as the Saxons.

Extrapolating from this figure, Mansberg came up with a total loss for the whole army of around 2,000. However, this ignored the fact that two

---

379 quoted in Forst de Battaglia, p.181.
380 The nearest comparable figures in the horse-and-musket era would be for the Prussians at Rossbach in 1757, who suffered 548 casualties out of 22,000 (for a casualty ratio of 2.5%, or over three times that of the allies in 1683 had they suffered so few as 500 casualties). No other battle that I know of was won so lightly. However, the Battle of Rossbach lasted barely 2 hours, because the Prussians' opponents collapsed with extraordinary speed. At Vienna, full-scale fighting lasted from 5 or 6 a.m. to 6 p.m. (12–13 hours) if the clearing of the approaches is excluded; given the gap with no fighting that preceded the clearing, it should add no more than an hour to the total, making a day of 14 hours' fighting. Even allowing for the possibilities that Ottoman use of firearms may have been inaccurate and that some fighting involved no contact due to the Germans' use of pikes and other defences, it is impossible to believe that the allies in 1683 suffered as few casualties in absolute terms, and a third as many relative to the numbers involved, in 14 hours of fighting as the Prussians of 1757 did in 2.
381 Karl Staudinger, *Das königlich bayerische 2. Infanterie-Regiment 'Kronprinz' 1682 bis 1882* (Munich: Oldenbourg, 1885–1887), p.81.

other contingents (the Imperialists and Poles, especially Sieniawski's Poles) had fought much harder than the Saxons and especially the Bavarians. On the other hand, it did match one of the more credible contemporary news reports, an Italian relation, cited by Mansberg,[382] which gave the casualties as 700 Poles, 400 Saxons, and 500 Bavarians and Franconians; the report failed to give a figure for the Imperialists, who had been in action the longest, so Mansberg suggested the addition of at least 600 for them, to give a total of 2,200. The figures for the Saxons and the centre do not match the specifics reported or calculated for these contingents, especially as the Franconian casualties can hardly have been higher than the Bavarians' (though the figure of 500 for the centre did crop up regularly in reports), but Mansberg's 600 for the Imperialists seems on the low side, and so, with these two considerations balancing each other out, 2,200 seems reasonable. In the nineteenth century, there developed something like a consensus amongst careful historians that overall casualties for the Germans were around 1,500; they were less sure about the Poles, but Renner[383] put their losses at 600 – for a total of 2,100. However, there has since then been a trend amongst Polish or Polish-inclined historians to increase the numbers, especially for the Poles; Forst de Battaglia estimated the allied *dead* at a maximum of 2,000, including 500 Poles, and 2,000–3,000 wounded; at one point, Wimmer was cited as putting the Polish casualties alone at 1,300, while in his *Entsatz* he put the overall allied casualties at 4,000 (including 1,500 dead), of which a good half were Poles, especially from Sieniawski's column.[384]

The safest statement therefore about the Christian casualties is that they suffered at least 2,000 dead and wounded, and the total was probably in that area but perhaps as high as 4,000. Naturally, no prisoners or missing are recorded for the relief army – as recorded above, the Ottomans had unhesitatingly killed the few prisoners they had taken during the army's approach march.

Few senior figures (as Le Bègue put it, 'people of consideration') amongst the allies were hit. The Imperialist FML Charles Eugène duc de Croy had been wounded but not seriously; his relative, the Prince de Croy, a major or captain in his infantry regiment, was killed.[385] The unlucky Casimir Freiherr von Königsegg of Lubomirski's dragoons died a few days later of the sword-cut that had penetrated his hat-protection, though curiously he was not deemed worthy of being mentioned by Le Bègue. Ferdinand Maximilian, Graf von Trautmannsdorff, a major in DR Schulz, was also killed, as was the Hanoverian colonel, Pallandt. Amongst the Poles, two officers commanding *pancerni* squadrons were killed during Sieniawski's advance: young Stanisław

---

382   p.112. Mansberg did not further identify the report.
383   p.437.
384   Forst de Battaglia, pp.180–181; Marian Zgórniak, 'Die Struktur des polnischen Heeres zur Zeit des Grossen Türkenkrieges (1672–1699)', *Studia Austro-Polonica*, 3 (1983), pp.381–399, here p.395 (citing Wimmer *Wojsko polskie*); Wimmer, *Entsatz*, p.205. Paradowski, pp.184–185, generally follows Wimmer, while stressing that the Poles also suffered heavy losses through sickness later in the campaign.
385   The name of the relative is usually specified as Maurice, but Le Bègue gave it in his Account as Thomas; the Diary suggested that they were brothers, as did Sobieski (in Plater, pp.77–78).

Potocki, and the Crown Court Treasurer Andrzej Modrzewski. The Counts of Fontaine (Imperialist GWM), Tilly (lieutenant-colonel of IR Baden) and Schallenberg (lt.col. of IR Wallis) were wounded, none of them mortally.[386]

In addition to the battle casualties, of course, note must be taken of the siege and civilian losses. In Vienna, from the garrison of about 11,000 men, by 12 September about 5,000 had been killed in action or died of sickness, and 3,500 more were sick or wounded in the city's various proper or makeshift hospitals (though some historians think that the figure of 5,000 dead, first recorded by the diarist Hocke and not supported by documentary evidence, is too high); 1,648 combatant civilians had been killed or died sick. The losses amongst the rest of the civilian population of the city are never recorded, but, given the indiscriminate Ottoman use of mortar bombs against the interior and the widespread sickness in the crowded and unsanitary conditions of the siege, must have run into thousands, though commentators are usually at pains to stress that they were nothing like the appalling death-toll the urban population had suffered in the plague of 1679–1680.[387]

Losses in the unprotected countryside outside Vienna south of the Danube were far worse – the inhabitants had Lorraine's vigilance to thank for the fact that the damage was not extended to the north bank as well. If losses were not as high as the 300,000 that Hocke[388] initially claimed or the half-million that later estimates reached, they were still appalling. Throughout the region, up to 5,000 villages and smaller unwalled towns had been sacked and burnt by the Tatars and the Ottoman army's robber-followers; official registers just for the territory of Lower Austria showed that of 47,994 houses in the Duchy, 13,368 had been destroyed, and well over half of these had no inhabitants to return and attempt to rebuild them. The official numbers for the people were around 30,000 killed; the figures for those carried off into slavery by the Tatars varied between 40,000 and 87,000, with 70,000 generally accepted as the most likely total by modern historians such as Wimmer. Thousands of those carried off from their homes found death in the Ottoman camp, either worked to death in the siege trenches or massacred in the slaughter of the prisoners ordered by Kara Mustafa, but the majority had already been taken off to Hungary and the interior of the Ottoman Empire by the slave-dealers, and a few did manage to return home over the succeeding decades. All of this was on top of the casualties of the plague of 1679–1680, which itself had hit a rural population not yet recovered from the terrible devastation of the Thirty Years' War. Much of Royal Hungary had been spared the ravages of the Turks because most of its lords had hastened to submit to the Ottomans' puppet princeling Thököly, but the few lords who remained loyal to their king, the Emperor Leopold, suffered as badly as the Austrians; their estates in the westernmost part of the Kingdom of Hungary (confusingly, these

---

386   Schallenberg is specified in Le Bègue's Account but not the diary; as an officer of IR Wallis that was serving under Schulz at Jedlesee, he should not even have been present on the battlefield.
387   For much detail on the siege casualties, see Renner, pp.439–440; Newald, vol. 1, pp.224–225, 230–231; *Das Kriegsjahr 1683*, pp.261–262; Hocke, pp.200–201. Most recent historians seem to be following one or other of these.
388   p. 201

are today mostly in Austria, not Hungary) were sacked as thoroughly as the unhappy Duchy of Lower Austria – on those alone of the Palatine, Pál Esterházy, 10,000 serfs were reported to have been killed or carried off into slavery, not counting those who had fled never to return, and similar figures were claimed for other estates and regions. Despite substantial immigration, it would be decades before Austria and Hungary recovered from the horror that was the Ottoman invasion.[389]

Ottomans

The Ottomans' camp, their siege works, and all the fields around were littered with their dead; the hills to the south were covered with the hordes of their fleeing warriors. Although the Christians were left in possession of the field, they were in no mood to start counting dead bodies, and we have only estimates for the Ottoman losses. Many contemporary reports quoted a round figure of 10,000 dead on the field, and most historians have tended to follow it; if the garrison really slaughtered 3,000 sick and wounded Turks the next day (see above), these would not be included in the total; nor would those men hiding in the suburbs who gave themselves up the next day; nor would the Ottomans killed or captured during the initial pursuit actions on the days immediately after the battle – most reasonably estimated at 2,000.[390] Some put the total of bodies on the field higher, at 15,000 (Mansberg) or even 20,000 (Dolleczek), the second of these adding further high figures for troops killed in the pursuit (8,000); but the higher totals do not command belief, and 10,000 for the battlefield, perhaps 15,000 including losses and men surrendering over the next few days, seems a reasonable estimate.[391] The nature of the battle, with the intermittent Ottoman rushes, the fierce fighting over strong-points that did not allow the involvement of very large numbers, and towards the end the easy collapse of Ottoman defence lines with minimal resistance, do not suggest a huge casualty list; this would have happened only if a full pursuit had been mounted of the fleeing Ottomans, or if they had been caught against a river during their retreat, or if Sobieski had got his wish and trapped the Ottoman army against Vienna or the Danube or the German half of the army, in which case Vienna could well have been the Cannae of the seventeenth century.

---

389 On the losses in the countryside, see Barker, pp.283–284; Renner, p.275 and fn.; *Das Kriegsjahr 1683*, p.204; Wimmer, *Entsatz*, p.143; Karl Gutkas, 'Das Jahr 1683 in Niederösterreich', in Waissenberger, Robert (ed.), *Die Türken vor Wien: Europa und die Entscheidung an der Donau, 1683* (Salzburg: Residenz Verlag, 1982), esp. pp.159–160; and Franz Theuer, 'Die Türken im Burgenland', in Waissenberger, pp.163–168.

390 Most writers referred only to the killed, but Sobieski mentioned to his wife late on the 13th that the Polish troops were bringing in 'an uncountable multitude of prisoners' (Plater, p.71).

391 Many give the 10,000 figure, which was also accepted by Joseph von Hammer-Purgstall, *Geschichte des osmanischen Reiches* (Pest/Vienna: Hartleben, 1827–1835), vol. 6, p.413; *Das Kriegsjahr 1683*, p.261, acknowledged that the total was variously given between 10,000 and 20,000; Wimmer, *Entsatz*, pp.204–205, accepts the 10,000 for the battlefield, gives the 2,000 figure for the pursuit, and the overall total of 15,000. For the higher estimates, see Mansberg, p.111; Dolleczek, 'Entsatzschlacht', p.170. Bizarrely, Dalérac, vol. 1, p.164, put the Turkish dead as low as 800.

A loss of 10,000 seemed small enough compared with Sobieski's dreams of a victory of annihilation, but with the extra losses inflicted over the following days, and the thousands of *yerli kulu* who would have deserted by the time the Ottoman army reached Hungary, and the fact that the army was by then in complete disarray, it was still a major blow to the Ottoman Empire. And on top of the battle casualties were the huge Ottoman losses of the siege itself – a cost that would have been worth paying if they had taken the city, securing their hold on Hungary for ever more and opening up central Europe to their raids for plunder and slaves, but a terrible waste of experienced troops on a failed attempt. The undated casualty list for the siege found in the Ottoman camp (see Appendix II) showed total losses of 48,543; apart from the officers, the numbers specified for each line in the list are suspiciously rounded, and in most cases even more suspiciously high, though on the other hand the Tatar casualties seem too low and *gönüllü* losses are not mentioned at all. If we assume that the list was compiled at about the same time as the census of the army, 7 September, it also omitted losses in the final four days of the siege down to the 11th; during these days the Ottomans lost heavily in unsuccessful assaults on the 8th, but then stopped trying to storm the breaches while they concentrated on preparations against the relief army, continuing (apart from the bombardment) only with the work of pushing approaches and mines which still cost many lives but nothing like as many as in the assaults. During the same days, however, losses to sickness continued to mount in the Ottoman camp. If we set the exaggerations in the list against these omissions, it seems reasonable to conclude that Ottoman losses in the siege had indeed been in the order of 40,000–50,000. Kara Mustafa's attempt to take Vienna had cost the Ottoman Empire very dearly.

Booty

The booty falling to the victors was massive. Most of the Ottoman non-combatants had packed up properly and left with all their property and slaves in the days before the battle, some even made their escape on the morning of the 12th; but those who stayed to fight made it away with only the clothes on their backs, their personal weapons and horse-gear, and, if they were lucky, whatever belongings they could seize and carry in their arms; everything else, reputedly down to food on the table, was left to the Christians.

The army itself lost its entire official equipment. Kara Mustafa's huge palace-tent complex, which Sobieski described to his wife with some exaggeration as being as large as Warsaw or Lwów,[392] together with its rich contents, fell into the hands of the Poles, along with the Grand Vizier's chancery including the sensitive documents of Ottoman dealings with the Hungarian rebels, and all the army's cash chests except for 10,000 gold pieces, the only money that Kara Mustafa's officials had managed to carry away. The fabulously decorated tents alone were conservatively estimated

---
392 Plater, pp.72–73.

as worth 30,000 Gulden, the value of the contents immeasurable. Large numbers of spare horses fell to the Christians, including the Grand Vizier's richly equipped ceremonial steed, already mentioned. As Sobieski drily told his wife, the Grand Vizier had escaped with only his coat and his horse, and 'I have established myself as his heir'.[393] Every last tent of the Ottoman camp was abandoned to the Christians, the final figure reliably estimated at 25,000, though Sobieski got carried away by his attempts to make out the Ottoman army was bigger than it had been and suggested that the total was nearer 100,000.[394] Ottoman culture still showed its origins as a people of nomadic herders and steppe-raiders in the considerable amount of personal wealth that could be sunk, especially by officials and officers, into the decoration and outfittings of campaign tents, which were made of expensive cloths and decorated with richly woven carpets and tapestries, all shot through with gold thread and decorated with jewels, and hundreds of these structures came into possession of Polish officers.[395]

As to the more serious military equipment: the entire artillery train, siege and field guns alike, was left at Vienna: the Imperialists subsequently brought into the Vienna arsenals 4 'full cannon' (48-pounders), and 106 or 107 other cannon of various calibres, including a number of 24-pounders but the majority of them smaller, and 10 mortars; and these were not the only guns taken, for we know that the Saxons kept the 6 cannon they had captured on the Krottenbach, and it is likely that the troops of the centre and the Poles also kept some of the pieces they had taken;[396] the total of Ottoman guns captured (the majority of them of light calibre) could well have been near the 170 or 180 total suggested by Le Bègue and the 'Baden account'.[397] Along with the artillery was a great mass of ammunition: this included 4,000 *centner* (approximately, hundredweight; see Glossary) of gunpowder, 4,000 *centner* of lead, 1,000 bombs ready to be loaded with powder, 2,000 fire-shot, and 20,000 hand-grenades, 18,000 solid cannon-balls of various calibres, and tons of all the equipment needed for siege works – 20,000 sandbags, at least 10,000 picks and shovels and 30,000 other pieces of mining tools, 50 *centner* of pitch and resin with 1,100 pans for burning it (necessary to illuminate night attacks or for attempts to set fire to the wooden parts of defences), 1,000 empty wool sacks and at least 1,000 sheep-skins (useful for helping to 'pad' entrenchments and help make them proof against enemy shot), 2,000 plates of iron for use in shielding, more iron and wood ready for working,

---

393 Plater, p.72.
394 Plater, pp.74–75.
395 The tents are illustrated in all their colourful glory in many modern works. See, for example, Waissenberger, p.113 (with a near-contemporary monochrome illustration of the whole main palace tent on p.112); Hubert Glaser (ed.), *Kurfürst Max Emanuel: Bayern und Europa um 1700* (Munich: Hirmer, 1976), vol. 2, plate opposite p.52 (this volume also includes, on p.77, a reproduction of a contemporary drawing of some of the tents from when Sobieski exhibited them at home in 1684).
396 Since Polish units led the initial limited pursuit, it is likely that the 'fifteen or so' guns that Sobieski described (Plater, pp.78–79) as abandoned by the Ottomans during their retreat never left Polish possession.
397 See Appendix I, 11.10, for discussion of the numbers of captured guns. Further detail on calibres is relevant to a history of the siege, which I may produce in future.

2,400 scythes or halberds, and 500 Janissary muskets, plus large amounts of oil, match, nails, saltpetre, canvas, and rope.[398] Significantly, there were also 8,000 empty ammunition wagons, explaining why the army was supplied so plentifully with *matériel*: an ammunition transport must have arrived only recently from Buda, too late for it to be sent back before the relief army approached (the Ottoman army had often struggled to keep itself fed but had never gone short of ammunition, and although the diarists of the siege do not record the arrival of any ammunition trains after August, the plentiful supply of powder and shot coupled with the empty wagons waiting to return do suggest a recent arrival). Sobieski remarked to his wife that he could not imagine how the Turks would manage for the rest of the campaign with so much lost ammunition.[399]

As has just been noted, and observed earlier (see Chapter 9), the Ottoman army had had difficulties keeping itself fed, but the Christians found substantial quantities of food in the camp, and equally generous stores of biscuit later in the Neugebäude south of the city: not counting the large amounts of lesser foodstuffs such as honey, rice and oil, there were 20,000 buffaloes, oxen, camels and mules in the camp (not all of these, admittedly, were edible), 10,000 sheep (which were), and allegedly 100,000 *malter* of grain[400] (a 'malter' was a measure of volume, at this time highly variable, but later established as equivalent to about 12 bushels, or 420 litres, so that 100,000 of them was a very considerable supply, and even if the exact figure is a mistake, there was clearly enough to have fed the Ottoman camp for a long time, suggesting Kara Mustafa had been hoarding provisions).

Scores, perhaps hundreds of Ottoman standards and rank insignia such as horse-tails fell to the Christians and ended up in arsenals and churches in Vienna and Poland. Perhaps most famous of all the official booty was the great red banner from Abaza Sari Hüseyin's wing, which Sobieski persisted in believing was the great Islamic religious symbol, the Standard of the Prophet (which was actually black but usually covered in green; see Glossary). The day after the battle the King sent the red banner in the hands of his secretary Tommaso Talenti to Rome as a gift to the Pope, accompanied by the message 'Veni, vidi, Deus vicit' (I came, I saw, god conquered), a play on the terse statement 'veni vidi vici' of Gaius Julius Caesar reporting one of his victories – if Sobieski had not been trying to be so clever, he might have remembered that the original quote referred to an exceptionally easy victory over a hopelessly inept opponent, which was hardly the image the King was currently striving for. The captured banner was displayed for a while in Rome then according to some accounts handed over by the Pope to the pilgrimage

---

398 See Appendix I, 11.10, for discussion of these figures.
399 Plater, p.78.
400 *Das Kriegsjahr 1683*, p.265; Renner, p.438; on the Neugebäude biscuit supply, Vaelckeren, p.106 (see Appendix I, 11.11, for doubts as to the accuracy of the figure). Some further details also in the report of the Brandenburg envoy Bernhard Ernst von Schmettau of 16 September, quoted in Mansberg, p.114 n.81, which lays particular stress on the thousands of Hungarian oxen which were brought into the city and sold at knock-down prices.

shrine of the Santa Casa (Holy House) at Loreto, but later returned to Rome, from where it disappeared a century later.[401]

In addition to all this 'public' property, the Christians also captured large amounts of private possessions, 'an infinity of all sorts of baggage' as Le Bègue put it: jewellery and cash, the tents and their furnishings, decorated horse gear and weapons, dining plate and knick-knacks in precious metals, even food on the table. According to Vaelckeren,[402] in the tents of the Grand Vizier and 'the pashas' alone the plundering soldiers (principally Poles) found cash and furnishings to the value of 'several millions' (of Gulden), so that some rankers got as much as 20,000–30,000 Gulden for their share – though we may assume that the majority got a lot less than this, and even amongst the Poles the bulk of the loot was claimed by senior officers, which may account for the impression some got that the Ottomans had escaped with all their most valuable possessions.

Despite Sobieski's strict orders, the plundering began almost at once for the Poles. They had entered the Ottoman camp at its biggest and richest part anyway, the King himself had laid immediate claim to the palace-tent complex of Kara Mustafa and all its riches, other Polish generals had laid claim to the 'next best' tents,[403] and throughout the evening they were encountering runaway Ottoman slaves who had absconded with what they could carry of their former masters' valuables; undisciplined and poorly paid Polish infantry had been over-worked and starved for days, so it is hardly surprising that they began to break ranks – and even with the noble hussars, the costs of equipping themselves far exceeded their pay, so attempts to recoup their losses were only to be expected.[404] Sobieski himself, who like many Polish magnates had contributed significantly to the costs of the campaign out of his own pocket, was keen to recoup his losses in any way possible – and he also had a wife greedy for rich things who had to be taken into consideration.[405] Meanwhile, the Germans obeyed orders throughout

---

401 The tag is sometimes rendered as 'Venimus, vidimus et Deus vicit' (we came, we saw and god conquered). According to Pastor, the banner spent over a hundred years in Rome until the city was sacked by the French at the end of the eighteenth century and it disappeared for ever – see Ludwig Pastor, *History of the Popes, from the close of the Middle Ages*, trans. by Ernest Graf (London: [Routledge &] Kegan Paul, 1949-53), vol. 32, p.183 n.1. There are suggestions that the banner may have survived in Rome and been returned to the Turkish government by Pope Paul VI, but this seems to be a confusion with the *Lepanto* standard that Paul returned to the Turks in 1967.
402 p.101. Many historians have followed this estimate. The Brandenburg envoy Schmettau estimated the value of everything found in the Grand Vizier's palace-tent complex at 'several tons of gold' (quote in Mansberg, p.114 n.81). Compare the estimates in Dudik, p.507.
403 Schmettau's report, in Mansberg, p.114 n.81.
404 Polish historians tend to insist that the looting by Poles did not begin until the morning of the 13th, but there can be no doubt that Sobieski himself started the process during the night (see the 'Baden account' in Röder, vol. 1, Urk., p.19), and Kuniz's experiences make it clear that the Poles started well before dawn. The argument about the hussars needing to recoup their costs is made by Wimmer, *Entsatz*, p.211.
405 This may account for some of the apparent inconsistencies in Sobieski's subsequent letter to his wife (see Plater, especially pp.73–74), which referred to the scale of the booty while at the same time describing its paucity in comparison with that acquired at the Battle of Chocim in 1673: the Polish army overall had secured a lot of booty, but the King had gained comparatively few of the personal baubles that he knew his Queen would expect.

the night and kept to their ranks; they were only released to join in the fun on the following morning; then, Sobieski, his desire for booty beginning to outweigh his military sense or else (as Stoye put it) 'intoxicated' by the scale of the success,[406] concluded that no full-army pursuit was going to take place on this day and, accepting from the reports of the limited pursuit that no sneak Ottoman counter-attack was to be expected, issued new orders permitting plundering. By then, the Germans were deeply embittered that the Poles had had so long to get to the plunder first. (The bitterness extended well into the nineteenth century, when the historian Newald, deeply and most of the time unfairly hostile to the Poles, pointed out that by remaining in order of battle during the night the Germans were effectively guarding the Polish looters against any possible Ottoman counter-attack.)[407] Even then, German plundering was carried out in a controlled manner, with several men released from each company to search the camp on behalf of their comrades.[408]

Not many hours of the 13th had gone by before the civilian population of Vienna had started to join in; even before the city's gates had been officially opened (many gates had been bricked up during the siege to prevent their being blown open by petards in surprise attacks), inhabitants were making their way out by the sally ports or clambering out through the breaches or over the walls and palisades, and scattering throughout the Ottoman camp, looking first of all for the food, cold-bloodedly ignoring the dying prisoners left behind by the Turks and the hundreds of bawling children besides the corpses of their dead and dying mothers. The Viennese could be completely indiscriminate: some of them even stole the horses of a detachment of Polish soldiers who had unwisely left their hungry animals to graze near the Stuben Gate.[409] The German soldiers were concentrating on money and valuables, but the Viennese civilians, hungry (though by no means reduced to starvation) by the end of the siege, competed with the Poles for the food supplies, both portable and on the hoof. One of the German complaints against the Poles was that they plundered Ottoman magazines that would have been useful in supporting subsequent military operations, but, in addition to the fact that the Viennese were as bad as the Poles in this, the hungry Poles needed food, their own supply trains were days away beyond the Wienerwald, they had asked the authorities of the city for bread and (not surprisingly given the long siege) been declined, and there was little else they could do to feed themselves – though equally, indiscriminate plundering was more wasteful, for it emptied the magazines much more quickly than controlled use would have done.[410]

Not everyone in Vienna was so cold-hearted as the civilian population. News of the Christian orphans in the camp came to Leopold Kollonitsch, Bishop of Wiener-Neustadt and unofficial President of the Hungarian

---

406 Mansberg, p.111, which puts the point much more harshly; Stoye, pp.265–266.
407 Newald, vol. 2, pp.113–114.
408 Rauchbar, vol. 2, p.270.
409 *Das Kriegsjahr 1683*, 265; Renner 438. Since the Stuben Gate directly faced the River Wien, the grazing horses were probably south of the Wien.
410 Stoye, p.268.

Chamber (treasury), who had served in Vienna throughout the siege. Kollonitsch, a fervent supporter of the Counter-Reformation and one of the few Hungarian nobles to be completely pro-Habsburg, was loathed by almost all his compatriots – by most of them for his persecution of Protestants, by even his brother Catholic bishops for his unstinting support of the absolutism of the Habsburg court. In 1681, the Hungarian Diet of Ödenburg had passed a law dismissing him as President of the Hungarian Chamber – but the government in Vienna took no notice. However, he was a brave and, in any matter not connected with Catholicism, intelligent man, capable of vigorous measures in defence of the city: he had brought provisions when he arrived, worked hard on hospitals, and had seized chestfuls of cash and jewellery belonging to Hungarian archbishops as they were being sent through the city to escape the advancing Ottomans, a measure that infuriated the wealthy archbishops and was hardly calculated to endear him to the Magyars but provided the city administration with valuable funds to aid the defence. Now, he acted to save the orphans: he went out of the city to the camp and collected around 500 of the unfortunate children, many of them badly wounded by the inept Ottoman attempts to kill them, a few infants still trying to suckle at the breasts of their dead mothers, and brought them back to safety in the city; some were so sick or injured that they had to be taken to the city's hospitals, but of the rest, as many as he could, he put up in his own house, and persuaded the City Council to quarter the rest in the Zuchthaus (prison) in return for his promise to feed them all at his own cost.[411]

As to the disputes between the Poles and the Germans over the Poles getting the lead over plundering, it must be acknowledged that despite starting late the Germans did not do too badly; an awful lot of the public and private property from the Ottoman camp, including many rich tents and bejewelled gear, ended up in the possession of senior German officers, such as Hermann of Baden, or of the Habsburg government; as already noted, the Imperialists certainly picked up the lion's share of the Ottoman artillery. And Sobieski, despite his inordinate enthusiasm for the valuables all around him, made generous gifts to the German commanders and to Leopold.[412]

---

411 Newald, vol.1, p.215; Joseph Maurer, *Cardinal Leopold Graf Kollonitsch, Primas von Ungarn: sein Leben und sein Wirken* (Innsbruck: Rauch, 1887), p.163. Most historians mention Kollonitsch's generous action.

412 Wimmer, *Entsatz*, pp.210–211; Plater, pp.81–82 for Sobieski's report of what he had given to the Saxons, and Dalérac, vol. 1, p.171 for gifts to the Elector of Bavaria (in neither case were they worth very much).

12

Aftermath

Although the story of the rest of the campaign, from the cultural clash that nearly broke the Imperialist-Polish alliance to the autumn successes and winter failures, is intrinsically fascinating, space limitations preclude a detailed account of these months, so we will end here with only a brief summary – Paradowski's book provides a recent account with more detail,[413] and the 'usual suspects' amongst the main works used for the battle also cover the subsequent events.

Kara Mustafa and the retreating Ottomans reached Raab on 14 September, joining there the Transylvanians and the Ottoman forces left there in July to contain the Imperialist fortress when the Grand Vizier advanced to Vienna. Keen to preserve his position with the Sultan by blaming someone else for the disaster, Kara Mustafa saw no better scapegoat than the man he already hated, the venerable *beylerbeyi* of Buda, Koca Ibrahim, who was promptly throttled, and replaced at Buda by Kara Mehmed, although as commander of the advance guard on the right wing he would in any just assessment have been considered at least as responsible for the defeat. A few other officers and officials were executed or imprisoned, but others, especially the Janissary Ağa Mustafa Bekri, avoided death through a combination of political clout and maintaining personal guards. More remnants of the Ottoman army came in to the Raab camp, but morale was naturally terrible and organising supplies difficult, while the Hungarian lords who had submitted in July were turning against them and it was by now obvious that Thököly was unreliable, so, despite the position's technically good strategic situation, on the 17th they set off for Buda, where the bulk of them arrived on the 21st. There, although the army continued to suffer from sickness and desertion, and approaching cold weather meant serious problems for troops mostly equipped only for fighting in the warm, there was a degree of recovery. The Sultan sent gifts indicating his continuing support for his Grand Vizier, so Kara Mustafa's authority was for now reinforced, and he waited to see what the infidels would do.

The Christian coalition had weakened in the days after the Kahlenberg, but not completely broken. An immediate major pursuit of the defeated

---

413 Paradowski, pp.154–184 (chapter 9 also deals with the fascinating story of separate Polish-Cossack actions in the east, in Podolia and Moldavia).

enemy could have made serious gains, but, to Lorraine's frustration, Sobieski for several days strangely lost all desire for such an action. The King's bull-headedness then caused a diplomatic setback when he insisted on entering Vienna on the 13th, before the Emperor could arrive, an action bound to cause offence; Leopold entered his battered capital on the 14th, ceremonially but with something of an air of anticlimax; and a meeting between Leopold and Sobieski along with a military review, carefully choreographed at Schwechat on the 15th, still managed to end badly with the Poles feeling insulted – there was a fair degree of cultural misunderstanding involved, but Sobieski did not help with his attempts to push forward his son as a candidate for marriage into the Habsburg dynasty, which he was never going to gain. Despite this, the Polish-Imperialist alliance managed to survive. On the same day, however, the Saxons without warning set off back home: the Elector John George had several good reasons for being unhappy with his treatment at the hands of the Imperialists, including the religious frictions between Protestant Saxons and Catholic Imperialists, and the fact that it was now clear he was not going to receive any financial recompense for the march of his army, though a brewing diplomatic crisis in northern Europe, the 'Baltic Crisis of 1683', may also have contributed to the decision. The Franconians were reluctant to advance beyond Vienna, but their reluctance was reinforced by serious sickness spreading through their contingent. From 21 September, the Bavarians also started suffering major outbreaks of disease, though these were greatly exaggerated by Maximilian Emanuel who, selfish to the core, was effectively withholding continuing co-operation in the hope of procuring an independent command for himself, so for some weeks the Bavarians remained inactive on the Marchfeld.

Inevitably, some of Leopold's ministers now wanted to turn the Monarchy's attention west against the continuing threat of France (French troops had entered the Spanish Netherlands during the last days of the siege of Vienna), but there was substantial support for at least some kind of counter-attack against Turkish Hungary. Although relations between the Imperialists and the Poles continued strained, because of both bad Austrian treatment of the Polish soldiers and Sobieski's attempts to intercede on behalf of Leopold's rebel Hungarian subjects, reports sent in by the commandants of the forward fortresses at Raab and Komorn indicated that, while the Ottomans were not destroyed, they were in considerable confusion, and the chances of recovering parts of Turkish Hungary seemed too good to pass up, especially to Sobieski who now longed to end the campaign with another great success. Sobieski himself had his eyes on Buda, capital of Turkish Hungary and key to their control of the entire province, capturing which would indeed be a fitting end to the year, but there were strong doubts about whether a siege of the city could be organised so late in the year (the 1684 campaign would prove such doubts completely correct) and other voices dickered between attacking the modern fortress of Neuhäusel, the Ottoman forward outpost on the north bank of the Danube inside Royal Hungary, and tackling the older fortified city of Esztergom on the Danube itself, key to opening up the river as a supply line for any future siege of Buda. On 17 September (the day that Kara Mustafa left the line of the River Raab to retreat to Buda), Sobieski, losing patience with the continuing discussions, set off east from Schwechat with just the Polish army; Lorraine followed him with the Imperialists on the 18th, leaving behind both the sulking Maximilian Emanuel and the continuing ministerial debate whether to turn against France. It soon became apparent that advancing through territory devastated by the Ottoman advance in July and retreat recently was not a viable prospect, so they decided to shift at Pressburg to the less-damaged north bank of the Danube, which necessitated a delay of nearly a week while a boat-bridge could be organised there, though this gave time for Lorraine's infantry to catch up with the faster-moving Poles and Imperialist cavalry. Both armies were on the north bank by the middle of the 27th. Imperialist-Polish relations remained tense due to Sobieski's continuing attempts to interceded on behalf of Thököly and the Hungarian rebels, but the advance east continued, through the soggy but prosperous great island known as the Schütt, hardly touched by operations until now; the Poles continued to pull ahead of their allies. At the far end of the Schütt, with their forces strung out behind them, on 3–4 October Lorraine and Sobieski agreed that Neuhäusel was not a practical target so they would proceed down the Danube to a position opposite Esztergom, to the city's north-bank bridgehead called Párkány, and assess the situation there.

Kara Mustafa at Buda had been kept informed of this advance. As it became clear that the Christians were heading against the important Ottoman fortress-city of Esztergom, loss of which would isolate their enclave at Neuhäusel north of the river but also open the infidels' way downstream to Buda, so the Grand Vizier sent the new *beylerbeyi* of Buda north to Esztergom and Párkány. On 7 October Sobieski, based on incorrect reports of Ottoman forces in the hills north of Párkány, rushed ahead with some of his Polish cavalry and ran into an ambush expertly laid by Kara Mehmed at the head of perhaps 8,000 Ottomans. In the first Battle of Párkány, the Poles were routed, Sobieski himself came within a hair's breadth of being hacked down and was for a while reported as killed, and only the timely arrival of FML Dünewald with Imperialist cavalry, sent on by Lorraine to help, saved the Polish cavalry from annihilation. Chastened, Sobieski submitted to Lorraine's insistence on waiting for the rest of the army to catch up before acting further. Elated at his success and ignoring advice to pull back over the Danube to Esztergom, Kara Mehmed also called up major reinforcements across the river and drew up to fight, facing west with the River Gran to his rear. Two days later, on 9 October, in the second Battle of Párkány, the full Imperialist-Polish army, at least 27,000 strong including a good 12,000 infantry, faced Kara Mehmed again, this time with about 14,000 cavalry and just 1,200 infantry – the Ottomans were also expecting Thököly, who was supposed to be a few miles up the valley of the River Gran, but the Hungarian rebel leader as usual failed to appear. Kara Mehmed could not use the same trick twice; the result was a foregone conclusion. The allies, formed closely without intervals between their units in exactly the same style as Lorraine in the Battle of the Kahlenberg, advanced and swept the Ottomans from the field in under an hour. Thousands fled east towards the River Gran, only to be trapped in its marshes and slaughtered by the pursuing Christians; thousands more fled south to Párkány and the boat-bridge over the Danube to the safety of Esztergom, only for the boat bridge (as these were wont to do in such circumstances) to break under the panicking throng. Allied troops easily stormed the feeble wooden fortifications of Párkány itself and cut down the troops trying to defend it, and then they swept on to the river bank against the crowds of Ottomans trapped there, who were slaughtered on dry land or forced into the river to drown. In terms of casualties, it was a disaster for the Ottomans as big as the Kahlenberg: at least 9,000 men were killed or drowned, 1,200 taken prisoner by the Christians at the end when their blood-lust abated, and only a few thousand made it over the River Gran or across the boat bridge before it broke.

Second Párkány was a major victory for the Christians. Ottoman morale collapsed: in the camp around Buda, soldiers resumed deserting in droves, and Kara Mustafa left to go to Belgrade with the core elements of the army, the *kapi kulu* and the *yerli kulu* of the major *beylerbeyi*s, leaving Kara Mehmed (although badly wounded in the battle) in charge of the frontier. The Grand Vizier had hoped to restore his personal influence with the Sultan by a personal interview, but Mehmed IV left Belgrade to return to Adrianople before he got there, and Kara Mustafa, still officially commander of the army, could not go beyond Belgrade without permission.

On the opposite side, the victory held the increasingly shaky Imperialist-Polish alliance together for a few weeks longer. Lorraine, discovering that Esztergom could completely control any river traffic going past it, recognised that no advance beyond it was possible while it remained in Turkish hands, and pressed a rather reluctant Sobieski into besieging the city, though for complicated political reasons the Poles would only remain in a supporting position on the north bank. The Imperialist army, now rejoined by the Bavarians under GWM Steinau, re-crossed to the south bank on 20–21 October, and despite increasingly bad weather started a siege of Esztergom on the 22nd. The city's fortifications were antiquated, though its position on a steep hill could have made it very difficult for the Germans to establish effective artillery positions (a problem that they would definitely encounter at Buda the next year), but fortunately there were hills close enough to place breaching batteries on, and cannon-fire plus mortars throwing bombs indiscriminately at the interior soon broke the desire of the defenders to hold out. A capitulation was signed on the 27th, and the next day 10,000 Muslim troops and inhabitants left the city with their belongings to board boats to take them down the Danube.

The capture of Esztergom was another big success for the Imperialists: a fortress-city of major strategic importance had been captured, and perhaps as important as the military value was the symbolic – for the first time in nearly ninety years, a Christian power had retaken one of its cities from the Ottomans. No-one could get too complacent, for Esztergom had already changed hands several times, but it gave cause for optimism, and this would turn out to be justified: Esztergom was only the first of many Hungarian cities to be recovered by the Christians in the ensuing years.

For now, Esztergom had to be the end of it; the season was too late to try further operations – and besides war had finally broken out between France and Spain, so all German attention was for the moment directed west. The

Bavarians went home, as did 3,000 Swabians who had marched up. This left only the Imperialists, and the Poles, who were insisting on winter quarters in Upper Hungary (which meant that they would be maintained at the expense of the Habsburgs or their unfortunate Hungarian subjects all winter) while at the same time continuing to try to persuade the Imperialists to negotiate with Thököly and his rebels. Leopold and his ministers were not averse to the Poles taking over territory currently in rebel hands, which would effectively mean the reconquest of such territory, but since Thököly himself had withdrawn south over the border of Turkish Hungary to Grosswardein, they would have preferred the Poles to take quarters beyond the River Theiss near Grosswardein and the Transylvanian border, effectively cutting the rebel-held towns of Upper Hungary off from any Ottoman or Transylvanian help. However, Sobieski was determined to have quarters in the Hungarian counties nearest Poland, so at the end of October off towards Upper Hungary he marched with his army, Lorraine trailing behind with the Imperialists, scattering his own regiments left and right into the quarters assigned to them; eventually, when he was done, he sent Dünewald with a small corps to continue after Sobieski to make sure that any towns that surrendered to him received Imperialist garrisons.

In fact, the Poles had a sorry time of it. They took only a few trivial forts on their way to the counties nearest Poland, and the deeper they marched into Hungary, the more they came into open conflict with the *kurucok*. The weakly disciplined Polish soldiers had a penchant for plundering at the best of times, and, as conditions worsened with food shortages and sickness accompanying them as they dragged themselves through the misery of an east European early winter in the open, control almost disappeared; it was inevitable that they would alienate the Hungarians. However, the Lithuanians had made absolutely sure of this. The Lithuanian army only joined Sobieski in mid-November, when it turned up at Rima-Szombat showing not the faintest hint of embarrassment at its disgraceful lateness, even after marching not on the heels of Sobieski through Moravia and Austria but directly from Cracow into Upper Hungary; entering Hungary in October, it had treated the inhabitants along its route with appalling savagery, plundering them whether loyal or rebel, and going out of its way to inflict terrible cruelties on any community suspected of being rebel. At least in part, the Lithuanians' vicious behaviour was deliberate: they knew that Sobieski was negotiating with the rebels and they intended to wreck the negotiation, solely because it was Sobieski's initiative and might redound to his credit. In this they succeeded. Relations between the Poles and Hungarians disintegrated; towns kept their gates firmly closed to the King who wanted to pose as their liberator, the countryside became full of ambushes of any Pole or Lithuanian who strayed from the march column. Walled towns were essential to any army for safe winter quarters, but in early December, when they reached their target counties, the Poles could take only one small town, Zeben (the Imperialists also besieged and took the slightly more substantial Leutschau, though they allegedly had to burn much of it to the ground to do so), so Sobieski decided to take the thousands of sick and the weakest units on across the border with him, leaving a garrison in Zeben and distributing the rest of the Polish army

NO MORE TIME TO LOSE

in the villages of the Zips region (Hungarian territory much of which had been pawned to Poland centuries earlier). On 13 December he re-crossed the Polish border, and by Christmas was reunited with his wife. As soon as he had departed, the troops left in the hostile Hungarian villages ran amuck: thousands deserted to go home, the rest behaved so badly that by January most of them were being recalled. The Polish army was in ruins. It was a desperately sorry end to the greatest page in its history.

The Ottomans had one last gift for the allies, however, a fine Christmas present. Kara Mustafa was stuck at Belgrade while his influence with the Sultan plummeted. With the fall of Esztergom, his fate was sealed: although he immediately executed several of the senior officers of the garrison, he could not execute or discredit every man who might report to the Sultan his own share in responsibility for the disasters of the campaign, and the more men he executed, the more he created enemies for himself desperate to ensure that they were not next. Besides, the court rivals who sought his position now sensed an opportunity and threw their influence into the scales. Many Ottoman troops returning home through Adrianople had been heard to declare that they would never serve again under Kara Mustafa, which not only acted directly as a factor weakening his position but also allowed his enemies to argue to Mehmed IV that an insurrection by the troops was possible if the Sultan insisted on standing by Kara Mustafa. Nevertheless,

Execution of Kara Mustafa. Caspar Luyken, 1689 (Rijksmuseum, Amsterdam)

for a while Mehmed IV continued to show confidence in his Grand Vizier, and the intrigues took a little longer to reach their inevitable conclusion as Kara Mustafa's enemies, joined even by members of the imperial family such as Koca Ibrahim's wife, Mehmed's sister, worked on the Sultan. On 14 December, two court officials with orders for his dismissal and execution left Adrianople heading back up the military road through stinking winter weather across the Balkans for Belgrade.

One could not simply hand such orders over to their victim, so the messengers on arrival at the camp outside the city conferred with the Janissary Ağa, Mustafa Bekri, and together on 25 December, after Mustafa Bekri's troops had secured every escape route, they presented themselves at the Grand Vizier's tent. Kara Mustafa took the news calmly, completed his noon prayers without a break in his voice, and asked only that the carpet be removed so that he could die with his feet on the ground – which technically in Islam meant that he would die a warrior and go to paradise – before raising his beard to allow the executioner's strangling rope easy access to his throat. A few minutes later, he lay dead in the dust, and his head had been removed from his body so that, according to standard Ottoman practice, the skin of the head could be flayed from the skull, stuffed, and sent to the Sultan as proof that his orders had been carried out.

The body was eventually taken to Adrianople for burial, but the skull was interred at Belgrade, where it would be found in 1688 by Christian soldiers just after their capture of the city and sent to Vienna; the Imperialists, who on occasion had a fine sense of irony, presented it to Bishop Kollonitsch, because during the siege of Vienna Kara Mustafa, learning of the bishop's energetic work in the defence of the city, had openly threatened to decapitate him when the Ottomans broke in.[414]

Despite the fact that Kara Mustafa's own ineptness had played a major part in the defeat at Vienna, he was the best of a bad lot, as would become clear in the following years when one ineffective politician after another succeeded to the seal of Grand Vizier; it is doubtful whether anyone could have held the Ottoman Empire together and resisted the Christian alliance that would form in 1684 against it, but if it were at all possible, Kara Mustafa was the only man for the task. Not until late 1689, after Mehmed himself had been overthrown in 1687 by an army revolt, would the Sultan find another competent chief minister. Richly deserved though the punishment was, the

---

414 The story of Kara Mustafa's death was widely reported. See Kreutel & Teply, pp.200–201, for the account of the Master of Ceremonies, and Cantemir, vol. 2, p.315, for some of the political scheming that secured the order for his execution; also, the account of the English commercial official ('factory chancellor') at Constantinople, Thomas Coke (Coke to unknown, 8 February 1684 OS) in British Library: Add.MSS 22,910, f. 227 v. – 228. Kreutel & Teply, pp.291–315, discusses the question of the skull found at Belgrade (formerly thought not to be Kara Mustafa's because his 'head' was sent to the Sultan); the conclusion of this paper, about the flaying of the skull and the sending of the stuffed skin, is supported by the witness Martelli (Johann Friedrich Esper, *C.A. de Martelli, Römisch Kaiserl. Generaladjutanten... Errettung in und aus der Türkischen Gefangenschaft* (Erlangen: Heyder, 1825), p.147) and other evidence of normal Ottoman practice.

intriguers of the Sultan's court did the Christians a substantial service when they secured the order for Kara Mustafa's execution.

Nevertheless, the details of Kara Mustafa's last moments offer us a perfect epitome of the hypocrisy that lay at the very heart of the Ottoman Empire, a fitting marker at this significant turning-point: the attempt to deceive his god with the removal of the carpet. Nothing demonstrates the corruption of the Ottomans so neatly, their use of literal interpretations of selected bits of religion, rather its totality and its spirit, when such an interpretation suited them.[415] The hypocrisy was not personal to Kara Mustafa, but typical of the Empire as a whole; one needs think only of the centuries-long practice of *devşirme*, the seizure and forcible conversion of subject children as recruits for the *kapi kulu* in flagrant breach of the rules of Islam. Vienna in 1683 was the Empire's high-water mark, the start of its decline; but the declining would not start the process of corruption, which had been at its heart from the very beginning.

The future

Encouraged by the victory at Vienna and even more by the recapture of Esztergom, the Ottoman Empire's enemies – its three most recent victims, the Emperor, Poland and Venice – formed a new alliance in March 1684 under the aegis of the Pope, a Holy League aimed at driving back the Ottomans in both central Europe and the Mediterranean. The Imperialists were uncertain at first, for France remained as big a threat to them as the Ottomans did, but they started operations in Hungary anyway, and when Louis XIV granted the Empire a formal truce in August, they were able to throw their entire weight into the effort. After a shaky start in 1684 covered in my forthcoming *Wilfully run our head against the wall* – scheming cavalry generals pushed Lorraine into a siege of Buda for which the Imperialist army was not ready, leading to a major defeat with massive casualties – the Imperialists went from strength to strength in Hungary, finally taking Buda in 1686 and reconquering almost the entire kingdom by 1688 then holding it against serious counter-attacks down to the peace in 1699. It was the first time ever that a whole land had been reconquered from the Ottomans, but further advances into the Balkans were prevented by the French attack on the Emperor in 1688, and liberation of the Balkan peoples was delayed for nearly two centuries. Venice meanwhile chose not to try to recover its most recent loss, the island of Crete, but concentrated on regaining its former stations at the entrance to the Adriatic and throughout the Aegean, as well as the Morea (the Peloponnese, that part of southern Greece so nearly an island); it kept them all at the peace settlement, though it lost them again within a couple of decades. Poland, after playing such a glittering part in the saving of European

---

415 Abrahamowicz, in Waissenberger, p.241, draws attention to the sham conduct at the moment of execution and describes other areas where Kara Mustafa ignored the strictures of Islam when it suited him.

civilisation, stumbled from stalemate to set-back as Sobieski's campaigns to recover the Coomonwealth's lost Ukrainian province of Podolia and conquer Moldavia collapsed in ruins under the double weight of their own over-ambitious objectives and the reluctance of the Polish magnates to support anything that might give him more prestige and thereby increase the power of the monarchy; Sobieski himself died in 1696 a failure, his dreams shattered and the credit of his truly great achievement forgotten, and that Poland did recover Podolia at the peace settlement of 1699 was due almost entirely to the efforts of its allies at the peace congress. Russia, which had joined the war in 1686, gained only a single base that gave it limited access to the Black Sea, Azov, which it would soon lose again, but it had started on the path that would turn it within a century from a victim of Tatar slavers into a power capable of conquering the Crimea and threatening the very existence of the Ottoman Empire.

Russia's setting off on the path to world power was only an indirect consequence of the relief of Vienna; the battle had a far more significant effect on world history than that.

13

Commentary

Criticisms

Many of the aspects of the campaign open to criticism have been addressed directly at the relevant point in the main account above. The broader issues surrounding the Battle of the Kahlenberg boil down to a small number of key questions, which have been argued over, usually with national fervour verging on the vitriolic, ever since; and I will address three of them here.

How important was the part played by the Poles in the victory?

Fiercest of the arguments was that over whether the Germans or the Poles were primarily responsible for the victory. This usually boiled down to attempts by German historians to diminish the role of the Poles, or by Polish historians to play it up. Some of the more extreme Germans in the nineteenth century even tried to reduce the numbers of Polish troops present in order to minimise the part that they played, often accompanied by snide remarks about the fact that, however many Poles made it to Vienna on 12 September, they were far fewer than Sobieski had committed to send under the terms of the alliance. The course of the battle could be presented in such a way as to support the German case, for there was no doubt that Lorraine and the Imperialist-Saxon left wing had borne the brunt of the fighting for many long hours before the Poles even appeared in action. In fact, the truth was that both nationalities played a significant part in the victory; it could not have been achieved without all the major contingents that had assembled on the Tulln plain.

To consider the Polish numbers first: it was true enough that, whether Sobieski had 17,000 as most historians concede, or 15,000 as Le Bègue asserted, or close to 21,000 as Wimmer would have it and as I am inclined to believe, the Polish army was well below the 40,000 that it was committed to bring under the Holy Alliance, the treaty of Warsaw of March 1683. However, this was hardly the fault of the Poles: despite the references to potential sieges of Vienna or Cracow in the treaty, and the occasionally feverish work on the fortifications of the city over the previous winter, no-one had seriously expected Vienna to be besieged, at least not in this first full year of the war – everyone thought that the Ottomans would first concentrate on the remaining fortresses protecting Royal Hungary like Raab, as indeed Kara Mustafa was ordered and originally intended to do – and the Poles had legitimately prepared for their own campaign in the Ukraine. Despite the initial westward shift of Sieniawski, the Poles were not prepared for marching to the Danube, so, when the Ottoman army reached Vienna and desperate Imperialist appeals for assistance raced across central Europe to Warsaw, Sobieski was compelled to rearrange all his campaign preparations from the ground up. Then, when Lorraine's calls for him to come to Vienna became ever more pressing, he responded gallantly and, setting out with just 26,000, pushed his troops through Moravia as hard as troops could ever be pushed if any of them were to arrive in fighting condition. Given the pressure the Poles were under and the speed of their march, it was to their great credit that as many of them arrived as did. Whether 15,000 or 21,000 paraded at Tulln, no more could fairly have been expected.

These Poles, even if below treaty strength, were playing a valuable part in the victory just by their presence, before they had even come to contact with the Ottomans. There can be no doubt that news of the King of Poland's union with the German forces was a very nasty blow to the Ottomans: it so alarmed the Grand Vizier that he could think of nothing to do against the allies, thereby contributing materially to Kara Mustafa's mental paralysis as the allied army approached his camp. There is not much doubt either that the same news was the primary cause of the Tatars' lamentable performance in the days leading up to the battle and of their early departure from the field of battle, leaving Kara Mustafa and his subordinates blind to the details of the approach of the Christians, paralysing even further the Grand Vizier's mind. On the other hand, Sobieski's arrival, with his personal reputation as a consistently-successful battle commander against the Ottomans to add to the troops who would make up not far short of a third of the overall allied army, boosted the confidence of all the other Christian contingents. Sobieski could have sat inactive throughout the 12th and still claimed a share of the credit for the victory.

His soldiers deserved more than that, however. It is true enough that Lorraine and the left wing were fighting almost unsupported for most of the morning and with no real Polish involvement until 2 p.m.; it is true that Lorraine and the left wing had driven the Ottomans before them for hour after hour until that point in the early afternoon, with all the credit for this going to the steadiness of the German troops and to Lorraine's own ability in learning the lessons of the clashes with the Ottomans in the early summer and adopting a formation with no gaps; and it is true that the final magnificent Polish cavalry charge took place just that little bit too late to be decisive, for the Ottoman army was by then already defeated and beginning to break up. Nevertheless, the grandeur of the last great charge in history of the winged hussars should not blind us to the fact that Poles had then been in action for several hours before it took place, in the less dramatic but more important fighting on the slopes of the Schafberg and around the Türkenschanz. And even if Sieniawski had not fought so hard and no Pole had drawn his sword or cocked his musket before 4 p.m., the mere advance of the Polish wing had kept Ottoman troops tied down that might otherwise have been thrown against the Germans. Indeed, if the Poles had not been present at all, the Germans would not have been able to fight as well as they did: they would have been compelled either to advance with their right flank completely open, or to extend their line much more thinly to cover the extra distance. If they had adopted the former, there can be no doubt that Kara Mustafa or his subordinates, their minds not paralysed by the advance of the 'Lion of Lechistan', would have been bound to exploit it and smash the Christian right flank, either by sending Abaza Sari Hüseyin into the Wienerwald or by hitting it as soon as it tried to leave the tree-line. If they had adopted the latter, with a long shallow battle-line, it is highly likely that the counter-attack launched by Osmanoğlu, which was only blocked by units coming up from further behind in the dense Christian formation, would have been a lot more dangerous than it already was, and might even have broken Lorraine's advance – that is, they would have stopped the relief dead in its tracks, repulsed it, ensured the fall of Vienna.

No-one ever pretends that the Poles relieved Vienna on their own, or has ever suggested that they could have done, but nor could the Germans have done it on their own; Vienna certainly could not have been saved without Sobieski and his exhausted soldiers.

Was Sobieski the effective commander-in-chief of the allied army?

It is an interesting tribute to the difference in outlook of the seventeenth century from our own that we can even ask this question. Humans of the contemporary age are actually every bit as status-obsessed as those of the baroque age, but in matters as important as military command they have long since accustomed themselves to recognised hierarchies, to strict rules establishing who has the right to issue orders to whom based on formally appointed ranks, rules that could be applied even in a multi-national force like the allied relief army. The new standing armies of the late seventeenth century were starting to develop such rules, but had not got there yet, and other, fuzzier rules of precedence involving kings and dukes came to the fore. If Sobieski wanted the supreme command, he had to fight for it.

Nominally, after the discussions at Stetteldorf Sobieski was supreme commander of the relief force; about this, there is no doubt. There is equally little doubt that the King himself thought that he was, believed to the end of his days that he had been the true commander of all the contingents present, that his was the primary responsibility for the greatest and most important victory of the age. But how true was this?

Quite a large part of Europe subsequently agreed with Sobieski; in many of the news reports that circulated, Lorraine was not even mentioned. It was not just those from afar who were capable of being deceived by Sobieski's nominal authority or by his subsequent frenetic public-relations activity; even the Brandenburg envoy to the Habsburg court, Johann Georg von Anhalt, an eyewitness of the battle, personally pro-Imperialist and representative of a government that, while currently unfriendly to the Habsburgs, was not on good terms with Sobieski, unequivocally stated that Sobieski 'commanded in chief'.[416] On the other hand, Le Bègue was constantly at pains to emphasise the independence of his master, that Lorraine made significant military decisions without regard to the King, as part of his personal conviction that the Duke was the man really responsible for the victory. Some of the assertions of Lorraine's catty secretary need to be taken with a pinch of salt, and he did sometimes go too far as with his virtually writing Sobieski out of the discussions at the Kahlenberg monastery on the 11th (see Chapter 8 above, and Appendix I, 8.1), but in this respect he was on the right track.

According to most conceptions of propriety in the seventeenth century (that is, to everyone except the electors), in the absence of the Emperor Leopold, Sobieski was right to claim the supreme command as the only king present, and he was supported in this by the terms of the Polish-Imperialist alliance; but those were not the true reasons why he was acknowledged as commander. Lorraine acknowledged his supremacy out of political wisdom, recognising Sobieski's need to be top dog and accepting that this was the best and quickest way to move forward in securing the relief of Vienna; in no way did this imply that he obeyed Sobieski as completely as a modern subordinate general obeys the commander-in-chief. The two electors meanwhile had an entirely different agenda: if one of them could not obtain the top position, they were determined it was not going to Lorraine. They knew that neither of them had a legitimate claim to supremacy that could be recognised by the other or by the rest of the contingents present, so, when it came to deciding to whom they should submit, faced with a choice between a despised elected king and a duke who was not only not an elector but also their subordinate in the traditional ducal hierarchy of Europe, they preferred the elected crown, which trumped the only card Lorraine had in his hand, his office as the deputy of an Emperor. (However, John George was prepared to serve *alongside* Lorraine in a role that could be presented as a partnership even if it was not.) Sobieski was accepted ultimately because Saxony and Bavaria could not consider serving under Lorraine. From their point of view as much as from Lorraine's, his command was far more nominal than effective. If the electors did indeed rush to congratulate Sobieski after the battle as he told his wife, they did so not out of genuine respect for him as commander but because they had no intention of going to congratulate poor Lorraine.

Not that the Duke seems to have cared: he did exactly what he wanted anyway. Lorraine had seen through Sobieski's vanity, played on it, allowed Sobieski to act the alpha male, had even let him have all the glory... and meanwhile had moved when he wanted, secured the plans that were most critical to his own aims, acted almost entirely according to his own judgement – aided, it must be admitted, by the fragmented nature of the

---

416 Quoted in Forst de Battaglia, p.181, and elsewhere. The full statement as quoted by Forst de Battaglia, its grudging tone eloquently demonstrating Anhalt's reluctance to give credit to Sobieski, runs: 'The King in Poland commanded in chief, and was everywhere where the greatest fire was. I must without flattery give witness to the King and both his field commanders that they, just as the other generals, were all the time to be found at the head of the army, and everything proceeded without the slightest confusion and [or] disorder.'

Wienerwald – and when Sobieski's wishes and his own clashed, had followed his own. Lorraine's deep concern that Vienna was close to falling dictated the actions of the allied army; Sobieski's desire for a victory of annihilation was passed over at every opportunity. The attack of the left wing on the morning of the 12th was entirely Lorraine's. The Duke was not, as his latest biographer Urbanski has suggested,[417] merely acting as Sobieski's executive officer, doing all the hard work of implementing Sobieski's broad plans.

About Sobieski, it must be acknowledged that, unless he was so dense as to fail to notice this, he had sense enough not to pick a quarrel over insubordination at such a dangerous moment: when the Duke flouted his orders, he was prepared to grin and bear it, both for the sake of allied harmony (whoever was right about when to start the battle and how to fight it, the worst thing to do was to create a breach in the allied unity over the issue) and because he must have known his own prestige would suffer badly if he reacted to Lorraine's independence and initiated an unseemly argument.

Most historians these days, even Polish ones, accept that the conditions of the action on 12 September, with a hugely wide battlefield too broken up by hills and woods to permit of command oversight, let alone close control, made it impossible anyway for one commander-in-chief to direct the battle as a whole in any degree that gave him a preponderant impact on the overall outcome. Sobieski certainly tried: he had his adjutants ready to carry his orders wherever he wanted, and he seems to have regarded himself as exercising control with an appropriate light touch, accepting Lorraine's reports and approving the Duke's actions, as noted above either oblivious to the fact that Lorraine was acting with complete autonomy or more likely turning a blind eye to it. But the left wing was dancing to Lorraine's tune, not Sobieski's, even before the King left to rejoin his Polish troops on the right. Since Sobieski ultimately let Lorraine do his own thing, perhaps he had recognised the situation and was merely preserving the semblance of his own overall control for use in his publicity operations later. If so, the King deserves as much credit for this willingness to give way when giving way was necessary as for his willingness to come to Vienna.

If Sobieski was not the effective commander-in-chief, nor was Lorraine; the Duke – despite the occasional references by Le Bègue to his issuing orders to Waldeck, and the arguments of his modern biographer that he was 'in a historical sense' the commander-in-chief and ultimately 'responsible for victory or defeat'[418] – made no serious attempt to control any part of the allied army beyond the left wing that had been assigned to him and that he had chosen to use to implement his own plan of breaking the siege of Vienna by a direct advance through to the city. Indeed, the fate of the direct appeals for help from the left wing to the Franconian FML von der Leyen show that no-one was providing effective overall control coordinating the centre and the wings at this stage. Such coordination as took place later in the day of the centre corps with the rest of the army was carried out more by the King than

---

417 Urbanski, p.135.
418 Wentzcke, p.214.

by the Duke. Sobieski and Lorraine commanded the allied army between them.

Ultimately, Sobieski and Lorraine shared not only the command but a great deal of the credit for the victory. Sobieski had brought a third of the allied army, his reputation for victory against the Ottomans, and a crowned head that helped to hold the allied army together. Lorraine brought a third of the allied army, a cool head coupled with a sturdy ability to apply lessons he had learned, an absolute determination not to be side-tracked from the immediate need into dreams of a victory of annihilation, and a willingness to overlook every affront to his status as long as he kept the allies working towards the common goal. We should not forget the others, however. Maximilian Emanuel acted out of motives far more selfish than he should have done, but he did the right thing. Waldeck deserved considerable credit for his ability to see beyond his own current *bête noire* of the French threat to recognise the Ottoman danger and for his hard work in moving the Franconians to action in time. Perhaps even more credit is owed to grumpy John George: Saxony was nowhere near as badly threatened should Vienna fall as were Bavaria or Franconia, but when the call came he responded valiantly, marched with his troops before the Imperialists had given him any assurances of recompense, arrived in time and did his duty with sturdy courage despite being heroically patronised, all for six bronze cannon and a few measly baubles. He may not have glittered in history like his fellow-elector Maximilian Emanuel, but John George deserves our respect far more than the Bavarian.

Could the Ottomans have won at the Kahlenberg if they had acted differently?

Once, this question would have been regarded with astonishment: the traditional view of a huge Ottoman army, outnumbering the relief force at least two to one, with Turkish ferocity counter-balancing their acknowledged lack of discipline, made it impossible to imagine an easy or inevitable Christian victory. However, once we understand that Kara Mustafa's field army in fact barely equalled the relief force, the question appears in a totally different light.

It seems safe to conclude that the Ottomans might very well have won if they had acted differently *before* the 12th. However, once that day dawned with the Christians flooding down the last line of hills and the Ottomans sitting at the foot of the slopes waiting passively to receive them, in insufficient numbers to outflank Sobieski or break through the dense German formations, they had few choices open to them. Unless the Christians had made some serious mistakes or had suffered some extremely bad luck or Kara Mustafa had shown extraordinary ability, their chances of victory were, though not completely non-existent, slim indeed – and Kara Mustafa's mental paralysis suggests that he knew this very well.

How were the Ottoman prospects of victory so much better with earlier action? Tied up with this question is that of how close Vienna was to succumbing. The publicity image created throughout Christendom of the victory was that Vienna had been relieved at the last possible moment, that it would have fallen if the relief had been delayed a day longer. In fact, expert witnesses who saw the state of the defences and the Ottoman siege works afterwards generally put the city's ability to hold out longer at between three and eight days. I am inclined to believe the lower figures: the mines in the curtain wall were ready to be exploded by the end of the 12th, and when these were fired, unless they created such chaos that the assault forces were able to overwhelm the remaining defences and break right through to the interior, the Ottomans would have faced further retrenchments set up by Starhemberg behind the expected breach points, and beyond these yet more defences such as chained and barricaded streets. These makeshift defences could have held up the besiegers for two or three days, but it is hard to imagine them keeping out the Ottomans for much longer. If the Ottomans had stormed Vienna, and been granted at least another day to take full possession and get their gear inside, the Christian relief force, with no serious military equipment at its disposal, would have been unable to winkle them out again, would have found its own position increasingly untenable – especially once the Ottoman victory encouraged their forces north of the Danube to traverse the River March, occupy the Marchfeld, and establish contact with the victorious army in Vienna, which now had the ability to cross the river that it had been struggling to acquire all summer, with access to the food resources of the north bank that the Christians had tried to preserve for their own forces, plus thousands more slaves and tons more plunder to inspire their reinvigorated troops to yet more devastation.

So the Ottoman army needed at least four days to have been reasonably sure of taking Vienna and putting themselves in a very strong strategic situation. If they had defended the Wienerwald, they had every possibility of gaining those four days.

Firstly, if sufficient forces had been sent beyond the hills to the Tullner Feld, they could have harassed the march of the Christians across the plain to the foot of the Wienerwald. Given that the south Germans were already coming down the right bank of the river, the Ottomans certainly could not have stopped Lorraine and Sobieski from crossing by the Tulln bridge, but by harassing the south Germans' advance they could have slowed it, and by the time it reached Tulln and cleared the bridgehead to allow Lorraine and Sobieski to cross, at least a day would have been gained for the Ottomans, more likely two. The Tulln crossing, which took long enough unopposed, might well have taken even longer when armed forces stood in the vicinity of the bridgehead, when Ottoman cannon-balls were falling on the rickety bridge, when the arguments amongst the Christian commanders were magnified by this evidence that the route chosen was not going to be easy. Admittedly it might not have taken so long, and the day of rest after crossing that actually took place on the 8th could have been abandoned, recovering a day. However, once the Christians were assembled on the Tullner Feld, they had to get across it; Turkish and Tatar light cavalry had plenty of experience in harassing Christian forces and would have had no trouble slowing their march to a crawl. It took the Christians (delayed by discussions and hesitations) a day to get across the Tullner Feld; with enemy harassment, it might have taken another day – the most likely course of events is that the commanders, instead of their afternoon plod across the plain on the 9th, would not have moved at all on their first day at Tulln, and waited until early on the next day to set out, probably reaching the foot of the Wienerwald that evening. Two or more days down, and already the Christians would have been tired and frazzled.

Then they had to get through the Wienerwald. This was difficult enough, as we know, when un-opposed; if they had had to fight for every step, it would at least have taken days longer – they might not even have managed to break through at all. Historians when discussing the fighting of the battle itself are unable to agree whether the conditions of the Wienerwald, the woods and hills and gullies that made the fighting so difficult in the early stages of the 12th, favoured the Christians or the Ottomans; one can find writers who argue that the broken terrain made things difficult for the Christians because it favoured the skirmisher tactics of the Ottoman irregular troops and especially delayed the deployment of the cavalry-heavy Polish army, and writers who argue the opposite, that it made things easier for them because it prevented the Ottomans using their best arm, the cavalry, to greatest effect. In fact, the terrain made things difficult for *both* sides: it hampered the Ottomans in their use of cavalry, which was undoubtedly the arm in which they were most skilled, while at the same time it prevented the Christians from deploying and fighting in disciplined, solid, close-order formations and it made the Poles almost worthless as a fighting force. When they fought at the exits to the Wienerwald on the 12th, neither side had a serious advantage (although once the Christians made it to open ground, the advantage definitely passed to them). But within the Wienerwald, if the Ottoman aim (whether its warriors were made aware of this or not) was merely to try to hold up the advance of the relief army, it did not matter who benefited tactically, only that the terrain favoured *delay*; whether the Ottomans were disadvantaged by their inability to use cavalry or the Christians by their inability to operate in formation, any action *at all* would have slowed the Christian advance dramatically. The advance through the woods was difficult enough with no opposition; opposition would have at least doubled the time taken to get through to the Vienna basin. Indeed, if the Ottomans had fought hard enough, they might have simply ground the Christians to a halt, exhausted them so much that they could not make it to the far side; if they had had only moderate good luck, they might even have defeated the relief force completely – it would only have taken one forceful leader driving into one of the gaps that were bound to have arisen between the different Christian contingents in the broken terrain, and the relief force would have been shattered. But this was not necessary, only that the Ottomans hold up the advance for an extra day to the Buchberg and another day or two to the far side of the Kahlenberg. If the Ottomans had created an abatis in the parts of the Wienerwald nearest their camp, as Koca Ibrahim had (probably) argued, at least another day would have been added to the total, and another factor added that the relief army might not have been able to get past at all, for after days of constant skirmishing in the woods an assault on an entrenched position may have been beyond them.

NO MORE TIME TO LOSE

This gives us the situation as laid out in the table below, comparing the actual stages of the relief army's advance with the best-case possibilities had the Ottomans fought to delay them in the Wienerwald:

Actual dates	Dates (best-case) with Ottoman delaying action
late 6th – 7th, crossing at Tulln; late 7th, arrival of Germans from Krems-Mautern	
8th, resting, reconnaissances, mass, review;	late 8th, arrival of Germans from Krems-Mautern
9th, crossing Tullner Feld;	late 9th – 10th, crossing at Tulln (assume no time spent resting afterwards)
10th, into Wienerwald, Lorraine to Klosterneuburg & camp on Buchberg, Poles no further than Kirchbach;	
11th, left wing to crest line at Kahlenberg, centre to Vogelsang-Hermannskogel, Poles to Dreimarkstein-Sauberg-Weidlingbach valley;	11th, crossing Tullner Feld
12th, battle	12th – 13th, into Wienerwald, Lorraine fights through to Klosterneuburg and the Buchberg; Poles no further than Kirchbach
	14th – 15th, left wing to crest line at Kahlenberg, centre to Vogelsang-H'kgl, Poles to Dreimarkstein-Sauberg-Weidlingbach valley (possibly not even that far);
	16th, depleted, worn-out left wing and centre attack abatis; Poles perhaps not even in action until 17th
	17th, battle in the open

It must be stressed that the dates on the right are the best possible for the Christians, and even so this gives the Ottomans five extra days to take Vienna, one more than they really needed. If, appalled at the prospect before them of fighting their way across the Tullner Feld and through the Wienerwald, the allied commanders had spent a further day at Tulln arguing, or if they had had to spend a whole further day fighting over the Kahlenberg (both of which are perfectly possible), then their chances of making it to the Vienna basin before the city fell were very slim indeed.

By failing to oppose the Christian crossing of the Wienerwald, the Ottomans reduced their chances of victory significantly. Victory was not impossible, however: the Ottomans might just conceivably have won if Kara Mustafa had not been so demoralised that he spent most of the day in complete inactivity but had instead provided some central control of the action – perhaps committing part of his reserve of regular troops from the centre, instead of just some of his own household troops, to support the three-pronged attack against Lorraine in the morning. This counter-attack, before the Christian left wing had formed its unstoppable line, was the closest to breaking Lorraine that the Ottomans came, and it was just within the bounds of possibility for the Ottomans at this stage to overwhelm his left flank, or to break through on his right cutting him off from the centre, if they had committed enough good troops and managed them with sufficient skill. Such an event might well have spelt defeat for the whole Christian army, though that was not inevitable, for Waldeck's centre might still conceivably have held on long enough for the massed cavalry of the Poles to be brought to bear.

Once Lorraine had won the open ground and formed his solid line, however, the battle was almost certainly lost for the Ottomans. The only hope they had of stopping Lorraine was if they had used artillery very skilfully in coördination with the *yerli kulu*, with cannon fire opening gaps in Lorraine's line and the warriors pouncing before the line could reform. However, the Ottomans had no notions of close artillery-infantry coöperation such as the Christian world had developed with the concept of battalion guns; artillery for the Ottomans was what it had been for centuries, a static arm intended to defend fixed positions or soften an enemy up in the initial stages of the battle – and even in this limited mode the Ottomans used it very badly at the Battle of the Kahlenberg. Beyond this, the Christians might conceivably have still lost the battle if their troops had performed especially badly, or if their commanders had committed some exceptionally stupid mistakes or failed to cooperate to a catastrophic degree and Kara Mustafa had been alert enough to exploit them; but otherwise, with Lorraine steadily advancing in a formation that the largest concentration of Ottoman troops could not break, they were bound to lose; if the Ottoman right and centre had been still holding by 5 p.m., the Polish charge would have been utterly decisive.

However, unfortunately for the Ottomans there were no such mistakes by the Christian commanders, no such failures to cooperate (with the possible exception of von der Leyen's refusal to support the Saxons). That Vienna was saved was due to a number of individuals: firstly to grim Starhemberg in the city and his tough management of the defence, and then, as Le Bègue stressed in his Diary (see Appendix IV) to all the commanders of the relief army who served so diligently and all the soldiers who fought so hard when they were called on. Any one of the commanders could have harmed the relief effort if they had failed to cooperate:

> Apart from the example that my lords the Electors of Bavaria and Saxony and that so many princes from all the great dynasties of the Empire gave to the army by their vigour and firmness, one cannot praise and esteem them highly enough for the ease with which they consented to all the proposed dispositions, concerning themselves solely with the relief of Vienna, and contributing everything to avert the delays that the competition and the competing jurisdictions of so many different units normally brings in such cases.

Importance of the battle

'Kings and battles' have not been in fashion amongst historians for many years. A few historians recognise that certain events are of major significance in determining human destiny,[419] but for most of them, it does not matter much in the development of humanity, they argue, whether (say) Marlborough took Lille from the French in 1708 or how he did it; so all history of events is consigned to the rubbish-bin.

The argument is intrinsically false, on both counts, the 'whether' and the 'how'. As for the 'whether': the individual event, even when tediously repetitive like a series of sieges, may be significant when it forms part of a wider effort that could fall down completely, taking the world down a very different road, at the failure of any individual step (as Marlborough's campaigns to break the hegemonic power of France could have fallen down if any major fortress like Lille had defeated him). And as for the 'how', this matters because *any* human actions in the past, most especially collective ones where many humans have to work together at different levels and in different ways to achieve a common goal they have been set or have set themselves, have a great deal to teach us about how humans behave, about how they succeed or fail in their endeavours, about how big a role their own petty rivalries or their failure to consider alternatives or their emotional weakness or external circumstances or just plain luck may play in deciding the outcome. Recent past or distant past, it does not matter: all events, all occasions when humans have acted with or against each other, can tell us something about the way we can behave today – the politics of Republican Rome in the first century B.C., for example, with its ambitious politicians espousing causes of principle for entirely cynical motives, are extremely

---

[419] Georg Wagner makes a strong case for the importance of the Christian victory over the Ottomans at St Gothard in 1664 as an event that determined the fate of European civilisation, though he was less explicit than I will try to be about why this was so. See Georg Wagner, *Das Türkenjahr 1664: eine europäische Bewährung* (Eisenstadt: Burgenländisches Landesarchiv, 1964), especially p.533.

informative to anyone considering British or American politics of the last few decades. Kahlenberg and the relief of Vienna tell us a great many things about how humans behave, and the story is worth telling on that account alone. But it is also worth telling for the other reason: that it was not even just an individual step in a series of events but a truly significant event in its own right – that it mattered very much indeed for the future shape of the world, right down to our own day, whether Vienna fell to the Ottomans or survived in Christian hands in that hot summer in 1683.

We have already commented on the ways that the Vienna campaign is instructive about human actions; for example, the threats to the Christians' common effort of the drive of so many alpha-males for dominance – the allies were fortunate indeed that the Imperialists were led by so level-headed a man as Lorraine who treated such power-games with the contempt they deserved, and that their ranks included other sane minds such as Waldeck. Or there are the power-games that were being played out on the other side of the Wienerwald in the Ottoman camp. No-one who has seen contemporary politics, whether in corporations or on the national stage, can fail to see their relevance. Since these have been covered at the relevant moments in the account above, we can proceed to that second reason for looking at the battle, its intrinsic significance.

Why was the relief of Vienna so important?

The relief of Vienna was a massively significant event in human history: it mattered enormously to the world in which we live today how the campaign ended, and therefore, in addition to the instructive reasons for reviewing its course, studying it is worth-while because of its intrinsic importance. On top of this, however, is the fact that this general lesson of the event's significance is itself an important one: that at critical junctures events do matter, and individual actions can have a massive impact on the whole future course of the culture.

Why then was the relief of Vienna so significant? Why did it matter, not just for the generation of 1683 in central Europe but for all the generations down to our own throughout Christendom, that those Austrians and Germans and Poles fought to defend their world against such a terrible enemy? Surely any effects of the battle had run their course within decades and European history had continued on the same groove it would have followed anyway.

Nothing could be further from the truth. To answer the question, it is necessary to consider an 'alternative history', to look at what would have happened if Kara Mustafa had won: if he had either taken Vienna before the relief arrived and then held the city against the allied army, or if Lorraine and Sobieski had failed in their attempt to relieve the city and the Ottomans had stormed in a few days after the relief force had been repulsed.

The direct short-term results for central and eastern Europe alone would have been considerable. Instead of the end of Turkish expansion and the start by the Imperialists of the drive to roll back the Ottomans that by 1699 would liberate at least most of Hungary, including Transylvania, from their corrupt rule, modern Austria would have been turned into a wasteland, a brand-new border territory on the centuries-old pattern of the Ottomans, over which Muslim looting bands, operating out of the new base in Vienna and backed up by regular troops making bigger forays from the same, would strike out at will as far as Salzburg and Bavaria in the west, Graz in the south, and Bohemia in the north. As already noted, the population of the Austrian countryside had not yet recovered from the devastations of the Thirty Years' War, and in reality decades would pass before it recovered from the destruction wrought by just that one Ottoman campaign in 1683; if those raids were being repeated all over Austria year after year, in all the areas untouched in 1683, with all the fortified refuges being whittled away as first the smaller walled towns and then the bigger ones fell to the supporting campaigns of the regular Ottoman troops also based in Vienna, then the 70,000 civilians killed or enslaved in the 1683 campaign would have been multiplied many times over, and Austria would have been turned into a semi-desert the way all East European lands had been if they tried to defend their independence against the Ottomans – most recently, as Podolia and the rest of the Ukraine had been within the last thirty years. With French support, the Germans might conceivably have recovered Vienna after a few years, but if the Ottomans had managed to hold on to the city for any length of time, the devastation would have slowly but remorselessly spread outwards further and further into southern Germany and the Czech lands. Regardless of whether the Christians eventually recovered Vienna, in the south the thin strip that was all that remained of Croatia would have become untenable, would have either joined willy-nilly to Thököly's vassal principality or been annexed by the Turks to Ottoman Bosnia, and Turkish raiders, who even when Croatia had been a viable defence line had shown themselves able to break through occasionally as far as the borders of Italy, would have had a free run through Carniola towards Venetia and the rest of the defenceless north Italian plain. The dream of Sultan Mehmed II, the captor of Constantinople, that he would also take Rome itself, might have been realised two centuries after his death. In the meantime, behind this new zone of destruction and booty, Hungary would of course have been lost completely to the Habsburgs and to Christendom; Thököly's control of all of Royal Hungary would have become permanent – for as long as it suited the Sultan, anyway.

Meanwhile, further back, the Ottomans would certainly have carried out what they had been wanting to do for a century: the annexation of Transylvania and the two Roumanian states, Moldavia and Wallachia; for in their great days of expansion it had been a rough-and-ready maxim of the Ottomans that vassal states were incorporated in full when further vassal states had been acquired beyond them so that they were cut off from all possibility of foreign intervention – and, with Poland knocked out of the running by a defeat at Vienna, the new puppet principality of Thököly would cut the three states off from Christian support very effectively. This great swathe of land would have provided fresh new estates and other sources of revenue for the Ottoman state and its officials, perhaps even enough to have rejuvenated the institution of the timariot cavalry or, more likely, to have allowed organisation of an effective substitute for that increasingly-outdated institution. Certainly, these two new massive sources of wealth, the border-lands for the slavers and thieves and the internal annexations for the rest, would have infused new life into the creaking Ottoman system, kept it going for perhaps centuries longer. Reinvigorated and with new centres of strength on the Hungarian plain, Constantinople could have renewed the attack on Poland, under pretext of revenge for its support for the Imperialists in 1683, whenever it chose: major offensives coming in from the east, supporting raids all along Poland's southern border – for Thököly would not have dared refuse passage and support to Ottoman raiders. Under such conditions, southern Poland was indefensible; Podolia would have become merely the first Turkish conquest on the Polish plain instead of the only one; the Ottoman reach might have extended as far as Cracow, and, unless France came to its aid, the suicidally selfish Polish nobility might have found its fate not in the partition by Russia, Prussia and Austria that it suffered a century later but in partition by the Turks and perhaps the Swedes within decades of the fall of Vienna. As for Muscovy, it could never have stood and expanded against the renewed power of the Ottoman Empire; it could at best have clung on to a precarious independence as a peripheral land – no Peter the Great could have turned it into the mighty Russian Empire when there was a strong still-expansionist Ottoman state to the south able to keep Moscow in check any time it chose by sending out the slavers of the Crimea.

After a certain point – the devastation of central Europe, the rejuvenation of the Ottoman Empire by new lands and new sources of slaves and plunder – it becomes impossible to predict with any certainty what would have happened in the east, especially with the possibility that devastated Austria might have been reconquered with French support. What France would choose to do would determine events throughout he region. For, curiously, it would be the consequences of the fall of Vienna in the *west* that would have had the most far-reaching and long-lasting effect on the history of the world.

One of the most important factors that in the couple of centuries after 1683 would bring Europe to world dominance was its diversity, its multiplicity of states that gave the continent overall such flexibility: if new ideas, whether in science or social conscience, were suppressed in one of its states, they could usually be taken to another state and flourish there, so that Europe's culture never stagnated but continued to develop all the time, went from strength to strength. It is often forgotten how fragile this diversity was, how rare it was in world history and how easy to crush in its early stages. If Vienna had fallen to the Ottomans, diversity would have been at an end. How was this possible?

To answer that, it is necessary to recall what really did happen in the west during the years after the relief of Vienna. In 1684, Louis XIV gave up for a while his ambitions to become Emperor, suspended his territorial expansion against the Empire, and let the Germans get on with fighting the Ottomans in Hungary, aware on the one hand that his hostile actions in 1683 had weakened his international reputation which he needed to restore by some insincere but carefully presented pro-Christian moves, and convinced on the other hand that the War of the Holy League would be a disaster for the Emperor and the princes who followed him into Hungary, that after a few years France would be able to move in and pick up the pieces, its dream of European hegemony merely postponed for a few years. Meanwhile, Louis sought to create absolute internal conformity within France by turning on the Protestants: in 1685 he revoked the Edict of Nantes that secured toleration for the Huguenots, and began a campaign of terrorisation against them, seeking to compel them to convert to Catholicism. In fact, the revocation only provoked occasional revolt and frequent emigration: skilled and hard-working Huguenots took their talents to enrich England, the Netherlands, Protestant principalities in the Empire (the Markgraf of Bayreuth, who served in the relief army as an FML in the Franconian contingent, settled many of them on his lands) – even far-off Brandenburg, once France's secret agent in eastern Europe but increasingly its committed enemy. As the next couple of years rolled by, Louis's mistake over the War of the Holy League became ever more obvious, with the Imperialists going from victory to victory: they regained most of the Kingdom of Hungary, re-incorporated the Principality of Transylvania into the Kingdom, and pushed the Ottomans back to Belgrade. Their army grew greatly in size and even more greatly in confidence, its veteran soldiers driving from one conquest to another, its commanders learning how to manage far-flung and difficult campaigns, its bureaucrats discovering – admittedly slowly, with great difficulty and much hardship for the men in the ranks – how to support those campaigns logistically and how to find the money to pay for them. In short, they were catching up with every advantage that France had once held over its enemies. And alongside the Imperialist soldiers were Bavarians, Franconians and Swabians, and smaller contingents from tiny German states, all turning themselves from new formations into experienced corps – even on occasion Brandenburgers, learning again to fight alongside the Imperialists instead of for the King of France as had seemed to be their destiny in the early 1680s. Every success of the Germans in Hungary brought, even to the princes of the Empire who did not join in themselves, new confidence that the Empire could fight and win – and not just against Turks. In the Netherlands, the politically powerful burghers of Amsterdam, whose rabid caution had dragged William III of Orange out of the war against France in 1678 and prevented him from acting against Louis's peace-time aggression in the years after, likewise began to take note of the way that the wind was changing, to consider that taking the field against France might in fact be the safer bet after all. And so in 1688, when Louis XIV finally decided he could not let the Empire go on any more winning victories against the Turks and sent the French army into the Rhineland, William III was able, with full support of the previously so-cautious Dutch burghers, to launch his astonishingly bold move to turn France's most important ally into its enemy, with his invasion of England. The gamble paid off: the Catholic James II was expelled, William III of Orange became William III of England, Scotland and Ireland, and England, united under its new Protestant ruler, began, even if reluctantly at first, to play a major role in Europe, the first steps that would take it to the position of a world power. To stop French aggression for good, England, the Netherlands, Spain, Empire and Emperor formed the Grand Alliance; in north Italy, which in the early 1680s had seemed set to fall under permanent French domination, the Duchy of Piedmont-Savoy turned against Louis XIV and joined the allies – not permanently, but long enough to break the chains that would have kept it and eventually the rest of Italy under the heel of Paris. Despite the Grand Alliance, the subsequent Nine Years' War of 1688–1697 would be a tough fight, especially since the Imperialists (with good reason) continued their operations against the Ottomans, keeping many troops in Hungary that could have been used against France; but the allies fought Louis XIV to a standstill, something no-one could have conceived was possible in 1682. And when the war resumed a few years later over the Spanish Succession, France would be brought almost to its knees, and the world-wide Spanish empire kept from falling entire into the hands of Louis XIV. French hegemony of Europe was thwarted.

None of this would have happened if Vienna had fallen to the Ottomans in September of 1683. Firstly, the loss of its capital, and central Europe's primary point of defence against the Turks, would have been a fatal blow for the Habsburg dynasty: this would have spelt the end of the Habsburg Monarchy itself and of the dynasty's hold of the imperial crown, and with that, the triumph of France. For Louis XIV had long desired to replace Leopold I as Holy Roman Emperor, and nothing now could stand in his way. With Austria itself wrecked, the last part of Hungary irrevocably in the hands of the Ottoman puppet Thököly, and all the Habsburgs' other provinces under threat of the sort of raids that the area round Vienna had suffered in the summer of 1683, Leopold's own conglomerated lands would have shattered. And with its prestige annihilated by the fall of Vienna, with no power base of its own, with no resources to allow it to prop up the line of defence against the Ottoman threat, the dynasty could not hold on to the imperial crown against the now-irresistible pressure and promise of Louis XIV – the pressure of France's super-power position on all the leaderless princes of the Empire, and the promise that its super-power resources, the only resources big enough to deal with the Turkish threat, would be thrown into the struggle to defend against the Ottomans if only the electors would chuck out the Habsburgs and elect the first Bourbon Emperor. Admittedly, the imperial crown was officially for life, and unless Leopold had been killed in the aftermath of the fall of Vienna he would still have been alive at this point, a considerable obstacle to electing Louis as Emperor; but ways could always be found round constitutional objections such as this (for example, in the 'real' 1688, England found just such a way round a very similar problem, by creating the fiction that James II had abdicated). Louis XIV ruled the Empire; France was dominant throughout Europe. There can be little doubt that with France's huge resources thrown into the scale a new defence line could have been erected against the Ottomans, limiting the area of real destruction to Austria and the areas close to it; perhaps a Franco-Reichs army might even have retaken what was left of Vienna a few years later and faced the Ottoman Empire across the buffer zone of the vassal state of Thököly's rump of Hungary, with Thököly playing the same old treacherous double game between the two powers. It is conceivable that Louis XIV, secure now in his pre-eminence as Europe's supreme ruler and no longer needing the Ottoman Empire as a check on his enemies, might even have sent his armies into Hungary in a French-led reconquest of the Kingdom and the rest of the Balkans – while at the same time his navy bombarded Constantinople as it had bombarded Genoa, landed troops in Egypt a century before

Napoleon tried it, and swept the Ottoman fleets from the sea, turning the Mediterranean into a French lake as Europe had been turned into a French backyard. France, had it wanted, could certainly have driven the Ottoman Empire back to be a purely Asiatic power.

However, this is taking speculation too far. No matter how successfully the French might have acted against the Ottomans, the fact remains that, had Vienna fallen, they would have been dominant throughout every part of Europe behind wherever the iron line of the Ottoman border was drawn. France, Catholic and absolutist, is now the super-power, the only power in Christian Europe; it is naturally dominant over all other states, and even if they are inclined to resist, the fact remains that it is now the only state capable of holding back the Ottomans; every other state toes the line set by Louis XIV. Brandenburg remains a French client in eastern Germany (though of course now it is merely acting as a loyal supporter of its French emperor) and Sweden abandons its brief period of anti-French policy to join it; Poland, if it is not already collapsing before an Ottoman onslaught or imploding in civil war and incapable of following a rational policy, has no choice but to follow suit. When Louis XIV turns on the Huguenots now, there is nowhere for them to flee, for no-one will take them, no-one will risk offending the new Caesar; and Catholicism begins to regain its absolute hegemony throughout Europe, the Counter-Reformation to drive back the diverse views of Protestantism and restore a deadly conformity across all parts of Europe not under the heel of the Ottoman Empire. Worst of all, perhaps, is the situation with England: when the pro-Catholic policies of James II drive his subjects to exasperation and they look abroad to William III for salvation, there is no Dutch fleet carrying an army of German contingents to Torbay, for the Dutch burghers – if they still exist at all, for Louis XIV may by now have annihilated the Dutch Republic as he had tried to do in 1672 – will not lift a finger against France, and there is no German contingent that is not subservient to the will of Paris. If England does not dissolve in its second ruinous civil war in half a century, it bends to James' surly will and heads back in religion towards Catholicism and in politics towards absolutism, the same oppressive belief systems as the rest of Europe. And when feeble Charles II of Spain finally dies in 1700, there is no War of the Spanish Succession, for, although there is no hesitation now in the sickly monarch's bequeathing his world-spanning dominions to France (indeed, in the present circumstances he might leave them directly to Louis XIV instead of to one of his relatives), there is no Habsburg Monarchy to contest the will and send its veteran troops into north Italy, no England to furnish a Marlborough who will lead the English and Dutch armies and all their German clients to union with the great Imperialist general Eugene of Savoy and at Blenheim finally shatter France's dreams of super-power dominance. Spain, and with it its world empire, falls to the Bourbons; the Americas, from Hudson Bay to Tierra del Fuego, are in their iron grip, absolutist, Catholic, French- and Spanish-speaking, with the miserable English colonies clinging on to the northern seaboard, existing only on sufferance of the Bourbon super-power as long as London bows to the will of Paris. There will be no American War of Independence and no United States; there will be no Latin American wars of independence and no republics of Mexico or Bolivia or Argentina; for all of these depend on the development of diverse ideas, and the support of autonomous foreign powers able and willing to help them in their struggles for independence – and who in the world will stand up to the colossus of Paris?

From the Elbe to the Philippines, a great huge swathe of the world forms a sterile uniform culture, for century after century its ideas in the iron rule of the pomp and the dead formalism and conformity of the second half of the reign of Louis XIV. If France decides to expand to the far east, to look to the wealth of India (as it did in reality in the eighteenth century), there is no English rival to stand in its way. As far as the Bourbons choose to extend their dominion, thus far do they extend it, and with it their monolithic culture. Europe and all its possessions become a second China, stultified, devoid of the diversity without which the culture cannot develop further.[420] In 'real history', China was forced to modernise by the pressure of vigorous outsiders as they scrapped with each other over the booty to be had in Asia, but in this Bourbon-dominated world there are no vigorous outsiders, and the two world powers of Europe and China may go on unchanged and unchanging for ever.

We cannot take the specific alterations in world history further than this, especially as it is impossible to predict what would have happened to the Ottoman Empire in this brave new world. Would it have survived as an empire, perhaps pushed out of Europe and redefining itself by deep-continental conquests as a more Asiatic power, or would it have clung on as one of the buffer states between the two super-powers into which the globe had divided, Bourbon Europe and China? In neither option would it offer the world any hope, for it would be as closed and inflexible a culture as the other two, hostile to new ideas, crushing the diversity that allows innovation and development to flourish. Maybe diversity will come from some source we cannot imagine; perhaps in this frightening monolithic world Mughal India will build on its brilliant arts to create a culture that is not only capable of withstanding French conquest but can also develop the variety of ideas that will break the dead grip of France and China on the world. All we can be sure of is that the ideas will not come from London or Philadelphia; the rights of man will not be formulated in Paris and exported throughout the globe; slavery will not be ended in the west in the bloodbath of Gettysburg; if anyone anywhere develops the great understandings of the way the world works, from evolution to the atom, it will not be in universities of Europe and the Americas. I would not be able to write this book, and even if I could, you would not be sat reading it, for what you think and how you think would be controlled by closed minds following dead rules laid down centuries ago.

At least one can hope that, if independent intellectual enquiry is sustained *somewhere* in this sterile world, when its practitioners come to study history and the catastrophe at Vienna in the summer of 1683, they will not be so foolish as to argue that events do not matter much in the history of the world.

---

420 Compare Jack A. Goldstone, *Revolution and rebellion in the early modern world* (Berkeley: U. of California Press, 1991), p.484, which stresses 'the rise of toleration and avoidance of rigid cultural conformity as factors in economic success.'

Colour Plate Commentaries

by Michal Paradowski

Plate A.   Ottoman *Kapi Kulu Sipahi* Cavalryman

This very well-armed and well-armoured soldier is from one of the *kapi kulu sipahi* units, the elite of the Sultan's cavalry. His *çiçak* helmet has feathers in its plume holder, indicating that the soldier serves in a guard formation. His mail, armour and shield clearly puts him equal to the Polish hussars and Imperialist cuirassiers – at least in equipment. His green garment is barely visible under his armour and the red waist scarf and boots add to the distinctive look. As well as his sword he is armed with a bow, with the bow case visible at his left side and a quiver of arrows on his right.

Plate B.   Ottoman Janissary

Soldier of one of Janissary *orta*, the core of the Ottoman Army at Vienna. In his left hand he is carrying *fitilli tüfek* (matchlock musket), with the long match cord in his hand and coiled around his lower arm. He has a typical Ottoman pattern sword with plain cross guard in his right hand. His headwear is famous ak börk cap, normally used for ceremonial purposes only – the Janissaries would wear it during parades, upon leaving Constantinople and during the musters in the presence of the Sultan. This soldier is wearing a long green kaftan, baggy red breeches and yellow leather shoes.

Plate C.   Polish Infantryman

During the 1670s, most of the foreign infantry units in the Polish army started to change from Western style of clothing to Polish styles. The soldier shown here has a blue outer garment over a yellow linen one – blue was the colour most commonly worn by the infantry in Poland. His cap is also of blue cloth, most likely purchased in the same order of cloth as his coat. He has managed to obtain good quality brown leather boots, possibly looting them from a battlefield. He is armed with musket and a *berdiche* axe, the latter used in a dual role of musket rest and highly effective hand-to-hand weapon. He would normally also have had a sword, carried at his left side.

Plate D.   Polish Winged Hussar

Well-equipped Polish hussar, with good set of armour, including vambraces (*karwasze*) and a *szyszak* helmet. He does not have a characteristic wing attached to his back, as many hussars did not wear them during the campaign. Over his armour he wears a pelt of an exotic cat. Hussars wore a great many different types of pelt and leopard, tiger, lynx and wolf are all recorded – much depending on personal taste and wealth. This hussar is wearing a lioness pelt, most likely purchased in Poland from Armenian merchants specialising in the import of such exotic items. He is wearing a red *żupan* and yellow saffron boots, often worn by Polish nobles. He is armed with sabre and pistol although these would be only part of his armament. He would most likely have also had another pistol, both carried in holsters at the saddle bow. Other weapon would probably be an *estoc* or *pallasch*, carried under the left side of the saddle and, of course, a long *kopia* lance.

Plate E.   Imperialist or Bavarian Grenadier

Grenades were by 1683 often used during the siege operations. We have the evidence of them being employed by the defenders of Vienna, as shown on the engravings by Romeyn de Hooghe. The soldier presented is most likely an Imperial or Bavarian grenadier from the relief army. These troops had the difficult duty of clearing the trenches of the remnants of the Ottoman besieging forces, and grenades would be very useful during in such a task. While different shades of grey, or even of white, seem to be most associated with the Imperial uniform coats, blue coats were in use in some German armies and were near universal in the Bavarian army. White stockings, brown shoes, black felt hat and white cravat were ubiquitous throughout western armies of the period.

Plate F.   Imperialist Cuirassier

Many cavalry units in the western Europe gradually abandoned the use of armour and helmets, but those in central Europe retained the protection of back and breast plates, and those who faced Ottoman cavalry also still used the *zischägge* helmets (as they continued to do until well into the late years of the next century when facing the Ottomans). The long sleeved buff coat provided additional protection to its wearer. He is wearing the characteristic high cavalry boots of the period and has protected his hands with leather gauntlets. He is armed with a sword, while the pair of pistols would be carried in holsters on his saddle. Many other allied cavalry in 1683, including Polish *arkabuzeria*, Lubomirski's mercenary cavalry and most if not all of the other German cavalry, would be equipped in a near identical fashion.

Plate G.   Ottoman Timariot *Sipahi* Cavalryman

The provincial timariot *sipahi* cavalry had once been a major component of the Ottoman army, but were seriously reduced by 1683, though other troop types would have been equipped similarly. His outer garment is a red *delia*, covering a blue *kaftan* and breeches. As with many other Polish and Ottoman horsemen, he had long brown boots. Instead of helmet, he had a turban; with his only protection being mail vambraces. He is armed with a sword (not visible here), a bow carried in its case at his left side, and a long-handled variant of the horseman's hammer, often used as an additional weapon by cavalry.

Plate H.   Ottoman Balkan *Yerli Kulu* Infantryman

The regular Ottoman units were supplemented by the retinues of the *beylerbeyi*s, which came under many names, such as *sarica*s or *seğmen*. This is a typical Balkan infantryman such as a *sarica*, armed with musket and sword. He has a red *kaftan* with a blue scarf and with dark green breeches and wears low yellow shoes. Instead of a turban (more likely in contingents from the Asian provinces such as the Syrians), he is wearing tall red cap decorated with feathers.

Glossary

Terms in bold refer to other definitions in the list.

abatis
: Barrier formed by cutting down trees and entangling them, with the branches turned to enemy. When formed along the edge of a wood, the tree-trunks also formed a breastwork for the defending troops. Advancing enemy troops could be shot down at leisure as they tried to cut or climb through.

Ağa
: Turkish for chief, master; used at this period most often for the officers of an official's household, although in general usage it had become reduced to a vague epithet of respect. Retained its original implication of high rank in various senior military offices; see e.g. **Janissary Ağa.**

askeri
: Lit., Turkish for 'the military'; in Ottoman practice, all those who were in state service, whether in the army, the bureaucracy or the clergy – the 'ruling institution', as opposed to the reaya, the ruled. They received salaries from the state, or from religious foundations established out of plunder taken by the state, and paid no taxes.

battery
: In the seventeenth century, a B. was an entrenched *position* for cannons, in any number, not a company-sized unit of artillery.

Beylerbeyi
: Lit., lord of lords; governor-general of a major Ottoman province, usually the overlord of several sancak-beys. His province was sometimes called a *beylerbeyilik*. The position was originally a very senior one within the Ottoman hierarchy, but by the late seventeenth century was somewhat devalued, and there was an implicit division between truly senior *beylerbeyi*s, such as those of Rumelia, Anatolia and Buda, who had **vizier**al status, and the more junior ones who were often barely above a *sancak-bey* – for nearly a century, any individual newly-conquered fortress had been made into a *beylerbeyilik*. There was a world of difference between a *beylerbeyi* of Buda, who headed a major province with authority over other *beylerbeyi*s and could conduct certain aspects of foreign policy, and a *beylerbeyi* of Neuhäusel, who headed a single fortress

and a small enclave of territory surrounding it. Their household troops were known as **yerli kulu**, and formed a significant part of the Ottoman army at this time. (Strictly speaking, the word should be spelt 'beglerbegi', and will be found thus in many reference works, but most though by no means all western Ottomanists for this and other titles with 'beg/bey' prefer the 'y' spelling, which reflects the word's pronunciation and the practice in recent Turkish dictionaries and Wikipedia, so I have followed suit.)

Buda — Capital of Hungary; since 1541, in possession of the Ottomans, who called it Budin, and for whom it was a significant forward base, a keystone of their control of most of Hungary. (In 1872, it would be united with the separate town of Pest on the opposite bank of the Danube to form the modern city of Budapest.)

Candia — Chief city of Venetian Crete (modern name: Iraklion), heroically defended against the Ottomans in a siege that lasted on-and-off for over twenty years, and continuously from 1667 to 1669 when it finally capitulated. Many Germans had participated in the final three-year siege, and this along with the Battle of St Gothard (see **Köprülüs' War**) formed the west/central Europeans' most recent experience of fighting the Ottomans.

çavuş — Ottoman palace official, not exactly translatable, with varied duties including state courier, sergeant (in the legal sense), herald, attendant, or on occasion even executioner.

cebeci — Lit., armourers; one of the salaried corps of the **kapi kulu**, arsenal troops responsible for maintaining all kinds of weapons and armour. At this time the entire corps (not all of which came to Vienna) was about 8,000 strong.

Centner — German measure of weight, roughly equivalent to the hundredweight (with which of course it shares its name from the Latin 'centum'); technically, the C. was slightly heavier – it was equivalent in modern measures to 56 kg., while the British hundredweight (cwt.) of 112 pounds equals 50 kg. In modern German, the spelling is 'Zentner', which clarifies how 'Centner' is pronounced.

chevaux-de-frise — lit., Friesian horses; actually, obstacles of spears or metal spikes sticking out from balks of timber, so-called because they were an effective barrier against cavalry and were supposed to have been invented by the Friesians, a people who had no cavalry of their own and especially needed such barriers against their mounted enemies. Sometimes known as 'Spanish riders'. Contemporaries occasionally distinguished between *chevaux-de-frise* as heavy permanent obstacles and '**Schweinsfeder**' as mobile obstacles carried by infantry and assembled by inserting boar spears into balks of wood when needed; but

GLOSSARY

	terminology was often used loosely – the lighter portable obstacles were often called *chevaux-de-frise* (and I so use the term in this book), although the heavier ones were rarely called Schweinsfeder.
Chocim	battle of 11 November 1673, in which Sobieski gained his greatest victory over the Ottomans; see **Sobieski Wars**. It was fought just south of the Dniester, in what was then northern Moldavia, and is now Ukraine; the form of name used here, accepted as the English form, is in origin a Polish corruption of the Roumanian name Hotin (in modern Ukrainian, Khotyn).
chorągiew	Polish for 'troop'; a unit of cavalry (literally, it meant 'banner' – compare with the Ottoman term 'sancak', as in **sancak-bey** below). See chapter 11, section 'Final attack', for a suggestion that the Poles used 'squadrons' for a level of organisation *above* the ch., so that is not a valid translation of the word.
Cossacks	Free-booters living in the open steppe border-lands between Poland, Russia and the Ottoman Empire, mostly in what is now the Ukraine (there were also Cossacks elsewhere on Russia's southern borders). In conjunction with the settled peasantry of the Ukraine oppressed by the Polish nobility, they had attempted to form an independent state in the middle of the seventeenth century, but had failed, and those of them who had not either fallen under Russian rule or been destroyed during the **Sobieski Wars** of the 1670s had reverted to a stateless peripheral existence in the steppes. They were considered excellent light cavalry.
Crimeans	See **Tatars**.
Croats	Natives of Croatia (then a part of Hungary, an autonomous kingdom within the greater kingdom); although repeatedly devastated by the Ottomans and losing much of its territory, it had resisted complete conquest. The Croat regiments in the Imperialist army were not *officially* hussars, nor any kind of light cavalry except insofar as the Imperialists regarded anything other than cuirassiers as 'light'; those regiments that survived to the end of the seventeenth century converted to dragoons, and they seem to have been considered more fit to be placed in the formal order of battle than Hungarian units, but they probably looked and acted a lot like hussars.
Crown…	In Polish practice, referred to the Kingdom of Poland as opposed to the Duchy of Lithuania (a geographical term rather than a constitutional one). See also **Hetman**; **Poland**.
defile	in military terms, any relatively narrow passage that would hinder troops from forming up properly; the classic

	example is a ravine or gorge, but in the seventeenth century a d. could be a gap between two woods, or between a hill and a river. Commanders of the period disliked them intensely: troops could be trapped if caught in a defile, or if an enemy was formed up just outside the exit he could prevent troops in it from deploying effectively, forcing them to come out in disorder, a guarantee of defeat.
Dragoman	Western corruption of Turkish 'tercüman', = interpreter, translator. The term was used in the Ottoman Empire to describe both their own interpreters and those of foreign ambassadors visiting Constantinople. From the late 1660s, the Ottoman government, whose leaders and Muslim officials refused to learn western languages, had been appointing Christians, usually Greeks, to a semi-ministerial post of Grand Dragoman, who played a significant part in diplomatic negotiations and the interrogation of important prisoners.
ducat	gold coin in general circulation across Europe, usually the highest-value coin in common use in any country; in Habsburg terms in 1683, roughly equivalent to two **Thaler**, or the value of three **Gulden**.
Dutch War	War in the west, 1672–1679 (often mis-dated 1672–1678 because the Netherlands and Spain withdrew from the war in 1678). Started by the treacherous Anglo-French attack on the Dutch Republic in 1672, it had come to involve most of western and central Europe in a major struggle to block French expansion, in which the Francophobe powers achieved only a qualified success (partly because the **Imperialists** were distracted by the **Kurucok** Revolt in Hungary). Many Imperialist officers had gained their main military experience in this war. Most states of the Empire had joined the struggle, but Bavaria had remained neutral. France had continued its expansion after the war by pseudo-legal means, and was still regarded as a very great threat by the Empire and Emperor.
Elector	Highest-ranking princes of the Empire, who had the right to elect a new **Emperor**, and precedence over all other princes in the Empire in matters of its government; in German, Kurfürst. There were at this time seven: the Archbishops of Mainz, Trier and Cologne (the 'spiritual electors'), the Count Palatine, the Margrave of Brandenburg and the Dukes of Saxony and Bavaria. The King of Bohemia (a crown held by the Habsburgs) counted as an Elector for imperial elections but not at other times, allowing the Habsburgs to vote for themselves but not influence the aristocratic running of the Empire. Electors were always very prickly about maintaining their

	precedence over other rulers of the Empire. The mark of an Elector was not a crown but a hat.
Emperor	Elected federal head of the Empire (see **Reichs**); in German, 'Kaiser' (though in 1683 the original Latin spelling 'Caesar', pronounced the same, was still in use). Habsburgs had held the title for centuries, but it had never been made hereditary; each Habsburg successor had to secure election by the **Elector**s (if elected while his father was alive, he was called the 'King of the Romans'). The Emperor was also a direct ruler of a number of dominions of his own (see **Habsburg Monarchy**), some of which were within the Empire and some of which (principally, the Kingdom of Hungary) were outside it; the Hungarians in particular, while understanding that their ruler held the title of Emperor and acknowledging it as a courtesy, in any important matter recognised him only as their 'king'.
Empire	See **Reichs**.
Feldzeugmeister	Lit., master of field equipment; a senior general officer; in a few years, it would come to mean nothing but 'General of Infantry', but in 1683 the term retained part of its original meaning and a FZM was expected to have special responsibility for artillery, and for most tasks of an engineering nature, especially building bridges.
Franconia	One of the **Kreis**e of the Empire, in south-central Germany on either side of the upper Main river (today, forming the northern part of Bavaria); its main states were the Bishoprics of Bamberg and Würzburg, and the Imperial Free City of Nuremberg, and it contained a number of other smaller principalities. Although the two bishoprics had substantial armies for their size, Franconia was not dominated by a single powerful state like some Kreise, and the 'federal' spirit of loyalty to the Empire and Emperor remained strong amongst its rulers.
Freiherr	German for 'free lord', or Baron – but not every 'Baron' in the Imperialist army was German, so both terms are used here.
General-Lieutenant	In Habsburg practice, not a 'lieutenant general' (which south Germans of the time called a 'Feld-Marschall-Lieutenant'), but more the equivalent of the English post of Captain-General; the Emperor's supreme 'deputy everywhere' in military matters, the Commander in Chief of the **Imperialist** army. Montecuccoli had held both this post and the administrative office of President of the **Hofkriegsrat**; Lorraine held only the former, weakening his ability to head the Emperor's armed forces.
Generalwachtmeister	Or, General-Feldwachtmeister; German general rank equivalent to Major General (literally, it is exactly the same title: it means 'sergeant-major-general', which

was the original full English form of Major General). Strictly speaking, the term used by the Habsburg government in 1683, and for some years after, was Obrist-Feldwachtmeister, but GWM later became the accepted form, and contemporaries used it more often than OFWM, so I have elected to standardise on GWM. There was no great consistency in contemporary practice, however: the Saxon Suttinger used 'General Major' for Imperialist officers but GWM for everybody else, while the Saxon publication *Aufrichtige und unpartheyische Relation* used 'General Major' for everyone, and the Franconian Schliz von Görz used both terms indiscriminately.

gönüllü — Lit., 'braves'; Ottoman warriors normally serving as volunteers, for booty and the chance to distinguish themselves and thereby win a position in the regular army (occasionally, they were paid by the state, and they were organised in units with salaried officers). Usually mounted, lightly equipped; effectively, bandits.

Graf — German for Count (or in English peerage ranks, an Earl), but, as with **Freiherr**, not everyone holding the title was German.

Grand Vizier — Chief minister of the Ottoman Empire; the **Sultan**'s absolute deputy in administration, justice and military affairs, subject only to the override of the Sultan or his right of approval should he bother to exercise them – or to the Sultan's right to dismiss or execute any G.V. at whim. Originally drawn from the **kapi kulu**, but this was changing in the late seventeenth century. Kara Mustafa was G.V. of the Ottoman Empire from 1676.

Gulden — Standard currency unit in the Habsburg Monarchy, although it was actually a 'unit of account' – there was no coin called a G. circulating, it was a term used in book-keeping, valuations, salary documents, and so on. Sometimes translated as 'florin'. It was equivalent to two-thirds of the **Thaler** (which was a real coin); see that entry for purchasing power. See also **Kreuzer**.

Habsburg Monarchy — A term created by modern historians for the various kingdoms and duchies directly ruled by the Emperor, as opposed to the Empire of which he was federal head; contemporaries used vague terms like the 'lands of the House of Austria', or the imprecise 'Hereditary Lands' (which did not officially cover the entire state, because the Habsburgs held Hungary by election, not by hereditary right). From about 1740, the whole monarchy (including the Kingdoms of Hungary and Bohemia) was referred to by the even less accurate name of 'Austria'. Legally, each kingdom and duchy was a separate state, connected only by the shared ruler, and their nobilities resisted attempts by the dynasty to link them together more closely by common institutions; the **Hofkriegsrat** was the only government body at this time with recognised authority over most of the Monarchy. Most of the lands of the Monarchy were within the Empire and were ruled by hereditary right; Hungary was outside the Empire, and the Habsburgs were Kings there by right of election by the Hungarian Diet (parliament). Troops etc. of the H.M. were referred to as **Imperialist**.

haiduk — In the context of this book, a Hungarian infantry unit of the Polish royal guard. The term is Hungarian (where it is spelt 'hajdúk') and had a chequered history: it originally meant a cattle-drover, then (since cattle-drovers were wild unruly men, just like the cowboys of the American West) it came to mean free-booter who might perform military service as a foot-soldier, and after the free-booters had been persuaded to settle down and granted land in free (non-serf) communities in return for more reliable military service, it came to mean a type of soldier; by the late seventeenth century, any native Hungarian infantry, whether they came from the H. communities or not, tended to be called H. (while cavalry were called hussars). Technically, in Hungarian, the singular is 'hajdú' and 'hajdúk' is already plural, but in English practice 'haiduk' has become established as a singular form and is pluralised again.

Herzog — German for Duke; in the Empire usually a reigning duke, the head of a state; in precedence the highest princes of the Empire apart from the **Elector**s.

Hetman — Polish commander. The two halves of the Polish-Lithuanian Commonwealth, the **Crown** (Kingdom of **Poland**) and Lithuania, each had two Hetmans, a Grand Hetman (commander in chief); and a Field Hetman (his deputy, but also with special responsibilities); in 1683, the two H. of the Crown were Jabłonowski and Sieniawski respectively. The post was an office, not a rank, and normally, once a man had been appointed to it, he held it for life. The word was probably borrowed from German 'Hauptmann'. When used in English, the plural is 'Hetmans'.

Hofkriegsrat — Lit., Court War Council; an Imperialist administrative body roughly analogous to a ministry of war, although strictly speaking it was not a ministry, since it was a collegiate body (making decisions collectively) and it had no budget of its own (every item of spending had to be referred to the treasury, known as the Hofkammer, for approval). It ran the administrative aspects of the Imperialist army (supply, recruitment, raising of new regiments, etc.), and tendered advice on operations to the Emperor *if* he asked for it. For much of the seventeenth century, it had also managed the *routine* aspects of Imperialist foreign policy towards the Ottoman Empire – since the Ottoman Empire regarded itself as at war with any Christian neighbour even when it had signed peace treaties with them, it was logical enough for such a neighbour to have foreign relations with it run by a military organisation. The 'Hof' prefix indicated a body of the Emperor's administration, not the Empire's. The H. was one of the few government departments of the **Habsburg Monarchy** with authority over most of the lands of the Monarchy: in finance, each kingdom and duchy had its own treasury, in law each kingdom and duchy had its own chancery, and so on, but the H. managed military matters for every kingdom and duchy except for the duchies of Inner Austria, which for convoluted political reasons had a H. of their own based at Graz, and for Hungary, where its authority was valid in practice but hotly disputed otherwise. The main H. was headed by a President, who normally had only a chairman's authority over the collective workings of the board but in emergencies could make decisions on his own authority, and obviously by his overall conduct set the tone for the whole board. Most seventeenth-century bureaucracies were slow and crude by modern standards; the H. was no worse than most, except for its complete lack of spending control, but even here, the main problem was not the H. itself but the Habsburg Monarchy's lack of sufficient revenue to pay for everything it needed to do. The H. has often been accused of hampering campaigns by trying to direct operations from afar, but for the late seventeenth century this is unfair: the H. advised the Emperor on strategy only when he requested it, and the bigger problem lay with field commanders (even quite good ones like Lorraine) who tried to avoid responsibility by requesting inappropriately explicit instructions. Of course, Presidents of the H. with political influence at court, such as Hermann of Baden, could affect policy decisions independently of their official position.

horse-tails	In Turkish, *tuğ*; standards used by the Ottomans as insignia of rank; sometimes with a crescent at top. The number of poles carried varied with the rank of the official; in 1683, the **Grand Vizier** had five, an ordinary **beylerbeyi** had two and a **beylerbeyi** of vizieral status, three.
Hungary	See **Royal Hungary**; **Upper Hungary**.
Imperialist(s)	Of or pertaining to the Emperor as distinct from the Empire; translation of the German 'kaiserlich(en)'. Armed forces of the Emperor raised in his own dominions (the

	Habsburg Monarchy) and serving his interests alone were 'Imperialist'; armed forces raised by other rulers of the Empire and organised within the framework of the Empire were called '**Reichs**' (those raised by other rulers on their own authority with no reference to the Empire were simply known by their names, e.g. 'Bavarian' or 'Saxon' – but see **Reichs** entry).
Inhaber	Colonel-proprietor ('owner') of a German regiment. In German practice, especially Imperialist, nobles contributed a great deal of their own resources to raising and organising new regiments, and were regarded almost as owners of the units. The I. sometimes commanded his regiment in the field as well, but often left this to the lieutenant-colonel or a colonel-commandant, especially since the I. was usually also a general with duties elsewhere (it was rare, though not unheard-of, for an I. to be a non-military man).
Janissaries	The biggest and most famous corps of the **kapi kulu**, the Ottoman regular infantry, equipped with muskets and swords, but no pikes or bayonets. Originally a small élite, in the fifteenth and sixteenth centuries they had become a large corps, and, as one of the few bodies of regular infantry in the world at that time, had played a large part in Ottoman victories. There had always been limits to their discipline, however, and their quality had declined considerably in the seventeenth century, despite a partial recovery under the Köprülüs; by 1683 the discipline and training of European armies had far overtaken that of the J., and although they were ferocious fighters in siege warfare and steady enough in open battle, they were not drilled to fight in formation and maintain controlled musket fire. The Polish royal guard also had a small unit of Turkish-style troops that were called Janissaries.
Janissary Ağa	Commander of the corps of **Janissaries**, a senior Ottoman officer, although by 1683 he was not necessarily a professional soldier. His role had always been as much to control the Janissaries on behalf of the Sultan as it was to command them in the field.
kapi kulu	The Ottoman standing army, lit., 'slaves of the Porte'. Comprised of the **Janissaries**, **Sipahis** of the Porte, **topci**s, **cebeci**s and a few other small corps. The term also encompassed all members of the provincial and central administration (except for Muslim-born bureaucrats and judges), right up to the Grand Vizier, all of whom were officially slaves of the Sultan and could be executed at his whim (even the growing numbers amongst them who were technically free-born Muslims, like Kara Mustafa). Originally a small élite formation of slave

guards (slave troops were quite common in all medieval Islamic cultures), the k.k. had become greatly enlarged in the fifteenth century, by the end of which it formed a third or more of the overall Ottoman army, and, as the only standing army then in existence, contributed greatly to Ottoman success against less disciplined European, Persian and Egyptian foes until the late sixteenth century. Until about the middle of the seventeenth century it continued to fill its ranks from Christian prisoners of war and (in flagrant breach of the laws of Islam) from older children seized from the subject Christian populations; both of these would be forcibly converted to Islam, and brutalised and browbeaten into submission to the Sultan, who retained absolute power over their lives, in return for which they had their salaries, booty from successful campaigns, a certain licence from the government in their behaviour towards the civilian population, and, for the brightest among them, the opportunity to reach the heights of power, for the entire administration up to the **Grand Vizier** was open to them. Despite this, they had shown 'Praetorian' tendencies since the late fifteenth century, and their interference in government became especially bad in the first half of the seventeenth, at the same time as their discipline declined seriously; the k.k. ceased to be the dominant element of the army and an increasing role was played by the **yerli kulu**. The k.k. corps enjoyed a brief renaissance from the mid-seventeenth century when the Köprülü dynasty restored some of their earlier discipline for a few decades. By this time, the ranks were increasingly filled by born Muslims, the sons either of former members of the corps or of civilians, who sought membership in the k.k. more for the salary and the tax benefits than from any desire for military service, but in 1683 they were still reasonably competent, although the government never forgot the risk that they might turn on their masters. The main problem by then was that the Ottoman Empire's European enemies had developed standing armies of their own, far better disciplined that the k.k. had ever been.

kethüda   A steward, lieutenant, deputy, or executive secretary, or prefect, or majordomo, of any official in Ottoman hierarchy, from **vizier**s, **beylerbeyi**s etc. down. Sometimes encountered in its alternative form 'kiaya'. (NB: Turkish does not have the English 'th' digraph, and the middle consonants are pronounced separately, 't-H'.

Khan   Title of the ruler of the Crimean **Tatars** (it was also one of the lower titles of the Ottoman **Sultan**). The word was of Turco-Mongol origin and harked back to the days of Genghis Khan, of whom the Crimean Khans saw

	themselves as the heir. All Khans of the Crimea came from the 'royal' Giray clan, hence all had the same surname 'Giray', which, by convention, was not dropped from their names like most dynastic names. The Khan in 1683 was Murad Giray, though older works often show Selim Giray – Selim, a distinguished Tatar leader, was Khan several times, but not in 1683. (NB: the word is pronounced 'HHaahn', not 'Karn' [see Pronunciation Note]; Khan is an English spelling of the word rendered in modern Turkish as 'Han'.)
kiaya	See **kethüda**.
Köprülüs' War	The war, or sequence of wars, from 1657 to 1664, in which the Ottomans under the two Köprülü Grand Viziers wrecked the Transylvanian move towards independence, inflicting massive casualties in Transylvania in the process, then repulsed some less-than-effective Imperialist attempts to support the Principality. They went on to attack the Habsburg Monarchy, taking Neuhäusel in the north (in present-day Slovakia) in 1663 and suffering a minor defeat in August 1664 at St Gothard before pushing the Imperialists to a humiliating peace at **Vasvár** shortly after.
Kreis	Lit., 'Circle'; a district of the Empire (see **Reichs**). In the sixteenth century the Empire had been divided into a number of Kreise as part of an attempt at improved local administration; by the late seventeenth century, with the increased separatism of the larger states of the Empire, those Kreise containing large states such as Brandenburg were moribund, but those containing many small states too weak to defend themselves on their own, especially **Franconia** and Swabia, continued to function, with Kreis meetings, substantial Kreis forces, and officials and officers appointed at the Kreis level. In the 1680s, their main problem was not the disparate nature of their forces, for their troops were strong, effective, accustomed to serving together; it was the collective nature of the command: firstly, the need for the various rulers of a Kreis or their representatives to get together before any major decision could be taken – although the sizes of the Kreise were set so that meetings could be held quite easily and, by seventeenth-century standards, quickly – and secondly, the tendency, familiar to anyone who has had to operate in a committee-run organisation, to avoid individual responsibility and adhere strictly to orders and collective decisions. This last was shown in the Battle of the Kahlenberg in FML von der Leyen's refusal to aid the Saxons, and would come up again many times during the ensuing war in Hungary.

	Kreuzer	Small, low-value silver coin in general circulation in the Habsburg Monarchy; there were 60 K. to the **Gulden**.
	Kurucok	Hungarian rebels; the word (which in Hungarian is technically plural) is usually regarded as meaning 'crusaders' (it was believed to have been used originally by the rebels' loyalist opponents as a derogatory reference to the peasant rebels of 1514 whose uprising had originated in a crusade), though this is questioned by some historians. The term appeared in around 1672, when the current revolt started, but was not *universally* adopted as a descriptor of the rebels of 1672–1685 (it would be used much more consistently for the rebels of 1703–1711 under Ferenc Rákóczi), though it is a label that is useful for modern historians. Hungarian rebels, who were all 'nobles' and their retainers, fought for a combination of decent and shabby motives: hostility to religious oppression by the Catholic Habsburgs and to the brutal military occupation of their country by Habsburg troops after the magnate revolt of 1670, and a desire to defend their native laws, but also the wish for a noble-dominated state in which they would be able to exploit their serfs without restriction – and some leaders were driven purely by the desire to be alpha-male. See 'Dramatis personae' above under the entry for Thököly.
	Lieutenant	This spelling in German ranks is correct; the form 'Leutnant', although occasionally encountered in the idiosyncratic orthography of the seventeenth century, was rare until it was promoted in the nineteenth century by Germans who wanted to remove any traces of French influence from their language but could not find an alternative word for the nakedly French-origin word 'lieutenant' (they could not use the literal German equivalent, 'Statthalter', because that already had a different meaning) and so chose to alter its spelling. Even then, however, the Habsburgs continued to use the original spelling with an 'i' into the twentieth century – despite an attempt by an Austrian officer in the 1820s to completely Germanise military terminology that would have turned 'Lieutenant' into 'Leitmann' (on this, see A. O***, 'Versuch zur Ausrottung fremder, in die deutsche Kriegssprache eingeschlichener Wörter', *Oestreichische Militärische Zeitschrift*, 1826 part 2, 44–78).
	line	military formation with one of more units side by side, overall wider than it is deep. A battle formation had one or more lines; in each line, the units could be several ranks deep.
	Lower Austria	There were several separate Austrian duchies; this was the one 'lowest' downstream on the Danube, including Vienna and the land between it and the Hungarian border.

müteferrika	A small élite corps of guards and pages of the **Sultan**, officially part of the **kapi kulu** but formed from sons of leading Muslim figures, therefore not technically slaves; also, a similar corps serving the Grand Vizier. (The term had several other meanings not relevant here; the Ottoman Empire did not believe in precision in the use of terminology.)
Neuhäusel	Fortress-enclave in Royal Hungary north of the Danube, captured by the Ottomans in 1663 and a serious threat to all Habsburg possessions north of the Danube; the Imperialists had tried briefly to besiege it in the late spring before being forced to move off and face the approaching juggernaut of the Ottoman main army.
Ottoman	From the Turkish 'Osmanli', = 'those of Osman', followers of Osman, the semi-legendary founder of the dynasty. All troops, officials and clergy of the empire were considered 'Ottomans'. The Ottoman Empire had been ethnically Turkish in origin; during the fifteenth century, it had become a multi-racial state, with large numbers of non-Turks in the army and administration (see **kapi kulu**) but was still regarded by Europeans as primarily Turkish – and by 1683, with the rise of ethnic Turks such as Kara Mustafa to the highest offices, it was starting on the path towards becoming politically 'Turkish' as well. In this book I mostly use the terms 'Ottoman' and 'Turkish' as interchangeable, though this is strictly incorrect as many O. officers or officials were non-Turkish (see the Dramatis Personae, for example Koca Ibrahim); on occasion, where it is necessary to consider Tatar and non-Tatar elements of the army, I use O. as a general term covering both and 'Turks' to mean 'non-Tatars'.
Palatine	In Hungary this meant the highest office in the Kingdom, with enormous political, administrative, military and judicial power, giving the holder almost royal authority. (It is also the Latin/English form of a Polish office, the *wojewoda*, one of which headed each major Polish province.)
pancerni	Polish medium cavalry, armoured (hence the name, from the German 'panzer', = armour) but in chain or scale, lighter than that of the **winged hussars**; in 1683 they also had lances, but shorter ones than the hussars'.
Pasha	Title of respect added to the name of senior Ottoman officials, especially **beylerbeyi**s and upwards; technically, an anglicised spelling of the Turkish 'Paşa'; it has no exact equivalent in English but might be thought of as 'my lord'. It was an honorific appended to a personal name, not an office – the occasional western practice of referring, say, to the 'Pasha of Buda', was formally incorrect (although

	Mavrocordato used something similar very occasionally, as recorded in Kreutel & Teply, e.g. p.72), since the correct form would have been 'Koca Ibrahim Pasha, beylerbeyi of Buda'.
Petronell	When Lorraine was retreating from the line of the River Raab towards Vienna at the start of the campaign, Ottoman forces had attacked his baggage train on 7 July, and when several cuirassier and dragoon regiments formed to drive them off, Turks and Tatars charged, broke their formation by exploiting the gaps between squadrons normal in European tactics, and routed them, though a subsequent counter-attack of fresh troops led by Lorraine eventually drove off the Ottomans. It was a nasty moment for the Imperialists, a reminder that their standard tactics were not necessarily suitable against the Ottomans, and a bad blow to their troops' morale, already hit hard by the retreat.
pocztowi	men of the second and third ranks of **winged hussars**, from lesser gentry; may be equated with 'squires'.
Poland	Its full title was the Polish-Lithuanian Commonwealth; technically, it was two joined states, the Kingdom of Poland (known as the 'Crown') and the Grand Duchy of Lithuania. Although headed by an elected king, it was thought of by its dominant nobility as a republic (which was another word for Commonwealth).
Porte	Short for 'Sublime Porte', a translation of various Ottoman terms used to refer to 'the government' (in the same way that 'Downing Street' is used as a synonym for the British government or 'Capitol Hill' for the American legislative branch). It may have referred centuries earlier to an actual entrance where the Ottoman ruler conducted public business and dispensed justice, but by 1683 any such meaning was purely symbolic, referring to the threshold of state power rather than a physical entrance. However, in the seventeenth century its meaning was in the process of shifting from the seat of the **Sultan**'s government to that of the **Grand Vizier**, who increasingly ran all day-to-day affairs.
Pressburg	Small Hungarian city, on the north bank of the Danube, just over the border from Austria (in present-day Slovakia); since the capture of Buda by the Ottomans in 1541, it had been the capital of Hungary. The name is German, as its inhabitants spoke German; the Hungarians called it Pozsony; the modern Slovak name of Bratislava was not even invented until the twentieth century.
pułk	Polish for regiment. In the cavalry, this bore no resemblance to a western-style regiment but was a formation of very variable size and normally containing a mixture of troop

	types (winged hussars, pancerni, light cavalry); I have retained this specialist term for cavalry formations, but translated it as 'regiment' for the infantry.
purse	translation of the Ottoman Turkish term *kes* or *kese*; a higher-level 'unit of account' in Ottoman finance, equivalent to 50,000 *akçe* (a small and extremely devalued silver coin that remained the lower-level unit of account). Contemporary English diplomats regarded 1 purse as equal to about £100; given the then exchange rate with Habsburg currencies, this made *about* 500 Thalers or 750 Gulden. In 2024 values, it may be *very* roughly equated with a sum of about £15,000–20,000 ($20,000–25,000), though the present-day 'Bank of England inflation calculator' declares that £1 of 1683 equates to £184 today, making the purse £18,400.
Raab	Fortress in Royal Hungary on the south bank of the Danube; Hungarian name, Győr. Apart from the island fortress of Komorn it was the 'front line' for the Imperialists in Hungary. It had been the original target of the massive Ottoman army in June 1683; when Kara Mustafa decided to go past it to besiege Vienna, he left Koca Ibrahim to blockade it.
rank	rows of soldiers side-by-side within a unit; a seventeenth century infantry battalion might be up to six ranks deep. That battalion of six ranks would then form part of one of the lines of the battle formation.
reaya	Lit., flock; the subjects of the Ottoman state, at this time both Christian and Muslim; those who paid taxes as opposed to the **askeri** who lived off taxes; like sheep, they were supposed to be protected by the Ottoman ruler, but were also to be fleeced by him. The Ottoman government preferred to keep them un-armed and to block entry to the askeri class, so as to preserve its tax base. (At the time of the siege of Vienna, the Ottoman Empire was *starting* a trend that would reach its culmination in the nineteenth century, of regarding only its *Christian* subjects as r. while all Muslims were treated as part of the ruling class.)
Reichs	Of or pertaining to the Empire, or, to give it its full title, the Holy Roman Empire of the German Nation. The Empire was a federal organisation under an elected Emperor who also directly ruled his own state (see **Habsburg Monarchy**) which was partly within the Empire and partly outside it. Germans carefully distinguished between institutions or troops of the Empire, which were referred to as Reichs, and those of the **Emperor** (Kaiser), which were referred to as 'kaiserlichen' (see **Imperialist**) or included the prefix 'Hof' (court) in their title, e.g. **Hofkriegsrat**. In military terms, Reichs should really be used only for forces raised

	through the **Kreis** mechanism, but is also used more loosely to designate any forces other than those of the Emperor. Given that the English language has only the one word-root 'imperial…' to translate the two German concepts, 'Imperialist' is normally used for 'kaiserlich(en)', and 'Reichs' is left in the original German. Historians who favour the nation state are fond of repeating Voltaire's feeble witticism that the Holy Roman Empire was not holy, nor Roman, nor an empire, but in the 1680s it was still a tolerably effective institution, recovering from a nadir in 1648 and under the astute low-key leadership of Leopold I seeking ways to develop in the interests and for the defence of its members. See also **Kreis**.
Reichsfürst	Prince of the Empire; a title of honour, giving significant precedence but no property – its holder was not necessarily Prince 'of' any territory, though it could be added to other lower territorial titles such as 'Graf' to raise the status of its holder.
Royal Hungary	The part of the medieval Kingdom of Hungary that was still ruled by the King (the Habsburg **Emperor**, Leopold); basically, the westernmost strip between Austria and Turkish Hungary, and the long stretch north of the Danube and parts east (roughly equivalent to modern Slovakia), including the region known as **Upper Hungary**. Since 1541, a big swathe of central Hungary had been occupied by the Ottomans, and to the east of this the Ottomans and their Magyar collaborators had separated Transylvania from the Kingdom and turned it into a semi-independent principality, a vassal state of the sultan's; R.H. was 'everything that was left' after these losses, and had been gradually whittled away by the Ottomans ever since. In 1682, Thököly had taken over most of the Slovakia part, and in the summer of 1683, as the Ottomans advanced to Vienna, nearly all of the rest of the country had submitted to him when faced with the alternative of Turkish-Tatar devastation if they tried to defend themselves.
Sancak-bey	Head of a 'sancak' (lit., banner), a division of the Ottoman Empire roughly equivalent to a county (pronounced 'sanjak'). The *sancak* was originally the band of warriors that served under the local commander's banner; from the fifteenth century, it was an administrative subdivision of the state, and from the sixteenth century a constituent part of the larger provinces of the **beylerbeyi**s, to whom the s.-b. was subordinate. (On the spelling of 'bey', see **beylerbeyi** entry.)
Schweinsfeder	Boar spear (plural: Schweinsfedern); short stout spears which could used by infantry for defence against cavalry, either on their own (e.g. stuck in the ground like stakes)

GLOSSARY

	or inserted cross-wise into portable balks of timber to create shoulder-high barriers. The term is often used interchangeably with **chevaux-de-frise**. These obstacles were more flexible than pikes, and were briefly popular, especially against the Ottomans with their numerical superiority in undisciplined light cavalry and their fondness for suicidal charges aiming to reach hand-to-hand combat, until the advent of the socket bayonet made such devices largely redundant.
Senators (Polish)	Generals, ministers, and the senior officials of Poland's provincial administration. The Polish Senate, like the Roman Senate which it consciously emulated, was neither elective nor representative, but an aristocratic body representing the nobility's interests.
serçeşme	An extremely obscure Ottoman title – its components literally mean 'commander-source' or 'commander-fountain'; defined by Kreutel & Teply and a few others as the commander of all *sekban*s (see **yerli kulu**). None of the lists show these as an independent corps at this time, for they were part of the **beylerbeyi** household units; either the S. had some kind of nebulous authority over the forces of the *beylerbeyi*s (if this were true, we would expect him to be mentioned a lot more) or he was an officer only of the *sekban*s of Kara Mustafa's own household troops. Given the role assigned to him in the reinforcements sent by Kara Mustafa to Koca Ibrahim at the start of the battle, the latter option seems the most likely.
Silahdar	Also spelt Silihdar, or in current Turkish, Silahtar. Lit., sword-bearer. Two meanings in Ottoman practice: 1. an official of the Sultan, who originally carried his sword but was now a moderately important government functionary (the Ottoman historian who wrote an account of the campaign known as S., or sometimes 'the Silahdar' was properly called Fındıklılı or Funduklulu Mehmed [Mehmed of Fındıklı] Ağa, though he was only a page in 1683, not becoming S. until 1703); and 2. one of the four corps of the **Sipahis** of the Porte, the second of the two senior 'regiments'.
sipahis	Lit., horsemen; a term for two types of Ottoman cavalry: 1. the **timariots**; and 2. the six regiments of the salaried cavalry of the **kapi kulu**, also known as the Sipahis of the Porte. The seniormost regiment of the S. of the Porte was also specifically and confusingly known as the S.; the other five regiments were the Silahdars and two regiments each of *Gureba*s and *Ulufeci*s. The Sipahis of the Porte carried lances, javelins, bows, scimitars and shields, almost never firearms; they may have been armoured (most likely, in

Sobieski Wars	chain mail) and worn helmets, but not necessarily – many, perhaps the majority, wore coloured robes and turbans.
	Name for the conflicts in and around the Ukraine from 1667 down to 1676, especially the open wars between the Ottoman Empire and Poland (1672, 1673–1676) but also conflicts involving the Cossacks and Tatars. Despite heroic fighting and many tactical successes, including Sobieski's crushing tactical victory at Chocim, the Poles had been forced to a comparatively humiliating treaty with the Ottomans at Żórawno in 1676.
Standard of the Prophet	A great Islamic relic, known in Islam (here using the Turkish spelling) as *sancak-i sherif*, or holy banner; usually believed to have belonged to the Prophet Muhammad. Technically it was black, but it was covered in so many protective layers of green, the Prophet's colour, that it was often described as green. There were actually several such banners, either because the ancient original had torn into several pieces or because copies had been made to help protect the original from theft.
Sultan	In western usage, the title of the Ottoman ruler. In Ottoman practice, this had not been his primary appellation since the middle of the fifteenth century, when more prestigious titles had been adopted, first 'Khan' and then 'Padishah'; by the seventeenth century 'Sultan' had been reduced amongst the Ottomans to a comparatively minor title of respect used for many members of the royal family, but it had 'stuck' in the Christian world as the word for the ruler – although a loose Italianate translation of Padishah, 'Grand Signor', was also used – and is still employed by historians today. At the time of the siege of Vienna, the Ottoman S. was Mehmed IV, usually seen as a dangerously immature *roi fainéant* obsessed with hunting and with filling his private treasury with cash and jewels, though his actions may have had some (mistaken) purpose in recovering the dynasty's prestige.
Tatars	A term used by westerners to refer *generally* to the mostly Turkic successor states of the western part of Genghis Khan's Asian empire, and *particularly* to the state centred around the Crimea, which had submitted as a vassal to the Ottoman Empire in the late fifteenth century. The Crimeans under their **Khan** were a robber state, enslaving and plundering the lands of their Christian neighbours for centuries, either on their own behalf or at the behest of the Ottoman **Sultan**. They fought on horseback as light cavalry, poorly armed and devoid of discipline, absolutely incapable of attacking any fortified position, but spreading destruction and great panic through their great speed and mobility, which also meant that their enemies always

thought that the Tatars fielded more warriors than they actually had. In the **Sobieski Wars** of the 1670s, they had been thoroughly defeated several times by the Poles under John Sobieski, and had learnt a very healthy respect for the King and his troops. During the Ottoman advance to Vienna, they had spread out ahead of the main army, and during the siege had operated all around the countryside, enslaving and destroying – invariably ruining food supplies that the Ottoman army at the siege would have found useful.

Thaler
A coin common throughout the German-speaking world; originally, short for 'Reichsthaler', after Reichsthal, the place where it was minted (via its corrupted Spanish form, 'dollar', it would cross the Atlantic to the Americas). It had a moderately high value, with greater purchasing power than the pound sterling or U.S. dollar of 2024; to give a rough idea of its value, according to the fixed prices declared for food within Vienna during the siege, one could get 17 pounds of beef or 4 'old hens' or two geese for a T. (at 6 Austrian kreuzers to the pound of meat and 102 kreuzers to the T.), though the startling disproportion between the beef and other prices here compared with modern values reminds us of the limitations in such comparisons. As an alternative comparison: the annual state tax burden in Hungary on a large peasant household grouping (a 'porta') in the mid-seventeenth century was 10 florins, or about 6 T., though on top of this peasants also owed large dues of cash, produce and labour to their landlords. Another equation (though the method is not very accurate): in 1684 the exchange rate for the Thaler to the English pound (another unit of account) was around 5:1, while the present-day 'Bank of England inflation calculator' declares that £1 of 1684 equates to £178 to-day, making the T. equivalent to £35.60. See also: **Gulden**.

timariots
Ottoman cavalry (**sipahis**) who served on the basis of a benefice (a 'timar') awarded to them by the state, providing them with a revenue of variable size (as opposed to the salary paid to the standing army of the **kapi kulu**). The *timar* is often equated to the fief of the western feudal system, but it was awarded bureaucratically, directly by the state, without the pyramid-like hierarchy of vassals that was a key feature of feudalism, and the holder had no right of permanent tenure – timariots could be moved around the Ottoman Empire at the will of the state. Once, t. had formed the bulk of the Ottoman army; by 1683 they were in serious decline. Those with a big revenue were expected to come armoured and with retainers; the majority of them were comparatively light cavalry. (The term as used

	here and by most English-speaking historians is an English word, a slight anglicisation of the Turkish word 'timarli'.)
topci	Ottoman gunners, one of the salaried corps of the **kapi kulu**.
towarzysz	Lit., comrade ('knight' might be a better translation); the men of the front rank of the **winged hussars** in the Polish army, usually leading nobles but sometimes from the lesser gentry; followed by squires (**pocztowi**).
Transylvania	Vassal state of the Ottoman Empire since 1541 (see **Royal Hungary**); ethnically, mostly Hungarian, with German ('Saxon') and Roumanian minorities. Its most recent attempt at independence had been crushed by the Ottomans in the Köprülü's War.
Turk(ish)	See Ottoman.
Turkish Hungary	The part of Hungary ruled by the Ottoman Empire. See **Royal Hungary**.
Upper Hungary	The north-eastern part of **Royal Hungary**; roughly equivalent to the eastern half of modern Slovakia. Its chief city was Kaschau.
Vasvár	Peace treaty between the Imperialists and Ottomans at the end of their previous war, the **Köprülüs' War**, in 1664. Hungarians mis-understood the pressures that forced Vienna to conclude the treaty and saw it as a betrayal of the struggle to defend Hungary against the Turks, leading some of them (paradoxically) to align with the Turks against the Habsburgs.
Vizier	In Ottoman parlance, one of the senior members of the Sultan's council (Viziers of the Dome), the highest of whom was the Grand Vizier; and, a title of respect accorded to very senior officials of the provincial administration, especially the uppermost **beylerbeyi**s such as that of Buda. Westerners occasionally used plain V. to refer to the Grand Vizier. The word is an anglicised form of an Arabic-Turkish word, spelt in Turkish 'vezir'.
winged hussars	élite Polish heavy cavalry, armoured and with feather-bedecked wooden slats attached to their backs; they fought with a variety of weapons, including a big medieval-style lance with a huge coloured pennant. (Paradowski raises some doubt whether the wings were used in this campaign.)
yerli kulu	In the seventeenth century, the Ottoman Empire had moved away from reliance on the classical elements of its army, the **kapi kulu** and **timariots**, and a new category of troops had come to play a significant role: the y.k., lit. slaves of the *bey*s, soldiers maintained by individual **beylerbeyi**s out of their substantial state salaries (this may also have applied to the lower-level **sancak-bey**s but for most of them *probably* did not). The term indicated the

origin of the men, the fact that they were household troops of the *bey*s, not exactly what type of soldier they were; y.k. were usually various kinds of irregular light cavalry, which might fight on foot, but they could also be fully infantry; all were of militia quality, not as trained, well-equipped or steady as the **kapi kulu**, but generally they were likely to have firearms. Christian eyewitnesses who saw them deploy at the foot of the Kahlenberg thought that the bulk of them came up mounted but dismounted to fight. An extraordinary variety of inconsistently-defined terms was used to describe the y.k. and their individual troop types: *seymen* or *seğmen* (for which the variant *sekban* or *segban* might also be encountered) could be a generic term for all of them, or a specific term for those amongst them who were firearm-equipped infantry (and even more confusingly, this term was also used for a sub-division of the Janissaries), while, if these names were used specifically, they might generally be called *levend*s (another term with many meanings); in the Benaglia list of the Ottoman army at Belgrade, the main troop type listed was *sarica*, which usually meant musket-equipped infantry or dragoons, with *deli*, light cavalry suitable especially for scouting and raiding, the next most common, but also mentioned were other types, as well as household officers and servants. Further difficulty is caused by confusion between the y.k. and the *serhad kulu* (lit., slaves of the border), who were troops assigned to border fortresses, often with the same names as the different categories of y.k.; some writers, including Marsigli, recognised only the *serhad kulu* and did not even mention the y.k., and it is possible that the contingents commanded by some of the border **beylerbeyi**s such as Koca Ibrahim of Buda included troops from the fortress in addition to those of their own households.

Appendix I

Points of uncertainty and dispute

The sections relating to chapter 1 also give references to other books on uniforms.

Chapter 1

1.1 The Imperialist army.

Sources: Mansberg, pp.30–36; Stöller, p.34, which is probably the basis for most lists by nineteenth century works, such as *Das Kriegsjahr 1683*, p.232, and Renner, p.419; Dolleczek 'Entsatzschlacht', p.173, has a similar list, which is occasionally a bit odd. Supporting information taken from Wrede, vols. 1 and 2 for the infantry, 3 for the cavalry. There are significant differences between Mansberg and the lists based on Le Bègue; I have generally accepted the number of companies specified in the Le Bègue list in preference to Mansberg alone but not when Mansberg is supported by Wrede; and I have included regiments not in Le Bègue.

On uniforms: two immensely valuable recent publications on the subject are no. 47 in this series, Bruno Mugnai, *Wars and soldiers in the early reign of Louis XIV. Volume 2 – the Imperial army, 1657–1687* (Warwick: Helion, 2019), and Robert Hall and Giancarlo Boeri, *Uniforms and flags of the Imperial Austrian Army, 1683–1720* (Farnham: The Pike and Shot Society, 2011). It should be noted that these two publications adopt different numbering systems for regiments (the Imperialist army never had official regiment numbering until the nineteenth century, and even then adopted two conflicting systems).

On the numbers of the Imperialist infantry: Mansberg (p.35) notes that figures on strengths vary from 6,400 (from the Venetian diplomat Contarini) to 9,900 (article in the *Neue Militärische Zeitschrift* of 1813), with most contemporary accounts including Vaelckeren giving 8,000, which for Mansberg (who gives the Imperialists 64 companies instead of the 54 here, because he includes units probably elsewhere) makes an average of 125 per company instead of the official 204. It is certainly possible to agree with Mansberg (pp.35–36) that new infantry regiments (Leslie, Croy, Daun) had probably not yet been completed, and others (Baden, Grana, Erbprinz of Lorraine) had reduced badly during campaign, so the figures offered by contemporaries seem probable.

On the numbers of the Imperialist cavalry: official strength of cavalry regiments was 800, in 10 companies of 80. The figures quoted by Le Bègue, when compared with the numbers of companies in his lists, would give 60 men per company or 600 men for a full strength regiment. This may be taken as the absolute maximum for the cavalry units, which had all been serving strenuously throughout the campaign. The listed numbers of squadrons are extremely unusual, since an Imperialist mounted regiment would normally have formed 5 squadrons, not 2 or 3; Mansberg, p.34, proposing an effective strength of an average of 50 men per company, argues that the companies were strong enough to form only 2 squadrons per regiment except for CRs Sachsen-Lauenburg, Taafe and Piccolomini with 3; he includes Lubomirski in this, making the Imperialists' total only 45 squadrons. I am not convinced by his argument, since even at 50 men per company it would have been possible to form 3–4 normal-sized squadrons per regiment; but it is an inescapable fact that the two main sources that specify squadron numbers, Suttinger and the fairly basic 'Forme de la Bataille' in the Schliz von Görz account (Newald, vol. 2, p.103), while they give a slightly higher total for the Imperialists than Mansberg, of 48, can only divide amongst the named regiments at small numbers of squadrons each. The total for the battle is sometimes given as high as 12,900, based on Le Bègue's figures; or as low as Mansberg's 10,500, based on contemporary historians such as Wagner.

1.2 The Bavarian army

Sources: *Das Kriegsjahr 1683*, p.234; Mansberg, pp.42–47; Staudinger, *Geschichte des kurbayerischen Heeres unter Kurfürst Max. II. Emanuel*, vol. 1, p.159; Bavarian regimental histories by Staudinger and Dauer (see Bibliography).

On uniforms: an invaluable recent addition to the literature on the subject is no. 38 in this series, Bruno Mugnai, *Wars and soldiers in the early reign of Louis XIV. Volume 7 – armies of the German states, 1655-1690, part 1* (Warwick: Helion, 2024), chapter 4, some colour plates, and pp.313–319 in his Appendix I. Conflicting details about some of the Bavarian infantry regiments (suggesting that only one was in the later-standard blue coats) is in *Die Türken vor Wien: Europa und die Entscheidung an der Donau 1683: 82. Sonderausstellung des Historischen Museums der Stadt Wien… 1983* (Vienna: the Museum, 1983), p.216.

On the Bavarian infantry and the attached units: Mansberg, p.46, argues that the Bavarians with their auxiliaries totalled only 11 battalions in the battle, including the Kreis battalion under Rummel, because the Salzburgers were assigned to join the Imperialists on the left wing (although they arrived with the Bavarians and count towards the overall totals). The Suttinger order of battle shows 12 battalions for the Bavarians. See following note on the debated units.

On the total numbers of Bavarian infantry: Mansberg, p.46, thinks that the Bavarians had suffered considerably in skirmishes with the Tatars since their arrival in the area. Such activity is not recorded in the Bavarian histories, and these specify very low casualties for the Bavarians for the entire campaign, so I believe a high strength is likely.

On the total numbers of Bavarian cavalry: Mansberg claims that the Bavarian cavalry had been suffering heavily since its arrival from its exertions and casualties in skirmishes with the Tatars, so that, given the companies still formed the 16 squadrons one would expect from their official strength, those squadrons must have been very weak. Later, p.46, he adds a company of Kreis cuirassiers of 101 men under Rittmeister Jakob Graf von Hamilton. Compare the end of chapter 11 for casualties, where it is suggested that Bavarian casualties throughout the campaign were minimal, and thus Mansberg's conclusions here are quite inappropriate.

On the question of the Bavarian artillery: different figures to those listed in the text are given in Staudinger, *Geschichte*, vol. 1, pp.159–160: he shows 26 battalion guns for the Bavarians and the attached Kreis troops (at two guns per battalion), though it is not clear whether this is from sources or from an assumption of two per battalion; he also states based on reports of Degenfeld that few experienced gunners came with the army, and gives some details of the field artillery that was left behind. Other writers agree on the total number of guns as 26. It is possible that this higher figure was due to inclusion of lent Imperialist artillery. The Capitulation of Passau had included the possibility of the Habsburgs' lending Bavaria ten guns in lieu of their bringing their own; it seems that the Imperialists did leave four 12-pounders and six battalion guns at the border, but without teams, without which they could not be moved – and since the Bavarians had managed to bring a reasonable number of their own pieces, they did not put any effort into bringing the loaned guns. Alternatively, the 16 'Bavarian' guns may have *included* some of the Imperialist pieces. The large number of personnel does suggest a bigger train than 16 gun, but against this is Degenfeld's suggestion that he had few gunners. As with so much of the details of the relief army, we cannot be certain.

1.3 On uncertainties surrounding the Neuburg and Beck regiments

The presence of these units is disputed. Bavarian works such as Staudinger, *Geschichte*, vol. 1, p.165, are certain that all the extra units served under Degenfeld.

Re. Beck: Staudinger explicitly states that the battalion, under lt.col. Jakob Sieghard von Gallenfels, on its way to join Lorraine from Styria in July, had been ordered to stand at 'Ennspasse' (from which may stem Mansberg's claim that *Neuburg*'s was on the Ens), and from there joined Degenfeld and the Bavarians at Krems, and was still with them in October; Mansberg, p.35, also thinks 3 companies under Gallenfels were under Lorraine; Wrede, vol. 1, p.531, has only the 7 companies of the regiment in Vienna, with no mention of companies outside.

Re. Neuburg: Mansberg, p.46, says that the Imperialist battalion of Neuburg IR was on the Ens; Wrede, vol. 1, p.259, gives IR Neuburg 5 companies in Vienna and 5 companies in the battle; the list in Hassel and Vitzthum von Eckstadt, p.138, includes a reference to '1 pfalz-neuburgsche Kompagnie zu Pferd' which suggests the possibility that references to Neuburg are not to the Imperialist IR but to troops of the Palatinate; Jochner, p.41, mentions the Franconians had trouble getting boats for the move downstream as salt barges were already needed for the '5 coys of Pfalz-Neuburg troops' (which could refer to Palatinate troops or the Imperialist IR).

1.4 The Franconians

Sources: *Das Kriegsjahr 1683*, p.234; Mansberg, p.39–42; Jochner, *passim*. List also in Hassel and Vitzthum von Eckstadt, p.138.

Although referred-to as 'Franconians' here, it must be remembered that these were not a single coherent army like the Bavarians and Saxons, but a mixture of Kreis troops and the small army of the then-combined bishoprics of Würzburg and Bamberg.

On uniforms: what little can be determined, about the Würzburg-Bamberg units, is in no. 126 in this series, Bruno Mugnai, *Wars and soldiers in the early reign of Louis XIV. Volume 7 – armies of the German states, 1655-1690, part 3* (Warwick: Helion, 2024), pp.192–193.

On the numbers of Franconian infantry: only 7 'Franc.' battalions are shown in the Suttinger order of battle, a figure which *Das Kriegsjahr 1683*, p.239, justifiably increased to 8; according to the figures of troops sent, there should have been at least 11; the order of battle included by the Franconian official Schliz von Görz in his 'Relation' (Newald, vol. 2, p.103), gave the Franconians 13 battalions, including 6 in the 3rd line (where Suttinger showed no Franconians at all); having so many units in the last line is so unusual as to excite suspicion. Mansberg, p.42, suggested (with absolutely no evidence) that the two Kreis regiments formed only a big battalion each in the order of battle, and thinks that several of their companies were amongst the troops left to guard the train. The latter seems more likely than the former. However, one is left wondering if the improbable-seeming figures for the Franconians given by Schliz von Görz might be more correct than they seem.

On the numbers of Franconian cavalry: only 7 squadrons appear in the Suttinger order of battle. There is a great deal of confusion about the units and numbers involved. I part company from Mansberg on the number of companies in the Kreis CR; the Kreis had decided (according to Jochner, p.33) to send only 6 companies, not 8 (which is why my total of 1,200 is lower than Mansberg's 1,300). Mansberg appears wrong in his general claim that all companies were 60 instead of 80, as only the Kreis regiments, not the Würzburgers, had decided to leave 20 men per company at home; but even so the units must all have been under-strength to form only 7 squadrons, so I assume that 60 men per company must have been a maximum. However, Jochner (pp.34–35) also mentions 2 'ritterschaftlichen Compagnien', 250 men under Rittmeister Redwitz, as setting off for Nuremberg; later (p.45) he lists a review of 10 August at the same place where the *two* Würzburg-Bamberg regiments were present and a DR 'unter Truchsess von Hedersdorf' [?] and *two* CR 'Hohenzollern', which included a company of the Teutonic Order under Rittmeister von Frankenstein. *Das Kriegsjahr 1683*, p.234, gives the cavalry only 7 squadrons but 2,500 men (in which it was probably following Le Bègue, in Stöller, p.34), which would give what would normally seem an improbably high average of 357 men per squadron, though, if Mansberg is correct, the Imperialist cavalry this year also went for small numbers of large squadrons per regiment.

1.5 The Saxon army

Sources: *Das Kriegsjahr 1683*, pp.232–233; Mansberg, pp.36–39; Hassel and Vitzthum von Eckstadt, pp.113–115; and Schuster and Francke, vol. 1, pp.102–103.

On uniforms: there are two recent Helion publications on the army: as with the Bavarians, there is no. 38 in this series, Bruno Mugnai, *Wars and soldiers in the early reign of Louis XIV. Volume 7 – armies of the German states, 1655-1690, part 1* (Warwick: Helion, 2024), chapter 5, some colour plates, and pp.319–324 in his Appendix I; but also Alexander Querengässer, *The Saxon Mars and his force: the Saxon army during the reign of John George III, 1680-1691* (Century of the soldier series: warfare c. 1618-1721 no.48) (Warwick: Helion, 2019)

A variant contemporary OB, of the Saxon army in its original camp at Dresden, formally dated 12 June, from the Wilhelmshöher Kriegskarten archive, Marburg, titled 'Campement welches Ihr Churfürst. Durch. von Sachsen bei Dresden gehalten und mit selbiger Armee wieder die Turcken nacher Wien um Entsatz marschiret ist. den 12. Junii 1683', with catalogue title 'Aufstellung des Feldlagers der Armee des Kurfürsten von Sachsen bei Dresden vor dem Zug gegen die Türken nach Wien, 12. Juni 1683', has been published on the internet currently at <https://www.digam.net/index.php?page=1&ID=2561>, accessed 29 Oct. 2024, though this has already moved at least once; this shows 13 battalions for the infantry with 3 for the Leib regiment (presumably, one battalion was left at home), along with 13 squadrons and cavalry and 3 of dragoons. It also identifies the 'Duke Christian' IR as Christian of Sachsen-Hall, which may have been an alternative courtesy title of the same man – almost certainly Christian, 1652–1689, a younger son of August, the current reigning Herzog von (Duke of) Sachsen-Weissenfels. The source is reproduced in black-and-white in Mugnai, Wars and soldiers..., vol. 7 part 1, p.211, but at a size difficult to read.

On the strengths of the Saxon cavalry: there are slight disagreements as to the exact official strength of a regiment. The Suttinger order of battle shows 12 squadrons for the Saxons; others suggest 13; the list would give 14 squadrons if we accept only 1 squadron in the Leib-Regiment (instead of the 3 shown by many), otherwise 16 squadrons. Mansberg, p.38, suggests that the discrepancy may be partly accounted for by some companies being amongst those left behind to cover the train at Krems and Altenberg.

1.6 Polish and Ottoman armies (note)

It is not practical to go here into the dress of the Polish and Ottoman armies; for these, readers can refer to excellent recent Helion publications by Michał Paradowski (no. 79 in this series) and Bruno Mugnai (no. 55 in this series) respectively, though for the Ottomans there are also two older volumes in Italian by Mugnai with more illustrations, and it must be noted that Mugnai does not recognise the *yerli kulu* a a category. Older but still valuable are Osprey books in the 'Men at Arms' series: two excellent volumes on the Poles by Brzezinski, and for the Ottomans a single volume by Nicolle, inferior only because it covers a huge time span of several centuries in just one slim book; for the winged hussars, there is also a recent publication in the 'Warrior' series by Brzezinski. For the Poles, see also the collection of plates by Wróblewski. (See Bibliography for full details of these publications.)

Chapter 3

3.1 The question of a council on 7, 8 or 9 September.

This council is much less clearly dated than the one at Stetteldorf on the 3rd. Some put it late on the 7th; Hermann of Baden, who really ought to have known, puts it before dinner (midday meal) on the 9th, immediately before setting off (Röder vol. 1, Urk., p.14); Sobieski, first thing in the morning on the 9th, told his wife that despite repeated discussions nothing definite had been decided yet *about the route* (Plater, p.58). Le Bègue in his entry for the 8th (Stöller, pp.99–100) explicitly describes the final formation with the Imperialists on the left wing; he could as usual be referring to the events of 'yesterday' (though in this instance I believe he is not, and that his 'yesterday' applies only to the first clause of his first sentence in that entry), but this explicitly excludes the 9th as the day for this decision. It is highly likely that discussions continued into the morning of the 9th, perhaps that the order of battle was settled on the 8th and the routes only the next day (though the early start of the Imperialists on the 9th would argue against this); but, as with the date of the religious service, the rest day of the 8th seems by far the most likely day for such discussions.

Chapter 4

4.1 Just what was Mercy's reconnaissance doing?

Le Bègue's clearest statement about Mercy's orders is in the 'Account' (Stöller, p.32), where he recorded that, immediately after the discussions on the 8th, Lorraine 'sent the Baron de Mercy to Maurbach [sic] with two thousand horse to observe from there what movement the enemies were making in their camp…'. In the Diary, the secretary merely mentioned Mercy's departure for Mauerbach. The target is too clearly named in both versions for there to be any doubt about it; and since neither version used the definite article (which would have referred to the stream of the same name), he meant the village. Either Lorraine and his staff were breathtakingly ignorant of the geography of the Wienerwald, or Le Bègue was wrong about the orders. By no stretch of the imagination could Mercy ascertain anything about Vienna and the Ottoman camp from Mauerbach, which stood a good five miles just from the crest line of the last hills before the Vienna basin, a couple of miles further from the Turkish camp – and the hills around were no higher than anywhere else, none offering a vantage point from which viewers could see the basin and what was going on around the city. A mistake in noting the orders seems far more likely, especially as a change of just one preposition produces intelligible objectives: 'to observe from there what movement the enemies were making *from* their camp', that is, to find out what Turkish or Tatar forces had been posted in the Wienerwald or were being sent out into the hills.

It is possible that this was merely part of a general attempt to understand the terrain and passages within the Wienerwald; perhaps guides had hinted at the possibility of easier routes if one went further south, and Lorraine was trying to find out if they were correct, either generally or on behalf of Sobieski, for to get to Mauerbach Mercy would have to traverse the entire part of the Wienerwald in front of the Polish wing. Mauerbach the village gave access to Mauerbach the valley, which led down into the valley of the Wien and thence to Vienna, ostensibly an easy enough passage especially once one reached the Wien valley, but one which could not be used without the army's cutting itself off from the Danube and its supplies, and one which the allies had already excluded from consideration. Lorraine was not inflexible, and might have been prepared to consider a change of plan, but Mercy was not ordered to go beyond Mauerbach the village, and did not do so, therefore the terrain *up to* Mauerbach was what Lorraine expected information on.

Plenty of other explanations are possible. Firstly, there is the undisputed fact that, again if Le Bègue is to be believed, Mercy reported only about what he had been able to discover on the state of the defence of Vienna; this could suggest the orders really were to scout out the Vienna basin – perhaps the Imperialist headquarters really *was* that ignorant of where Mauerbach was and what could be seen from it. However, Lorraine's secretary seems to have found the business of reconnoitring terrain boring, for he made no mention of the other reconnaissances sent out to establish routes into the Wienerwald and we know about these only from other sources such as the Franconian official Schliz von Görz; maybe Mercy conscientiously reported back on the state of roads and the absence of Tatar parties in the hills, and Le Bègue just failed to record these reports in favour of noting what was incidental to Mercy's mission, the news that he sent back about Vienna from prisoners taken.

It is even possible that Lorraine's secretary got it completely wrong, and nineteenth-century historians were correct in ignoring him, reporting as they did that Mercy was sent to feel out the terrain in front of *Lorraine's* path, especially with a view to finding passages for artillery, and to work with Heissler at Klosterneuburg in reconnoitring Turkish dispositions from vantage points nearer the Danube, as Heissler had already done.

Chapter 5

5.1 How reliable was Silahdar's story?

The story told by Silahdar of Khan Murad Giray's diatribe against Kara Mustafa is recounted in the text. Silahdar, it must be remembered, was not present, though he may have been writing information given to him by men who were; and we know from other situations (see my forthcoming *Wilfully run our head against the wall* on the 1684 campaign) that he was capable of reproducing nonsense. Many details of the story do not ring true: Silahdar explicitly stated that the incident took place on the 9th, but by that day the Christians were already safely over the bridges and advancing across the Tullner Feld (although against this, we must accept the possibility that Silahdar might have simply got the story right but the day wrong); the pose adopted by Murad Giray in Silahdar's story was practically a cliché; and the idea that a canny politician such as Murad would have declared openly to a religious official, even one of his own household, his willingness to betray his religion, stretches credulity to its limits. There is no hint of the story in the diary of the Master of Ceremonies, which is accepted as a genuine diary compiled at the time, and Silahdar may well have been setting up Murad Giray as a scapegoat for the defeat. Nevertheless, he may equally well have been building his story out of a foundation of eyewitness reports available to him that no-one had dared record at the time when Murad was still Khan, and there may be some substance behind the story, in terms of Ottoman *suspicion* of Murad, a belief that the Khan and his followers were definitely up to something.

5.2 Could the Tatars have prevented the Christians from crossing the Danube?

There is no doubt that many officers in the Ottoman army *expected* the Khan to have done much more to disrupt the Christian army during such a dangerous operation as crossing the Danube up to and including the 8th. In fact, the Khan and his depleted Tatar horde would have found it very difficult to act effectively against the Danube crossing: European armies knew how dangerous a river crossing could be (it was only a variant of the familiar problem of the defile) and were very experienced in organising such operations to keep any danger at bay; the bridgehead at Tulln had been fortified so that troops could come off it and deploy in safety, Poles (who were well trained and experienced in dealing with Tatars) led the way over the bridge, and anyway thousands of regular German troops were already on the south bank and marching up from Krems-Mautern to Tulln on the day of the crossing. Murad, even if he had been present on the Tullner Feld with the entire 20,000 Tatars attributed to him by the Ottoman army list (which is unlikely), could have done little to *stop* the crossing if he had tried. The suspicions of Kara Mustafa's entourage on this point, while understandable, were not justified. However, Murad had also done nothing to *delay* the Christians: to slow the march of the Germans down from Krems-Mautern, and then to hinder the allied advance across the Tullner Feld, both of which lay within his power. Tatar harrassment could at least have reduced the Christians' march to a crawl, and Murad did nothing but observe the Christians once they entered the Wienerwald. Admittedly delaying tactics would have been a lot easier if the Tatars had been supported by trained Ottoman troops or thousands of the *yerli kulu*, but there is no doubt that the Ottomans had justifiable reservations about Khan Murad Giray.

5.3 How many Tatars were present in the battle on 12 September?

The reference to Murad's entourage of 200 brings us to this final mystery surrounding Crimean involvement in the battle. If we believe the list of 7 September, Murad had 20,000 Tatars. That figure is improbable. The Tatars had *joined* the Ottoman army at Székesfehérvár at the start of the campaign with a claimed 20,000.[421] The total was certainly exaggerated even then, and the number of Tatars was bound to have decreased since: they had lost heavily in the various battles and actions of the campaign, especially the Bisamberg (the Ottoman casualty count for the campaign of 7 September had given 2,000 Tatars dead, and this number seems for once an under-estimate rather than an exaggeration, or else was not intended to include losses beyond the Danube); more Tatars were still north of the Danube somewhere; and many had slipped off home with their booty. Even the most conservative estimate based on the original figure of 20,000 could give Murad Giray no more than 15,000, possibly as few as 10,000 men. Thus, those 200 men with him were merely his personal entourage, while the rest of his army should have been already in position alongside Abaza Sari Hüseyin or in the parties that we know were scattered throughout the Wienerwald scouting.

However, there is also, as we will see, the fact that no-one from either side, Ottoman or Christian, had a word to say about fighting Tatars on the day of battle apart from some minor clashes with the Polish flank guards in the Wien valley – and given the unusual nature of Tatar tactics, we would expect some western witnesses to have remarked upon them if they had seen any Tatars in action. Dalérac[422] suggested that the Tatars had departed before the battle, apparently referring to the morning of the 12th.

---

[421] Ernst D. Petritsch, 'Die Tatarish-Ottomanischen Begleitoperationen in Niederösterreich', *Studia Austro-Polonica*, 3 (1983), pp.207–240, here p.219.

[422] vol. 1, pp.153, 154. He also noted that stories had spread amongst the Christians that Sobieski had secured the Tatar departure by secret negotiations (in the same way that the King had secured the changing sides of the Moldavians and Wallachians before Chocim in 1673), but acknowledged these stories were nonsense.

On the Ottoman side, Mavrocordato[423] did refer in general terms to the Khan and Tatars serving on the left wing, and later to their taking flight; he did not indicate how large were the forces with Murad, and could have been referring to minimal forces as concluded in the text. The Master of Ceremonies explicitly stated that the Khan gave no help at all to Abaza Sari Hüseyin; and in his later review of the causes of the defeat commented firstly that Tatars were no good in open battle anyway and secondly that they were so burdened down with their booty and slaves that they were incapable of fighting; he also asserted that the Khan did nothing in the battle. Mehmed Giray in his chronicle made several key statements and one significant omission:[424] he made no mention of any part played in the battle by the bulk of the Crimean army, which we would expect if Murad Giray had had 10,000–15,000 men present, but he did record distinguished service by the recently-arrived Hacci Giray with his 500–600 Tatars; and he stated that Murad himself took no part in the battle (this does not necessarily clash with the Ottoman diarists' description of the Khan's *personal* intervention at the very end of the day). Most significantly, Mehmed Giray stated, after his account of the defeat: 'The army of the Tatars [was located] at a rest-place two days distant, all their tents and their train were there. Around the Khan were few people.' From the context and wording, this is not apparently intended as a reference to where the Crimeans were two days after the battle, but that they were at two days' distance from Vienna at about the time of the battle, where Khan Murad rejoined them after the battle. Even if we do not accept this reading, the key element remains: the Tatar tents and train were intact. On 12 September, the Ottoman army would lose its entire camp and baggage in the rout at the end of the day, but the Tatars got theirs off safely. There was only one way they could have done this: they had left before the battle. (Other sources confirm that the Tatars were at Raab by the 13th at the latest; see Chapter 12 above. The Tatars moved very fast when on their own, and might even have made it from Vienna to Raab by the 13th if they had left on the 12th – but not with their baggage.)

All these hints combined (the strange reference to Murad's having only 200 followers, the complete absence of any mention of Tatar involvement in the battle by Christian, Ottoman or Tatar writers, the explicit statement that the Crimean army was camped intact at some distance from Vienna) strongly suggest that most of the Tatars left before the battle and very few were present at the Battle of the Kahlenberg: just Murad's small personal entourage (which Murad apparently kept out of action anyway), Hacci Giray's 500–600, and the various small scouting parties known to have been still in the Wienerwald on 10–11 September, who *presumably* rejoined their Khan on the 12th (though it is equally possible that they followed their compatriots in heading for Hungary). Khan Murad may have had as few as one or two thousand Tatars with him on 12 September.[425] The figures given for the Tatars in the order of battle in chapter 10 assume that this is correct.

---

423 in Kreutel & Teply, p.88; the Master of Ceremonies: Kreutel & Teply, pp.189–190, 197.
424 Köhbach, pp.155–156.
425 Wimmer, *Entsatz*, p.194, appears to agree in some degree with this argument.

Chapter 6

6.1 The loan of the four German battalions to the Poles.

The loan of these four battalions is widely attested, and although no explanation is ever given for the choice of one battalion per contingent instead of sending four from the Centre which was already nearest the Poles, the reason is almost certainly political: no corps commander would agree to lend a unit unless everyone did. It is less clear *when* they left to join the Poles: it is often suggested, based on Le Bègue's 'Account' (Stöller, p.36) and a misunderstanding of Sobieski's letter of 12 September to his wife, that this took place as late as the night of 11–12 September; but if this had been so, the units would never have made it all the way across the battlefield, and I follow here the Franconian account of Schliz von Görz (Newald, vol. 2, p.99) and the 'Baden account' (Röder, vol. 1, Urk., p.15); the Saxon account in *Aufrichtige und unpartheyische Relation*, p.10, also stated that the loan was made 'before one climbed the Kahlenberg'. The loaning of units had been foreseen in Sobieski's original 'Order of Battle' document (see box in Chapter 3), which leaves the question, why had the loaning not been done before, as the army left Tulln? Possibly the idea of loaning had been lost in the rejection of parts of Sobieski's Order of Battle, and were revived by the King here. If the timing of the loan is uncertain, even greater uncertainty surrounds the questions of what the four battalions did when they joined the Poles; see Chapter 11.

6.2 The question of a blessing on 11 September.

It is often suggested that the blessing, or even a full mass attended by Lorraine and Sobieski, took place on the Leopoldsberg, or perhaps the Kahlenberg. This is unlikely. If Sobieski had climbed either of the hills, he would undoubtedly have seen the terrain of the Vienna basin twenty-four hours before he actually discovered what the ground was like (see below). Le Bègue actually stated (Stöller, p.100) that Lorraine returned from the night reconnaissance, heard mass, then went to see Sobieski, and showed him 'from the heights of Weidling' the plan for the day, 'and then was given the benediction to the army, Father Marco having for this climbed the mountain'. Although calling it a mountain is overstating the case somewhat, this can only refer to the Buchberg hill, right above the army in the Weidlingbach valley – even Marco d'Aviano would have found it difficult to bless the army from the top of the Leopoldsberg two miles away.

Chapter 8

8.1 Sobieski and the 11 September meeting at the monastery.

There is no doubt about the meeting involving Sobieski at the Kahlenberg monastery, or the role of Dupont in the discussions, as there is plenty of evidence on it (see other footnotes to Chapter 8). From Le Bègue, however, we might doubt that it even existed: the 'Diary' mentions it not at all, and the 'Account' (Stöller, p.36) is exceedingly brief. The secretary is throughout striving to downplay the role of the King, to present Lorraine as doing all the work while Sobieski merely approved it afterwards. There seems no doubt that Lorraine was indeed doing a great deal of the detailed work necessary for the movements of each day, and that he was determined to follow his own plans while continuing to kowtow to the King; but Le Bègue went too far in almost writing Sobieski out of the account altogether.

Chapter 10

10.1. Were any Hungarian troops in the relief army?

As noted in Chapter 10, apart from the general acceptance that Pál Esterházy was present, and the dubious counting of CrR Kéry and CR Pálffy, it is not generally recorded that any Hungarian troops were with the relief army. Official loyalist Hungarian forces had effectively disbanded with the collapse of the line of the River Raab at the start of July. Esterházy, as Palatine and one of the richest magnates of the kingdom, would normally have had at least several hundred armed men permanently at his command, private troops and others required by his office (the unusual Hungarian system of armed forces at this time is covered in my forthcoming *Wilfully run our head against the wall*, on the 1684 campaign), but these, or at least the majority of them, would have been left to try to defend his estates and castles against *kurucok* attacks. Hungarian historians occasionally argue that he may still have had some troops with him, maybe up to a thousand (a few try to go higher even than that), but such efforts are never convincing.[426] Given contemporary prejudices against any soldiers not organised into proper regiments, a few *may* have been present and overlooked by witnesses, but it stretches credulity to claim that no witness would have recorded a thousand or more Hungarians in their unusual dress and equipment.

---

426 See particularly János J. Varga, *Válaszúton: Thököly Imre és Magyarország, 1682-1684-ben* (Budapest: História / MTA Történettudományi Intézete, 2007), p. 146, especially n.44.

Chapter 11

11.1 Identification of Osmanoğlu

'Osmanoğlu' is an epithet, not a full name, normally requiring a given name to be complete (e.g. Mustafa Osmanoğlu); alone, it means merely 'son of Osman', and is the same as 'Osmanpashazade' the Persian '-zade' suffix being, for the Ottomans, simply a more sophisticated expression for 'son of' than the Turkish '-oğlu'. No such person appears anywhere in the Ottoman diarists, least of all in their lists of the forces assigned to Kara Mehmed and Koca Ibrahim. There is a strong temptation to regard this individual as being identical with Ahmed Pasha Osmanpashazade, the *beylerbeyi* of Anatolia, especially since Kütahya was the latter's seat, and this is supported by references in Mavrocordato earlier in the campaign to Ahmed Osmanpashazade as 'Pasha of Kütahya in Anatolia'. However, both this man and an 'Osman Ogly bey of Chiuta' appear in the 7 September census, and there is support in the Benaglia list for an Osmanoğlu in addition to the *beylerbeyi* of Anatolia, so there seems no doubt that he existed separately from Ahmed. However, the Ottoman diarists (Kreutel & Teply, p.189) were clear that the Ottoman forces in action at the start were from Kara Mehmed's advance guard, which did not include any Osmanoğlu, and which was formed entirely of troops from Syria and neighbouring areas, not west-central Anatolia where Kütahya lay. It is just possible that Osmanoğlu was a bandit chief from Anatolia taken into government service with his followers; this was a not uncommon practice with the Ottomans, and there is evidence from the 1690s of just such a chieftain, known as Osmanoğlu, who founded a provincial dynasty known as the Karaosmanoğlu that held sway in parts of Anatolia into the nineteenth century. On the family, see F.W. Hasluck, *Christianity and Islam under the Sultans* (first published Oxford 1929, here citing the edition edited by Margaret M. Hasluck, 2 vols., Istanbul: Isis Press, 2000), vol. 2, pp.478–482. The rather aristocratic Ottoman diarists might well have chosen to avoid mentioning such a disreputable figure.

11.2 The question of Sobieski's mass on 12 September.

This mass, whether it took place at all and if it did, where, have been debated at inordinate and pointless length; Le Bègue is quite clear that Sobieski went to mass in the chapel immediately after the discussions with Lorraine, and that the Duke was not present; there is no mention of the King traipsing all the way from the Kahlenberg to the Chapel of St Leopold, so the location must have been the former, not the Leopoldsberg as is sometimes suggested (possibly basing on Dalérac, vol. 1, pp.154–155, who did explicitly put it at the Chapel of St Leopold). Since the Duke was a Catholic, and the officer of a devoutly Catholic Emperor, it is unthinkable that he did not attend mass before a battle, therefore reasonable to assume that he had already taken communion earlier in the day, and that d'Aviano had officiated; this version, with two separate masses at which d'Aviano officiated, also matches the Bavarian letter of 17 September in Newald, vol. 2, p.96, which Newald viewed as disproving the existence of the mass.

11.3 Did John George III command at the left wing?

The reference in the text to John George's commanding 'by the left wing' was a rather odd claim for John George to make given that he was not its commander. There was never any doubt about his personal courage, so he cannot have been using this as an excuse for avoiding danger, even though, as a ruler, he had perfectly valid reasons at his disposal for not putting his life at risk had he wanted them. Perhaps Lorraine had been buying his cooperation by giving him the impression that he was the direct commander of the left wing; or perhaps by 'left wing' he meant the column on the road, the left-most element of the left wing. However, it may be significant that the version of this account quoted by Mansberg (pp.91–92 n.58), probably from an earlier edition than the one I have used, phrased this thus: '…while he however held the command *at another place*' (emphasis added), which could mean anything – although the correction to 'left wing' could well have been a change made by the original witness, and thus an intentional clarification.

11.4 The repulse of Heissler's dragoons.

Mansberg's text appears to suggest that this took place on the *right*; given that the Heissler DR was explicitly located on the far left of the line at the start of the day by Le Bègue, it is hard to see how or why it had been shifted all the way across to the far end of the left wing. As always, the reference in the source to 'Janissaries' should be read as 'Ottoman infantry of some kind', although, since Koca Ibrahim did have Janissaries in his wing, it is not impossible that these really were men of that corps. It is however slightly worrying how similar this action sounds to the events recorded by Le Bègue for Heissler at the *start* of the day. A variant version of events is offered by Dalérac (vol. 1, p.151), though since he was nowhere near the left wing and was probably recounting second-hand information from a man of Lubomirski's corps, not too much reliance can be placed on it: according to him, the action was warming up in the 'villages and the bottoms', with the Turks firing dismounted then remounting, and it was this which 'one of these corps of dragoons' mistook for a flight, leading to its incautious advance and destruction. Dalérac places the death of Königsegg here rather than later. He then (p.152) goes on to recount how the Marchese Parella repeatedly requested permission from Lorraine to attack the Turkish post (something on the near side of the Nussdorf – Kahlen?) with his volunteers, but Lorraine, pretending not to hear the Italian, assigned the task to his trusted compatriot Mercy, though stressing three times that he put on his cuirass first; Mercy carried out the mission 'with as much skill as valour' and gradually the Turks spread back out over the hilly terrain.

11.5 Who commanded the Syrian counter-attack around Kahlen?

Mansberg, p.92, puts the counter-attack under a veteran but luckless commander called Harun Pasha the Unfortunate of Damascus, 'vizier of Suristan', a concatenation of inconsistencies so close as to lead one to doubt his very existence. 'Suristan' was a form of name for what we call 'Syria', but this did not exist in the Ottoman Empire as a single entity, but was divided into three main provinces (not counting the regions that are in the east of modern Syria): Aleppo in the north, Damascus in the south, and Tripoli between them, with Damascus the one most likely to be thought of as plain 'Syria'. But we know without a doubt that the *beylerbeyi* of Damascus, Abaza Sari Hüseyin, was in command of the *left* wing of the Ottoman army at this time, facing where the Poles would be appearing. The *beylerbeyi* of Aleppo is a more likely candidate, for he was in Kara Mehmed's advance guard – but his name was Deli Bekir. No *beylerbeyi* of Tripoli (in Ottoman Turkish, Tarabulus, or Trablus-i Şam) is recorded as serving at the siege of Vienna; no Harun of any kind appears in the index to Kreutel & Teply.

11.6 Issues surrounding the fall of Heiligenstadt.

Many historians put the fall of Heiligenstadt before the pause; some (for example, Wimmer, *Entsatz*, p.190) even suggest that the Saxons took it at about the same time as the Imperialists took Nussdorf. The first point is flatly contradicted by Le Bègue in his Account, and the whole sequence is in itself extremely improbable. Heiligenstadt is very nearly due south of Nussdorf; to attack it, the Saxons would have had to do one of two things, neither of them likely. Firstly, they could have shifted a bit to their left and then crossed the lower Schreiberbach to advance southwards – leaving both flanks but especially their left in the air. Secondly, they could have pivoted in between the Schreiberbach and the Nesselbach to advance south-east and attack Heiligenstadt from that angle – leaving their right not only completely in the air but also facing Koca Ibrahim's forces behind the Nesselbach and the bulk of the Ottoman army beyond. On top of these improbabilities, there is the fact that, if the Saxons took Heiligenstadt at the same time as the Imperialists took Nussdorf, the Ottoman defenders of Nussdorf would have found their line of retreat to the south cut off, would have been trapped and either massacred in large numbers or forced to surrender; if such a dramatic turn of events had taken place, it would assuredly have received some mention in the sources, even in the laconic Le Bègue. This argument also takes care of the possibility that some Imperialist battalions might have gone past Nussdorf to continue the advance *while* the attack on Nussdorf continued behind them, thereby covering the Saxons' left flank, for even if the Imperialists had been willing to go beyond a major fortified point leaving a substantial Ottoman force to their rear, such a move would likewise have put them across the garrison's line of retreat. It is next to certain that Heiligenstadt fell *after* the Imperialists had taken Nussdorf and the surviving Ottomans of the garrison had retreated thence to the Nesselbach line.

11.7 The Potockis.

The Potockis were a powerful magnate family, and like most such families could sometimes be more concerned with their own power or personal vendettas than with the common good, but many of them served honestly and courageously. Andrzej had been left behind at Cracow as effective head of the government in Sobieski's absence, and would succeed Sieniawski as Crown Field Hetman the following year; Szczęsny (Felix), his brother, was fighting at Vienna, and Stanisław his 24-year old son (Szczęsny's nephew) was on his last moments of life. The brother's name as used by the man himself was probably the Latin Felix or its slightly Polonised form Feliks, but modern Polish practice *generally* prefers the literal translation of the name into Polish, Szczęsny (lit., 'happy', in its original sense of 'possessed of good fortune').

11.8 Matczyński's charge.

Details of the charge are very obscure: in some histories, it is omitted completely; in others, its events are 'merged' with those of the reconnaissance-charge by the Potockis, and its commander is variously given as Atanazy Miączyński (who was actually serving in Jabłonowski's wing) and Matczyński. It is never clear if the attack was part of a final attempt to disengage the Potockis or was launched in its own right; given the distance it had to traverse, it may well have started as the former but been completed as the latter because by the time it reached the enemy the Potockis had already disengaged – Sieniawski, as eager for action as his troops, was hardly the man to call it off at the last moment. Paradowski, p.139, describes this as a counter-attack against Turks pursuing the defeated reconnaissance. I have accepted Wimmer, *Entsatz*, p.198, as the authoritative history. This is supported by the Account of Le Bègue which described, after the saving of the initial charge by the Bavarian infantry: 'The effort of ours having slowed the pursuit of the enemy, the King, who saw what was happening, wanting to recreate the disorder which had happened, had the first line of his hussars advance promptly against the enemy, and Graf Rabatta had the Imperialist dragoons join this, as the King had asked. This main body of Turks separated from their troops, not daring to sustain the shock of ours, withdrew with more diligence than they had advanced, towards a little height, where there were some infantry and some cannon.'

11.9 Timing of Baden's clearing of the siege works.

Some siege diarists put this as early as 5 p.m., and this was followed by Dolleczek; Le Bègue put it as late as 7.30 (which would require Lorraine to take at least two and a half hours to advance less than two miles unopposed); between 6 and 7 seems the most likely time. There is also confusion over the regiments that Baden had: no two sources agree exactly (except for DR Heissler which appears in all lists), and I have formed a composite list from the differing units mentioned by Vaelckeren, Hocke, Ruess, the *Aufrichtige und unpartheyische Relation*, the anonymous siege diarist in Stöller, p.138, and the 'Baden account'; Le Bègue is silent about the regimental names, making only a confusing reference to Mercy that I have interpreted as in the text. The gate used is almost always specified as the Schotten, but Le Bègue in his Diary refers to the 'Danube Gate' (and to getting troops into the city, not attacking the trenches); there was no gate in Vienna with this formal name, and though three gates (Oberfall, Unterfall and Fischertürl) faced the Canal, none was appropriate for getting troops in under the present circumstances *or* for linking up with the garrison to attack the trenches; the Schotten, which was the land-facing gate nearest the Danube on the north, fitted the bill perfectly. Baden's use of music is from Hocke, p.197; I have assumed the reason.

11.10 Numbers of captured Ottoman guns and other gear.

The Imperialist figures in the text are from Vaelckeren, p.108, and Hocke, p.221, with *Theatrum Europaeum*, vol. 12, p.556, following (although Hocke puts the number of mortars at 16). These numbers are based on what Starhemberg brought in to the Imperialist arsenals on the 15th. Le Bègue in his Account (Stöller, p.40) gave 180 cannon or mortars, and the 'Baden account' (Röder, vol. 1, Urk., p.19) made it 170 cannon and 26 mortars. (Le Bègue in the Diary specified that 80 pieces were found in the siege works, which by his reckoning would put 100 guns in the army that faced the relief force.) There are suggestions in contemporary news reports (Dudik, pp.444, 445) that the heaviest guns and mortars were not collected from the Ottoman camp and counted in the first days after the siege, and more were being found all the time; but it is unlikely that Vaelckeren and Hocke omitted any from their lists – they had had plenty of time to include the latest figures by the time their accounts were published. Dupont, p.146, provided a much more detailed breakdown, with 14 60-pounders, 26 48-pounders, 35 24-pounders, 42 18-pounders, 74 of 4–12-pounders (making 191 cannon), and 26 mortars of different calibres; apart from the complete divergence between his figures and those of Hocke-Vaelckeren, our suspicions are aroused by the way the list reads like a west-European recommendation for a siege train; I suspect that Dupont (who was on the way to Poland by the time the artillery was being counted) made up the list. Vaelckeren also included in the 'ammunition' section of his list what his English translator rendered as 200,000 'great musquets to shoot small granadoes' (p.108); comparing with other lists (Hocke, p.221; Dudik, p.444), both of which give the 200,000 figure, it seems that this was a translation of 'Brandt-Röhren für grosse und kleine Granaten', and while 'Brandröhren' *could* be a term for a kind of firearm, 200,000 'grenade-launchers' beggars belief, and in this context I believe it refers to a 'fire-reed', the tube placed in the hole of the grenade to carry the fuse with the flame into the interior (Paradowski, p.218, from a Polish edition of Vaelckeren, gives 20,000, but even this is an improbable number for such equipment.)

On other captured equipment: details based on a comparison of the lists in Vaelckeren, pp.107–108, and Hocke, pp.219–220, with a little common sense applied to some of the figures – I do not believe, as Hocke's lists states, that the Ottoman army had a million filled wool-sacks – the camp would have been drowning in wool if there had been so many. Not all of this military gear made it into the Imperialist arsenals when Starhemberg sent out 1,000 men on the 15th to collect it; the figures for what was brought in show (for example) 983 *centner* of powder and 1,500 *centner* of lead (see Renner, p.439, and *Das Kriegsjahr 1683*, pp.265–266, citing a document in the Vienna Kriegs-Archiv). Other lists of booty may be found in Staudinger, *Das königlich bayerische 2. Infanterie-Regiment*, p.82 n.2; Dolleczek, 'Entsatzschlacht' p.179, which includes a column of suspiciously high figures from a Polish source; and, with some even more improbable numbers, in Dudik, pp.444, 507. Compare versions of the Vaelckeren list and another by Dalérac from his *Polish manuscripts* book of 1700 (a variant of his *Anecdotes* book that I have relied on, which does not contain such a list), in Paradowski, pp.217–219.

11.11 How much grain was captured in the Ottoman camp?

Unfortunately, the grain figure of 100,000 *malter* is quoted in a measure of *volume*, whereas calculations of military bread production and consumption tend to be in *weights*, and translating volume to weight even of a known substance such as wheat grain is not an exact science (it can vary according to the exact type of grain, its growing conditions, and many other factors) even when the volume measure is stable – and the *malter* was a very variable (though always a large) measure. Some extremely rough calculations are possible: Siemienowicz (in calculations which *appear* to translate volume to weight for grain) suggests that the German *malter* was equal to 600 pounds weight, which would give the Ottoman store 60 million pounds, or 27.1 million kg., which would come out at 485,360 *centner*. According to the calculations of Perjés, 20,000 *centner* of grain would keep an army of 90,000 (60,000 combatants and 30,000 support) fed for a month; this means that the 485,360 *centner* could have kept the entire Ottoman army and its camp-followers fed for two years! Assuming that Siemiennowicz's conversions are correct, I strongly suspect that the Imperialist documents got a decimal point in the wrong place and the real amount must have been 10,000 *malter*. See: Kazimierz Siemienowicz, *The great art of artillery of Casimir Simienowicz* [sic] (London: Tonson, 1729; republished with a new foreword by O.F.G. Hogg, London: S.R. Publishers, 1971), p.67; and Géza Perjés, 'Army provisioning, logistics and strategy in the second half of the seventeenth century', *Acta Historica Academiae Scientiarum Hungaricae*, 16 (1970), pp.1-51; here, pp.5–6.

Appendix II

The Ottoman army census of 7 September and the casualty list

Census based on the copy in Vaelckeren, pp.89–91, checked against the more modern German versions published in Hammer-Purgstall, *Geschichte des osmanischen Reiches*, vol. 6, pp.734–735, and Toifel Beilage III; there is also Le Bègue's version in Stöller pp.35–36, mostly the same as Vaelckern but with some strange additions (Ahmed Pasha of 'Melie' with 5,000), omissions (such as Thököly) and increases in figures (the most notable being 22,000 for the *Sipahi*s), though he gives the correct figure of 1,500 for the *topci*s, giving lines that add up to 174,500 (not the 154,500 specified by Le Bègue); Barker (p.430 n.105) mentions a version from Kuniz with this same 174,500 total, notes its oddities, and remarks that the original of it has never been found.

In the version here, the original order has been modified to be more logical, with generally silent correction of personal and provincial names and clarification of official positions, and correction of the typographical error by Vaelckern's English publisher who added an extra zero to a line and increased the size of the *topci* corps ten-fold (the German original got the right number of 1,500, without which the Vaelckern quoted total does not match the figure one gets by adding his individual lines). Some of the more obvious errors and anomalies are addressed in the notes, but there are far too may of these to cover all of them.

For comparison/correction: columns added for:

- the *Benaglia figures* from Belgrade in May;[427] Mavrocordato's figures for May, from Kreutel & Teply, 70, where specified, are added in parentheses; a hyphen is given if the corps was known not to be in the camp at Vienna

- the *Master of Ceremonies / Silahdar figures* where appropriate (see below for details of these);

---

[427] Giovanni Benaglia, *Ausführliche Reiss-Beschreibung von Wien nach Constantinopel und wider zurück in Teutschland… dess Hoch-Gebohren Grafen Hern Albrecht Caprara* (Frankfurt: Wagner, 1687), pp.122–126; this list also reproduced in Toifel, pp.645–647, with a discrepancy in the total quoted.

The comparison is not perfectly valid, because changes had occurred in the governors and their household troops between May and September: some had died, been dismissed or moved to new offices, and at every such alteration the man's *yerli kulu* would have changed as well. We do not know whether *yerli kulu* normally moved with their master to his new post or remained with the new holder, or a mixture of the two, or whether the bands of warriors were broken up and joined other governors at will; but we do know that the composition of these units was fluid, impermanent. In addition to such changes, individual reinforcements may have joined some governors; *gönüllü*s who had distinguished themselves in action may have been taken onto a governor's payroll. It is also a matter of concern that Benaglia did not include in his list the household forces of the Grand Vizier himself, although we know full well that Kara Mustafa brought a substantial corps of his own troops. However, the overall impression is important: the numbers so carefully counted by Benaglia at Belgrade, widely accepted as reliable, were at the start of the campaign, when units were most likely at their peak strength, and the majority of them would only have reduced as the siege progressed – but, with a few notable exceptions, Benaglia's numbers are all *lower* than the figures of 7 September, in some cases markedly so. The comparison gives a clear indication of just how misleading the listed figures were.

		Vaelckeren	Benaglia etc. (Mavroc. figs. in brackets)	MofC/Silahdar
Kara Mustafa, his court & Janissaries		6,000	[not mentioned]	
Kapi kulu				
	Mustafa Bekri, Janissary Ağa	16,000	15,000*	5,000 (to right wing)
	Osman Ağa of the Sipahis	12,000		3,000 (4 regts)†
	Topci başi (master of the ordnance, i.e. gunners)	1,500	5,000‡	
	Cebeci başi & the *cebeci*s (armourers)	4,000		1,500
	Egyptians (*Misirli*)	3,500	3,000	1,000
	Miners (*laguncilar*)	5,000		
'Villa' or 'Dilly' Ağa of the timariot *sipahis*§		5,000		
Ali Ağa of the Volunteers (*gönüllü*)		5,000		
Kara Mehmed, BB of Diyarbekir (Mesopotamia)		5,000	1,500 (2,500)	2,000
Hizir, BB of Bosnia		6,000	1,540 + 800	2,000

THE OTTOMAN ARMY CENSUS OF 7 SEPTEMBER AND THE CASUALTY LIST

Ibrahim, BB of Buda	5,000	2,065 + 800	4,000
Abaza Sari Hüseyin BB of Damascus	3,000	1,520 + 480 + 300	
Çirkeşli Celeb Hasan Efendi, BB of Temesvár¶	1,000	900	
Mustafa P. (of Mytilene), BB of Silistria	1,500 (108)	- [left at Raab	
Sheyh Ogli Ahmed, P. of Manisa [Saruhan]	1,000		300
Hasan Arnaut Hocazade, BB of Rumelia	6,000**	3,300 + 1,200	
Deli Bekir, BB of Aleppo	1,000	950	1,000
Ahmed Osmanpashazade BB of Anatolia	1,000	(1,500)	
Harmos, B. of Menteşe	500		200
Ahmed, B. of Tire ('Cyra')	600		
Hasan P. 'the treasurer', s-b. of Hamid	500	770	400
Binamaz Halil, BB of Sivas	1,000	530	1,500
Ali, B. of Ankara	500		
Arab Ali, s-b. of Teke††	500	340	200
Ahmed, BB of Maraş‡‡	1,000	710	1,200
Ali, 'B.' of Karaman§§	1,000		1,000
Mustafa P., s-b. of Hercegovina ‖	500		300
Hussein, B. of Bolu	600	326 (ca. 500)	300
Mehmed Pasha Deli Emir, BB of Adana¶¶	500	450 (700)	900
Aslan, B. of Nicopolis	1,000		
Hasan, P. of Nigde	500		
Ali, B. of Brusa	300		
Hasan, B. of Chernomen (Turkish Çirman, in Bulgaria)	300		
'Jurigi', or 'Yurek' BB of Erlau***	600	- [570+400 Jans]†††	
Sahib Deli Ömer, s-b. of Karahisar	1,000		200
'Osman Ogly', s-b. of Kutahya‡‡‡	1,000	300 + 210	
Ibrahim, BB of Gwdn [actually, Mehmed Gürcü]	600	-	
Servants, not in pay but capable of bearing arms§§§	20,000		
Tatar Khan, Murad Giray	20,000 ‖‖‖		
Thököly & Hungarians¶¶¶	15,000		
Michael Apafi Prince of Transylvania	6,000		
Şerban Cantacuzeni, Pr. of Wallachia	4,000		
George Duca, Pr. of Moldavia	2,000		
Total according to the muster:	168,000		

* Possibly referring to the entire *kapi kulu*, since Benaglia made no mention of *Sipahi*s; however, Benaglia elsewhere referred to 12,000 Janissaries. NB: whether the number when the campaign started was 12,000 or 15,000, the number at 12 September must have been much lower, because the Janissaries had suffered very heavily during the siege.

† The four junior regiments of the *Sipahi*s of the Porte (see Glossary) served under Koca Ibrahim and were assigned this 3,000 figure by the diarists. The two senior regiments, normally much bigger than the junior four, served in the centre under Kara Mustafa and a reliable count for them is not available. No figures were given at Belgrade for the *Sipahi*s of the Porte, but the two regiments could have up to 9,000 men on the books. However, a massive discrepancy had arisen in the seventeenth century between the numbers of men listed in the *kapi kulu* and those actually serving, as Muslim civilians acquired *kapi kulu* status for various reasons usually connected with tax evasion; and besides, the casualty list gave huge losses for *Sipahi*s 'and other cavalry', and many volunteers from the two regiments continued to serve in the trenches during the battle. The estimate in Chapter 10 of 4,000 for the two senior regiments may be taken as an absolute maximum.

‡ Benaglia probably included the *cebeci*s with the *topci*s in this figure; and the 5,000 *may* have been included already in the 15,000 specified by Benaglia as under the command of the Janissary Ağa.

§ Hammer puts *deli*s here, but most versions favour the timariots. The real name of the commander is unconfirmed; no name like these is given in the Kreutel & Teply index. See the note at the start of chapter 10 about timariots vs. *yerli kulu*.

| Occasional references to Egypt in this context are inexplicable.

¶ There is considerable confusion over the governor of Temesvár. The name here is correct: see Kreutel & Teply, pp.181–182, for the appointment of the extraordinarily reluctant bureaucrat Çirkeşli Celeb Hasan Efendi to the post, after the death of the previous holder, on 3–4 September.

** Hammer version says 600

†† Toifel version says, of Erzerum, which is nowhere near Teke (a *sancak* on the south coast of Anatolia).

‡‡ Ahmed Pasha Kethüda Sarhoş had in fact ceased to be *beylerbeyi* of Maraş on 25 August, when he was moved to Erlau, and was replaced by Ömer Deli.

§§ the original in Vaelckeren has 'Aly, B. of Caramania'; the contingent size is that for a *beylerbeyi*, but the governor of Karaman at this time was Ibrahim Şişman; it is not impossible that this refers to the *sancak-bey* of the sub-province (*sancak*) of Karaman, though this was known as Larende at the time and was not the 'capital' of the province (Konya was), plus, it would have been very odd for the *sancak-bey* but not the *beylerbeyi* to be present at the head of a *beylerbeyi*-sized contingent.

|| Identification of the correct name of this province (in Turkish, Hersek; in Serbian, Hercegovina), from the bizarre variants in the originals of the muster, is uncertain. Another viable candidate would be the Mustafa P. *sancak-bey* of Esseg listed by Benaglia, with 460 soldiers; Benaglia has no Mustafa of Hersek, but there is one such in the Kreutel & Teply index etc.. It might even be 'Ersek Ujvar' (Neuhäusel) though there is no Mustafa of this province in the Kreutel & Teply index.

¶¶ Commonly referred to as just 'Emir Pasha'. Mansberg gives him 600.

*** The Ottomans had been getting through *beylerbeyi*s of Erlau at a fair rate: according to western sources (not confirmed in Kreutel & Teply), one of this unusual name was killed in action in fighting on the Danube islands mid-July as part of the Ottoman operations to isolate Vienna. According to Kreutel & Teply, the next governor, Abaza Kör Hüseyin Pasha, fell in action at the Bisamberg on 24 August; the current tenant of the post was Ahmed Kethüda Sarhoş, previously *beylerbey* of Maraş.

††† some confusion with Manisa

‡‡‡ no trace in Kreutel & Teply index. Assumed to be the same as the 'mounted Osman Pasha' in the Benaglia list.

§§§ Term as given in Vaelckeren. Mansberg tried identifying these as *azeb*s of the *serhad kulu*, and Le Bègue's version (Stöller, p.36) did define them as 'La milice non payée du Sultan' (the unpaid soldiery of the Sultan) which could have been a description of *azeb*s; but all other source versions give them as some form of non-combatants.

||| See the discussion of Tatar numbers in Appendix I, 5.3.

¶¶¶ The bulk of Thököly's *kurucok* were with him north of the Danube; a force of 1,000–2,000 Hungarians *may* have been in the camp at Vienna, but even if they were, Kara Mustafa could have placed no reliance on them, and indeed, like the Roumanians, they took care not to participate in the battle.

General notes

Other versions of the Muster.

Cf. the versions in Dudik pp.505-506; Boethius, vol. 1, pp.139-140. *Das Kriegsjahr 1683*, pp.242–243, has a cut-down version of this, with many of the individual beys lumped together as 'contingents of 22 pashes with 300 to 2000'. Dolleczek, 'Entsatzschlacht', p.176, gives what is presented as a version of the Muster, which even includes Vaelckeren amongst its cited sources, but which is significantly different (his listed units produce a total of over 285,000). Mansberg pp.69–72 also has a version of 'Muster', heavily modified and so 'annotated' with the author's mistaken beliefs about the structure of the Ottoman army as to be worthless (for examples, he confuses Kara Mustafa's guard with the *kapi-kulu sipahi*s, omits the 5,000 for the timariots because he thinks the various 'bey' figures are the timariots, and he does some grouping, e.g. of all Asian *beylerbeyi*s, Buda with Grosswardein and Erlau, etc.).

How was the muster carried out?

Vaelckern (p. 94) claimed that the muster was carried out by marching soldiers two by two past the Grand Vizier whose officials then counted them, in contrast to what westerners thought of a muster (whole formations being drawn up in the open and remaining stationary while they were counted); this made fraud so much easier, by allowing the same men to be re-used, marched past again and again. A western-style muster, which would have made abuses more difficult to conceal, would of course have been impossible in a siege where many troops had to be kept in the works. However, Vaelckern's story is inherently improbable: if the soldiers had marched past two by two past a single point, assuming no more than two seconds for each pair to go by, it would have taken an hour for 3,600 to be counted, and 46 hours for the supposed 168,000 – nearly two solid days and nights. This is not likely. It is fractionally more probable that several different officials supervised such a march-past simultaneously. The only slight evidence in favour of Vaelckern's story is a gap in the record kept by the two Ottoman diarists between 4 and 8 September, the days between the first alarming news that the Christians were coming and the arrival of Koca Ibrahim. The diarist who was actually present was a court official (the Master of Ceremonies); was he spending those missing days, up to and including 7 September, carrying out a long and tedious muster, too busy to write his diary? Against this we may note that the Ottoman minister Mavrocordato made absolutely no mention of a muster; his own account of the siege is much shorter than those of the diarists, but as a government official he might have been expected to have noted a major bureaucratic effort if one had taken place. It is also not without significance that the journal of a member of the staff of the captive Imperialist ambassador Kuniz, who observed events in the Ottoman camp throughout the siege, likewise made no mention of a muster being held (though he did incorporate the list into his account). The inclusion in the list under several posts of persons who had recently been replaced suggests that it was compiled from slightly out-of-date records. From all this evidence combined, the most likely conclusion is that the Ottomans held a bureaucratic census, not a muster: officials compiled the list, starting out from their own salary registers but then relying heavily on the various corps commanders and provincial governors handing in figures for their contingents, maybe even guesswork for irregulars such as the volunteer *gönüllü*s. There would have been little or no verification by eye. Such paper fantasies had long been the norm in the Ottoman bureaucracy.[428]

The casualty list.

Another document purportedly found in the Ottoman camp and published in the same works was a casualty list, even more suspicious than the supposed muster. This is reproduced from Vaelckeren, pp.93–94, modified by comparison with the version of the anonymous diarist of Kuniz's staff in Firnhaber, p.507, with that in Hocke, p.200, and the modern edition of Toifel, Beilage III. It clearly refers to the whole siege, not just the battle, but even so, many of the figures seem excessive, though the entries for Tatars and other cavalry, reflecting casualties in the field actions north of the Danube, look reasonable. The list presumably does not include losses of the *gönüllü*s, who were not in pay – the Tatars were not paid either, but the Khan was more likely to have handed in records of casualties for political reasons (to confirm the contribution of his people to the campaign) than was the commander of the *gönüllü*s.

Pashas	3
çorbacis of Janissaries	15
captains of Egyptian troops*	25
officers of the timariots (possibly including zaims)	500
Janissaries	10,000
miners	16,000
Sipahis & other cavalry	12,000
engineers & workers	6,000
Tatars	2,000
Timariots	2,000
Total	48,544
	(actually, 48,543)

*The Kuniz diarist and Hocke called these 'captains of the assault troops' [*serdengeçti*?], not Egyptians.

---

428 On standards in the Ottoman bureaucracy, including its regular throwing out of the documentation intended to act as a check on corruption, see Joel Shinder, 'Ottoman bureaucracy in the second half of the seventeenth century: the central and naval administrations' (unpubl. PhD thesis, Princeton U., 1971).

Appendix III

Ottoman discussions: did Koca Ibrahim oppose Kara Mustafa?

Did Kara Mustafa hold another council of war as the infidels closed in during the final days of the siege? and if so, did Koca Ibrahim of Buda oppose him? The matter is much in dispute.

Historians before the middle of the twentieth century were in no doubt, for they relied on the account of the Roumanian statesman and historian Dimitrie Cantemir in his history of the Ottoman Empire, first written in his native tongue in 1714–1716 and subsequently translated into several European languages. This included a detailed quote of a discussion about tactics on the eve of the battle, in which Koca Ibrahim took part, arguing in favour of fortifying the edge of the woods, and Ibrahim was probably also intended to be understood by readers as the voice of 'the pashas' quoted opposing Kara Mustafa. Cantemir, though twice Prince of Moldavia during his life, was not an eyewitness to the siege of Vienna (he was only 10 years old at the time), but later moved in the circles of people who had been present, so was assumed to be reliable; the exact words that he put into the mouths of Kara Mustafa and his opponents were probably made up, but they were assumed to represent accurately the existence of the debate and its general thrust. However, Cantemir was not the first to present this story: Lorraine's first biographer La Brune delivered a very similar account in his history of the Duke first published in 1691, just after Charles's death.[429] La Brune himself was no more in the Ottoman camp in the days leading up to 12 September 1683 than Cantemir was, but as a member of Lorraine's entourage he had every opportunity to meet people who had been, especially someone like Kuniz, who had spent the entire siege as an Ottoman semi-prisoner and kept himself well informed of what was going on around him. Except in the matter of the date for the big debate with Koca Ibrahim's argument for entrenching the edge of the woods (Cantemir placed it late on the 11th, from La Brune it could have been on an earlier day), the two accounts supported each other well. Since they agreed with each other, and since there was never

---

429 see La Brune, p.279.

any reason to believe that Cantemir had copied La Brune, they seemed to be independent works each broadly confirming the story told by the other; not direct evidence but accounts that had to be taken seriously.

But then everything was overturned when, starting in 1967, the chronicles of the Ottoman diarists were translated and published in western languages; for in these accounts there is not a word of any council of war after the brisk one-hour discussion on 9 September, at which Koca Ibrahim was not even present, and whose very brevity precludes the possibility of fierce debates on how to fight the battle. Cantemir and La Brune seemed completely discredited, although some historians such as Barker tried to salvage something of what they had offered.[430] However, the key Ottoman diarist, the Master of Ceremonies, was not exactly impartial: he was from Kara Mustafa's clientele, and, especially in the days after the battle when he would have written up his account of the end of the siege, the most important motive for him was to present Kara Mustafa in a good light and his opponents in a bad light. Kara Mustafa intended to put the entire blame for the defeat on Koca Ibrahim, so his followers were hardly likely to remember or record that Koca Ibrahim had presented cogent arguments for a different conduct of the battle that might have produced a victory where Kara Mustafa's plan had clearly failed to do so. It is perfectly possible that the Master of Ceremonies would have simply failed to record a debate that did take place.

Is there any internal evidence in the Cantemir-La Brune accounts that supports their veracity? The Cantemir version is reproduced below, and analysis of this allows a cautious 'yes' in answer to this question. As far as the exact words are concerned, they are clearly made up: not only is it improbable that a debate would have run on the lines of a proposal by Koca Ibrahim followed by two long and so coherently-presented arguments with no interruptions of any kind, but also, the calm rational words put into Kara Mustafa's mouth are hardly those of the man whose bullying was legendary, the man who only a week before, when faced by a senior official known as the Defterdar who declined an appointment as *beylerbeyi* of Jenő, had pulled his beard (an extreme insult in itself), then boxed his ears, knocked him further round the head, dismissed him from his present office, and a day later still forced the unwanted *beylerbeyilik* on him.[431] Kara Mustafa did not cope well with opposition to his will; any debate, any contrary opinion offered by Koca Ibrahim, whom he already disliked, would have provoked an unpleasant reaction – although the Grand Vizier would probably have had enough self-control not to treat the venerable *beylerbeyi* of Buda in quite the same way as the unfortunate Defterdar, especially on the eve of battle, no matter what his personal feelings.

In addition to the obvious untruth of the actual words, the mere presence of Koca Ibrahim at a meeting, when he had been so ostentatiously excluded from the earlier debates recorded by the Ottoman diarists, might also be seen as evidence against Cantemir – would Kara Mustafa have invited someone he detested? In short: yes. The Christians were approaching, the non-

---

430 see Barker, pp.319–320.
431 Kreutel & Teply, pp.181–182.

combatants were packing up and leaving, the situation of the Ottoman army was beginning to look a lot less secure than Kara Mustafa would have liked, his nerves were becoming frayed (witness the repeated calling the troops to arms and then standing them down again); now was the time to see if *anyone*, even someone that he detested, could come up with a way for him out of the mess. And if a scape-goat were needed later, it would be much more difficult to blame Koca Ibrahim if he had never been present in any council of war before the battle.

Beyond this, if we look *below* the calm words supplied by Cantemir at some of the arguments underneath, they are as psychologically convincing as Kara Mustafa's willingness to turn to his old enemy at this late stage. In particular, Kara Mustafa's contradictory references both to the 'innumerable and invincible forces of the Othman Empire' and to 'our weakness' strike the reader very forcefully as arguments genuinely dredged up in the course of a long and acrimonious discussion by a man under increasing stress, about his situation and about how strong the Christians were and how they would attack. They do not sound like arguments dreamt up by a Roumanian Prince-historian 30 years later. They suggest a man who sees the operation that should have made his political power unassailable slipping from his control and who vacillates between hope and fear or clings on to straws – he has seen only enemy troops on the Kahlenberg chain so far, perhaps the reports of Poles and other Germans are false and the troops he sees are the only enemies he must fight, in which case he is saved, but on the other hand he has seen the true size of his own army, the enemy would surely not be advancing unless they have more than these… and then there is the great agonising question of whether to fight on two fronts, facing the woods and the city. We know from accounts of the siege of Czehryń, that Kara Mustafa was a man who vacillated under pressure, moved from depression in adversity to excessive confidence under the persuasion of others.[432]

The one weakness I see in accepting Cantemir's account is the suggestion attributed to Koca Ibrahim of creating an abatis in the near stretches of the woods. Such an action was impossible for him by the time he was supposed to have made it: by the evening of the 11th, Koca Ibrahim's right wing no longer controlled even the nearest parts of the woods in front of it, and could in no way hope to construct an abatis there. It seems incredible that Koca Ibrahim was unaware of this: he knew that his men had already been skirmishing with the Christians along a line at or beyond where any abatis would be created. Perhaps the timings are out by a little: if the council of war took place earlier than the late evening, perhaps Koca Ibrahim did not know that his men were even as he spoke losing control of the tree-line. After all, the Christians did get the impression that the Turks were trying to entrench in some way before the skirmishing drove them off – perhaps Koca Ibrahim had issued orders to start an abatis before he left to go to the council. Perhaps he knew of the loss but thought that his strong right wing could hold on,

---

[432] See the account of this siege in La Croix, [Édouard] Sieur de, *Mémoires du Sieur de La Croix, ci-devant secrétaire de l'ambassade de Constantinople* (2 parts, Paris: La Veuve A. Celier, 1684), vol. 2, pp.239–257.

and was proposing an abatis only for the centre and left wing, both of which still had access to the tree-line and could have created an abatis in plenty of time before the Christians approaching them arrived. Or just possibly the date of the discussion was incorrect in Cantemir and the council, with Koca Ibrahim's proposal, occurred a day earlier when the entire Ottoman army still had the ability to construct an abatis.

Curiously, the Ottoman Master of Ceremonies in his discussion of the causes of the defeat did make a suggestion that the Ottoman army should have entrenched itself thoroughly against the relief force, though he was talking not of an abatis in the woods but of trenches and batteries some way back from the tree line, with enough open ground in front to permit cavalry counter-attacks when these were appropriate. He did not state that this option was discussed, but it was clearly something within the range of possibilities for the Ottoman mind.[433] Historians have occasionally dismissed the idea that the Ottomans would have discussed entrenching on the grounds that this was not then a tactic used by the Ottoman army – but not only had an Ottoman army entrenched its camp at Chocim in 1673, but also here was a participant making the very suggestion soon after the battle. Perhaps Koca Ibrahim made a suggestion like this, and Cantemir misinterpreted what he had been told and turned it into an abatis.

Ultimately, all this is so much speculation. However, there are some aspects about which we can be reasonably certain: despite the silence of the Ottoman diarists, there would inevitably have been more discussions after 9 September; those discussions would certainly have covered the questions of how to oppose the relief army and whether to try to continue the siege at the same time. Even if we accept no more than that (and I believe we *can* accept more than that), the account of Cantemir does at least summarise some (not all) of the tactical issues facing the Ottoman commanders on the eve of battle, the issues that, even if they were not raised in council, would have been very much at the front of their minds.

Cantemir's account

After stressing increasingly poor morale amongst the Ottoman troops as the siege wore on, and claiming that the failure to prevent the junction of the Polish relief force with the Germans was due to this inertia, the Roumanian historian began his account of the discussions preceding the battle:[434]

> Shortly after, when they were assured the enemy's forces were marching against them, the night before the battle almost a fourth part of the army dispersed themselves, and the rest, whose religion engaged them to remain, showed so little

---

433 Kreutel & Teply, pp.196–197.
434 Cantemir, vol. 2, pp.308–310; original paragraph numbering and random italicising omitted, but the original translator's contemporary spelling practices (Othman) and idiosyncrasies (use of both 'Basha' and 'Pasha') retained, as is the excellent original punctuation which, even after all these centuries, is a model of how to use punctuation to ensure clarity.

resolution and ardor [sic], that they did not seem willing even to try the fortune of a battle.

The Bashas themselves are struck with dread at the desertion of their soldiers; the [Grand] Vizir alone, whom these things ought to have convinced of the vicissitude of human affairs, continues fearless, and imagines nothing insuperable by his power. However, he assembles the other officers, and asks them, what course they thought should be taken. Ibrahim Pasha, Beglerbeg of Buda, first declares his opinion, and advises the raising of the siege, the marching of the troops against the enemy, the cutting down of the neighbouring woods, and making a rampart with the trees, and fortifying it with cannon, in order to receive the first and warmest attack; and that afterwards the horse should fall upon the enemy in flank as they retire. This method, if rightly pursued, would, it was to be hoped, gain an easy and speedy victory. He added, the Othman [Ottoman] army being already weakened by the toils of a long siege, could not be divided, nor part of it left in the works without great danger, much less should a passage be open to the enemy as far as the very camp, the extent of which would render the defence of it more difficult to the Othman forces, and the attack more easy to the assailants.

All the Pashas, except a few, approve this advice, and entreat the Vizir not to abuse his authority, nor be the occasion of great detriment to the Othman Empire. The Vizir alone opposes the admonitions, and says,

> I know not what fatal calamity threatens the Othman affairs, that so many persons of eminent prudence should almost be hurried into perverse and unreasonable opinions. You advise the abandoning of Vienna, which we have besieged for three months [actually two], and now reduced to such extremities, that it can scarce hold out so many days. But if you voluntarily suffer it to escape out of your hands, what do you else but willfully resign, without a battle, the wished for victory to a small body of the enemy, which scarce deserve the name of an army, if compared with the innumerable and invincible forces of the Othman Empire? Will not the garrison, if they see our soldiers quitting their trenches and works, attack them as they retire, repair their walls, which we have demolished, recover what we have taken, destroy the ramparts raised against them, and render the siege more difficult to us when we return? Will not our own soldiers, if after so many labours in vain sustained, so many of their companions killed unrevenged, when they are just ready to seize the wished for prize, we should lead them farther from it, will they not (I say) sink in their courage, and fight with less vigour, and, as the proverb expresses it, do their business only with the ends of their fingers? Will not the enemy's army, when they find the siege raised by us, refuse to try the fortune of a battle, which in their present circumstances they cannot avoid, without hazarding their all; and victoriously retire without the loss of a man; and leave us thus deluded to engage with much more cruel enemies, for the autumnal rains are approaching, which formerly obliged Soliman,[435] in other respects an invincible Emperor, to abandon the siege. But if it should happen otherwise, and the Germans,

---

435 Süleyman the Magnificent, the Ottoman Sultan who started the conquest of Hungary and besieged Vienna in 1529.

pushed by their evil genius, be induced to fight, which of you will venture to promise that the Janizaries, even after a victory, will return to the siege, and again enter those trenches, where they have hitherto sustained so many fatigues, and lost so many companions? You are sufficiently acquainted with their obstinacy by their seditious expressions, which deserve indeed to be punished, but that the present situation of affairs renders it necessary to oppose the rebels to the enemy, rather than the sword of the executioner. I do not deny, these turbulent men have greatly abated of their former ardor; but they will grow still more indolent, if you remove them out of their trenches, and tacitly command them to despair of taking the city. It may be easy to recover what the enemy shall seize during the battle; but consider, it is much easier to defend what we are already possessed of, than to recover it. The desire of revenge will animate the Janizaries to return to the siege; but take care, lest their fury, if the garrison should make a vigorous defence, be not turned against our heads. We are now in a situation, that we must either live or die. But to overcome, after we have abandoned a city besieged by us so many months, has the appearance rather of a defeat than a victory. The Sultan daily expects from us an account of our success, and has already made preparations for a triumph. If the event shall prove contrary, it is easy to imagine what danger hangs over your heads as well as mine. If you consider these things, and weigh them in the balance of prudence, you will perceive, it is in vain to lead the army into the field, in vain to fight for victory, unless the greatest part of the Janizaries be left to defend the works and carry on the siege. It will terrify the enemies, if they find we are ready in our camp for battle, and at the same time prosecuting the siege as vigorously as before; it will conceal our weakness; prevent the garrison from attacking our rear; inspire our soldiers with courage; and in short, is the only method by which we can obtain not only an easy, but a compleat victory.

When the Vizir had ended his speech, the Bashas answer,

There is nothing to be feared from the garrison, who being equally, if not more exhausted by sickness and labours than the Othman soldiers, will be more sollicitous about the defence of the fortifications still left them, than the recovery of what they have lost: besides, the trenches and other works are much stronger than the city, and if one or two regiments are left to defend them, it will be more difficult for the garrison of Vienna to seize them, than for the Janizaries to take the city. The other Janizaries now employed in the trenches, may be much more advantageously opposed to the enemy, whose army is not to be contemned [viewed with contempt], since it contains not only the forces of almost all Germany, but also a considerable body of auxiliaries from Poland. It is certain the Janizaries sometimes obstinately refuse to obey the commands of their generals, and even threaten their lives; but it is no less certain, they are easily softened by some little presents, and promises of increasing their pay; nor is it probable, that after so many fatigues, they will leave the reward of them to others, when they are just at the end of their labours. The dividing of the battle in two parts will be more inconvenient to the Othman army, than to the enemy; and there is reason to apprehend the terror, which this method is expected to strike into them, will render the Germans desperate, since the contest is not for one city, but for the safety of all Christendom; and so may bring destruction to the whole Othman army.

But neither could these remonstrances divert the Vizir from his purpose, who alledged, the management of this expedition was committed to him by the Sultan; that an account of it would be expected from him; that if any misfortune happened, it would be imputed to him, and not to them; and he could not suffer it to be said, he had gone through so many hardships, and lost so many men, without any advantage.

Appendix IV

Le Bègue's accounts of the battle

Translated from Stöller, pp.37–40, and 101–103. All references to simply 'the Duke' mean Lorraine; all references to 'H.H., = His Highness (in the original French, S.A., = *Son Altesse*) also refer to Lorraine.

The Account

[Begins after references to the start of work on Leslie's battery]

One laboured all night on this work, but before it was finished, the enemy, noticing it at 5 in the morning of the 12th, advanced some troops to prevent it. They took post quite close to this work behind a screen, and behind planks which almost closed off the terrain of the descent from the mountain before our battery.

The Count de Fontaine, who was put in command of this post, was quick to oppose their efforts, and immediately stopped work, assembled what people he had, and formed two battalions; he positioned them then between this fence and the battery he was making, at a distance however which gave him room to be able to take some measures to prevent himself from being enveloped by the enemy, who were extending at the same time to right and left to gain the flank.

The Duke who was observing from St Joseph's Chapel[436] the enemy movement, had several battalions from the closest regiments march to the aid of these first units. This reinforcement, led by the Duke of Croy, arriving in time, our people extended the frontage of their line and took the decision to attack the enemy who were posted behind the screen.

---

436 Le Bègue's Austrian editor in 1933, Stöller, consistently corrects this as the Chapel of St Leopold (i.e. the Leopoldsberg). There is no reason for this; it is clear that the writer refers to the chapel of the monastery of St Joseph on the Kahlenberg.

The thing was carried out with such vigour that the enemy, not being able to hold off this effort, abandoned their post and withdrew behind another screen, where was standing the main body of their troops.

In this action the Duke of Croy was wounded on the shoulder by a musket-shot, which passed right through, which obliged him personally to withdraw. The Count de Fontaine held firm, arranging all that was necessary to hold this post, which the enemy seemed to want to attack afresh. Nevertheless they did not do so and contented themselves with firing on our people from the hedges that they had occupied. Ours did the same from their side, and the fire continued on both sides.

However the Duke, who had seen what was happening, having noticed that the enemy were moving up their entire corps which was camped on this side of Nussdorf to support their advanced troops, first of all started the march of all the left wing, and a little after gave orders to the Prince of Waldeck and the Duke of Sachsen-Lauenburg to come out of the wood by the avenues which were at the head of their camp.

He sent to inform the King of all these things and, having learnt that he was coming to St Joseph's Chapel, he went out to meet him, and showing him the movements that were taking place, told him the dispositions he had made in this encounter.

The King agreeing on everything, he entered the Chapel to hear Mass there, and the Duke went to the head of his troops who were advancing.

The orders of the Duke having been carried out, the infantry took position at the exit of the wood; one then sent down the dragoon regiments of Heissler and the Saxons, which Count Caprara posted on the left at the foot of St Leopold's Chapel [Leopoldsberg].

Heissler's regiment received orders around 8 o'clock to go and attack the enemy who were occupying [low] ground[437] on the left from which they were firing on the rear of our people, and the infantry likewise had orders to advance on the enemy who were posted behind the screens and in the hollow ways.

This movement was made on both sides at once; the Turks made some resistance, but it was not strong enough to prevent our people advancing and making them retire behind another ravine.

Count Leslie, who had got the artillery down, had it advance in this location at the head of the infantry; the Duke of Croy also returned there after having had an initial dressing of his wound, and had the strength to continue serving the rest of the day.

This advantage gained time and ground to extend the front of the left wing bit by bit as it descended and exited from the defile. Nevertheless our first line of infantry who, marching against the enemy, never stopped making a continuous fire of musketry mixed with that of artillery, captured another

---

437 In the original French: 'occupaient un terrain'; the 'terrain' *might* come from Le Bègue hearing Germans refer to a 'Grund' which he rendered in French as 'terrain' unaware of or overlooking the fact that the German word has implications of a low-lying quality – it can mean a 'bottom', a valley floor or even a ravine.

post, and a screen which extended almost from the Danube as far as opposite the Camaldulensian [monastery].

The Duke called a halt here towards 10 o'clock, and although the rest of the left wing filled the ground that we had just occupied, and although Count Caprara extended to the bank of the Danube, he sent orders to the Prince of Waldeck, who was appearing already on the first heights to the right, and to the Duke of Sachsen-Lauenburg, who also had exited from the wood, to continue their march until they had come into line level with us, and to advance extending to the right until they would be in reach of supporting the Poles at the exit from the defiles of their route, which was on the right of the whole army.

These dispositions being made, the Duke returned to the head of the left wing to set in motion all together this great body of German troops, the Elector of Saxony came to join him and remained always at his side in the most exposed positions.

The King, who had remained at St Joseph's Chapel, having seen all that had happened, sent orders to his troops to march, and after having heard mass, went to make them advance, with such diligence that towards noon he [Sobieski and the Polish army] joined our right wing [i.e. came level with Sachsen-Lauenburg].

However, the Duke took care that, our army marching in [order of] battle against the enemy, the junior generals should re-establish order in the places where it was broken by the difficulty of the passages, and that one should keep up there by all means a steady advance making a continuous musket and cannon fire.

One advanced in this manner albeit quite slowly, as much through the difficulty and unevenness of the ground as through the enemy opposition. Our left which advanced along the Danube took from them the village of Nussdorf, after a quite considerable resistance. There was the same on our right to occupy, on the same line, a height held by the enemy who, by the vigour of their defence, had shaken one of our battalions, but having been supported by the Styrum Dragoons which Count Dünewald sent there, this battalion rallied, it then occupied this height and one continued to advance.

The soundness of this advance, that of our order of battle, and the situation of the area which made our troops appear as if in a type of amphitheatre, presented to the viewer in this movement a great and formidable object, and I have no doubt that it appeared so to the Turks, and that it was one of the causes of the victory.

The King being still behind, the army halted quite close to [level with] Nussdorf, until the Duke noticed that we were everywhere just about level, he continued his march, and our left, advancing, took without much resistance the post that the enemy held at Heiligenstadt. The Prince of Waldeck on his side obliged those facing him to withdraw.

However, the enemy troops who had formed up in their camp made some movements which seemed to intend come at us, but perceiving the army of the King joining up with our right on the height, the greatest proportion of their troops threw themselves on that side so that the Poles and Turks found themselves facing each other both almost in the same order, making more depth than front [i.e. deeper than they were wide]. The Poles seemed to support themselves on a wood and the Turks on their camp.

The King, who was marching at the head of his troops, detached several squadrons of his hussars, who charged with great vigour, lances lowered, to attack the Turks frontally. They overthrew at first those who were opposite them, but penetrating too far, they drew so great a number of enemies onto them that they were forced to turn their backs. The Turks pursued them as far as a position where the Prince of Waldeck had sent forward very opportunely several Bavarian battalions, with the Mercy Regiment in an advantageous post from where they could support them.

The effort of ours having slowed the pursuit of the enemy, the King, who saw what was happening, wanting to recreate the disorder which had happened, had the first line of his hussars advance promptly against the enemy, and Count Rabatta had the Imperialist dragoons join this, as the King had asked. This main body of Turks separated from their troops, not daring sustain the shock of ours, withdrew with more diligence than they had advanced, towards a little height, where there were some infantry and some cannon.

After this success the King continued his advance with all the army, the enemy for their part resisted in all the different posts that they had occupied. The fire of their musketry and of their cannon did us some damage, but our troops not being shaken advanced always and continued to gain ground. However the Duke having got close with the left to the enemy camp so as to distract the effort that they were making on the right, the Turks formed up in order of battle at the ravine before their camp, and, turning several pieces of cannon against us, they fired with them several shots and gave the impression of wanting to hold this post [the line of the Döblingerbach??], which was the strongest of all the ground and which served as a retrenchment for their camp. But their firmness did not last long, and our people having advanced to musket range, they abandoned this ravine at five o'clock in the evening, and we seized the opportunity [laissèrent toute la commodité] to get over it without hindrance and to enter their camp.

It was thus that the Duke, profiting from this advantage, had the entire left turn, and instead of marching as previously along the Danube, he had it bear to the right passing through the enemy camp, without a single soldier breaking ranks to plunder the baggage that the enemy had left scattered around, nor their raised tents. This movement being seen by the Turks who were facing the Poles, succeeded in disconcerting them, and, afraid of being taken in flank, they began to withdraw.

The King subsequently crossed the ravine with his troops despite the fire of the Janissaries who defended it, and pursuing the enemy troops, he entered around seven o'clock a little after the Prince of Waldeck who had already entered it with the Bavarians and Franconians.

The Duke having reached with the Emperor's army about half past seven in the evening the suburb and the counter-scarp, Prince Louis of Baden was ordered to advance towards the enemy trenches with some troops that the Baron de Mercy led, but one could get there so quickly only under cover of night which fell, the body of Janissaries who were there did not have the opportunity to complete the retreat that they had already begun as soon as they saw us approach their camp. Their casualties were low and their steadiness was still considerable right up to evening, because, before abandoning their trench, they tried a new attack against the city, and not succeeding in this, they turned against the army the cannon that they had in their batteries, from which they made several discharges. Night having suspended the drive for victory, we were obliged to make a halt in this part of the camp which was between the Danube and the River Wien, the enemy having retired beyond this river. The Duke sent to compliment the King on the success of the day, as if we owed it to his presence. The King returned the compliment, sending to him to say that it was true everyone had had his share in it but one owed the action to his conduct and the firmness of the German troops who had been the first to enter the camp and the works of the enemy.

Besides the compliment, the Duke had sent to His Majesty to discuss the march of the 13th, to which he replied that he would arrange with him on the morrow, after having rendered thanks to god for the good success of the day.

During the night the enemy passed the River Schwechat, making their retreat their last military action, and abandoned their camp with such precipitation that they left in the quarters of the Grand Vizier the Great Banner of the Ottoman Empire, and the horse-tails which are the everyday insignia of command and of the dignity of the Grand Vizier, all their tents, and the majority of their gear, all their ammunition and provisions of which they had an extraordinary amount, all their artillery amounting to a hundred and eighty pieces of cannon and mortars, and they hastened their retreat with so much diligence that already on the 13th their leading troops were already re-crossing the Raab [river], as we learnt from the governor of Raab [fortress].

We lost, of people of consideration, Prince Thomas de Croy, Count von Trautmannsdorff, and the lord Potocki, captain of a company of hussars amongst the Poles. Of wounded, apart from the Duke of Croy, we had the Counts de Fontaine, Tilly and Schallenberg, but only lightly, and they did not stop serving for the rest of the day.

The Diary

From the camp of the Ottomans before Vienna, 12th September '83.

Notwithstanding the difficulty of the marches made by the army, that one had believed impracticable, all the troops arrived yesterday in the camp, apart from those of Poland, who remained about an hour behind. Our artillery, which had to double and triple the teams on account of the steepness of the mountain, arrived towards six o'clock in the morning, so that we were awaiting only the arrival of the King to begin descending the mountain and reach a screen that the enemy occupied at a quarter of an hour from Nussdorf, and other heights level with this, where the *corps de bataille* and the German right wing and the Poles should advance and take position;

this was what had been proposed to do today. And as H.H., having noticed already yesterday that the largest part of the enemy force was placing itself on the Danube side, he had ordered already in the night to take post at the foot of the height of the Camaldulensian Monastery [Kahlenberg] to make easier the defile of the descent, which was very tight, and had ordered that in the night five battalions should march there and that a battery be established there. The Count de Fontaine who was charged with this command was not able to finish his entrenchment, [and] the Turks, seeing that he was working, came towards 7 o'clock to prevent it; this started the action of the day, which ended only in the occupation of the posts above [qui se fût terminée sans cela à occuper le postes cy dessus].

The Turks having thus advanced around 7 o'clock in the morning with sufficient force to drive our people from the post, and being covered by a sort of palisade, from which they were firing on our infantry; the Prince de Croy and the Count de Fontaine had the infantry advance to drive the Turks from their post, from which they drove them, and ours held on there. However, H.H. had other infantry advance under these screens to support these five battalions; the Turks advanced on it from their side likewise, and the action began; the advance of the infantry of the entire left wing, and of the dragoons, with the cavalry[,] having been ordered.

The infantry being posted in the space behind this palisade below this monastery, and the dragoons of Heissler and Saxony [DR Reuss] having descended, Heissler was ordered to charge a battalion of Janissaries, which were the most pushed forward on the left, and the infantry, to cross in order of battle the palisade and to attack the Turks in the little valleys on the right.

This movement and the fire of our musketry forced the Turks to abandon the post, and their retreat gave room to our people to win another post, from where, by continuous fire they obliged the enemy to retire equally, with the result that we occupied the height of Nussdorf, where we stopped to give time for the Prince of Waldeck and the right wing to come up level with us; which they did without much opposition from the enemy.

The King of Poland who saw from the height of Kahlenberg the order of march of the German troops, their firmness and the retreat of the Turks, quickly went to his army, with the result that towards eleven o'clock the entire army had descended and was in order of battle, on the same line as Nussdorf. After this the general advance began, the enemy always retiring under the musketry of our infantry, which forced them to abandon the Danube and make an effort against the right wing, where the Poles had only cavalry. Some units of Poles were repulsed and forced to retire, there were also several battalions which gave way, but that was nothing, and the King having had his hussars advance, and H.H. having pressed the advance of the left right up to their camp, they withdrew everywhere.

We entered their camp on our left towards five o'clock in the evening. The right wing entered it a little later after having broken the Janissaries of the Guard of the Grand Vizier. In this manner at 7 o'clock of the evening we were in all of their camp, full of their tents and their baggage. It was ordered that no-one should pillage, which was fully obeyed, no-one leaving their ranks. The left wing advanced in order of battle close to the city to start getting some infantry in by the Danube Gate; which was done, and then we continued to advance on the enemy which were in order of battle away from their camp. When we advanced towards the approaches, the Janissaries tried an assault on the city, and afterwards withdrew by their galleries to the right of their army; here there was a lot of firing by our dragoons with them and they [Turks?] suffered some casualties.

The army stopped the action and the advance towards ten o'clock in the evening, while the Turks crossed the Schwechat, having abandoned their artillery and baggage, which was pillaged throughout the night.

The loss of men in the two armies was not great, the enemy having always given ground. After having given up their posts from the left wing to the right, near their camp there was a greater fire, but this killed few people; there were only 200 men of the Emperor's army out of action, and 150 Poles. Amongst the Poles there were two or 3 people of consideration killed, amongst others my lord Potocki. Amongst the Germans there was the Prince de Croy killed, the Duke his brother wounded in the shoulder, the Count von Trautmannsdorff major in [DR] Schultz killed, the counts of Fontaine and Tilly wounded in the leg. We took the Great Standard of the Turkish Empire and some horse-tails, which are the command insignia of the Grand Vizier. We found 80 pieces of cannon in the approaches, and in the camp provisions of war and mouth [food] in great amounts, all their rich tents and an infinity of all sorts of baggage. The King in person was always under fire and in the most dangerous places, showing by his conduct and the wisdom of his commands the boldness of a great captain. H.H. did the same, and everyone acknowledges that we owe to his care and to his dispositions the relief of Vienna and the success of the enterprise. My lords the electors of Bavaria and Saxony were always under fire and have given much proof of their valour and of their greatness. The Prince of Waldeck has done everything that could be expected of a good general. The Polish hussars did extremely well, having forced some very difficult passages in the teeth of the fire of the Janissaries. Some battalions of Bavarians and the Schultz and Styrum Dragoons also did very well on the right. On the left we owed to the regiments of Grana and Baden the occupation of the first posts, from which all the rest ensued, having done very well there and with such firmness that all the rest of the infantry followed their example and acted like veteran troops. The Heissler Dragoons and those of Saxony were the first which acted vigorously; and generally all the generals and officers of the Emperor, Saxony, Franconia and Bavaria did very well. The order of battle, the conduct of the march, the precision of the difficult movements [des mouvements ayant fort], show that, if the dispositions were good, the execution was extremely well done by the generals. Apart from the example that my lords the Electors of Bavaria and Saxony and that so many princes from all the great dynasties of the Empire gave to the army by their vigour and firmness, one cannot praise and esteem them highly enough for the ease with which they consented to all the proposed dispositions, concerning themselves solely with the relief of Vienna, and contributing everything to avert the delays that the competition and the competing jurisdictions of so many different units normally brings in such cases.

Appendix V

The 'Baden account'

Translated from the French original in Röder, vol. 1, Urkunden, pp.13–19; this extract, pp.15–19, beginning with nightfall on the 11th. Beese (p.238 and n.175) notes that it was part of a much larger report 'La campagne de 1683…' and confirms that it was probably written by someone in Hermann of Baden's entourage. The account was found in the Carlsruhe archives with annotations by Hermann indicating it had his approval. Paragraph breaks have been added as the original has none, and a few of the author's interminable sentences broken down into two or more shorter ones; I have also inserted a certain amount of punctuation to clarify meaning. It is noticeable that Lorraine, Hermann's political enemy, gets just two mentions in this account, both of them assigning him an unimportant role in the action.

With night, the Turks made a prodigious quantity of fires all around their camp, yet without budging nor undertaking the slightest thing. One detached several battalions to go and take position at the foot of the mountain and one had the cannon moved forward to place it advantageously so it could be used the next day.

Day came and the enemy not only continued to batter the besieged city from their works even more strongly than ever, but [also], being further reinforced before us and posted with about 1,200 Janissaries behind the planks which surrounded a vineyard at the foot of the mountain, they were the first to recommence firing on ours, who responded at first diligently with cannon and musket shots.

The King of Poland, who was camped on the right, came at this time to our camp to observe there and to consider the enemy camp, whose situation seemed advantageous, as much from the height with which it was surrounded as from the screens which covered it and which from a distance resembled entrenchments. However, the combat of the Turks at the foot of the mountain against our battalions posted there under the command of the Duke of Croy, warmed up in such a manner that Prince Louis of Baden, who was at the head of the dragoons posted at the inclination, seeing the enemy constantly reinforced, advanced to support the Duke of Croy, who showed to the entire army the proofs of his valour by the vigorous resistance that he made. Prince Hermann of Baden, who was with the King of Poland and other generals high up, seeing his nephew engaged in a combat dangerous by the strength of the enemies who were all running to this place and of whom several detachments, flowing along the bushes, intended to envelop him, descended at the head of the rest of the infantry that he made follow him in haste, and having found there Count Leslie, general of infantry [FZM], one saw this combat redoubled with a great fury, so that, notwithstanding the fire of the enemies who were assuredly the most redoubtable in this place, after having had the planks that served them for an entrenchment forced sword in hand, one obliged them to fall back; Prince Louis having even had a party of dragoons that he was leading dismount to achieve this. Several battalions of Saxon infantry who, in courageously repulsing the enemy had opened the passage and the descent on the right, were led by their officers to this attack with much leadership and courage.

These having been followed by everyone, those of Bavaria and of Franconia with the rest of those of the Emperor, one began to extend and to occupy the height that the enemy had just abandoned. The rest of the German infantry having arrived with the cavalry, the Duke formed the [order of] battle and, having the artillery move in front, he had this army advance, encouraged by this start with a happy success, towards a second height, where the enemies were massed in large numbers giving the appearance of wanting to fight. But seeing that we were going with cries of joy straight at them, they descended to the low ground, not being able to sustain the fire of our cannon, and ceded to us even this height, on which our generals found it appropriate to make a halt, while awaiting the arrival of the Poles, who, having a camp a little further off, could not descend so soon.

We halted there more than a good half hour, with much impatience, so that everyone had his face turned towards this side, and seeing suddenly appear the pennants that the Polish cavalry carry attached to their lances, one heard so formidable a cry from our troops that even the Turks positioned opposite us appeared to be moved by it. The soldiers, some leaning on their arms to relax, leapt up with precipitation, with neither drum nor command; one was even forced to drive back with blows from the flat of the sword those who, through too much excitement, scattered in crowds to go at the enemy. They, perceiving the advance of the Poles, had advance against them a part of the troops opposed to our left. Against them, for lack of his cannon, the King sent a party of his hussars, who, charging them flat-out with lowered lances, repulsed them first-off, but [they] having been reinforced by troops which came out of the camp, the Poles turned face and fled at top speed towards their own, pursued by the enemies sword in hand with terrifying noises and howlings. The Poles, having joined up with the reinforcement that the King sent to them, stopped and pursued the Turks, who once more saved themselves before them with precipitation, so well that this game having continued up to three times, to the great contentment of the spectators, the Poles, outraged at such time-wasting, finally forced the enemies to cede this mountain, on which the King at once took position, placing there his cannon and infantry.

This action, which at the start seemed strange to the eyes of those who had never seen anything like it, did not fail to make a big effect and to cause consternation amongst the enemy: the Grand V[izier], who right up to this time to avoid recognising the trouble he was in had remained in the approaches to continue there battering the city with fury, turned up there in person, but seeing the situation half-desperate, he left command with the V[izier] of Buda and returned to the approaches, undoubtedly intending to try to save the cannon, [but] having been prevented from this by the bad news that he received a little after, he withdrew with precipitation towards Petronell to reassemble there the runaways of his army and cover their retreat.

The Poles, after having gained this height, being put in line with us, the front of all this army occupied a very considerable extent, [and] marched right against the enemy posted on the height which remained between us and their camp, on which, especially on the side of the Poles, they had brought up cannon to defend it. They made a great noise at our arrival and came up in disorder sword in hand, seeming as if they wanted to fall right amongst our battalions; but not being able to sustain the fire of our infantry and of our pieces, they were overthrown and forced to retrace their steps in confusion faster that they had come, knowing that they were abandoning to us this height, the same as the one where their camp was positioned. The approach, being steep, seemed quite difficult, as much on our side as on that of the Poles, who were the closest to their great camp [the southern part of the overall Ottoman camp] where was the tent of the Grand V[izier], which was defended with much stubbornness; but the Vizier of Buda who commanded there, seeing the left wing enter the camp and fearing to be surrounded, abandoned it with all the cannon that were there to the Poles, who, being the closest to the great camp, entered it the first, and got the greatest part of the rich booty that was there. The Turks at the head [northern end?] of the said camp gave the impression of wanting to resist but seeing the German troops advance, they disappeared little by little, abandoning to pillage their camp where all the tents were up, the terror and consternation in which they found themselves not having permitted them to carry anything except what they could put in haste on their horses and a few camels.

Notwithstanding the unhappy state to which the enemies saw themselves reduced, they continued to batter the city with stubbornness and despair, with cannon balls and bombs, even more strongly than they had done during all the siege. The Duke of Lorraine decided to send there Prince Louis of Baden with the Heissler Dragoons and three battalions of infantry, to clear out the trenches and seize the cannon and ammunition that were there. They went there at once, and having warned the Count von Starhemberg to have a part of the garrison sortie at the same time, they constrained them [the Ottomans] to leave them [the trenches], with a loss of 170 pieces of cannon, 26 mortars, and a prodigious quantity of all sorts of ammunition and of instruments for moving earth.

Thus the entirety having been abandoned by the precipitate and shameful flight of the enemy, night fell, which prevented our troops, exhausted with the fatigue of 24 hours of march and continual skirmishing, from pursuing them. The King, after having taken possession during the night of the tent of the Grand V[izier] with its silver plate, and all other very rich and valuable equipages that were there, and even a good part of the treasure of the Janissaries that their treasurer had left behind, entered the city the next day; and the Emperor, having been informed of everything, went there the day after....

Appendix VI

Two German accounts of the battle

Saxons: the 'Honest and impartial relation'

Translated from *Aufrichtige und unpartheyische Relation von der Victoria der Christen...* (see Bibliography for full details) pp.6–13, including the final indignant paragraph on p.13, which is presented in the original in a large bold type, expressing the Saxon unhappiness at how their role had been omitted from the initial news accounts of the battle. Punctuation has been modernised, with rather more full stops than provided by the original author, who was fonder of inordinately long sentences than is the norm even in German – for the most part, the author's rare full stops have been taken as paragraph marks, as the original is also without paragraph breaks of any kind between its first and last pages. I have not indicated the occasional use of abbreviations and French or Latin words in the German original (except for the quote of Lorraine's words to Goltz), but rendered them into plain English. The only ranks mentioned are 'Feld-Marschall' and 'General Major', which are so close to their English equivalents that I have chosen to translate them.

As however the day broke, which was the 2nd (12th) September,[438] the Saxon infantry moved somewhat down the hill, and took position at a location where they could see everything and could take position advantageously, since along the foot of the hill a screen of stone, man-high, was placed, and on this a board partition of wood was found, which the battalions of the first line had used very conveniently to their advantage. Field Marshal von der Goltz was also in the process of having a battery constructed at a suitable

---

[438] The Saxons, as Protestants, were still using the Julian calendar, the 'Old Style', as opposed to the Catholics who for more than a century had been using the more accurate Gregorian calendar, which was at this point 10 days ahead of the Julian. Literate Protestants were aware of the difference between the calendars and often quoted both versions when specifying a date.

point, through which to inconvenience the enemy, but as one was working on this, suddenly one saw the enemy advancing in great numbers in the bottom, which lay opposite the part of the hill on which the Saxons were posted; one also became aware at the same time that the enemy which stood opposite the lower part of the hill, on which the Imperialists were posted, behind a palisade, somewhat further down the hill than the Saxons, attacked these [Imperialists] furiously. At this, the Saxon battalions likewise had to throw themselves down from the height, neck over head, and from those that came down in such speed were formed as fast as possible 2 battalions, thereby to oppose the enemy, so as to prevent him from taking post in the hollow way lying below on the hill and in the bottom, which would have served him as a great advantage.

Meanwhile the other battalions came after, and were likewise posted in the best positions against the enemy; the enemy, as he saw this, desisted from advancing further in the bottom, but his infantry sought nothing but covered places wherein they could stand in safety, from which they now and then fired pot-shots at the Saxon infantry, which for their part held firm in their position, until one perceived that the greatest force of the enemy was coming more to the left-hand, where the Saxon grenadiers and Imperialist infantry had taken position behind a board partition along the hill. On this then the Saxon infantry of the first line swung to the left to face [lit., make front against] the enemy that were strongly attacking the grenadiers and Imperialist infantry. The enemy now stood in the hollow way pretty much under cover, having before him scrub and stones for his concealment, and was firing heavily on the Saxons, who were standing completely in the open and could be seen from foot to head.

While this was going on, one saw above on the hill the Franconian infantry standing completely still; to there Major General Reuss sent to request the commanding Major General to advance with his battalions, because the enemy could easily have got in against the Saxon rear; he indicated that he was willing himself, but represented that the Prince of Waldeck, who had the supreme command over the Franconians, had forbidden him most explicitly to move from the spot until he himself should indicate this to him. On this then the Saxon battalions of the second and third line advanced against the bottom, where the first line had stood before, in order to keep a watch on this, so that the enemy could try nothing from there, so that thus the Saxon infantry, for their security, were forced to form out of their 5 lines only one with two fronts.[439]

Meanwhile, the enemy with firing did much damage to the battalions of the first line, without that they could be repaid in equal coin, because, as aforesaid, he [the enemy] was under cover and they on the other hand stood completely in the open. It appeared therefore to be more beneficial and better to dislodge the enemy from such an advantage. After one now a little viewed [recognoseiret] the enemy's position, the Saxon infantry promptly advanced on it, attacked the enemy simultaneously in front and flank, they

---

439 I suspect that the '5' is a typo for '3'; there is no other reference to the Saxons being in five lines.

fell into confusion, turned, and hurried to the hill behind them, with the Saxons pursuing all the time, and never letting them come to a halt, also, even as they tried to re-assume position on the same [hill], hurried up after them, and drove them from the aforementioned great, wide-stretching hill (which would have been very advantageous for them, if they had been able to establish on it) and forced them to retire.

In the meantime the Saxon battalions which were, as already reported, placed opposite the bottom, also advanced, and had repulsed the enemy standing before them, which however established several companies [Fähnlein] in a ditch in the aforementioned bottom, where there was a substantial plain which stretched along around the hill and on to the first Turkish camp [this can only refer to the lower Schreiberbach], and by a continuous fire from there hindered the same [Saxons] from advancing further or from coming level with those on the hill.

As one perceived this, one immediately detached some men from the same, which fell on the enemy from the side, and compelled them thus to completely decamp from there, through which the somewhat held-back battalions gained room to join with the others on the hill.

His Electoral Highness of Saxony came at once in person to the hill, and declared publicly to his generals, who in this action had always been in the forefront and had led the infantry, that he was very satisfied with their actions, and wished that he himself could have been with them in person; as he however held the command by the left wing, he was required not to absent himself from there.

What meanwhile was going on at the Imperialist infantry with the enemy, one had not been able to observe so exactly from the Saxon point of view; impartial viewers [witnesses] report that the Turks, which stood opposite them, as they saw their comrades pushed back and pursued, also began to waver and to turn away, on which 2 battalions of Imperialists led by the Duke of Croy pushed forward, and finally drove them up the hill. However the Turks hotly disputed the descent on the far side of the hill with the Imperialists, until Prince Louis of Baden with the Saxon dragoons, which he took out of the second line of the left wing, advanced there, had them dismount, and thus completely drove the enemy from the hill,[440] in which then 2 Saxon battalion guns, which were brought on the hill, and by which quite a lot of damage was inflicted on the enemy, contributed in no small amount. On this the entire Imperialist infantry had drawn up the hill and taken position there.

Up to now, which was already about 2 hours before midday, not the least had happened on the right side, where stood the Bavarian and Franconian infantry, nor on the right wing, and only a part of the Imperialist and then the Saxon infantry had been in action. However, in the meantime the Bavarian and

---

440 The German verb 'chargiren', borrowed from French, at this time could mean either 'to charge' or 'to fire'; neither makes sense in this sentence, and I have chosen to translate as 'drive'. Whatever is meant, we may be sure that Louis of Baden took care not to get to close quarters with the Turks, where all the advantages of western discipline would be lost, especially not after dismounting the regiment.

Franconian infantry, together with the right wing, had gradually advanced, and moved closer. However, one saw thereupon at once strong Turkish units march towards the right wing, likewise also some Turks, which had been pushed into the aforementioned bottom [middle Schreiberbach?], turned, together to attack the right wing. Against these a part of the Poles made a fresh attack, but were repulsed by the enemy, and retired on the 4 battalions of infantry, which had been given by the Imperialists, Bavarians, Saxons and Franconians to the King of Poland at [his] request before we climbed the Kahlenberg, and subsequently placed in an advantageous position before the right wing. These sustained the Poles on 3 different occasions, and at that time it seemed as if the right wing would get into difficulties, which is why the Saxon Field Marshal [Goltz] then sent several officers to the Bavarian and Franconian infantry which stood closest to the right wing to request them to go to the aid of the right wing, to which the Franconian Major General then again showed himself perfectly willing but was countermanded by the Prince of Waldeck, on the pretext that there no-one but he had the command. Finally the hussars advanced forward, and they brought the enemy to flight, and in this one had not been able to see any sign that any infantry apart from the aforementioned 4 battalions had anything to do with the enemy, much less repulsed them as the gazetteers [newspapers] report.

During this time the Duke of Lorraine, together with other Imperialist generals, came to the Saxons on the forementioned hill and observed the action on the right wing right to its end, and as one saw the enemy flee, the Duke of Lorraine asked the Field Marshal Goltz whether one was satisfied with the honour and great advantage that had been won over the enemy this day; to which Field Marshal Goltz gave the answer: As it appears that the enemy is terrified, so he thought it good that one should pursue them and further prosecute the victory. The Duke of Lorraine said to this, 'Marchons donc' [let us march then] and together with the other generals with him rode back to the Imperialists.

The Saxon infantry thereupon immediately advanced down the hill, with the Imperialists following, and the whole [order of] battle began to move. Those Turks which were still in the bottom, as they saw this, retired to their first camp, and one saw, that they had assembled many thousands above at their camp on the left side, where was a great open field. On the corner of this height the enemy had thrown up something rather like a redoubt, and placed in it 6 bronze cannon, from which they gave fire on those advancing, but always shooting too high.

One held it assuredly for certain at this time that the enemy would dispute this height, as nothing was to be seen from the bottom of what was happening on the height. Both the Imperialists and the Saxons steadily advanced to the height, and everyone was busying himself climbing this while keeping in good readiness to fight. Finally, as one got to the top expecting to meet the enemy, they had already cleared off, retreating for the last camp.

The Saxons were thereby the first [in], and therefore they also received the 6 bronze guns as booty, as their standards had been the first to be seen flying in the enemy camp. Subsequently the Saxon dragoons helped attack the enemy approaches [siege works], where substantial resistance was encountered and a good part of the dragoons remained [on the field]. Following this the cavalry was moved in front of the infantry and sent off after the flying enemy.

What now further occurred, as night fell, one has nothing to note from the Saxon side, and thus nothing more to report here, especially since the gazettes are in any case full of these [later events].

All this that has been presented in this Relation truly took place, and such is conceded by all impartial onlookers, and no less by all Imperialist generals which were on the left wing. Therefore it is unjust that one assigns to the Saxons in the gazettes not one the least part of this action, nor wishes to even mention them with a word.

Franconians: Schliz von Görz

Translated from 'Relation von der Bataille, welche sich den 12./2. Septembr. dieses lauffenden 1683. Jahres, bey Entsezung der Kays. Residenz Statt Wien begeben…', in Newald, vol. 2, pp.98–102; this extract, pp.100–102. This was written by an eyewitness, a privy councillor of the Würzburg bishopric, Johann Freiherr von Schliz genannt von Görz, then an envoy of the Franconian Kreis to the Imperialist court, as a report to the members of the Kreis. The author's own punctuation and use of abbreviations have usually been preserved, but long sentences have sometimes been broken down, and it has occasionally been necessary to use quite loose translations of some of the more convoluted sentences. Most ranks specifically mentioned do not have immediately obvious English translations and, in contrast to the preceding source, I have left them in German.

The 12th, as one went to the conference, towards daybreak Lord Count Leslie had a battalion of infantry march from the hill of the Calenberg Monastery, on which the Turks made a heated attack, so that, notwithstanding one met them with equal resistance, yet it was necessary to bring up two more battalions, and to support them, which caused that one became further engaged with the enemy. The Imp. and Sax. troops took their posts proportionately to their strength, the Elector of Bavaria with his own and the Franc. troops took positions likewise, up to the 10 squadrons [of Sachsen-Lauenburg], and these on as far as the Poles, the Poles however took the field towards the mountain, as far as they could. As now neither time nor the situation allowed a formal order of battle to be formed, the generals employed the troops according to the circumstances as they arose, and reinforced each other where it was necessary. The infantry, which was mixed with some cavalry, went ahead, the rest followed immediately after, now in three lines, now in more. The Turkish attack on the Imp. was absolutely furious, and after this had lasted a good hour and encountered equal resistance, they became impatient and made such an attack with drawn swords in their hands that the Imp. were obliged to mêlée with them, yet through the good care of the generals this was immediately remedied and the enemy driven back. The Sax. troops also so set about the enemy that they drove him to flight, the Bav. and Franconian infantry took meanwhile the height next to that which the Imp. and Sax. had mastered, and drove back the Turks they found there. The cavalry followed meanwhile the infantry, and the Allied [cavalry] were commanded by His Highness the Lord Markgraf of Bayreuth, General Feldmarschall Lieutenant, together with the General Wachtmeisters Münster and Bavois [Beauvau]. After now the most part together with the Poles turned to the right, and the Turks noticed that the Poles were not provided with sufficient infantry, threw themselves upon them in such a way that one was forced to reinforce them with 2 battalions and 2 regiments of dragoons. After this the whole army began to advance on a parallel front, foot by foot, and supported each other where necessary, also the artillery came up bit by bit, which was immediately put in action, and drove the enemy from the hills and crossways which they had occupied right up to their camp. Then the enemy began to throw themselves on the Imp. on the [their] right and on the Poles on the left, but while the land on this side from the hill opened up, one drew with the infantry more to the right and aided the Poles. Then the Imp. on the left wing fell on the Turkish trenches and took the guns.

The Bavarian infantry, commanded by the General Feldmarschall Lieutenant Degenfeld together with other Major-Generals, meanwhile attacked the hill on which the Grand Vizier stood, in order to take the cannon with which the Turks were playing on them from three locations; the enemy however had the advantage of the height, and the Janissaries inconvenienced the Poles greatly with their muskets. The aforementioned Poles showed great valour however, and during this fight several battalions commanded by General Feldmarschall Lieutenant Leyhen [von der Leyen] and Major General Thüngen were sent against their [Turks'] flank. The Bavarians promptly climbed the hill, withstanding all fire from the Janissaries, on which the Turks became wavering and were forced to abandon this post, and driven further back under steady firing up to the gate, even to the approaches before Vienna. It appeared however as if the Grand Vizier then rallied, in that in sight of the entire Christian army he would not leave the approaches, and even continued to bombard the city. When the King of Poland saw this, he advanced against the enemy followed by a large number of Germans, and drove him out of the camp. Subsequently the Imp. generals gave orders to attack the Turks even in the trenches, and the troops of Prince Lubomyrsky began to shoot down those who were in the trenches and ran out. About 600 Turks remained on the field here, all artillery, all tents, the magazines of provisions and ammunition, together with much fine furniture, fell to the Christian army. The horse on which the Grand Vizier himself had ridden, which was very richly decorated, his standard, and both field insignia which he was accustomed to have carried before him, fell into the hands of the Poles. And thus the city of Vienna, so closely pressed for over 2 months, which had been so opened in two locations by mines that one could ride a horse through the [defences], and for which 180,000 Turks had ventured their everything, had we liberated, with an army of 70,000 men, comprised of Imper., Polish, Bavarian, Saxon and Franconian troops, through unanimous agreement and admirable good order, also to the incomparable pleasure [good conduct?] of the soldiers, during the combat, so that the hand of God was visible in this struggle, in that heart, courage and intelligence were taken away from his enemies.

Appendix VII

Sobieski's letters to his wife

Translated from the French translations of Plater, pp.64–80 (the eighth and ninth letters). The originals were in Polish, except for occasional snatches of French, which were marked in Plater by use of italics; I see no reason to mark them in any way here, except for one untranslatable phrase that I have left in the original. Plater's foot-notes, which were sometimes absurdly inaccurate, are omitted. As Dalérac noted (vol. 1, p.408), the grandiloquence and tendency towards circumlocutions, and the sometimes outrageous self-praise, were typical of Polish culture of the period – though it must be admitted that in this Polish culture matched Sobieski's personality very closely. The 'from' address that Sobieski assigned to the first of these letters was pretty wide of the mark but probably reflected that those around him knew the names of few of the localities they were traversing, and he used the only name he had heard used by the Imperialists.

Eighth letter

> At the mountains of Calemberg [Kahlenberg], near a burnt monastery, opposite the Turkish camp
> 12 September, at 3 o'clock in the morning

Sole joy of my soul, charming and well-loved Marysieńka!

Although there is no doubt that business is pressing us more and more, that the post will only leave tomorrow [and] that it must have difficulty in getting through because of the Tatars who scour the countryside, nevertheless, to avert your worries as much as I can for my part, I put everything to one side and I take up my pen to tell you that we are here, since yesterday evening, opposite the Turkish camp. The rest of our army will arrive, if God wills it, this afternoon [après-dinée]. It would be difficult to describe everything that has happened here. We had all the difficulties of the world in our crossing of the Danube. The bridges broke down under the artillery and the baggage. The majority of the carts had to seek fords, and luckily found some via several branches of the Danube, except for the main arm of the river, where the current was too rapid; for there is no river to compare with the Danube for force. Last Thursday, that is the 9th, we saw the Elector of Bavaria arrive, and here is his portrait: He is of the height of our Comte de Maligny, chestnut-brown hair, not bad features; the lips and chin in the Austrian style,[441] but not unattractive; the eyes a little lowered, [his] manner French. He joined us almost by post. He dresses better than the others. He has fine English horses; the King of France sent him a dozen with saddles and harness; otherwise neither pages nor lackeys. He has manners and good breeding, although he is very young. He has got to know Fanfan [Prince Jakub] so well and is on such familiar terms with him that people say they are tied since childhood; he [Maximilian Emanuel] often calls him my dear brother; also, I must admit that Fanfan has become quite changed from what he was; the poor little thing puts up with a lot and is no longer fed up. He carries himself well, thanks be to God.

The two Electors initially kept themselves at some distance from me. Now that we are approaching the enemy, they are less under observation; they come themselves always to take the word of the day from me, and ask ten times at once whether I do not have anything to command them. The Elector of Saxony is a decent man, with a true heart; he suffered a fall from his horse yesterday and has scratched his face. Both Electors keep near me several of their cavaliers to bring my orders. Last night, they sent a detachment of cavalry to guard my tent. Share all this with the Bishop of Łuck. He claimed that I would have much to endure from them and their German coolness. These princes have reinforced my Polish troops with four big regiments of infantry which form the right wing, and the lowest officer could not be more flexible nor more complaisant than they are with me. This is why we can hope to succeed, with the aid of God, albeit not without great efforts; for we have found affairs very different from what we had been led to believe, especially with the localities and the terrain. And so, after this famous crossing of the Danube, about which I have just told you, we had to cross the mountains where, to put it literally, we did not go up but climbed. Since last Friday, we have not eaten or slept any more than our horses. I was separated, that day, from my army, in order to be present at a council of war, and I was for the space of twenty-six hours without my own [people]. They had fallen behind, because of these cursed river [?] crossings, so much so that among the subalterns some had already begun to fear the worst. Luckily, some of them saw me at the head of the Hungarian infantry [haiduks of the guard]. I had sent it on ahead, because the German troops were already too exposed [aventurées]; but God, in his infinite goodness, preserved us from all confusion; not a man perished, despite the Tatars who attacked us on all sides. As for the Turks, one brings us to them like dogs. My dragoons and the Cossacks have taken from them a lot of cattle. Oh Menzynski! Menzynski!

---

441 Probably meaning, 'like the notorious Habsburg lower lip', which due to relentless in-breeding by the dynasty had reached a very noticeable size by this time. The observation was trivial but true: portraits of Maximilian Emanuel show a distinct though muted version of the Habsburg lip – the Elector's paternal grandmother was a Habsburg.

What was very extraordinary, was that there arose, ten hours ago, a violent wind which blew right in our faces. The cavalry had difficulty keeping on their horses; we were talking about the aerial powers being unchained against us; for the [Grand] Vizier has a reputation of being a great magician.

It was thus yesterday at noon that I rejoined my army, and we clambered up these wooded mountains of which I have told you. What a blessing of Providence that we have been able to pass these defiles without loss or delay. We left our baggage at a league from here, near the Danube, in a position strong and provided with entrenchments. I have here with me only two of my carts, and those the lightest; the rest of my effects are on mules; but even those, we have not seen for forty-eight hours. As for the rest, that is not important[;] what is more [important], is that we had been misled. The Generals themselves had assured us that once we crossed the mount Calemberg, the difficulties would all be smoothed away, and that from there the road to Vienna would be nothing but a gentle slope along the vineyards. On arriving here, we perceived first of all the immense camp of the Turks and the city of Vienna in the distance; but far from being separated by fields, there are forests, precipices, and an enormous mountain that we have before us and about which no-one had told us. So, it will hardly be within two days from now that we will be able to get to grips with them. We must change for now our order of battle and make war in the manner of Maurice[,] Spinola and others, who advanced *à la secura*, gaining ground little by little. Nevertheless, humanly speaking and besides putting all our hope in God, it is to be believed that an army chief who has thought neither about entrenching nor about concentrating, but who is camped there as if we were at a hundred leagues from him, is predestined to be beaten.

The Commandant of Vienna has already noticed us, because he lets off rockets and fires cannon incessantly. As for the Turks, they have done nothing up to now, except that they have detached fifty or so squadrons with several thousand Janissaries towards our left wing, where are the Prince [Duke] of Lorraine and the Elector of Saxony, established in the Camaldulensian Monastery. The Turks give the impression of wanting to defend this defile; I want to go there myself later, and that is why I finish this letter; for it is a matter of knowing whether they have made some entrenchment there; this would be very unfortunate for us, since it is on this side that I want to attack them. Our army occupies the space of a good half-league across the mountains and woods, in a terrain so cut up that it is only by little footpaths that one can get from one wing to the other.

I have spent the night on the extreme right, close to the infantry. One can see from here the entire Turkish camp, and the cannon do not allow closing one's eyes. We have so much abstained from meat these two days, Friday and Saturday, that any of us could hunt the stag on these mountains. The horses have had the worst of it; they have had nothing to eat but tree-leaves. The provisions and forage that we were promised have not been supplied; however, the people have very good will; the German regiments of infantry who have been joined to ours serve with a docility that I have never seen in mine; ours only watch the Turkish camp with a covetous eye and are full of impatience to get in there. The Tatars still do not show themselves; I do not know where they have gone.

I have received, my heart, your letter of 6 September; it was just at the moment when we were preparing to climb the mountains. Do not brag so much about its being your no. 6 [letter], for this is my no. 8; it has kept me up until daybreak. But I must finish at last, embracing a million times my loveable and incomparable Marysieńka.

My kisses to my sister and to M[onsieur] the Marquis; I tenderly embrace the children.

Pass this letter to Drion; that will provide him with materials for argument.

Ninth letter.

In the tents of the Vizier, 13 September, at night

Sole joy of my soul, charming and well-loved Marysieńka!

God be thanked for ever. He has given the victory to our nation; he has given it such a triumph that past centuries have never seen the like. All the artillery, all the camp of the Muslims, infinite riches, have fallen into our hands. The environs of the city, the fields all around are covered with the dead of the infidel army, and the rest fled in consternation. Our people are constantly bringing us camels, mules, cattle, ewes, that the enemy had with him, and besides an uncountable multitude of prisoners. Moreover, a large number of deserters are coming in, the majority renegades, well dressed and well mounted. The victory was so sudden and so extraordinary that, in the city as in our camp, there were constant alarms; people were thinking they were seeing the enemy returning all the time. He [the enemy] left, in powder and munitions, to the value of a million florins.

I have witnessed this night a spectacle that I have wanted [to see] for a long time. Our train personnel set fire to the powder in several places; the explosion was like the last judgement, but without injuring anyone. I was able to see on this occasion in what manner the clouds formed in the atmosphere; but it is a misfortune: there was undoubtedly more than half a million in losses.

The [Grand] Vizier abandoned everything in his flight; he kept nothing but his coat and his horse. I have established myself as his heir; for the greatest part of his riches have fallen into my hands.

Advancing with the first line and pushing the Vizier before me, I met one of his servants who guided me into the tents of his private court; these tents alone occupy a space as wide as the city of Warsaw or Lwów. I have seized hold of all the insignia and flags that are customarily carried before the Vizier. As for the great standard of Muhammad, that his sovereign entrusted to him for this war, I have sent it to the Holy Father by Talenti. Moreover, we have rich tents, glorious equipages, and a thousand other very beautiful and very rich toys. I have still not seen everything; but there is no comparison with what we saw at Chocim. Nothing but four or five quivers mounted with rubies and sapphires equivalent only to a few thousand ducats. So you will not say to me, my heart, like the Tatar women to their husbands when they return without booty, 'You are not a warrior, since you have brought me nothing; for it is only the man who pushes to the front who can catch something.'

I also have a horse of the Vizier with all the harness. Himself has been pursued very closely [referring to the last moments of the battle]; but he escaped. His Kihag [kethüda] or first lieutenant was killed as well as many others of the principal officers. Our soldiers have seized hold of many swords decorated with gold. Night put an end to the pursuit, and besides, even when fleeing, the Turks defend themselves ferociously. In this respect, they have made the finest withdrawal in the world. However, the Janissaries were forgotten in the trenches, and in the night they were cut to pieces. Such were the pride and the presumption of the Turks that, while one part of the army offered us battle, another was assaulting the city. However they had the means to provide for all that. I estimate them, excluding the Tatars, at three hundred thousand combatants, others have counted three hundred thousand tents, which would make a number of men beyond any known proportion. For me, I count near enough a hundred thousand tents; for they occupied three immense camps. For two nights and a day, anyone who wants is plundering; even those of the city have come to share in the booty; I am sure they have [enough] of it for eight days. The Turks in fleeing have left many local captives, especially women, but after having massacred as many of them as they could. Consequently there were many killed women; but also many were only wounded and they could still recover. I came across yesterday a child of three years, a charming little boy, to whom one of these cowards had hideously cleaved the head by the mouth. The Vizier had seized in one of the Emperor's castles a fine living ostrich; but he had even cut off the head of this to prevent it falling back into the hands of the Christians. It is impossible to describe in detail all the refinements of luxury that the Vizier brought together in his tents. There were baths, little gardens with fountains, rabbit warrens, even a parrot, which our soldiers chased but could not catch.

Today, I went to see the city; it could not have held out more than five days. The imperial palace is riddled with shot; these immense bastions, cracked and half caved in, have a dreadful appearance; one would say they are like great areas of rock.

All the troops have done their duty well; the victory is attributed to God and to us. At the moment when the enemy began to give way (and the greatest shock took place there where I was, opposite the Vizier), all the cavalry from the rest of the army moved towards me on the right wing, the centre and the left wing having very little at all to do [!]; I saw then running up the Elector of Bavaria, the Prince of Waldeck and others; they embraced me, they kissed my face; the generals kissed my hands and feet; the soldiers, the officers, on foot and on horse, cried 'Ah! unser brave Konig!' [our gallant King]. All obeyed me even better than my own [troops].

It was only this morning that I saw again the Prince [Duke] of Lorraine and the Elector of Saxony; we were not able to meet yesterday, because they were on the far left; I had given them several squadrons of our hussars, commanded by the Marshal of the Court [Lubomirski]. The commandant of the city, Starhemberg, also came to see me today. All of them embraced me, calling me saviour. I was in two churches, where the people kissed my hands, feet, clothes; others who were too far away to touch cried out: Ah, give us your victorious hands to kiss! They seemed as if they wanted to cry out *vivat*; but they were held back by the fear of the officers and other superiors. However, a large number of people made a kind of *vivat*. I noticed that the superiors watched this with a bad eye; so, after having dined with the commandant, I hastened to leave the city and return to the camp. The crowd accompanied me back as far as the gates. I see that Starhemberg is on bad terms with the council of the city. In receiving me, he did not present to me any of the civilian employees. The Emperor has informed me that he was a league from here…. But now the day is beginning to break; I must finish this letter. I no longer have the ability to write and to enjoy any longer this dear tête-à-tête with you.

We lost many of our own in the battle; we mourn especially two people of whom Dupont will tell you. Among the foreigners, the Prince of Croy has been killed; his brother is wounded as are still several other persons of note.

Father d'Aviano embraced me a million times in the outburst of his joy; he claims to have seen during the battle a white dove soaring above our armies.

We are going to set off on the march, today already, to pursue the enemy in Hungary. The Electors have told me that they will accompany me.

It is truly a great blessing of God. Honour and glory be to him now and for ever!

As soon as the Vizier perceived that he could not hold on any longer, he summoned his sons to him and started to cry like a child. He said then to the Khan of the Tatars: 'Save me, if you can.' The Khan replied to him: 'We know well, the King of Poland, it is impossible to resist him; take care rather of getting us out of this.'

We have such oppressive heat that we exist now only by dint of drinking. We have just discovered yet another great quantity of ammunition. Truly I do not know how much they can have left and with what they will make a campaign. I have just this moment received the report that the enemy has abandoned about fifteen small cannons in his flight.

I am at the point of mounting my horse to march into Hungary, and I hope, as I said to you when I left you, to see you again in Stryj [southern Poland, quite a way east; due south of Lwów]. Wyszynski should make repairs to the roads there and prepare accommodation.

This letter is the best news-sheet, and you can use it for that purpose, making clear that it is the letter of the King to the Queen.

The Princes of Bavaria and Saxony have decided to follow me to the ends of the earth.[442] We must march double-speed for the first two leagues, because of the intolerable stench of the bodies, both of men and of horses and camels.

I have written to the King of France; I have told him that it was to him in particular, as the Most Christian King, that it was proper for me to make my report on the battle won and on the saving of Christendom.

---

442 The most blatantly inaccurate statement in a letter full of inaccuracies.

The Emperor is a league and a half away. He is coming down the Danube in a row-boat; but I detect that he has no great desire to see me, perhaps on grounds of etiquette. He is hurrying to arrive as Vienna so as to have the Te Deum sung. This is why I cede him the place. I am quite happy to avoid all these ceremonies; we have had nothing else up to today. Our Fanfan is brave to the highest degree.

End note. As Sobieski requested, this letter was published throughout Europe. An account of the campaign drawn from the two letters was published by the Queen, in Polish and Latin, and subsequently translated into French[443]. Extracts of the letters themselves were circulating in France by October. However, variant copies were in circulation. The Moravian monk Pater Brulig from the Raygern monastery, who witnessed Dupont riding past on his way back to Poland with the King's letter, incorporated a version of it (Dudik, pp.439–443) in his account of the events of the summer (he noted that it was available in French, Polish and German, presumably, copies either hand-written by the royal secretariat for distribution by Dupont during his journey or even hastily printed – or maybe hastily copied down by the monks as Dupont rested for an hour). That version has some interesting differences to the one reproduced here, including references to Maximilian Emanuel sending some of the captured jewels to his sister, Maria Anna, who resided at the French court as the wife of the Dauphin, clearly as a subtle reproach to the King of France for his support for the Ottomans and as a means of rubbing his nose in the German victory; this version also included a story that when Louis XIV had asked Maria Anna whether her brother would help the Imperialists, she had tartly replied that he would do his duty to the Emperor and the fatherland. Neither of these stories is in other published versions of the letter, such as that in Boethius, vol. 1, pp.164–168, but they reflect the public hostility to Louis XIV for his betrayal of the Christian community. If they had appeared in versions of the letter published in Poland, one might attribute them to the vindictive nature of Sobieski's Queen, who might well have added such anecdotes to her husband's letter for her own reasons; but since they seem to have been incorporated into Brulig's chronicle on the 15th, that explanation is not possible. Perhaps the letter did include the anti-French remarks, passed on to Sobieski by Maximilian Emanuel, and were suppressed by Sobieski's nineteenth-century translator, the Comte Plater.

---

443   Reproduced in Dalérac, vol. 1, pp.408–424.

Bibliography

Aufrichtige und unpartheyische Relation von der Victoria der Christen so sie beym Entsatz der Stadt Wien gegen die Türcken erhalten… zur Vertheidigung der Sächsichen Tapfferkeit (s.l.: s.n., [1683 or 4?]) (Sometimes attributed to Daniel Suttinger. The bulk of this publication was reproduced in *Theatrum Europaeum*, vol. 12.)

Baden account. See Röder.

Barker, Thomas Mack, *Double eagle and crescent: Vienna's second Turkish siege and its historical setting* (Albany: SUNY, 1967)

Beese, Christian, *Markgraf Hermann von Baden (1628-1691): General, Diplomat und Minister Kaiser Leopolds I.* (Stuttgart: Kohlhammer, 1991)

Benaglia, Giovanni, *Ausführliche Reiss-Beschreibung von Wien nach Constantinopel und wider zurück in Teutschland… dess Hoch-Gebohren Grafen Hern Albrecht Caprara* (Frankfurt: Wagner, 1687)

Boethius, Christoph, *Ruhmbelorberter, triumphleuchtender und glantzerhöhter Kriegs-Helm Dero Röm. Kaiserl. auch zu Hungarn und Böhmen Kön. Maj. und dero… Bunds-Verwandten wider den… Türckischen Tulband….* 6 vols. (Nuremberg: Lochner, 1686–1698)

Braubach, Max, *Prinz Eugen von Savoyen: eine Biographie* (Vienna: Verlag für Geschichte und Politik, 1963–1965), vol. 1

Broucek, Peter, Erich Hillbrand, and Fritz Vesely, *Historischer Atlas zur zweiten Türkenbelagerung, Wien 1683* (Vienna: Deuticke, 1983)

Brzezinski, Richard, *Polish armies 1569-1696.* colour plates by Angus McBride. 2 vols. (Men at arms 184, 188) (London: Osprey, 1987)

Brzezinski, Richard, *Polish winged hussar, 1576-1775*, illustrated by Velimir Vuksic (Warrior, 94) (Oxford: Osprey, 2006)

Cantemir, Demetrius, *The history of the growth and decay of the Othman Empire…*, transl. by A. Tindal . 2 vols. (London: Knapton, 1734–1735)

Dalérac, François Paulin, *Les anecdotes de la Pologne, ou, Mémoires secrets du règne de Iean Sobieski III du nom*. 2 vols. (Paris: Aubouyn & Clouzier, 1700)

Dauer, Joseph, *Das königlich bayerischen Infanterie-Regiment Prinz Ludwig* (Ingoldstadt: Ganghofer, 1892), vol. 1

Dolleczek, Anton, 'Die Entsatzschlacht vor Wien am 12. September 1683', *Organ der Militärwissenschaftlichen Vereine*, 26 (1883), pp.149–180 + 1 fold-out

Dolleczek, Anton, 'Die polnische Armee im XVII Jahrhundert: ihre Einrichtung, Gliederung und Kampfweise, mit besonderer

Berücksichtigung der... bei dem Entsatze von Wien betheiligt gewesenen polnischen Truppen', *(Streffleur's) Österreichisches Militärische Zeitschrift*, 24:3 (1883), pp.105–130

Dudík, Bela (ed.), 'Pater Bernard Brulig's Bericht über die Belagerung der Stadt Wien im Jahre 1683', *Archiv für Kunde Österreichischer Geschichts-Quellen*, 4 (1850), Heft 2, pp.255–296, and Heft 3/4, pp.397–508

Dupont, Philippe, *Mémoires pour servir à l'histoire de la vie et des actions de Jean Sobieski III du nom roi de Pologne, par Philippe Dupont, attaché à ce prince en qualité d'ingénieur en chef de l'artillerie* (Warsaw: Nakładem Świdzińskich, 1885)

Esper, Johann Friedrich, *C.A. de Martelli, Römisch Kaiserl. Generaladjutanten... Errettung in und aus der Türkischen Gefangenschaft* (Erlangen: Heyder, 1825)

Evliya Çelebi, *Narrative of travels in Europe, Asia and Africa in the seventeenth century* [translated anonymously from the German translation of] Joseph von Hammer-Purgstall (London: Oriental Translation Fund, 1834-1850, 2 vols., reprinted in one volume, New York/London: Johnson Reprint, 1968), vol. 1 (the author is identified as 'Evliya Efendi' in the work)

Feigius, Johann Constantius. *Wunderbahrer Adlers-Schwung, oder fernere Geschichts-Fortsetzung Ortelii Redivivi et Continuati: das ist, eine ausführliche historische Beschreibung von mancherleyen vorgefallenen Staats-Händeln... und von allem was von anno 1664 in politicis und civilibus so wohl bey dem Käyserl. Hof zu Wienn, als in Ober- und Nider-Ungarn, auch Sibenbürgen... vorgefalle* ([Vienna]: Voigt, 1694), vol. 1

Firnhaber, Friedrich (ed.), 'Diarium, was sich vom 7. Juny anno 1683 biss zu End der Belagerung Wienns bei der Türkischen Armee zugetragen', *Archiv für Kunde Österreichischer Geschichts-Quellen*, 4 (1850), pp.496–507

Forst de Battaglia, Otto, *Jan Sobieski* (überarbeitete Neuauflage, Graz: Styria Verlag, 1982)

Glaser, Hubert (ed.), *Kurfürst Max Emanuel: Bayern und Europa um 1700* (Munich: Hirmer, 1976), vol. 2

Goldstone, Jack A., *Revolution and rebellion in the early modern world* (Berkeley: U. of California Press, 1991)

Hammer-Purgstall, Joseph von, *Geschichte der Chane der Krim unter osmanischer Herrschaft: aus türkischen Quellen...* (Vienna: K.K. Hof- und Staatsdruckerei, 1856)

Hammer-Purgstall, Joseph von, *Geschichte des osmanischen Reiches* (Pest/Vienna: Hartleben, 1827–1835), vol. 6

Hassel, Johann Paul and Carl Friedrich Vitzthum von Eckstädt, *Zur Geschichte des Türkenkrieges im Jahre 1683: die Betheilung der kursächsischen Truppen an demselben* (Dresden: Haensch, 1883)

Hocke, Nicolaus, *Kurtze Beschreibung, dessen was in wehrender türkischen Belägerung der kayserlichen Residentz-Statt Wienn... passiret* (Vienna: Voigt, 1685)

Janko, Wilhelm von, 'Zur Geschichte des Entsatzes von Wien', *(Streffleur's) Österreichisches Militärische Zeitschrift*, 24:3 (1883), pp.3–22

Jochner, Georg Maria, *Zur Geschichte des Türkenkrieges im Jahre 1683: Teilnahme des frankischen Kreises an der Befreiung Wiens* (Bamberg: Historisches Verein, 1885)

Köhbach, Markus, 'Der Tārīh-i Mehemmed Giray – eine osmanische Quelle zur Belagerung Wiens durch die Türken im Jahre 1683', *Studia Austro-Polonica*, 3 (1983), pp.137–164

Kreutel, Richard Franz, ed. *Kara Mustafa vor Wien: 1683 aus der Sicht türkischer Quellen*. stark vermehrte Ausgabe besorgt von Karl Teply. (Osmanische Geschichtsschreiber 1) (Graz: Styria Verlag, 1982) (cited as 'Kreutel & Teply')

Das Kriegsjahr 1683: nach Akten und andere authentische Quellen dargestellt in der Abtheilung für Kriegsgeschichte des k.k. Kriegs-Archives (Mittheilungen des k.k. Kriegs-Archivs) (Vienna: Generalstab, 1883; published as part of the *Mittheilungen des k.k. Kriegs-Archivs* but with separate pagination, as individual work)

La Brune, Jean de, *La vie de Charles V duc de Lorraine* (Amsterdam: Garrel, 1691)

Laskowski, Otton, *La campagne de Vienne, 1683* (Warsaw: Institut des Sciences Militaires, 1933)

Laskowski, Otton, *Sobieski, King of Poland*, translated by F.C. Anstruther (Glasgow: Polish Library, 1944)

Le Bègue. See Stöller.

[Mansberg, Karl Wilhelm], *Der Entsatz von Wien am 12. September 1683* (Berlin: Rathenow, 1883)

Marczali, Henri (ed.), 'Relation du siège de Vienne et de la campagne en Hongrie 1683 [by the Conte di Frosasco]', *Revue de Hongrie*, 3 (1909), pp.34-66, 169-198, 276-292

Marsigli, Luigi Ferdinando, *L'état militaire de l'Empire Ottoman, ses progrès et sa décadence = Stato militare dell'Imperio Ottomanno...* (Hague: Gosse & Neaulme, 1732), 2 vols.

Maurer, Joseph, *Cardinal Leopold Graf Kollonitsch, Primas von Ungarn: sein Leben und sein Wirken.* (Innsbruck: Rauch, 1887)

Murphey, Rhoads, 'The functioning of the Ottoman army under Murad IV (1623–1639/1032–1049): key to the understanding of the relationship between centre and periphery in seventeenth century Turkey' (unpubl. PhD thesis, U. of Chicago, 1979)

Newald, Johann, *Beiträge zur Geschichte der Belagerung von Wien durch die Türken im Jahre 1683: historisch Studien* (Vienna: Kubasta & Voigt, 1883–1884), 2 vols.

Ottoman diarists. See Kreutel.

Paradowski, Michał, *We came, we saw, God conquered: the Polish-Lithuanian Commonwealth's military effort in the relief of Vienna, 1683* (Century of the soldier series: warfare c. 1618-1721 no.79) (Warwick: Helion, 2021)

Pastor, Ludwig, *History of the Popes, from the close of the Middle Ages*, trans. by Ernest Graf (London: [Routledge &] Kegan Paul, 1949-53), vol. 32

Petritsch, Ernst D., 'Die Tatarish-Ottomanischen Begleitoperationen in Niederösterreich', *Studia Austro-Polonica*, 3 (1983), pp.207–240

Plater, Stanisław, comte de (ed.), *Lettres du roi de Pologne Jean Sobieski, à la reine Marie Casimire, pendant la campagne de Vienne* (Louvain: Vanlithout & Vandenzande, 1827)

Przyboś, Adam, 'Die Waffenbrüder König Jans III. Sobieski im Jahre 1683', *Studia Austro-Polonica*, 3 (1983), pp.241–256

Rauchbar, Johann Georg von, *Leben und Thaten des Fürsten Georg Friedrich von Waldeck*. [ed. by] L. Curtze and A. Hahn (Arolsen: Speyer, 1867–1872), vol. 2

Renner, Victor von, *Wien im Jahre 1683: Geschichte der zweiten Belagerung der Stadt durch die Türken im Rahmen der Zeitereignisse: aus Anlass der zweiten Säcularfeier verfasst…* (Vienna: Waldheim, 1883)

Röder von Diersburg, Philipp, *Des Markgraf Ludwig Wilhelm von Baden Feldzüge wider die Türken…* (Karlsruhe: Müller, 1839–1842), vol. 1

Ruess, Johann Georg Wilhelm, *Wahrhaffte und gründliche Relation über die den 14. Julii Anno 1683 angefangene, den 12. Septembris aber glücklich auffgehobene Belägerung der Kays. Haupt- und Residentz-Stadt Wien* (Vienna: Ghelen, 1683)

Schuster, Oscar, and F. A. Francke, *Geschichte der sächsischen Armee, von deren Errichtung bis auf die neueste Zeit* (Leipzig: Duncker & Humblot, 1885, reprinted [Munich?]: LTR Verlag, 1983), vol. 1

Schliz von Görz. See Newald.

Schröder, Gustav, 'Der Kampf um Wien 1683: sein Verlauf und seine Bedeutung für die Geschichte des Festungskrieges', *Archiv für die Artillerie- und Ingenieur-Offiziere des deutschen Reichsheeres*, 47. Jhg., = Vol.90 (1883), pp.305–382

Shinder, Joel, 'Ottoman bureaucracy in the second half of the seventeenth century: the central and naval administrations' (unpubl. PhD thesis, Princeton U., 1971)

Sichart, Luis Heinrich Friedrich von, *Geschichte der königlich hannoverschen Armee* 5 vols. (Hanover: Hahn, 1860-1898), vol. 1

Staudinger, Karl, *Geschichte des kurbayerischen Heeres unter Kurfürst Max II. Emanuel, 1680–1726* (Munich: Lindauer, 1904–1905), part 1

Staudinger, Karl, *Das königlich bayerische 2. Infanterie-Regiment 'Kronprinz' 1682 bis 1882* (Munich: Oldenbourg, 1885–1887), 3 parts (no more pub.)

Stöller, Ferdinand (ed.), 'Neue Quellen zur Geschichte des Türkenjahres 1683', *Mitteilungen des Instituts für Österreichischen Geschichtsforschung, Ergänzungs-Band*, 13, Heft 1 (1933), pp.1–138. Contains: François le Bègue's 'Journal de la premiere campagne de Hongrie en 1683' and his 'Récit du secours de Vienne en l'année 1683'; as well as 'Relation du siège de Vienne par un officier de la garnison'.

Stoye, John, *The siege of Vienna* (London: Collins, 1964)

Suttinger. See *Aufrichtige und unpartheyische Relation* above for the textual account sometimes attributed to him; see Broucek, Hillbrand & Vesely above for the best modern reproduction of the famous Suttinger map/order of battle.

Theatrum Europaeum, oder, Aussführliche und warhafftige Beschreibung aller und jeder denkwürdiger Geschichten… (Frankfurt am Main: Görlin, 1691), vol. 12. NB: I cite this semi-periodical volume by its recognised standard title, used by most authors and in library catalogues, but the titles of some individual volumes varied, and for volume 12 was technically *Theatri Europaei continuati* – the fact that it then called itself 'zwölffter Theil' confirmed that it was intended as part of Theatrum Europaeum.

Thiel, Annemarie, 'Johann Heinrich Graf von Dünewald', unpubl. PhD thesis, U. of Vienna, 1941

Toifel, Carl, *Die Türken vor Wien im Jahre 1683* (Prague/Leipzig: Tempsky/Freytag, 1883)

Die Türken vor Wien: Europa und die Entscheidung an der Donau 1683: 82. Sonderausstellung des Historischen Museums der Stadt Wien… 1983 (Vienna: the Museum, 1983) [not the same as the 1982 publication of the same main title edited by Waissenberger]

Uechtritz-Steinkirch, O. von, *Heinrich Tobias Freiherr von Haslingen: ein Beitrag zur Geschichte der Befreiung Wiens im Jahre 1683* (Breslau: Korn, 1883)

Urbanski, Hans, *Karl von Lothringen: Österreichs Türkensieger* (Vienna: Amalthea, 1983)

Vaelckern, Johann Peter von, *Relation or diary of the siege of Vienna…* (London: Nott & Wells, 1684)

Varga, János J., *Válaszúton: Thököly Imre és Magyarország, 1682-1684-ben* (Budapest: História / MTA Történettudományi Intézete, 2007)

Wagner, Georg, *Das Türkenjahr 1664: eine europäische Bewährung* (Eisenstadt: Burgenländisches Landesarchiv, 1964)

Waissenberger, Robert (ed.), *Die Türken vor Wien: Europa und die Entscheidung an der Donau, 1683* (Salzburg: Residenz Verlag, 1982)

Waliszewski, Kazimierz, *Marysieńka: Marie de la Grange d'Arquien, Queen of Poland and wife of Sobieski, 1641-1716*, translated from the French by Lady Mary Lloyd (London: Heinemann, 1898)

Wentzcke, Paul, *Feldherr des Kaisers: Leben und Taten Herzog Karls V. von Lothringen* (Leipzig: Koehler & Amelang, 1943)

Wimmer, Jan, *Der Entsatz von Wien 1683* (Warsaw: Verlag Interpress, 1983)

Wimmer, Jan, *Wiedeń 1683: dzieje kampanii i bitwy* (Warsaw: Wydawnictwo Ministerstwa Obrony Narodowej, 1983) (used only for order-of-battle information)

Woliński, Janusz, 'König Johan III Sobieski und die Schlacht bei Wien 1683', In *La Pologne au XIIe Congrès International des Sciences Historiques à Vienne* (Warsaw: Państwowe Wydawnictwo Naukowe, 1965), pp. 49–62

Wrede, Alphons Freiherr von, *Geschichte der k. und k. Wehrmacht* (Vienna: Seidel, 1889–1905, reprinted Starnberg: LTR Verlag, 1985), 5 vols.

Zgórniak, Marian, 'Die Struktur des polnischen Heeres zur Zeit des Grossen Türkenkrieges (1672–1699)', *Studia Austro-Polonica*, 3 (1983), pp.381–399

Works only dealing with armies generally and their uniforms

Dolleczek, Anton, *Geschichte der österreichischen Artillerie* (Vienna: Selbstverlag [the author], 1887)

Hall, Robert and Giancarlo Boeri, *Uniforms and flags of the Imperial Austrian Army, 1683–1720* (Farnham: The Pike and Shot Society, 2011)

Kannik, Prebben, *Military uniforms in colour* (Poole: Blandford, 1968)

Knötel, Richard, *Uniforms of the world: a compendium of army, navy and air force uniforms, 1700-1937*, revised, brought up to date, and enlarged, by Herbert Jr Knötel and Herbert Sieg (London: Arms & Armour Press, 1980)

Mugnai, Bruno, *L'esercito Ottomano da Candia a Passarowitz (1645-1718)* (Venice: Filippi, 1997-1998), 2 vols.

Mugnai, Bruno, *Wars and soldiers in the early reign of Louis XIV. Volume 2 – the Imperial army, 1657–1687* (Century of the soldier series: warfare c. 1618-1721 no. 47) (Warwick: Helion, 2019)

Mugnai, Bruno, *Wars and soldiers in the early reign of Louis XIV. Volume 3 - the armies of the Ottoman Empire, 1645-1719* (Century of the soldier series: warfare c. 1618-1721 no. 55) Warwick: Helion, 2020.

Mugnai, Bruno, *Wars and soldiers in the early reign of Louis XIV. Volume 7 – armies of the German states, 1655–1690, part 1* (Century of the soldier series: warfare c. 1618-1721 no. 113) (Warwick: Helion, 2024)

Nicolle, David, *Armies of the Ottoman Turks, 1300-1774* colour plates by Angus McBride (Men at arms 140) (London: Osprey, 1983)

Querengässer, Alexander, *The Saxon Mars and his force: the Saxon army during the reign of John George III, 1680-1691* (Century of the soldier series: warfare c. 1618-1721 no.48) (Warwick: Helion, 2019)

Sapherson, C. A., *The Imperial cavalry 1691-1714* (Leeds: Raider Books, 1989)

Sapherson, C. A., *The Imperial infantry, 1691-1714* (Leeds: Raider Books, 1989)

Wróblewski, Bohdan, *Wojsko Polskie w dobie Króla Jana III w trzechsetną rocznicę wiktorii wiedeńskiej 1683-1983* (Warsaw: Wydawnictwo Interpress, 1983)

Other titles in the Century of the Soldier series

No 39 *In The Emperor's Service:* Wallenstein's Army, 1625–1634

No 40 *Charles XI's War:* The Scanian War Between Sweden and Denmark, 1675–1679

No 41 *The Armies and Wars of The Sun King 1643-1715:* Volume 1: The Guard of Louis XIV

No 42 *The Armies Of Philip IV Of Spain 1621–1665:* The Fight For European Supremacy

No 43 *Marlborough's Other Army:* The British Army and the Campaigns of the First Peninsular War, 1702–1712

No 44 *The Last Spanish Armada:* Britain And The War Of The Quadruple Alliance, 1718–1720

No 45 *Essential Agony:* The Battle of Dunbar 1650

No 46 *The Campaigns of Sir William Waller*

No 47 *Wars and Soldiers in the Early Reign of Louis XIV:* Volume 2 - The Imperial Army, 1660–1689

No 48 *The Saxon Mars and His Force:* The Saxon Army During The Reign Of John George III 1680–1691

No 49 *The King's Irish:* The Royalist Anglo-Irish Foot of the English Civil War

No 50 *The Armies and Wars of the Sun King 1643-1715:* Volume 2: The Infantry of Louis XIV

No 51 *More Like Lions Than Men:* Sir William Brereton and the Cheshire Army of Parliament, 1642–46

No 52 *I Am Minded to Rise:* The Clothing, Weapons and Accoutrements of the Jacobites from 1689 to 1719

No 53 *The Perfection of Military Discipline:* The Plug Bayonet and the English Army 1660–1705

No 54 *The Lion From the North:* The Swedish Army During the Thirty Years War: Volume 1, 1618–1632

No 55 *Wars and Soldiers in the Early Reign of Louis XIV:* Volume 3 - The Armies of the Ottoman Empire 1645–1718

No 56 *St. Ruth's Fatal Gamble:* The Battle of Aughrim 1691 and the Fall Of Jacobite Ireland

No 57 *Fighting for Liberty:* Argyll & Monmouth's Military Campaigns against the Government of King James, 1685

No 58 *The Armies and Wars of the Sun King 1643-1715:* Volume 3: The Cavalry of Louis XIV

No 59 *The Lion From the North:* The Swedish Army During the Thirty Years War: Volume 2, 1632–1648

No 60 *By Defeating My Enemies:* Charles XII of Sweden and the Great Northern War 1682–1721

No 61 *Despite Destruction, Misery and Privations..:* The Polish Army in Prussia during the war against Sweden 1626–1629

No 62 *The Armies of Sir Ralph Hopton:* The Royalist Armies of the West 1642–46

No 63 *Italy, Piedmont, and the War of the Spanish Succession 1701–1712*

No 64 *'Cannon played from the great fort':* Sieges in the Severn Valley during the English Civil War 1642–1646

No 65 *Carl Gustav Armfelt* and the Struggle for Finland During the Great Northern War

No 66 *In the Midst of the Kingdom:* The Royalist War Effort in the North Midlands 1642–1646

No 67 *The Anglo-Spanish War 1655–1660:* Volume 1: The War in the West Indies

No 68 *For a Parliament Freely Chosen:* The Rebellion of Sir George Booth, 1659

No 69 *The Bavarian Army During the Thirty Years War 1618-1648:* The Backbone of the Catholic League (revised second edition)

No 70 *The Armies and Wars of the Sun King 1643-1715:* Volume 4: The War of the Spanish Succession, Artillery, Engineers and Militias

No 71 *No Armour But Courage:* Colonel Sir George Lisle, 1615–1648 (Paperback reprint)

No 72 *The New Knights:* The Development of Cavalry in Western Europe, 1562–1700

No 73 *Cavalier Capital:* Oxford in the English Civil War 1642–1646 (Paperback reprint)

No 74 *The Anglo-Spanish War 1655–1660:* Volume 2: War in Jamaica

No 75 *The Perfect Militia:* The Stuart Trained Bands of England and Wales 1603–1642

No 76 *Wars and Soldiers in the Early Reign of Louis XIV:* Volume 4 - The Armies of Spain 1659–1688

No 77 *The Battle of Nördlingen 1634:* The Bloody Fight Between Tercios and Brigades

No 78 *Wars and Soldiers in the Early Reign of Louis XIV:* Volume 5 - The Portuguese Army 1659–1690

No 79 *We Came, We Saw, God Conquered:* The Polish-Lithuanian Commonwealth's military effort in the relief of Vienna, 1683

No 80 *Charles X's Wars:* Volume 1 - Armies of the Swedish Deluge, 1655–1660

No 81 *Cromwell's Buffoon:* The Life and Career of the Regicide, Thomas Pride (Paperback reprint)

No 82 *The Colonial Ironsides:* English Expeditions under the Commonwealth and Protectorate, 1650–1660

No 83 *The English Garrison of Tangier:* Charles II's Colonial Venture in the Mediterranean, 1661–1684

No 84 *The Second Battle of Preston, 1715:* The Last Battle on English Soil

No 85 *To Settle the Crown:* Waging Civil War in Shropshire, 1642–1648 (Paperback reprint)

No 86 *A Very Gallant Gentleman:* Colonel Francis Thornhagh (1617–1648) and the Nottinghamshire Horse

No 87 *Charles X's Wars:* Volume 2 - The Wars in the East, 1655–1657

No 88 *The Shōgun's Soldiers:* The Daily Life of Samurai and Soldiers in Edo Period Japan, 1603–1721 Volume 1

No 89 *Campaigns of the Eastern Association:* The Rise of Oliver Cromwell, 1642–1645

No 90 *The Army of Occupation in Ireland 1603–42:* Defending the Protestant Hegemony

No 91 *The Armies and Wars of the Sun King 1643-1715:* Volume 5: Buccaneers and Soldiers in the Americas

No 92 *New Worlds, Old Wars:* The Anglo-American Indian Wars 1607–1678

No 93 *Against the Deluge:* Polish and Lithuanian Armies During the War Against Sweden 1655–1660

No 94 *The Battle of Rocroi:* The Battle, the Myth and the Success of Propaganda

No 95 *The Shōgun's Soldiers:* The Daily Life of Samurai and Soldiers in Edo Period Japan, 1603–1721 Volume 2

No 96 *Science of Arms: the Art of War in the Century of the Soldier 1672–1699:* Volume 1: Preparation for War and the Infantry

No 97 *Charles X's Wars:* Volume 3 - The Danish Wars 1657–1660

No 98 *Wars and Soldiers in the Early Reign of Louis XIV:* Volume 6 - Armies of the Italian States 1660–1690 Part 1

No 99 *Dragoons and Dragoon Operations in the British Civil Wars, 1638–1653*

No 100 *Wars and Soldiers in the Early Reign of Louis XIV:* Volume 6 - Armies of the Italian States 1660–1690 Part 2

No 101 *1648 and All That:* The Scottish Invasions of England, 1648 and 1651: Proceedings of the 2022 Helion and Company 'Century of the Soldier' Conference

No 102 *John Hampden and the Battle of Chalgrove:* The Political and Military Life of Hampden and his Legacy

No 103 *The City Horse:* London's militia cavalry during the English Civil War, 1642–1660

No 104 *The Battle of Lützen 1632:* A Reassessment

No 105 *Monmouth's First Rebellion:* The Later Covenanter Risings, 1660–1685

No 106 *Raw Generals and Green Soldiers:* Catholic Armies in Ireland 1641–1643

No 107 *Polish, Lithuanian and Cossack armies versus the might of the Ottoman Empire*

No 108 *Soldiers and Civilians, Transport and Provisions:* Early Modern Military Logistics and Supply Systems During The British Civil Wars, 1638-1653

No 109 *Batter their walls, gates and Forts:* The Proceedings of the 2022 English Civil War Fortress Symposium

No 110 *The Town Well Fortified:* The Fortresses of the Civil Wars in Britain, 1639-1660

No 111 *Crucible of the Jacobite '15:* The Battle of Sheriffmuir 1715

No 112 *Charles XII's Karoliners Volume 2 -* The Swedish Cavalry of the Great Northern War 1700-1721

No 113 *Wars and Soldiers in the Early Reign of Louis XIV:* Volume 7 - Armies of the German States 1655–1690 Part 1

No 114 *The First British Army 1624–1628:* The Army of the Duke of Buckingham (Revised Edition)

No 115 *The Army of Transylvania (1613–1690):* War and military organization from the 'golden age' of the Principality to the Habsburg conquest

No 116 *The Army of the Manchu Empire:* The Conquest Army and the Imperial Army of Qing China, 1600-1727

No 117 *French Armies of the Thirty Years' War 1618–48*

No 118 *Soldiers' Clothing of the Early 17th Century:* Britain and Western Europe 1618–1660

No 119 *Novelty and Change:* Proceedings of the 2023 Helion and ompany 'Century of the Soldier' Conference

No 120 *Peter The Great's Disastrous Defeat:* The Swedish Victory at Narva, 1700

No 121 *Royalist Newark 1642-1646:* Sieges and Siege Works

No 122 *The Battle of Fribourg 1644:* Eughien and Turenne at War

No 123 *Science of Arms: the Art of War in the Century of the Soldier 1672–1699:* Volume 2: Cavalry, Artillery & the Conduct of War

No 124 *Supplying the New Model Army:* Logistics, arms, ammunition, clothing, victuals and the matériel of war, 1645–1646

No 125 *Wars and Soldiers in the Early Reign of Louis XIV:* Volume 7 - Armies of the German States 1655–1690 Part 2

No 126 *Wars and Soldiers in the Early Reign of Louis XIV:* Volume 7 - Armies of the German States 1655–1690 Part 3

No 127 *Confrontation of Kings, 1656:* The Three-Day Battle of Warsaw in the Swedish Deluge, 1655-1660

No 128 *The Battle of Lens 1648:* Condé beats the Spanish

No 129 *Ukrainian Cossacks from the late 16th century to the early 18th century:* Organisation, Clothing, Equipment, Armament

No 130 *Wars & Soldiers in the Early Reign of Louis XIV:* Volume 8 - The Armies of Denmark-Norway, Courland and Danzig, 1655–1690

SERIES SPECIALS:

No 1 *Charles XII's Karoliners:* Volume 1: The Swedish Infantry & Artillery of the Great Northern War 1700–1721